Lecture Notes in Artificial Intelligence   1266

Subseries of Lecture Notes in Computer Science
Edited by J. G. Carbonell and J. Siekmann

Lecture Notes in Computer Science

Edited by G. Goos, J. Hartmanis and J. van Leeuwen

T0190004

Springer
Berlin
Heidelberg
New York
Barcelona
Budapest
Hong Kong
London
Milan
Paris
Santa Clara
Singapore
Tokyo

David B. Leake   Enric Plaza   (Eds.)

Case-Based Reasoning Research and Development

Second International Conference
on Case-Based Reasoning, ICCBR-97
Providence, RI, USA, July 25-27, 1997
Proceedings

Springer

Series Editors
Jaime G. Carbonell, Carnegie Mellon University, Pittsburgh, PA, USA
Jörg Siekmann, University of Saarland, Saarbrücken, Germany

Volume Editors

David B.Leake
Indiana University, Computer Science Department
Lindley Hall 215, Bloomington, IN 47405, USA
E-mail: leake@cs.indiana.edu

Enric Plaza
Campus Universitat Autonoma de Barcelona, CSIC
E-08193 Bellaterra, Catalonia, Spain
E-mail: enric@iiia.csic.es

Cataloging-in-Publication Data applied for

Die Deutsche Bibliothek - CIP-Einheitsaufnahme

Case based reasoning research and development : second
international conference ; proceedings / ICCBR-97, Providence, RI,
USA, July 25 - 27, 1997. David Leake ; Enric Plaza (ed.). - Berlin ;
Heidelberg ; New York ; Barcelona ; Budapest ; Hong Kong ;
London ; Milan ; Paris ; Santa Clara ; Singapore ; Tokyo : Springer,
1997
    (Lecture notes in computer science ; Vol. 1266 : Lecture notes in
    artificial intelligence)
    ISBN 3-540-63233-6

CR Subject Classification (1991): I.2, J.4

ISBN 3-540-63233-6 Springer-Verlag Berlin Heidelberg New York

© Springer-Verlag Berlin Heidelberg 1997
Printed in Germany

Typesetting: Camera ready by author
SPIN 10548898   06/3142 – 5 4 3 2 1 0   Printed on acid-free paper

Preface

In 1995, the first International Conference on Case-Based Reasoning (ICCBR) was held in Sesimbra, Portugal, as the start of a biennial series. ICCBR-97, the Second International Conference on Case-Based Reasoning, was held at Brown University in Providence, Rhode Island, on July 25–27, 1997. The goal of the conference was to achieve a vibrant interchange between researchers and practitioners with different perspectives on fundamentally related issues, in order to examine and advance the state of the art in case-based reasoning and related fields.

ICCBR-97 featured a selection of mature work and new ideas from case-based reasoning research and applications. Researchers and developers from 19 countries submitted a total of 102 papers to the conference. Out of these submissions, 28 were presented as talks and 31 were presented as posters.

The conference was chaired by David Leake of Indiana University and Enric Plaza of IIIA-CSIC (the Spanish Scientific Research Council). They gratefully acknowledge the careful effort of the Program Committee and additional reviewers during the paper selection process. Members of the Program Committee and additional reviewers are listed on the following pages.

The Chairs give special thanks for the assistance and generous support ICCBR-97 received from the American Association for Artificial Intelligence (AAAI), the Catalan Association for Artificial Intelligence (ACIA), IJCAI Inc., Inference Corporation, LEXIS-NEXIS, and the European Network of Excellence in Machine Learning (MLnet).

The Chairs would also like to thank Alfred Hofmann, Computer Science Editor at Springer-Verlag, for his assistance in publishing these proceedings; Thomas Dean, of the Computer Science Department of Brown University, for his sponsorship of the conference at Brown University; Patricia Henry, Director of Conference Services at Brown University, for making the local arrangements for the conference; and the Indiana University Conference Bureau for administering the conference registration process.

July 1997
David B. Leake
Enric Plaza

Program Chairs

David B. Leake, Indiana University, U.S.A.
Enric Plaza, IIIA-CSIC (Spanish Scientific Research Council), Catalonia, Spain

Program committee

Agnar Aamodt	University of Trondheim
David Aha	Naval Research Laboratory
Klaus Althoff	Fraunhofer Institute
Kevin Ashley	University of Pittsburgh
Ray Bareiss	ILS, Northwestern University
Brigitte Bartsch-Spörl	BSR Consulting
Carlos Bento	University of Coimbra
Karl Branting	University of Wyoming
Ernesto Costa	University of Coimbra
Michael Cox	Carnegie Mellon University
Boi Faltings	EPFL, Lausanne
Ashok Goel	Georgia Institute of Technology
Kristian Hammond	University of Chicago
James Hendler	University of Maryland
Thomas Hinrichs	ILS, Northwestern University
Eric Jones	Alphatech, Inc.
Mark Keane	Trinity College of Dublin
James King	LEXIS-NEXIS
Philip Klahr	Inference Corporation
Janet Kolodner	Georgia Institute of Technology
Ramon López de Màntaras	IIIA-CSIC
Robert Macura	Medical College of Georgia
Michel Manago	AcknoSoft
William Mark	National Semiconductor Corp.
Ashwin Ram	Georgia Institute of Technology
Michael Richter	University of Kaiserslautern
Christopher Riesbeck	ILS, Northwestern University
Edwina Rissland	University of Massachusetts
Hideo Shimazu	NEC
Evangelos Simoudis	IBM Almaden Research Center
Derek Sleeman	University of Aberdeen
Ian Smith	EPFL, Lausanne
Gerhard Strube	University of Freiburg
Katia Sycara	Carnegie Mellon University
Shusaku Tsumoto	Tokyo Medical and Dental University
Manuela Veloso	Carnegie Mellon University
Angi Voss	GMD FIT
Ian Watson	Salford University
Stefan Wess	TecInno GmbH

Additional Reviewers

Josep Lluís Arcos
Ralph Bergmann
Piero Bonissone
Amílcar Cardoso
Brona Collins
Vincent Corruble
Carl-Helmut Coulon
Mark Devaney
Khaled El Emam
Susan Fox
Anthony Francis
Christoph Globig
Paulo Gomes
Marc Goodman
Christiane Gresse

Harald Holz
Andrew Kinley
Mario Lenz
Héctor Muñoz-Ávila
Bart Netten
Ruediger Oehlmann
Klaus Schmid
Gordon Shippey
David Skalak
Barry Smyth
Brendon Towle
Wolfgang Wilke
David Wilson
Mark Winter
Chris Wisdo

Conference Support

ICCBR-97 was supported by the American Association for Artificial Intelligence (AAAI), the Catalan Association for Artificial Intelligence (ACIA), IJCAI Inc., Inference Corporation, LEXIS-NEXIS, and the European Network of Excellence in Machine Learning (MLnet).

     MLnet

Table of Contents

Application Papers

Scientific Papers

Representation and Formalization

Indexing and Retrieval

Adaptation

Case-Based Reasoning in Color Matching

William Cheetham (cheetham@crd.ge.com),

John Graf (graf@crd.ge.com),

GE Research & Development Center, 1 Research Circle, Niskayuna, NY 12309

Abstract - A case-based reasoning system for determining what colorants to use for producing a specific color of plastic was created. The selection of colorants needs to take many factors into consideration. A technique that involved fuzzy logic was used to compare the quality of the color match for each factor. The system has been in use for two years at a growing number of GE Plastics sites and has shown significant cost savings.

1 Introduction

A case-based reasoning (CBR) application for coloring plastics is in use at multiple General Electric Plastics sites. GE will produce plastic in whatever color is needed by the customer. When a customer orders plastic they include a sample of the color needed, called the standard. GE will then color match the plastic to the customer's color standard. This color match process involves selecting colorants and their respective amounts so when combined with the plastic they generate a color that matches the customer color standard. This paper describes how the CBR process [1, 2, 4] applies to color matching and how different requirements of the color match are evaluated in order to select the optimum color formula.

2 Prior Art in Color Matching for Plastics

Selecting the colorants and loading levels for a color formula was previously either accomplished by using human working experience or computationally expensive computer programs. There are commercially available computer programs that can calculate the colorant loading proportions for a color formula that matches a color standard. Since these programs perform an exhaustive search, they require a user to select a subset of the allowable colorants. Usually five to seven are selected out of thirty to fifty possible colorants. The final formula will usually consist of four or five colorants. Having users make the critical decision of which colorants to select for the search often produces a non-optimal solution. Furthermore, it does not take into consideration other important attributes of a color match.

In order to convert a set of colorants and loadings into a single color Kubelka-Munk theory [3] is used. This theory describes how the absorption and scattering of colorants in a material are related to the visible color of the material. Each colorant contributes to the absorption and scattering of the material and its contribution is proportional to the amount of it present in the system multiplied by an absorption and scattering coefficient for that colorant. Our system uses Kubelka-Munk theory.

3 Color Matching Process

The color matching system consists of a spectrophotometer attached to a personal computer. The spectrophotometer is used to determine a numerical representation of a color, called a reflectance curve, see Figure 1. The reflection curve shows the percent-

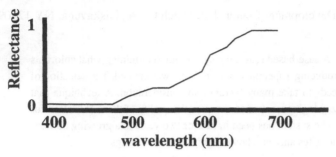

Figure 1: Reflectance Curve

age of light reflected by a color at each wavelength of the visible spectra (i.e. 400nm to 700nm). A spectrophotometer reads the reflectance of an object at 31 points equally spaced along the visible spectrum. Comparing two spectra is done by calculating the sum of differences or sum of squared differences between two curves over all 31 points in the visible spectrum. The personal computer contains the case-base and case-based reasoning software, called FormTool. Each case in the case-base contains a reflectance curve and a list of pigments and loadings used to create that color. FormTool is described below.

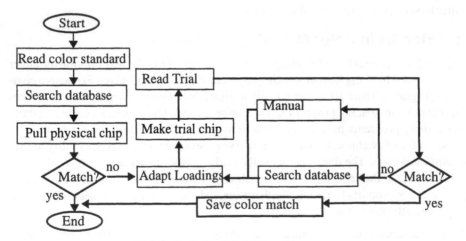

Figure 2: Color Matching Process

The color matching process developed is shown in Figure 2. The color matcher places the physical color standard in the spectrophotometer and reads the spectrum of the color standard into the color matching system. Next, the color matcher enters key information such as the resin and grade of material in which to generate the match. FormTool then searches its case-base of previous matches for the "best" previous match and adjusts those previous matches to produce a match for the new standard. There are multiple criteria which the color match must satisfy

- the color of the plastic must match the standard under multiple lighting conditions,
- there must be enough pigments to hide the color of the plastic,
- the cost of colorant formula should be as low as possible,
- only a limited amount of light can be transmitted through the plastic (optical density), and
- the color should not change when the plastic is molded at different temperatures.

The color matcher looks at the physical standard from this previous match and determines if it is acceptable for the application and customer. If the match is not acceptable, FormTool then adapts this previous match so that it more closely matches the requested color and application. The color matcher then makes a physical chip using the adapted formula. If this new match is acceptable then the adapted loadings are saved into the database and the match is finished. If the match is not acceptable then the user can decide to do one of three things:

1) manually or automatically adjust the color loadings (manual), or
2) switch to a different previous match as the starting point for this color match (search database)

After one of these is done the cycle continues until a match is found. When the "End" oval is reached a formula has been obtained that gives the "best" color match and balance of all other important properties.

4 The Case Selection Process

This section describes a method to evaluate the quality of a specific color formula. A selection process that uses this method to evaluate a formula can be used to find the formula that will reproduce a specified color and meet all desired attributes for the application of the specified color. A nearest neighbor [1] retrieval is used. However, the nearest neighbor must be determined by evaluating the degree of match in all of the attributes described above. This evaluation needs to provide a consistent meaning of an attributes similarity throughout all attributes. The consistency is achieved through the use of fuzzy linguistic terms, such as Excellent, Good, Fair, and Poor, which are associated with measured differences in an attribute. Any number of linguistic terms can be used. A fuzzy preference function [5] is used to calculate the similarity of a single attribute of a case with the corresponding attribute of the subject, see Figure 3.

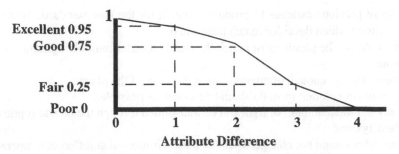

Figure 3: Fuzzy Preference Function for Metamerism

In this figure, a difference of 1 unit in the values of that attribute for the subject and comparable would be considered excellent, a difference of 2 would be good, 3 would be fair, and 4 would be poor. This rating is then transformed into the fuzzy preference function in Figure 3.

The result of using fuzzy preference functions is a vector, called the fuzzy preference vector. The vector contains a fuzzy preference value for each attribute. The values in this vector can be combined, through weighted aggregation, to produce a robust similarity value. The use of fuzzy preference functions allows for smooth changes in the result when an attribute is changed unlike the large changes that are possible when step functions are used.

A fuzzy preference function is used to transform a quantifiable value for each attribute into a qualitative description of the attribute that can be compared with the qualitative description of other attributes. A fuzzy preference function allows a comparison of properties that are based on entirely different scales such as cost measured in cents per pound and spectral curve match measured in reflection units. Based on discussions with experts and work to classify previous matches into various sets of linguistic terms we found that there was enough precision in our evaluation of the similarity of the attributes to have four linguistic terms. Table 1 shows the linguistic terms and the numeric similarity score that corresponds to each term.

Table 1: Global Preference Function Scale

Fuzzy Rating	Maximum Score	Minimum Score
Excellent	1	0.95
Good	0.94	0.75
Average	0.74	0.25
Poor	0.24	0

Fuzzy preference function were created for each of the following attributes of the color match

- color similarity,
- total colorant load,
- cost of colorant formula,
- optical density of color, and
- color shift when molded under normal and abusive conditions.

The remainder of this section describes how the fuzzy preference functions were constructed for each attribute.

4.1 Color Similarity

Two different ways of rating the quality of a color match are the spectral color curve match and metamerism of the color. Matching the spectral curve is the best way to match a color for all possible lighting conditions. Minimizing metamerism reduces the color difference under the most common lighting conditions. Minimizing metamerism is the traditional way a color match was done before there was a spectrophotometer that could read the reflectance of a color. Both of these methods are useful in matching a color.

The spectral color curve match is a rating of how closely the color of the formula created matches the color of the standard. A spectral curve is a representation of the amount of light that is reflected from an object at each wavelength of the visible spectrum. Comparing spectral curves of objects is the best way to compare their color, because if the two objects have the same spectral curve, then their colors will match under all lighting conditions. Other color matching techniques only match colors under one lighting condition, so the colors can look quite different under other lighting conditions.

The spectral curve match is characterized by the sums of the squared differences in the reflection values at 31 wavelengths from 400 to 700nm at a 10nm interval. Table 2

Table 2: Match Quality Rating

Fuzzy Rating	Maximum Sum of Squares Difference
Excellent	0.000124
Good	0.000496
Fair	0.001984
Poor	0.007936

shows the value of that sum of squares that is needed for an Excellent, Good, Fair, or Poor match. These values are determined by having an expert rate the curve matches in the case-base and then finding the minimum value for each of the ratings, excluding a few outliers.

For example, a sum of square difference of 0.000124 is the maximum difference for an excellent rating, from table 2. The score corresponding to this would be 0.95, the minimum score for excellent from table 2. Sum of square values between the minimum and maximum values have scores that are linearly interpolated from the minimum and maximum values for that rating. Figure 5 shows the fuzzy preference function for curve match.

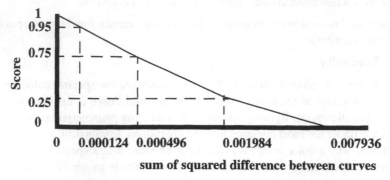

Figure 4: Fuzzy Preference Function for Curve Match

A second measure of the curve match is the metamerism index. Metamerism takes place when two objects are the same color under one lighting condition, but different under another lighting condition. Figure 5 shows that two color chips can look the same

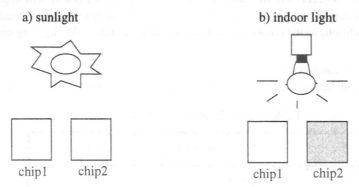

Figure 5: Metamerism

under one lighting condition (sunlight) and different under another (indoor light). This is the effect of metamerism. There are specific lighting conditions that are more common than others. If the spectral curve match is good, there can still be metamerism among the primary lighting conditions. This metamerism should be as small as possible.

The metamerism index is measured in dE* units using the International Commission on Illuminations L*a*b* color scale [Billmeyer-81]. In order to calculate dE*, the stimulus color is determined from the multiple of the spectral power curve of a light source

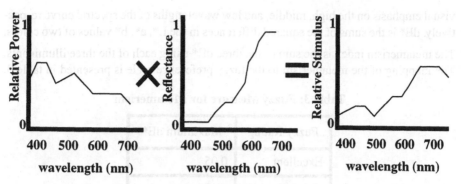

Figure 6: Calculation of Stimulus Color

and the reflectance of the object in question, see Figure 6. The stimulus color curve can be used to determine the L*a*b* values of the color. Figure 7 shows the L*a*b* scale which is a three-dimensional space for representing color with L (lightness) on the up-down axis, a (red-greenness) on the left to right axis, and b (yellow-blueness) on the front to back axis. This color space represents color under one lighting condition (spectral power curve), unlike the spectral curve that represents color under all lighting conditions. The difference in L*a*b* values is computed by determining the difference in the L*, a*, and b* values of the two colors. These differences are called dL*, da*, and

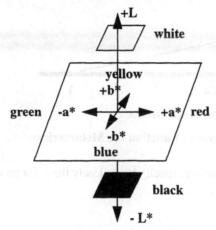

Figure 7: L*a*b* Color Space

db* respectively. Then, dE* is calculated using the following formula:

$$dE^* = \sqrt{dL^{*2} + da^{*2} + db^{*2}}$$

In order to use the L*a*b* color scale an illuminant needs to be selected. The standard illuminants that we selected are C (overcast-sky daylight), D65 (normal daylight), and F7 (florescent light). These represent the most common lighting conditions and give visual emphasis on the high, middle, and low wavelengths of the spectral curve respectively. dE* is the sums of the squared differences in the L*, a*, b* values of two colors.

The metamerism index is the sum of the three dE* using each of the three illuminants. The mapping of the metamerism to the fuzzy preference scale is presented in table 3.

Table 3: Fuzzy Measure for Metamerism

Fuzzy Rating	Maximum dE*
Excellent	0.05
Good	0.15
Fair	0.4
Poor	1.0

This table and all other similar ones are generated from an analysis of the case-base. The fuzzy preference function generated from table 4 is given in figure 8. These two

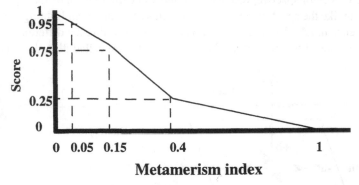

Figure 8: Fuzzy Preference Function for Metamerism

properties, curve match and metamerism, specify how closely the color produced by a formula matches the color of a standard.

4.2 Total Loading

The total colorant load is total volume of all colorants used for a set volume of plastic. It is best to use the least volume of colorants that makes an acceptable match, for reasons relating to the manufacturing of the plastic.

The quality of the remaining properties depends on the color that is being matched. For example, a cost that is good for a red color might be poor for a white because reds are much more expensive. In order to use fuzzy preference functions for these attributes the case-base must be subdivided into portions that have consistent values for the prop-

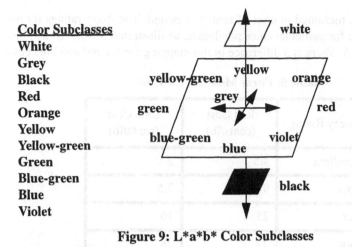

Color Subclasses
White
Grey
Black
Red
Orange
Yellow
Yellow-green
Green
Blue-green
Blue
Violet

Figure 9: L*a*b* Color Subclasses

erties. We have divided the case-base into eleven classes. Figure 9 lists those classes and shows where they are in the L*a*b* color space. For each attribute, the fuzzy ratings needed to be calculated separately for each subclass.

An attribute that uses these subclasses is the total loading of colorant in the formula. The total colorant loading of the formula can be characterized in parts per hundred (pph) parts of base material such as plastic. The total colorant loading is dependent upon the color to be made. Table 4 shows the fuzzy ratings for total colorant loading

Table 4: Fuzzy Measure for Total Colorant Loading

Fuzzy Rating	White pph	Green pph
Excellent	3	0.4
Good	5	0.7
Fair	7	1.1
Poor	11	3.2

for the white and green color subclasses. The rest of the subclasses are similar to the ones presented. Historically, whites tend to require much more colorant than a green color. This is because it takes more of the white colorant to hide the color of the plastic. The difference in typical loadings is accounted for by using separate tables for separate colors. A fuzzy preference function can be easily constructed for each subclass.

4.3 Cost

The cost of the colorants in the formula should be kept to a minimum to maximize the profitability of the manufacturing process.

The attribute cost is measured in units of cents per pound. The fuzzy ratings for this attribute are specific for particular color subclasses, as illustrated for the red and blue subclasses in Table 5. There is a difference in the mapping for the red and blue color

Table 5: Fuzzy Measure for Cost

Fuzzy Rating	Red Cost (cents/lb)	Blue Cost (cents/lb)
Excellent	4.5	2
Good	9	3.5
Fair	25	10
Poor	72	28

families because the cost of colorants to make a red tend to be more expensive than the colorants used to make a blue.

4.4 Optical Density

The optical density of plastic is the thickness of plastic that is required to stop all light from radiating through the plastic. A specific optical density is required for many applications. For the majority of color formulas, it is desired to make the material opaque to prevent light from transmitting though the material. Optical density can be used to characterize how much light is transmitted through a sample. The type of colorants used in a formula and the loading level of the colorants determine the optical density of the material. The qualitative values of optical density are color dependent. For example, it is easier to obtain the needed optical density in an opaque grey color formula than in a red color. Table 6 shows fuzzy rating of optical density for a grey and a red color.

Table 6: Fuzzy Measure for Optical Density

Fuzzy Rating	Grey dE*	Red dE*
Excellent	5.9	5.9
Good	5.8	5
Fair	5.5	2
Poor	4	1

4.5 Hide Color Shift

The color shift when molding under normal and abusive conditions comes from the fact that the plastic can be molded at low and high temperatures. The same plastic is a slightly different color when molded at different temperatures, because plastic tends to yellow at higher temperatures. In order to minimize the color shift, extra colorant loadings need to be used. A formula must also be robust enough to hide these color changes in the base plastic. One way to characterize this attribute of hiding variations due to process conditions is to measure the color of the material under normal processing conditions and under abusive processing conditions. The difference in color between these two processing conditions is then measured in dE* units using the CIE L*a*b* color scale. Table 7 shows the process color change in dE* units mapped between the

Table 7: Fuzzy Measure for Color Shift

Fuzzy Rating	Grey dE*	Yellow dE*
Excellent	0.05	0.05
Good	0.10	0.15
Fair	0.2	0.4
Poor	0.5	1.0

grey and yellow color subclasses. Visually, a larger change in color due to processing conditions can be tolerated in a light yellow color than a grey color as shown by this mapping based on historical data.

4.6 Aggregate Fuzzy Preference Values

Each of the above properties including spectral color match, metameric index, loading level, cost, optical density, and color shift due to processing conditions, is based on different scales of units. By mapping each of these properties to a global scale through the use of fuzzy preferences and linguistic terms such as Excellent, Good, Fair, and Poor, it becomes possible to compare one attribute with another.

The next step is to create a summation of the preference value of each attribute. This can be done with a weight of unity for each attribute or the end user can supply weights of their own if they desire to emphasize one attribute over another. Dividing this summation term by the summation of the weights gives the global preference value for the system.

5 Adaptation

Most formulas that are retrieved need some adaptation. The similarity calculation described above is used to guide the adaptation. Adaptation is done by performing a search which repeatedly varies the loadings of the colorants in the formula retrieved and evaluates the new similarity. Kubelka-Munk theory is used as part of the similarity calculation and provides a formula for predicting the color change from modifying the loadings of the colorants. Having a function that can accurately evaluate the effect of an adaptation is the key to performing the correct adaptation.

6 Benefits and Future Work

The General Electric company has been using the color formulation tool (FormTool) at one factory since 1995 and has seen significant cost savings. Two other factories in the US are also now using FormTool. When FormTool was introduce in 1995, the similarity algorithms were used to optimize the formulas for of historical colors. Since colorants are the most expensive portion of the plastic by weight, these new formulas produced a significant cost savings. There was additional savings from new color matches done during 1995 and 1996 using FormTool.

When use of FormTool was started in 1995 the case-base contained 1700 previous matches. FormTool is now used for approximately 2000 color matches per year. By the end of 1997 we expect the case-base to grow to over 10,000 color matches. The majority of these new cases will be obtained from historical records of sites which have started using FormTool. The remainder of new cases will come from successful color matches where FormTool was used and the matches were automatically added to the case-base.

FormTool is now the primary tool for creating color matches at GE Plastics sites in the United States. There are plans to move the system to GE Plastics sites in Europe, Asia, and Australia. There is also work going on to connect the case-bases from each of these sites into a single global case-base which can be updated from any of the global sites.

The U.S. Patent and Trademark office has issued a notice of allowability for the patenting of the color matching process described here. A European patent has also been filed.

7 References

[1]   Aamodt, A., Case-Based Reasoning: Foundational Issues, Methodological Variations, and System Approaches, AICOM, Vol. 7, No. 1, March 1994.

[2]   Althoff, K-D., A Review of Industrial Case-Based Reasoning Tools, AI Intelligence, United Kingdom, 1995.

[3]   Billmeyer, F., Principles of Color Technology: Second Edition, John Wiley & Sons, New York, 1981.

[4]   Kolodner, J., Case-Based Reasoning. Morgan Kaufmann, 1993.

[5]   Mendel, J., Fuzzy Logic Systems for Engineering: A Tutorial, Proceedings of the IEEE, Vol. 83, no. 3, March 1995.

Estimating Software Development Effort with Case-Based Reasoning

G.R. Finnie*, G.E. Wittig* and J-M. Desharnais**

School of Information Technology
Bond University, Gold Coast
Queensland 4229, Australia
gfinnie@Bond.edu.au
gwittig@Bond.edu.au
** *Software Engineering Laboratory in Applied Metrics*
7415 rue Beaubien Est, suite 509
Anjou, Quebec, Canada H1M 3R5
(Address Correspondence to Dr. G.R.Finnie)

Abstract

Software project effort estimation is a difficult problem complicated by a variety of interrelated factors. Current regression-based models have not had much success in accurately estimating system size. This paper describes a case based reasoning approach to software estimation which performs somewhat better than regression models based on the same data and which has some similarity to human expert judgement approaches. An analysis is performed to determine whether different forms of averaging and adaptation improve the overall quality of the estimate.

Introduction

Estimating the size and development effort required for a software project remains one of the most complex problems in managing software development. A software development project involves a number of interrelated factors which affect development effort and productivity. The factors include the development environment, skills of the development staff and complexity of the system to be developed. As factors interact in unforeseen and unpredictable ways accurate forecasting has proved difficult.

A number of models, primarily regression-based, have been proposed to assist software estimation. Results have generally been disappointing. Heemstra (1992) concluded that estimation models have not shown that they can be used as a reliable estimation tool. In practice most pragmatic software estimation appears to be based on various forms of expert judgement, usually anchored in the experience of prior software projects. As a result the use of case-based reasoning for estimation is intuitively appealing.

Software estimation based on expert judgement relies on adaptation of existing knowledge of prior software development projects. Earlier research by the authors (Finnie and Wittig, 1996; Finnie et al, 1997) has investigated the use of artificial intelligence techniques for software estimation and has contrasted case based reasoning (CBR) and artificial neural networks with other models in use. The research discussed in Finnie et al (1997) focused on these alternative approaches while the research discussed below deals specifically with the CBR issues of adaptation and combination of results.

The current paper evaluates the effectiveness of CBR for software estimation and investigates the merit of different adaptation and estimation strategies for the estimation model. A data set of 299 software development projects was used to establish a case base (of 249 cases) which was then used to test alternative CBR strategies on the remaining 50 test cases. The CBR approach was also compared with a regression model. The prediction accuracy of the CBR approach appears to be at least as good as other techniques in use and outperformed the regression model used. Averaging of several adapted cases using a geometric mean provide the best estimates for software development effort.

Problems with Software Estimation Models

A wide range of models have been proposed for software size estimation with a commonly used technique being Function Point Analysis (FPA) (Function Point Counting Practices Manual, 1994). However no model has proved to be outstandingly successful at effectively and consistently predicting software development effort. Most models are based on regression analysis of some set of past cases. Matson et al (1994) review some of the problems associated with regression models, specifically as applied to FPA. All the models presume the ability to estimate system size early in the life cycle which is a major weakness of the lines of code models. FPA estimates can usually be generated reasonably accurately at an early stage of the development.

Kemerer (1987) performed an empirical validation of four algorithmic models (SLIM, COCOMO, Estimacs and FPA), using data from projects outside the original model development environments without re-calibrating the models. Most models showed a strong over estimation bias and large estimation errors with the mean absolute relative error (MARE) ranging from an average of 57 percent to almost 800 percent. Ferens and Gurner (1992) evaluated three development effort prediction models (SPANS, Checkpoint and COSTAR). The prediction error is large, with the MARE ranging from 46 percent for the Checkpoint model to 105 percent for the COSTAR model.

Jeffery and Low (1990) conducted a study to investigate the need for model calibration at both the industry as well as the organization level. Again the MARE was high, ranging from 43 to 105 percent for the three companies which were used in the study. Jeffery et al. (1993) compared the SPQR/20 model to FPA using data from 64 projects within one organization. The models were re-calibrated to the local environment to remove over or under estimation biases. The estimation errors are considerably less than those of previous studies with MAREs of approximately 12 percent which reflects the benefits of model calibration.

Case based reasoning has attracted little attention as a software estimation technique although Mukhopadhyay et al. (1992) developed a model (Estor) based on the judgement of a single expert which was evaluated against expert judgement, COCOMO, and Function Point Analysis (FPA). In this research none of the models were able to improve on the performance of the expert. The estimation error of the expert and of Estor were considerably less than FPA and COCOMO. Despite the improvement the errors are still large with Estor's MARE greater than 50 percent. In the Estor CBR model the system size is based on elapsed time (for previous cases) and any adaptation of this time is done on the basis of rules extracted from a protocol analysis of an expert estimator's performance on an actual estimation task.

Function Point Analysis

Function Point Analysis is a two stage process (Function Point Counting Practices Manual, 1994). In the first phase unadjusted function points (UFP) are computed on the basis of an estimate of the number of inputs, outputs, inquiries, internal files and external files in the system. Each of these in turn is assessed as simple, average or complex and assigned a weight accordingly. The total UFP count is the sum of all these weighted components. In the second phase the unadjusted function point count is adapted by the use of 14 general system characteristics (gsc) which attempt to compensate for differences in technical complexity between system developments e.g. in terms of data communications or on-line data entry requirements.

General system characteristics (gsc) are rated on a score of 0 (no influence) to 5 (essential). The total gsc score is called the Total Degrees of Influence (TDI) and can therefore range from 0 to 70. The UFP count is modified to calculate function points (FP) as follows:

$$FP = UFP \times (0.65 + 0.01 \times TDI)$$

A CBR Model for Software Estimation

The case-based reasoning paradigm has an intuitive appeal for use in software effort estimation as it has the capability to model the way expert estimation is performed as well as explaining the reasoning applied to adapt past cases. The current analysis was performed to evaluate the effectiveness of CBR for software development effort estimation. The primary questions to be answered were:

(1) Does CBR perform significantly better than regression models
(2) How does the use of averaging a number of CBR estimates for a project affect the accuracy of the prediction.
(3) Is the use of CBR better than choosing a random mix of projects as a basis for comparison i.e. does matching cases on similarity improve the quality of the estimate.
(4) Does the use of adaptation of past case data improve the quality of the estimate

In order to develop a suitable CBR system for software estimation it was necessary to establish those factors which could be used for adaptation i.e. if the current problem differs in some way from a stored case how can one adapt the effort estimate. The test data available was divided into 249 "training cases" to be held in the case base and 50 test cases to evaluate the quality of the model. The key concept used to determine case adaptation was to identify factors which contributed to significant differences in productivity between cases.

The gsc's were analysed in the training cases to determine whether there were any significant differences in productivity (using a simple independent two tailed t-test) between those with a low rating on the gsc (a score of 0-2) and those with a high rating on the gsc (3-5). Only 6 of the gsc's in fact showed any significant difference (at $p<0.05$). As these tests were primarily used to establish suitable heuristics it was not felt necessary to adjust alpha levels for the number of tests. The six factors were:

Performance	$(t=3.59,$	$p=0.0002)$
On-line data entry	$(t=-2.16,$	$p=0.02)$
End-user efficiency	$(t=1.88,$	$p=0.03)$
Complex processing	$(t=3.50,$	$p=0.0003)$
Multiple sites	$(t=4.42,$	$p=.00001)$
Facilitate change	$(t=4.27,$	$p=0.00001)$

A CBR system was developed based on Remind 1.3. Remind is a commercially available case based reasoning tool produced by Cognitive Systems Inc. Nearest neighbour retrieval was used to identify the cases most similar to a given problem case, based on the significant gsc, system size (in unadjusted function points) and the ratios of inputs, outputs, inquiries, internal files and external files to the total UFP count. The latter were included when it was noted that the relative proportions of factors such as inquiries in the total UFP count appeared to significantly influence productivity. Ten cases were initially kept out of the sample of 249 in order to provide a test set to allow experimentation with different retrieval and adaptation combinations. Adaptation rules were developed based on the differences in productivity for each significant gsc. This was done by developing a simple linear regression model (using the 239 cases) for each of the six significant gsc with productivity as the independent variable. Adaptation rules then adjusted the software development effort estimate by a multiplier based on the differences in score for any significant gsc.

As an example, suppose that project A stored in the case base has a performance rating of 0, a function point count of 200 and a development effort of 1000 hours. Project B for which the effort is to be estimated has a function point count of 150 and a performance rating of 5. If the multiplier has determined a 5% difference in productivity for each point on the gsc scale, there will be a 25% difference in productivity between the cases and project B will be estimated to take

$$(150 + 200) \times 1000 \times 1.25 = 937.5 \text{ hours.}$$

All adjustments are combined into a single multiplier before the final estimate is determined. Combination is by multiplication of the factors e.g. if a 20% increase in productivity due to one factor is matched by a 20% decrease in productivity due to another factor the final multiplier should remain unchanged.

The adaptation approach used assumes a linear relationship between the FP count (i.e. system size) and development effort primarily for simplicity. Although the relationship is non-linear in practice (in general more effort is required per function point with increasing system size), the system size in FP was a major factor (fairly heavily weighted) used for the nearest neighbour matching. As a result most similar cases extracted were of similar size. Further work on adaptation strategies would need to consider the use of non-linear adjustment. .

Research Data

This database is the result of a compilation of 299 projects from 17 different organisations (Desharnais et al, 1990). The standard deviation and the skewness of the data suggests the possible presence of outliers, but none of these were excluded from the analysis. Table 1 below gives the mean for each statistic (e.g. the project development effort), the maximum and minimum values as well as the skewness of the data. The table refers to the actual project data recorded.

Table 1 Summary of Project Data

	Description	Mean	Min.	Max.	Skew.
Effort	Effort in hours	7086	247	86478	4.75
UFP	Unadjusted FP	298	48	1257	1.81
FP	Adjusted FP	267	40	1182	1.86
UFP/Hour	Productivity	0.071	0.008	0.696	3.99

Size in function points and project effort was determined for each project on completion. This has the advantage in an ex post facto analysis of removing any difficulties caused by changes in project specifications. The very large range of productivity is typical of data from software development projects and illustrates the difficulty of establishing models which can predict effort with any consistency.

Performance Evaluation

Different error measurements have been used by various metrics researchers, but for this project the main measure of model performance is the Mean Absolute Relative Error (MARE). MARE is calculated as follows:

$$MARE = \left(\sum_{i=1}^{n} \left| \frac{estimate - actual}{actual} \right| \right) \div n$$

where:

  estimate is the model estimate for each observation
  n is the number of observations
  actual is the observed development effort value.

MARE is strongly influenced by the effect of any significant outliers. To obtain a second perspective on the effectiveness of the prediction, the percentage of predictions which fell within 10%, 25% and 50% of the actual figure were also determined.

Research Methodology

The test data available was divided into 249 "training cases" to be held in the case base and 50 test cases to evaluate the quality of the model. The CBR model discussed above was used to retrieve cases most similar to the test case (using nearest neighbour matching). To determine the effect of averaging the estimates, the five nearest neighbours of each test case were retrieved. A comparative analysis was performed with results based on adaptation of a single case, adaptation and averaging of three cases and adaptation and averaging of five cases. Averaging using both arithmetic and geometric means was compared. As discussed below, the three case and five case average based on geometric rather than arithmetic means had similar prediction accuracy and both performed somewhat better than other approaches. The results for models using these averaging techniques are given in Tables 2a and 2b below. Given the similarity of the three and five case models it was decided to use the three case geometric mean model (3GEO) for further analysis as this simplified the overall processing required.

In order to assess whether nearest neighbour retrieval gives a better estimate than a purely random retrieval, the 3GEO CBR model was compared with estimates based on a random selection of cases. Each test case development effort was estimated as the geometric mean of three estimates calculated from the productivity of three randomly selected cases. The results are given in Table 3 below and the significance of any difference in Table 6.

In order to compare CBR with the use of regression models, a model based on a log-linear transformation of unadjusted function points together with the 14 general system characteristics was used. This had been shown in earlier research (Finnie *et al*, 1997) to be the best estimation model for the data set. In the earlier work, regression was performed on the 249 training cases with a variety of models to estimate development effort. The six models used were based on:

> unadjusted function points (UFP)
> function points (FP i.e. UFP adjusted by the general system characteristics)
> log-linear transformation of UFP and development effort
> log-linear transformation of FP and development effort
> multiple regression with UFP and the 14 general system characteristics
> multiple regression with log-linear UFP and the 14 gscs.

The regression model was used to predict development effort for each of the fifty test cases and the results compared with the best of the CBR models. The results are given in Table 4.

Table 2a : CBR prediction

	CBR (One Case)		CBR (3 cases, Arithmetic mean)	
Absolute Estimation Error	Freq %	Cum %	Freq %	Cum %
0-0.1	24%	24%	18%	18%
0.1-0.25	16%	40%	24%	42%
0.25-0.5	26%	66%	32%	76%
>0.5	34%	100%	24%	100%
MARE	0.426		0.362	

Table 2b : More CBR prediction

	CBR (3 cases, Geo. mean)		CBR (5 cases, Geo.mean)	
Absolute Estimation Error	Freq %	Cum %	Freq %	Cum %
0-0.1	20%	20%	24%	24%
0.1-0.25	24%	44%	22%	46%
0.25-0.5	32%	76%	38%	84%
>0.5	24%	100%	16%	100%
MARE	0.332		0.341	

Table 3: Comparing Nearest Neighbour with Random Selection

	CBR(3 cases, nearest neighbour, Geo. mean)		CBR(3 cases , random, Geo. mean)	
Absolute Estimation Error	Freq %	Cum %	Freq %	Cum %
0-0.1	20%	20%	6%	6%
0.1-0.25	24%	44%	18%	24%
0.25-0.5	32%	76%	42%	62%
>0.5	24%	100%	38%	100%
MARE	0.332		0.800	

As discussed above, the Remind CBR model included a number of rules to adapt the predicted effort in an attempt to account for any significant identified differences between the retrieved and the target case. The significant differences were in those gsc's which had been shown to have a significant influence on productivity in an analysis of the case base. The results of this comparison are given in Table 5.

Table 4 : CBR vs Regression

	CBR (3 cases, nearest neighbour, Geometric mean)		Regression	
Absolute Estimation Error	Freq %	Cum %	Freq %	Cum %
0-0.1	20%	20%	10%	10%
0.1-0.25	24%	44%	26%	36%
0.25-0.5	32%	76%	36%	72%
>0.5	24%	100%	28%	100%
MARE	0.332		0.623	

Table 5: Effect of adaptation

	CBR (3 cases, nearest neighbour, Geometric mean with adaptation)		CBR (3 cases, nearest neighbour, Geometric mean without adaptation)	
Absolute Estimation Error	Freq %	Cum %	Freq %	Cum %
0-0.1	20%	20%	24%	24%
0.1-0.25	24%	44%	26%	50%
0.25-0.5	32%	76%	22%	72%
>0.5	24%	100%	28%	100%
MARE	0.332		0.372	

Table 6 : Pairwise comparison of prediction accuracy

Comparison	t value (one tail - paired samples)	p
Regression vs CBR (geometric mean of 3 NN cases)	2.48	0.008**
CBR (one NN case) vs CBR (arithmetic mean of 3 NN cases)	1.16	0.12
CBR (one NN case) vs CBR (geometric mean of 3 NN cases)	1.844	0.03*
CBR (geometric mean of 3 NN cases) vs CBR (arithmetic mean of 3 NN cases)	1.55	0.06
CBR (geometric mean of 3 NN cases) vs CBR (geometric mean of 3 random cases)	2.88	0.003**
CBR (Adaptation) vs CBR (no adaptation)	1.0	0.16
CBR (geometric mean of 3 NN cases) vs CBR (geometric mean of 5 NN cases)	0.22	0.41

* significant at p<0.05
** significant at p<0.01

Discussion of Results

Overall the case-based reasoning paradigm appears to have significant potential for application to the software estimation problem. (All statistical results discussed in this section are based on paired sample two tailed t-tests). It performs much better than a regression model (MARE of 0.332 vs an MARE of 0.623, difference significant at p<0.01) based on the same data. As discussed by Finnie et al (1997), the CBR model appears to perform as well as a model based on neural networks but has an added advantage of some explanation capability.

The use of averaging appears necessary to improve the quality of the estimate. The estimates based on the single best case had an MARE of 0.426 while the estimate based on the geometric mean of the three nearest neighbour case estimates had an MARE of 0.332 (The difference is significant at p<0.05). Interestingly the geometric mean appears to produce better estimates than the arithmetic mean (an MARE of 0.332 vs 0.362). The difference is fairly strong but just not significant at the 0.05 level. (t=1.5, p=0.06). Lootsma (1997) has argued that the geometric mean is a powerful technique for aggregating ratio scale information, particularly when dealing with the relative values of criteria. Moving from an estimate based on the geometric mean of three nearest neighbours to five nearest neighbours has little impact on the MARE although there is a slight improvement in the number of predictions within 10% and within 25% of the actual.

The use of CBR is clearly better than an estimate based on a random selection of stored cases. The comparative MARE of 0.332 vs 0.8 (t=2.88) is significant at p < 0.005. Selecting those cases which are similar to the target provides a far more satisfactory estimate than one based on the productivity determined from random prior cases.

For this analysis rule-based adaptation of estimates does not appear to have a major effect. Although the MARE is somewhat better for the adapted sample (0.332 vs 0.372) the difference is not significant. However it is important to realise that the adaptation rules were to some extent based on the perceptions of the researchers and it is possible that different heuristic adaptations could be more effective. In addition the adaptation of these cases is based on a pure analysis of the data rather than the expert judgement of an individual familiar with the environment.

Conclusion

Case based reasoning has the potential to model the approach taken by human experts in software effort estimation. Expert judgement is a process of adaptation from experience of earlier software projects i.e. by reasoning from stored cases where the storage is human memory. The prediction accuracy of the CBR technique is at least as good as any of the other models in use.

As discussed in the section dealing with problems with software estimation models, estimation errors using existing techniques are large with the cited studies showing that MARE rates of 50% to 100% are common. The current CBR approach has an MARE of around 35% for the given data. Although the prediction is not particularly good, the noise in the data set is considerable. In addition the data was not calibrated for specific environments.

Case Based Reasoning has the advantage that the actual cases used in the estimation process can be retrieved and if necessary adapted further by any individual involved in the estimation process i.e. it allows the added use of human intuition and judgement. Although not adequately tested by this data a CBR system deployed as an expert estimation assistant would require more information relevant to the adaptation process, probably from analysis of human expert approaches. CBR allows the development of a dynamic case base with new project data being automatically incorporated into the case base as it becomes available.

References

Desharnais, J.M., et al. Adjustment Model for Function Points Scope Factors - A Statistical Study, *IFPUG Spring Conference*, Florida (1990) .

Ferens, D.V. & Gurner, R.B. An Evaluation of Three Function Point Models for Estimation of Software Effort, *IEEE National Aerospace and Electronics Conference – NAECON92*, Vol. 2, 625–642, (1992).

Finnie, G.R. & Wittig, G.E. AI Tools for Software Development Effort Estimation, *Proceedings of the Conference on Software Engineering : Education and Practice*, University of Otago, 113-120, (1996).

Finnie, G.R., Wittig, G.E. and Desharnais, J-M. A Comparison of Software Effort Estimation Techniques: Using Function Points with Neural Networks, Case Based Reasoning and Regression Models, to appear in *Journal of Systems and Software*, 1997.

Function Point Counting Practices Manual, Release 4.0 *International Function Point Users Group*, Blendonview Office Park, 5008–28 Pine Creek Drive, Westerville, OH 43081–4899, USA, (1994).

Heemstra, F.J. Software Cost Estimation, *Information and Software Technology*, vol. 34, no. 10, pp. 627–639, 1992.

Jeffery, D.R and Low, G.C.   Calibrating Estimation Tools for Software Development, *Software Engineering Journal*, 215–221, (July 1990).

Jeffery, D.R., Low, G.C. and Barnes, M. A Comparison of Function Point Counting Techniques, *IEEE Transactions on Software Engineering*, vol. 19, no. 5, 529–532, (1993).

Kemerer, C.F., An Empirical Validation of Software Cost Estimation Models, *Communications of the ACM*, vol. 30, no 5, 416–429, (1987).

Kemerer, C.F., Reliability of Function Points Measurement: A Field Experiment, *Communications of the ACM*, vol. 36, no 2, 85-97, (1993).

Lootsma, F.A., The Relative Importance of the Criteria in the Multiplicative AHP and SMART, to appear in *European Journal of Operations Research*, 1997.

Matson, J.E., Barrett, B.E. and Mellichamp, J.M., Software Development Cost Estimation Using Function Points, *IEEE Transactions on Software Engineering*, vol. 20, no. 4, 275–287, (1994).

Mukhopadhyay, T., Vicinanza, S.S. and Prietula, M.J., Examining the Feasibility of a Case-Based Reasoning Model for Software Effort Estimation, *MIS Quarterly*, vol. 16, no. 2, 155–171, (1992).

Srinivasan, K. and Fisher, D., Machine Learning Approaches to Estimating Software Development Effort, *IEEE Transactions on Software Engineering*, vol. 21, no. 2126-137, (1995).

Applying Case-Based Reasoning to Automated Deduction

Marc Fuchs[1] and Matthias Fuchs[2]

[1] Fakultät für Informatik, TU München, 80290 München, Germany
fuchsm@informatik.tu-muenchen.de
[2] Center for Learning Systems and Applications (LSA), Fachbereich Informatik,
Universität Kaiserslautern, 67663 Kaiserslautern, Germany
fuchs@informatik.uni-kl.de

Abstract. The use of CBR has been very profitable for many areas of artificial intelligence. Applying CBR to automated deduction, however, is a very intricate problem. The premise "small changes of a problem cause small changes of its solution" is definitely not satisfied by automated deduction. Therefore, case adaptation by means of symbolic proof transformation techniques is very limited.
In view of the fact that automated deduction essentially is a search problem, we propose to utilize case adaptation for selecting and configuring a search-guiding heuristic based on known cases. This also allows us to elegantly integrate methods for learning search-guiding heuristics which can significantly improve performance. The evaluation step of CBR corresponds to an attempt of the theorem prover at hand to solve a problem employing the heuristic provided by case adaptation. Experimental studies demonstrated that this approach is viable and actually produces promising results.

1 Introduction

Problems in automated deduction (AD) pose some of the hardest search problems. In view of the central role learning plays in human problem solving it was recognized very early that some form of machine learning would be crucial for improving the performance of AD systems. However, while in other areas of artificial intelligence machine learning has greatly contributed to the progress of research, in AD so far learning has not had a comparable impact on research. Most approaches have appeared only very recently (e.g., [17, 10, 14, 8, 7, 9]).

The main difficulty of learning in connection with AD is the fact that tiny variations of a problem often lead to significantly different solutions (*proofs*). This circumstance severely limits the applicability of analogous proof transformations by means of deterministic procedures. These procedures basically attempt to *compute* a proof of a (novel) *target problem* based on the known proof of a *source problem* and some kind of analogy or similarity detected in the specifications of target and source problem (e.g., [5, 10, 14]). Sophisticated patching strategies are required to enhance performance (e.g., [5]). Under these conditions, CBR does not appear to be a suitable machine-learning technique for AD since case adaptation—at first sight—amounts to proof transformation.

In [17] and more recently in [8], [7], and [9] it was demonstrated that it is also possible to *learn search-guiding heuristics*. A search-guiding heuristic learned from a source problem is used for searching for a proof of a target problem. This approach has proven to be quite successful and has several advantages. The most prominent advantage is that source and target problem do not have to be as similar as for proof transformation. Moreover, patching strategies are in a way integrated because the search for a proof is more flexible than a deterministic proof transformation. Therefore, search can compensate for (moderate) differences between source and target problem that proof transformation cannot cope with without falling back on specific patching strategies (cp. [5]). In this context, CBR can be used to configure (and learn) a search-guiding heuristic which then can be employed to search for a given target problem. Thus, CBR can be used to automate a crucial task usually performed by an *experienced* user.

2 CBR for Automated Deduction

We shall consider CBR for problem solving, i.e., solutions of new problems are derived using old solutions as a guide. Thus, we assume that a case base $CB = \{C_1, \ldots, C_n\}$ is given. Each case $C_i = (P_i, S_i)$ contains a problem P_i and a solution S_i of P_i. In order to solve a new *target problem* P_T via CBR we chose a process model similar to [12] that includes five steps: retrieval, adaptation, criticism, evaluation, and memory update.

In the context of AD, the problems to be solved are *proof problems*. A proof problem $\mathcal{A} = (Ax, \lambda_G)$ is specified by a set Ax of facts (*axioms*) and a fact λ_G (*goal*). We want to show that λ_G is a logical consequence of Ax (i.e., $Ax \models \lambda_G$). A fact may be a clause, or a general first or higher-order formula. It is construed using a set $\mathcal{P}$ of predicate symbols, a set $\mathcal{F}$ of function symbols, and a set $\mathcal{V}$ of variables. $\tau(p), \tau(f) \in \mathbb{N}$ denote the arity of each $p \in \mathcal{P}$ and $f \in \mathcal{F}$, respectively. Hence, the signature $sig = (\mathcal{P}, \mathcal{F}, \tau)$ contains syntactic information on predicate and function symbols that will play a role in retrieval and case adaptation. A *proof* $\wp$ of a proof problem $\mathcal{A}$ is a solution of $\mathcal{A}$.

Applying CBR to solving proof problems confronts us with the following task: Given a case base CB of solved proof problems (i.e., $C_i = (\mathcal{A}_i, \wp_i)$) and a target problem $\mathcal{A}_T$, find a source problem $\mathcal{A}_S$ in CB so that the solution $\wp_S$ of $\mathcal{A}_S$ can be used to solve $\mathcal{A}_T$, i.e., to find a proof $\wp_T$. Commonly, a proof is a symbolic representation of a reasoning process. Assuming such a proof representation, a first approach to case adaptation is to attempt to manipulate $\wp_S$ on a symbolic level so as to obtain $\wp_T$. As discussed in section 1, such a proof transformation involving little or no search is severely limited in the area of AD.

But when considering AD as a search process controlled by heuristic means, other kinds of adaptation than proof transformation become possible. Usually, an AD system has a variety of heuristics at its disposal. Choosing the "right" heuristic for the problem $\mathcal{A}$ at hand is crucial. The knowledge which heuristic to choose is in general not available a priori. CBR, however, can alleviate this difficulty by suggesting heuristics based on the cases in CB.

Thus, instead of providing (symbolic) proofs, CB provides search-guiding heuristics. In other words, instead of providing solutions, CB provides ways to obtain solutions. The advantages of this approach have already been outlined in section 1. Note that commonly heuristics are (extensively) parameterized. Case adaptation hence may include appropriately configuring parameters, possibly by employing machine-learning techniques. Taking all this into account, instead of $\wp_i$ the solution slot S_i of a case $C_i = (A_i, S_i)$ contains the heuristic $\mathcal{H}_i$ that was used to solve A_i and the decisions $\mathcal{D}_i$ made by $\mathcal{H}_i$. $\mathcal{D}_i$ is divided into positive and negative decisions P_i and N_i, respectively. The positive decisions P_i essentially correspond to $\wp_i$ and comprise the decisions that contributed to finding $\wp_i$. The negative decisions N_i basically represent redundant search effort, i.e., decisions that finally proved useless for finding $\wp_i$. These decisions P_i and N_i made in the past can be used to appropriately configure a heuristic usable for the target (cp. section 5). In summary, we employ the following CBR approach which we merely sketch here. Details will be addressed in the subsequent sections.

In the *retrieval* step a target problem $A_T = (Ax_T, \lambda_T)$ and its signature sig_T are used as search keys to find a case suitable for solving A_T. We use an explicit similarity measure sim_T defined on proof problems in sig_T for judging the similarity between A_T and the problem description of a case.

Adaptation corresponds to configuring a heuristic. The case selected in the retrieval step supplies information that can be used to configure a search-guiding heuristic. Usually, there will be the possibility to configure several different heuristics. After choosing the configuration possibility that appears to be most promising, learning techniques that support and agree with the chosen configuration method can be applied. That is, the adaptation step is the interface allowing us to integrate methods for learning search-guiding heuristics with CBR.

Criticism merely checks whether source and target problems A_S and A_T are "sufficiently" similar. This form of criticism may be coupled with the retrieval step: No case is returned if there is no sufficiently similar case.

In the *evaluation* step the heuristic configured in the adaptation step is used by the AD system at hand to search for a proof of the target problem A_T. Furthermore, some feedback is collected in order to allow for updating existing cases or for creating a new case. This feedback is used during *memory update* to modify the case base and possibly introduce new cases.

3   The Similarity Measure

A central point in CBR is the notion of similarity which is employed to find appropriate source cases from the case base CB. Basically, there are two different techniques for judging similarity: the *representational approach* (e.g., [11]) and the *computational approach* (e.g., [1]). In this paper we shall employ the computational approach, i.e., an explicit similarity measure sim_T.

In order to compute the similarity between a source problem A_S and the target A_T defined over sig_S and sig_T, respectively, it is necessary to become independent of specific names for symbols. To this end we employ a so-called *signature match* σ. σ is an injective, arity-preserving function that maps the function/predicate symbols of signature sig_S to function/predicate symbols of signature sig_T. σ can be easily extended to formulae and proof problems over sig_S. It is possible that none or several signature matches exist. We successively enumerate all signature matches σ from $\mathcal{A}_S$ to $\mathcal{A}_T$ and compute the similarity $sim_T(\sigma(\mathcal{A}_S), \mathcal{A}_T)$. Thus, we obtain similarity values between a case and the target w.r.t. different signature matches.

Using these similarity values we can construct an ordering $>_T$ defined on proof problems in sig_T (to be described shortly). $>_T$ will be defined so that $\mathcal{A}_1 >_T \mathcal{A}_2$ if $\mathcal{A}_1$ is more similar to the target $\mathcal{A}_T$ than $\mathcal{A}_2$. $>_T$ allows us to determine the cases most similar to the target. More exactly, with $>_T$ we can compute the cases $C_1, \ldots, C_m$ of CB and the matches $\sigma_{i1}, \ldots, \sigma_{in_i}$, $1 \le i \le m$, such that there is no other case $C = (\mathcal{A}, S)$ in CB and no signature match σ with $\sigma(\mathcal{A}) >_T \sigma_{ij}(\mathcal{A}_i)$. In order to simplify the notation, in the sequel we shall assume that a source problem $\mathcal{A}_S$ is given in the signature sig_T.

sim_T assesses the similarity of the problem descriptions of two proof problems. The design of sim_T is motivated by the fact that a target problem $\mathcal{A}_T = (Ax_T, \lambda_T)$ is proved by virtue of a proof of a source problem $\mathcal{A}_S = (Ax_S, \lambda_S)$, if all axioms of Ax_S are subsumed by axioms of the target problem, and the target goal λ_T is subsumed by the source goal λ_S. Hence, subsumption criteria like this will play the major role in our approach. Furthermore, refinements by using other criteria are reasonable (see below). These refinements have proven their usefulness in experiments, although naturally a simple proof replay often is impossible if Ax_S and Ax_T are similar in such a "weaker" way.

To realize measure sim_T we introduce a similarity rating sim_T^{form} defined on formulae. Let ax_1 and ax_2 be two formulae. We define $sim_T^{form}(ax_1, ax_2) \in [0; 1]$ by $sim_T^{form}(ax_1, ax_2) = \max\{rating(\rho_i) : \rho_i(ax_1, ax_2), 1 \le i \le N\}$. $\rho_1, \ldots, \rho_N$ are similarity criteria (predicates) defined on formulae. The function $rating$ reflects the reliability of a predicate for judging similarity between two formulae. Possible similarity criteria are the relations $\lhd$ and $\lhd_A$, where $\lhd$ denotes "plain" subsumption, and $\lhd_A$ subsumption modulo the theory given by a set of formulae A. (Here, we shall always use $A = AC$, i.e., associativity and commutativity). We employed $rating(\lhd) = 1$ and $rating(\lhd_A) = 0.8$. Note that we actually refined sim_T^{form} by adding further similarity criteria, thus increasing the ability to produce distinctive measures. But a description of these technical details is beyond the scope of this paper.

With the help of sim_T^{form} we are able to construct a similarity measure sim_T defined on proof problems. In the following let $\mathcal{A}_T = (Ax_T, \lambda_T)$ be a target problem and $\mathcal{A}_S = (Ax_S, \lambda_S)$ be a source problem (both given over sig_T). Let $Ax_T = \{ax_1, \ldots, ax_m\}$, $Ax_S = \{ax'_1, \ldots, ax'_n\}$ $(n, m > 0)$. The similarity of target and source problem is $sim_T(\mathcal{A}_S, \mathcal{A}_T) = (s_1, s_2, s_3) \in [0; 1]^3$, where

$$s_1 = \frac{1}{n} \cdot \sum_{i=1}^{n} \max\{sim_T^{form}(ax, ax'_i) : ax \in Ax_T\}$$

$$s_2 = \frac{1}{m} \cdot \sum_{i=1}^{m} \max\{sim_T^{form}(ax_i, ax') : ax' \in Ax_S\}$$

$$s_3 = sim_T^{form}(\lambda_S, \lambda_T)$$

Thus, s_1 judges the degree of "coverage" of Ax_S through similar axioms of Ax_T. For example, we have $s_1 = 1$ if all source axioms are subsumed by target axioms. s_1 decreases if only weaker similarity criteria are fulfilled. The value s_2 represents the percentage of target axioms that have a similar counterpart in Ax_S. Additional axioms in Ax_T do not prevent the source proof from being applicable (in the case $s_1 = 1$), but may complicate the search for this proof. Finally, s_3 measures the similarity between target and source goal λ_T and λ_S. We have $s_3 = 1$ if λ_S subsumes λ_T ($\lambda_S \lhd \lambda_T$) or $s_3 = 0.8$ if $\lambda_S \lhd_A \lambda_T$.

With sim_T we can define $>_T$. Let $\mathcal{A}_1$ and $\mathcal{A}_2$ be two proof problems in sig_T. Let $sim_T(\mathcal{A}_1, \mathcal{A}_T) = (s_1, s_2, s_3)$ and $sim_T(\mathcal{A}_2, \mathcal{A}_T) = (s'_1, s'_2, s'_3)$. We define $>_T$ by $\mathcal{A}_1 >_T \mathcal{A}_2$ iff $s_1 > s'_1 \wedge s_2 > s'_2 \wedge s_3 > s'_3$. $>_T$ is a rather weak ordering, but it has proven to be adequate in our experiments.

4 The Structure of the Case Base

Since we have chosen a computational approach for similarity assessment in order to find a case most similar to the target, organizing the case base as a simple linear list (denoted by CB_L) will in general be insufficient. The unsatisfactory performance of CB_L (especially for retrieval) is due to the fact that we did not compile knowledge on the similarity of cases into the case base, thus allowing for more efficient retrieval mechanisms. Therefore, in the following we shall introduce a hierarchical storage scheme that—unlike CB_L—very often circumvents the exhaustive examination of the whole case base. Furthermore, we want to emphasize that the storage scheme offers the potential to speed up the examination of certain cases by utilizing information on previously examined cases.

The central idea is to collect the cases in so-called *case classes*. Let $CB = \{C_1, \ldots, C_n\}$. We define an equivalence relation $\approx$ on cases by $C_i \approx C_j$ iff $C_i = (\mathcal{A}_i, S_i)$, $C_j = (\mathcal{A}_j, S_j)$, and $\mathcal{A}_i \approx^A \mathcal{A}_j$. We define $\mathcal{A}_i \approx^A \mathcal{A}_j$ iff $\mathcal{A}_i = (Ax_i, \lambda_i)$, $\mathcal{A}_j = (Ax_j, \lambda_j)$, and there exists a bijective signature match σ such that $\sigma(Ax_i)$ and Ax_j are equal modulo renaming the (implicitly universally quantified) variables. Using $\approx$ we can divide CB into disjunct case classes $CB = \cup_{i \in J}[C_i]_{\approx}$, $J \subseteq \{1, \ldots, n\}$. Note that—because of the bijectivity requirement—it is sufficient to compute the values s_1 and s_2 for only *one* representative C of a case class w.r.t. $\mathcal{A}_T$ in order to obtain the values for all cases $C' \in [C]_{\approx}$. Thus, a significant speed-up of the computation of sim_T can be achieved.

Furthermore, we can represent hierarchical relations between the classes by using a subset relation $\sqsubseteq \subseteq 2^{CB} \times 2^{CB}$. We say $[C_1]_{\approx} \sqsubseteq [C_2]_{\approx}$ iff there exists a signature match σ such that $\sigma(Ax_1)$ is a subset of Ax_2 (modulo renaming variables). The information on subset relations between case classes can be used to compute sim_T more efficiently. On the one hand it is possible to use *positive* information on similarities between axioms from Ax_1 and Ax_T in order to compute the similarity between problem A_2 and A_T. On the other hand *negative* information can be utilized. E.g., if there is no signature match from A_1 to A_T then there is also no signature match from A_2 to A_T.

We represent this semantical information with a directed acyclic graph $G = (V, E)$. Each node $v \in V$ represents a case class. Furthermore, an edge $(v_i, v_j) \in E$ iff the case classes associated with v_i and v_j are in subset relation. This hierarchical case base will be denoted by CB_H.

5 Realization of the Process Model

In this section we shall describe in some more detail how the different steps of the process model sketched in section 2 are realized.

Retrieval: In the retrieval process the nodes of the graph representing CB_H are examined. Naturally, this examination is done in a pre-order style to reuse the information obtained from predecessor nodes in the graph. As mentioned previously, we spare ourselves the examination of successors of a node v (representing case class $[C]_\approx$) if no signature match exists from the case signature to the target signature. Furthermore, we pass information on similarities between axioms of case C w.r.t. a signature match to the successor nodes of v.

After examining the case classes, possibly a lot of different cases (with more than one signature match) are identified to be most similar to the target. We randomly select one of these cases (and a signature match) to be the "best" case for the target. In the future other criteria for selecting a case can be employed.

Adaptation: Adaptation corresponds to configuring (learning) a heuristic (cp. section 2). The solution slot S of a case contains the heuristic $\mathcal{H}$ and the decisions D made by $\mathcal{H}$ in order to solve the respective problem.

Basically, there are two different machine-learning techniques to configure a heuristic using $\mathcal{H}$ and D. (Recall that D is subdivided into positive and negative decisions P and N.) On the one hand *implicit approaches* are applicable where a heuristic is learned using the decisions D, but no explicit use of D is made during the application of the heuristic to solve the target. E.g., in [8] parameters of a general heuristic (e.g., $\mathcal{H}$ itself) were tuned in order to speed up the search for a source proof. On the other hand *explicit approaches* are applicable where the information D is explicitly taken into account by a heuristic (e.g., [9]). In this context, designing a heuristic amounts to the construction of a similarity measure so as to force decisions similar to those from P. Besides these two machine-learning approaches, it is of course also possible to simply use the "source heuristic" $\mathcal{H}$ (kind of a memory-based configuration method).

Among all the configuration possibilities one must be chosen. There are certain (heuristic) criteria which can be employed to facilitate this choice. For instance, the method introduced in [8] works best if the signature of the target problem comprises many symbols. (Technical details on this issue are beyond the scope of this paper.) The chosen configuration method is executed, and finally the signature match that comes with the source case selected during retrieval is applied to those parts of the configured heuristic that are linked with the signature of the source problem. For time-consuming methods which are independent of a target problem (like [8]), it is advisable to pre-process new cases during memory update. Thus, so to speak pre-configured heuristics are provided which then only need to be adapted to the target signature with the signature match.

Criticism: In the criticism phase we check whether the source problem $\mathcal{A}_S$ (given over sig_T) and the target problem $\mathcal{A}_T$ fulfill a *minimal similarity predicate ms*. Let $sim_T(\mathcal{A}_S, \mathcal{A}_T) = (s_1, s_2, s_3)$. We check if ms is fulfilled with $ms(sim_T(\mathcal{A}_S, \mathcal{A}_T))$ iff $c_1 \cdot s_1 + c_2 \cdot s_2 + c_3 \cdot s_3 \geq min$, where $c_1, c_2, c_3 \in \mathbb{R}$, and $min \in \mathbb{R}$ is a threshold. Actually, we use $c_1 = 3$, $c_2 = 1$, $c_3 = 2$, and $min = 1$. Hence, a subsumption of one third of the axioms of Ax_S, or no superfluous target axioms, or a subsumed target goal each suffice alone to reach the threshold.

Evaluation: The heuristic configured in the adaptation step is used by the AD system at hand. If a given time-out T is exceeded, the search is considered a failure. The feedback 'failure' is used in the memory update phase. If a proof of $\mathcal{A}_T$ could be found, the feedback is 'success', and the positive and negative decisions made during the search for the proof are identified. These decisions constitute $\mathcal{D}_T$ which is then utilized during memory update.

Memory Update: The case memory is updated according to the feedback obtained in the evaluation step. If the feedback 'success' is returned, the decisions $\mathcal{D}_T$ are analyzed in order to determine whether a new case should be created. Essentially, if the target problem could be proven very easily (rather few negative decisions or redundant search effort), then there is no need for a new case because the cases in CB_H seem to be sufficient. Otherwise, a new case is added to CB_H. This can entail the creation of a new internal structure of the graph representing the case base by generating a new node and new edges. If the feedback 'failure' is returned the source case is examined. A source case that shows a bad reuse behavior (high failure rate) is deleted from the case base. In order to provide more general mechanisms to learn from misleading retrieval results, it is reasonable to develop mechanisms for adapting the similarity measure in the future (e.g., learn the relevance (ratings) of the similarity criteria, cp. [2])

6 Experiments

In order to estimate the usefulness of our approach to using CBR in the area of AD, we performed several experiments with the DISCOUNT system ([3]) on a SPARCstation 10. DISCOUNT is a prover for pure equational logic based on the unfailing completion procedure (cf. [4]). We experimented with problems from the TPTP library v1.2.0 ([16]), a standardized problem library for AD. In this section we shall present the results we obtained in the area of groups and lattice-ordered groups (GRP domain). The efficiency of our approach will be demonstrated by comparisons with conventional heuristics of DISCOUNT and with the prover OTTER in its "autonomous mode" which automatically selects an appropriate search-guiding heuristic based on simple built-in selection mechanisms (cp. [13]). Since OTTER has won the CADE-13 theorem prover competition

([15]) in the category "Unit Equality Problems" (to which the GRP domain belongs) a comparison with the current state-of-the-art is provided. In the sequel, we present the principles of our solution process and experimental results.

Solution Process: In order to use CBR techniques to solve the problems in the GRP domain we need at first a case base CB_H containing some solved problems. To this end, in the *initialization phase* we start with $CB_H = \emptyset$ and add all those problems (cases) to CB_H that two "conventional heuristics " Υ_1 and Υ_2 of DISCOUNT which proved very profitable for problems of the GRP domain (and do not use CBR) can solve within a given period of time. (Technical details on this issue are irrelevant to this paper. See, e.g., [6].) We use the time-out $T = 1$ minute to keep the time for the initialization phase rather small.

Starting with this initial CB_H we attempt to solve the problems that are still unsolved by using CBR. Since a change of CB_H by inserting a solved problem can influence the CBR process it is sensible to choose a cyclic solution process to solve the unsolved problems. In each cycle all of the problems that are still unsolved are tackled with CBR in the lexicographical order of their names. But DISCOUNT tries to solve a problem again only if CB_H has changed since the most recent attempt to solve the problem. Therefore, the solution process stops as soon as there is no change of CB_H during a cycle. Since applying this cyclic process entails that a problem is possibly often tackled with different source proofs, we chose quite small a time-out T_{cbr} when using CBR to minimize the time for unsuccessful proof runs. For our experiments we set $T_{cbr} = 3$ min, whereas the time-out is 10 min for OTTER and DISCOUNT employing Υ_1 and Υ_2.

Experimental Results: In the initialization phase DISCOUNT proved 99 of 125 problems which were inserted into CB_H. The first three rows of table 1 show the three problems solved during the initialization phase which were later used as sources. The remainder of table 1 displays the problems DISCOUNT could then solve by using CBR. (Problems not listed here and not solved during the initialization phase could also not be solved by OTTER.) The table is organized as follows: The first two columns list the names of the target problems and the names of the source problems suggested by CBR, respectively. The third column shows the run-time of a successful DISCOUNT run using CBR. This run-time only comprises the time needed to retrieve a similar source problem and to find a solution in the following deduction process (retrieval time < 3s for the hierarchical CB_H). Depending on the way CBR is viewed, the one minute of each failed attempt with Υ_1 or Υ_2 during the initialization phase may or may not be taken into account. Note that it does not make sense to consider the time needed for solving a source problem in CB_H nor the time spent on updating CB_H, because this effort is made only once for each new case and from then on a case in CB_H can be utilized over and over again at no additional cost. Finally, columns 4–6 show the run-times of OTTER and DISCOUNT (using Υ_1 or Υ_2, respectively). The entry '—' denotes exceeding the time-out of 10 minutes.

The clustering of the rows indicates the cycle during which CBR succeeded. (The initialization phase is cycle 0.) Note that during a cycle not only the problems of previous cycles can become source problems, but also problems of the

Table 1. Experiments in the GRP domain.

Target	Source	CBR	OTTER	DISCOUNT Υ_1	DISCOUNT Υ_2
GRP190-1			2s	3s	2s
GRP191-1			2s	2s	2s
GRP179-1			—	—	12s
GRP169-1	GRP191-1	36s	4s	—	—
GRP169-2	GRP190-1	38s	4s	—	—
GRP179-2	GRP179-1	37s	—	—	—
GRP179-3	GRP179-1	38s	—	—	—
GRP183-1	GRP179-2	40s	—	—	—
GRP183-2	GRP183-1	42s	—	—	—
GRP183-3	GRP183-1	40s	—	—	—
GRP183-4	GRP183-1	42s	—	—	—
GRP186-1	GRP179-1	41s	—	—	—
GRP186-2	GRP179-1	40s	—	—	—
GRP167-3	GRP183-1	129s	—	—	—
GRP167-4	GRP183-1	130s	—	—	—
GRP167-1	GRP167-3	32s	—	—	—
GRP167-2	GRP167-4	35s	—	—	—

same cycle: E.g., in cycle 1 (second cluster of rows), target problems GRP183-i ($i > 1$) can be proved using source problem GRP183-1 which was proved in the same cycle. This is possible because GRP183-1 precedes GRP183-2 etc. in the lexicographic order of names. GRP167-3 and GRP167-4 can also be proved with GRP183-1. But their names precede GRP183-1 and therefore they "have to wait" until cycle 2. A problem proved in cycle $i > 1$ caused $i - 1$ failures before. Even if we added $(i - 1) \cdot 3$ min to the run-times of CBR (possibly also adding the 2 min stemming from the initialization phase) the total time would still be less than the time-out of 10 minutes for OTTER and DISCOUNT without CBR.

We can observe a significant improvement of the success rate comparing CBR with OTTER and DISCOUNT (without CBR). CBR solves 113 problems (90%), whereas OTTER and DISCOUNT solve 93 (74%) and 99 (79%), respectively.

7 Discussion

Applying CBR to automated deduction is a difficult task. In this paper we proposed to use CBR to configure a search-guiding heuristic based on previous cases in order to tackle a given target problem. Thus, CBR in a way supplies instructions on how to conduct the search. When employed in this manner, CBR flexibly automates a crucial task that is usually performed by the user or some rigid built-in mechanism as in the renowned theorem prover OTTER. Compared to proof transformation techniques, this approach has the advantage of having a wider range of applicability because the similarity demands are not so high.

Nonetheless, the similarity measure plays a central role in the retrieval phase of our CBR model. The intuitively sensible design of the similarity measure and our experimental results support the viability of our approach. We believe that the similarity measure can (and needs to) be improved by adapting it based on failure/success statistics. Furthermore, our current mechanisms for deciding whether a solved problem should become a new case are very crude first ideas which nevertheless work quite well.

References

1. **Aha, D.W.:** *Case-based Learning Algorithms*, Proc. Case-based Reasoning Workshop, Morgan Kaufmann Publishers, 1991.
2. **Althoff, K.-D.; Wess, S.:** *Case-Based Knowledge Acquisition, Learning and Problem Solving in Diagnostic Real World Tasks*, Proc. EKAW, 1991, pp. 48–67.
3. **Avenhaus, J.; Denzinger, J.; Fuchs, M.:** *DISCOUNT: A System For Distributed Equational Deduction*, Proc. 6th RTA, 1995, Springer LNCS 914, pp. 397–402.
4. **Bachmair, L.; Dershowitz, N.; Plaisted, D.:** *Completion without Failure*, Coll. on the Resolution of Equations in Algebraic Structures, Austin, TX, USA (1987), Academic Press, 1989.
5. **Brock, B.; Cooper, S.; Pierce, W.:** *Analogical reasoning and proof discovery*, Proc. CADE-9, 1988, Springer LNCS 310, pp. 454–468.
6. **Denzinger, J.; Fuchs, M.:** *Goal-oriented equational theorem proving using teamwork*, Proc. 18th KI-94, 1994, Springer LNAI 861, pp. 343–354.
7. **Denzinger J.; Schulz, S.:** *Learning Domain Knowledge to Improve Theorem Proving*, Proc. CADE-13, 1996, Springer LNAI 1104, pp. 62–76.
8. **Fuchs, M.:** *Learning proof heuristics by adapting parameters*, Proc. 12th ICML, 1995, Morgan Kaufmann, pp. 235–243.
9. **Fuchs, M.:** *Experiments in the Heuristic Use of Past Proof Experience*, Proc. CADE-13, 1996, Springer LNAI 1104, pp. 523–537.
10. **Kolbe, T.; Walther, C.:** *Reusing proofs*, Proc. 11th ECAI '94, 1994, pp. 80–84.
11. **Kolodner, J.L.:** *Retrieval and Organizational Strategies in Conceptual Memory*, Ph.D. Thesis, Yale University, 1980.
12. **Kolodner, J.L.:** *An Introduction to Case-Based Reasoning*, Artificial Intelligence Review **6**:3–34, 1992.
13. **McCune, W.W.:** *OTTER 3.0 reference manual and guide*, Techn. Report ANL-94/6, Argonne Natl. Laboratory, 1994.
14. **Melis, E.:** *A model of analogy-driven proof-plan construction*, Proc. 14th IJCAI, 1995, pp. 182–189.
15. **Sutcliffe, G.; Suttner, C.:** *First ATP System Competition* held on August 1 in conjunction with the 13th International Conference on Automated Deduction (CADE-13), New Brunswick, NJ, USA, 1996; Competition results available via WWW at http://wwwjessen.informatik.tu-muenchen.de/~tptp/CASC-13.
16. **Sutcliffe, G.; Suttner, C.B.; Yemenis, T.:** *The TPTP Problem Library*, Proc. CADE-12, 1994, Springer LNAI 814, pp. 252–266.
17. **Suttner, C.; Ertel, W.:** *Automatic acquisition of search-guiding heuristics*, Proc. CADE-10, 1990, Springer LNAI 449, pp. 470–484.

A Case-Based Approach for Elaboration of Design Requirements

Paulo Gomes[1,2]

[1] ISEC - Instituto Superior de Engenharia
de Coimbra

Quinta da Nora, 3030 Coimbra
pgomes@sun.isec.pt

Carlos Bento[2]

[2] CISUC - Centro de Informática e
Sistemas da Universidade de Coimbra

Polo II - Universidade de Coimbra, 3030
Coimbra

{pgomes|bento}@eden.dei.uc.pt

Abstract

The process of Case-Based Creative Design comprises: problem specification, problem elaboration, case retrieval, case adaptation, and verification. Problem specification and elaboration are crucial stages in the design process. Notwithstanding most of the current systems do not address this phase, assuming that the problem is well defined and complete, which is not a valid assumption for most of the situations.

In this paper we propose a case-based method for problem elaboration. Old design episodes are used for problem specification and elaboration. Through the use of a graphical editor the user explores a set of alternative problem specifications. This helps the user in the problem specification task. If the problem still remains ill or incompletely defined, a problem elaboration method is used to complete the problem specification based on a library of cases and domain knowledge.

1. Introduction

Design is a complex activity that is generally ill-structured and requires a great amount of different types of knowledge (Reich 1991). It comprises creation of a structure complying with a set of functional specifications and constraints (Tong & Sriram 1992).

Design can be divided into routine and non-routine design (Gero 1994). We use the term *routine design* when the designer is *a priori* acquainted with the necessary knowledge. In this way routine design comprises parametric variations of old designs. *Non-routine design* involves two sub-classes: (1) innovative and (2) creative design. In *innovative design* a new artifact is generated from a known class of designs, but differs from previous class artifacts in some substantive way. This can occur, for instance, in terms of value(s) assigned to the design variables which are specific to the new solution. In *creative design* the space of possible design alternatives is expanded through the use of new design variables. This takes place when the space of potential designs is extensive and is not entirely defined by the knowledge available to the user. In creative design the process of specifying the design requirements is also viewed as an important phase (Tong & Sriram 1992 , Kolodner & Wills 1993).

In this paper we present the problem specification and problem elaboration phases in CREATOR, which is a case-based reasoning shell for creative design. In the problem specification phase a graphical editor is used to help the user identifying the desired design functionalities. CREATOR uses its memory structure to perform problem elaboration in order to complete the design requirements. Two types of knowledge represented in the memory structure are used for problem elaboration: a hierarchy of functionalities and the problem descriptions of cases in memory.

In the next section we present the case representation we adopted in CREATOR. Section three shows the memory structure that supports the whole process. Section 4 presents how the graphic editor assists the user to carry out the problem specification. We describe the algorithm for problem elaboration, and show how CREATOR uses cases for problem elaboration. In section 5 we give an example in the domain of specification of room configuration. Section 6 describes related work. In section 7 we present some conclusions and future work directions.

2. Case Representation

Within our framework *design episodes* are represented in the form of SBF models (Goel 1992, Stroulia et al. 1992). These models are based on the component-substance ontology developed by Bylander and Chandrasekaran (Bylander and Chandrasekaran 1985). A case comprises three different parts: Problem Specification (Function); Explanation (Behavior); Design Solution (Structure).

The problem specification comprises a set of *high level functionalities* (HLF) and *functional specifications* (FS) that must be exhibit by the design. The explanation is in the form of a causal structure, representing the design behavior. The case solution describes the design structures that accomplish the desired functionalities described in the target problem.

A design problem is represented by a tree of functionalities, where leaves are FSs and the high levels in the tree represent HLFs. HLFs are abstract functionalities, used to help the user in specifying the design problem. Each leaf in the tree represents a Functional Specification in a schema comprising the following slots:

- *Given*: The initial behavior state.
- *Makes*: The final behavior state.
- *By-Behavior*: Behavior constraints.
- *Stimulus*: External stimulus to the design.
- *Provided*: Structural constraints.

Figure 1b specifies functionalities associated with the bedroom sketched in figure 1a. The abstract goal is to design a bedroom. This HLF comprises two FSs: Sleeping1 and Resting1, meaning that the bedroom must allow people to sleep and rest. For example, functionality Sleeping1 comprises the final behavioral and initial behavioral states (*Makes* and *Given* slots). The *Makes* slot describes that exist a Person, located in Bed1, laid, and with mental state asleep. The *Given* slot defines the initial conditions, which comprise the existence of a Person with awake mental state.

The *design solution* is in the form of a hierarchy of device structures. Each structure can be viewed as a set of device structures where substances can flow through. The structure schema is as follows:

- *Is-a-part-of*: the super structure of the structure.

- *Consists-of*: the sub-structures of the structure.
- *Is-a*: the class of the structure.
- *Relations*: structural relations with other structures.
- *Properties*: structure properties.
- *Functions*: the structure primitive functions.
- *Modes*: the operation states of the structure.

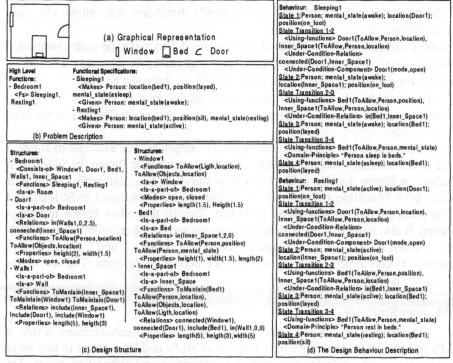

Figure 1 - Case representation of a bedroom.

Figure 1c describes the bedroom structure which comprises a door, a window, the walls, a bed, and the inner space. The first structure described is the Bedroom1. It consists in Window1, Door1, Bed1, Walls1, and Inner_Space1. The class of Bedroom1 is Room. In the description of the other structures is defined the superstructure (Is-a-part-of slot), in this case Bedroom1, the class of the structure (Is-a slot), the primitive functions performed by each structure (Functions slot), relations with other structures (Relations slot), properties of the structure (Properties slot), and the functioning states of the structure (Modes slot). For example, one of the functions of Door1 is to allow the location of Person to change (ToAllow(Person,location)). Relations comprise a predicate functor representing the relation name, and a list of arguments describing relation parameters. Properties describe structure characteristics, for example height(2) represents that Door1 is 2 meters high. Modes are represented by a word describing the possible operation modes. For example, Door1 has two functioning modes: open or closed. Most of the times modes are treated as constraints.

A *case explanation* describes the causal behavior of the design in terms of directed graphs (DGs). The nodes of a DG represent behavioral states and the edges represent state transitions. A *behavioral state* can be composed by one or more substance schemas. A *substance schema* characterizes the properties and the property values of a substance. A *state transition* represents the conditions under which the transition between behavioral states occurs. A state transition is represented by a schema with the following slots:

- *Using-functions*: The primitive component's functions that allow the state transition.
- *Under-condition-relation*: structural relations needed to make the state transition.
- *Domain-principle*: domain principles or laws responsible for the state transition.
- *Under-condition-component*: component conditions that must be met.
- *Under-condition-substance*: substance conditions that must be met.
- *Under-condition-transition*: other state transitions that are influential to the state transition.

Figure 1d presents the Sleeping1 and Resting1 behaviors. For example in figure 1 there is one substance schemas representing the properties of Person, in State1. It is a substance Person, located in Door1, with position on_foot, and with mental state awake. State Transition 1-2 says that the transformation from State1 to State2 is due to the primitive functions of Door1 and Inner_Space1, that allow Person to change location. It also states that the transition is constrained by the relation that represents the existence of a connection between Door1 and Inner_Space1 (connected(Door1,Inner_Space1)), and that the door must be open. The rest of the description is analogous.

3. Memory Structure

The memory structure comprises two interconnected substructures: a tree of HLFs and FSs, and a graph of cases. The tree of HLFs and FSs is used in two ways. One is in providing help for the problem specification and elaboration phase. The other role is in retrieving the starting cases. The starting cases are all the cases with at least one FSs in common with the new problem. These cases are used as starting points in the graph of cases for exploration of the episode memory, making possible for the searching mechanism to incrementally retrieve neighbor cases

The tree of HLFs and FSs comprises three different types of nodes and three types of links (see figure 2). Nodes are of type: HLF class, HLF instance, and LF node (a LF node comprises a list of HLFs and/or FSs). Connections between nodes are of type: hlf_ako, hlf_isa, and lfs_comp links. A hlf_ako link represents that a HLF class is a kind of a HLF superclass. A hlf_isa link represents that a HLF instance is a HLF class. A lfs_comp link connect a list of functionalities (HLFs and/or FSs) to a HLF instance. This kind of connection represents a partonomic relation between a HLF instance and the list of HLFs and FSs in the LF node.

In the graph of cases nodes represent episodes, and edges represent functional differences between cases. In figure 2 *Case1* is connected to *Case2* by the link *Differences1-2*. This link represents the functional differences between *Case1* and *Case2* problem descriptions.

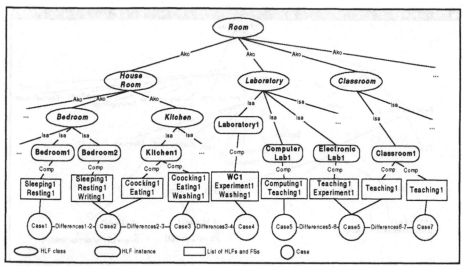

Figure 2 - Example of a memory structure in the domain of room configuration.

A difference link is created only when the cases that it connects have at least one Functional Specification in common. A difference link connecting two cases, comprises three parts:

• The set of FSs that belong to the first case but do not belong to the second one.
• The set of FSs that belong to the second one but do not belong to the first one.
• The set of differences in the FSs common to both cases.

Case links are automatically generated, when a new case is stored in the case library.

4. Problem Elaboration

Design specifications are often ill-defined or incomplete. This is particularly common in creative design. The process of problem elaboration tries to create a full description of the design requirements. Kolodner & Wills (Kolodner & Wills 1993) call it the process of "designing the design specification". Defining the design problem takes place in two phases. The first step is done by the designer, and the second one is performed by the system.

4.1 Helping the user specifying the problem

In our system the first step comprises the definition by the designer of the HLFs and FSs in the new problem. She/he makes use of the graphical editor which shows the relevant part of the memory structure for the elaboration process. The memory structure presented to the user is a hierarchy of HLFs and LF nodes, like in figure 2, with the difference that it does not show cases and connections between them (see figure 3).

The user can perform several operations on the nodes and each type of node has associated a set of available operations.

High Level Function classes can be expanded (e.g. subclasses and/or instances are displayed), collapsed (e.g. subclasses and instances are hidden), and new High Level Function instances can be linked to a class.

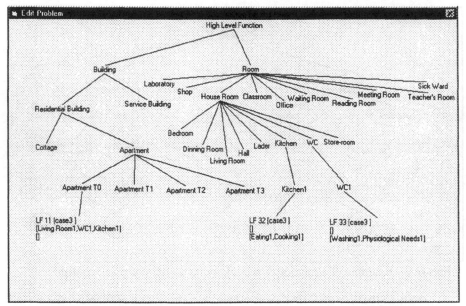

Figure 3 - CREATOR's graphic editor with a problem description.

High Level Function instances can be expanded (e.g. LF nodes are displayed), collapsed (e.g. LF nodes are hidden), new LF nodes can be linked to it, and it can be added to the new problem specification.

LFs can be added to the new problem specification, and can have its contents modified. When a user selects a LF node the lfs_comp link and High Level Function instance associated to it are automatically added to the new problem specification. The problem specification phase results into a set of High Level Function instances, LF nodes, and lfs_comp links. At the beginning, the graphical editor shows only the root node.

As we denoted before a problem specification may be incomplete. A High Level Function instance belonging to the problem specification is said to be incomplete if:

(a) does not have any lfs_comp link connecting it to a LF node; or

(b) occurs in a LF node, and does not have any corresponding complete High Level Function instance in the problem (a complete High Level Function has at least one non-empty LF node).

As an example, *Problem1* in figure 4 is incomplete because the High Level Function Bedroom1 satisfies condition (a). *Problem2* is also incomplete because WC1 satisfies condition (b). *Problem3* is complete because all the High Level Function instances and High Level Functions in LF nodes are completely specified.

The problem specification can be more general or more specific depending on the number of complete HLFs it comprises. The more complete HLFs incorporated in the new problem, the more specific the problem description becomes. On the opposite side, selecting a higher number of incomplete HLFs results into a more general problem. This defines a relation between the number of incomplete HLFs and the number of alternative solutions for the problem. In this way when the problem is completely defined the system generates solutions for a single problem. On the other hand, when the specification is incomplete, the system creates solutions for a class of problems. In the framework of creative design incomplete specifications result into a richer set of alternative solutions with the drawback of increasing the computational demands of the system. In the next section we describe the elaboration process that takes place when the problem is not completely specified.

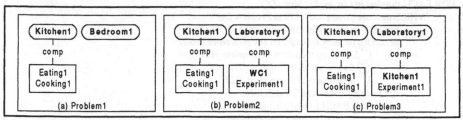

Figure 4 - (a) and (b) incomplete problem specifications, (c) a complete problem specification.

4.2 Algorithm for problem elaboration

When the problem specification comprises incomplete HLFs the system uses the algorithm described in figure 5 for problem elaboration.

The system will try to elaborate all the problems in *List_of_Problems* (step 1 of figure 5). A problem is elaborated until it comprises only complete HLFs (step 2). If a High Level Function is incomplete, the algorithm searches for the respective node in the memory structure (step 3 and 4). If the node has lfs_comp links (step 5), the system creates a new copy of the problem specification for each link (step 7) and adds the LF node (that one the lfs_comp link connects) to each problem copy (step 8). Each new problem is added to *List_of_Problems* (step 9). If lfs_comp links are not found in memory (step 11), the algorithm searches for subclasses of the *Incomplete_HLF*. If subclasses are found (step 12), the system creates a new copy of the problem for each subclass (step 14) and replaces in each copy the *Incomplete_HLF* by the subclass in memory (step 15). The new problems created are appended to *List_of_Problems* (step 16). If no subclasses are found (step19), the superclass of the *Incomplete_HLF* replaces it in the problem (step 20). After all High Level Function instances are complete, several design problem alternatives are generated by the system.

5. Example

CREATOR evolved from IM-RECIDE (Gomes et. Al. 1996), an independent domain reasoning shell. The domain chosen for tests, was the building/room configuration. The case library has 36 cases describing various buildings comprising various rooms. Like schools, restaurants, etc. We present an example in CREATOR from the beginning of the problem specification till the alternative problem specifications produced by the system.

We consider a decorator who wants to design the displacement of furniture in an apartment. So, She/he uses CREATOR's graphic editor to help her/him in the problem specification task. After using the graphic editors she/he establishes the problem specification (see figure 3). Note that in the figure it is not possible to distinguish the kinds of nodes. This happens because in the editor types of nodes are drawn using different colours.

```
1. FOR EACH Problem in List_of_Problems DO
2.        WHILE there are incomplete HLFs in Problem DO
3.            SELECT an incomplete HLF (Incomplete_HLF)
4.            Search the memory structure for (by preference order):
                  1st Lfs_comp links from Incomplete_HLF
                  2nd Subclasses of Incomplete_HLF
                  3rd Superclasse of Incomplete_HLF
5.            IF Lfs_comp links were found THEN
6.                FOR EACH Lfs_comp link DO
7.                    Make a copy of the Problem
8.                    Complete the Incomplete_HLF using the list of HLFs and list of FSs in the LF
                          node connected by the lfs_comp link
9.                    Add New_Problem to List_of_Problems
10.               END FOR
11.           ELSE
12.               IF subclasses were found THEN
13.                   FOR EACH subclass DO
14.                       Make a copy of the Problem
15.                       Replace the Incomplete_HLF by the subclass
16.                       Add New_Problem to List_of_Problems
17.                   END FOR
18.               ELSE
19.                   IF superclass was found THEN
20.                       Replace the Incomplete_HLF by the superclass
21.                   END IF
22.               END IF
23.           END IF
24.       END WHILE
25. END FOR
```

Figure 5 - Algorithm for Problem Elaboration.

The problem specification comprises three High Level Function instance nodes, and three LF nodes. High Level Function instance nodes are: Apartment T0, Kitchen1, and WC1. LF nodes are: LF11 [Living Room1, WC1, Kitchen1], LF32 [Sleeping1, Resting1, Storing1], and LF33 [Washing1, Physiological Needs1]. All LFs belong to case3, because this case is the most similar one to the problem. The problem is not completely specified, because Living Room1 is incomplete. So, CREATOR began the problem elaboration process trying to complete Living Room1. It starts by searching for lfs_comp links, and it found seven links. Seven problems are generated using the specification of Living Room1 in seven different cases in the episodic memory.

Figure 6 presents the problems generated by CREATOR. Problems 2, 3, and 4 have the same FSs for Living Room1, but they differ at the Functional Specification description level. The same happens to problem 6 and 7.

The decorator selected *Problem1* because it has the most adequate description for an apartment without bedroom (sleeping). He could have also modified any problem in order to arrange it, or could have selected more than one problem.

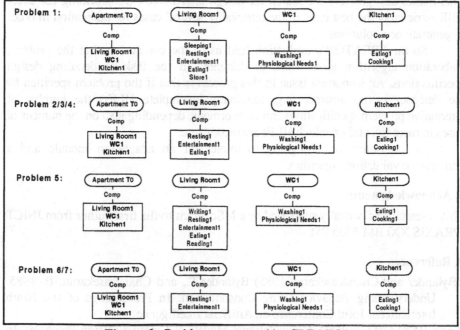

Figure 6 - Problems generated by CREATOR.

6. Related Work

Few work in the area of problem elaboration in creative case-based design has been done in the past. This is due probably to the fact that most of the systems in this area focus on other design phases, considering that the problem is well-defined and complete.

The predecessor of this system (IM-RECIDE) does not aid the user in the problem elaboration phase as CREATOR does. It relies on the user abilities to define the problem. Goel's work on KRITIK (Goel 1992) does not address this issue also.

A system with a similar approach to problem elaboration is SUPPORT (Nakatani, Tsukiyama, and Fukuda, 1993). Problem specification is performed using a graphic editor, allowing the user to build a hierarchical function tree. While in CREATOR a memory structure comprising domain knowledge and old design cases are used to make problem elaboration, SUPPORT uses only the cases

7. Conclusions and Future Work

In this paper we address the problem specification and problem elaboration phases of the design process. We present a case-based approach for problem elaboration. In the basis of our work is the SBF model representation of cases, and the memory structure used in CREATOR. We have also presented an example of the problem elaboration process.

We defend that ill and incomplete defined problems have a strong link with creative design. This happens because these types of designs specifications give the chance for the system to explore rich sets of alternatives in the problem specification. This makes also possible the search for design alternatives, transforming the usual CBR retrieval of the best case, in the retrieval of several cases for adaptation in order to generate new solutions.

So far CREATOR's evaluation lead us to the conclusion that the problem elaboration algorithm saves work to designers in the task of detailing design specifications. An important issue in this process is that if the problem specified by the designer is too abstract (e.g. too many incomplete HLFs) the number of alternative problem specifications can be enormous, depending also on the number of cases in memory, and on which HLFs are incomplete.

In the future we are going to implement an adaptation module and a verification/validation algorithm.

8. Acknowledgments

This research was partially supported by a MSc. grant to the first author from JNICT (PRAXIS XXI BM 6563 95).

9. References

(Bylander and Chandrasekaran 1985) Bylander,T., and Chandrasekaran, B. 1985. Understanding Behavior Using Consolidation. In Proceedings of the Ninth International Joint Conference on Artificial Intelligence.

(Gero 1994) Gero, J. 1994. Computational Models of Creative Design Processes. In T. Dartnall (ed.), *AI in Creativity*. Kluwer, Dordrecht, pp. 269-281.

(Goel 1992) Goel, A. 1992. Representation of Design Functions in Experience-Based Design. *Intelligent Computer Aided Design*. D. Brown, M. Waldron, and H. Yoshikawa (eds.). Elsevier Science Publishers.

(Gomes et al. 1996) Gomes, P., Bento, C., Gago, P., and Costa, E. 1996. Towards a Case-Based Model for Creative Processes. In Proceedings of the 12th European Conference on Artificial Intelligence. John Willey & Sons.

(Kolodner and Wills 1993) Kolodner, K., and Wills, L. 1993. Case-Based Creative Design. In AAAI Spring Symposium on AI+Creativity, Stanford, CA.

(Nakatani, Tsukiyama and Fukuda 1993) Nakatani, Y., Tsukiyama, M., and Fukuda, T. 1993. Reuse of Conceptual Designs for an Engineering Design Group. In *Reuse of Designs: an interdisciplinary cognitive approach*. De. Willemien Visser. Proceedings of the Workshop of the 13th IJCAI, France.

(Reich 1991) Reich, Y. 1991. Design Knowledge Acquisition: Task Analysis and a Partial Implementation. *Knowledge Acquisition: An International Journal of Knowledge Acquisition for Knowledge-Based System* 3(3):234-254.

(Stroulia et al. 1992) Stroulia, E., Shankar, M., Goel, A., and Penberthy, L. 1992. A Model-Based Approach to Blame Assignment in Design. In Proceedings of the 2nd International Conference on AI in Design.

(Tong and Sriram 1992) Tong, C., and Sriram, D. eds. 1992. *Artificial Intelligence in Engineering Design*, Vol. I. Academic Press.

Case-Based Reasoning in an Ultrasonic Rail-Inspection System

Jacek Jarmulak[1,2], Eugene J.H. Kerckhoffs[1], Peter Paul van't Veen[2]

[1] Delft University of Technology, Faculty of Technical Mathematics & Informatics,
P.O. Box 356, 2600 AJ Delft, The Netherlands,
[2] TNO Institute of Applied Physics,
P.O. Box 155, 2600 AD Delft, The Netherlands,
jarmulak@tpd.tno.nl

Abstract: Non-destructive testing (NDT) is often used for periodical inspection of infrastructure (e.g. railroads, pipelines). The inspection results in huge amounts of data which usually has to be analysed by an operator (or a team of operators) for occurrence of defect indications. This paper presents an example of use of case-based reasoning in interpretation of data from non-destructive testing, namely, a prototype for classification of images from an ultrasonic rail-inspection system. The reasons for the choice of case-based reasoning instead of statistical classification or a rule-based expert-system approach are explained. The overall design of the prototype is described and observations and conclusions relating to the prototype and generally to the use of CBR for NDT are presented.

Key words: non-destructive testing, ultrasonic inspection, rail inspection, image interpretation.

1   Introduction

Since 1986 Dutch Railways use an Ultrasonic Rail-Inspection System (URS) to inspect the railway tracks [Roos 1990]. The result of the inspection is a series of images which represent a sort of cross-section of the rail. The images have to be interpreted in order to recognise images of possible defects. Currently, the interpretation is done partly using an expert system with a simple set of rules and the remaining images have to be analysed by a human operator.

To increase the length of the rail track that can be inspected per year and to reduce the workload on the operator it has been decided to improve the automatic interpretation subsystem. Of the many requirements that the new system should fulfil probably the most important is that it should be easily adaptable to the planned increase in the number of ultrasonic sensors. After analysis of the problem, case-based reasoning came up as the most promising methodology.

This paper first presents the way the ultrasonic images are obtained and how the current interpretation system works. Next, some reasons for the choice of the CBR approach and against the choice of other methodologies are discussed. Then, the way the CBR prototype application has been implemented is described. The results obtained with the prototype are presented, discussing what has to be done to make the prototype suitable for real-world use. The paper ends with conclusions and some general remarks about applicability of CBR in NDT.

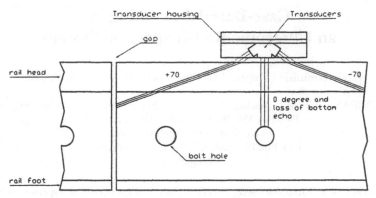

Fig. 1. Schematic view of the ultrasonic transducer assembly placed over one half of a fish-plated joint.

2 The Current Inspection System

The rail inspection is done using a special coach. The coach has two assemblies of ultrasonic transducers (one per rail). In an assembly the transducers are placed at 0° and ± 70° angles (see Fig. 1), providing information in 4 channels: 0° echo, loss of bottom echo, and ±70° echoes. The measurements are made every 2 mm along the rail.

Knowing the time elapsed from the send-pulse till the reception of an echo, the positions of the echoes are calculated. When indications coming from a section of the rail are put together an image as shown in Fig. 2 is obtained. Similar images are common in ultrasonic testing and are called B-scans, see for example [Hopgood et al. 1993] where a method of interpreting ultrasonic images of welds is described.

Once B-scan images of the rail are available, they have to be interpreted in order to detect any abnormalities which could point to possible defects (e.g. cracks).

In the current URS system some of the B-scan images can be interpreted automatically. The goal of the automatic interpretation is mainly to recognise noise and rail-construction images (no attempt is made to recognise defects). Before the classification can be done the data has to be processed. First, the points are grouped into clusters. Clustering is done by combining points (belonging to one transducer channel) which are within certain horizontal distance from one another. For 0° echo clusters, the system additionally attempts to fit circles corresponding to bolt holes in the rails.

Fig. 2. B-scan image from the URS system (vertical placement of the bottom-echo-loss indications is arbitrary).

The data obtained from the clustering is processed by a simple rule-based expert system which has rules for recognition of certain types of noise images as well as bolt holes and simple construction elements. The images not recognised by the rules (about 1/3 of the initial images) have to be interpreted by the operator.

One of the limiting factors in the current system is the image clustering algorithm which is not capable of extracting enough information from the image. For example, in some situations it is important to know the orientation of the line formed by a group of points. This information is in the current system not available, which means that whenever the orientation is a distinguishing factor, the images could be confused. Up till now, the problem was solved by excluding such cases from automatic interpretation.

It was clear that a better interpretation system needed a better image clustering algorithm. Such an algorithm has been implemented and is described in [Jarmulak 1996]. The points in the image are combined to form lines, parabolas or regions of noise with known parameters. In the prototype described in the rest of this paper the new clustering has been used.

The second limiting factor, as far as the improvement of the interpretation is concerned, has to do with the use of an expert system for the classification and, in particular, with the difficulties with the knowledge acquisition. These problems are discussed in the next section describing the choice of methodology for image interpretation.

3   Choice of Methodology

3.1   Reasons Against Choice of Statistical Classification

Many automatic NDT interpretation systems make use of statistical classification. Recently, use of neural networks has become popular, see e.g. [Udpa & Udpa 1990]. (Most of the neural networks used can be considered as statistical classifiers, see [Sarle 1994].) In the case of URS data statistical classification does not seem to be a viable choice for two main reasons.

First, most of the statistical classification methods require representation of the problem in form of a feature vector which is fed to the classifier. Such a feature vector should have manageable dimensions and should fulfil the requirement of continuity, i.e. images from the same class should have similar feature vectors (the distance between them should be small) and feature vectors from different classes should be sufficiently different. Describing URS images by such a vector would be very difficult if not impossible.

Second, a classifier requires training with examples which are representative for all the classes it has to recognise. Collecting such a representative and exhaustive training set is a problem common in NTD. Obtaining a good training set can often be very expensive. It may be also difficult to guarantee that the set is exhaustive, as is the case with URS. Training with a non-exhaustive training set can result in dangerous misclassifications when the system encounters data it does not "know".

3.2   Problems with Rule-Based Expert-System Approach

After analysis of the rules in the existing expert-system classifier, it has become clear that improving the performance of the system could not be easily done just by adding additional rules to its rule base (even given that the improved image clustering is used).

The first problem is of a practical nature and has to do with the complexity of the rules describing positional relationships of elements in the image. This makes it difficult to debug the rules. Especially, the discussion of the rules with an expert becomes a problem. While the problem of rule complexity does not itself prevent a construction of an expert system, it would still make the maintenance of the system difficult.

The second difficulty with the expert-system approach is related to the knowledge acquisition. The normal images are relatively easy to describe. However, often the whole ultrasonic system does not work perfectly and this results in images missing some indications or having some indications extraordinarily large. Strictly speaking, such images are not good, but because they contain nothing which would point to the presence of a defect, they are classified as images of good constructions. So, if an expert is asked how an image of e.g. a fish-plated joint looks like he will tell how the image *should* look like. He may recall some of the aberrations, but certainly not all possible ones. Therefore, during knowledge acquisition sessions much of the interesting information is obtained more or less by accident, e.g. when while going through the recorded data a certain special image is encountered.

The third, and possibly in our case the most important, problem which speaks against the expert-system approach is the fact that the system is to be expanded from 4 to 8 ultrasonic transducers per rail. So far, no images obtained with the new set of transducers are available. This means that any rule-base developed now would be unusable in the near future without an almost total update. The update would be made difficult both by the even greater complexity of the rules and by the knowledge acquisition problems. The current experts will need some time before they become experts in interpreting images from new transducers.

3.3   Reasons in Favour of CBR Approach

Use of CBR for classification of URS images has several advantages.

First, it relates better to the natural way the operator interprets the images. This is best illustrated if we think about the new 8-transducer system. Before the system goes into use we can only have a vague idea about how the images of the rail constructions will look like. (Though knowledge of the physics of the scanning process could be used to develop a model of how the images are obtained, this is not trivial because the look of the images is largely influenced by settings of various detection thresholds, which means that the model would contain strong nonlinearities.) Only when the first scans are made, then the operator will know what, e.g. a thermit weld will precisely look like. Later classifications will be made on the basis of similarity to previously seen images. Only when some anomalies are observed then the operator has to use his knowledge of the acquisition system to explain them; afterwards, he will simply know that e.g. images of insulated joints can have missing indications from some transducer(s) on one side of the joint.

Second, when CBR is used, the problem of the knowledge acquisition is largely reduced. As already mentioned, the knowledge about URS images is not well formalised making rule-based classification difficult. When CBR is used, the knowledge needed can be split into two main types. First, we need knowledge about what features of the images are important when comparing them. This knowledge is much easier to acquire from the expert than the knowledge described in the previous section. The second type of knowl-

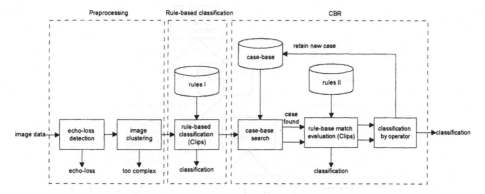

Fig. 3. Schema of the combined rule-based and CBR classification system.

edge is contained in the already classified images. These are readily available because all the images acquired by the system are stored together with their classifications. These images can be used to build the initial case-base.

Third, the case-based system is capable of learning. This can be done by simple retaining of new cases, but it is also possible to let the system acquire knowledge about types of incidents it should pay attention to because they could be possible defects. The ability to learn largely solves the problem of adapting the interpretation system to the data from the new 8-transducer acquisition system. Some changes will have to be done to the matching algorithms and to the rules evaluating the retrieved matches, but they are much simpler then rewriting almost the whole rule-base as would be necessary if an expert system was used instead. This means that using the CBR approach the whole interpretation system can be designed and tested on the existing URS system, and then, with relatively little effort, adapted to handle the data from the new acquisition system.

Fourth reason in favour of CBR is that the system will always work in co-operation with an operator, which seems to be an almost "classical" setting for CBR systems. In our case the operator is responsible for evaluation, when the automatic system cannot reach a conclusion, and for adaptation when necessary.

Other reasons in favour of CBR include better acceptability and easier justification of system results compared to an expert system.

4   Outline of Prototype System

The design of the prototype system combines the rule-based classification of the already existing system with the new CBR approach. The flow schema is shown in Fig. 3. After image has been processed the system attempts to classify the image using the already tried-and-tested rules (Clips expert-system shell is used for this purpose [Giarratano & Riley 1989]). The images which cannot be classified this way pass to the CBR system. A similar case is retrieved from the case-base and then the differences between the current and the retrieved image are analysed by another set of rules. If images are judged to be sufficiently similar, then the classification is done automatically; otherwise, the image is shown to the operator who can accept or change the suggested classification. Such cases are then stored in the case-base.

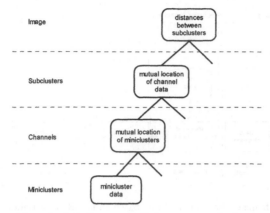

Fig. 4. Image hierarchy (subclusters are distinct groups of points, e.g. a bolt hole; miniclusters are described by their position, size, angle and dispersion).

Use of a rule-based classification allows for quick recognition of typical images which can be well described by an expert. CBR part allows the system to gather and apply knowledge about the images not described by the rules. Cases in the case-base can at some later stage be analysed in order to derive new rules which can be used in the rule-based part. The use of rules has the advantage of faster processing but only if individual rules are applicable to a reasonable fraction of (typical) images; otherwise, huge size of the rule base will result in degrading of the performance. It is also obvious that well chosen rules in the rule-based classifier will contribute to the reduction of the case-base size and a further increase in the speed of the system.

A discussion of an approach combining rule-base (for typical situations) and CBR (for exceptional situations) can be found in [Surma & Vanhoof 1995].

4.1   Case Representation and Matching

In the prototype system a case contains the representation of the problem (the image to be classified) and the solution (the final classification). The final system will probably also store explanations (locations of defects in images) for cases containing defects. We may also use some context information (e.g. proximity of a railroad crossing) as it has been observed to influence image interpretation done by the operator.

As already mentioned in section 2, the original image consisting of incident points situated at the co-ordinates where they were detected is clustered in order to combine neighbouring points into elements like lines, parabolas, or regions of noise. The results of clustering are stored in a hierarchical structure (Fig. 4) which closely corresponds to the layout of the elements in the image.

The structures are matched top-to-bottom and the allowed differences in the parameters are expressed as fuzzy membership functions in such a way that an exact match results in a value of 1 and with increasing difference it decays to zero. The results of the matches are combined using a fuzzy AND operator. Matching can be broken off if it becomes clear that the result will be worse then some required value.

Inexact matching is done whenever the number of elements differs or elements can be matched in various combinations, e.g. matching of miniclusters within a channel is done using inexact graph matching.

4.2   Case-Base Organisation and Case Retrieval

The initial experiments have shown that the case-base of the final system will have to store in the order of tens of thousands of cases. With that many cases the design of the case-base and of the retrieval and matching becomes critical to the success of the whole system.

All cases considered during retrieval will be matched; however, matching of two images can be broken off as soon as it becomes clear that the case currently being matched will have a worse match than e.g. the best match so far. It is therefore important that the case matched as first should have a high probability of good match, this way many matches on the latter cases will not have to be done in full and will cost less time.

The case-base is organised hierarchically. Based on the channels present, the number of subclusters and the length of the cluster, an array of cases in the leaf of the hierarchy tree is reached. (Distinction on length is done because rail constructions usually have certain fixed length.) Cases in the leaf array are then sequentially matched.

If the search does not stop on the first array of cases then other leaf arrays are searched, this includes also branches with a different number of subclusters or different channels present. Usually, the so retrieved cases will have a match too bad for automatic classification but still they can be used to suggest a correct image type (see section 6.3)

In the current prototype only one best matching case is retrieved and passed to the evaluation stage. In the next version of the prototype two best matching cases will be retrieved: one with and one without a defect. Non-defect and defect cases will be stored in two separate case-bases.

4.3   Case Evaluation and Adaptation

The evaluation of the match between the problem case and the retrieved case is done by a set of rules. The most important heuristic here is that the defects will usually manifest themselves as extra indications not present in the retrieved case. In the prototype, there are only a few rules which analyse the differences between the two images. Addition of more rules is made difficult by the fact that, at the moment, the image classification is limited to simple stating the presence or absence of a defect. With an extra information specifying the type of the construction visible in the image it would be possible to use rules specifically applicable to those types of constructions (e.g. fish-plated joints and thermit welds would require use of distinct rules). This problem will be further discussed in section 6.3.

If, as result of evaluation, the match between images has been deemed insufficient for automatic classification then the image is shown to the operator for either confirmation of the suggested classification or for adaptation.

In our system no automatic adaptation is done. The solution to a problem consists here of a single classification (there is no possibility of gradual adaptation), and the system has not been designed to change the classification automatically (e.g. from a bolt hole to a bolt hole with a defect). Any change of the classification has to be done by the operator (adaptation is for the user, see [Mark et al. 1996]).

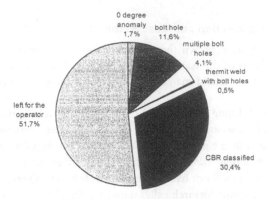

Fig. 5. Classification results on 96 data files beginning with an empty case-base. (100% does not include echo-loss images. First four classifications are done by the rule-base.)

5 Results of Experiments

Several experiments with the prototype system have been done using available data files. The files have been scanned and the images have been classified. In one of the experiments 96 data files were scanned beginning with an empty case-base. The 96 files contain ca. 60000 images, 35000 of which contain only echo-loss indications. The classification results in Fig. 5 are for the remaining 25000 images. The rule-based classifier could classify 17.9% of these images into four classes. We can notice that the more complex rules (for thermit welds with bolt holes) can classify relatively few images. It means that if we want to improve the results of the rule-based system much effort will be necessary to achieve even small percentage gains.

In this experiment the CBR classifier contributed more to the total percentage recognised images than the rule-based classifier. When we analysed the results we could see that, as expected, the percentage of images recognised by the CBR classifier increased with an increasing number of cases in the case-base (at the end of the experiment approximately 12000 cases were stored).

6 Discussion

The results of the experiments are encouraging but also point to several problem areas which have to be dealt with in order to obtain a fully satisfactory system. In the following, three most important observations are discussed.

6.1 Case-base searching speed

In its current implementation the search speed in the case-base is too slow. The limiting factor here is the inexact matching of the miniclusters. Some speed gain can be reached by optimising the matching algorithm (the one currently used is relatively simple). But even when the matching is optimised the expected size of the case-base (several tens of thousands of cases) will necessitate the use of reasonably fast hardware and possibly doing parallel retrieval. Current estimates are that, e.g. a PC with 2 or 4 Pentium Pro™ CPUs should be sufficient.

It is possible that the average search time will not grow proportionally to the size of the case-base. That is because in a larger case-base it will be more probable that the first cases being matched will have a good match and the search will be broken off.

The size of the case-base can be reduced by a periodic removal of cases which never had a good match, e.g. noise images.

6.2   Number cases vs. complexity of evaluation rules

There is a clear relation between the complexity of evaluation rules and the number of cases in the case-base necessary for satisfactory performance of the system. To achieve the same performance one can use either a small case-base and more complex evaluation rules or a large case-base with a small set of simple rules. At the moment, our preference goes to the use of a large case-base in combination with simpler evaluation rules; such a system should be more reliable and easier to maintain. Its results should also be easier to justify to the user.

6.3   Lack of detailed classification

As already mentioned, the images currently classified by the operator have only two possible classifications: there is a defect or there is none. The limited number of classifications has a practical reason: it would simply take too much time if, for every image seen, the operator had to enter the classification. However, the lack of a more detailed classification limits the capabilities of the CBR system (as mentioned in section 4.3). A more detailed classification would also be advantageous for other purposes, e.g. for doing detailed statistics of data, retrieval of certain types of images for operator training, etc.

Fortunately, use of a case-base offers a possibility to assign detailed classifications to all the images. We have observed that the cases retrieved from the case-base have almost always the same type as the image being analysed (though the differences may be too big to do automatic classification reliably). The type of the retrieved case can be used as the default classification shown when the image is presented to the operator. If the type is correct, and almost always it will be, then the operator does not have to do anything and the image will be assigned the default classification.

7   Conclusions and Future Work

This paper has presented the idea of the use of CBR for the interpretation of images from the ultrasonic rail-inspection. The CBR approach has been shown to have some theoretical advantages over the use of a rule-based expert system. To check if they translate into real results a prototype system has been implemented which combines the advantages of rule-based and CBR systems. The obtained results are encouraging and work is being done towards a final realisation. To obtain really satisfactory results special attention will have to be paid to the implementation of fast search and match algorithms. Also the need to store more detailed classifications of images has become clear.

We see the following as the main advantages of the CBR system (as compared to the rule-based classifier):
- the knowledge acquisition is simplified,
- the system will be able to learn,
- the whole system will be easier to adapt to the new 8-transducer data acquisition.

Another advantage which may also prove to be important is that the results of the system should be easier to analyse and to justify; this is especially important in case of any misclassifications made by the system.

Still, use of a rule-based classifier has advantages (as far as the processing speed is concerned) if significant percentage of images can be described by relatively small amount of rules. Because this is the case with URS, we have opted for a hybrid system combining rule-based and CBR classifiers.

We see CBR as being potentially interesting to other problems from the NDT. For many NDT problems no reliable statistical classifiers can be constructed. The problems are also often not well formalised so that rule-based classifiers are difficult to design. Still, the problems are successfully solved by the operators. If we can record the data and the solutions, and if there is enough knowledge how to index the data so that different cases can be reliably distinguished, then use of CBR can be a viable alternative. For example, we have successfully used ideas of CBR in development of an automatic interpretation system for data from eddy-current heat-exchanger testing.

In the nearest future the work on the URS system will include, first of all, optimisation of the case-base retrieval. We are also going to add a second case-base with only defect cases, so that apart from the best matching non-defect case a best matching defect case will be retrieved. If the match evaluation is done for both cases this should improve reliability of the system (especially if defect cases contain information locating the indications corresponding to the actual defect - the explanation for the classification as a defect). Experiments will have to be carried out which make clear to the users the advantage of the use of more classification classes (see sections 4.3 and 6.3) and the addition of explanations to the images with defects (see section 4.1).

References

Giarratano, J. and Riley G. (1989): *Expert Systems: Principles and Programming*, PWS-KENT, Boston

Hopgood, F.F., Woodcock, N., Hallam, N.J. and Picton, P.D. (1993): Interpreting ultrasonic images using rules, algorithms and neural networks, *European Journal of NDT*, Vol. 2, No. 4, pp. 135-149.

Jarmulak, J. (1996): B-scan Image clustering and Interpretation in Ultrasonic Rail-Inspection System, in *ASCI'96 Proceedings of the second annual conference of the Advanced School for Computing and Imaging, Lommel, Belgium, June 5-7, 1996*, Kerckhoffs, E.J.H., Sloot, P.M.A, Tonino, J.F.M. and Vossepoel, A.M. (eds.), ASCI, Delft, pp. 190-195.

Mark, W., Simoudis, E. and Hinkle, D. (1996): Case-Based Reasoning: Expectations and Results, in *Case-Based Reasoning: Experiences, Lessons & Future Directions*, Leake D.B. (ed.), MIT Press, Cambridge, MA, pp. 269-294.

Perner, P. (1993): Case-Based Reasoning for Image Interpretation in Non-Destructive Testing, in *Proceedings of the First European Workshop on Case-Based Reasoning EWCBR-93*, University of Kaiserslautern, Germany, pp. 403-409.

Roos, J. (1990): Het ultrasoon railinspectie systeem, *NAG Journal*, Nr. 105, Nov., pp. 21-34

Sarle, W.S. (1994): Neural Networks and Statistical Models, in *Proceedings of the Nineteenth Annual SAS Users Group International Conference*, April 1994.

Surma, J. and Vanhoof, K. (1995): Integrating Rules and Cases for the Classification Task, in *Proceedings of the First International Conference on Case-Based Reasoning ICCBR-95*, Portugal, pp. 325-334

Udpa, L. and Udpa. S.S. (1991): Neural networks for the classification of nondestructive evaluation signals, *IEE Proceedings-F*, Vol. 138, No. 1, February, pp. 41-45.

CBR in a Changing Environment

D. Y. Joh
Handong University
Pohang, Kyoungbuk 791-940, Korea
dyjoh@han.ac.kr

Abstract

Case-Based Reasoning (CBR) has been proposed for design tasks in which past experience is exploited to solve the current problem. Based on a study of experts, it is believed that a case based approach would be appropriate as the basis for computer aided decision support system for internetwork design. However, certain characteristics of the internetwork design domain require that the state of the art in CBR be extended before it could be applied to internetwork design.

A *knowledge revision* mechanism is proposed to extend the use of previous cases. Knowledge revision updates information about design components and uses that information to augment the case base, enabling the retrieval mechanism to select both from actual experiences and from experiences which might have occurred had current devices been available at the time. A computer program, CIDA, implements key portions of the model.

An empirical experiment was performed to validate the model. The results, blinded, were graded by three evaluators. A statistical analysis of the evaluations indicates that CIDAs performance is between that of experts and intermediates, but is significantly better than that of human novices. An ablation experiment shows the extended CBR approach has advantages over both existing state-of-the-art CBR systems and constraint satisfaction systems.

1 Introduction

Schank (1982) proposed CBR (Case-Based Reasoning) as a model of human reasoning. CBR is known to be superior to rule-based reasoning and model-based reasoning such domains as design where past cases are used to solve current problems (Kolodner, 1991). Until now, however, little research has been done concerning how well perform in a domain characterized by rapid information obsolescence, where computer-aided decision support is attractive.

In this paper, we discuss the algorithm and the evaluation of a new CBR system, CIDA (Joh, 1996), which addresses the above problems in the area of designing internetworks. Experimental evidence from the evaluation indicates that an extension of the CBR approach is capable of problem solving at a level comparable to that of skilled humans.

2 The Domain - The Internetwork Design

2.1 A View of the Internetwork

While there is a widely known view (OSI Model) of the internetwork in telecommunications society, we observed that the network design expert sees it from an entirely different point of view (Joh, 1996). In order to understand a large complex network, the expert concentrates only on important points, where many network connections are merged, based on their geographical locations. When the expert designs an internetwork, he first tries to divide the whole network into pieces, according to their geographical location.

According to such geography-centered view, network nodes such as PCs, printers, etc. first go into a place called a Wiring Closet (WC). Media from WCs are merged together in a place called a Building Entrance (BE). Several BEs go to a place called a Hub Place (HP). An internetwork, therefore, consists of a number of WCs, BEs, and HPs, as well as subnetworks to be connected. Based on this view, the expert interprets the internetwork design task as the problem of configuring a set of devices for those geographical junction points.

2.2 An Example of the Internetwork Design

In this section, we present an example of the internetwork design problem. We restrict our focus only on WCs to show the problems involved avoiding any unnecessary complexities.

The First WC of ABCNet

Initially, a typical WC of the ABCNet, a running campus network of a University, had several multiport repeaters (MRs), that have 8 BNC ports each. A multiport transceiver (MT) that provides 8 AUI ports was installed to connect these MRs through AUI ports, using drop cables. One AUI port of the MT was connected to a fiber optic transceiver (FOT), also. A fiber optic cable from FOT then goes out to the nearest BE. (Figure 1).

Introduction of a New Device: A Hub

Later, the expert has learned about a new device, a hub. A hub integrates terminal servers, bridging and routing functions, and network management, as well as repeating function, within a single box. One hub can have several boards each of which has one type of multiple ports on it so that one hub could supply a large number of the same type ports by using same boards, or it could supply various type of ports by using different boards. A particular hub, for example, can support up to 192 BNC ports, while an MR has only 8 BNC ports. It also supports level 5 unshielded twisted pair (UTP) wire.

The Second WC of ABCNet

Based on the newly acquired knowledge that one hub could replace several MRs and MTs together in a WC, the network designer tested several vendors' physical products to see how they work in a real network environment. Then, it was decided to use hubs instead of the combination of several MRs and one MT (Figure 2).

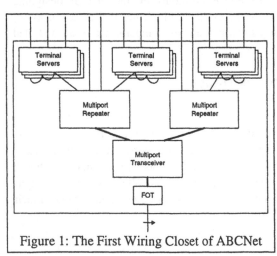

Figure 1: The First Wiring Closet of ABCNet

Because hubs now supported fiber optic ports, FOTs could be removed from WCs, also. Nonetheless, because the fiber optic port was very expensive, FOTs were still used. Notice that there are capabilities of the hub that are not used.

The Third WC of ABCNet

As the additional capabilities of a hub were realized and became familiar, they were tried and used. One was the RJ-45 ports that a hub supported. Previously, thin Ethernet cable

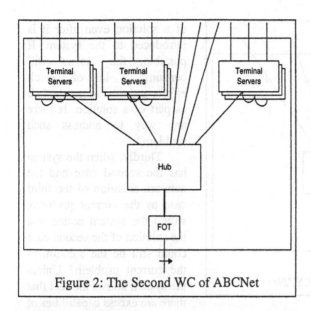

Figure 2: The Second WC of ABCNet

was the only medium used from network nodes to a WC. After the hub was introduced, level 5 UTP was installed for trial purposes. (see Figure 3). This is an example of the phenomenon in which the rationale of the internetwork design is dependent upon the available internetworking devices.

The WC of XYZNet

Afterwards, the expert consulted with XYZ University to design an internetwork (XYZNet, hereafter). XYZ University had already installed fiber optic cables between buildings, but they were going to use level 5 UTP wire within a building from network nodes to BEs. So a WC would have many UTP wires coming in and one UTP wire going out to a BE (Figure 4).

Issues

Let us now think about the retrieval problems in such a situation. In order to find a closely matched case, the network design expert adopts the method of giving weights to features. Such features as MAC layer standards, physical layer standards, OSI functions, and port types are used. Assume that the system has the above three cases of ABCNet, and the XYZNet situation as the current problem. Based solely on the above features, no case in the system can be retrieved because no case use 10BaseT as its physical standard exclusively, which the current problem requires. Remember that a portion of media used in the third case is level 5 UTP. Then, isn't the third case similar enough to the current problem that it could be retrieved and used to produce a solution?

Furthermore, there is another problem. Let us assume that the system has the first case and some other cases that do not have a hub as a component to their solutions. Because the hub has never been implemented, it would be very unlikely for the hub to become a component

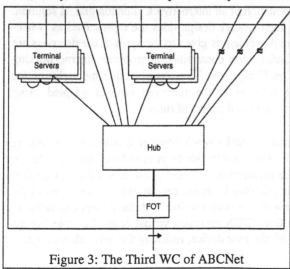

Figure 3: The Third WC of ABCNet

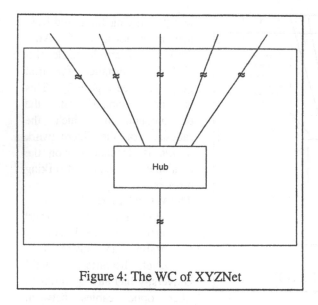

Figure 4: The WC of XYZNet

of a solution even after it is introduced to the system. If possible, the system will consume a lot of search efforts and time to get the hub as part of a solution. Is there any way to address such problem?

Thirdly, when the system has the second case and the network situation of the third case as the current problem, would the system notice that the solution of the second case could still be the solution to the current problem? Unless the system knows the fact that there are excess capabilities of the hub that could solve the current problem, considerable amount of time and effort could be wasted before the system find that a hub could still be the solution. How can such issues be addressed?

3 CIDA: A Computer Implementation

In this section, we discuss algorithms implemented in CIDA (Conceptual Internetwork Design Assistant), a prototype system that captures salient features of the cognitive model of an internetwork design process and that addresses the problems discussed above (Joh, 1996).

3.1 CIDA

CIDA was implemented using GoldWorks III™, a development environment based on Golden Common LISP™, and run on a Pentium PC (for details, see Joh, 1966). A case, in CIDA, consists of the representation of an internetwork situation and its solution. They are represented using frames. Internetwork design rules are represented as 'when-modified' daemons. When the current problem is given to the system, the daemons are triggered to generate constraints. Under these constraints, appropriate internetworking devices are selected from the Design Component Tree, an objective hierarchy of the internetworking devices. Then the solution to the retrieved case is adapted using adaptation knowledge which is represented in the form of rules.

3.2 Virtual Case Generator

The virtual case generator creates virtual cases whenever a new internetworking device is introduced into the system. Once a new device is introduced into the Design Component Tree, CIDA retrieves the previous design cases, and inserts the new device, in combination with the other existing devices if necessary, into the solution parts of the retrieved cases to see whether the new device is compatible with the network situation of the cases. If the new device works fine, CIDA generates virtual cases, by replacing the solution part of the retrieved case with the new device, retaining the network description part of the case. Figure 5 shows the pseudo code that introduces a new device into the system and generates virtual cases.

3.3 Expanded Case Generator

The expanded case generator makes expanded cases when a device chosen as part of a solution has functionality beyond that is required to solve the current problem. Once a design task is done, the system checks to see if any device has any extra functionality. If so, the network description part of the current problem is modified. This modified version of the network description and the solution forms an expanded case. Figure 6 shows the pseudo code of generating expanded case.

3.4 CIDA's Behavior

In this section, CIDA's behavior is described using two different campus internetworks: ABCNet and XYZNet.

Virtual case

Observation of the cognitive behavior of the expert reveals that when a new internetworking device, a hub for example, was introduced, the expert tried it in his most recent case, and performed a mental simulation to see if it works fine. As a result, he noticed that it is much better to use a hub than an MR. He was now willing to use a hub instead when there is a situation where an MR is required.

In CIDA, when a hub is introduced, the device is added to the auxiliary knowledge of internetworking devices. Assume that the current problem is similar to that of the first case. But it requires 40 thin Ethernet cables instead of 8, because more PCs has been added to the first case. Then, CIDA retrieves the first case and triggers the adaptation

```
Input: Information on a new internetworking device
Output: A frame for the new device, Virtual Cases

procedure generate-virtual-cases
    (information-on-new-device design-component-tree case-library)

while there is a device yet to compare on the design-component-tree
    do retrieve a device from the design-component-tree
        if the function and the standards of the new device are same
            as those of existing device
            then repeat do     ; retrieve another device to compare
            else go to the next step ; a real new device is found
        end if
    end do
end while

create a new device frame for the new-device

while there is a case yet to be tried with the new-device
    do retrieve a case from the case-library and
        generate the network requirements from the network description
        of the case
    do generate a new solution for the case with the new-device
        if the new solution can satisfy all the requirements
            then generate a case with the previous network description
                and the new solution
                            ; generate a Virtual Case
            else repeat do      ; the new device is no help
        end if
    end do
    end do
end while
```

Figure 5: Pseudo Code for Generating Virtual Cases

mechanism to modify the solution to the first case. The system calculates the number of MRs required for the current problem and generates the solution of five MRs, one MT and one FOT.

As shown above, if the adaptation mechanism is used, there is no possibility for a hub to be included in the solution, even though a hub is superior to the combination of several MRs and a MT in all respects. The adaptation mechanism alone could lead to an inferior solution. This is because the system does not have a case with a new device and, as a result, cannot retrieve a case that has a newly introduced device as its solution. The concept of a virtual case is introduced to address such problem. A virtual case is a case that has a new device as its solution, but has never been actually implemented.

Auxiliary Knowledge Revision: Component Dependency Network

Auxiliary knowledge revision is a way of updating changes in the system's preferences among design components, due to technology development or any change to the system's knowledge. It is implemented using a the concept of data dependency network. Assume that there are two cases in the case library; the first case and the virtual case that is generated based on the first case that has a hub as its solution. And the current situation is same as that of the second case. In such a situation, both cases in the library could be retrieved as being similar to the current problem because their situations are exactly same. Then, the question is which one to choose?

Most CBR systems contain an auxiliary knowledge in the form of a hierarchy structure, especially a tree structure. The links of the hierarchy are the only way the nodes can be related. There is no direct relationship among nodes.

Based on the expert's cognitive behavior, we noticed that he uses a preference structure to determine which internetworking device to select when more than one solution is possible. The preference structure is based on the internetworking devices' capability; their various functions, their support for various media, and standards they support.

The Design Component Tree, CIDA's auxiliary knowledge of internetworking devices implements such preference structure. For example, when a virtual case, with a

```
Input: The final solution for the current case
Output: An Expanded Case

procedure generate-expanded-case
            (final-solution current-network-description)

get the functions and standards of the design components of the final-
  solution
get the required functions and standards of the current-network-
  description
calculate excess functions and standards of the final-solution

if there are excess functions and standards of the final-solution
   then
        do   generate a case with the same network description of
               the current-network-description and the final-solution
             calculate network description based on the excess
               functions and standards of the final-solution
             add the calculated network description to the
               network description part of the case
        end do
   else stop
end if
```

Figure 6: Pseudo Code for Generating an Expanded Case

hub as its solution, is generated, CIDA notices that a hub is superior to an MR. This preference structure is added to the auxiliary knowledge. Each internetworking device object has two special slots called, 'replaced-by' and 'replace' that implement the obsolescence of a device. When CIDA notices that an MR becomes obsolete because of the introduction of a hub, the system adds a hub as the value of the 'replaced-by' slot of an MR and adds an MR as the value of the 'replace' slot of a hub. The existence of those slots enables CIDA to search for a substitute device when an inferior device might otherwise be selected as a solution to an internetworking design problem. Now CIDA is able to select which solution to adopt for the current problem. The 'replaced-by' link and 'replace' link make CIDA choose a hub instead of several MRs.

Case Expansion

A WC of XYZNet uses only UTP wires (Figure 4). Using design knowledge, the system generates the constraints that RJ-45 ports are required. In the case library, there is no such case that is similar to this one. CIDA, therefore, has to solve this problem from scratch by performing blind search through the entire internetworking device tree. CIDA acquired the information that a hub is able to deal with up to 192 UTP wires when a hub was first introduced to the system. Nonetheless, because this knowledge is not included in the cases, the system can not retrieve the case even though it has the capability to provide the solution for the current problem.

Case expansion is a way of updating a case with information that has not yet been used, but which might be useful for future problem solving. For example, when a hub was selected as a solution for the second case, CIDA updated the problem description part of the second case with the unused extra capability of a hub, so that the case can be retrieved as being similar to a future problem such as XYZNet case.

4 Validation

4.1 Empirical Experiment

For the experiment, nine subjects were selected and categorized into three groups according to their internetwork design related work experience and knowledge: experts, intermediates, and novices. Two experimental tasks are devised with different levels of difficulties. Each task consists of two parts: a network description and a list of available internetworking devices. Both tasks were given to each subject and to CIDA to generate solutions. All solutions from the human subjects and from CIDA were submitted, blinded, to three evaluators.

Hypotheses And Evaluation

The null hypotheses used in evaluating the performance of CIDA in comparison with humans are as follows:

H1: The average performance of groups with different level of knowledge (novice, intermediate, expert, and CIDA) is the same.

H2: The average performance within each group is the same for both levels of task difficulty.

H3: The evaluations made by the different evaluators about the average performance are the same.

We wish to reject null hypotheses H1 and H2 in favor of CIDA. Acceptance or rejection of H3 will shed light on the perceived quality of both human and computer designs as interpreted by different types of evaluators.

Data collection from human subjects in the pilot test and the main study was performed by following Ericsson & Simon (1984). The solutions for the tasks were judged by three evaluators: evaluator V1, a practitioner, evaluator V2 who has both academic credentials and practical experience, and evaluator V3 who has strong research credentials. The evaluators were asked to evaluate the designs with their own criteria but the same 100 point scale grading scheme; 90-100: excellent design, 60-90: acceptable design, 40-60: poor design, 10-40: not acceptable design, 0: no design. The solutions were blinded and given to the evaluators for grading.

Analysis

Multi-factor ANOVA output for the main effect only model show that the test statistics for all three main effects are statistically significant at the 0.05 level (Table 1). Performance is affected by the level of the knowledge and the level of the difficulty of the task. And there is a significant difference among evaluators.

Table 1: The Result of Multi-factor ANOVA with Main Effects Only (n=9)

Source	F Values	Pr > F
Knowledge Levels	2.97	0.0401
Tasks	6.44	0.0141
Evaluators	5.73	0.0056

The average scores (Table 2) shows that the performance of CIDA appears to be between the expert group and the intermediate group for two evaluators, and superior to the expert group from the third evaluator.

Table 2: Average Scores of each group

Group	Evaluator V1	Evaluator V2	Evaluator V3	Average
Expert	86.5	62.7	79.6	76.3
CIDA	83.4	59.2	83.7	75.4
Intermediate	76.4	55.6	77.2	69.7
Novice	57.5	37.5	64.7	53.2

ANOVA contrasts (Table 3) shows that for "average scores", only the contrast between the novice group and the expert group is significant. The "average score" contrast between novice and model turns out to be less significant than those between novice and expert and novice and intermediate, perhaps because the solutions generated by CIDA range from expert to novice quality. The "highest score" contrast between the novice group and CIDA is also highly significant.

Table 4 shows each group's performance difference across the two tasks. As knowledge level goes from expert to novice, the performance difference between the two tasks, within each group, gets larger.

Table 3: Scheffe's Contrasts between Groups ($\alpha = 0.1$)

Know. Comparison	Highest Score	Average Score
Novice : Expert	3.282 ~ 49.107**	0.296 ~ 45.743*
Novice : CIDA	4.462 ~ 62.427**	-6.549 ~ 50.937
Novice : Intermediate	-1.725 ~ 36.614	-2.505 ~ 35.519
Intermediate : Expert	-12.987 ~ 30.487	-15.045 ~ 28.070
Intermediate : CIDA	-12.062 ~ 44.062	-22.143 ~ 33.518
Expert : CIDA	-23.490 ~ 37.990	-31.312 ~ 29.662

* Statistically significant at $\alpha = 0.1$,   ** Statistically significant at $\alpha = 0.05$

Table 4: Mean Difference between Two Tasks

Group	Mean Difference
Expert	6.6
Model	9.4
Intermediate	15.1
Novice	24.3

4.2 Ablation Experiment

An ablation experiment evaluates the contribution of a component to the performance of the overall system by removing the component (Cohen & Howe, 1988). We have performed an ablation experiment to determine how different components in CIDA affect its efficiency and competence.

In this experiment, the most interesting issue to look at is whether the addition of Virtual Case and Expanded Case generating capability and the Component Dependency Network to an existing CBR system could result in any efficiency comparing to CBR system alone or CBR system and Constraint Satisfaction Problem Solving techniques combination.

To establish this, we first disabled all the functions but the CBR function and ran two internetwork design tasks. Under this circumstance, the system retrieved the most similar case solely based on the features of the case and the similarity calculation function. Once the most similar case was retrieved, the case was adapted to generate the solution for the current task. It turned out that this system could not solve task #1 because it was not able to retrieve a similar case from the case library. It is because the features of the current task is so different that none of the case in the case library could be matched with. For task #2, it retrieved one case and adapted it as a solution.

Next, we added Constraint Satisfaction problem solving capability to the CBR system. When CBR system failed to solve the task, Constraint Satisfaction problem solving part is triggered to solve the problem. CIDA implements the Constraint Satisfaction capability in a more local sense. When CIDA calculates the constraints from the network description, the constraints that should be met in every local places are propagated so that there won't be any conflicts among constrains for different local places. Protocols and LAN standards used in designing an internetwork are the examples. Once it finds design components for local places, such as WC, BE, and HP, it combines them to form a global solution checking a handful of global constraints discussed later.

Finally, Virtual Case and Expanded Case generating function and Component Dependency Network capability were added to the CBR system. The reason CIDA with all components generated much smaller number of solutions than the CBR plus Constraint Satisfaction system did (12 vs. 54 for task #1 and 17 vs. 260 for task #2,

Table 5: Number of Designs Generated under the Ablation Experiment

Tasks	CBR only	CBR + CS	CBR + VC + EC + CDN
Task #1	None	54	12
Task #2	1	260	17

Table 5) is as follows. While combining local solutions into a global solution, CIDA considered several global constraints: consistencies among internetworking devices, consistencies between the data processing capacities of devices, scaling constraints and growth related constraints. These features in CIDA made the solutions optimal in a global sense while the Constraint Satisfaction function in CIDA made the solutions optimal only in a local sense.

5 Conclusion

Human problem solving behavior is sufficiently complex that case-based reasoning alone is not likely to be an adequate model for it. Our results show, however, that a skillful implementation of CBR can perform the internetworking task at a level high enough to be relied upon for an intelligent assistant. In addition, Joh (1996) shows that while human problem solvers tend to generate fewer alternative solutions for a harder problem than for an easier problem, perhaps due to a heavier cognitive load, CIDA was able to generate more alternative solutions than did the experts, did even for the more difficult task. That implies that CBR might serve as the basis for a helpful decision support tool in such a domain where the complexity of the problem limits a human decision maker's problem solving capability.

References

Cohen, P. and Howe, A. (1988). "How Evaluation Guides Research, " *AI Magazine*, 9(4), 35-43.
Ericsson K. A. and Simon, H. A. (1984). *Protocol Analysis: Verbal Reports as Data*, Cambridge, MA, MIT Press.
Joh, D. (1996). *"Knowledge Revision in Case-Based Reasoning: A Cognitive Model of the Telecommunications Internetwork Design Process,"* Ph.D. Dissertation, Joseph M. Katz Graduate School of Business, University of Pittsburgh.
Kolodner, J. (1991). "Improving Human Decision Making through Case-Based Decision Aiding," *AI Magazine*, 12(2), 52-68.
Schank, R. C. (1982). *Dynamic Memory*, Cambridge University Press, Cambridge, UK.

Case–Based Reasoning
for Information System Design

Dirk Krampe and Markus Lusti

University of Basel, Department of Computer Science / WWZ
Petersgraben 51, CH–4051 Basel, Switzerland
Phone/Fax: ++41-61-26-73251
email: krampe@ifi.wwz.unibas.ch

Abstract. We present a process model that applies case–based reasoning techniques to information system design. Describing the process model we focus on similarity and case adaption aspects. We are currently implementing the process model in a research prototype called CBModeler.

The CBModeler project shows how the development of information systems can be supported by reusing design specifications from former projects. It assumes that all designs are derived from a reference model that describes the most important aspects of a specific information system domain. Thus we are also integrating schema–based and model–based reasoning techniques.

We introduce the notion of design and design component, similarity and adaption process. Furthermore, we describe how a meta–model can be used to preserve system wide consistency and a reference model to preserve consistency in a domain. Finally, we give a simple design scenario.

Keywords: case–based reasoning, information system design, reference model, meta–model

1 Introduction

Most people associate software reuse with the implementation level of software development. Our work is focused on the early steps of system development, especially the reuse of design specifications. Design specifications are independent of a specific programming language or development environment. They are therefore easier to discuss than implementation aspects.

Case–based reasoning is a technique which proves successful in a wide range of application areas [9]. A case based system "solves new problems by adapting solutions that were used to solve old problems" [14]. In order to design a new information system we look in a library of existing designs, select one and adapt it. When applying case–based reasoning techniques the following problems arise:

- What is a design specification? Dozens of design methods and notations exist to describe software specifications.
- Can we find useful and enough cases? A useful case is a design specification which is general enough to be applicable to more than one software system and concrete enough to describe real world applications.

- What does retrieving, reusing, revising and retaining design specifications mean (see [1])?

Our notation has been introduced by Scheer [15]. He describes design specifications using entity types, functions, events, organization units and relations between these design component types. The notation enables us to generate different kinds of models which are important during the design of information systems, for example entity–relationship diagrams, function trees, event driven process chains and organization hierarchies.

There are several reasons to use this notation. We had to find a popular method which offers enough useful design examples. Next, we needed design specifications stored in databases (and not hand written or stored using other imprecise techniques). Finally, we needed general design specifications applicable to more than one information system.

Scheer's company has developed a CASE-Tool and offers databases which contain reference models either for different information system domains – such as furniture or car industry – or which describe the general architecture of existing information systems such as the SAP/R3 software system[1].

The case–based design process model of Section 2 is based on the assumption that all designs can be derived from a general reference model describing the most important aspects of an information system domain. The reference model we use is imported from Scheer's CASE–Tool database. Thus, the information system domain **CBModeler** works on is defined by the domain the imported reference model describes.

Design problems are normally open world problems [13,3]: We have only weak design theories and no complete domain model. Usually, a design solution has to meet many different design requirements, which may be incomplete and contradictory. Furthermore, the requirements may lead to more than one solution. In addition, it is difficult to decide wether a suggested solution is correct or wrong. Finally, while solving a design problem, the needed components may not exist and have to be created from scratch or by adapting existing components.

The design process can not be fully automized. An intelligent design tool can only *suggest* solutions:

- It acts as an intelligent design assistant proposing solutions that have to be evaluated by a human designer.
- It carries out routine tasks to relieve the human designer.
- It helps structuring the design experience and makes it accessible to future design processes.
- It stores design alternatives and decisions. Future developers should be able to access the applicability of the alternatives (i.e. advantages/disadvantages, decision context) [8].

These requirements are taken into account by the process model presented in Section 2.

---

[1] SAP/R3 is a commonly used standardized information system that is customizable to different application domains.

1.1 Case–Based, Schema–Based and Model–Based Reasoning

Bartsch–Spörl discusses the integration of case–based, schema–based and model–based reasoning techniques to support complex design tasks[6,5] (see Table 1). She focuses on the architectural design of complex buildings, but the integration of the three reasoning techniques is also useful for other design domains.

The process model presented in Section 2 uses the same classification: *Model–based* reasoning guarantees design consistency on the meta–model level (see Example 8). A *schema–based* approach is indicated if a reference model provides a general framework for design specifications of an information system domain. This approach compensates for a well defined domain model and the lack of case examples. Parts of a reference model can be viewed as "topological schemata which represent reusable design components equiped with knowledge how they can be embedded in an actual design context" [6]. Furthermore, design templates are used to instantiate design components during the design adaption phase (see Example 9). We also use reference model rules to preserve consistency in the domain. Finally, *case–based* reasoning techniques are used to benefit from design experience made in former projects. A reference model offers the general design framework and design cases are used to fill in missing details.

Whereas model–based reasoning is done on an abstract meta–model level, schema–based reasoning is more specific because it focuses on the domain description of the reference model. Case–based aspects provide reasoning on the most specific level of concrete design case examples (see Table 1).

Table 1. Comparing Case–Based, Schema–Based and Model–Based Reasoning

	Cases	Schemata	Models
CBModeler usage	design specifications	reference models	meta–models
Generality	low	intermediate	high
Context Dependency	high	intermediate	low

2 A Process Model for Case-Based Design

This section introduces some fundamentals necessary to understand our design process model. We will then describe the design process model and focus on similarity and case adaption aspects. We are currently implementing the process model in a research prototype called **CBModeler**. The reader interested in further details – for example other knowledge based approaches in system design and implementation aspects – may refer to [11,12,10].

2.1 Definitions

Definition 1 (Meta–Model, Meta–Components). System designers need a *meta–model* to describe the functions, the data and the control/process flow

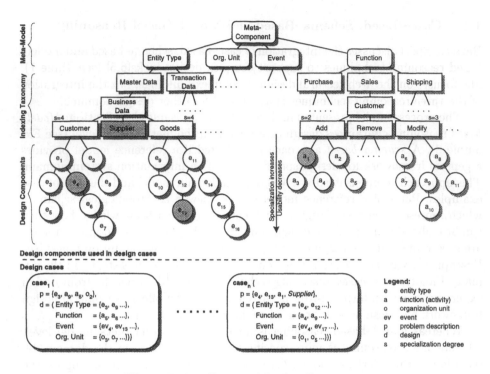

Fig. 1. Design Cases and Design Components

of the software to be designed. It contains *meta–components*, relations between meta–components and integrity rules. Our meta–model contains meta–components such as entity types, functions, organization units, events and relations and is based on [15].

Definition 2 (Design, Design Components, Problems and Features).
A *design d* is a design of an information system in terms of the meta–model. Each design contains several *design components*, which are instantiated meta–components. Examples are the entity types Customer, Supplier and the functions Add Customer, Modify Customer in Figure 1. *d* contains a set of entity types, functions, organization units, events and relations. Figure 2 shows the connections between various design components. Each hyperlink points to another design component.

A *design problem* $p = \{f_1, \ldots, f_m\}$ describes the requirements for a new design using the design features $f_1, \ldots, f_m$. A *design feature* f_i is defined either as an existing design component or as a leaf in the indexing taxonomy. The latter is used to specify a design feature which is needed but not stored in the case base yet. Examples for design features are the shaded items in Figure 1. *design(p)* or *d* is the solution for *p*.

Definition 3 (Case, Case Base). The tuple $c = (p, design(p)) = (p, d)$ is called a *case*. We say $design(p) =?$ or $c = (p, ?)$ if the design problem p is not

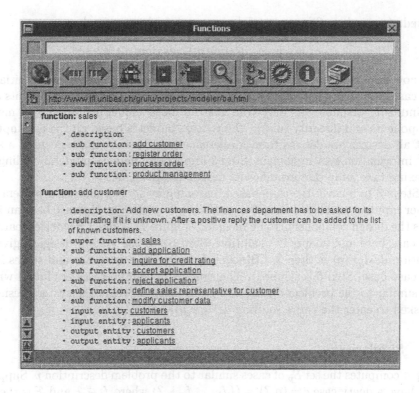

Fig. 2. Hypertext View of Design Components

1. $\mathcal{CB} = \emptyset$
2. Import a reference model and its indexing taxonomy
3. **While** a new case example $c = (p, d) = (p, design(p))$ is available:
4.   Compute $S_p = \{c' = (p', design(p')) \in \mathcal{CB} \mid sim(p, p') > 0\}$
5.   **If** $S_p = \emptyset$ **Then** read $design(p)$
6.   **If** $design(p) =?$ **Then**
         (a) Compute $c_{max} = (p_{max}, design(p_{max})) \in S_p$
         (b) $design(p) := design(p_{max})$
         (c) Adapt $design(p)$ internally:
             i. Read all unknown design components
             ii. Add design components from other $c' \neq c_{max} \in S_p$ to $design(p)$
             iii. Apply integrity rules and reference model rules
         (d) Adapt $design(p)$ externally:
             i. Present $design(p)$ to the system designer
             ii. System designer modifies $design(p)$
             iii. If necessary adapt integrity and reference model rules
7.   Define the state of c: $state \in \{checked, not\text{-}checked, designed, failed\}$
8.   Adapt indexing taxonomy
9.   Add c to $\mathcal{CB}$
10. **EndWhile**

Fig. 3. A Case–Based Design Process Model

solved. A *case base* CB is a set of design cases with known solutions:

$$CB = \{c_1, ..., c_n \mid c_i = (p_i, design(p_i)); design(p_i) \neq ?; i = 1, ..., n\}$$

We now discuss the process model shown in Figure 3. The first two steps initialize the case base. The empty case base contains no cases, no design components and no indexing taxonomy. It only contains the meta–model definition (i.e. meta–components and integrity rules). The process model is based on the assumption that all designs are derived from a reference model describing aspects of a specific information system domain. Step 2 imports a reference model including an indexing taxonomy that classifies its design components.

Steps 3 to 9 cover the case–based reasoning cycle. Normally, the system designer inputs a problem description p: He browses through the case base and selects the design components to be included (Figure 1). Then, CBModeler searches the case base and adapts the solution (Step 6). If the system designer gives a solution $design(p)$ in Step 3, CBModeler acquires the new case and stores it in the case base (Step 6 is skipped). The same is done if no cases are found which are similar to the problem description p (see Step 5, where the system designer is asked to enter the entire solution $design(p)$).

2.2 Similarity

Step 4 computes the set S_p of cases similar to the problem description p. Suppose you have a query case $c = (p, ?) = (\{f_1, ..., f_m\}, ?)$ where $f_i \in \mathcal{F}$ and $\mathcal{F}$ is the set of all possible design features in CB. We can now define the set S_p of all cases matching the query case c:

$$S_p = \{(p', design(p')) \in CB \mid p' \cap M_p \neq \emptyset\} \text{ where}$$

$$M_p = \bigcup_{i=1}^{m} M_{f_i} \qquad \text{(global matching set)}$$

$$M_{f_i} = sub(index(f_i)) \qquad \text{(local matching sets)}$$

$sub(index(f_i))$ is the subtree of all design components belonging to the same indexing taxonomy than f_i, including the index itself.

Example 4. Suppose the query case is $c = (p, ?) = (\{e_4, e_{13}, a_1, \text{Supplier}\}, ?)$ (see Figure 1). The local sets of matching design components M_{f_i} are

$$M_{e_4} = \{\text{EntityType.MasterData.BusinessData.Customer}, e_1, \ldots, e_8\}$$

$$M_{e_{13}} = \{\text{EntityType.MasterData.BusinessData.Goods}, e_9, \ldots, e_{16}\}$$

$$M_{a_1} = \{\text{Function.Sales.Customer.Add}, a_1, \ldots, a_5\}$$

$$M_{\text{Supplier}} = \{\text{EntityType.MasterData.BusinessData.Supplier}\}$$

and the global matching set is $M_p = M_{e_4} \cup M_{e_{13}} \cup M_{a_1} \cup M_{\text{Supplier}}$. The set S_p of all cases matching the query case are those which have at least one of the design components with the global matching set M_p in common.

Definition 5 (Local Similarity). A local similarity measure is a function sim_l which compares a design feature f of the query case with existing design components:

$$sim_l : \mathcal{F} \times \mathcal{F} \to [0,1]$$

$$(f,f') \mapsto sim_l(f,f') := \begin{cases} 0 & : \quad f' \notin M_f \\ 1 - d_f \dfrac{1}{s(s+1)} - d_{f'} \dfrac{1}{s+1} & : \quad f' \in M_f \end{cases}$$

where d_f and $d_{f'}$ is the distance to the *most specific common abstraction* of f and f' ($msca(f,f')$), and s is the specialization degree of the corresponding design component tree.

When using a taxonomy, the term of the most specific common abstraction is useful to compute the degree of similarity (see [9, p.346f] and [16, p.60,p.128]). The similarity measure we use has been introduced by Bergmann & Eisenecker to compute the similarity of Smalltalk classes [7].

The similarity of two design components increases with the generality of the most specific common abstraction. General design component are more useful than specific ones[2].

Example 6. Let us compute the similarity of e_4 and e_5 in Figure 1. $msca(e_4, e_5)$ is e_1 because e_1 is the first or most specific common abstraction we can find in our taxonomy. The distance d_f of e_4 to e_1 is 1 and the distance $d_{f'}$ of e_5 to e_1 is 2. As the highest degree of specialization in the customer taxonomy is $s = 4$ the similarity of e_4 and e_5 computes to $sim(e_4, e_5) = 0.55$. The similarity of e_4 and e_8 is $sim(e_4, e_8) = 0.5$ because $msca(e_4, e_8)$ is Customer. Finally, the similarity of e_4 and e_9 is 0 because $e_9 \notin M_{e_4}$, where M_{e_4} is the local matching set of e_4 (see example 4).

Definition 7 (Global Similarity). Using this local similarity measure, we can now define a global one, which describes the similarity degree of the query case c, and a case $c' = (p', design(p')) = (\{f'_1, ..., f'_{m'}\}, design(p')) \in S_p$, which matches the following query case:

$$sim : \mathcal{F}^m \times \mathcal{F}^{m'} \to [0,1]$$

$$(c,c') \mapsto \frac{1}{m+m'} \sum_{i=1}^{m} \sum_{j=1}^{m'} sim_l(f_i, f'_j)$$

sim allows to compute the set S_p of matching cases (Step 4), after which the best matching case $c_{\max}$ is selected (Step 6(a))[3]. Its design is taken as a first approximate solution to problem p and is copied to $design(p)$ (Step 6(b)).

---

[2] Wether the usability increases or decreases with higher specialization depends on the actual domain. Fur further details see [9, p.346f] and [16, p.128].

[3] If more than one case matches best with the problem description p some case is randomly choosen. It does not matter which one it is because during the adaption the other cases found are taken into account as well.

2.3 Adaption

We distinguish between the *internal adaption* (Step 6(c)), which is done by CBModeler itself and the *external adaption* (Step 6(d)), which has to be accomplished by the human system designer.

The first internal adaption Step 6(c)i reads the unknown design components CBModeler knows about. In our scenario of Section 3, this concerns the unknown Supplier entity type. CBModeler asks the system designer for such components and adds them to the new design.

Next, CBModeler adds design components which have not yet been included but which can be found in other designs (Step 6(c)ii).

Finally, in Step 6(c)iii integrity and reference model rules are applied. Integrity rules belong to the meta–model definition and define the criteria for a consistent design in general. Reference model rules apply domain dependent knowledge about the information system domain, i.e. the reference model. They preserve consistency in the domain.

Example 8 (Integrity rules). Examples of integrity rules are "Each function has to use at least one entity type as input or output", "Each organization unit is responsible for at least one function" or "Each event triggers at least one function". If such rules are violated, CBModeler examines other designs to repair the new design. If, for example, there is an event that does not trigger any function, CBModeler investigates other designs using this event and includes the function to the new design which is most commonly triggered by this event.

Integrity rules are independent of the domain defined by the reference model. They only assure a consistent design on a meta–model level.

Example 9 (Reference model rules). Examples of reference model rules are "Each master data needs at least functions for adding, modifying and removing a data entry" or "Functions that support the shipping of goods need entity types for a stock". These rules depend on the domain the reference model describes. If such rules are violated, CBModeler tries to include design components from other existing designs or tries to instantiate the necessary design components from so called design templates (for example a design template for functions that operate on master data).

Next, the external adaption starts. The solution *design(p)* is presented, and the system designer modifies it (Step 6(d)i and 6(d)ii). The intention of the external adaption is twofold. First, the design has to be adapted to match the needs of the information system. Second, CBModeler needs a feedback for the solution generated so far. For example, the system designer may find further reference model rules or integrity rules to be stored in CBModeler's rule base (Step 6(d)iii). He may also say wether the solution is useful for a real world design or not (Step 7).

2.4 Learning

The remaining steps concern learning: The system designer defines the state of the new design (Step 7) and adapts the rules (Step 6(d)iii) and the indexing taxonomy (Step 8).

Finally, the new case is stored in the case base, and CBModeler is ready for solving a new design problem.

3 A Simple Design Scenario

We will now give a simple design scenario. Suppose we want to design a sales system. We use CBModeler's navigation module to identify the design components (see Figure 2). First, we specify the entity types Customer, Supplier and Goods. Starting on the meta–model level, we select EntityType and navigate through the indexing taxonomy stored in the case base (see Figure 1). The indexing taxonomy is defined by the reference model we use and may be modified each case–based reasoning cycle. We are offered components for customers ($e_1 \ldots e_8$) and and goods ($e_9 \ldots e_{16}$) and finally select e_4 and e_{13}. Design components are complex objects belonging to an object hierarchy and inheriting the properties of more general components. The customer entity type e_4, for example, is a specialization of e_1 and has the specializations e_6 and e_7.

A supplier entity type does not exist. Therefore, we add a new indexing category Supplier and select it in order to express the need for a new entity type component. Finally, we navigate through the function taxonomy and select a function responsible for adding new customers (a_1). The selections made so far are stored as a problem description p ($case_n$ in Figure 1).

Now, CBModeler looks for designs that use the selected or similar design components. The search is easy because all design components point to the cases which use them. Let us say, S_p is the set of all cases that match the problem description p. CBModeler chooses the best matching case $c_{\max} \in S_p$ and suggests its design as approximate solution d to the new design problem p.

The design d is now adapted. First, CBModeler asks for the properties of the new Supplier entity type and adds it as a new design component under the Supplier indexing category. CBModeler knows that master data (i.e. supplier) need at least one function for adding, modifying and removing a data entry. It therefore modifies the function taxonomy and adds a taxonomy for suppliers similar to the existing one for customers. The functions are initialized from design templates for functions that operate on master data.

The next adaption step completes d by examining the existing design components and the solution space S_p of the other matching cases. For example, the solution d contains the selected customer entity type e_4 but the system designer did not select a function that modifies e_4. There exists a function a_9, that points to entity type e_4 and is responsible for updating the customer entity type e_4 (see Figure 1 and 2). This function is added to the design d. The solution space S_p contains other cases which may have design components that are also useful in the given situation. These components are added to the solution d too. Next, the system designer himself adapts d, which is finally stored in the case base.

4 Conclusion

The process model presented in Section 2 distinguishes between three reasoning techniques: *Model–based* reasoning guarantees design consistency in general on the meta–model level. A *schema–based* approache is indicated if a reference model provides a general framework for design specifications of an information system domain. Finally, *case–based* reasoning techniques are used to benefit from design experience made in former projects which is used to fill in missing design details. Only the integration of different reasoning techniques can tackle complex design tasks such as information system design.

The similarity measure introduced in Section 2.2 focuses on the notion of the most specific common abstraction. Similar design components belong to the same indexing taxonomy. The measure states that reusability of design components decreases with higher specialisation degree. Thus, a specific design component is supposed to be less useful than a general one. The similarity measure could be improved by defining weights for different meta–component types. For example, it is more important to emphasize the similarity of entity type components than of different organization unit components.

Our research prototype is beeing implemented with SICStus Prolog on a UNIX platform. The representation of design cases and components uses the object–oriented extension of SICStus Prolog. SICStus Objects support logic programming in large applications and flexible sharing and reuse of knowledge. They combine logic programming in Prolog style with object–oriented techniques. We use a WWW browser to navigate through the design components and the indexing taxonomy and to specify new design problems. The browser is connected with the case base using TCP/IP and client/server technology.

For the future, our main concern will be the case adaption, especially the automated adaption of different design models such as entity–relationship models and event driven process chains. Furthermore, we want to store design alternatives and decisions made by the human designer to make them accessible to future design processes. This includes advantages, disadvantages and applicability of a design alternative and the context of each design decision.

References

1. Agnar Aamodt and Enric Plaza: Case–based reasoning: Foundational issues, methodological variations and system approaches. AI Communications, **7(1)** (1994) 39–59.
2. Agnar Aamodt and Manuela Veloso, ed.: Case–Based Reasoning Research and Development First International Conference on Case–Based Reasoning (ICCBR-95), Sesimbra/Portugal, (1995).
3. Klaus-Dieter Althoff and Brigitte Bartsch-Spörl: Decision Support for Case–Based Applications. Wirtschaftsinformatik, **38(1)** (1996) 8–16.

4. S. Bakhtari and B. Bartsch-Spörl: Bridging the Gap Between AI Technology and Design Requirements. Third International Conference on Artificial Intelligence in Design (AID-94), (1994) 753–768.

5. Brigitte Bartsch-Spörl: KI-Methoden für innovative Design–Domänen. Beiträge zur 3. Deutschen Expertensystemtagung (XPS-95), (1995) 137–151.

6. Brigitte Bartsch-Spörl: Towards the Integration of Case–Based, Schema–Based and Model–Based Reasoning for Supporting Complex Design Tasks. In Aamodt and Veloso [2], (1995) 145–156.

7. Ralph Bergmann and Ulrich Eisenecker: Fallbasiertes Schliessen zur Unterstützung der Wiederverwendung von objektorientierter Software: Eine Fallstudie. Beiträge zur 3. Deutschen Expertensystemtagung (XPS-95), (1995) 152–169.

8. Dieter Holz: Über das Entwerfen von Gebrauchssoftware: Lehren aus dem Entwurfsprozeß einer Arbeitsumgebung für einen Lexikographen. Dissertation, Universität Basel, Institut für Informatik, (1995).

9. Janet Kolodner: Case–Based Reasoning. Morgan Kaufmann Publishers, Inc., (1993).

10. Dirk Krampe: Conceptual Modelling via System Analysis. Artificial Intelligence in Design 1996, Stanford University, USA; Workshop Notes on 'New Directions in Case–Based Design Systems', (1996).

11. Dirk Krampe: Ein wissensbasiertes Werkzeug zur Unterstützung des konzeptionellen Entwurfs betrieblicher Informationssysteme. WWZ-Discussion Paper 9604, Wirtschaftswissenschaftliches Zentrum der Universität Basel, (1996).

12. Dirk Krampe and Markus Lusti: Towards a Case–Based Assistant for the Conceptual Modelling of Information Systems. Information and Classification: Proceedings of the 20th Annual Conference of the "Gesellschaft für Klassifikation e.V.", University of Freiburg im Breisgau, Springer (1996).

13. Pearl Pu: Issues in Case–Based Design Systems. AI EDAM, **7(2)** (1993) 79–85.

14. Christopher K. Riesbeck and Roger C. Schank: Inside Case–Based Reasoning. Lawrence Erlbaum Ass., Hillsdale, (1989).

15. August-Wilhelm Scheer: Business Process Engineering: Reference Models for Industrial Enterprises. Springer (1994).

16. Stefan Wess: Fallbasiertes Problemlösen in wissensbasierten Systemen zur Entscheidungsunterstützung und Diagnostik. Dissertationen zur künstlichen Intelligenz, Infix–Verlag (1995).

Applying Memory-Based Learning to Indexing of Reference Ships for Case-Based Conceptual Ship Design

Dongkon Lee[1], Jaeho Kang[2], Kwang Ryel Ryu[2], and Kyung-Ho Lee[1]

[1] Shipbuilding System Department, Korean Research Institute of Ships and
Ocean Engineering, P.O. Box 101 Yusung-Ku, Teajeon 305-600, Korea
email: {dklee, khlee}@mailgw.kimm.re.kr
[2] Department of Computer Engineering, Pusan National University
San 30 Jangjeon-Dong, Kumjeong-Ku, Pusan 609-735, Korea
email: {jhkang, krryu}@hyowon.cc.pusan.ac.kr

Abstract. This paper presents a method of applying a memory-based learning (MBL) technique to automatic building of an indexing scheme for accessing reference cases during the conceptual design phase of a new ship. The conceptual ship design process begins with selecting previously designed reference ships of the same type with similar sizes and speeds. These reference ships are used for deriving an initial design of a new ship, and then the initial design is kept modified and repaired until the design reaches a level of satisfactory quality. The selection of good reference ships is essential for deriving a good initial design, and the quality of the initial design affects the efficiency and quality of the whole conceptual design process. The selection of reference ships has so far been done by design experts relying on their experience and engineering knowledge of ship design and structural mechanics. We developed an MBL method that can build an effective indexing scheme for retrieving good reference cases from a case base of previous ship designs. Empirical results show that the indexing scheme generated by MBL outperforms those by other learning methods such as the decision tree learning.

1 Introduction

The conceptual ship design phase, which is the first step of a whole ship design process, determines the overall dimensions of a new ship based on selected, previously designed reference ships of the same type with similar sizes and speeds. From the viewpoint of case-based reasoning, the selection of reference ships corresponds to the indexing step and the determination of design parameters corresponds to the adaptation step. This paper presents a method of applying a memory-based learning (MBL) technique to automatic building of an indexing scheme for accessing reference ships from a case base during the conceptual design phase of a ship. The reference ships are used for deriving an initial design of a new ship and then this initial design is kept modified and repaired until the design reaches a level of satisfactory quality (Andrews 1981). The selection of good reference ships is essential for deriving a good initial design, and the quality of the initial design directly affects the efficiency and quality of the whole conceptual design process. The selection of reference ships has so far been done by design experts relying on their experience and engineering knowledge of ship design and structural mechanics. We developed an MBL method that can build an effective indexing scheme for retrieving good reference ships from a case base of previous ship designs. For learning, we used 122 bulk carrier data of past designs with the record of reference history showing the reference ships used for designing each ship. Empirical results show that the indexing scheme generated by MBL outperforms those by other learning methods such as the decision tree learning. In one previous research result reported in (Schwabacher et al. 1994), a decision tree learning method has been shown effective for deriving an indexing scheme for case-based yacht design. However, we observed in this research that the decision tree sometimes misses an important condition and thus recommends inappropriate reference ships, seemingly because the learning algorithm attempts to minimize the size of the derived tree too severely for making it noise tolerant.

2 Reference Ship Selection

The design of a new ship follows the customer's order which usually specifies the type, the required *DWT* (Dead Weight), and the speed. The designer then selects from the database of previous ship designs the reference ships of the same type with similar *DWT*'s and speeds. The most similar one among these reference ships is called a mother ship. The designer determines the major parameters of a new ship's dimensions which are *LBP* (Length Between Perpendiculars), *B* (Breadth), *D* (Depth), and *t* (draft). Using the mother ship as the basis model, the designer considers the tendency of these parameters to differ among the other reference ships, depending on their varying *DWT*'s and speeds.

Figure 1 shows the correlation between the *LBP* and the *DWT* of 122 bulk carrier designs. We can see that the ships are clustered into many groups of similar sizes where some of the ships in the same group are close to each other, but the boundaries between different groups are not always very clear. The selection of reference ships for designing a new ship of given requirements may have to be done first by identifying the group the new ship should belong to, and then by selecting those ships whose design requirements are similar to those of the new ship. Although Figure 1 shows that the *LBP* increases roughly in proportion to the *DWT*, there are some irregularities and exceptions due to the customer's additional requirements and other factors such as the ship's navigation route and voyage condition. Moreover, close examination reveals that the rate of *LBP* change is actually different from group to group. Therefore, we need a learning method that can capture not just the global tendency but the local tendency as well.

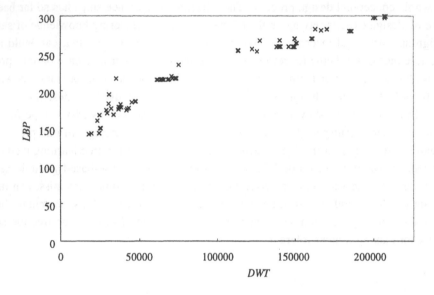

Fig. 1. *LBP* vs. *DWT* of 122 bulk carrier designs.

3 Building an Indexing Scheme by MBL

3.1 MBL for Retrieving Reference Ships

Since memory-based learning algorithms just save training instances in memory and the inductive process actually takes place at the time a test instance is given, they are often called *lazy learning* algorithms. In contrast, the *eager learning* algorithms such as neural networks and decision tree learning algorithms try to induce the best classification rules or hypotheses at the time of training (Aha 1997; Friedman et al. 1996). One generally known strength of lazy learning over eager learning is that the former can derive solutions that are more sensitive to the context of a given problem, because it can reflect the local tendency or case-specific characteristics as well as the global tendency or average characteristics (Atekson et al. 1997; Friedman et al. 1996).

Most lazy learning systems use nearest neighbor (NN) algorithms (Cover and Hart 1967) for finding past cases similar to a given problem (Stanfill et al. 1986; Aha 1991; Cost and Salzberg 1993; Atekson et al 1997). In this paper, we retrieve reference ships for a new design by using an NN algorithm. The reference ships to be retrieved are those of the previously designed ships that satisfy the requirements of a new ship the most closely. Unlike most other NN algorithms which are usually used for identifying a single most similar case to a given instance, our NN algorithm should retrieve multiple reference ships similar to a given new ship. Moreover, it should be able to recommend the most similar one as a mother ship among the reference ships.

Figure 2 shows how MBL can be used for selecting the reference ships, given a new ship of specified speed and *DWT* requirement. In the figure, ships of past design are designated by the x's and each of them is enclosed by a boundary that represents the range within which the ship is worth referencing. A new ship of specified speed and *DWT* is shown in the figure as a point indicated by an arrow. For a new ship q_1, x_1 becomes a reference ship. For q_2, both x_2 and x_3 are worth referencing, while the one closer to q_2 under a certain similarity measure becomes the mother ship. For the ship q_3, there is no reference ship available because none of the previous ships is similar to this one at all. Note that x_2 is worth referencing to a wider range than any others, and x_4 seems exceptional and thus it is never referenced for a new ship design. Note also that the range of reference for x_4 is sensitive to speed, and in general the boundaries for the ships are not necessarily in regular or symmetric shapes. The two important tasks of our learning algorithm are to determine the range of reference for each ship and to provide a way to measure the degree of similarity between two given ships.

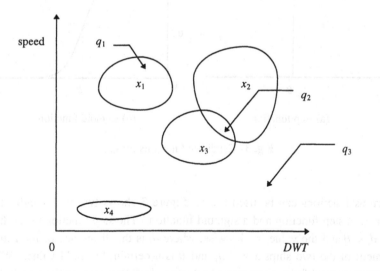

Fig. 2. An MBL approach to reference ship selection.

3.2 Similarity Metric

We calculate the similarity between a previous ship x and a new ship q by the following similarity function:

$$S(x,q) = \prod s_i(x,q) \tag{1}$$

where s_i is the kernel function (Atekson et al. 1997) to compute the similarity of the two ships in terms of the i-th design requirement (either speed or DWT in our problem). We let S and s_i have values in the range from 0 to 1 so that they can be considered as the probabilities measuring the likelihood of a ship being referred to by another. By doing so, we can easily determine with a uniform measure whether a ship is qualified as a reference ship; in this research the ships with the similarity values of 0.5 or higher are always qualified. With the usual distance measure of most nearest neighbor algorithms, however, it is not easy to set a uniform threshold value for reference ship qualification. Multiplication is used in this function instead of summation because the two ships should not be considered similar when the similarity of the two ships in any one of the design requirements is not high enough. For example, however similar the speeds of the two ships are, one cannot refer to the other if the DWT difference between the two exceeds a certain limit.

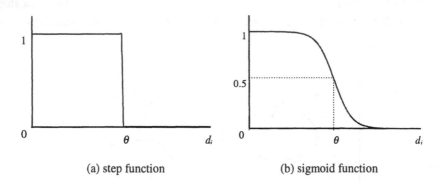

(a) step function   (b) sigmoid function

Fig. 3. Candidate functions for s_i.

Various functions can be used for s_i. Figure 3 shows two such candidate functions for s_i: a step function and a sigmoid function. The step function takes the value 1 when $d_i < \theta$ and the value 0 otherwise, where d_i is the difference of the i-th design requirement of the two ships x and q, and θ is a certain threshold value. When the step function is used for s_i, the range of reference is determined by the threshold value θ and the similarity is represented simply by binary values 1 and 0. Under this scheme, we cannot tell how much a ship is worth referencing and thus we do not have a way to select a mother ship among the retrieved reference ships. To provide a notion of degree of similarity we need a function having a slope nearby the threshold value. The sigmoid function is one such function that we decided to use as the kernel function s_i in this research. The threshold value θ for the sigmoid function is determined such that s_i becomes 0.5 at θ.

An advantage of using the sigmoid kernel function comes from the fact that the slope change does not affect the threshold value as demonstrated in Figure 4. The threshold corresponds to the range of reference and the slope to the mechanism of providing the degree of similarity, and these two are to be learned for each ship for later reference. Since the threshold and the slope of the sigmoid function can be adjusted independently of each other, the learning algorithm can search for their values much more easily.

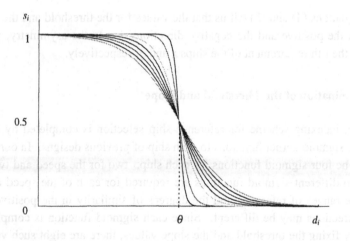

Fig. 4. Sigmoid functions with varying slopes at a fixed threshold.

The similarity metric that we need for reference ship retrieval can be said to have an asymmetric property (Ricci and Avesani 1995). For example, a previous ship with the *DWT* w may be worth referencing when the *DWT* of a new ship to be designed is $w + \alpha$, but not when it is $w - \alpha$. Therefore, for both the speed and the *DWT* the threshold and the slope in both directions should be learned separately.

We conclude this section by giving the equations regarding the similarity metric. The kernel function s_i which computes the similarity of x and q in terms of the i-th design requirement is expressed as a sigmoid function of the difference d_i of the i-th design requirement of x and q, the threshold θ_{x_i}, and the slope k_{x_i}.

$$s_i(x,q) = K\!\left(d_i(x,q), \theta_{x_i}, k_{x_i}\right) \qquad (2)$$

$$K(d,\theta,k) = 1 - \frac{1}{1 + e^{\frac{d+\theta}{k}}} \tag{3}$$

$$q_{x_i} = \begin{cases} q'_{x_i} & \text{if } x^{(i)} - q^{(i)} \geq 0 \\ q''_{x_i} & \text{if } x^{(i)} - q^{(i)} < 0 \end{cases} \tag{4}$$

$$k_{x_i} = \begin{cases} k'_{x_i} & \text{if } x^{(i)} - q^{(i)} \geq 0 \\ k''_{x_i} & \text{if } x^{(i)} - q^{(i)} < 0 \end{cases} \tag{5}$$

The equations (4) and (5) tell us that the values for the threshold and the slope are different in the positive and the negative directions due to the asymmetry, where $x^{(i)}$ and $q^{(i)}$ are the i-th requirement of the ships x and q, respectively.

3.3 Determination of the Threshold and Slope

Building an indexing scheme for reference ship selection is completed by assigning appropriate sigmoid kernel functions to each ship of previous designs. In our problem, there must be four sigmoid functions for each ship: two for the speed and two for the *DWT*. Two different sigmoid functions are required for each of the speed and *DWT* because the ranges of reference and the degrees of similarity in the positive and the negative directions may be different. Since each sigmoid function is completely de-termined by fixing the threshold and the slope values, there are eight such values that should be determined for each ship. Given a record of reference history, what we want is to find the optimal threshold and slope values for each of the design require-ments (*DWT*, speed) that minimize the following error E_x for a given ship x:

$$E_X = \left(\sum_j \left(S_{EX}(x, x_j) - S(x, x_j) \right)^r \right)^{\frac{1}{r}} \tag{6}$$

where $S_{EX}(x, x_j)$ is the value of similarity between x and x_j given from the examples in the record of reference history, and $S(x, x_j)$ is the similarity value computation based on the equations (1) - (5), with the threshold and slope values assigned to certain ini-tial values at the beginning. The goal of learning from the examples in the record of reference history is to search for optimal values for the thresholds and slopes which minimize E_x. We tried several heuristic search methods for this optimization and found that genetic algorithms gave the best result.

4 Experimental Results

We used 122 bulk carrier data designed from 1974 to 1995 with the record of reference history, of which the earliest 100 ships were used for training and the remaining 22 for testing. We compared the performance of MBL with those of a simple heuristic, a decision tree learning, and a neural network. The design requirements are the *DWT* and the speed. Designing a new ship of certain requirements, in the conceptual design phase, involves determination of the major parameters which are *LBP*, *B*, *D*, and *t* as mentioned in section 2. A good initial design derived from the reference ships promises efficiency and quality of the whole design process. Therefore, we tried to evaluate different learning methods by deriving an initial design by performing linear regression on the reference ships recommended by each method, and compared the results with the real test ship data.

Table 1 compares the correctness (% of correct reference ships retrieved) and the completeness (% of reference ships actually retrieved among all the reference ships) of the reference ships retrieved by different methods. *DWT*(5%) and *DWT*(10%) in the table respectively represent the simple heuristics by which all the ships within 5% and 10% differences of the *DWT* value of the target ship are retrieved as reference ships. These heuristics are tried because the *DWT* is considered the most important among all the design requirements. As more ships are retrieved and thus the completeness becomes higher, the proportion of the correct reference ships among all those retrieved gets smaller (low correctness) because more irrelevant ships tend to be selected. The result of decision tree learning by C4.5 program (Quinlan 1993) exhibits low correctness although its completeness is high. We found that the reason for this low correctness is that a few rules derived by C4.5 were missing the most important feature *DWT* from its condition part, apparently as a result of attempting to derive a minimal decision tree. The learning strategy of C4.5 to minimize the decision tree is generally good for capturing a global tendency of the training data in noisy environments. As argued in section 2, our problem prefers a method which can capture a local tendency as well as the global tendency. We can see in the table that the result by MBL reveals the highest correctness with reasonably compromised completeness. In our experiment, a ship is qualified as a reference ship if the ship's similarity to the new ship computed by our similarity function is greater than or equal to 0.5. Note also that C4.5 cannot rank the reference ships but our MBL can, and thus only the MBL can recommend a mother ship among the retrieved reference ships.

Table 1. Comparison of correctness and completeness of various methods.

Method	Correctness	Completeness
DWT(5%)	55.2%	58.0%
DWT(10%)	39.9%	99.2%
Decision Tree	49.8%	100.0%
MBL	81.8%	75.6%

Table 2 compares the qualities of the initial designs (where *LBP*, *B*, *D*, and *t* are determined) derived by performing linear regressions on the reference ships retrieved by various methods. The first row shows the result by regressing on all the ships with respect to the *DWT*. The neural network on the second row is an exception; instead of a linear regression, the parameter values are derived by directly training the neural network on each of the parameters. The row *DWT(5%)* means that all the ships within 5% difference of the *DWT* value of the target ship are used for regression. For the rows Decision Tree and MBL, the reference ships retrieved by each method are used for regression. The last row shows the result of the regression on the actual reference ships obtained from the record of reference history. We can see that MBL consistently provides the values with the lowest average errors for each of all the parameters.

Table 2. Average errors of major parameter values derived by various methods.

Method	LBP(m)	B(m)	D(m)	t(m)
All Ships	6.75	0.70	0.50	0.59
Neural Network	3.04	0.59	0.21	0.17
DWT(5%)	6.41	0.79	0.34	0.21
Decision Tree	1.81	0.31	0.27	0.32
MBL	1.51	0.31	0.11	0.10
Ships in the record	0.14	0.05	0.09	0.10

5 Conclusion

We showed that an MBL technique can be effectively applied to indexing of reference ships for the conceptual design of a new ship. The similarity metric we proposed in this paper is based on the concept of joint probability of independent events rather than the concept of summation of distances of each features, as is usually found in most other nearest neighbor algorithms. Our similarity metric can easily represent cases where a ship cannot refer to another due to the difference in a single feature exceeding a certain limit, despite the similarities in most of their other features. The probabilistic nature of our similarity metric also allows us to easily determine whether a ship should be qualified as a reference ship; for example, a ship of similarity greater than or equal to 0.5 is qualified. The kernel function we used is a sigmoid function to take advantage of the fact that the threshold and the slope can be controlled independently of each other, and thus the learning algorithm can search for the optimal values more efficiently. One other distinctive aspect of our application is that our similarity metric should be asymmetric due to the nature of referencing in the conceptual ship design. The asymmetry causes more parameters to appear in learning, thus increasing the search complexity although the number of training examples available were relatively small. However, empirical results still showed that the indexing scheme generated by our MBL technique outperformed those of other learning methods including C4.5 and neural networks.

References

Aha W. D., (1991) Case-Based Learning Algorithms, *Proceedings of the 1991 DARPA Case-Based Reasoning Workshop*, pp. 147-158, Morgan Kaufmann.

Aha W. D., (1997) Editorial on Lazy Laerning, to appear in *Artificial Intelligence Review* Special Issue on Lazy Learning.

Andrews D., (1981) Creative Ship Design, *The Royal Institution of Naval Architects*, Nov., 1981, pp. 447-471.

Atekson C., A. Moore and S. Schaal, (1997) Locally Weighted Learning, to appear in *Artificial Intelligence Review* Special Issue on Lazy Learning.

Cost S. and S. Salzberg, (1993) A Weighted Nearest Neighbor Algorithm for Learning with Symbolic Features, *Machine Learning*, 10, pp. 57-78.

Cover, T. and P. Hart, (1967) Nearest Neighbor Pattern Classification, *IEEE Transactions on Information Theory*, 13, pp. 21-27.

Friedman, J.H., R. Kohavi, and Y. Yun, Lazy Decision Trees, (1996) *Proceedings of the Thirteenth National Conference on Artificial Intelligence*, Portland, Oregon.

Ricci F. and P. Avesani, (1995) Learning a Local Similarity Metric for Case-Based Reasoning, *Preceedings of the First International Conference on Case-Based Reasoning* (ICCBR-95), pp. 23-26, Sesimbra, Portugal.

Schwabacher M., H. Hirsh and T. Ellman, (1994) Learning Prototype-Selection Rules for Case-Based Iterative Design, *Proceedings of the Tenth IEEE Conference on Artificial Intelligence for Applications*, San Antonio, Texas.

Stanfill C and D. Waltz, (1986) Toward Memory-Based Reasoning, *Communication of ACM*, 29, pp. 1213-1229.

Quinlan J. R., (1993) C4.5:Programs for Machine Learning. Morgan Kaufmann, San Mateo, CA.

CBR for Document Retrieval: The FALLQ Project

Mario Lenz, Hans-Dieter Burkhard

Dept. of Computer Science, Humboldt University Berlin, Axel-Springer-Str. 54a, D-10117 Berlin, Germany, Email: {lenz,hdb}@informatik.hu-berlin.de

Abstract. This paper reports about a project on document retrieval in an industrial setting. The objective is to provide a tool that helps finding documents related to a given query, such as answers in *Frequently Asked Questions* databases. A CBR approach has been used to develop a running prototypical system which is currently under practical evaluation.
Keywords: Hotline support, document retrieval, case-based reasoning.

1 Introduction

Today it is becoming more and more difficult to sell products without a reliable and efficient customer support. This is true both, for industrial equipment as well as for highly complex software systems. The reason for this is that maintenance costs often exceed the initial value and thus become a decision criterion of customers ([6]).

In this paper, we report about the FALLQ project which aimed at applying a CBR approach to build a tool for supporting Hotline staff. This project has been performed in cooperation with LHS Dietzenbach, a market leader on the telecommunications software market (see Section 2).

The structure of the paper is as follows: In Section 2 we will sketch the application area and the requirements on an information system. Section 3 explains why a CBR approach was adopted and what design decision have been taken. Section 4 goes into detail about the development methodology and the structure of the implemented system itself. Then, Section 5 gives an evaluation of the system before alternative approaches and open issues are discussed in Section 6.

2 The Application Area

LHS is a company developing and selling a customer care and billing system for providers of telecommunications services. Currently, this system has more than thirty projects and installations world-wide. Because of the dynamics of the telecommunications market, the complexity of the application software is steadily growing. Also, the number of installations and customers is growing considerably. Hence, there is an urgent need for an information system which helps

- keeping track of customers' enquiries;

- finding answers to problems that have already been solved before, either for another customer or by different staff members;
- maintaining information useful for internal purposes, e.g. descriptions of defects which might be useful for the system developers.

Within the company, information and knowledge are stored in many different places using various types of documents, e.g.

- descriptions of *defects* and problems during the development of modules;
- specifications of modules summarizing the functionality provided;
- *Frequently Asked Questions*–like documents
- documentations delivered with the products, training material etc.

Last but not least, a wealth of knowledge is kept by the experienced staff members which have been developing the software for several years. Because of the rapid growth of the company, however, more and more new staff are employed who lack this historical knowledge.

To cope with the market's demands, an information system had to be developed that helps to find information related to a certain topic in the various knowledge sources and document databases.

2.1 Hotline characteristics

A first implementation aimed at a tool supporting the Hotline staff while more general applications should be kept in mind for future versions. The Hotline itself can be characterized as follows:

- The term *Hotline* might be misleading. There is no strong demand for handling customer enquiries within minutes or even seconds. Rather, finding the answers to problems usually involves a complex problem analysis and thus may take some time. Nevertheless, questions concerning problems that have been solved before should, of course, be answered rapidly.
- Nearly the entire query is given in free text, possibly with abbreviations and misspellings. Only some minor information, such as the customer ID, the release number etc. are given in a formatted style.
- All questions deal with a specific customer care system. Hence, a general world understanding is not required – rather all descriptions can be interpreted in the context of that system. Also, a number of highly specific terms will be used such as names of functions and modules.
- The tool is designed to *support* the Hotline staff, not to *replace* them: The system should search for similar past problems, suggest solutions and let the Hotline staff decide.

3 CBR for Supporting Hotline Staff

After having analyzed the requirements on an information system, it seemed most promising to apply a CBR approach. In particular, the following key properties of CBR appear to be highly useful:

- CBR does not require a fixed structure of cases, thus customer enquiries can be encoded as a mixture of free text and attribute-value based representation.
- The idea of similarity is central to CBR, hence there is no need to express queries to the system in exactly the same terms.
- New cases can be added to the system at any time.

Nevertheless, a number of problems had to be solved which appear to be specific for the design of CBR applications. These are:

1. What constitutes a case? What components does a case have?
2. How is an appropriate similarity measure defined?
3. How is the case memory structured in order to assure efficient retrieval?
4. How can cases be acquired? How is the system maintained?

In the following we will describe in detail the decisions that have been taken for the FALLQ project.

3.1 Case structure

Since the objective of the FALLQ project was to support the Hotline staff, the structure of cases has been defined according to the given documents. More precisely, a case consists of three parts:

Question-Text: the question asked by the customer in free text (English);
Attributes: additional attributes provided in a structured form – these include information about the customer ID, the current release number etc.;
Answer-Text: the answer given by the Hotline staff, again in free text;

Note that this is the structure of cases as they occur in the source documents. In order to make the information contained in the plain texts accessible, each case is *parsed* for some kind of *keywords*. However, a *keyword* here is more than usually considered for example in the Information Retrieval community: In the FALLQ system a *keyword* is considered to be an *Information Entity* (IE, see Section 3.3) which helps finding cases for which this IE had been relevant.

In this approach, the term *parsing* actually refers to a $n : 1$ mapping from strings to IEs, that is *parsing* includes identifying a word (or a phrase) itself, grammatical variations, abbreviations of it, and even foreign language expressions of that word. All these are mapped to a single IE which is some kind of symbol capturing a certain meaning. This mapping will be useful for defining similarity as it is sufficient to specify similarity between IEs instead of all possible strings and variations that might occur. What's more, a classification of the IEs is performed during this process which determines whether the IE represents a general English term, a system-specific term, a system attribute etc.

For this procedure, a list of keywords has to be given. Note that both, constructing the list of keywords as well as classifying the IEs can be performed automatically to a great extend (see Section 4.2).

3.2 Similarity measure

In general, two cases should, of course, be similar if they contain the same expressions. Hence, we decided to apply a composite similarity measure SIM where the similarity of a case F to a query Q is defined as:

$$SIM(Q, F) = \sum_{e_i \in Q} \sum_{e_j \in F} sim(e_i, e_j)$$

where e_i and e_j are the IEs that have been extracted from the free texts of the query Q and the case C, respectively, during parsing.

Based on the above discussed $n : 1$ mapping from strings to IEs, we can now define the *local* similarity function *sim* which compares any two IEs, that is two symbols representing a certain meaning in the domain. Doing so, two cases may also be similar if they are both expressed in completely different words which, however, can be mapped to similar IEs.

The verbs `bill` and `charge`, for example, are two different strings which one could imagine being mapped to the two IEs _BILL_ and _CHARGE_, respectively. Using a thesaurus, these two IEs can then be considered as similar to some extend as they are synonyms. Since we compare IEs and not strings in terms of similarity, this mapping also covers the strings `billing` and `charged`.

The *local* similarity function *sim* has been defined on the basis of linguistic similarity of words obtained from a thesaurus (cf. Section 4.2).

3.3 Case memory and retrieval

In order to allow for an efficient yet flexible case retrieval process, we implemented the model of *Case Retrieval Nets* ([3, 4]) in the FALLQ system:

- The keywords of a case will make up the *Information Entities* (IEs).
- Every case node represents a single entry in one of the FAQ documents.
- The *similarity* of IEs has been defined as explained above.
- The *relevance* of an IE for a case is either 1 or 0 depending on whether the IE occurred in that case or not.

Using this model, retrieval for a given query case is performed by:

1. Parsing the query text for keywords and identification of IEs.
2. Activation of those IEs which appear in the query.
3. Similarity propagation among IEs in order to consider similar keywords.
4. Relevance propagation to case nodes in order to access cases in which the same or at least similar IEs occurred, and establishing a a preference ordering based on the achieved activations.

3.4 Case acquisition

Acquisition of cases can be performed by simply extracting the relevant parts from a traditional database where all documents mentioned before are stored in electronic formats. New cases can be entered as soon as a new question has been sent by a customer and answered by the Hotline staff. Whether a *steering committee* will be responsible for deciding about usefulness of cases, is still a matter of evaluation.

4 The FALLQ Implementation

As a result of the research project reported about in this paper, a prototypical system has been developed which runs on PCs under Windows 3.x. This section will explore the general architecture as well as some details of development.

4.1 General system architecture

Figure 1 sketches the general process model of the FALLQ system. Most notably, one can distinguish two phases: (1) Building the structures when starting the system and (2) actually using the system. While the first phase may take some time for larger case bases (remember that cases have to be parsed from text files), the retrieval itself is fast (see Section 5) and is performed in a continuous cycle.

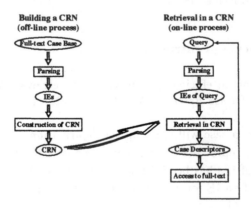

Fig. 1. General process model of FALLQ system.

4.2 Methodology of development

As mentioned in Section 3.1, a list of IEs has to be provided in order to parse English text documents and construct a structured case memory from these. In general, at least the following approaches are possible for establishing this list:

(1) brute force: Simply use all words occurring in the documents as IEs.

(2) statistic-oriented: Select keywords based on statistics of all documents.

(3) knowledge intensive: Let a domain expert specify meaningful keywords.

When developing the FALLQ program, all three approaches have been unified: The majority of all the words in the documents have been used (1), however, some of these which are obviously of no use (such as articles and other expletives) have been discarded (2), and additional knowledge sources have been used to add keywords highly specific to the system (3). This strategy kept the effort for the knowledge acquisition phase at a minimum.

A further question of system development concerns the problem of similarity. As mentioned in Section 3.2 we distinguished between general and system-specific terms. For the former, a general purpose thesaurus of English has been utilized in order to identify groups of similar words. For system-specific terms, additional documents like training material and a glossary have been used to construct an ontology of terms which has been the basis for defining local similarity as defined in Section 3.2.

4.3 Future Requirements

The objective of the FALLQ implementation was to test whether a CBR approach is really applicable for the considered task. For a full running system, some extensions would be required which, however, do not concern the retrieval functionality but mainly the integration within the existing IT structure. Some of these extensions will be mentioned here briefly:

Integration in a Client-Server-Environment: The FALLQ system should be integrated into the Client-Server-Environment existing at LHS. It is intended to provide a WWW-Interface to the system which can be used by customers to access a CBR server performing the retrieval task for a specific set of documents.

Utilization for internal purposes: Currently under investigation is the utilization of the FALLQ system for LHS-internal purposes. For example, system developers want to re-use the knowledge encoded in the various documents. A major advantage is that the vocabulary is nearly the same as that for the FAQ documents because all types of documents deal with the same customer care system. Consequently, only minor changes will be required to internal structures.

5 Experimental results

Currently, the implemented prototype is under evaluation at LHS. In preliminary tests, case bases with up to 1.000 documents have been loaded (approximately 2.6 MB of text data) while the keyword list (cf. Section 3.1) contained about 2.500 entries.

5.1 Evaluation criteria

Following the methodology of CBR and Information Retrieval ([8]), we evaluated the system according to the following criteria:

Speed of retrieval: The time required for performing retrieval.
Recall: How many of the relevant documents are found?
Precision: How many of the found documents are relevant?

Note that the case base provided for the prototype is quite small compared to the huge amount of data that will have to be dealt with in reality. Hence, only very preliminary statements about these criteria can be given in the following.

Speed of retrieval: In initial experiments retrieval was performed extremely fast, that is running on a PC no delay could be recognized between starting the search and getting the answers. On a SPARCstation-10, retrieval time varied between 0.01 and 0.20 seconds depending on the size of the query case[1]. What's more, about 50% of that time is required to parse the input text.

Recall and Precision: In the initial experiments, 3 different situations could be observed:

1. Exactly the same case has been retrieved (if a query equaled one of the cases): This should, of course, be expected.
2. None of the cases retrieved seemed to be useful: In these situations, the queries really seemed to express somewhat new situations since searching the documents manually did not yield any success either.
3. Cases describing related topics have been found: This is, of course, the most interesting situation. According to the feed back from the domain experts, the top ranking cases could have been very helpful to the Hotline staff for answering the posed question.

Summarizing we may state that the recall of the FALLQ system is probably (note the preliminary character of the experiments) very high.

Precision, on the other hand, crucially depends on the query posed to the system. As the FALLQ system has been designed to always retrieve the best k cases, precision will be high if (nearly) k similar cases exist; precision will be low, on the other hand, if only few (or even none at all) similar cases exists. Here, a different scheme might be more desirable such as introducing a kind of similarity *threshold* to avoid that cases are retrieved which, by pure coincidence, share a minor part with the query.

5.2 An example query

To give an illustration of the system's behavior, consider the following question asked by a customer:

---

[1] Note that complexity of retrieval in Case Retrieval Nets does not directly depend on the size of the case base but on the size of the query case.

Query:
Explain the difference between special numbers and the friends and family numbers.

Given this query, the FALLQ system retrieves the following entry as the top case:

Found case:
Is it possible to assign special (low-rate) numbers to subscribers (friends & family)?

The IEs that have been found in both texts have been underlined. As can be seen, there is no direct mapping between the used keywords. For example, in the query the string "special numbers" is used while in the found case the two strings "special" and "numbers" appear isolated. Here the similarity of IEs helps to relate these keywords. While in the example one string is merely a substring of the other, the same model also works for completely different words having a similar meaning.

6 Discussion

A number of questions that did arise during the development of the FALLQ system have already been mentioned above. Here we will focus on unsolved problems and on a comparison with alternative approaches.

6.1 Open issues

Automatic extraction of IEs: As mentioned before, the list of keywords can be extracted from the documents nearly automatically. This is true for IEs representing single words. A problem that has to be solved, however, is how groups of words can be recognized automatically — for example, how does the system realize that "Customer Administration Module" should be represented by a single IE instead of three. Up to now, IEs of this type have to be entered manually.

Adjustment of similarity or relevancy: In the initial version, the relevancy of all IEs has been chosen to be equal for all cases. Of course, there might be IEs playing a more important role than others — and this may even be case-dependent. Since a manual setting of these *weights* is not feasible, research is required about automatic tuning mechanisms.

Handling of misspellings: Currently, FALLQ is not able to deal with misspellings and errors caused by scanning documents. As this is a crucial problem in the application under investigation, methods for dealing with it are required.

Structuring of IEs: For building the FALLQ system, manuals and other materials have been used to gain a basic understanding of the system. This knowledge has been *translated* into a flat structure, namely similarity of IEs. As has been shown in [5], it is possible to utilize more structured knowledge for representing similarity in CRNs. This should be applied in the FALLQ system, too.

Classification of query types: At an early stage of the FALLQ project, we considered to use certain words and phrases to identify the type of query, that is to decide whether the query expresses a simple question, the need for a broader explanation, a question about future functionality etc. For this, a simple method like *Speech Acts* ([9]) could have been applied. However, we did not follow that direction of research as some initial tests did not show an improvement of the retrieval accuracy. This might have been due to the limited size of the case base and needs further exploration.

6.2 Why not *Information Retrieval?*

At first sight, the approach described in this paper may look very similar to traditional approaches from *Information Retrieval* (IR, [8]). What's more, LHS even tested some of the available IR tools before considering CBR. The major disadvantages of IR are:

- IR is mainly based on statistics over document sets, it will be hard to integrate a user-specific similarity measure with a reasonable amount of effort.
- Similarity in most IR approaches is mainly based on common keywords and (sub-)strings. It is not clear how domain-specific knowledge, like system-specific synonyms and abbreviations, can be utilized.

6.3 Why not *Natural Language Processing?*

An alternative to parsing the documents for IEs might be to use more sophisticated *Natural Language Processing* (NLP) techniques. When taking a closer look, again some severe disadvantages for the task at hand can be identified:

- A crucial component of any NLP system is the dictionary. For this, not only the words themselves but also linguistic knowledge about these words is required. Since a number of system-specific terms are required, building this dictionary would involve too much man power.
- Also, robustness of many NLP systems is an open question: What happens if an unknown word occurs which is quite likely in the given environment?
- Analyzing texts in a NLP fashion is surely computationally expensive. Also, mapping the NLP representation of one text to another may be hard. How could similarity of the examples in Section 5.2 be determined? Probably mainly based on the observed keywords — hardly based on the structure.

Nevertheless, we are currently investigating whether it might be helpful to integrate some ideas from the *Information Extraction* community ([7]) in order to obtain a certain amount of structure from the documents.

6.4 Related work from the CBR community

Because of the close relationships between CBR and IR, a number of approaches have been suggested for merging the two. Recent work includes the use of *Terminological Logics* ([2]) which provide a clear semantic and a formal model for handling concept descriptions. For the work reported here, however, it is not clear how the required *TBoxes* and *ABoxes* can be obtained from the plain text documents. Probably, this requires a lot of manual effort and would result in a sophisticated structuring of documents similar to [1].

7 Summary

In this article, we have presented results from the FALLQ project which aimed at applying a CBR approach to the domain of document retrieval. The research carried out in this project resulted in the FALLQ system which can be used to answer a given query by retrieving related documents from domain specific document databases such as *Frequently Asked Questions* archives. The system has been evaluated positively and a follow-up project is currently being established.

Acknowledgments

The authors want to thank all those people who contributed to the success of the FALLQ project, in particular staff members of LHS involved in the project as well as Ralf Kühnel, Mirjam Kunze, Andre Hübner and Thomas Röblitz from Humboldt University and Dirk Wieczoreck, now at Technical University Berlin.

References

1. K. L. Branting and J. C. Lester. Justification structures for document reuse. In Smith and Faltings [10], pp. 76–90.
2. G. Kamp. On the use of CBR in corporate service and support. In M. T. Keane, J. P. Haton, and M. Manago, editors, *2nd European Workshop on CBR (EWCBR-94)*, pp. 175–183
3. M. Lenz and H.-D. Burkhard. Case Retrieval Nets: Basic ideas and extensions. In G. Görz and S. Hölldobler, editors, *KI-96: Advances in Artificial Intelligence*, pp. 227–239, LNAI 1137, Springer Verlag, 1996.
4. M. Lenz and H.-D. Burkhard. Lazy propagation in Case Retrieval Nets. In W. Wahlster, editor, *Proc. ECAI-96*, pp. 127–131, John Wiley and Sons, 1996.
5. M. Lenz, H.-D. Burkhard, and S. Brückner. Applying Case Retrieval Nets to diagnostic tasks in technical domains. In Smith and Faltings [10], pp. 219–233.
6. M. Lenz, H.-D. Burkhard, P. Pirk, E. Auriol, and M. Manago. CBR for Diagnosis and Decision Support. *AI Communications*, 9(3):138–146, 1996.
7. E. Riloff and W. Lehnert. Information extraction as a basis for high-precision text classification. *ACM Transactions on Information Systems*, 12(3):296–333, 1994.
8. G. Salton and M. McGill. *Introduction to Modern Information Retrieval*. McGraw-Hill, New York, 1983.
9. J. Searle. *Speech Acts: An Essay in the Philosophy of Language*. Cambridge University Press, New York, 1969.
10. I. Smith and B. Faltings, editors. *Advances in Case-Based Reasoning*, LNAI 1186. Springer Verlag, 1996.

Combining Medical Records with Case-Based Reasoning in a Mixed Paradigm Design -- TROPIX Architecture & Implementation

A. Sunny Ochi-Okorie, C.Eng., MNSE, MIEE
Visiting Scholar (Senior Lecturer- [1]FUTO),
Center for Advanced Computer Studies (CACS),
The University of Southwestern Louisiana,
2 Rex Street, PO Box 44330, Lafayette, LA 70504-4330; Email: aso@cacs.usl.edu

Abstract

The design architecture, case representation of actual medical cases, and the implementation of *TROPIX*, a tropical disease diagnosis and therapy tool are presented. *TROPIX* is intended to be bundled with laptop computers for rural health centers and semi-urban hospitals in developing countries. Our model uses the *ideal domain knowledge* to build a *decision matrix, DM* from disease *features* against which new cases are measured using the *MVF (Matched Vector Functions)* algorithms. The result of the diagnosis stage provided by the *MVF* procedure and other parameters of the features are then used for CBR case retrievals, verification, and case validation. The final stage in the design yields the selection of 1 or 2 competing cases presented for reuse and perhaps for subsequent *repair* and *adaptation*.

The solution for the new case solved is either one or more actions, a therapy plan or recommendations. The design demonstrates how we can integrate domain knowledge and (medical) records with *CBR, statistical pattern recognition*, and *abductive reasoning* to build a knowledge based system.

1. Introduction

[2]*TROPIX* is an expert systems tool for the diagnosis and treatment of some 22 tropical diseases that are prevalent in Nigeria and other tropical / developing countries.

For its goals, *TROPIX* is to i) act as an advisory tool to novice users, specifically senior nurses in rural hospitals / health centers with limited or no *doctors*; ii) act as a decision support tool for medical diagnostics and therapy for doctors in solo practice or in under staffed hospitals / clinics; iii) provide an alternative way (e.g. CBR) to reach a reasonable tentative diagnosis, and hence early commencement of clinical management of patients in the absence of laboratory facilities in many rural and semi-urban hospitals.

The burden of tropical diseases on many developing countries is astronomical. This may be seen from the populations at risk, the millions infected annually, especially in Africa, the limited trained manpower (World Bank in[12]) and the socioeconomic impact suffered from most of these debilitating diseases.

According the World Health Organization (W.H.O.), global control of Onchocerciasis (river blindness disease due to black flies) is expected to cost over US $15 million per

---

[1]FUTO - Federal University of Technology, Owerri, P.M.B. 1526, Owerri, Imo, Nigeria
[2]Part of the Ph.D. research effort of the author at the FUTO with benchwork done at the CACS (1993-97).

year for next 10 years [WHO Web page]. The economic burden from Malaria is worse.

Taken together, there are over 50 tropical diseases, and whatever studies or applications developments that can be done to improve their diagnosis and therapy, identify pre-disposing factors or new disease vectors (e.g. ticks or black flies) etc., will in the long run contribute significantly towards their control and possible eradication. *TROPIX* is one such system with this objective in mind.

Most tropical diseases have good *symptomatic / attribute* value set that is amenable to *symbolic* or *numeric* processing. This is what makes the methods we use in *TROPIX* quite successful in solving this problem.

TROPIX is a multi-strategy approach involving: statistical pattern recognition or cluster analysis, and abductive inference using the decision matrix in concert with CBR methods. It further integrates medical (domain) records with the CBR library design using a unique strategy for discriminating retained cases from other regular cases that form part of the patients' records in the system [7]. It reaches a tentative diagnosis by invoking some abductive inference [11] using the novel MVF algorithms and the domain's associative knowledge encoded in the disease decision matrix, *DM*. Definitely, our *DM* design model clearly shows the flat association between disease symptoms/signs and pre-disposing factors (pdf's) of a patient which in turn help us establish the *ERF* (*Evidence Ratio Factors*). *ERF*'s are derived from counts of present features and their prior probability contents. The initial diagnosis using the *DM* against the new case data in vectored form are special *associative memory* operations. This offers a minimized search space for a solution considering the size of attributes for all 22 diseases. Following the *tentative disease* determination, it then uses the cases in the case base to perform the validation. Case weights generated by *Singular Value Decomposition* (*SVD*) help to ensure sharp *orthogonality* between classes, and also show the similarities within a disease type and across different disease types. In contrast to work done by some researches like Opiyo in [9], a major goal in *TROPIX* is the diagnosis and therapy of tropical diseases with CBR methods used primarily for validating that diagnosis because of limited lab (test) facilities.

In this paper, we describe the details of its design, and implementation methods used. Much of our efforts have been devoted to the diagnostic side of this problem.

As a result, therapeutic details following past or "ideal" solution retrievals are not given.

Knowledge elicitation was from over 5 medical experts on tropical diseases.

2. Related Work

To our knowledge, there are few applications oriented research that have handled as many disease diagnosis and therapy as we have done in TROPIX, limited to tropical diseases. A few researchers have done work on diagnosis of one or two tropical diseases within the last 3 years, This includes the research of Flaubert and Esae, [3] on malaria.[3]Beatriz Lopez's Ph.D. work on *Case-based Reasoning applied to learning*

---

[3] Beatriz Lopez's Ph.D. work directed by Enric Plaza, a researcher at the IIIA (AI Research Inst.) of the Spanish Scientific Research Council - Source of information: CBR Newsletter Vol. 6 No.2, 1997.

control knowledge in pneumonia diagnosis at the Univ. Politecnica de Catalunya is a recent work of interest, though *pneumonia* is not categorized as a tropical disease.

Opiyo in [9] deals with expertise relocation in support of rural health workers in developing countries. The prototype is called MERSY (a Medical Reference SYstem) with some diagnostic capabilities using CBR case retrieval method based on the *k-nearest neighbor (k-NN)* algorithm. The emphasis of that design is on "reference, rather than diagnosis", and thereby "only acts as source of previous experience" if that experience is already available in its knowledge base or medical records.

Early promising work of Myers and Pople on *Internist*, was briefly described in [5] by Mishkoff. *Internist* (a *rule-based* system) was said have the capability to diagnose some 500 diseases; but was unable to track some inter-relations between disease symptoms. It was later improved as *Caduceus* using a *model-based expert system designed to correct the problems* in its predecessor. Jack Ostroff, et al [10] have also contributed good work in their advisory expert system called "EXPERT" for consultative-decision making for *primary eye care* in *developing countries*.

Another good application project that integrates Case-Based retrieval with a relational DBMS for Aircraft Technical Support was done by J. Allen, et. al reported in [1]. Their work integrates *ReMind* (a CBR shell), Microsoft Access for the relational DBMS to record other important aircraft data, and Visual Basic for the user interfaces.

In assessing *probabilistic similarity* between the new case and the other cases in the case-base, research reported in [6] on *massively parallel case-based reasoning* uses the *inner product* moment (*k-NN algorithm*) and prior probabilities to build similarity ranks. While this vectored approach is advantageous, however it will pay a high price in computation time because of the attempt to literally match "millions of stored cases" in its search for a solution, especially when string features are used.

In order to provide a similarity ranking for a new case, researchers in [1, 2, 6, 9] have matched or propose to match the new case, say $c_{new} = \{c_{new1}, c_{new2}, \ldots, c_{newn}\}$, with the retained (or any cases) in the case-base, $c_x = \{c_{x1}, c_{x2}, \ldots, c_{xm}\} \in \Re$, with the case set elements being some case features, or derived indexes.

Following this reasoning, the authors in [6] suggest the implementation of *"massively parallel connectionist architecture"* which will be suitable for *memory-based* or *instance-based* reasoning in applications like speech-speech translation .

They then derive a *similarity function* (SF) [4] from the *inner product* of c_{new} and c_x, i.e. $S(c_{new}) = F(c_x \, c_{new}) = F\Sigma \, \{c_{new1} c_{x1}, \ldots, c_{newn} c_{xm}\}$.

The idea of *competitors* in diagnosis is said to be related to the *parsimonious covering theory* [11], or *differential diagnosis set* in [7]. In the real-world, a good diagnostician would like to have all available explanations to observable problem symptoms.

Thus, the solution to a diagnostic problem is the *set of all explanations* for the case features present (from symptoms / signs to pdf's and their root causes).

3. TROPIX Architecture and Design Considerations

First, we present an overview and general description of its architecture, with some design considerations. An important feature of the design in *TROPIX* is the way in which it integrates *medical records* within the knowledge based system.

The representation of this design is shown in the *TROPIX* architecture in Fig.1 below.

The ovals represent data repositories, or transitional data packets, while the rectangles mean processes. The logical operation of the system may be appreciated from Fig.1. When new case is received, its *CSI* (Case Similarity Index) is immediately determined, before the diagnosis, and validation steps are performed.

The Case-Base is shown with other patients' records within the larger dashed frame as well as the *DM* which is an associative memory of *ideal* disease classes with their associated symptoms, and the pdf's from patients' environment and background. Additionally, some diagnostic decision rules in the form of constraints are included to check the validity of proffered diagnosis results in the *MVF* matching algorithm.

A new case entry made in *TROPIX* may be thought of (conceptually, as a new branch to a tree) or a "box" full of attributes, having several case indexes. The indexes are, namely -

1. *CaseIRN*, Case Internal Record Number (a function of the patient's id, and the number of cases the patient has had with the hospital or clinic).
2. *CSI* - points to candidate cases, and helps with internal clustering as well as retrieving differential diagnosis set. $CSI = f$ (*symptoms slot#, pdf slot#, $f(ASW)$*). ASW stands for age, sex, weight, respectively.
3. cWt_{dj}, Case Weight (zero for new case until diagnosis / *SVD* operations performed) - helps with case-base selection / validation.
4. d_j (unknown until diagnosis performed); will lead to therapy selection from case-base, or indexing to ideal therapy table $Th(d_j)$.
5. *cCovWt* (covariance value of the case weight - zero until case is classified).
6. *cMeanWt* (case mean weight - zero until case classified).

Fig. 2 below shows this representation. Each case is made up of n real-valued attributes,

$$c_x = \{c_{x1}, c_{x2}, \ldots, c_{xn}\} \in \Re,$$

while the ideal case for each category in *DM* is given by

$$cdj_x = \{cdj_{x1}, cdj_{x2}, \ldots, cdj_{xn}\}^T \in \Re.$$

The case attributes or features form the vector, S_j^T, P_j^T. The features are organized into slots that map each disease in *DM* where it is normally present and depicts the inherent ambiguities in an associative memory-based reasoning. S_j^T for example may be present in disease D_1, and D_{12}. Thus, fever, or headaches as a feature may be present in more than one disease, e.g. *Malaria* has fever, headaches, etc. By the same token, *Yellow Fever* has headaches, fever, and a few other features that might be more distinctive or peculiar to Yellow Fever, but not for Malaria. Although features are grouped and assigned slot values in the prototype design of *TROPIX*, it is very easy to add new features to the design with very minor program changes.

Principal Concepts / algorithms in TROPIX - general scheme

The *DM* consist of dichotomous data representing present (1) or absent (0) attributes. Currently, the system has 129 attributes, and 21 diseases, giving a search space of 2709.

Most of the work reviewed does not use a multi-strategy in their problem solving as is done in TROPIX. Further, among those designs that use the CBR methods [1, 2, 7, 10], TROPIX differs significantly in that it does not match a new case with other existing cases prior to determining its class. Thus, our approach searches the *ideal case* definition classes in *DM* to find the best match, then computes the weight of the new case used in case retrieval (*selection*) from the case library.

This strategy is better because (i) it uses the domain's associative memory to quickly generate a hypothetical answer, and then (ii) uses the CBR method to validate it, or otherwise contest it. It is not affected significantly by any growth in the case-base size.

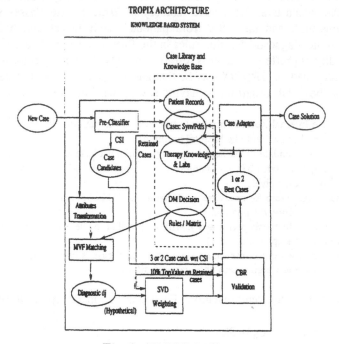

Fig. 1 - TROPIX Architecture

Further, the *MVF* algorithm incorporates data *dissimilarity* analysis (after the Hamman SF in [4]) between the new case features, and those of the ideal case, and minimizes the effect of *irrelevant* features. Following the targeting of a tentative (plausible disease, or disease *competitors*) the retrieval of cases is then done with a threshold value of ±10% of the case weight determined with the *SVD* method for the next level of decision - validation of diagnosis, or otherwise.

MVF Algorithm

The *MVF* procedure is designed to search the *DM* space for the best match. Thus, it analyzes for places where features are *present* in both new case and *DM*, *absent* in both (*irrelevant*), or where they differ (*present* in one, but *absent* in the other).

Consequently, we perform several matrix operations on *DM* and S_j^T & P_j^T (transposed new case features). For space constraints, and completeness, we abridge the algorithm as following.

1. *Begin Function MVF( )* /* lst Pass new features & determine size of vector / matrix
2. Extract SM (sym/signs) and PM (pdf's) form *DM* prototype;
3. Loop:

$$SN_{kj} = \sum (S_j^T \bullet SM_{ij}) \qquad \text{/* computes similarities in } SM$$
$$PN_{lj} = \sum (P_j^T \bullet PM_{ij}) \qquad \text{/* using the inner products}$$

$SQ_{kj} = \Sigma \mid SM_{ij} - S_j^T \mid$ /* computes dissimilarities

$PQ_{lj} = \Sigma \mid PM_{ij} - P_j^T \mid$

$SB_{kj} = \Sigma \{(1 - S_j^T) \bullet (1 - SM_{ij})\}$ /*computes where both have absent features

$PB_{lj} = \Sigma \{(1 - P_j^T) \bullet (1 - PM_{ij})\}$

$n_s' = \Sigma$ s_new   /* determines actual syms/signs present for validation

$n_p' = \Sigma$ p_new   /* determines actual pdfs present

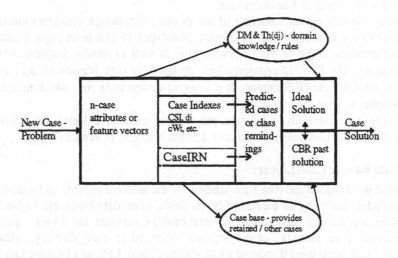

Fig. 2 - A Case Representation as Box Container and Case Interactions

$ESF (d_j) = \chi = \frac{3}{4} n_s' (SN_{kj} + SB_{kj} - SQ_{kj}) + \frac{1}{4} n_p' (PN_{lj} + PB_{lj} - PQ_{lj})$

/* Extended similarity function *(the ¾ and ¼ are domain constants derived from experts opinion on the relative influence of symptoms / signs and pdf on symptomatic or clinical diagnosis)*

$cur\_MVF_1 = 1 - \chi$ (Decreasing function) ⎰ (mirror image)

$cur\_MVF_2 = 1/(1 + \varepsilon^{-x})$ (Sigmoidal function) ⎱ cur_MVF

$s_k = \Sigma RM(n, j)$ /* sums the a priori probabilities of the Rule Matrix from *SM*

$p_t = \Sigma RM(m, j)$ /* sums the a priori probabilities of the Rule Matrix from *PM*

Compute $ERF_j = \frac{1}{2}[(n_s'/n + n_p'/m) + 2(c_1 s_k + c_2 p_t)]$ /* ERF's of dj given its features present.

Use the ERF score to reconcile tie in diagnosis; with *MVF constraint rules* (given in details in [8]), and the highest *ERF* value select *"Best"* of *competing disease category*, d_j, keeping the 2nd or 3rd contender for *differential diagnosis*.

End Loop

4. Compute the case weight by *SVD*:

     Using known d_j Substitute *ideal features* in DM with S_j^T & P_j^T;

     Multiply *DM* by DM^T for data reduction (129x21* 21x129 reduces to 21x21);

     cWt_{dj} = pick value {$SVD(DM)$ for the jth column, and j^{th} row}/*(trace of egenvalues)*

Return (*prev_MVF* , *cur_MVF* , ERF_j, *dj*, cWt_{dj})

End <MVF function>

4. TROPIX Implementation and Methodology

The user interface was built with *Microsoft Access 2.0 / Access Basic®*; while the internal diagnostic algorithms / statistical processing was done with *Matlab®* 4.0 for Windows. The case library was implement on *Access/Jet®* 2.0 database engine.

The hardware used was a 486/DX IBM PC with 16 MB of ram, 50 MHz CPU clock, and over 10 MB of free disk space.

After the conceptual modeling of the project, our design consideration included an easy to use system that can be quickly prototyped to enable us begin evaluation of its performance in the shortest possible time as well as handle frequent developmental changes. The *TROPIX* prototype built on the *Microsoft Windows®* 3.11 environment has full GUI and OLE support. It is an event-driven software - which means that it will respond to what the user wants to do.

There are essentially 3 parts to the system, namely: a Relational DBMS / Case-Library; the User Interface Screens; and the Numeric Inference Engine.

Data base & Case-Library

First we designed the data base schema for the medical records and case-library. This includes specifying all the record types, fields, sizes, data-types, etc. in the data base.

Next we defined and tested the relationships between the tables - patient person record, case records, case_symptoms, case_pdfs, case_Therapy, ideal_Therapy, case_Lab (tests used if ordered by physician), ideal_Lab, and Disease List (holds vital domain data). The relationships include one-many, many-many, and one-one between tables. Based on the tables, we designed several simple query skeletons used as *data source* for the user interface screens -- the Forms. A special protected field called *"Retained"* is added to the *CaseBase* table to segregate retained cases of the 'true' case-library from regular case records of the patient's information system.

User Interface

The Forms (Screens) were then created and populated with the needed controls of various types - regular fields, check-box fields, combo/list box fields, etc. Fig.3 shows the screen for *TROPIX CBR-Main for Case Validation*. Other screens are left out for space constraints. Some controls have attached *event codes* written in *Access Basic* to execute specific actions required.

Some Special Screen Features

Many of the controls on the *TROPIX* screens have prompt capabilities.

Thus, when you point to, or click a mouse on the control, or tab into it, you will be prompted for what to do. This may be a validation text /message on the status bar at the bottom of the screen. This feature became very vital in the question / answering screen of Case-Symptoms and Case-Pdfs during history taking. A click or tab movement onto any attribute question selection will give user possible causes of those manifestations, i.e. suggesting or *explaining* possible disease associations to guide the user's reasoning with the system. Attributes may be selected by clicking the check-box (indicating it is present in patient's case), or not selected (unchecked). Pressing the space-bar key also toggles the check-box in these screens.

CSI values are generated and updated for the case each time the Case-Symptoms and Case-Pdf screens are used. Also, the system creates some 2 special files for data persistence between the *User Interface*, and the *Inference Engine* each time these history taking screens are visited, or used.

Further, we provided a few *Pop-Up* dialog boxes that will present the Disease list, case or patient profiles on-the-fly; thus enabling the user to check consistency or think about vital questions to ask patient in other to capture the right features. Necessary navigation buttons were added with attached *Access Basic* event codes in *procedures* for those controls in order to respond to the events that are *user-driven*.

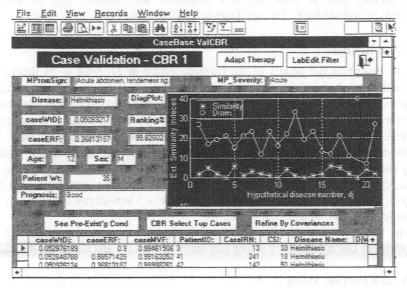

Fig. 3 - CBR-Validation Screen - launched from Case Screen

A few typical reports were created from data base queries for medical case records tracking in the system and routine or exception reporting generally used in overall information management.

The Inference Engine

Accordingly, we built *Access Basic* procedures to activate, link / pass data to *Matlab* when the user presses the *diagnose* button on the Case-Form Screen.

Following the specified algorithms given above, we created the *Matlab* programs - *Diagnose.m*, and CaseCov.m files. The first one carries out the *MVF* procedure to reach a tentative diagnosis, returns result to the controlling program within the user interface for validation to begin. Prior to validation, *Diagnose.m* also generates a plot of current diagnosis which typically will reveal all valid *contending* classes in the diagnosis.

This is a very useful tool in *differential diagnosis* discussed in detail in [8]. Provision has been made in the design to embed this plot to the *Case-Validation Screen* which has an OLE control to receive this generated plot. Typical plots for Yellow fever and Typhoid fever cases are shown in [8].

The validation uses a series of SQL query to search and retrieve cases from the case-base. The search criteria includes the diagnostic, d_j and the case weight, cWt_{dj} returned from invoking *Diagnose.m*. The case weight values for retrieved qualifying cases are then extracted, and passed back to Matlab for *CaseCov.m* to generate covariance's, mean, and standard deviations of those values as a refinement step in the selection process and future statistical learning. The case description (complaints) and the MPS (Most Prominent Signs) fields may be also be matched against those of the retrievals if the user *double clicks* the field in the main form.

Finally, the best case within the d_j class bubbles to the top, and becomes the case whose solution pair is used. In some instances, the solution may be changed (adaptation) using the ideal_Therapy knowledge in the data base.

5. Conclusions

We have described the details of the research effort in *TROPIX* -- its design and implementations showing the underlying reasoning mechanism as a mixed-paradigm used in concert with Case-based Reasoning. The vector-based case representation and the diagnostic abductive reasoning used as a basis for reaching tentative diagnosis are presented. The development of this model as a way of dealing with case manifestations and causes, and the intuitive way to capture these during patient's history taking is a significant accomplishment in this domain.

Further, the integration of medical records data base seamlessly woven with the case-library is shown to be a practical way to combine a knowledge-based system with information systems management.

The user interfaces described illustrate the ease of use of the system with lots of built-in knowledge that dynamically assists user through prompts and status-bar messages.

Results and Further Work

At the time of writing, *TROPIX* has a test case-base of 38 retained cases and some 50 case / medical records of patients - including personal profiles.

Laboratory test results of the prototype have shown approximately 95% accuracy in diagnosis when compared with the selected cases from the hospitals used in the research. The two mis-diagnoses were due to i) incomplete data in DM, and ii) some logic error in the current *MVF* implementation in which it could not resolve some score ties among 3 winning classes. However, the visual plots showed the winning class better than the numeric values. This problem is being addressed to improve system. We also see the need to perform clinical tests of the system to determine its performance - both with novice users (a nurse, or paramedical staff), and with experts (physicians in tropical medicine and parasitology). This will be finished by mid-1998.

Further, the research can use published, or proven test cases to re-evaluate performance of the system, not only in terms of diagnosis, but also on the therapeutic side. Future work includes the idea of implementing a regionally based case-library *servers* equipped with more knowledge content, or additional reasoning techniques like "*smart voting agents*" that would assist several hospitals in very geographically dispersed areas. This seems very feasible on the *Internet / Web*, and would likely be an important tool for doctors to diagnose and treat travel related disease transmissions, disease outbreaks among US troops deployed overseas, or get a second opinion with the ability to access dispersed case-bases for regions of interest.

6. Acknowledgments

The author gratefully acknowledge the support given to this work by Prof. Michael Mulder, and Harold Szu, the current director of CACS for the research facilities arrangements. In addition, many thanks go to Dr. R. Loganatharaj, Dr. T. Maida, and V.J. Raghavan for their useful suggestions and support.

We are also grateful to the many medical experts in Nigeria and the USA who have contributed their ideas and expertise to this work, especially, Dr. J. Osondu - Medical Director of Janet Memorial Hospital Aba; and Don Langford, M.D. (former medical missionary for over 20 years in the tropics, now at) Amelia Industrial Clinic, Amelia Louisiana who helped review the prototype.

The paper reviewers are also appreciated for their valuable comments.

Finally, the work would not have been possible without the initial funding provided by the World Bank's Staff Development Programme of the Nigerian Universities Commission at the FUTO.

I remain indebted to Eng. Prof. C.O.G. Obah, the Vice-Chancellor of FUTO, also my mentor, who charted a course for me in academic endeavors.

7. References

1. Allen, J., Patterson, D., et al, Integration of Case Based Retrieval with a Relational Database System in Aircraft Technical Support, in LNAI 1010 -Veloso M. & Aamodt A., (Eds.) CBR R & D, First Int'l Conf., ICCBR-95, Portugal, Proceedings, pp. 1-10, 1995.

2. Berger, J. *"ROENTGEN: Radiation Therapy and Case-Based Reasoning"*, pp. 171-177, Proc. of the Tenth Conf. on AI for Applications, IEEE Computer Society Press, 1994

3. Flaubert, B.S. and Esae, T.D., *Expert Systems as a useful tool for tropical diseases diagnosis: the case of malaria*, Health Informatics in Africa (HELINA-L) '93, Ile-Ife, Nigeria; Conf. Proceedings, Elsevier Science Publishers, Amsterdam, The Netherlands.

4. Joly, S. and Le Calve', G., *"Similarity Functions"* in Van Cutsem, B. (Ed.), *Classification and Dissimilarity Analysis*, LN in Statistics, Springer-Verlag, New York, 1994.

5. Mishkoff, H.C., *Understanding Artificial Intelligence*, Texas Instrument Inc., Dallas, TX, p3:17-25; 1986.

6. Myllymäki, Petri and Tirri, Henry, "Massively Parallel Case-Based Reasoning with Probabilistic Similarity Metrics", pp. 144-154 in Topics in Case-Based Reasoning, Ed. Stetan Wess, et al, Vol. 837, LNAI, Springer Verlag, 1994.

7. Ochi-Okorie, A.S. *Disease Diagnosis Validation in TROPIX Using CBR*, Accepted to appear in The Journal of Artificial Intelligence in Medicine, Elsevier, January, 1998.

8. Ochi-Okorie, A.S., and Dr. J. Osondu, *Musing With Case Pre-Classifiers As Diagnosis Predictors in a CBR System*, Jan. 1997, Technical Report, TR-97-2-001, The Center for Adv. Computer Studies, The Univ. Of Southwestern Louisiana, Lafayette, LA., USA.

9. Opiyo, E.T.O., *Case-Based Reasoning for Expertise Relocation in Support of Rural Health Workers in Developing Countries*, in LNAI 1010 -Veloso M. & Aamodt A., (Eds.) CBR R & D, First Int'l Conf., ICCBR-95, Portugal, Proceedings, pp. 77-86, 1995.

10. Ostroff, J.H., Dawson, C.R., et al, *An Expert Advisory System for Primary Eye Care in Developing Countries*, in Expert Systems in Government Symposium, ed. K. N. Karna, IEEE Computer Society, pp. 490- 495, 1985.

11. Reggia, J. A., *Abductive Inference*, in Expert Systems in Government Symposium, ed. K. N. Karna, IEEE Computer Society, pp. 484-489, 1985.

12. World Bank, *World Development Report 1993: Investing in Health*, Oxford University Press,1993.

Ocram-CBR:
A Shell for Case-Based Educational Systems

Marco Papagni, Vincenzo Cirillo, and Alessandro Micarelli

Dipartimento di Informatica e Automazione
Università di Roma Tre
Via della Vasca Navale 79, 00146 Roma, Italy
{papagni, cirillo, micarel}@inf.uniroma3.it

Abstract. This paper presents a case-based authoring system for training and educational applications. The system, called Ocram-CBR and developed in JAVA™, can plan lessons for any application domain whatsoever. Ocram-CBR contains a User Modeling module, capable of building a representation of the user objectives and characteristics, that allows personalizing the teaching interaction. A distinguishing feature of the User Modeling module is the use of a hybrid approach, in which case-based components and an artificial neural network are integrated into one coherent system so that each component performs the tasks for which it is best suited. The Training module of Ocram-CBR plans lessons using a library of cases indexed and successively retrieved by means of a discrimination search and serial search. The system has been adapted for a training course in "Information Systems" and for a second application which will teach learners to write business letters more effectively.

1 Introduction

Computer Based Training (CBT) systems can play a crucial role in tutoring quickly and cheaply. In the last few years some researchers (see for example [2], [3] and [8]) have already explored the Case-Based Reasoning approach for educational applications. In this paper we describe Ocram-CBR, a case-based shell system explicitly conceived and developed to allow for authoring both the domain to be taught and the way in which the material is taught. The system plans a training session in a generic domain, customised with the user's preferences and objectives. To achieve this, the system bases itself on past training sessions with similar users and objectives and takes advantage of a User Modeling component.

Ocram-CBR has been adapted for a training course in "Information Systems". While application software already exists, company trainees often need to become aware of what concepts lie behind project management and how planning a project should be approached. Since not all trainees have the same educational background, it would be tiresome to offer all of them the same set course. Our system permits learners to see a series of "slides" so chosen as to correspond to the specific learning needs determined (i) by a user model created through an initial interview; (ii) by the history of the learner with characteristics most similar to those of the user; (iii) by the specific choices the user makes as the course proceeds (learners may skip slides or ask for more details). The System is readily adaptable to teaching any other subject for which a case library and the appropriate training material (a library of slides) has been created. To show how flexible the System is, it has been used also for a second apparently quite different application designed to help users learn how to write effective business letters in English, whether or not they are native speakers of that language.

Ocram-CBR, implemented in JAVA™ and composed by 23,000 lines of code, 164 classes (external libraries not included), 1.13 MBytes of byte-code, is realised in a Client/Server architecture.

2 The General Architecture of the System

Figure 1 shows the architecture of the system. It consists of the following elements:

- a User Modeling component, realised by means of case-based approach, capable of building a representation of the user characteristics and goals (User Model) as desumed by the system through the dialogue;
- a Training component, capable of planning lessons on a specific domain according to the user characteristics, represented in the User Model, and the user objectives ;
- a User Interface, that manages the interaction between user and system.

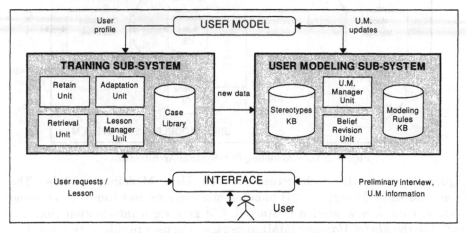

Figure 1: Global architecture.

The system allows any type of user to get different functionalities: student, teacher and administrator. The student can submit some teaching problems as planning lesson, request of example, request of exercise, etc.

The teacher can insert new cases, teaching material, new topics, and can easily define an original solution to a teaching problem.

Finally the administrator, through user-friendly interface, can set all system parameters and the current case structure; this functionality allows one to use the system in different tutoring domains.

In the following sections we give an overview of the anatomy of the system components.

3   The User Modeling Sub-System

The user model is a frame whose slots are basically attribute-value pairs, called components, that describe some interesting aspects of the user knowledge.

The user modeling process entails the following activities:

1. Identifying current user.
2. Retrieving the proper user model, if any, or performing a preliminary interview.
3. Updating the model in order to insert or remove information about the user.
4. Retrieving data from the model to answer explicit request from the host system.

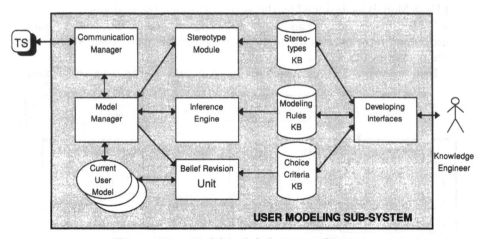

Figure 2: User Modeling Sub-System Architecture.

Figure 2 shows the architecture for the User Modeling module. The *Communication Manager* (CM) handles messages to and from the training system. Once a new session is started, CM gets login information that are useful to the *Model Manager* (MM) to retrieve the user profile, if the user has already been modelled (otherwise a preliminary interview is performed). The MM eventually updates the current User Model whenever the host system asks data to be inserted into or removed from the model. When the model is updated, MM activates in turn the *Stereotype Module* and the *Inference Engine*. The former will be exploited later on in this section, the latter simply searches for firing rules in the modeling rules *Knowledge Base* (KB), i.e. for rules whose left hand side pattern matches with a component already present in the model, and inserts the right hand side of those rules into the model. At the end the *Belief Revision Unit* (BRU), based on ATMS is activated if any inconsistency is found within the model; BRU solves the inconsistencies according to the criteria coded into the *Choice Criteria KB*.

The User Modeling system uses an approach for user modeling based on *stereotypes* [6]. A *stereotype* can be viewed as a description of a prototypical user.

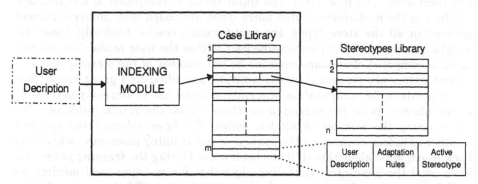

Figure 3: Case-Based Approach to User Modeling.

We have used a method for the integration of symbolic Artificial Intelligence (AI) and artificial neural networks for the task of automatically inferring user stereotypes during the user modeling phase. In particular, in our approach we integrate an artificial neural network in a case-based reasoner. A possible case-based approach for the selection of the most suited stereotype, on the basis of the user behaviour, is represented in Figure 3. The case library contains the old cases (gathered from experts in the domain) in the form of frames, whose slots are the "user behaviour" (a pattern constituted by the actual values of the attributes for a particular user), the "selected stereotype" (that can be viewed as a pointer to the Library of Stereotypes) and a *demon*, i.e. a procedural attachment, that is activated when the old case is indexed, which triggers the knowledge base of adaptation rules which adapt the selected stereotype to the content of the User Model. When the system is presented with a pattern of attributes relative to the particular user, the indexing module tries to find the old case that closely matches (according to a specific metric) the new case. The selected old case contains all the relevant information useful for classifying the user, i.e. the most suited stereotype and the demon that activates the adaptation rules, starting from the selected stereotype and the actual pattern representing the user behaviour. One problem posed by this approach is in the determination of a metric to be used in the indexing module: in fact we have noticed that this type of classification of users must be made in the light of incomplete and often conflicting information. Our proposed solution (which has already been successfully experimented in the domain of *adaptive hypermedia*, see [4]) consists in the use of a *function-replacing hybrid*, where an artificial neural network implements (i.e., is functionally equivalent to) the module represented in bold line in Figure 3. The old cases present in the library of cases are used as *training records* for training the network. The metric of the indexing module of Figure 3 is in that way replaced by the *generalisation* capability of the network. One advantage of this choice is that the distributed representation and reasoning of the neural network allows the system to deal with incomplete and inconsistent data and also allows the system to "gracefully degrade" [7]. Since this kind of classification problem is in general not linearly separable, a Multi-Layer-Perceptron [7] with three distinct layers has been used. The first layer, the input layer, is composed of the neurons relative to the n attributes-value pairs (that are coded into numeric values) present in all the stereotypes; the input values comes, basically, from the weight associated the attribute-value pair within the user model. The output layer is composed of as many neurons as the number of the stereotypes. The output values are computed by the network according to a given input; this corresponds to the computation of a rank-ordered list of stereotypes present in the library. As for the hidden layer, there are no theoretical guidelines for determining the number of hidden nodes. We have selected the optimal number of hidden neurons in the context of the training procedure, where the backpropagation algorithm ([7]) has been used. During the training phase, we have used the Simulated Annealing algorithm for avoiding local minima as well as escaping from them when necessary (see [5] for more details concerning the authoring phase of the network). In our first experiments we have measured the efficacy end the efficiency of the user modeling component (which is actually a shell system currently used in an information filtering system as well, see [1]). The proposed architecture proved to be more precise than the traditional approach to stereotype recognition via triggers.

4   The Training Sub-System

The architecture of the training sub-system is shown in Figure 4. By describing a sample session, we will explain the interaction and the roles of the modules present in the figure.

The student, by using the *Student Interface*, selects one training problem to submit to the system (e.g., "Lesson Planning", "Details Request", etc.), and then characterizes the request. For example the student selects "Lesson Planning" and then inputs the *primary topic* of the lesson (e.g., "Project Management"), and, if desired, a list of *secondary topics* to be included in the lesson (e.g., "Business Process"), along with the objective of his training (acquire new knowledge or procedures, refresh some concepts, etc.).

The *User Modeling* sub-system retrieves the model of the particular user who is using the system; the model contains: (i) information about the user knowledge of system topics (this knowledge is represented by means of a semantic network; a value for each concept pinpoints the user's expertise with respect to that knowledge); (ii) data regarding the user (e.g., grades given by the system, average difficulty of requested training, etc); (iii) a list of attribute-value pairs, that tells the system the user's preferences about each section of a lesson (introduction, exercises, examples, images, etc.), and gives the program the ability to present topics in a suitable manner. Four procedures are then activated using the information about the user. These are: 1) definition of Learning Context; 2) Case Retrieval and Adaptation; 3) Lesson Presentation; 4) Case Retain. A lesson is an ordered sequence of slides, hyperlinked and retrieved from the *Training Material Library,* which appears on the screen; presentation order is based on past cases.

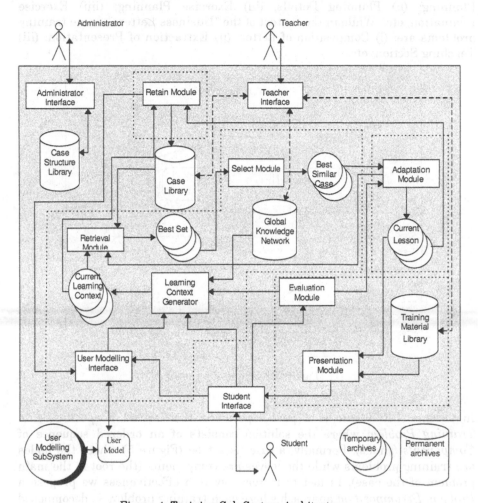

Figure 4: Training Sub-System Architecture.

A user-friendly *Administrator Interface* allows the administrator to set all the system parameters (e.g., case information, user features, training problems, etc.) for a particular training context.

As in any authoring system, the *Teacher Interface* allows the teacher to introduce the solution for a case that describes a training problem.

4.1   Problem Decomposition approach and Case Library

Ocram-CBR is capable of solving a general *training problem*, that is, a problem described by a sequence of *attribute-value* pairs, preliminary defined by the administrator. For instance, in the case of the training course on "Information Systems", examples of training problems are: (i) Lesson Planning; (ii) Planning Details; (iii) Exercise Planning; (iiii) Exercise Evaluation, etc.. While in the context of the "Business Letters", some training problems are: (i) Composition of Letter; (ii) Extraction of Presentation; (iii) Teaching Section; etc..

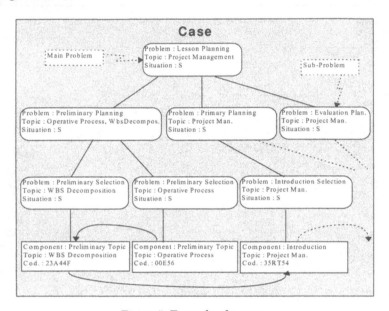

Figure 5: Example of a case.

In Ocram-CBR a *case* is a past experience that solved a specific *Main Training Problem* where the solution consists of an ordered sequence of *Components* (slides). Formally, a *case* is a tree (Figure 5) where the nodes are training problems while the leaves are components (the root is the main problem of the case). In fact to increase system effectiveness we propose a *Problem Decomposition* approach where each training problem is decomposed into sub-problems, each of which is then decomposed in the same way, until an elementary problem (solution component) is reached. This method allows the teacher to define the solution of a problem in a creative mode (there is not a pre-defined structure of the solution) and allows the system to reuse old case parts when needed. To permit the system to solve new problems, by reusing old case-decompositions that have been proposed in situations similar to the new one, each *case* in the *Case Library* is stored as linked set of *Case Elements*. A *Case Element* represents a two-level sub-tree (decomposition) of the *case*. Each level is defined by a *<Training Problem, Solution>* pair (Figure 6). A *Training Problem* sums up the context where the

Solution has been proposed, and thus contains the *Problem Descriptor* and the *Situation*. Figure 6 shows an example of a *Training Problem* described by a specific set of *attribute-value* pairs, the *Problem Descriptor*, and other sets that define the *Student Learning Status* (user's knowledge status before the lesson), *Student Features* (grade, cultural level, interests, etc.) and *Lesson Preferences* (user's preferences regarding lesson arguments; e.g., presentation, topic depth, exercises, etc.).

The *Solution* is a set of *sub-problems* (each one with its own type and description) or is a set of *components*.

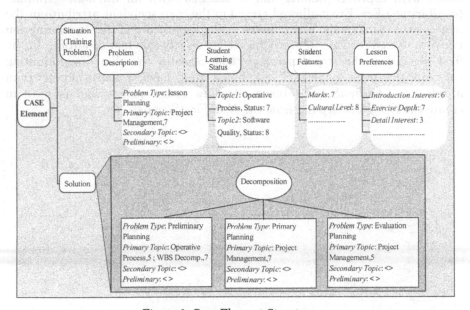

Figure 6: Case Element Structure.

The Case Library stores each case by recording its case-elements indexed with a discrimination network and retrieved with the DSR algorithm (Figure 7). When Ocram-CBR faces a new problem, it uses the DSR algorithm to retrieve from the *Case Library* the *Case Element* that best matches the new training problem; then it defines the solution for the last problem adapting the solution of the retrieved *Case Element*. If it is an elementary solution the process ends, otherwise each sub-problem of the new solution is solved in the same way (the solution is a decomposition). According to the capabilities, knowledge and goals of the user (that are stored in the user model), the *Adaptation Module* modifies this decomposition and communicates to the *Retrieval Module* all not elementary sub-problems that need decomposition.

4.2 The Retrieval Algorithm

The retrieval algorithm *DSR* (Discrimination and Serial Retrieval) we propose (Figure 7) makes a discrimination search only on the most important attributes (each attribute is weighted by a relevance factor p_i), that must necessarily match with the new case values, while other attributes are analysed by a serial search. Therefore only the case that best matches with the new one (and needs low adaptation effort) is retrieved. The similarity metric $(Similarity(x_i,y_i)=1-d(x_i,y_i))$ used in the algorithm is based on the distance metric shown in Figure 7 where D_i is the i-th attribute domain and $w_i(x_i,y_i)$ is the distance between symbolic attributes x_i, y_i in the semantic network; this network holds correlations between every topic known to the system and is implemented in the *Global Knowledge Network*. *PartialSelection()* is used to create the *NodeFirstStep* list that contains all nodes with depth=*DepthMax* and is labelled with an *attribute* "similar" (similarity>1-Err, Err = allowed error) to the correspondent attribute in the new case. A case is a list of attributes in the same order of the discrimination network: weight order. All preceding nodes satisfy this last condition. In the first algorithm, the step *PartialSelection()* creates the list discriminating between the most important attributes that have a depth lower than *MaxDepth*. *ChildrenSet(n)* returns all cases under node *n* and is used to create the *CaseFirstStep* list from the *NodeFirstStep* list.

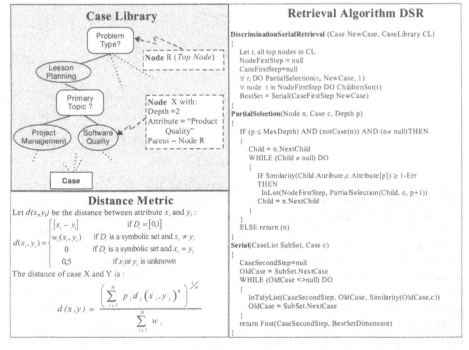

Figure 7: The Case Library with the Distance Metric and
the Retrieval Algorithm DSR.

Serial() orders all cases in the *CaseFirstStep* list considering all attributes that create an ordered list (*CaseSecondStep* list) and returns the first *BestSetDimension* elements (using *First()*). These will constitute the *BestSet* (*InTidyList(l,e,mis)* inserts in the list *l* the elements *e* in the proper position using the weight *mis*). This method finds the case that best matches the new one in an efficient and effective manner.

5 Conclusions

This paper has described Ocram-CBR in which the User Modeling sub-system is based on a hybrid architecture. This choice guarantees *fault tolerance* to noise in the data which represent user behaviour, a capability that allows the system to "gracefully degrade". The Training sub-system can plan lessons independently of the application domain. In this context a teacher can easily insert new topics and cases from which the system can generate automatically new lessons using its own training experience. Moreover the teacher can easily custom the system to different training domains. The retrieval algorithm used in the Training sub-system is based on a combination of discrimination and serial searches.

The system, functionally operative, will now be tested from the standpoint of user satisfaction.

References

1. Ambrosini, L., Cirillo, V. and Micarelli, A.: "A hybrid Architecture for User-Adapted Information Filtering on the World Wide Web". In *Proceedings of the 6th International Conference on User Modeling UM-97*, Chia Laguna (In press) (1997).
2. Chandler, T.N.: "The Science Education Advisor: Applying a User Centered Design Approach to the Development of an Interactive Case-Based Advising System". *In Journal of Artificial Intelligence in Education*, **5**(3) (1994) 283-318.
3. Kolodner, J.L.: "From Case-Based Reasoning to Scaffolded Electronic Notebooks: A Journey". In J. Greer (ed.) *Proc. of AI-ED 1995*, Charlottesville: AACE (1995) 25-35.
4. Micarelli, A. and Sciarrone, F.: "A Case-Based Toolbox for Guided Hypermedia Navigation". In *Proc. of the Fifth International Conference on User Modeling UM-96*, Kailua-Kona, Hawaii (1996a) 129-136.
5. Micarelli, A. and Sciarrone, F.: "A Case-Based System for Adaptive Hypermedia Navigation". In: I. Smith and B. Faltings (eds.) *Advances in Case-Based Reasoning*. Lecture Notes in Artificial Intelligence, Springer-Verlag, Berlin (1996b) 266-279.
6. Rich, E.: "Users are individuals: individualizing user models". *International Journal of Man-Machine Studies*, **18** (1983) 199-214.
7. Rumelhart, D.E. and McClelland, J.L. (eds): *Parallel Distributed Processing*. MIT Press, Cambridge, Massachusetts (1986).
8. Schank R. C.: "Case-Based Teaching : Four Experiences in Educational Software Design". In *Interactive learning Environments* **1** (1990) 231-253.

From Troubleshooting to Process Design: Closing the Manufacturing Loop

C. J. Price, I. S. Pegler, M. B. Ratcliffe, A. McManus

Department of Computer Science, University of Wales, Aberystwyth
Ceredigion, SY23 3DB, United Kingdom
email: cjp@aber.ac.uk

Abstract. This paper describes the dual use of a case base for diagnosis and for improving the design of a manufacturing process. In the short term, the case base is used to provide past experience in dealing with similar problems during the manufacture of aluminum components. In the longer term, it is used to feed that experience into the design of the manufacturing process for new components.

This is achieved by having a case base of previous manufacturing process problems and solutions. For diagnosis, case base matching is done in a fairly straightforward manner. In order to use the cases in design analysis, the case information about process type and problems with a particular process is fed into a process failure mode and effects analysis (FMEA), and provides details of possible problems and their likelihood.

1 Introduction

The use of cases for troubleshooting problems has been one of the success stories of case-based reasoning (CBR), for example [1, 2]. This paper describes a case-based assistant for troubleshooting process problems in an aluminum foundry. This work extends the use of CBR for troubleshooting in two significant ways.

Firstly, the storing of cases for use in troubleshooting is done implicitly, rather than by an explicit software maintenance action as is usually the case. The reason why this is practical are discussed.

Secondly, and more significantly, the cases are used as a way of closing the loop back to design, in an attempt to improve the manufacturing process by reducing the incidence of similar problems in the future.

2 Troubleshooting the foundry with cases

A brief description of the pressure die casting process

The parts produced by aluminium die-casters are typically *finished products*. The process of casting the metal is only one of a long list of operations such as clipping, milling, drilling, powder coating, inspection, storage, transportation. Each of these processes is subject to different kinds of failures.

The machines used to cast the metal vary in the way they operate. Most machines inject the metal from the side, others from the top. In addition, a vacuum system can be used to drain air from the cavity prior to casting, in order to lessen the effect of air pockets in the casting. Larger machines would be used to cast heavier or more complex parts. The characteristics of the die can also vary, from a simple die of two halves, to a more intricate system with sliders and cores that allow more complex shapes to be cast. Some dies contain multiple impressions of the same part, so that several can be made during one casting cycle.

Although the kinds of problems that occur in the die casting process are similar from one foundry to another, the methods used to tackle the problems can be foundry-specific. Because there are different approaches to casting, building a general rule-based troubleshooting system for foundries would be difficult. Troubleshooting requires detailed knowledge of design constraints, customer requirements and the manufacturing process as implemented at the particular foundry. This means that troubleshooting information is often foundry specific, and best expressed as cases.

Recording foundry problems

The foundry process troubleshooting system was based on an existing paper-based process concern report (PCR) quality control system, where process problems were recorded on paper and tracked until they were solved. In the worst cases, a truckload of aluminum components might be returned from a customer because of some problem such as bad surface finish. The foundry staff would need to:

- record the return of stock
- check the quality of further components of the same type made since the delivery
- identify whether the problem was still occurring and fix it
- decide what could be done with the returned stock
- plan what to do to avoid repetition of the problem in future

The computerised version of the PCR system records problems in a database, and has links to other foundry databases in order to make entry of information as painless as possible, e.g. by entering a component name, the PCR system pulls in customer details. The problem is described by selecting the process name from a list of processes, and then selecting a problem type from a list of possible problems with that process. In addition, free text may also be used to describe the problem.

An example of a problem specification is given in figure 1.

Matching past problems

When the basic problem description has been entered, the user can choose to perform case based matching against previous similar problems. Cases in the PCR system are flat database records. Case matching is done by nearest neighbour, and produces a list of possibly relevant cases by a weighted match on:

116

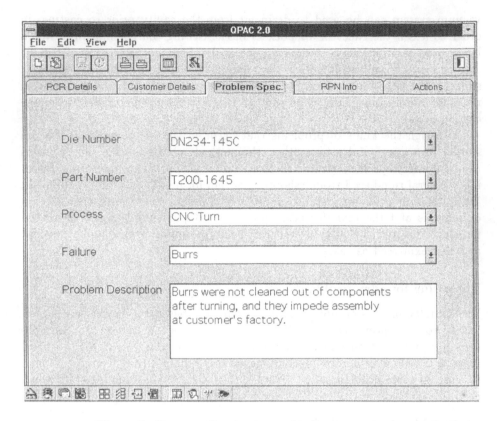

Fig. 1. Problem specification in troubleshooting system

- type of the process in which the problem occurred
- specific problem with the process
- component category
- component attributes
- recentness of past problem

A list of matches like the one shown in figure 2 is produced. The user can look through this list and examine the detailed record of each past case, using their judgement to select the most appropriate of the matches. The component category matching is based on a component hierarchy, and is used to order the cases in such a way that the most likely cases will be those as close as possible in the hierarchy to the problem.

Classifying the components manufactured at the foundries involved investigation of the quality demands required of different types of component. Different categories with identical quality demands were merged. The process of building the classification tree was an iterative process requiring a great deal of consultation with quality managers.

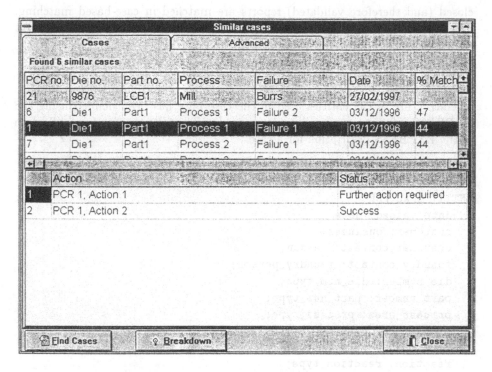

Fig. 2. Matching problem to past cases

When a good match with a past case is found, details of the actions taken last time can be imported to the present case, providing information on matters such as the appropriate team of people to deal with the problem, the actions needed to solve the problem, and the most efficient way to handle the faulty components already made.

As well as providing painless entry of information, the foundry staff have been encouraged to use the PCR system by provision of facilities such as automated faxing of problem report acknowledgements to customers, and problem tracking facilities for quality managers to monitor the progress of solutions to problems.

The PCR system has been installed at three aluminum foundries which run similar computing facilities. Each foundry presently has a three figure number of cases recorded, and uses the system to record, track and help fix all problems that occur.

One of the notable features of the PCR system is that no outside support for case base maintenance is needed. All problems are eventually fixed, and when they are, the foundry quality manager *closes* the problem report. The act of closing a problem report essentially validates the case associated with that problem report, saying that an acceptable solution has been found. Only closed (and therefore validated) reports are matched in case-based matching. The foundry quality managers are validating the casebase while carrying out their normal function.

2.1   Structure of case

The structure of the entities used in the case base has been defined using the EXPRESS information modelling language [3]. The following is a simplification of the EXPRESS description for a case.

```
(* definition of abstract PCR *)
ENTITY QPAC_PCR
   date_raised: date;
   customer: business;
   customer_contact: person;
   foundry_contact: foundry_person;
   die_number: die_num_type;
   part_number: part_num_type;
   process_area: process_type;
   problem: problem_type;
   severity: severity_type;
   reaction: reaction_type;
   occurrence: percentage; -- percentage of parts affected
   quantity: whole_number;-- number of parts affected
   description: strings;
   actions: LIST [1:?] OF action;
WHERE
   problem_ok:
      applicable(problem,process_area);
END_ENTITY; -- end of top level PCR entity

(* entity to define a simple action *)
ENTITY action;
   action_by: foundry_person;
   action_taken: action_taken_type;
   action_status: action_status_type;
END_ENTITY;

action_status: (for_information_only,
further_action_required,
success,
failure);
```

The cases are stored using a DBASE3 database, and case retrieval is done by database access and the weighted match described earlier.

3 Feeding cases into process FMEA

One of the tasks often carried out when designing the manufacture of a new aluminum component is a process Failure Mode and Effects Analysis (FMEA) [4]. Process FMEAs are often carried out by design engineers rather than staff in day to day contact with what happens on the foundry floor. In theory, they are supposed to be a live document, reflecting the latest experience of problems on the factory floor. In practice, that is seldom the case.

The Process Concern Report case base contains a history of process problems that can be used to feed practical experience into the process FMEA exercise. In this way, the case based experience that has been built up can help to eradicate those process problems during the design stage of a new component.

The key to the use of the case base in this way is a process flowchart system that enables an engineer to describe the processes that are carried out during manufacturing. This is done by selecting process names from a drop down list. This list contains the same processes as are used in the troubleshooting system. By enumerating all of the processes used to manufacture the part, a list of process/failure combinations can be generated for use in FMEA (see figure 3).

The validated case base can be used to supply real data on the problems that can occur with each process. The severity and frequency information about related past cases can be used to attach significance values to each possible problem, highlighting for the engineers the most important problems to tackle.

The case base also includes the foundry staffs best advice on precautionary steps for avoiding such problems in the long run, feeding that experience into the design process.

Again, the relevance of such past cases is decided not just by matching similar processes, but by a more complex match including component attributes and similarity in the component hierarchy.

Process FMEAs are intended to be live documents, i.e. continually referenced and updated. In practice these documents are produced to satisfy customer requirements and are rarely utilised to their full potential. Typically they are referenced as a last resort when troubleshooting. Using case-based reasoning to integrate FMEA generation with problem logging, troubleshooting and quality-related tasks maximises the potential for the re-use of design and troubleshooting knowledge within the foundry.

4 Summary

Figure 4 illustrates the central role that the PCR case base plays in troubleshooting and in design. Case-based reasoning provides the cornerstone for allowing troubleshooting knowledge to be built up and re-used for quality-related procedures. It provides excellent data for creating a realistic process FMEA report, and even beyond that, for deciding on inspection and control checks in the foundry itself.

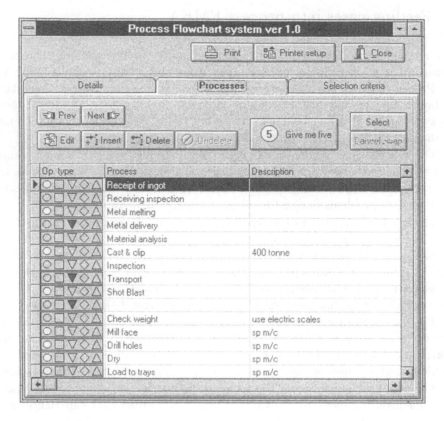

Fig. 3. Process flowchart for making a new component

The largest of the foundries where the case based system described in this paper has been implemented has less than 400 employees. Even in companies of this size, CBR provides a valuable repository of past decisions, and feeding that experience into future designs is proving valuable. The potential for this kind of system should be even greater in large companies where knowledge is more widely diffused through the organization.

Acknowledgements

This work has been carried out on the UK EPSRC funded project GR/K/81829, with the cooperation of Kaye (Presteigne) Ltd, Morris Ashby Ltd, and Burdon and Miles Ltd. Building the cases was possible due to the assistance of the three Foundry Quality Managers, Stuart Lewis, Ken Hawkes and Barry Clayton.

References

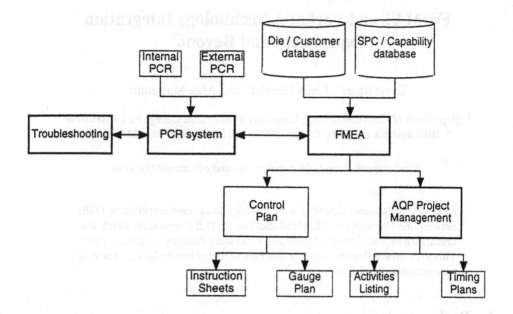

Fig. 4. Overall troubleshooting/design perspective

References

1. Acorn. T. L.. Walden, S. H.: SMART: Support Management Automated Reasoning Technology for Ccmpaq Customer Service. In Innovative Applications of Artificial Intelligence 4, eds: Scott, A. C., Klahr, P; AAAI Press (1992) 3–18
2. Dattani, I. Magaldi, R. V., Bramer, M. A.; A Review and Evaluation of the Application of Case-based Reasoning (CBR) Technology in Aircraft Maintenance. Applications and Innovations in Expert Systems IV. SGES Publications (1996) 189–203
3. Schenck, D. A., Wilson, P. R.; Information Modeling the EXPRESS Way. Oxford University Press (1994) ISBN 0-19-508714-3
4. Failure Mode and Effects Analysis Handbook. Ford Motor Company Ltd (1995)

ForMAT and Parka: A Technology Integration Experiment and Beyond*

David Rager[1], James Hendler[1], and Alice Mulvehill[2]

[1] Department of Computer Science, University of Maryland, College Park MD 20742
[2] BBN Systems and Technologies, 10 Moulton Street, Cambridge MA 02138

Email: rager@cs.umd.edu, hendler@cs.umd.edu, amm@bbn.com

Abstract. This report describes a Technology Integration Experiment (TIE) between the University of Maryland and The MITRE Corporation which was undertaken as part of the (D)Arpa/Rome Laboratory Planning Initiative (ARPI). This work led to an integration of the UM Parka-DB tool into the MITRE ForMAT transportation planning tool.

1 Background

In case-based planning (CBP), previously generated plans are stored as cases in memory and can be reused to solve similar planning problems. CBP can save considerable time over planning from scratch (generative planning), thus offering a potential (heuristic) mechanism for handling intractable problems. The CaPER system [8], focused on new approaches to CBP. In particular, one drawback of CBP systems has been the need for a highly structured memory that requires significant domain engineering and complex memory preindexing schemes to enable efficient case retrieval

In contrast, the CaPER CBP system used the Parka high performance knowledge representation system [9] to retrieve plans quickly from a large memory that was not preindexed. Thus, it was relatively inexpensive to access memory frequently, and memory could be probed flexibly at case retrieval time. CaPER issued a variety of queries that resulted in the retrieval of one or more plans (or parts of plans) that were combined to solve the target planning problem. These plans could be merged and harmful interactions among them resolved using annotations on a plan to capture interdependencies among its actions [8, 7, 5, 9].

Transportation Logistics Planning The United States Transportation Command (US-TRANSCOM) is responsible for generating and maintaining the plans by which United States military forces are deployed. This responsibility includes determining the transportation needs for missions short and long, small and very large. For large missions, the

* This research was supported in part by grants from NSF(IRI-9306580), ONR (N00014-J-91-1451), AFOSR (F49620-93-1-0065), the ARPA/Rome Laboratory Planning Initiative (F30602-93-C-0039), ARPA I3 Initiative (N00014-94-10907), ARPA contract DAST-95-C0037 and the Army Research Laboratory. Dr. Hendler is also affiliated with the UM Institute for Systems Research (NSF Grant NSF EEC 94-02384).

process by which these transportation plans are constructed can be very complex and time consuming. Representatives from the various services and commands involved in a plan must collectively decide how best to allocate the limited transportation resources (aircraft, ships, trucks and trains) to achieve the many military goals of the mission. The end result of this process is an Operational Plan (OPLAN) which specifies where and when the forces involved in a mission are to be moved. Associated with an OPLAN are one or more Time Phased Force Deployment Data (TPFDD) which describe what, when, and how the forces for a mission will be deployed. The OPLAN and TPFDDs are stored and maintained until their execution is called for. At that time, the plan will generally have to be modified to fit the particular details of the current situation.

ForMAT (Force Management and Analysis Tool) provides an environment in which a force development and planning specialist can view, modify, and create the basic structures of TPFDDs (called force modules, or FMs). FMs prescribe a force or set of forces that can be used to satisfy some planning requirement. The FM is typically a grouping of combat, combat support, and combat service support forces, and ranges in size from the smallest combat element to the largest combat group. It may specify accompanying supplies and the required movements, resupply, and personnel necessary to sustain forces for a minimum of 30 days. The elements of a FM are linked together so that they may be extracted from, or adjusted as, an entity to enhance the flexibility and usefulness of a plan. One or more FMs for use in a given plan are stored in a TPFDD. In theory, FMs form a library which can be drawn upon to quickly build a new plan. In a crisis, new TPFDDs will be built, at least in part, from FMs within one or more existing TPFDDs.

The force modules that compose TPFDDs are themselves composed of smaller units called Unit Line Numbers (ULNs). A ULN identifies a force, support for a force, or a portion of a force. A ULN is often described by its Unit Type Code, which can span a wide range of items from tactical fighter squadrons and army battalions to dog teams, or even a Catholic chaplain. Finding appropriate ULNs (and therefore FMs) in previous TPFDDs is a complex task, similar to case-retrieval in case-based planning.

2 High Performance Support for ForMAT

The integration of ForMAT and the University of Maryland system began from a Technology Integration Experiment (TIE) which examined whether the "structure matching" system developed for supporting the case-based reasoning in CaPER could also handle retrieval in ForMAT. Before we describe this integration, we review the approach to structure matching in CaPER and the parallel versions of the algorithms that provided the original speedup needed to support a knowledge base as large as ForMAT required. (Note that we eventually were able to support ForMAT on a single processor using a data-based version of Parka. This work is described in Section 3.)

2.1 Representing Structures for Matching

Our description of the problem of structure matching follows that given in [12]. A knowledge base (KB) defines a set, P, of unary and binary predicates. Unary predicates have the form $P_i(x)$ and binary predicates have the form $P_j(x_1, x_2)$, where each x_i is a variable on the set of frames in the KB. An existential conjunctive expression on these predicates is a formula of the form $\exists x_1, \ldots, x_m : P_1 \wedge P_2 \wedge, \ldots, \wedge P_n$, where $n \geq 1$. Our task is to retrieve all structures from memory which match a given conjunctive expression. Therefore, we would like to find all such satisfying assignments for the x_i.

We can view the problem of matching knowledge structures in two ways. The first is as a subgraph isomorphism problem [3]. We view variables as nodes and binary predicates as edges in a graph. We want to find structures in memory which "line up" with the graph structure of the query expression. The other way to view the matching problem is as a problem of unification or constraint satisfaction. If we can find a structure in memory which provides a consistent assignment to the variables x_i (i.e., unification), then that structure matches the conjunctive expression.

Overview of the Algorithm. The structure matching algorithm operates by comparing a retrieval probe, P, against a knowledge base to find all structures in the KB which are consistent with P. This match process occurs in parallel across the entire knowledge base. A Parka KB consists of a set of frames and a set of relations (defined by predicates) on those frames. Most relations are only implicitly specified and so must be made explicit by expanding the relation with the appropriate inference method. By computing inherited values for a relation, all pairs defining the relation are made explicit. We currently allow only unary and binary relations.

A retrieval probe is specified as a graph consisting of a set of variables $V(P)$ and a set of predicates (or constraints) $C(P)$ that must simultaneously hold on frames bound to those variables. The result of the algorithm is a set of k-tuples, where each k-tuple encodes a unique $1 - 1$ mapping of frames to variables in $V(P)$, that unifies with the description of the structure in memory with $C(P)$. The set of frames that can bind to each variable is initially restricted by a set of constraints indicated by unary predicates. Each unary constraint may only constrain the values of one variable. Examples of these constraints are "X is a dog" or "the color of X is yellow". We allow set theoretic combinations of the unary constraints, for example "X is a dog and the color of X is yellow", or "X is a dog but X is not yellow"[4] The domains for each variable are maintained throughout the match process and are further restricted as more constraints are processed.

Constraints between frames bound to variables are specified by a set of binary constraints. For example, we can say "the color of X must be Y", or "X is a part of Y", for some X and Y in $V(P)$. Binary constraints are processed by "expanding" the binary relation given in the constraint. By expansion we mean that all pairs participating in a relation R in the KB are made explicit by invoking the inference method for the associated predicate. The pairs allowed to participate in the expanded relation

---

[3] More specifically, this is a problem of Directed Acyclic Graph (DAG) isomorphism with typed edges, the edges being the relations in the KB between frames.

[4] Variables in the query probe which do not appear in a unary constraint are treated differently. Variables not contained in a unary constraint are still able to be constrained by intersecting the instances of the range and domain of the predicates in binary constraints in which the variable appears.

are restricted to those in the domains of the variables related by R. For example, a binary constraint may be expressed as (Color X Y). In this case the values for each concept in the domain of X are computed for the color predicate and pairs that have values outside the domain of Y are excluded. Two additional binary predicates, "eq" and "neq" are provided to provide codesignation and non-codesignation of variables. These constraints act as a filter, eliminating any tuples from the result for which the constrained variables are(not) bound to the same frame.

The result of a structure match is a set of k-tuples, where each tuple corresponds to a satisfying assignment of the k variables. Alternatively, the result can be viewed as a relation. Initially, the matcher begins with an empty set of relations. During the match, several intermediate relations may be constructed. Simple binary relations result from the expansion of a binary constraint. These are later fused (via a relational join operation) or filtered (via codesignation or non-codesignation) until a single relation remains. The algorithm selects binary constraints to process using a greedy algorithm based on a simple cost model stored in the metadata.

3 Integrating ForMAT and PARKA

Based on our successes in the creation of the single processor version of PARKA, we focused our effort on the design of a new version which would optimize single-processor performance using a database system to provide both efficiency and scalability. The resulting system, PARKA-DB was used in the actual support of ForMAT described below. (For convenience we drop the "DB" and refer to the system by the original name "PARKA" in the remainder of this report.)

3.1 TPFDD Casebase

Initially, we encoded one of the ForMAT casebases into the PARKA knowledge representation system. MITRE provided the casebase of TPFDDs, and at UMCP a program was written to recode it into the database tables used by PARKA. The casebase contains 15 TPFDDs, consisting of a total of 319 FMs and about 14,000 ULNs. The corresponding PARKA knowledge base consists of 54,580 frames, 31,314 structural links, and 607,750 assertions. In addition, a domain-specific ontology was created containing approximately 1,200 frames for domain concepts such as "FM", "ULN", service branch, capabilities, functions, geographic locations, etc. Frames in the base ontology are organized in an abstraction ("is-a") hierarchy.

The initial casebase was tested using a graphical interface front end to PARKA (see Fig. 1). Through this testing we developed the base ontology and ensured that the PARKA casebase could handle the retrieval tasks required by ForMAT. Two addition features were added to PARKA to support ForMAT queries, string matching and variable restrictions. String matching provides the ability to search for values that contain a substring, such as searching for a description string that contains the substring "dog." Variable restrictions allow the user to restrict results to a set of values. In ForMAT it is used to restrict the search space of a query to a specific set of FMs instead of the entire casebase.

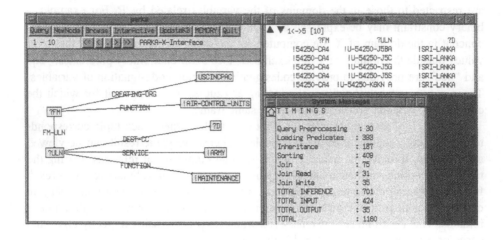

Fig. 1. The PARKA front-end graphical representation of a ForMAT query.

3.2 How ForMAT Uses PARKA

PARKA was designed as a knowledge base with a simple application program interface (API). Any program that conforms to the API can use the PARKA back-end. The PARKA browsing and quering tools are a graphical interface front-end accessing the PARKA back end using the same API. Code was added to ForMAT to allow it to access PARKA. By conforming to the PARKA API, ForMAT can use any back-end version of PARKA, such as our recently developed distributed version or any of the parallel versions, transparently to the user.

The ForMAT system from MITRE used a similar API to access its casebase retrieval system. To integrate ForMAT and PARKA, the ForMAT casebase code was removed and replaced by code to connect the two APIs. This code uses the ForMAT query specification to create the PARKA query. Because ForMAT is written in LISP and PARKA is in C, the LISP foreign function interface was used to communicate between the two languages.

When a ForMAT user wants to search the casebase, they build a query using the ForMAT FM Query interface (See Fig. 2). When the query is executed, the query is converted into a PARKA query which is passed to the back-end where the retrieval is done. The results are passed back to ForMAT where they are displayed to the user.

ForMAT supports two types of retrieval, exact and general. An exact query searches for FMs with specific features, while a general query searches for FMs with similar but not necessarily exact features. An exact ForMAT query is very much like a PARKA query. The ForMAT interface allows the user to specify some FM and ULN features. These features are then converted into the binary predicates used in the PARKA casebase. The query shown in Fig. 2 searches for a force module with three features. The corresponding PARKA query includes those features as binary predicates plus a predicate that specifies the object with those features is a force module.

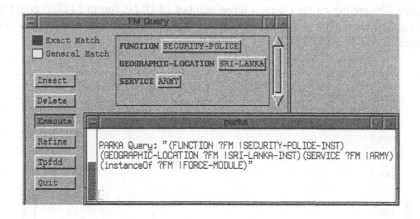

Fig. 2. An example of the ForMAT query window and a PARKA query.

For general queries, PARKA needs to perform multiple queries, each more general than the previous one. For example, a query may look for FMs with a geographic-location in Saudi Arabia. An exact match would only return FMs with the exact value of Saudi Arabia. If no such FMs exist, none would be returned. A general match would perform a second query if no FMs were found. The second query would relax the constraints on geographic-location and search for any values under Middle East in the base ontology. This generalization would continue until results are found.

ForMAT also allows users to specify queries that include OR and NOT, but Parka only does conjunctive queries. For disjunction, the query is converted into multiple queries and the results are combined. (A and (B or C)) becomes the two queries (A and B) and (A and C). NOT is handled by doing two queries, first the query is done without the predicates within the NOT. The results are saved and the query is done again to find the FMs to remove from the previous results. For example (A AND (NOT B)) would become A set-difference (A AND B).

3.3 Comparisons

We used a set of 379 queries to compare the two retrieval methods. The queries are actual ForMAT queries done by users during testing and military planning exercises (taken from history files). The queries were run 10 times each as exact queries and the times were averaged. Both methods returned the same FMs for all queries.

The timing results are graphed in Fig. 3. The speeds of the two methods are roughly the same, with PARKA having some advantage on larger queries. On average, across the 379 cases, the PARKA results are 10ms faster than the original ForMAT algorithm. Most of the queries take less than 100ms using either retrieval method. These are queries that only search FM features. The slower queries are ones that also search for a combination of FM and ULN features. ForMAT's algorithm is based on a linear search algorithm that searches all the ULNs that belong to the FMs returned by the FM part of the query. Depending on the query, a large number of ULNs (up to 14,000) could be searched. The more FMs searched by the query, the better the PARKA algorithm does in comparison to ForMAT's search of all the ULNs.

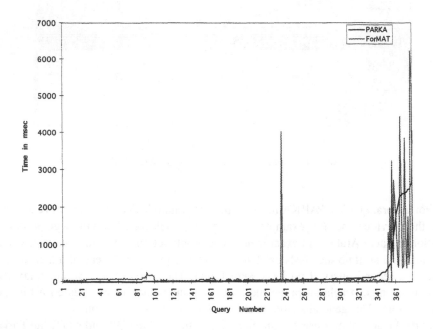

Fig. 3. Graph of ForMAT and PARKA query times sorted by PARKA times.

One problem with these results is that the queries were very varied, and were collected across many uses of ForMAT. However, the PARKA algorithms were developed so that memory caching would provide a significant improvement on queries which were related to each other as was expected would happen in a typical ForMAT use. Therefore, for a more concise comparison, we needed a set of specific queries representing a "typical" use of ForMAT. MITRE provided a set of queries for this purpose. In particular, as part of the Joint Warfare Interoperability Demonstrations (JWID), ForMAT was configured to communicate with the TARGET system[11]. One set of queries in this experiment required 17 different searches of the casebase with a wide range of queries including both FM and ULN features.

Our comparison tests showed that the FMs returned by the two systems were the same, but PARKA was significantly faster than ForMAT. Figure 4 shows the results of this test. The total time of the TARGET query is 73.9 seconds for ForMAT and 8.1 seconds for PARKA. Thus, we see that for this query set PARKA is about 9 times as fast as ForMAT alone.

We are able to demonstrate from this experiment that PARKA does much better at casebase queries that include ULN features. This is because including the ULNs increases the search space from 319 FM structures to 319 FM plus 14,000 ULN structures. This shows that the PARKA algorithm will do better than the ForMAT algorithm as the size of the casebase grows.

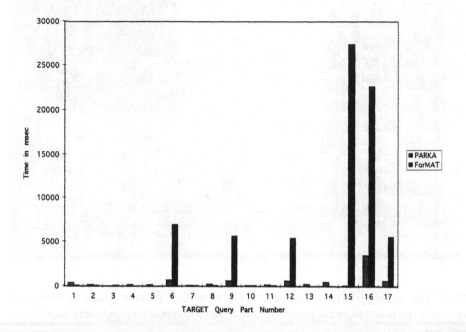

Fig. 4. Graph of ForMAT and PARKA query times for the parts of a TARGET query.

Although ForMAT and PARKA are fully integrated, there is still room for improvement. Currently, PARKA only returns the names of the FMs that were retrieved from the casebase. The LISP structures corresponding to these names are then retrieved from a hash table of FMs. The time it takes to do this is included in the PARKA timing results. A closer integration which allowed ForMAT to use the data stored within the PARKA KB would eliminate the need for the separate LISP structures and improve the overall system performance and memory requirements.

4 Continuing Work

The integration of ForMAT and PARKA is continuing as part of a Phase III ARPI project. One significant improvement made recently is that an integration of the PARKA system and another UM system was exploited to allow ForMAT to become significantly more interoperable with external data sources. In particular, ForMAT users may find additional information such as aircraft and vehicle specifications, airport capacity, maps, or weather information helpful when creating new TPFDDs. The HERMES system[10] was developed at the University of Maryland by VS Subrahmanian to

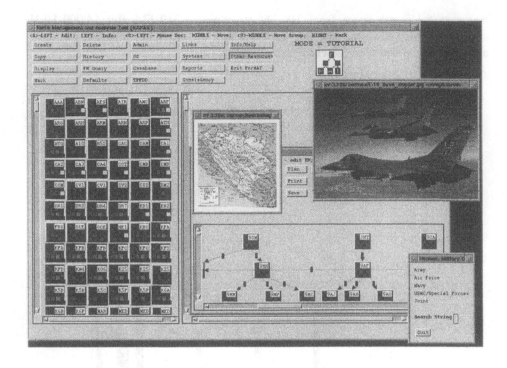

Fig. 5. The working prototype combines ForMAT's interface, PARKA's inference engine and Hermes access to web pages and graphics to provide a unified system for case-based transportation planning.

provide for the semantic integration of different and possibly heterogeneous information sources. We have added an interface to the HERMES server to the ForMAT tool. Through a hierarchical menu the user has access to a number of online factbooks, maps, and weather information. HERMES returns a list of information sources that can be viewed in Netscape or a graphics viewer. Figure 5 shows the integrated ForMAT/PARKA/HERMES system in use for a Bosnia scenario developed as part of the Phase III case-based planning cluster.

Currently, we are looking at implementing a new system which will be a successor to ForMAT written to more completely exploit PARKA's capabilities as well as to greatly extend the coverage of ForMAT. We currently plan that this system will be jointly implemented by BBN and the University of Maryland with the goal of transitioning the resulting system into military use.

5 Conclusion

We believe that the joint ForMAT/PARKA system was one of the successful demonstrations that the technology base for Arpa provides approaches that can be exploited by the military. The new version of ForMAT, via the integration of PARKA, is more capable, faster, and more usable than the earlier version. The University of Maryland team profited by use of real data and a specific knowledge base to focus our optimization efforts on. The ForMAT system gained by use of this new technology. Final experiments proved that the system had gained a significant speedup (in the experiment with the TARGET query the integrated system was nearly 10 times as fast as the unaugmented ForMAT system). In addition, this effort is now continuing, with a joint tool under development that is expected to surpass the original in speed, size and, most importantly, functionality.

References

[1] Andersen, W., Evett, M., Hendler, J. and Kettler, B. "Massively Parallel Matching of Knowledge Structures," in *Massively Parallel Artificial Intelligence*, Kitano, H. and Hendler, J. (eds.), AAAI/MIT Press, 1994.

[2] Evett, M.P., Hendler, J.A., and Spector, L., "Parallel Knowledge Representation on the Connection Machine," *Journal of Parallel and Distributed Computing*, 1994.

[3] Evett, M.P. *PARKA: A System for Massively Parallel Knowledge Representation*, Ph.D. thesis, Dept. of Computer Science, University of Maryland, College Park, 1994.

[4] Evett, M.P., Hendler, J.A., and Andersen, W.A., "Massively Parallel Support for Computationally Effective Recognition Queries", *Proc. Eleventh National Conference on Artificial Intelligence*, 1993.

[5] Hendler, J. High Performance Artificial Intelligence, *Science*, Vol. 265, August, 1994.

[6] Lenat, D.B. and Guha, R.V., "Building Large Knowledge-Based Systems", Addison Wesley, Reading, Mass., 1990.

[7] Kettler, B.P., Hendler, J.A., Andersen, W.A., Evett, M.P., "Massively Parallel Support for Case-based Planning", *IEEE Expert*, Feb, 1994.

[8] Kettler, Brian "Case-based Planning with a High-Performance Parallel Memory," Doctoral Dissertation, Department of Computer Science, University of Maryland, October, 1995.

[9] K. Stoffel, J. Hendler and J. Saltz, High Performance Support for Very Large Knowledge Bases, *Proc. Frontiers of Massively Parallel Computing*, Feb, 1995 (Extended Abstract).

[10] VS Subrahmanian, Sibel Adali and Ross Emery, A Uniform Framework For Integrating Knowledge In Heterogeneous Knowledge Systems, *Proceedings of the Eleventh IEEE International Conference of Data Engineering*, March, 1995.

[11] Walker, E. and Cross, S. eds. *Proceedings of the ARPA-Rome Laboratory Planning Initiative Annual Workshop*. San Mateo, Ca., Morgan-Kaufmann Publishers, 1994.

[12] Watanabe, L., and Rendell, L., "Effective Generalization of Relational Descriptions", AAAI Eighth National Conference on Artificial Intelligence, 1990.

Encouraging Self-Explanation Through Case-Based Tutoring: A Case Study

Michael Redmond
Computer Science
Rutgers University
Camden, NJ 08102
(609) 225-6122 Fax: (609) 225-6624
E-mail: redmond@pizza.rutgers.edu

Susan Phillips
Chemistry
Holy Family College
Philadelphia, PA 19114
(215) 637-7700
E-mail: phillips@pizza.rutgers.edu
Keywords: case-based education, self-explanation

Abstract. This paper presents a case-based tutor, CECELIA 1.1, that is based on techniques from CELIA, a computer model of case-based apprenticeship learning [Redmond 1992]. The teaching techniques include: interactive, step by step presentation of case solution steps, student predictions of an expert's actions, presentation of the expert's steps, student explanations of the expert's actions, and presentation of the expert's explanation. In addition, CECELIA takes advantage of a technique from VanLehn's [1987] SIERRA – presenting examples in an order so that solutions only differ by one branch, or *disjunct*, from previously presented examples. CECELIA relies on its teaching strategy encouraging greater processing of the examples by the student, rather than on embedding great amounts of intelligence in the tutor. CECELIA is implemented using Hypercard on an Apple Macintosh, and has been pilot tested with real students. The tests suggest that the approach can be helpful, but also suggest that eliciting self-explanations from students who normally do not self-explain may be challenging.

---

[1] This research follows from work on CELIA which was supported by the Army Research Institute for the Behavioral and Social Sciences under Contract No. MDA-903-86-C-173, and Contract No. MDA-903-90-K-0112 and by DARPA contract F49620-88-C-0058 monitored by AFOSR. Work on CECELIA was partially supported by Rutgers University and Holy Family College. Thanks to Janet Kolodner for her advice and guidance concerning CELIA, and to Justin Peterson and Joel Martin for helpful discussion. Colleen Griffin did some of the development of the initial version of CECELIA.

1 Introduction

Research dealing with models of learning can be examined from the opposite direction – implications for teaching. Redmond [1992,1990] presented a case-based computer model, CELIA, that shows how a student can learn by observing an expert and explaining the expert's actions to himself. CELIA was inspired and influenced by protocol studies [Lancaster and Kolodner 1988]; empirical experiments with the program suggested that the model was an effective learning method [Redmond 1992]. The success of CELIA suggested several educational implications [Redmond 1994]. We have developed a case-based tutor, CECELIA (Chemistry Education CELIA) based on some of the learning techniques that made CELIA successful, along with another tactic. The framework used in CECELIA is an iterative, presentation of the steps in the correct solution of a case. There are four central features of the teaching strategy:

- student predictions of an expert's actions. This helps a student to identify when they need to learn something.
- student (self-)explanations of the expert's actions. Self-explanation [Chi, Bassok, Lewis, Reimann and Glaser 1989; Chi, de Leeuw, Chiu, and LaVancher 1994; Renkl 1996] involves the student trying to explain how the expert's current action fits into the overall problem solving. This helps both in identifying the need to learn and in more fully understanding the expert's problem solving.
- focus on step by step (iterative) problem solving. This helps both by simplifying credit and blame assignment and by illustrating procedural knowledge.
- problem sets that isolate one *disjunct* (or branch) at a time [VanLehn 1987]. This helps the learner identify the important difference from known solution methods.

It should be noted that CECELIA in *not* an *intelligent* tutoring system (ITS) [Wegner 1987; Farr and Psotka 1992]; it is a tutoring system that uses a teaching strategy based on successful case-based learning research. ITSs know how to solve the problems being presented, know about common errors, follow the student's problem-solving, and diagnose the student's failures. In many cases, even the choice of problems presented to the student is determined by the tutor's assessment of what the student knows. CECELIA does not attempt to model what the student knows; it does not try to debug what the student is doing wrong; it does not adapt the problems to the student; and it does not know how to solve the problems.

While a full intelligent tutoring system is a potentially powerful teaching tool, the investment of effort to produce these systems is a significant obstacle, especially since much of the effort involves domain-specific and especially task-specific engineering. In fact, building ITSs subsumes the task of artificial intelligence; being able to solve problems in a cognitively plausible manner is just the beginning. This means that for each new task to be tutored, person-months of (sophisticated) effort is required to develop the tutor.

While CECELIA cannot present personalized instruction, it is built under the hypothesis that the greater initiative CECELIA asks of the student will lead to successful learning outcomes. Other recent research efforts have come to the same conclusion. Nathan and Resnick [1995] have shown that robust learning can occur without the tutor "understanding" students' actions. Their system instead promotes active learning and engages the student in generating and evaluating possible solutions.

CECELIA is implemented using Hypercard on a Macintosh, since Hypercard provides good support for developing a user friendly interface, and this environment is highly available, making future educational use practical. The current version focuses on teaching "balancing equations", a task involving choosing the correct coefficients for a chemical equation. This was chosen since it is the first task requiring multi-step problem-solving in general chemistry. In initial pilot testing, while some students' learning gains were encouraging, many students did not show signs of doing self-explanation and did not benefit from the tutor.

We first discuss the teaching strategy sketched above, then briefly discuss the balancing equations task. Then we show how CECELIA implements the teaching strategy, and discuss the results of initial pilot testing.

2   Features of the teaching strategy

When presented with a case, prediction of an expert's actions helps a student identify their weaknesses and gaps in their knowledge. When a student incorrectly predicts the expert's actions, that shows the student that his own problem-solving would have been incorrect for that step in the case. Prediction is useful even when the student is doing self-explanation. It takes greater understanding to actually come up with the correct action on one's own than to understand why an observed action was done. Prediction gives the student a test of their procedural knowledge.

Self-explanation can help a student detect a lack of knowledge or help the student better understand the expert's actions. Chi et al [1989] found that good students identified a lack of knowledge more frequently than did poor students, who remained unaware of what they didn't know. In addition, Tarmizi and Sweller [1988] found that studying worked out examples can be an even more successful learning technique than actually solving problems. Prompting the student to do self-explanation increases the possibility that the student will recognize the gaps in their knowledge, and try to learn something. Also, successful explanation of the expert's actions allows the student to come to a better understanding of the expert's problem solving, and may also help the student remember this example for future use. From a case-based perspective, the case that is more thoroughly explained to themself by the student is more useful in the future since it is a more fully elaborated memory, and more likely to be retrieved at an appropriate time since it is more likely to be appropriately indexed.

A focus on step by step, iterative, problem-solving provides advantages over approaches that focus on only problems ("given" information) and solutions. One, is that it illustrates more detailed, procedural expertise. Showing the process of finding a solution in a step by step manner, instead of simply showing a solution, provides a student correct steps to a solution, which he can use to produce future solutions. The cases thus contain the process necessary to get the solution instead of just the solution. From a case-based perspective, this gives the student exposure to the snippets [Kolodner 1988; Redmond 1990] that make up the details of the case. Second, perhaps more importantly, when student predictions are made on a step by step basis, credit and blame assignment is simplified. Incorrect predictions of *steps* (rather than whole solutions) isolates the problem to that step. Anderson and his group's intelligent tutors [Anderson, Boyle, Corbett, and Lewis 1990; Koedinger and Anderson 1990] make use of such a step by step focus as part of their model-tracing approach – giving feedback after each step taken by the student. Although not without controversy, they have found that it speeds the learning process. Our approach also provides the step by step focus but initially leaves it to the student to try to understand why the expert would take the step. From a case-based perspective, this step-by-step focus, in conjunction with self-explanation, could help students to retain justifications with the steps in the case [Carbonell 1986; Carbonell and Veloso 1988], and/or develop better indices.

The final aspect of CECELIA's teaching strategy is VanLehn's [1987] "one disjunct at a time" convention. Examples are presented in an order such that the solutions only differ from the procedure that the student knows by one difference. This teaching strategy actually has a long history in artificial intelligence, going back to Winston's induction program [Winston 1970], and it works with people too; VanLehn [1983] found that human teachers frequently implicitly follow this constraint though they aren't aware of the convention. CELIA did not benefit from this teaching strategy because of differences in domain. However, since CECELIA operates in a domain in which a wide variety of examples can be generated on demand, CECELIA takes advantage of this teaching strategy. From a case-based perspective, this strategy could facilitate storing difference links [Bareiss 1989] with case steps.

3 Balancing Equations

Chemical equations describe reactions, showing what elements or compounds react, and what products are formed during the reaction. The following equation is not balanced:

$$H_2O \quad \texttt{-----}\texttt{>} \quad H_2 \quad + \quad O_2$$

Integer *coefficients* are placed in front of compounds to show (relatively) how many atoms of each are involved in the reaction. Coefficients are used to *balance* the equation, so that the same number of each element appear on both sides of the equation. Chemical equations must always be balanced if they are to represent a real reaction. The above equation is not yet balanced since the left side has one oxygen atom, but the right has two.

How can this be corrected? A coefficient of "2" in front of the water molecule makes the oxygen atoms equal, but this causes the hydrogen atoms to be unequal, 4 on the left side and 2 on the right side. If a coefficient of "2" is put in front of the H_2, the equation will be balanced:

```
2 H O  ----->  2 H   +  0
   2         2      2
```

The initial simple general method taught by CECELIA in initial lessons is:

1. Find an element that only occurs once on each side of the equation, and choose coefficients so that the element will have equal numbers of atoms on both sides.
2. From the remaining compounds without coefficients, find an element that occurs in only one. That compound's coefficient is now fully constrained; calculate the value.
3. Repeat step two until all coefficients have been assigned.

4 CECELIA

CECELIA presents cases to the student in groups, called *lessons* following Van-Lehn [1987]. The examples within each lesson all are solved using the same steps; the only differences are surface features (such as which particular elements are involved, and what the subscripts are). Each lesson contains two cases in order for the student to be able to isolate and understand the extension to the previously understood process (the new disjunct). Note that because of this strategy, CECELIA does not attempt to choose which cases to present to the student at which time; the order is pre-determined. For teaching the balancing equations task, seven lessons are sufficient.

Each case is presented in a simple iterative manner: for each step in the solution, four screens (*cards* in Hypercard) are presented in order:

1. a prompt for the student to predict the next action
2. presentation of the correct action (with an option to see other acceptable alternatives, if any). The student is then asked to self-grade their answer.
3. a prompt for the student to explain why the correct action is appropriate
4. presentation of an expert explanation of the correct action.

Figure 1 shows these types of cards for the start of a simple case. Figure 1(a) shows the prompt asking the student for a prediction; predictions which involve choosing coefficients can be made by filling the numbers directly in the equation. Figure 1(b) shows CECELIA's presentation of the correct action. If an alternative action is possible, the student can click to see the alternative. So that CECELIA doesn't have to either understand natural language or force the student into some pre-set language for responding, the student is asked to mark the correctness of his prediction by clicking on a button. The student's predictions are captured in a file so the student's marking can be checked later if necessary.

Next, the student is asked for an explanation of the expert's action. This prompt is skipped if the student has made greater than N predictions with greater than X percent correct, and has marked their current prediction as correct. N and X are adjustable parameters, currently set to 10 and 80. Figure 1(c) shows the prompt asking the student for an explanation. The student can choose to give their explanation by 1) typing into the field on the screen, or 2) by clicking on boxed items at the top of the screen (such as "CH4", "the left side",

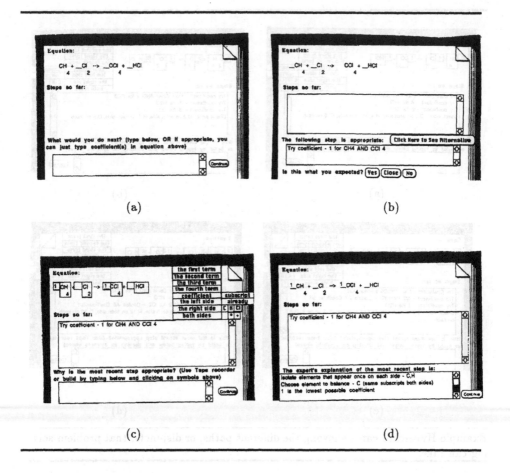

(a)

(b)

(c)

(d)

Fig. 1. CECELIA 1.1: Example student interaction.

etc), in conjunction with typing, or 3) by talking into a tape recorder (no students in the pilot test chose to tape record explanations). This explanation is also captured into a file for further analysis. Note, that as problem solving in an example continues, the student can see the previous steps taken in the problem. Thus, short term memory is not an obstacle to prediction or self-explanation. This reduces the cognitive load on the student, making it more likely the student can learn by studying the example [Tarmizi and Sweller 1988].

Finally, the student is given the explanation of the expert's action (Figure 1(d)). This explanation is detailed, showing reasoning behind which coefficients were filled in, and the algebra behind the numbers chosen (pilot testing with CECELIA 1.0 showed that the algebraic manipulations are an important step to the pilot audience).

Figure 2 illustrates some of the disjuncts involved in teaching the balancing equations task by showing the self-explanation card for the final steps of examples

138

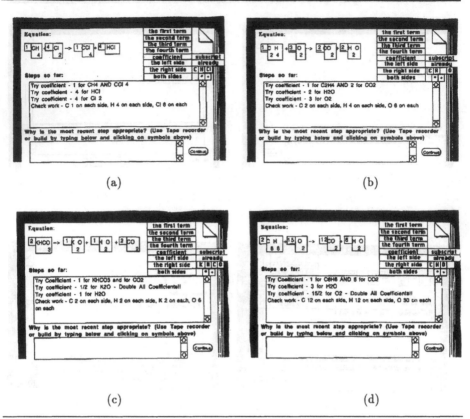

(a)   (b)

(c)   (d)

Example Hypercard cards showing the different paths, or disjuncts, that problem solving can take.

Fig. 2. CECELIA 1.1: Examples of solutions to problems presented to student.

from each of the early lessons. The first case (Figure 2(a)) solution has no complications. In the second lesson (Figure 2(b)), in the first step, instead of just choosing "1" as the coefficient (done in (a) since the element had the same subscript on each side), different coefficients must be chosen on the two sides since carbon (C) has different subscripts in the two terms.

A more significant increase in complexity is encountered in the third lesson (Figure 2(c)). Here the disjunct arises in the 2nd step – the initial coefficient choice for the terms involving carbon (C) leads to later calculation of a coefficient of 1/2. Since this is not valid, all coefficients are doubled to get all whole number coefficients. The fourth lesson (example in Figure 2(d)) teaches that the two preceding disjuncts can occur together in the same problem. In step 1, different coefficients must be chosen on the two sides; in step 3, all coefficients must be doubled. The fifth lesson involves doubling coefficients twice. Further lessons introduce greater complexity, eventually leading to the most difficult problems where backtracking is required.

5 Pilot Testing

We have carried out pilot testing of CECELIA to obtain initial feedback on the effectiveness of the tutor, and to get qualitative feedback from students. The hypothesis was that students could gain significantly with a tutor using the teaching strategies presented above, without putting intelligence into the tutor. Due to the small number of subjects, and some ceiling effect, we cannot draw statistical conclusions about CECELIA's effectiveness, but several students demonstrated performance gains, as well as increased confidence in their abilities.

5.1 Method

Subjects were students of Introductory Chemistry at Holy Family College. The subjects were recruited after the material (balancing equations) had been completely presented in class; they participated in exchange for extra-credit. The students were given a pre-pre-test; this was used to assign students of relatively equal distribution of prior abilities to the control and test groups. During the next week they had a second session in which they took a second pre-test, used the tutor, and then took a post-test. Though this immediate post-test does not give the student a chance to reflect on and integrate their experience with the tutor, it was done due to previous reviewer concerns about a Hawthorne effect. The subjects were also given a post experiment questionnaire to obtain subjective feedback on the tutor. A total of 13 students participated (a previous pilot study with CECELIA 1.0 involved 11 students).

Pre and post-tests were given on paper. Each test included twelve questions, which were counter-balanced – several versions of the test were constructed so that questions appeared equally on each of the three tests for each of the control and test groups. The students were given 30 minutes to do the pre-pre, pre and post-tests. All of the students completed these tests. Partial credit (1/3 correct) was given to students for problems in which the coefficients balanced the equation but were not the lowest possible values. The tutor's problems were a separate pool, not appearing on any of the paper tests. The control students used a standard practice or drill tutor on the same problems as used in CECELIA. The students were scheduled for 1 hour to use the tutor; this was held constant to ensure equal time-on-task for test and control groups. If students finished before an hour, they were re-presented the same problems again (this happened with several students). If an hour was up before the students were done, they were cut-off (this happened with most of the self-explanation tutor test students).

5.2 Results

The performance improvements of subjects with CECELIA was only 4 percent (due partially to one subject who had a decline, and also partially due to 4

Student	Pct Correct Pre	Post	Diff					
SA	55.0	59.2	4.2	s	= sqrt(s) = 7.88811			
SB	83.3	91.7	8.4	D	D			
SC	94.2	94.2	0.0					
SD	75.0	66.7	-8.3	t	= 2.571 (5 degrees of freedom)			
SE	77.5	83.3	5.8	.025				
SF	31.7	46.7	15.0					
				Difference	=	4.167 + (2.571 * 7.888) / 2.4495		
	----	-----	----			-		
Means	69.44	73.61	4.167		=	4.167 + 8.279407		
						-		

Table 1. CECELIA 1.1: Self Explanation Tutor Results from Pilot Study.

other subjects who did well on the pre-test (75 percent or above)). This was not statistically significant (statistically discernable) at the 0.05 level, and in fact was similar to the improvement for those using the control tutor. This was actually a smaller improvement than found in the pilot test with CELIA 1.0 (a 20 percent gain, under different experiemental conditions, *e.g.* students completed the tutor problems regardless of the time it took).

5.3 Discussion

There are several things that can be learned from the limited success of this prototype. One, the self-explanation literature identified a strategy that was used by the students who learned more (the "good" students) [Chi *et al* 1989]. In this experiment, we were working with students who may not normally use these self-explanation techniques. In [Chi *et al* 1994], students, whether they normally self-explain or not, when prompted to self-explain, were able to get benefits from that self-explanation. In the current tutoring effort, the program asked the students for self-explanations, however, it did not have a way of checking that explanation was really done. In fact, studying the logs captured by the program, frequently the students had little or no explanation (for example, a single space character). Thus, this tutor was not necessarily eliciting self-explanations from subjects who were not prone to do so otherwise. It is possible that the typing modality was too slow for the subjects. The opportunity to respond verbally for tape recording was offered and not taken. This may have been due to self-consciousness – the room where subjects worked had 3-5 subjects working at the same time. The point and click method of building explanations may have not been clear; the subjects only had one screen of introduction to the technique. The self-explanation literature was developed with verbal protocol studies, where a human experimenter prompted a subject to speak, and perhaps indirectly to think. It may be that a computer tutor may not be as compelling a prompt for promoting self-explanation. Some solution may be necessary for this problem.

Chi *et al* [1989] also found that one of the benefits that good students obtained by self-explaining was a better recognition of when they needed to learn something (they had more incidents when they identified that they didn't understand something). In the current experiment there were many situations where students who self-graded their predictions marked their answer incorrectly (usually marking "correct" when they were actually incorrect). These subjects were not getting an accurate idea of their skills.

It is possible that the subjects were pursuing goals of completing the extra-credit task, rather than learning goals. They, in fact, were not told that they would spend an hour with the tutor no matter how far they got. Some students appeared to try to race through the tutor as fast as possible.

Another problem, at least as far as getting noticeable improvement, was the level of difficulty of the task. This task is learned early in the first semester of college chemistry; almost all of the students had had some high school chemistry, where they most likely had been previously exposed to the task. Between that, and that the tutor was used after the material was presented in class, some students already could solve many of the problems. This, in part, explains the ceiling effect in which many students were already fairly successful at pre-test time. In fact, one student had a clear algorithmic method from high school that differed from the method demonstrated by the expert cases (and scored 94 percent correct on the pre-test). Future harder tasks being considered include Stoichiometry from chemistry (also covered in high school, but still challenging at the college level), and teaching the use of PERT charts to MBA students.

It is worth discussing the changes from CECELIA 1.0, and their impact. These changes were largely made in response to qualitative survey responses ro CECELIA 1.0. The extra choices for self-explanation modality were added; the presentation of expert explanations was added, the cases were divided into steps in a courser granularity - frequently two to three steps in CECELIA 1.0 became 1 step in CECELIA 1.1. This coincided better with the way the students perceived a step. However, it tended to gloss over the details of how to perform the steps – these substeps only appeared in the presentation of the experts explanation of a step. Thus, the students may not have learned the heart of the process implicit in the expert's case solutions. This could have been a factor in students achieving less of a gain with CECELIA 1.1 than with CECELIA 1.0. An improvement in strategy in the tutor, however, could be to initially show very detailed steps, and later *fade* the detail into fewer steps.

An additional comment should be made. The textbook introduces the balancing equations task as a heuristic task (not in those terms, of course). However, the tutor, in presenting examples one disjunct at a time, is actually teaching an algorithmic approach. In fact, only one in 50 problems in the chapter required backtracking when following the tutor's method for solving the problems. Some students found this systematicity very helpful, since they did not have to rely on intuition. CECELIA seemed to be most helpful to those students with weak skills but strong motivation. For instance, some older students, and students with math anxiety, were able to not only improve their ability to balance equations, but were also able to increase their self-confidence, something that would carry over to later material.

6 Conclusion

We have presented the ideas behind the initial version of CECELIA, a case-based tutoring system that relies on a cognitive teaching strategy based on the results of learning research. CECELIA relies on encouraging greater processing of cases by the student, rather than on embedding great amounts of intelligence in the tutor. Thus, CECELIA trades off student initiative for a significant amount of domain and task-specific development effort.

The teaching techniques presented here can be applied in tutorials for any task in which

- solutions are multi-step procedures for which the steps can be identified by an expert
- cases can be obtained that differ from each other by a single new branch.

The development involved in teaching a new task consists only producing case "data" for CECELIA's program. This data includes: steps in getting the answer, explanations, and alternative steps. CECELIA 1.1 can almost be considered a "shell' for case-based self-explanation tutors.

CECELIA has been pilot tested with limited success. Some students showed very important gains, but many students did not. Future work will focus on 1) more difficult tasks; 2) greater motivation of students to self-explain; and 3) more effective monitoring of student progress (without trying to produce an intelligent tutor).

References

[Anderson et al., 1990] Anderson, J. R., Boyle, C. F., Corbett, A., & Lewis, M. W. (1990). Cognitive modeling and intelligent tutoring. *Artificial Intelligence*, 42:7–49.

[Bareiss, 1989] Bareiss, R. (1989). Exemplar-based knowledge acquisition: a unified approach to concept representation, classification, and learning. Academic Press, New York, NY.

[Carbonell, 1986] Carbonell, J. (1986). Derivational analogy: A theory of reconstructive problem solving and expertise acquisition. In Michalski, R., Carbonell, J., & Mitchell, T., editors, *Machine Learning: An Artificial Intelligence Approach, Volume II*. Morgan Kaufmann, Los Altos, CA.

[Carbonell & Veloso, 1988] Carbonell, J. & Veloso, M. (1988). Integrating derivational analogy into a general problem solving architecture. In *Proceedings of a Workshop on Case-Based Reasoning*, Clearwater, FL. Morgan Kaufmann.

[Chi et al., 1989] Chi, M., Bassok, M., Lewis, M., Reimann, P., & Glaser, R. (1989). Self-explanations: How students study and use examples to solve problems. *Cognitive Science*, 13:145–182.

[Chi et al., 1994] Chi, M., de Leeuw, N., Chiu, M., & LaVancher, C. (1994). Eliciting self-explanations improves understanding. *Cognitive Science*, 18:439–477.

[Corbett & Anderson, 1990] Corbett, A. T. & Anderson, J. R. (1990). The effect of feedback control on learning to program with the lisp tutor. In *Proceedings of the Twelfth Annual Conference of the Cognitive Science Society*, pages 796–806, Cambridge, MA. Lawrence Erlbaum Associates.

[Farr & Psotka, 1992] Farr, M. J. & Psotka, J. (1992). Intelligent instruction by computer: Theory and practice. Taylor and Francis, New York, NY.

[Koedinger & Anderson, 1990] Koedinger, K. R. & Anderson, J. R. (1990). Abstract planning and perceptual chunks: elements of expertise in geometry. *Cognitive Science*, 14:511–550.

[Kolodner, 1988] Kolodner, J. (1988). Retrieving events from a case memory: a parallel implementation. In *Proceedings of a Workshop on Case-Based Reasoning*, Clearwater, FL. Morgan Kaufmann.

[Lancaster & Kolodner, 1988] Lancaster, J. & Kolodner, J. (1988). Varieties of learning from problem solving experience. In *Proceedings of the Tenth Annual Conference of the Cognitive Science Society*, Montreal, Canada. Lawrence Erlbaum Associates.

[Nathan & Resnick, 1995] Nathan, M. J. & Resnick, L. B. (1995). Less can be more: Unintelligent tutoring based on psychological theories and experimentation. In Vosniadou, S., Corte, E. D., Glaser, R., & Mandl, H., editors, *Psychological and Educational Foundations of Technology-Based Learning Environments*.

[Redmond, 1990] Redmond, M. (1990). Distributed cases for case-based reasoning; facilitating use of multiple cases. In *Proceedings of the National Conference on Artificial Intelligence (AAAI-90)*, Boston, MA. Morgan Kaufmann.

[Redmond, 1992] Redmond, M. (1992). *Learning by Observing and Explaining Expert Problem Solving*. PhD thesis, Georgia Institute of Technology, Atlanta, GA.

[Redmond, 1994] Redmond, M. (1994). Educational implications of celia: Learning by observing and explaining. In *Proceedings of the Sixteenth Annual Conference of the Cognitive Science Society*, Atlanta, GA. Lawrence Erlbaum Associates.

[Renkl, 1996] Renkl, A. (1996). Learning from worked out examples: A study of individual differences. *Cognitive Science*, 20.

[Tarmizi & Sweller, 1988] Tarmizi, R. A. & Sweller, J. (1988). Guidance during mathematical problem solving. *Journal of Educational Psychology*, 80(4):424–436.

[VanLehn, 1983] VanLehn, K. (1983). Felicity conditions for human skill acquisition: validating an ai-based theory. Technical Report CIS-21, Xerox Parc, Palo Alto, CA.

[VanLehn, 1987] VanLehn, K. (1987). Learning one subprocedure per lesson. *Artificial Intelligence*, 31:1–40.

[Wegner, 1987] Wegner, E. (1987). Artificial intelligence and tutoring systems. Morgan Kaufmann, Los Altos, CA.

[Winston, 1970] Winston, P. (1970). *Learning Structural Descriptions from Examples*. PhD thesis, Massachussetts Institute of Technology, Cambridge, MA.

Lessons Learned from Deployed CBR Systems and Design Decisions Made in Building a Commercial CBR Tool

Hideo Shimazu and Yosuke Takashima

Information Technology Research Laboratories, NEC Corporation,
4-1-1 Miyazaki, Miyamae, Kawasaki, 216, Japan
{shimazu, yosuke}@joke.cl.nec.co.jp

Abstract. This paper reports our experiences in several CBR system building projects. Based on the lessons learned in these projects, we have developed a help desk support tool, Help Desk Builder. It consists of a knowledge management tool and a customer information management tool. The knowledge management tool includes case-based retrieval functions. This paper focuses on the design decisions and architecture of the case-based functions in Help Desk Builder.

1   Introduction

Since beginning our CBR-related research activities several years ago, we have developed several CBR systems, including large-scale corporate-wide and medium-scale department-wide corporate memories.

When we first began to apply CBR technologies [3] to designs, we tended toward sophisticated knowledge-intensive systems whose architectures were CBR-centered and isolated from other information systems. However, as these systems were deployed and accessed by different types of users for diverse purposes, requirements placed on these systems increased, and the revision, operation and maintenance of such systems became increasingly difficult. We gradually learned lessons from these projects. Our recent CBR systems have generally been much simpler and easier to operate, with CBR technologies playing a smaller role, tightly integrated with other parts in the systems.

In 1996, we developed a commercial help desk support tool, Help Desk Builder. It consists of a knowledge management tool and a customer information management tool. The knowledge management tool includes case-based retrieval functions, and the design decision and architecture of Help Desk Builder has been strongly influenced by the lessons learned from our past experiences.

In this paper, we introduce our past projects and report important lessons learned from them. We also explain the design decision and architecture of Help Desk Builder, focusing on the CBR functions in Help Desk Builder.

2 Deployed CBR Systems

2.1 SQUAD

Our first widely deployed CBR system was SQUAD [1][2], a software-quality-control advisor system. SQUAD is a large-scale, corporate-wide CBR system for software quality control. A user inputs a problem related to software design or development to the system, and SQUAD retrieves cases with similar problems and their solutions. Each case corresponds to a software-quality-control activity done by software engineers.

Before the SQUAD system was developed, each case was reported as a two-page-long paper in free-format Japanese. We started the SQUAD project in collaboration with the SWQC (Software Quality Control) group. First we defined case representation to cover all the problems related to software design and development in reported cases. A paper form corresponding to the case representation was designed. Then, the SWQC group ruled that the paper form must be submitted with the conventional report. After that, thousands of cases were reported to the SWQC group, and these cases were stored in the SQUAD case base.

The SQUAD architecture is simple. Cases are stored in a home-made case base, and a nearest-neighbor similarity metric is used to retrieve similar cases. The similarity-based retrieval refers to similarity definition shown in Figure 1.

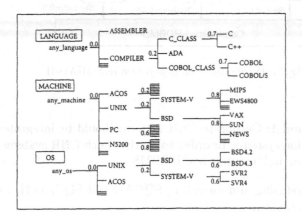

Fig. 1. Example of abstraction hierarchy used for nearest-neighbor retrieval

While we were operating the SQUAD system, we found the following problem.

Problem 1: Accessibility of case bases. The SQUAD case base has a specialized file format, and the case data can be accessed only via the SQUAD GUI system. Engineers and managers in corporate-data processing divisions and other administrative divisions pointed out that using a RDBMS (Relational Database Management System) as the storage of case base is necessary. Important reasons for this include the need for security control, case independence, and integrity management.

2.2 SQUAD-II

In order to solve Problem 1, we developed the SQUAD-II system [5]. The most significant difference between this system and SQUAD is the use of a commercial RDBMS as the case base manager. Each case is represented as a record in a relational database table. Because SQL does not have any similarity-based retrieval features, SQUAD-II carries out the nearest-neighbor retrieval by generating SQL specifications in varying degrees of similarity and dispatching the generated SQL specifications to RDBMS (Figure 2).

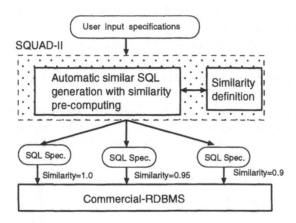

Fig. 2. Automatic SQL generation in SQUAD-II

Lesson Learned 1: Corporate CBR systems should be integrated into other information systems. In order to do this, such CBR systems must be built on open architectures like RDBMS.

While we were developing and operating SQUAD and SQUAD-II, we encountered the following problem.

Problem 2: Revision of case representation. After we defined a case representation for SQUAD, we soon found many new types of cases which could not be described by the case representation. We often had to revise the case representation. The SQUAD-II system internally has several independent case bases of different case representations as shown in Figure 3. When a user describes a problem, it is translated into several different query specifications and dispatched to corresponding case bases. The maintenance of the SQUAD system became harder as the number of the different case bases increased. In addition, we had to revise similarity definitions, and the revision caused similar problems. For example, when new technical terms like "ActiveX" or "Java" appear in reported cases, we have to revise similarity definition used for similarity-based retrieval. The maintenance of similarity definition becomes harder as the number of new technical terms increase.

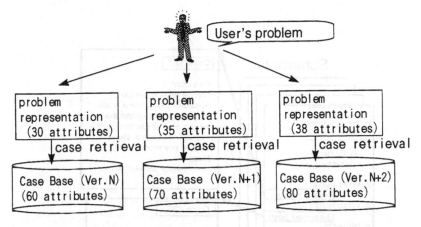

Fig. 3. Several different versions of case-bases in SQUAD-II

2.3 CARET

In the next project, we found a promising solution to Problem 2. CARET (CAse REtrieval Tool) [6][7] is a help desk support system for a commercial on-line service operated by NEC. When help desk operators receive repreated requests, CARET shows them similar previous customer inquiries and the operator replies.

In order for the help desk operators to be able to respond to inquiries in a reasonably short time, CARET must provide an easy and rapid interface for similar-case retrievals, but the fact that customers tend to explain their problems in widely varying ways was a serious obstacle to achieving rapid retrievals.

We analyzed that there exist typical categories of customer approaches to explaining their inquiries. They include step-by-step action-based explanation like "After writing body, selecting SEND, ...", diagram-description-based explanation like "Can I move this email from MAIL-BOX to my folder?", and physical-appearance-based explanation like "The upper-left switch is blinking. What does it mean?". An analysis of customer problems taught us that the majority of problems arise when a customer acts almost correctly, but makes some minor mistakes, and/or simply misunderstands a situation to a slight degree. Based on these analyses, we developed a new case indexing method using schemata and nearmiss points. For each of the above categories a set of predefined schemata is prepared, each of which describes a situation likely to arise as an inquiry. For example, step-by-step action-based schemata correspond to the step-by-step action-based category and consist of individual lists of the complex combinations of operations required to accomplish the most typical customer goals. A step-by-step action-based schema is similar to Schank's script [4]. If a customer's problem case is that he/she acts almost correctly, but makes some minor mistake, the case can be simply indexed with a set of a predefined schema and one or a few slight disparities (nearmiss points) between the schema and the case.

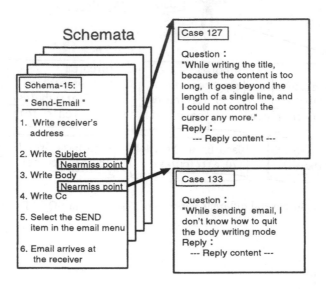

Fig. 4. Case indexing with a schema and nearmiss points

Figure 4 shows the "send-email" step-by-step schema, Schema 15, which represents typical and correct sequences of actions taken when a customer sends an email. Case 127 holds a question whose goal and actions are similar to those for Schema 15, but has a nearmiss point which causes this question. A pair of Schema 15 and the nearmiss point becomes the index for Case 127.

When an operator retrieves cases while listening to a customer's inquiry, the operator selects a corresponding schema. The schema is displayed on the terminal. When he/she points at one or a few problem points in the schema, if there are cases whose nearmiss points are equal or similar to those specified problem points, the cases are displayed on the terminal.

The most significant design decision of CARET was to separate its situation assessment mechanism from case representation. In SQUAD and SQUAD-II, the situation part of a case is represented in the case. When a user describes a problem, it is translated into an internal representation, and the nearest-neighbor mechanism calculates the similarity between the problem situation and the situation part of each case in a case base. To enable a computer to calculate similarity between different situations, the situation part of each case must be translated into a machine-readable internal representation. However, as pointed out at Problem 2, it is difficult to define case representation that can cover a wide range of existing and potential future cases and their situations. Repeated revision of case representation makes case base management difficult. Consequently, an essential solution against Problem 2 is to separate situation assessment mechanisms from case representations as shown in Figure 5.

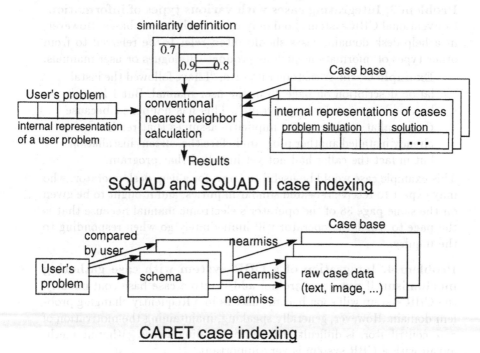

Fig. 5. Separation of situation assessment mechanisms from cases

In CARET, the situation of a case is represented in a pair of a schema and nearmiss links between the schema and the case. When a user problem is given, the situation of the user's problem is compared with corresponding schemata. Here, it is not a computer but a user that assesses the user's problem situation.[1] With this separation, cases do not have to be translated into internal representations because situation assessment is not done by CARET. Gathered cases are stored in raw forms. And, CARET only helps a user assess his/her problem easily and rapidly.

The revision of a case base also becomes much easier. In SQUAD and SQUAD-II, the revision task of a case base is to redefine the internal representation of cases. In CARET, the revision task of a case base is to add or modify schema structures. Because the number of schemata is much smaller than that of cases, the case base management becomes much easier.

---

[1] Because CARET does not calculate the similarity between a problem and cases automatically, it is doubtful whether CARET can still be categorized in case-based retrieval systems.

Lesson Learned 2: If a problem domain changes frequently, it is easier to separate the situation assessment mechanism from cases representations.

While we were operating CARET, we recognized new problems.

Problem 3: Integrating cases with various types of information. Conventional CBR systems hold only cases in their case bases. However, in a help desk domain, cases should often refer to/be referred to from other types of information, such as product catalogues or user manuals.

> **Example Case:** A customer reports, "I have followed the installation description on page 38 in the user manual. But I haven't been able to install the program". This has happened because the installation description implicitly assumes that readers have already installed another program before the current installation, but in fact the caller had not yet installed that program.

This example case would be useful to know for a help desk operator, who may expect to receive repeated similar inquiries, and it ought to be given on the same page 38 of the operator's electronic manual because that is the page to which the operator will immediately go when responding to the inquiry.

Problem 4: Integration of a CBR system with case gathering mechanism. If new cases are not added into a case base continuously, the CBR system will soon become useless in a frequently changing problem domain. However, generally speaking, maintaining the motivation of case contributors is difficult. Therefore, building a case gathering mechanism with a CBR system is very important.

3 Help Desk Builder

In 1995, we started designing Help Desk Builder, a general-purpose help desk support tool. Though our core technology is CBR, we understood that we had to build various non-CBR modules to put the CBR technology to practical use. Moreover, because customer support became an increasingly important market, we chose the help desk domain as its major market.

Help Desk Builder consists of a knowledge management tool and a customer information management tool (Help Desk Builder/CS). The knowledge management tool includes case-based retrieval functions. It consists of a multimedia knowledge authoring tool (Help Desk Builder/AT) and a knowledge content browsing tool (Help Desk Builder/BT) as shown in Figure 6.

3.1 Design Decision

This section describes major design decisions made in developing Help Desk Builder. Here, we focus on the design decisions related to CBR functions in Help Desk Builder.

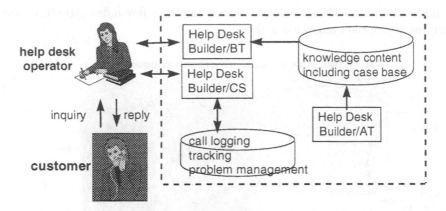

Fig. 6. Help Desk Builder /AT, /BT and /CS

Separating situation assessment mechanisms from cases: Based on Lesson Learned 2, we separated the situation assessment mechanism from cases representations. Cases are stored in raw form and are not translated into internal representations.

Providing various indexing mechanisms: A schema and nearmiss link is not the only indexing mechanism. More varieties of indexing mechanisms must be provided to express potential situation descriptions. Details will be described in the next section.

Integrating cases with various types of information: To solve Problem 3, we designed Help Desk Builder/AT as a general-purpose multimedia knowledge content authoring tool that can generate not only case bases but also other types of information such as product catalogues and user manuals. These varieties of information chunks can refer to one another.

Integrating a CBR system with a case gathering mechanism: To solve Problem 4, we built a customer information management tool, Help Desk Builder/CS. It facilitates logging incoming calls, tracking requests, and problem management. It stores every user's inquiry and an operator's reply as a raw case, counts which cases are repeatedly received, and advises which cases should be defined and stored as persistent multimedia cases using Help Desk Builder/AT.

3.2 Indexing mechanisms of pages

Domain experts create a knowledge content file using Help Desk Builder/AT. A knowledge content file consists of a set of multimedia pages and a set of index structures. Multimedia pages represent various types of information such as product catalogues, user manuals, and cases. A set of index structures discriminate pages into different categories. Help Desk Builder/BT shows a user the list of index structures. Then, the user chooses one or a few index structures and retrieves appropriate pages using them.

multiple outline menus

index structure

multi-media page

Fig. 7. Screen of "multimedia weed dictionary and weed-extermination casebook" using Help Desk Builder/BT

A knowledge content is based on a "book" metaphor. Figure 7 shows a screen image of Help Desk Builder/BT. The right-hand side of the window shows a multimedia page. The page contains text, OLE objects, and hyperlinks to other pages. The left-hand side of the window shows index structures. There are two types of index structures.

Outline menu index: Outline menu index is a tree of item nodes. Each leaf-item node links to a page. A knowledge content file can have any number of outline menus. An outline menu is used to discriminate a set of pages from a specific viewpoint. Another outline menu discriminates another set of pages from a different viewpoint.

Schema menu index: A step-by-step action-based schema, a diagram schema menu, and a physical-appearance schema menu are provided. They are the same as those in CARET.

Help Desk Builder/BT provides five page-retrieval mechanisms using these index structures.

(1) Outline menu Search: A user browses an outline menu. If the user chooses an intermediate item node, its children item nodes are listed. If the user chooses a leaf item node, a page linked from the node is shown at the right-hand side of the window.

(2) Multi-link page retrieval: When a user selects an item node in an outline menu, a list will be displayed of pages linked to the leaf nodes that are

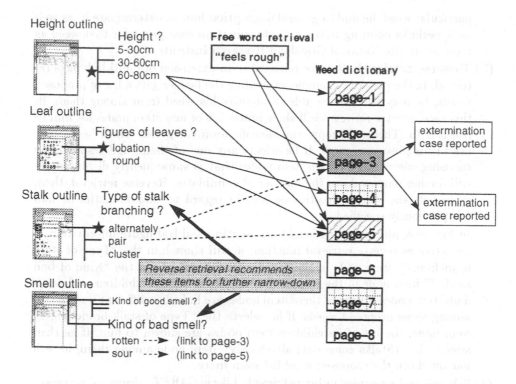

Height outline

Height ?
- 5-30cm
- 30-60cm
- ★ 60-80cm

Free word retrieval
"feels rough"

Weed dictionary

Leaf outline

Figures of leaves ?
- ★ lobation
- round

Stalk outline

Type of stalk branching ?
- ★ alternately
- pair
- cluster

Reverse retrieval recommends these items for further narrow-down

Smell outline

- Kind of good smell ?
- Kind of bad smell?
  - rotten ---▶ (link to page-3)
  - sour ---▶ (link to page-5)

page-1
page-2
page-3
page-4
page-5
page-6
page-7
page-8

extermination case reported

extermination case reported

Fig. 8. Multi-link page retrieval

descendant from the selected item node. When the user adds to this the selection of another outline menu, another set of pages will be similarly generated, and the list of pages displayed will include only those pages whose characteristics satisfy both requirements.

Figure 8 shows an example of such multi-link page retrieval. This is a CBR-system, created using Help Desk Builder/AT by the National Grassland Research Institute in Japan to help in the extermination of exotic weeds. It's front page screen is shown in Figure 7.

The knowledge content consists of a multimedia weed dictionary and a weed-extermination casebook. When a farmer finds an exotic weeds in his field, he consults the dictionary. After he finds the name of the weed, he accesses related cases linked to that weed page. If the farmer is unfamiliar with an exotic weed, his observation of its individual characteristics may be less than definitive, but if he uses multi-link page retrieval to combine more general observations of a number of different characteristics, he will gradually be able to narrow down the number of possible candidates.

In Figure 8, a farmer selects the "60 cm - 80 cm" item node in the "Height" outline menu and the "lobation" in the "Figure of leaves ?" item node in the "Leaf" outline menu, and then he inputs the words, "feels rough". He, then, gets a list of proposed weed pages, reads the description on each weed, looks at each weed picture, and identifies his weed. On the page for that particular weed, he finds a general description how to exterminate it, as well as hyperlinks pointing to several extermination case pages for that weed as reported to the National Grassland Research Institute.

(3) **Reverse retrieval:** Reverse retrieval is an extension of multi-link page retrieval. In the previous example, even after the farmer gets a list of proposed weeds, he may still not be able to identify his weed from among them. In this case, reverse retrieval will show him a list of new item nodes for him to respond to. These will represent identification categories which he did not use in his previous search. If he selects any one of them, and responds by choosing one of the children item nodes that is subsequently displayed, he will further narrow down the number of candidates. Reverse retrieval, then, represents the system questioning him in regard to characteristics he had not previously specified.

In Figure 8, after inputing height information and leaf figure information, if he activates reverse retrieval function, it will show him the "Type of stalk branching ?" item node in the "Stalk" outline menu and the "Kind of bad smell ?" item node in the "Smell" outline menu because children or descendant item nodes of each of these item nodes are linked to different weed pages among these proposed weeds. If he selects the "Type of stalk branching ?" item node, the list of its children item nodes are shown to him. If he then selects the "(Stalks come out) alternately" item node among them, he will narrow down the proposed weed list even more.

(4) **Schema and nearmiss point retrieval:** Like in CARET, schema and nearmiss-point retrieval is used as general purpose retrieval mechanisms. Schema structures such as step-by-step schema and diagram schema appear on the left-side hand of the window of Help Desk Builder/BT, and a nearmiss link points to a specific page which appears on the right-hand side of the window. In the weed-extermination casebook shown above, a step-by-step schema example is "Steps to maintain fields after harvesting rice". Cases related to these steps are linked from this schema.

(5) **Nearest neighbor retrieval:** We implemented the nearest neighbor-retrieval functions in Help Desk Builder/BT. Similarities are defined among item nodes in outline menus. However, the nearest-neighbor retrieval function is rarely used when building large-scale multimedia contents because the definition and maintenance of similarity definition is hard.

4 Summary

We have developed several CBR-related systems. Our early systems used sophisticated CBR techniques invented in CBR communities. Then, we developed our first large-scale CBR system, SQUAD. We adopted a simple method for nearest-neighbor retrieval. While we were operating SQUAD and SQUAD-II, we understood corporate CBR systems should be integrated with other information systems (Lesson Learned 1).

When we developed the CARET help desk support system, we solved a situation assessment problem by treating it as a user interface problem. We did not translate raw cases into internal representations in the project. Instead, we concentrated on inventing various retrieval mechanisms for cases (Lesson Learned 2).

When we designed and developed Help Desk Builder, we built not only a CBR tool but also non-CBR modules including case-gathering mechanisms for everyday operations. We extended the tool from a CBR tool to a knowledge management tool that integrates various types of multimedia information including cases. The motivation behind this decision came from the fact that cases were found to be only one type of knowledge chunks and cases should refer to/be referred to from other types of information such as product catalogues, user manuals, or multimedia dictionaries. We invented multi-link page retrieval and reverse retrieval. They are used as general purpose mechanisms for information retrieval, including case base retrieval.

References

1. Kitano, H., Shibata, A., Shimazu, H., Kajihara J., Sato, A., Building Large-Scale Corporate-Wide Case-Based Systems: Integration of Organizational and Machine Executable Algorithms. In Proceedings of the National Conference on Artificial Intelligence, 1992 (AAAI-92)
2. Kitano, H and Shimazu, H, The Experience Sharing Architecture: A Case Study in Corporate-Wide Case-Based Software Quality Control, In Case-Based Reasoning Experiences, Lessons, & Future Directions, ed D.B. Leake, AAAI Press/The MIT Press, 1996
3. Kolodner, J., Case-Based Reasoning, Morgan Kaufmann, 1993.
4. Schank, R., and Abelson, R.P., 1977. Scripts, Plans, Goals, and Understanding, Erlbaum, Hillsdale. N.J., 1977
5. Shimazu, H., Kitano, H., and Shibata, A., Retrieving Cases from Relational DataBase: Another Stride Towards Corporate-Wide Case-Based Systems, In Proceedings of the International Joint Conference on Artificial Intelligence, 1993 (IJCAI-93)
6. Shimazu, H., Shibata, A., and Nihei, K., Case-Based Retrieval Interface Adapted to Customer-Initiated Dialogues in Help Desk Operations, In Proceedings of the National Conference on Artificial Intelligence, 1994 (AAAI-94)
7. Shimazu and Takashima, Detecting Discontinuities in Case-Bases, In Proceedings of the National Conference on Artificial Intelligence, 1996 (AAAI-96)

Using Case-Based Reasoning for Reusing Software Knowledge

Carsten Tautz and Klaus-Dieter Althoff

Fraunhofer Institute for Experimental Software Engineering
Sauerwiesen 6, D-67661 Kaiserslautern, Germany
E-mail: {tautz, althoff}@iese.fhg.de

Abstract. Reuse of software knowledge is a principle for improving productivity and reliability of software development. To achieve this, reuse must be done systematically. This means that processes for retrieving, reusing, revising, and retaining have to be defined. At the same time organizational issues (such as the establishment of a separate organizational unit responsible for organizational learning) must be considered. In this paper we compare software knowledge reuse models to the CBR cycle of Aamodt and Plaza [1] and show that the approaches are very similar. We suggest to extend the CBR cycle by including organizational issues explicitly and conclude that CBR is a promising technology for realizing software knowledge reuse if our suggested organizational extensions are considered.

Keywords. Organizational View on CBR, Organizational Learning, Experience Factory, Quality Improvement Paradigm, Software Knowledge Reuse

1 Introduction

Reuse practice appears to exhibit considerable potential, far more than other ongoing activities, to enhance the software development process and to restructure not only the process of software construction, but also the actual software development departments. To accommodate for and to exploit software reuse, the management and organization of these departments are to be restructured not just locally and in isolation, but also in the context of the entire organization. [18, p. 167]

The reuse of all kinds of software knowledge is one of the main pillars of the approach used for transferring software technologies by our institute. The transfer is based on the Quality Improvement Paradigm (QIP) describing the activities of continuous improvement, the Goal/Question/Metric (GQM) approach for goal-oriented measurement and evaluation, and the Experience Factory (EF) concept describing the organizational structure for implementing a process improvement program which includes an experience base where all knowledge relevant to software development is stored [8].

QIP, GQM and EF have been applied successfully in several environments. Their successful application within NASA's Software Engineering Laboratory (SEL) has been recognized with the first IEEE/SEI Process Achievement Award. Currently, these approaches are the basis of improvement programs in many companies covering all branches of industry and ranging from small to midsize and large companies. [15, p. 13]

At this point, we are looking for technical support for realizing the experience base. We decided to explore case-based reasoning (CBR) for this purpose. CBR has already been used for software reuse in the past [10, 11], however, in this paper we discuss how well the CBR approach and our reuse approach match with respect to the conceptual knowledge level [4] and the organizational structure. There are other approaches which use similarity-based retrieval such as AIRS [13] and faceted classification [14], but the approaches do not offer a model on the conceptual knowledge level for using and learning from past experience.

The work described here has been inspired by a paper of Althoff and Wilke [6] where they introduce an organizational view[1] on the "CBR cycle" described by [1]. Such an organizational view is more helpful in order to understand the potential uses of CBR in software development and process modeling support. We strongly support this organizational view on CBR by detailing the correspondences between the CBR cycle and the reuse of software knowledge. We will show on an interesting level of detail that CBR is a very promising technology for developing an EF. Here the importance of CBR goes beyond realizing particular EF mechanisms, but supports the realization of an EF on a more general knowledge level [4].

The remainder of the paper is structured as follows. The next section gives a short introduction to the reuse of software knowledge. Based on this, we compare the reuse process with the CBR task-method decomposition model as introduced by [1], a detailing of the CBR cycle (section 3). Since the reuse process is very similar to the CBR cycle and organizational issues have long been considered as part of a successful reuse program, it seems natural to extend the interpretation of the CBR cycle to include organizational issues explicitly (see [17] for details here). Such issues have been considered in ongoing project case studies where CBR is used for realizing EF's (section 4). We will shortly describe our planned activities in this direction and point to issues that are still open (section 5).

---

1. We subsume two aspects under the term "organizational view": activities performed by humans rather than by machines, and the organizational structure, e.g., an organization may be subdivided into several project organization units and a unit responsible for organizational learning.

2 Reuse of Software Knowledge

The benefits of software reuse are manifold. Among them are improved productivity, improved reliability, better estimates, and faster time-to-market [16]. Traditionally, the emphasis has been on reusing code. However, reuse does not have to stop there. All kinds of software-related knowledge can be reused, including products (documents created by a software development project), processes (activities or actions aimed at creating some product) [9], and anything else useful for software development, e.g., effort prediction and productivity models or models of the application being implemented.

Reuse can be applied both to the planning of a software development project and to the performance of the project.

2.1 Reuse for Planning a Software Development Project

Before software development can start, the development project has to be planned (with respect to cost, schedule, effort, resource demands, etc.). At the same time, indicators for detecting deviations from the project plan are defined.

Unlike manufacturing where production is a repetitive task, software development has creative elements. This does not mean, however, that software knowledge reuse cannot be applied. Similar processes (project plans) can be used for similar software systems. Hence, planning a project can be based on plans of projects already terminated. This fact led to the development of the quality improvement paradigm (QIP) [8]. It divides the planning process into three steps, and takes into account that the lessons learned from the performance of the project (were the predicted cost, effort, resource demands, etc. correct?) have to be saved in order to improve the planning of future projects.

The planning steps are as follows:

- *Characterize.* The environment, in which the software development takes place, is described using the project characteristics as input. The characterization of the environment can be thought of as a set of models used in similar projects to the one to be planned. Models may describe possible project plans, the document structure of the software system, expected duration or effort distribution. In addition, suitable measurement goals are part of the characterization.
- *Set goals.* Based on the characterization and the capabilities of strategic importance to the organization, a set of measurement goals is defined. Measurement goals may be project-specific or of general interest to the organization. A project-specific goal might be the adherence to the predicted effort while the reduction of development cost in the long run is of interest to the organization as a whole. Thus, measurement goals define the successful project and organization performance. Reasonable expectations with respect to the goals are derived from the baseline provided by the characterization step.
- *Choose models.* Depending on the goals set, the right set of models from the characterization step has to be chosen or created. Usually, the chosen models have to be

tailored to the specific needs of the project. For instance, the effort distribution model might express the percentage of effort spent in each phase (requirements, design, code, test). If the total effort is known, the effort distribution model can be instantiated by replacing the percentiles with concrete effort numbers. Other models can be constructed using building blocks, e.g., a project plan can be constructed using building blocks for each phase.

The planning phase is followed by the actual performance of the project (step 4 of the QIP). During the performance the project is monitored to make sure that it uses its resources in the best possible way. For example, if the effort model predicts 400 hours for the design phase, and the actual design has taken 350 hours even though it is only to 50% complete, then obviously a problem has occurred for which a solution should be sought. At this point, reuse for performing the project comes in (see next subsection).

After the project has been completed, an evaluation takes place:

- *Analyze.* At the end of the project, the collected data and problems which occurred (and their solutions) are analyzed. The results of this analysis are lessons learned and improvement suggestions for future projects. For example, if a new technique for writing software requirements was applied in the project, one would like to know whether this requirements technique was helpful in the subsequent phases. Probably, some improvement suggestions regarding the technique will be provided by the project team.

- *Package.* The project feedback has to be consolidated into new, updated and refined models. For instance, if tutorial material exists describing the requirements technique, it can be updated using the lessons learned and the improvement suggestions from the analysis phase. This way, improvement suggestions find their way into future projects.

2.2 Reuse for Performing a Software Development Project

The project plan constructed in the planning phase can be used to guide the performance of the project. Each activity produces deliverables, usually some kind of document. Humans, however, start very seldom from scratch. Typically, something is reused. For example, instead of writing an informal application for a business trip (where we might forget lots of important information for the administration), we use an application form. The same is true for the development of software. Large deliverables can be assembled by reusing old pieces. To exploit reuse to the fullest extend possible it is necessary to provide support, e.g., in the form of an experience base where all reusable objects are stored. Both technical activities and project management (e.g., for replanning) is supported by the experience base. Again, any kind of knowledge can be reused, not just code. For example, if a schedule slippage is detected, the experience base may be consulted for possible actions like reducing the number of reviews (which will, however, increase project risks).

Reuse for the performance of a software development project is typically described by a reuse model such as the one proposed by Basili and Rombach [9]. Given a system S where a new object is to be integrated, a specification $\bar{x}$ of an object x is defined. The next step is to identify a set of reuse candidates $x_1, ..., x_n$. These candidates are evaluated. Eventually the best suited candidate x_k is selected. Depending on how close x_k is to x, x is created from scratch, or x_k is modified in a suitable way. Then, the new object is integrated into S resulting in a new system S'. An alternative to modifying x_k in such a way that it satisfies $\bar{x}$ is to modify S (and consequently $\bar{x}$) so that x can be integrated more easily. The last step of the process is to record the project-specific experience (e.g., x along with an evaluation whether x was successfully integrated into S) in order to improve the reuse support. The integration of the new experience into the experience base is referred to as "packaging". Integrating new experience may require to restructure parts of the experience base. This is referred to as "repackaging".

The experience base may not only be populated by experience gained by the software development organization itself, but also through transferring existing experience from outside the organization. Such experience can be found, e.g., in literature.

3 Comparison of the CBR Approach and the Reuse Approaches

For comparing both the QIP and the reuse-oriented software development model with the CBR approach, we use the task-method decomposition model proposed by Aamodt and Plaza [1] for four main reasons. First the task-method decomposition model bases on Aamodt and Plaza's CBR cycle which does not differ from other CBR cycles described in the literature with respect to its basic contents [12]. Second the combination of CBR and knowledge level analysis [4] is very helpful for our problem at hand (namely to find a technological basis for an EF). Third the task-method decomposition model has been successfully used within the evaluation of the Inreca CBR system as a means of analysis and comparison [3, 4, 2]. Fourth the CBR cycle of Aamodt and Plaza appears to be widely accepted in the literature (see [17] for examples).

We now shortly introduce the four top-level (sub)tasks "retrieve", "reuse", "revise", and "retain" of the CBR task-method decomposition model.

- *Retrieve* is decomposed into "identify features" (identifies relevant set of problem descriptors), "search" (returns a set of cases which might be similar to the new case), "initially match" (chooses a set of cases that are similar to the new case), and "select" (chooses the most suitable case from the set).
- *Reuse* is decomposed into "copy" (takes the selected case as the basis) and "adapt" (transforms the solution of the selected case to a solution for the new case).
- *Revise* is decomposed into "evaluate solution" (evaluates the success of the solution constructed in the reuse task) and "repair fault" (detects defects in the current solution and generates or retrieves explanations for them).
- *Retain* is decomposed into "extract" (identifies the information which must be stored), "index" (identifies the types of indexes needed for future retrieval as well as the structure of the search space), and "integrate" (updates the knowledge base with the parts of the actual experience likely to be useful in future problem solving).

3.1 Comparison of the CBR Approach and the QIP

The steps of the QIP compare to the CBR approach as follows:

- *QIP step 1 (characterize)*. In this step project characteristics are used to retrieve a set of relevant models. This corresponds to "identify features", "search" and "initially match" of the task "retrieve". Since no best candidate is selected at this point, the "select" task is not part of QIP step 1.
- *QIP step 2 (set goals)*. In this step measurement goals for the software development projects are chosen. This can be interpreted as "selecting goal cases"[1], i.e., the responsible manager looks for strategic improvement goals and/or combinations of them (e.g., "reduce the software development effort by 30%"). Therefore, QIP step 2 corresponds to the task "select" with respect to measurement goals (a subset of all relevant models returned in QIP step 1).
- *QIP step 3 (choose models)*. Here, the rest of the relevant models (describing products, processes, expectations for the goals) is selected in accordance with the goals selected in QIP step 2. Therefore, QIP step 3 corresponds to the task "select" with respect to everything but measurement goals. In addition, a project plan is assembled, i.e., the relevant models are integrated. This typically requires modification of the retrieved models. Hence, QIP step 3 corresponds also to the "reuse" task.
- *QIP step 4 (perform)*. During this step the project is performed. Even though the CBR process implies, that the solution is applied between the tasks "reuse" and "revise", it does not provide an explicit task for this. Therefore, there is no correspondence to QIP step 4. One of the reasons is that the project is usually not executed by the people responsible for running the CBR system. In terms of the EF concept, CBR specialists work in the EF, while the project is performed by the people in the project organization. Nevertheless, a model describing the CBR approach should also consider organizational issues, meaning that it should include the case application explicitly.
- *QIP step 5 (analyze)*. In this step the project performance is analyzed. Lessons learned and improvement suggestions with respect to the knowledge applied are written. Hence, QIP step 5 corresponds to the task "revise", but also to "extract" of the task "retain", because the output of QIP step 5 is exactly what has to be packaged in the next step.
- *QIP step 6 (package)*. Here, the lessons learned and improvement suggestions are integrated into the experience base. This includes formalizing the experience as well as restructuring the experience base. Therefore, QIP step 6 corresponds to "index" and "integrate" of the task "retain".

---

1. Another correspondence here is between defining similarity (as a special kind of general knowledge usually done by a domain expert) in CBR and defining goals (as concrete improvement goals derived from strategic business goals usually determined by the responsible manager) in QIP [6]. In both cases the resulting definition guides the later selection process and, thus, is of crucial importance for the whole procedure.

Table 1 summarizes the correspondences.

Table 1. Summary of the comparison between the CBR cycle and the QIP

CBR		QIP 1	QIP 2	QIP 3	QIP 4	QIP 5	QIP 6
retrieve	identify features	X					
	search	X					
	initially match	X					
	select		X (goals)	X (other)			
reuse	copy			X			
	adapt			X			
revise	evaluate solution				X		
	repair fault				X		
retain	extract				X		
	index					X	
	integrate						X

3.2 Comparison of the CBR Approach and the Reuse-Oriented Software Development Model

Reuse within a software development project basically consists of seven steps which are related to the CBR approach as follows:

- *Specify.* In this first step the need for a new object is recognized, and the needed object is specified. This step corresponds to "identify features" of the task "retrieve".

- *Identify.* An initial set of possible candidates is identified. This corresponds to "search" and "initially match" of the task "retrieve".

- *Evaluate and select.* The most suitable candidate is selected. This step corresponds to "select" of the task "retrieve".

- *Modify or create.* Either the most suitable candidate is modified to fulfill the initial specification or a new object is built from scratch. Both correspond to the task "reuse". However, the creation of a completely new case is only indirectly covered by the CBR cycle.

- *Integrate.* The new object is integrated into its surrounding system. Again, as the CBR cycle does not include the application of cases explicitly, this step has no correspondence. In terms of the EF concept, integration work is done in the project organization. Usually, the EF people are not involved in this step.

- *Record experience.* The success of using the new object is evaluated. This corresponds to the task "revise" as well as to "extract" of the task "retain".

- *(Re-)package.* This involves the integration of the experience into the experience base. Hence, this step corresponds to "index" and "integrate" of the task "retain".

Table 2 summarizes the results of this comparison.

Table 2. Summary of the comparison between the CBR cycle
and the reuse-oriented software development model

CBR		specify	iden-tify	evaluate and select	modify or create	inte-grate	record experi-ence	(re-)pack-age
retrieve	identify features	X						
	search		X					
	initially match		X					
	select			X				
reuse	copy				X			
	adapt				X			
revise	evaluate solution						X	
	repair fault						X	
retain	extract						X	
	index							X
	inte-grate							X

The result of the two comparisons carried out in this section is twofold. First we have shown that there are many commonalties between the CBR cycle and the two software knowledge reuse models. This can be viewed as a successfully passed plausibility test for CBR as a candidate technology for realizing software knowledge reuse. Second in both comparisons there is one basic correspondence missing. For the same reason already seen with the perform step of the QIP, the CBR cycle does not include any explicit correspondence for the "integrate" step of the reuse model. The consideration of the underlying reasons leads to the organizational issues of using CBR systems (see [17] for further details).

4 Current Status

Our current work bases on the general framework described in [4, 5], and [3]. [7] describes the analysis of a collection of experiences with respect to the application of CBR and the development of CBR systems, gathered by several questionnaires. These experiences have been made reusable by means of CBR technology, i.e., each questionnaire has been represented as a structured case. For instance, for a concrete application problem it can be searched for a similar problem or a similar CBR tool (i.e., a CBR tool that in principle can deal with the problem).

There are a number of ongoing industrial, research and in-house projects at our institute in the context of EF development. Currently the main effort here has been on identifying and capturing experiences (data, information, and knowledge) for potential reuse. Up to now CBR has not been used for their realization.

5 Summary and Outlook

We showed that the CBR approach as described by Aamodt and Plaza [1] is similar to the models used in the area of software engineering for reusing knowledge both on the project planning level and the project performance level. In the second part, we introduced an organizational structure for reusing software knowledge.

We plan to use a CBR system for software knowledge reuse and evaluate its benefits. For this purpose a common model incorporating the CBR process model and the reuse process models is being developed. Such a model will describe CBR-based reuse of software knowledge in sufficient detail. The organizational model described in [17] can be used as a basis for further evaluation with respect to useful support by using CBR systems.

6 Acknowledgements

We would like to thank Günther Ruhe and Frank Bomarius for the fruitful discussions. Jürgen Münch and Martin Verlage raised many issues we had to think about. Thanks also to Christiane Gresse and the anonymous referees for reviewing the submitted paper. They all have contributed to this final version in a constructive way.

7 References

[1]   Agnar Aamodt and Enric Plaza. Case-based reasoning: Foundational issues, methodological variations, and system approaches. *AICOM*, 7(1):39–59, March 1994.

[2]   K.-D. Althoff, E. Auriol, R. Barletta, and M. Manago. *A Review of Industrial Case-Based Reasoning Tools*. AI Intelligence. Oxford (UK), 1995.

[3]   Klaus-Dieter Althoff. Evaluating case-based reasoning systems: The Inreca case study. Postdoctoral thesis, University of Kaiserslautern, July 1996. (submitted).

[4]   Klaus-Dieter Althoff and Agnar Aamodt. Relating case-based problem solving and learning methods to task and domain characteristics: Towards an analytic framework. *AICOM*, 9(3):109–116, September 1996.

[5]   Klaus-Dieter Althoff and Brigitte Bartsch-Spörl. Decision support for case-based applications. *Wirtschaftsinformatik*, 38(1):8–16, February 1996.

[6]   Klaus-Dieter Althoff and Wolfgang Wilke. Potential uses of case-based reasoning in experienced based construction of software systems and business process support. In R. Bergmann and W. Wilke, editors, *Proceedings of the 5th German Workshop on Case-Based Reasoning*, LSA-97-01E, pages 31–38. Centre for Learning Systems and Applications, University of Kaiserslautern, March 1997.

[7]   Brigitte Bartsch-Spörl, Klaus-Dieter Althoff, and Alexandre Meissonnier. Learning from and reasoning about case-based reasoning systems. In *Proceedings of the 4th German Conference on Knowledge-Based Systems (XPS97)*, March 1997.

[8]   Victor R. Basili, Gianluigi Caldiera, and H. Dieter Rombach. Experience Factory. In John J. Marciniak, editor, *Encyclopedia of Software Engineering*, volume 1, pages 469–476. John Wiley & Sons, 1994.

[9]   Victor R. Basili and H. Dieter Rombach. Support for comprehensive reuse. *IEEE Software Engineering Journal*, 6(5):303–316, September 1991.

[10]   R. Bergmann and U. Eisenecker. Case-based reasoning for supporting reuse of object-oriented software: A case study (in German). In M. M. Richter and F. Maurer, editors, *Expert Systems 95*, pages 152–169. infix Verlag, 1996.

[11]   C. Fernández-Chamiso, P. A. Gozales-Cálero, M. Gómez-Albarrán, and L. Hernández-Yanez. Supporting object reuse through case-based reasoning. In I. Smith and B. Faltings, editors, *Advances in Case-Based Reasoning*, pages 135–149. Springer-Verlag, 1996.

[12]   Janet Kolodner. *Case-Based Reasoning*. Morgan Kaufmann, 1993.

[13]   Eduardo Ostertag, James Hendler, Rubén Prieto-Díaz, and Christine Braun. Computing similarity in a reuse library system: An AI-based approach. *ACM Transactions on Software Engineering and Methodology*, 1(3):205–228, July 1992.

[14]   Rubén Prieto-Díaz and Peter Freeman. Classifying software for reusability. *IEEE Software*, 4(1):6–16, January 1987.

[15]   H. Dieter Rombach. New institute for applied software engineering research. *Software Process Newsletter*, pages 12–14, Fall 1996. No. 7.

[16]   Wilhelm Schäfer, Rubén Prieto-Díaz, and Masao Matsumoto. *Software Reusability*. Ellis Horwood, 1994.

[17]   Carsten Tautz and Klaus-Dieter Althoff. Using case-based reasoning for reusing software knowledge. Technical Report IESE-Report No. 004.97/E, Fraunhofer Institute for Experimental Software Engineering, Kaiserslautern (Germany), 1997.

[18]   Mansour Zand and Mansur Samadzadeh. Software reuse: Current status and trends. *Journal of Systems and Software*, 30(3):167–170, September 1995.

New Technology Bliss and Pain in a Large Customer Service Center

Helen Thomas
Thomson-Consumer
Electronics
7225 Winton Dr.
Indianapolis, IN 46268
ThomasH@indy.tce.com
ph. (317) 415-3242

Richard Foil
Thomson-Consumer
Electronics
7225 Winton Dr.
Indianapolis, IN 46268
FoilR@acsc.indy.tce.com
ph. (317) 415-2102

Jim Dacus
Inference Corp.
490 S. Orlando Ave
Cocoa Beach FL 32931
dacus@inference.com
ph. (407) 799-1724

Paper type: Application

Abstract

The evolution of customer support centers in the early and mid-90's typically grew from industry technicians providing technical support to technical people. During this same time frame, the consumer electronics industry introduced significant changes in products available to the public, products that were technically complex. Digital Satellite Systems, Digital Video Disc, home theater systems and high definition television, all quite appealing to the average American consumer, all presented to the buyer as easy to set up and use and all technically beyond the comprehension and basic understanding of the average consumer. At the same time, manufacturing costs had to be reduced due to significant price erosions at the retail level, caused by retailer profiles which shifted towards high volume mass merchants and discount stores with "carry home today, enjoy tonight " marketing efforts.

Thomson Consumer Electronics (TCE) manufactures consumer electronics products under the brand names of RCA, GE, and ProScan. The TCE Consumer Support Center currently supports 3,500 unique consumer electronic products. In order to supply the huge demand for consumer service, TCE is the first large such manufacturer to embrace the leading edge of technology in so many way and at the same time. TCE is integrating: AT&T GE Switch, Answer Soft Computer Telephony Integration (CTI), Quintus Call Tracking System, Inference Case Based Reasoning (CBR), Adobe Acrobat Viewer, Fulcrum Full Text Search, integrated FAX, Mainframe interface, and Image Document Management. These technologies were brought together in order to provide a consistent and high quality technology-assisted customer service support to a non-technical customer, which resulted in both bliss and pain to the TCE Customer Support Center. The results are summarized in this case study paper.

Keywords: Case Based Reasoning, CBR, Customer Service Center, large scale integration, technology-assisted technical support, consumer electronics industry.

Why CBR Technology

Resources for staffing and supporting end consumer technical support began by utilizing electronics technicians and their skills, translating the technical hook-up and operation techniques, technical design capabilities and troubleshooting events with John Q. Public. As call volumes increased, customer support staffing resources with electronics savvy became more and more difficult to find. The solution was to teach basic electronics theory of operation to customer service people and provide them access to ASCII text keyword search files to support their efforts. Keyword search systems and documents were created in a mainframe environment and paper user guide manuals were ordered and stocked in hundreds of desks each year. As the keyword search files increased, successful and timely location of appropriate information decreased. Agent talk times on 800 numbers increased in direct proportion to the ready availability of information to support the call. Agents placed callers on hold while they traveled across acres of floor space to find the manual, only to find that the last manual in the library was already in use by another agent. Clearly, a better solution was needed.

Our quest for a high technology solution began with a virtual cornucopia of functional requirements. The solution must offer common English presentation and programmed logic conducive to technically complex troubleshooting by non-technical people. The tool also needed to be relatively easy to load and maintain, offer a high degree of flexibility for content changes as well as being capable of supporting a product array of a minimum of 5,000 unique and highly featured models in a dynamic environment carrying nearly 10 million inbound calls annually. High resolution color graphic presentations of literature attached to solutions with options to attach help files with hyper-text links, provide an entry point to other applications, as well as interfacing elegantly with a front end call tracking application would be required as well. Lastly, Case Based Reasoning, Inference Case Point and CBR Express met the requirements.

Project Objectives

- *First Call Resolution* - Reduction if not elimination of repeat contacts resulting in an overall reduction of caller hold times and caller frustration.
- *Quality Resolution* - Improved caller perception of the quality, thoroughness and usefulness of the contact.
- *Exchange Avoidance/Service Call Avoidance* - Elimination of unnecessary warranty exchange and warranty service costs.
- *Supplement Agent Training* - Skill building and agent expertise development. Education through use of knowledge base content.
- *Issue Tracking and Reporting* - Storage of Question/Answer pairs and solutions used to support products after the sale. Trend reporting and feedback to business components on product integrity in the field.

How we organized the project

Call content and prioritization of the value of content was identified through analysis using a combination of methods. Call volume reports by product type and reason for the call were used for initial segmentation of the content to identify subject matter volume areas at the highest level. An overlay of these to the return on investment objectives showed clear areas of high value in the subjects of Digital Satellite Systems, television and communications products.

Digital Satellite System and television support seemed to be the most logical starting point for building the knowledge base however, through the case base design and data modeling phase, product-to-product interconnection issues clouded what seemed so clear during the content data collection efforts. The practical application of television knowledge had great potential for interfacing with alternate audio and video signal source subject domains. Even though television was clearly a big hit area of need, the risk of an agent working towards a solution for television product and ultimately needing diagnostics for interconnect or alternate signal source diagnostics was very high. A 'back end forward' approach to video case base building was the most viable option and least likely to deliver a knowledge user to a dead end. User perception of the value and usefulness of the knowledge base was a critical success factor in the implementation. Warranty fulfillment methods were taken into consideration as well and specific subject domains grouped product families into two types, manufacturer exchange and field serviceable.

Initial load criteria for subject domains were modified to include starting simple, identifying product families that were exclusive by nature where calls were received by an exclusive community of agent users having a single warranty fulfillment type. Digital Satellite Systems met the new criteria as well as the high volume, usefulness and 'back end forward criteria.

Second level subject matter architecture analysis and design led to segmentation of case base types. Product operation/hookup, component failure diagnostics, procedures and general information sub-domains became the model for full implementation architecture.

Positions and responsibilities

Just as functional and technical requirements define the needs for technology to support business operations, new technology in a business defines process and organizational functional changes. Work flow, positions and areas of responsibilities require re-engineering in order to make the technology effective. The best technology in the world is worthless without the acceptance, support and active interaction of humans. This is especially true for artificial intelligence applications.

The immediately obvious restructuring of organizations includes such positions as knowledge base authors, document engineers, project managers and physical or logical data engineers. Less obvious organization changes in roles, skills and responsibilities within the business community can be just as critical, if not more so, than those required for the creation and implementation of artificial intelligence.

Skill set and core competency requirement changes begin at the agent level, and continue throughout the organization. Recruitment techniques, advertisements and sources for potential agent employees shift somewhat from areas with a preponderance of technical skills and capabilities to techniques and sources that are more heavily weighted with customer service interpersonal skills. Deductive reasoning skills remain in focus to support agent contribution and sanitizing of artificial intelligence tools and PC skills come more clearly into focus, creating a fresh and more plentiful pool of potential candidates.

While agent candidate pools can become more plentiful, the reverse is true for artificial intelligence authors, document engineers, subject domain experts and logical subject matter architects to support the agent community, the artificial intelligence database and the business, particularly if the agent community had been the primary resource and fertile breeding ground for these positions in the past. Preserving a career path structure within the agent community that maintains a breeding ground for subject matter experts cannot be overlooked.

Going from organization dependence on subject matter experts to artificial intelligence tools readily available to all, tends to surface a group of people who previously may have been overlooked. The 'almost experts' who have been quietly and proudly providing shoulder-to-shoulder advise to their peers in the agent community suddenly emerge and become noticed. These people, during the transition period, are likely to outwardly and totally reject, criticize and undermine the implementation of artificial intelligence. They see their valuable expertise being threatened by a computer. The very foundation of their existence in the workplace is being shaken.

Authors, supervisors, trainers and managers can have a tendency to ignore or brush aside the rumblings from this group of people, expecting them to adjust, conform and stop making waves. However, without the proper attention to these people, they are quite likely to succeed at causing an implementation to fail, or worse yet, leave the organization to join one where they can once again feel the gratification of being the best. Finding a channel to tap into their skills and their sense of self worth in the new environment is the challenge. Tapping into their skills and value by appointing responsibilities to act as knowledge contributors and artificial intelligence quality editors providing the much needed feedback to the knowledge base authors can match their skills, value and self worth to a new environment and preserve the training, tenure and business specific expertise investment that has been made in them, as well as providing them with a channel and a new niche in your organization rather than driving them through the doorway of your recruiting opponent businesses.

How we developed the Case Bases

On site training was done by a representative of the Inference Corp. Training lasted the better part of three days and covered in total the operation of the authoring software. Training also included one exercise in case building and discussed briefly how to organize information into something called a "Cluster".

It was decided that the initial case base development should support a fairly new and independent division of the organization whose functions employed a wide range of skills found in many other organizational segments.

Next we interviewed several call center agents to get their input on the wording of our highest level case questions which would serve to focus their search into a specific area. We found the input of a brand new temporary who had absolutely no product training or experience, to be our best source of information on how to pose our opening questions. More experienced employees had been brain washed to use our internal terms and jargon to classify call content, whereas the fresh perspective of a new person highlighted the need for intuitive operation.

Armed with almost 20 hours of training, a new Pentium PC and visions of rapidly producing a fully functional case base, a lone author sat down in front of a blank screen. Within hours he realized as the screen was still blank that the content of the case base was not going to come through divine inspiration. Some process for data collection and organization was definitely needed. One suggestion was to have agents write common problem symptoms and the appropriate solutions on index cards. An author could then group the cards into stacks of common symptoms and use them as a basis for case building. The cards started coming in and stacks started growing, and growing, and growing, but still the screen was blank. Case building should be a simple matter of defining a particular situation by the answers to a series of questions, yet the concept of a complete knowledge base was so abstract that the task seemed insurmountable. The next tool used was a flowcharting application but soon learned that the decision tree styling of a flowchart does not fit well with the dynamic structure of a knowledge base. An Inference consultant was brought in. He worked on-site for six weeks, and introduced case authors to a Microsoft's Excel spreadsheet program. The column headers became case titles and the cells below held the question - answer pairs that would define the symptom referenced in the title. The bottom row of the case column held the appropriate action to correct the situation and the path or location of any documents that would explain or provide more in-depth information. This form did work well for recording case information, but we found that as common symptoms were placed into adjacent columns that the result was a wonderful graphic depiction of the structure of each cluster of cases. This new way of looking a the case base made missing information stand out quite clearly and helped to streamline the list of questions needed to identify each situation. All the information needed to input in the case authoring software was now well organized into one location. It was a major advancement in the way we started to build our knowledge bases from that point forward.

Throughout the authoring process we kept in mind that as we have an increasingly technical consumer base, we also had a decreasingly technical employment base. Scripted items and testing procedures need to explained in depth by the supporting documentation. We tried to always use what became known as the 'Mail Room Test'. If an employee from the mailroom could be given a few minutes of training on the operation of our case retrieval software but no training or familiarization with the actual products, could they complete the functions normally done by an experienced agent? If the answer is yes them we have succeeded. At the same time, the case structure must allow the more experienced agents to reference materials and reference documents quickly without step by step guidance. As a final step prior to deployment of a newly developed case base, we recognized the need for testing from a non-technical point of view. Again holding up to the 'Mail Room' standard, this phase would insure that the case information was written free of inside terminology and flowed logically to a conclusion.

How we deployed CBR

Provided with a control group of sorts, a pilot release of the DSS diagnostic case base as a stand alone application was initiated to approximately 15 users. These users were each newly trained CSR's. Feedback was positive, yet very little unresolved search information was being, nor could have been retrieved from the inexperienced agents.

The case base was then introduced and released to as many as 60 CSR's of all levels and tenures. The resulting increase in case base usage (as reported by the Oracle Server) and new case material was surprisingly low, even non-existent. Net usage of the knowledge base tool had stayed fairly constant for almost two moths. It was in the search for answer to that question that led to the identification of the "High Incentive" group. The realization that artificial intelligence can be taken as an insult to intelligence by some individuals in the organization. Approaching the members of this group directly to solicit their expert opinions on content and structure of the knowledge base has promised positive returns. The previous "nay sayers" are now strong advocates of the system and excited about being involved in the process of knowledge collection.

Computational Architecture & Supporting Technology
Software Applications

ComputingArchitecture

How Callers Interact with the System

Seamless guided integration of multiple applications becomes priority as 'best of breed' stand alone application solutions are identified.

Avoidance of the "oh what a tangled web we weave" steered us towards tightly integrating Skills based routing from the switch, Computer Telephony software integrating telephonic call delivery (both inbound and outbound) with a call tracking application that interfaces with legacy systems and artificial intelligence applications linked to help files and graphic image viewing as well as full text retrieval applications.

Processing searches and delivering screen pops simultaneously with the inbound call is governed before the call or the data become interactive with the agent. Automatic Number Identification (ANI) or collected digits are passed from the switch to the telephony server, the telephony server interacts with the call tracking application systematically affecting a search against the database. Search results are synchronized and delivered simultaneously to the agent as the call is delivered.

How Users Interact with the System

Presenting front line application users with a barrage of applications, icons and file locations could defeat the purpose of simplifying and streamlining their work environment with technology. On the other hand, second and third tier users could become frustrated if they were forced to follow a structured path to obtain the contents of an on-line document image or help file.

Structured access for front line users was accomplished through creation of a standard user profile on the server, that users would pull down at their NT log on. The profile incorporates a start-up group that is programmed to sequentially and automatically launch a series of applications and log ons. Higher end users were provided with a standard Program Manager affording them the flexibility of launching applications as needed as well as utilization of File Manager.

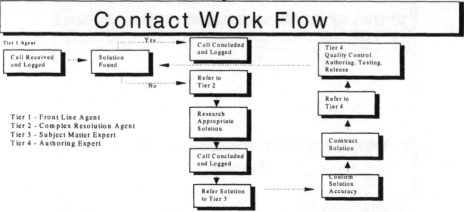

Contact Work Flow

Examples

A search through a diagnostic case base goes through several questions to yield a specific action.

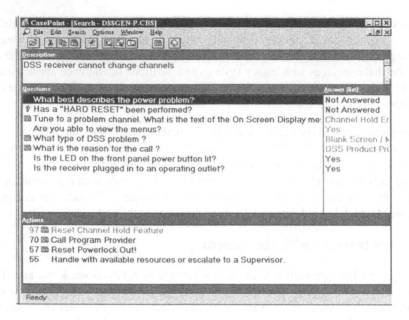

Searches in a reference case base place higher weight on the description and should yield an

action after a response to a single confirming question.

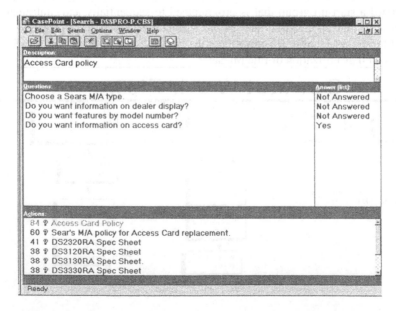

All actions and most questions provide an icon that will launch a supporting application or text browse to explain in depth the information referenced.

Graphic displays of product menus hotspotted to provide navigation simulation on the terminal.

Instruction books for all products are available on line.

Benefits Received

On-line dynamic logical situation analysis clearly enabled us to realize the benefit objectives of first call quality resolution, service call avoidance, warranty cost reduction and issue tracking. These firmly established returns were further supplemented by unforeseen benefits of back end integration with other software applications, streamlining the entire contact handling process.

Diagnostic and internal handling procedures (recipes for applying diagnostic and repair procedures and the 'how-to's' of internal processes) were easily attached to

CBR solutions as help files. Existing documents, graphics and manuals were attached to solutions taking the user to the precise document and page required to support the CBR solution.

Additionally, it became possible to capture snapshots of on-screen displays and menus not included in consumer support publications by combining the use of software designed to capture these images with help file software and facilitate television receiver menus many layers deep with hyper-text links and hot spots applied to the snapshots. The days of an agent asking a caller to describe which menu they were seeing during a set-up operation were over, along with the need to house, store and update hundreds of copies of dog-eared procedural manuals and publications.

Lessons Learned

A significant amount of effort to market internally and educate members of the business outside of the immediate call center environment became an obvious necessity early on. The understanding level of those business managers of the magnitude and potential of the new applications was not easily accomplished. Through a number of site visits and demonstrations resulting in an audience reaction that was substantially low key caused us to take a second look at how their reaction could possibly be so nonchalant. The solution was found to be a lack of comparison. They simply did not understand what the new technology was replacing. The dog-eared manuals and worn library cabinets became in integral part of our demonstrations. Side by side comparisons of old world to new world accomplished the level of amazement and positive reaction that was needed.

Gaining the understanding of call center management of the required resources to develop the knowledge was equally challenging. Devoting much needed call answering resources to activities taking them away from addressing the 'calls at hand' to develop and cleanse the knowledge for the calls not yet received. Our first approach was to assign authoring responsibilities to our subject matter experts asking them to create the knowledge during less busy call volume hours. As call volume priorities shifted and consumed the agent/authors time, their authoring responsibilities had a tendency to become less critical. Tenacity of keeping the long term benefits in focus and several missed deadlines finally resulted in recognition that a full time development staff would be necessary. In order to facilitate the long term objective, an increase of human resources would be necessary.

Agent acceptance of the new technology was easy only for those agents with no tenure. The new hires adapted to the new environment quite easily. Agents with advanced skill levels rejected the introduction of artificial intelligence and actively lobbied to lead the mid-term agents to follow their cause. If it were possible to turn the clock back and start over again, our first concentration of efforts would have proactively identified the lobbyists and assigned their support positions from the start.

Winning the support of internal Information Systems (IS) staff members who were born and bread in a main frame environment posed challenges as well. The IS main frame designers and developers of programs had a tendency to be protective and non-supportive of client server applications with potential of retiring their CICS application babies. Once converted, however, the tried and true standards of operations for design, development, testing and cut over in a main frame environment offered an element of stability that was not necessarily previously found in our client server application environment. The marrying of these two worlds-apart technology approaches resulted in the blended benefits of client server application flexibility with main frame development and testing technique stability, and put 'end user developers' in direct contact with company DBA's and computer room support people with an end result a lesson in greater understanding of the needs and urgencies from both perspectives.

Future Plans

Initial development efforts target internal support of call center agents, thereby supporting end consumers in their quest for information and support. Design and development from the beginning included making the case bases 'net ready' by design.

Phase 2 will include call deflection via web site access to knowledge and contact tracking applications, followed by Phase 3 integrating web applications and switch applications for 'call me' outbound automatic call distribution, blending inbound call distribution with outbound support calls resulting from web site call requests.

Proactive product and accessory sales case bases that launch automatically from new purchase support calls are planned, as well as publication of technical repair diagnostics and intelligent dispatch logic to support in-home field repairs.

Considering the benefits and future plans that have been identified after only a few months of artificial intelligence development, it is clear to see that a new media for creative business enhancement is at hand, positioning us for many more opportunities as we enter a new century and leave behind the technologically constrained paradigms of this century.

An Engineering Approach for Troubleshooting Case Bases

James R. Trott, Boeing Commercial Airplane Group, *jtrott@atc.boeing.com*
Dr. Bing Leng, Inference Corporation, *bing.leng@inference.com*

Abstract

Troubleshooting is a common application of case base technology. Often in these cases, the goal is to capture the approaches of troubleshooting experts and put these troubleshooting best practices in the hands of lesser experienced analysts. Effective knowledge capture is the primary bottleneck to creating a good troubleshooting case base. We used the KADS knowledge modeling methodology to guide the knowledge acquisition to create such a case base. KADS helped us to validate the logic of the entire case base before writing one case and to implement it more quickly than normal and with no errors. This paper illustrates our experience in the use of KADS to help build case bases effectively.

1. Introduction

This paper presents a systematic approach to the entire process of building case bases. It is rooted in theory and has proven successful in a case base development effort. We believe that other case base designers and builders can use this same approach to guide their work. Our approach:

- Uses the KADS knowledge modeling methodology to guide knowledge acquisition. KADS (Knowledge Analysis and Design Support) is a methodology developed by the ESPRIT consortium for creating Knowledge Based Systems [Tansley93]. We supplement this with Mager's process model for expert troubleshooting [Mager82].
- Enabled us to create and deploy a robust, medium-sized case base in only 9 weeks.
- Helped 3 levels of Subject Matter Experts (SMEs) to agree on the logic of the troubleshooting approach in the case base before a single case was entered.
- Allowed us to create a case base with *no* logic errors right from the start. And, in spite of long chains of questions, we could "tune" the performance of the case base in a matter of *minutes* rather than days.

2. Assumptions

First, we must state our assumptions that determine when this approach is appropriate.

- *Troubleshooting Case Base.* There are many kinds of case bases (such as informational, planning, diagnostic). We are focused on *troubleshooting*. [Mager82] describes troubleshooting as "(a) hunting for or locating causes of malfunctions and (b) acting to eliminate or clear them. It includes both locating and clearing." For any particular system, one or the other may be more important.
- *Existence of Expert Performance.* Case bases are more than just a collection of features (that is, questions) and solutions (that is, answers). They describe an approach to solving problems. Often, there are people who solve problems significantly better than others. It is this expertise—these "best thinking practices"—that we seek to capture and distribute to others.
- *Experts Have a Hard Time Describing What They Know.* Often, experts are willing to share their knowledge, if for no other reason than to reduce their work load. However, it is often hard to get this knowledge out of their head, especially as logic gets complex. Perhaps they have compiled years of experience so that they can make leaps in their reasoning that others cannot. They need someone to help them model what they know in a form that others can also use.

- *Knowledge is More than Information and Facts.* It is not enough simply to capture the *things* these experts know; we must also describe how these experts *use* what they know to solve problems.
  —How do they select between different and competing bits of information?
  —How do they manage risk and effort?
  —What procedural tasks do they perform?
  —What logical leaps do they make to deduce a solution from a complaint?
- *Complexity.* Knowledge acquisition requires a significant amount of effort. The SME's troubleshooting approach should be complex enough to warrant this effort.

3. The "PC/Host Case Base" Example

Throughout the paper, we will illustrate the KADS method with examples from a diagnostic case base—the "PC/Host Case Base"—we recently fielded. This case base is designed for "Level 1" analysts (those people directly answering customer calls) at a central help desk to troubleshoot problems with a commercial software package that connects PCs to mainframes, UNIX servers, and other hosts.

We took 6 weeks to analyze the problem and acquire knowledge from SMEs, and 1 week to implement a pilot case base in our CBR engine (CBR Express for authoring; CasePoint for searching, both from Inference Corporation). In this analysis phase, we conducted 14 interviews of SMEs with different levels of expertise and a variety of geographic and organizational boundaries. We took an additional 2 weeks to refine the logic with other SMEs and implement the final production case base.

4. The KADS Method

KADS (Knowledge Analysis and Design Support) is a methodology developed by the ESPRIT consortium for developing Knowledge Based Systems (KBS). It melds various knowledge acquisition theories into an integrated whole. In the United States, KADS has been used in a variety of ways [Gardner97]: KBS, use case design, object-oriented analysis and design, technical architecture, process modeling. In Boeing, KADS has proven effective on several projects, including CBR, KBS, and training development [Trott95]. KADS is available in the public domain and is also supported by consultants. Modeling can be done with standard office productivity tools although Object-Oriented analysis tools can help on larger projects.

The most frequently used piece of KADS is the "KADS Model of Expertise". It describes expert problem solving knowledge with four different models:

- *Domain Model.* Describes the most important concepts and objects in a system and how they relate to each other. They correspond to what the SME has in mind as he solves a problem. Examples include *is-a* and *part-of* relationships.
- *Inference Model.* Shows the roles that concepts play in an expert's reasoning as he seeks to complete a major step in the problem solving process. A major premise of KADS is that there are standard, generic, reusable templates that describe the approaches experts use to perform these steps. For example, experts follow similar approaches when diagnosing problems with an automobile's electrical system and with a human's digestive system: the domain-level concepts are different but the

diagnostic approach is similar. KADS provides a library of dozens of generic templates that describe problem-solving behavior. These become ready-made, customizable frameworks for structuring knowledge coming from an SME.

- *Task Model*. Describes the procedural nature of the expert's problem solving knowledge. This includes tasks and steps, sequencing and control, inputs and outputs, and operators.
- *Strategy Model*. Describes how the SME remains flexible and how he deals with uncertainty when trying to solve problems. It is the SME's higher level plan. Kinds of strategic knowledge we try to capture include: effort management, risk reduction, and choosing between alternatives.

By separating these types of expertise, KADS provides a common framework, methodology, and vocabulary for both knowledge engineers and SMEs; it is both formal and understandable. One SME, upon seeing his first KADS model, remarked, "That's my brain on the page!"

5. KADS Applied to Troubleshooting-type Case Bases

The KADS CBR project has 5 main phases, which can be done in concurrent pieces:

1. *Familiarization*. Gain an overall understanding of the domain, the problem(s), the expert, the user, and the system environment. This phase usually takes about 5% of total project time. The main deliverable is the Knowledge Engineering Plan that describes how the work will be organized.
2. *Conceptualization*. Develop the *logical, conceptual* model of expertise and understand the roles of the users and the system. This is the most difficult and the most important stage of development. This is where the details of the expertise are captured. This phase will take the majority (maybe 70%) of the project time. The main deliverable is the KADS Model of Expertise.
3. *Design*. Make editorial decisions about wording, select methods to deliver content (Web, CBR, work card), design and test user interface, review the content to ensure adherence to authoring guidelines.
4. *Implementation and Testing*. Implement the logical models in the CBR engine. Due in large part to our analytical approach, it took less than a week to implement.
5. *Maintenance and Expansion*. Add cases to the models and the case base.

5.1 Familiarization

During Familiarization, it is important to develop overall awareness of the project and to assess the complexity of the task and potential SMEs. Major activities include:

- Conduct an orientation meeting to educate SMEs, project team members, management, and users on CBR and knowledge engineering.
- Perform initial interviews to gain overall understanding of the experts, domain, intended users, and intended environment of the case base.
- Develop Knowledge Engineering Plan to summarize findings from the initial interviews. Components of the Knowledge Engineering Plan include project definition, identified risk and risk mitigation approaches, staffing requirements, knowledge acquisition tasks, and project schedule.

Putting it into Practice

- As part of initial interviews, observe the users' troubleshooting environment.

- Use overview, unstructured interviews. Go for breadth, not depth.
- The analyst's job is to identify risk factors; the management steering team must solve them. Use a risk checklist to ensure uncovering as many factors as possible.
- Plan to use both Level 1 SMEs and end users in case base verification. Identify who these will be and bring them into the process early.

5.2 Conceptualization (Develop Models of Expertise)

The Model of Expertise is built in the Conceptualization Phase. As described above, the KADS Model of Expertise is composed of four models. These are illustrated below for building a troubleshooting case base. These models guided our knowledge acquisition; however, we chose to use case-flow diagrams to show logic to the SMEs.

5.2.1 KADS Task Model (Process Model)

[Mager82] describes a general Task Model that troubleshooting experts use to solve problems. Figure 1 shows the flow chart that serves as our KADS Troubleshooting Process Model. He argues that expert troubleshooters run through 4 main tasks:

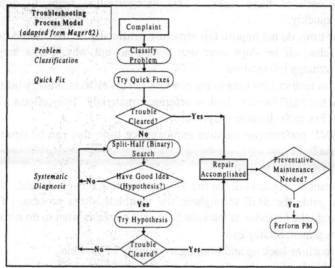

Figure 1: Process Model for Troubleshooting

1. *Classify the Problem.* Talk with the actual user. Verify the symptoms. Categorize the general nature of the problem. This task is mapped to the Problem Classification Inference Model (see Figure 2).
2. *Try Quick Fixes.* Even before locating the trouble, attempt solutions that are fast and cheap to try, even though their relevance may not be immediately apparent. If they work, time and effort are saved; if they do not, only a moment is lost and at least the analyst know what is *not* wrong. Often, experts are unaware that they are doing it (and so a key focus for knowledge acquisition). This task is mapped to the Quick Fix Inference Model (see Figure 4).
3. *Step by Step Search.* The last resort of competent troubleshooters is to take a systematic approach, eliminating large chunks of the system from suspicion at each point of testing. Hopefully, the SME will have hypotheses of what might be wrong

and will start testing these. If not, the good SME will perform what troubleshooters call a "Split Half Search" or a "Binary Search" which involves successively testing the system at or near its midpoint. When a test shows normal operation, then the portion of the system preceding that point is considered OK. The search stops when an hypothesis is found that makes sense to test or the trouble is found. This is more efficient than random search. This task is mapped to the Systematic Diagnosis Inference Model (**Figure 6**below).

4. *Perform Preventative Maintenance.* Clear other troubles before they happen. This is easier to do for troubleshooters who are on-site than for troubleshooters working over the telephone. Since we were focusing on case bases for help desks, we did not focus on this task for this type of task. However, whenever SMEs suggest appropriate preventative maintenance activities, they should be included as actions for the Level 1 analyst or notes to be included on a dispatch ticket.

Putting it into Practice

- As the SME describes his troubleshooting approach, identify when he is performing each of these tasks. This categorization helps to organize his knowledge quickly.
- At the same time, do not impose this structure artificially on the SME if he is doing something else. If he skips over one task, find out why. This may identify significant strategy information.
- What policies restrict how long to try one task? This reflects strategy information.
- When does the SME begin to look at reference material? This reflects a transition from Quick Fix to Systematic Diagnosis.
- Does the SME perform preventative maintenance tasks that can be described over the telephone?

5.2.2 KADS Strategy Model

Several important strategies underlie the Troubleshooting Process Model. To varying degrees, they guide the SME throughout the troubleshooting process. Thus, they should also guide the behavior of the case base as it suggests what to do next.

- Effort Management Strategies
  —Get the machine back up and running as quickly as possible.
  —Stop troubleshooting when the user becomes anxious or irritated.
  —If the problem cannot be fixed, include good guesses on the dispatch ticket.
  —Follow policy constraints that dictate when to stop.
- Information Utility Strategies
  —If there is an error message, give preference to that over other symptoms.
  —In the absence of other information, diagnose problems between the Virtual Print Session and the printer and then between the VPS and the host.
  —Only ask for information that the analyst can get from the user over the telephone or that the Level 1 analyst can discover directly using diagnostic tools.
- Risk Reduction Strategies
  —Avoid actions that will cause the user or other users to lose work.
  —Prefer actions and repairs that are less costly (but *understand what cost means*).
  —Prefer first actions that the Level 1 analyst can perform directly and then actions that the user can perform without fear of making mistakes.

Putting it into Practice

- In developing diagnostic case bases, listen for each of these strategies as the SME has to decide what to do next, when to stop, and how to deal with uncertainty. These strategies are almost never stated explicitly but are always present in the SME's mind at these junctures.
- When does one strategy overrule another?
- How does the SME know when to stop troubleshooting and dispatch a technician?

5.2.3 KADS Domain Model

For a diagnostic case base, the most important Domain Model to create is the description of system components, their attributes, and their relationships. Other items include: the list of synonyms and keywords and the set of available diagnostic tools.

Putting it into Practice

- Create a schematic of the system environment right at the start. Our SMEs used this to recall scenarios and important cases. It was done during Familiarization.
- In performing tests, the Level 1 analyst often has to use diagnostic tools.
  —Are analysts constrained from using tools by competence, availability, or policy?
- Keep the list of synonyms current to insure consistency in the case base.

5.2.4 KADS Inference Models: Problem Classification

The goal of Problem Classification is to place the user's complaint into one of several large buckets of problem types. Knowing the problem type narrows the set of likely quick fixes to try first. Figure 2 illustrates this Inference Model.

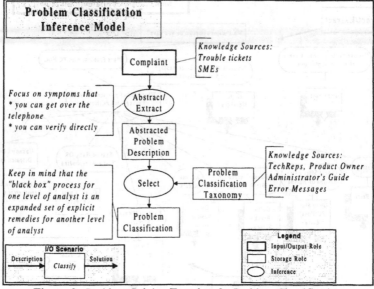

Figure 2: Problem Solving Template for Problem Classification

Problem Classification may be easy or difficult, depending on the domain. One expert recently said that just classifying the problem correctly is 60% of the battle! In such cases, it is likely that a fair amount of expertise lies in being able to abstract or "step back" from the complaint to understand just what the user is trying to say. In other cases, one can simply ask the user what his general problem is.

During knowledge acquisition, the most important concepts to focus on, as shown in Figure 2, are:
- the Problem Classification Taxonomy
- the Abstract/Extract inference that turns the complaint into a general problem description. Look for synonyms the SME uses to create the Problem Description.

Putting it into Practice
- Spend time identifying the major problem types.
  —Talk to SMEs from different levels and different geographic homes. Sometimes, these outsiders have a better idea of important or upcoming problems.
- In the process of Abstract/Extract, what are the keywords that the SME looks for?
  —What error messages and status messages is a user likely to see?
- People who actually go out to work on the machines may be the most helpful here.
- Knowledge acquisition techniques to identify and categorize the taxonomy include Concept sorting with the SME, clustering algorithms (such as Inference's Generator or induction). [Scott91] and [Gardner97] discuss these techniques well.

PC/Host Case base Example
Figure 3 shows a graphical depiction of problem classification.

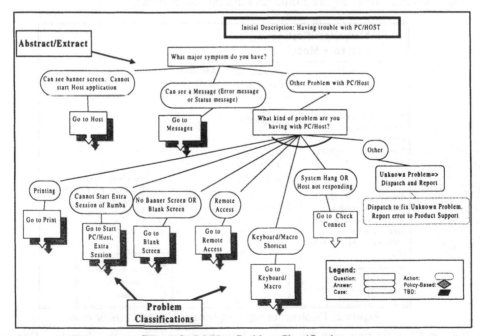

Figure 3: PC/Host Problem Classification

5.2.5 Inference Models: Quick Fix
The goal of Quick Fix is to attempt solutions that are fast to try or easy to carry out.

These tend to be broad-brush, low-cost actions that the Level 1 analyst can perform directly or describe to the user over the telephone. Generally, the order in which quick fixes are applied is not important. Figure 4 shows the Inference Model for Quick Fix.

During knowledge acquisition, the most important concepts to focus on, as shown in Figure 4, are:

- **Set of Quick Fixes** that are appropriate for the type of problem. These will turn into actions or questions in the case base.
- **Constraints** that limit applicability of the fix. Under what circumstances is it allowed/disallowed. These will turn into questions to ask in the case base.
- **Select**. How the SME decides to apply a fix. Does order matter? What does he do in case of a tie? Does he need more information? Do he pick the cheapest first? The one that does the least damage?

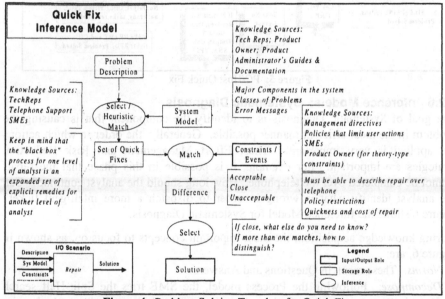

Figure 4: Problem Solving Template for Quick Fix

Putting it into Practice

- Move Quick Fixes towards the top of the graph.
  - —Sometimes, experts forget about the order of actions. If a SME moves a "quick fix" lower in the graph, investigate why: is it an important strategy.
- *Not all Quick Fixes are created equal.* Be careful when an SME describes a fix as "simple" or as "black box." How familiar is the SME with the details involved? Is it harder or easier than he thinks?
- *Not all constraints are real.* We found that certain SMEs assumed that a "Quick Fix" could not be done due to policy restrictions. However, when the next highest SME reviewed it, he encouraged it.

PC/Host Case base Example

Figure 5shows the PC/Host graph that illustrates Quick Fix.

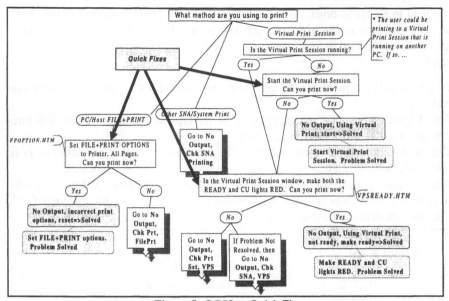

Figure 5: PC/Host Quick Fix

5.2.6 Inference Models: Systematic Diagnosis

The goal of Systematic Diagnosis is to identify the component that is causing the problem in the most efficient manner possible. Generally, the order in which actions are applied is very important. Thus, Effort Management and Risk Reduction strategies are important. For example, it is possible in this phase that the repair cannot be completed over the telephone. How long should the analyst continue? Can the analyst identify what is wrong in order to dispatch a more intelligent ticket? Figure 6 shows the Inference Model for Systematic Diagnosis.

During knowledge acquisition, the most important concepts to focus on, as shown in Figure 6, are:

- *Norms*. These result in Questions and Answers
- *Decompose*: Following the Process model, the SME tries the Split-Half search through the system until he finds an hypothesis ("good idea to try") at which point he tries that hypothesis.
- *Set of Hypotheses*. What reference books does the SME access?
- *Heuristic Match*. What does the SME do if there is not an exact match? This might result in:
  —additional information fields in questions
  —refining questions
  —actions which have more detailed steps embedded in their "additional information" fields.

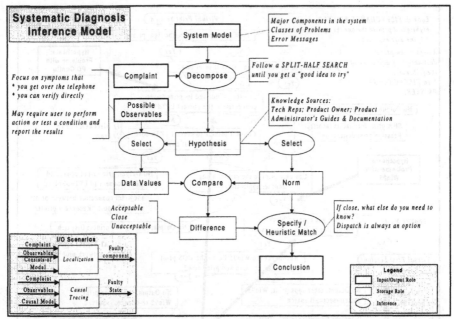

Figure 6: Problem Solving Template for Systematic Diagnosis

Putting it into Practice
- Many of the issues in Quick Fix apply here as well. Pay even more attention to the order of questions because they have to be done "systematically".
- If the SME gives several tests to try, consider making this "additional information" rather than making several Question/Answer steps out of it.
- Move systematic diagnosis activities lower in the graph than quick fixes.
- How do strategies and constraints in the Strategy Model limit systematic diagnosis?
  —Does the SME use "Causal Tracing" (to find a faulty component) or "Localization" (to find a faulty state in a component)? What is the SME's goal in this case?

PC/Host Case base Example
Figure 7 shows the PC/Host graph that illustrates Systematic Diagnosis. The SME is following a localization strategy, trying to get down to the offending component as quickly as possible.

5.3 Design
Since a case base solution and the choice of CBR engine is already determined, design issues are greatly reduced. The design must respect the knowledge in the graphs as well as the needs of the users. Areas to address include:
- Allocate knowledge content to different search methods. Not everything in the contents of the graph needs to go into a case base. Working with end users, we allocated knowledge content to HTML documents, work-cards, and the case base.
  —Using the same knowledge we modeled, we have implemented several different search methods to allow different levels of users access to the same material.

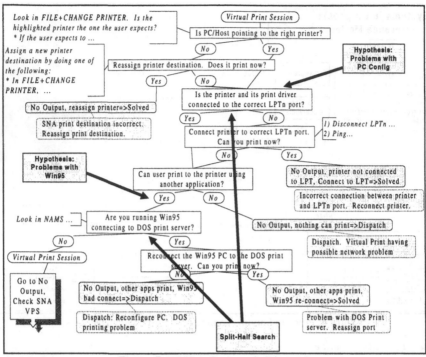

Figure 7: PC/Host Systematic Diagnosis

- Case Base Architecture
  - —The Strategy Model influences the architecture of the case base. It describes how the SME chooses what to do next and how he addresses flexibility. If a goal of the case base is to provide expert approaches to solving problems, then the Strategy Model should guide decisions about how much flexibility to give the user and how much control to impose.
  - —Example. When diagnosing problems with the Virtual Print Session, let users decide whether to diagnose "down to the printer" or "up to the host" first.
- Different levels of expertise
  - —Experienced users do not want to be bothered with "obvious quick fixes" whereas inexperienced users need to see them.

5.4 Implementation and Testing

A common difficulty during implementation is getting the right set of cases to come to the top for the user's consideration. Our CBR engine uses a system of weighting on the description and questions to control a case's score. When a case score crosses a certain threshold, then it is flagged as a match. Usually, the process of weighting questions is considered an "art"; it can take a long time to get right. However, our analytic approach gave us enough structure to program an algorithm to optimize weight selection automatically, despite complex chains of questions..

6. Conclusions

What if we had not used KADS to build the case base? What if we had just drawn flow charts? Depending on our analytic abilities and our SMEs' abilities to articulate the troubleshooting process, we might have built a similar case base. Probably it would have taken longer as we tried different approaches and structures (rather than having KADS guide us with an underlying theory). We might not have dealt explicitly with the division between quick fix and systematic diagnosis.

Of course, the major benefit of this engineering approach is the big picture view it gives to all team members. This helps in several ways:

- The SMEs grasp what is going on in the case base more easily with these models and graphs than by looking at hundreds of cases. It is easy for them to spot holes in logic and opportunities to streamline the troubleshooting process. They feel more comfortable when they need to approve the case base.
- The knowledge engineer can spend more time with knowledge acquisition (the important part) and less time with case base mechanics (the easy part). The latter can even be automated.
- Maintenance is much easier when SMEs can analyze the impacts of a new case directly in the logic graph and identify exactly where to place it.

We have often heard it said that modeling is fine to do for academic exercises; however, in the "real world" of applications, there is simply not enough time. Results must come quickly! Just start building the case base as quickly as possible and fix it along the way. For troubleshooting case bases, our experience and results argue against this mind-set. "The most important thing about modeling is the clearer communications and thinking of the project team"—analysts and SMEs [Rothkopf96]. It promotes careful thought about the problem before committing to a solution. Rather than slowing the process down, it should speed delivery of something the users really want. KADS helps the team think about the cognitive parts of the problem to be solved.

7. References

- **Gardner97** Building Cognitive Frameworks for Object-Oriented Systems. Gardner, Rush, et.al, SIGS Books, Inc., New York, NY, 1997.
- **Gardner96** A Cognitive Basis for Object-Oriented Analysis. Proceedings of Object World 96.
- **Mager82** Troubleshooting the Troubleshooting Course. Robert F. Mager. Lake Publishing Co:Belmont, CA, 1982. ISBN 0-8224-9370-5
- **Rothkopf96** Models as Aids to Thought. Michael H. Rothkop. In Interfaces, Volume 26, Number 6. The Institute for Operations Research and the Management Sciences.
- **Scott91** A Practical Guide to Knowledge Acquisition. Scott, Clayton, and Gibson. Addison-Wesley, 1991. ISBN 0-201-14597-9
- **Trott95** Knowledge Modeling to Capture, Analyze, and Transfer Expert Thinking. Trott, Norwood, & Murphy. Proceedings of the 1995 Best Practices in Training, American Society for Training and Development.
- **Tansley93** Knowledge-Based Systems Analysis and Design: A KADS Developer's Handbook Tansley & Hayball. rentice Hall, 1993. SBN 0-13-515479-0

A Large Case-Based Reasoner for Legal Cases

Rosina Weber-Lee

Ricardo Miranda Barcia

Marcio C. da Costa

Ilson W. Rodrigues Filho

Hugo C. Hoeschl

Tania C. D'Agostini Bueno

Alejandro Martins

Roberto C. Pacheco

Federal University of Santa Catarina

LIA - Production Engineering

rolee@eps.ufsc.br

Abstract. In this paper we propose a large case-based reasoner for the legal domain. Analyzing legal texts for indexing purposes makes the implementation of large case bases a complex task. We present a methodology to automatically convert legal texts into legal cases guided by domain expert knowledge in a rule-based system with Natural Language Processing (NLP) techniques. This methodology can be generalized to be applied in different domains making Case-Based Reasoning (CBR) paradigm a powerful technology to solve real world problems with large knowledge sources.

1. Introduction

Court decisions stored in large databases need efficient retrieval mechanisms to improve jurisprudence research. We have been working with a database that contains 90,000 legal texts (court decisions). The bottleneck is to convert these texts into cases to build the CBR system's case base from where the cases can be retrieved. We present a knowledge-based methodology to convert legal texts into cases, showing that it is possible to automatically model cases from texts. We demonstrate this within the specific domain of decisions of a State Court in Brazil. The fact that these legal texts are highly stereotypical is one of the reasons of the accomplishment of such task. Although the key principle is knowledge -- domain expertise, this is what makes feasible the automatic information extraction of these texts.

Our project refers to a large case-based reasoner in which the task is to provide the user with the most useful cases to support one legal input problem. The intended contribution is to show how to create case-based reasoners to solve real world problems that require large case bases.

1.1 Background

The attempts in developing intelligent systems in the domain of law were boosted by HYPO -- a CBR system that creates legal arguments from a case base on the domain of trade secret law (Ashley & Rissland, 1988a,1988b). In this program, dimensions are used to dynamically perform indexing and relevancy assessment of past cases.

Most importantly, the system demonstrated how to handle arguments and lessons present in legal cases. However, the hand-coding required in the development of such systems prevented them from becoming a paradigm for real world problems.

Considering different approaches to the automatic treatment of legal texts and documents, Branting and Lester (1996) describe the design task of document drafting that requires complex adaptation for case reuse. In their approach, they demonstrate the illocutionary and rhetorical structures of self-explaining documents.

Daniels and Rissland (1995) built a hybrid CBR and Information Retrieval (IR) system where the CBR technology plays the role of improving the query presented to the IR system, improving the results. This alternative stems from their claim that texts are not amenable to knowledge-based methods, therefore they do not benefit from the ability of retrieving relevant cases what is the main strength of CBR technology.

SALOMON (Uyttendaele, 1996) project proposes the improvement of access to legal texts through automatically generating summaries of court decisions of criminal cases. The summary represents court decisions through nine attributes in which the values are extracted from the texts. The approach combines statistical and knowledge-based techniques. Although it deals with indexing, they do not explore CBR technology.

All these efforts point to the necessity of developing tools to link the CBR usefulness in retrieval and real world domains.

1.2 Goals

The main goal is to develop a large retrieval-only case-based reasoner to retrieve the most useful cases to support jurisprudence research. In order to accomplish this goal we propose a knowledge-based methodology to automatically convert legal texts into cases. The intended result is to obtain cases modeled with descriptors extracted from legal texts. One major benefit from the development of large CBR systems in the legal domain is to make possible reusing the knowledge embedded in jurisprudence that is used to reference new court decisions. Improving the access of past legal cases enlarges the horizon from where new decisions are grounded, consequently raising the quality of the results of the judicial system.

Next section presents the domain of the application. Then we introduce our CBR system project. In section 4, we demonstrate the methodology to convert texts into cases. Finally, the conclusion is in section 5.

2. The Domain

Legal cases along with general principles, laws, and bibliographical references are the traditional sources of Law. Law is predominantly implemented by lawsuits, which refer to disputes of parts that advocate conflicting arguments. The universe of information comprehended by the subject where the conflict takes place is unlimited. The extent of the information embedded in the subject of lawsuits sometimes goes beyond the human capability of reasoning and understanding. This makes the law domain a fertile area for intelligent-based applications. Artificial Intelligence literature points to several efforts on modeling legal reasoning based on CBR technology as the most appropriate tool to reason within this domain, (Bench-Capon, 1995).

This paper focuses on the application of the CBR technology to retrieve legal cases that describe court decisions. The importance in choosing this part of the domain lies on the fact that these legal cases are referenced as foundations of petitions and decisions.

Brazilian professionals have two sources to search for past legal cases to ground new decisions: books and database systems. The available database systems consist of data from abstracts of legal decisions. These systems are limited to a recall that provides around 25% of relevant cases, (Blair, 1985).

Facing this dearth of resources, we are pursuing a system that makes feasible the search for relevant legal cases enlarging the reach of the research results. Achieving such goal will enhance the tasks of these professionals, representing an improvement to the judicial system in contributing to a better society.

The State Court of Justice (SCJ) records have around 90,000 machine readable complete descriptions of legal cases (not only the abstracts). These descriptions are the basic entity of our application. They describe the experiences that are the cases in the CBR system. Our methodology to convert these legal texts into legal cases is presented in section 4.1.

3. The CBR Application

The project's final purpose is a retrieval-only CBR system that plays the role of an intelligent researcher. The task to be performed by the system is the same as judges and their assistants perform: search for legal cases in the jurisprudence. The human experts guide the search by some hint they might have about the case but there are no effective means to guarantee the efficiency and the reach of the results. This CBR system aims at guaranteeing an efficient search, that is providing useful recalls. Also, the system aims at providing a better reach in terms of ensuring that every relevant case is actually recalled.

Initially we have developed a prototype using only court decisions on *habeas corpus* petitions in homicide crimes to evaluate the potential of a case-based reasoner to retrieve legal cases. The descriptors that indexed the cases were chosen attempting to capture strengths and weaknesses of the texts to provide usefulness to the retrieval. The hand-coded initial descriptors are the following: manslaughter (Boolean), qualification (list), status (list), conspiracy (Boolean), application (list), legal foundations (list), subject foundations (list), arguments (list), unanimity (Boolean) and result (list), as well as identification descriptors such as data, place and reporter; petition type and category were default to *habeas corpus* and homicide.

The response from legal experts motivated us to develop a reasoner able to embody all types of legal decisions. The legal experts suggested relevant descriptors and some features to the interface. They have also suggested a feature to perform new retrievals based on a smaller set of descriptors to be chosen by the user. The requirements of domain expert knowledge became evident in the development of many CBR problem areas. The implementation of the reasoner is essentially guided by expert domain knowledge.

```
petition type: habeas corpus
reporter: Des. José da Silva
city: Lages
number: 10.282          page: 06          date: 25/03/92
category: homicide
result: accepted
unanimity: yes
active part: defense attorney
passive part: district attorney
subject foundation: insanity
foundation concerning procedures: annulling
application: abatement
laws cited: articles 26 & 97 of Penal Code
argument 1: first offender          argument 2: non compos mentis
argument 3: negligence          argument 4: circumstantial evidence
manslaughter: yes
qualification: simple
status: consummated
conspiracy: no
corpus delicti: yes
```

Figure 1. Surface features and dimensions representing a case.

The prototype described above gave us an idea of the type of descriptors required to index cases to retrieve relevant legal cases. In the new reasoner, we use two types of descriptors: surface features and dimensions. Surface features are easily assigned from a specific part in the text. Although initially inspired by HYPO's dimensions we use this term to refer to the attribute[1] part of a descriptor, whose values have to be inferred from the text with the use of domain knowledge. A case in the new reasoner is modeled with the initial descriptors according to Figure 1.

The dimension *category* represents a delict (if within the criminal area) or the subject of the lawsuit. Law categorization is provided by the national penal and civil codes (and other sources of laws) that we have represented through a *tree of categories*. When filling out the input case, the end-user provides a category that may be at any level of the tree. The intelligent interface identifies the category in the tree and shows the upper levels to the user asking for confirmation, (see Figure 2). Suppose the end-user enters *theft*, the interface shows: level 1: *criminal*; level 2: *crimes against property*; level 3: *theft*, that represents the categorization according to the Brazilian criminal code.

The main result of the development of this large CBR system equals furnishing a human expert with the memory capacity and speed of a computer.

---

[1] Dimensions are called the attribute part of an attribute-value pair of a descriptor, (Kolodner, 1993, chapter 9).

Figure 2. The interface searches for the categorization in a tree of categories

4. Legal Cases

The knowledge representation in a large CBR system is the main issue to be resolved. The cases that comprise the case memory describe legal texts. These texts are converted into cases through the definition of attribute-value pairs that describe and index the cases. Next, we describe a methodology to perform this conversion automatically.

4.1 Methodology

The methodology to convert texts into cases was developed with the knowledge elicited from domain experts. There are two distinct phases, the development of the methodology and its implementation. Figure 3 illustrates these two phases and the steps they comprehend. Next, these steps are described regarding the development and implementation phases.

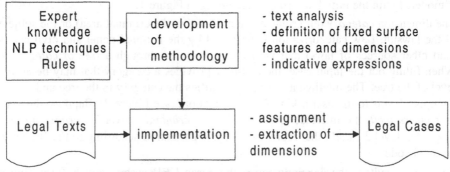

Figure 3. Phases and steps of the methodology.

4.1.1 Text Analysis

The development of the text analysis is required only at the beginning of the process when the domain is chosen. The type of texts from where the cases will be converted are analyzed by domain experts. The goal is to define the rhetorical structure of the texts and identify the parts in which the illocutionary expressions are present. We have performed sample tests to ensure that each substructure is actually present in every legal text. The rhetorical structure of the legal texts is described through the following substructures.

1. Identification: surface features such as date, city, reporter and petition type.
2. Abstract: varies in its length, starts after the end of the *identification* and ends with two paragraphs, the first indicates the applicant and the second presents the result.
3. Body: in its conclusion it is usually the court decision and its foundations. This is where the search for illocutionary expressions takes place. Upper paragraphs describe details of the situation, indicating the laws that categorize the subject, and points to foundations.
4. Closing: starts with one paragraph about votes followed by date, place and names of participating attorneys.

The implementation of text analysis consists of running a Natural Language Processing program that reads legal texts and identifies parts of the text that will be used in other steps.

4.1.2 Definition and Assignment of Fixed Surface Features and Dimensions

The development of this second step started with the knowledge elicitation from domain experts who have defined a small set of attributes to describe all legal texts. Experts expect them to be valued in all cases. These attributes are illustrated and exemplified in Figure 1.

surface features/dimensions	substructure
petition type	identification
reporter	identification
date	identification
city	identification
number	identification
page	identification
category	abstract and body: categorization
outcome	abstract: result
active part	abstract: applicant paragraph
passive part	abstract: applicant paragraph
application	abstract and body
foundation concerning procedures	body
subject foundation	body: conclusion
legal foundation	body: conclusion
arguments	body
first offender	body
laws cited	body: categorization

Table 1. Position of attribute values in the structure of the legal text.

It is important to point out that the definition of the attributes do not require the experts to examine a significant amount of texts. Their capability of pointing out these attributes relies on their expert knowledge of the domain. Next, experts were asked to point the substructure where the value of each attribute is informed. Results are shown in Table 1.

The knowledge acquisition process elicits from experts how the values appear in the texts. Rules were developed to be applied on each substructure to extract values for the attributes. The resulting rules are programmed in Prolog in a Natural Language Processing system that reads the substructure and assigns values to the attributes.

Given an attribute, the rule-based system is supposed to find its proper value. These are some guidelines to accomplish the task:

- identify in what part of the text to apply the rule, (it may be more than one part);
- check the existence of any useful information relevant in the dimensions and features already assigned;
- check the existence of general domain knowledge from where to obtain useful information, e.g., the tree of categories;
- check the existence of a limited list of possible values to assign to a dimension;
- identify the format of the value (e.g., list, number, sentence; single or multiple, etc.) if one is recognized.

These guidelines orient rules and strategies that are employed by the system. One of the strategies employed in this search is the use of word lists. The sentences within the proper paragraph are represented by lists of words and the system checks whether certain words or combinations of words occur in the lists. Let us illustrate this process with the assignment of the dimension *outcome*, that represents the result for the petition. The first requirement for the rules related to the result is the petition type; because depending upon it, the result may be expressed with different terms. For instance, in petitions for *habeas corpus*, the verb used to express its acceptance is '*conceder*' (concede, accept), whereas the verb '*denegar*' (refute, reject) is used to reject the petition. In different types of petitions, other verbs are employed to express acceptance, such as the verb '*prover*', which is a synonym of accept although it is not used in certain types of petitions. This information is obtained by the knowledge acquisition step. It narrows the problem in a such a way that we can draw rules as, "If petition type is *habeas corpus* then search in the substructure abstract:result for the verbs '*conceder*' and '*denegar*'". In Figure 4 the interface[2] shows two instances of substructure abstract:result where the outcome is informed. In Figure 5, the command '*resultado*' stands for triggering the rules that return the value for the outcome that is '*denegado*' when rejected (10881) and '*concedido*' when accepted (10886). This example demonstrates the use of expert knowledge in orienting the search for the proper values in the text. In assigning values for dimensions involving facts of the domain, the complexity of the rules increase. The system is designed to return a warning if a value is not found. Whenever a new expression is used by a reporter avoiding the system to trigger any rule, the system informs this failure and a new rule is created. This device guarantees efficiency and aids the maintenance of the system. The development phase ends when rules are provided to value all attributes.

---

[2] Amzi!Prolog 3.3Mar96 Copyright ©94-95 Amzi!inc.

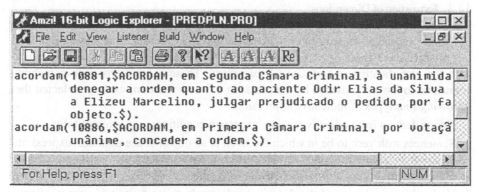

Figure 4. Portions of two legal texts where the outcome is read.

4.1.2.1 Testing Rules

The procedure for testing rules is the same for all attributes. To test the rule set oriented to extract the result of habeas corpus cases, we have gathered 684 texts – referring to all cases of this type from 1990 to 1996. The first rule set stemmed from a sample of 17 texts. Applying this rule set on the 684 texts, generated a 63% rate (434) of proper assignments. Two new rules were added and the execution of this new rule set resulted in 678 assignments. Out of the 6 cases left without values, 5 of those referred to cases where no result has been decided – the court relegated the decision to another court; only one (1) case provided no information about the decision in the substructure abstract:result. We consider this 99% (678 out of 684) good enough.

The implementation of the assignment phase can be performed since all rules are tested. In this phase, the rule-based system receives the texts and assigns values for all surface features and dimensions.

At this point, we already have cases to the reasoner, however we understand that case descriptions can be improved, and this is what we pursue with the dynamically extracted dimensions.

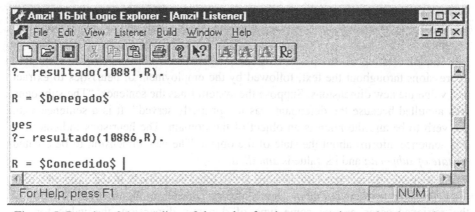

Figure 5. Results of the reading of the value for the outcome in two legal texts in Amzi!Prolog.

4.1.3 Extraction of Dimensions

The analysis of samples of legal texts by domain experts resulted in the observation of some repeated expressions that were usually present indicating relevant information about the case. This is how the development of this step has come up, with the identification of *indicative expressions*. These expressions were somehow connected to lessons provided by the cases. In a first evaluation, we have selected the following four types of indicative expressions.

1. Nouns derived from adjectives: they express a condition; e.g., impossibility.
2. Sentences with verb to be in which the noun is an object of the domain: express an information about the state of the object; e.g., custody is, victim has been, evidence was, perpetrator is, defendants were, etc.
3. Verbs that are objects of the domain: indicate facts; e.g., certify, arrest, allege, prove, etc.
4. Adverbs meaning *for this reason*, indicate conclusive lessons; e.g., therefore, ergo, hence, thus, therefore, accordingly, consequently, so.

When experts were asked about how to use these expressions, they suggested heuristics. One example is the noun *impossibility*. According to experts, nouns derived from adjectives indicate the presence of a lesson. Suppose the legal case reads, "...the impossibility of penalizing the defendant stems from the fact the defendant is under legal age and therefore his imprisonment constitutes a misfeasance...". This sentence clearly teaches the lesson that the defendant who is under age cannot be kept imprisoned. The sentence following the expression impossibility will usually inform about an illegal fact, whereas the sentence following therefore can either inform an illocutionary expression or expose reasons for the assertions, i.e., reveal the grounds for such impossibility. From this fact we can determine another dimension concerned to the grounds of the condition. Hence, the dimensions extracted from this first example would be: *penalizing condition* and *penalizing condition grounds*; and the values would be respectively *impossible* and *defendant is under legal age*. These observations usually hold, guiding the definition of heuristics and rules to extract dimensions. Another instance is in the text, " ..It is characterized the inadmissibility of the evidence when the means for its acquisition are illicit." The resulting dimensions are evidence condition and evidence condition grounds.

The implementation of this phase is accomplished first with a search for indicative expressions throughout the text, followed by the employment of heuristics to extract and value the new dimensions. Suppose the system finds the sentence, "The subpoena was annulled because the defendant was not properly served." It is a sentence with the verb to be and the noun is an object of the domain. The heuristics indicate that this sentence informs about the state of the object. The new dimension to be created is *state of subpoena* and its value is *annulled*.

These dynamically extracted dimensions are defined exclusively in the cases in which the originating text contain them. Hence, during a search in the reasoner, if many of the retrieved cases present some type of dynamic dimension, the value for the dimension is asked to the user in order to improve retrieval. If the user has no information or there are not many instances of a given dimension, then it is not included in the similarity assessment because the purpose of these dynamic dimensions is only to improve similarity.

5. Conclusions

It has been demonstrated an approach to automatically convert texts into cases to minimize the bottleneck of knowledge representation in large CBR systems. This approach can be generalized to be applied in different domains making CBR a powerful technology to the treatment of real world problems with large knowledge sources.

The rule-based text classification techniques employed in the very restricted domain of knowledge have limitations and advantages. The expert knowledge orientation makes it necessary a knowledge elicitation step. On the other hand, the limited domain guarantees that once the rules are elicited, they work for most texts, what has been demonstrated by our first experiments.

The development of a large retrieval-only CBR system in the domain of Law represents a solution to the search for jurisprudence, improving the quality of its results.

6. References

Ashley, Kevin D. & Rissland, Edwina L. (1988a). Compare and Contrast, A Test of Expertise. Proceedings of a Workshop on Case-Based Reasoning, 31-36.

Ashley, Kevin D. & Rissland, Edwina L. (1988b). Waiting on weighting: A symbolic least commitment approach. Proceedings of AAAI-88. Cambridge, MA: AAAI Press/MIT Press.

Bench-Capon, T.J.M. (1995) Argument in Artificial Intelligence and Law. JURIX 1995.

Blair, D.C. & Maron, M.E. An Evaluation of Retrieval Effectiveness for a Full-Text Document-Retrieval System. *Communications of the ACM*, 28 (3), 289-299, March 1985 in Daniels & Rissland , 1995.

Branting, L. Karl & Lester, James C. (1996) Justification Structures for Document Reuse *Advances in Case-Based Reasoning: third European Workshop*; proceedings/ EWCBR-96, Lausanne,Switzerland, November 14-16, 1996. Ian Smith; Boi Faltings (ed.)-Berlin; Springer,1996.

Daniels, J. J. and Rissland, E. L. (1995). A Case-Based Approach to Intelligent Information Retrieval. Proceedings of the SIGIR '95 Conference SIGIR '95 Seattle WA USA 1995 ACM.

Kolodner, J. (1993). Case-Based Reasoning. Morgan Kaufmann, Los Altos, CA.

Klahr, Philip (1996). Global Case-Base Development and Deployment. *Advances in Case-Based Reasoning: third European Workshop*; proceedings/ EWCBR-96, Lausanne, Switzerland, November 14-16, 1996. Ian Smith; Boi Faltings (ed.)-Berlin; Springer,1996.

Uyttendaele, Caroline, Moens, Marie-Francine & Dumortier, Jos. SALOMON: Automatic Abstracting of Legal Cases for Effective Access to Court Decisions. *JURIX 1996*.

A Scalable Approach for Question Based Indexing of Encyclopedic Texts

Christopher Wisdo

The Institute for the Learning Sciences, Northwestern University
1890 Maple Avenue
Evanston, Illinois, USA
wisdo@ils.nwu.edu

Abstract. This paper describes a tool set developed to aid a human content analyst index texts for use in a particular form of structured hypermedia known as an ASK System. The tool set assists the content analyst by employing a library of *question templates* to represent the types of questions the output ASK system might contain. Question templates provided roughly a six-fold increase in the rate with which texts are indexed compared to manual techniques. Indexing progress is linear throughout, indicating that the methodology can be used to effectively index a large body of texts.

1 Introduction

Case retrieval in CBR has classically focused on moving from a problem description to a best-matched case relevant for solving the problem. However, people often reason by following chains of remindings from case to case, collecting the information they need to solve a problem from many different sources. Inter-case links have been used in PROTOS [Bareiss 1989, Bareiss & Slator 1992] to facilitate categorization, and generated dynamically in HYPO [Ashley 1990] to support legal reasoning. The inter-case links of these systems support their specific problem-solving tasks by highlighting the relevance of certain key features. In less well-defined domains inter-case links can be used to directly support end-user browsing of a case-base.

ASK Systems[1] [Ferguson, et al. 1992, Osgood 1994] are a form of structured hypermedia organized on a model of the exploratory conversations which occur between a novice and an expert. In particular, after reaching an initial text, the user interacts with an ASK System by asking questions, receiving answers and then asking follow-up questions.

---

[1] ASK Systems have been created with video content as well as text content. Since this work is concerned with the creation of a text based system the word *text* will be used to denote the content of an ASK System node. The reader is reminded that ASK Systems are not constrained to be of any particular media type.

Users browse through an ASK System by selecting follow-up questions from those arrayed graphically around a central text [see Figure 1.]The questions which are used to navigate through an ASK System concisely inform the user as to the content which will be found by following the link, and how this content relates to what is currently being viewed.[2] Navigation by question is *informed* navigation, in contrast to navigation via search engine, and navigation via the opaque semantics of embedded phrases. Such systems place the burden for determining the relevance of information on the reader. The structure of an ASK System anticipates the avenues which a reader might want to explore and then labels links to this information with the question which is answered, clearly explaining the potential relevance to the reader.

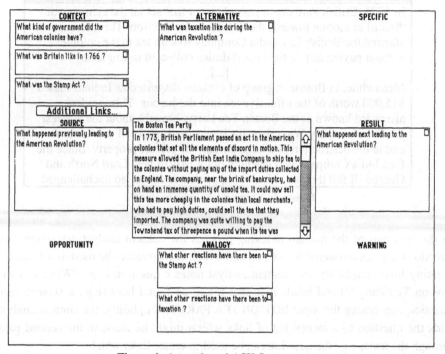

Figure 1: A text-based ASK System screen

The groupings of questions are based on the cognitive/associative categories (CACs) first described in [Schank 1977]. Each CAC describes a particular kind of conversationally coherent topic shift from the current focus.

---

[2]There are several reasons for having the user select follow-up questions rather than type them in. The most obvious is the difficulty in parsing free text and then deciding how to answer it. A second, less obvious, reason is that in many cases the system won't have an answer to a novel question. Instead of having the user use trial and error to find questions which the system can answer, the user is given these questions up front.

2   Manual Indexing of ASK Systems

Manual indexing of ASK systems involves two separate passes through the texts to be included in the ASK System. In the first pass the content analyst notes the questions which are answered by each text and categorizes them by topic and CAC so that they can be found later. Then, in the second pass the analyst attempts to remember these questions; retrieve them; and use them as a basis for creating links.

Consider a content analyst confronted with the text in Figure 2:

The Boston Tea Party[3]
In 1773, British Parliament passed an act that set all the elements of discord in motion towards the American Revolution. This measure allowed the British East India Company to ship tea to the colonies without paying any of the import duties collected in England. [...] Meanwhile, in Boston, a group of citizens disguised as Indians tossed $15,000 worth of the offensive tea into the harbor. This incident, afterward known as the Boston Tea Party, brought about the greatest pre-Revolutionary War crisis, for it was the first act of resistance to end in the destruction of a large amount of private property. Since the East India Company was carrying out a British law, Lord North and George III felt that the colonial opposition must not go unchallenged.

Figure 2: A typical text to be indexed

In the first part of the manual indexing process the content analyst determines the questions that are answered by a texts, and which can therefore be used as a basis for creating links. Explicitly, the content analyst notes a question (e.g., "What was the Boston Tea Party?") and labels it so that it can be found later (e.g., a *Description* question concerning the topic BOSTON TEA PARTY). Implicitly, the content analyst adds the question to a mental list of links which might be made in the second pass through the texts, e.g., the question can be used to create links which:

- Describe the Boston Tea Party

- Elaborate on events in Boston

- Describe the beginnings of unrest before the American Revolution

- Provide an example of an early political protest

This mental list of potential links which can be made to this question enables the content analyst to notice the potential for creating ASK system links later on; as such, it constitutes a *model of desired links* for the ASK System. This model, used by

[3]This text was taken from the "Revolution, American" article of Compton's Online encyclopedia 1991 edition.

content analysts in the manual construction of ASK Systems, is an implicit model, created incrementally as the analysts inspect the content of each text to be included in the ASK System.

The problem with the manual indexing process is that the implicit modeling of desired links does not scale up well enough to allow for the creation of large ASK Systems. Manual indexing is a time consuming, expertise intensive process which becomes unstable as more people become involved and as more time is spent indexing.

3   Question Template Based Indexing of Encyclopedic Texts

The indexing methodology presented here is based on the hypothesis that most of the questions which might serve as a basis for links in an ASK System of *encyclopedic* content are instances of general questions which can be anticipated in advance.

The questions which people bring to encyclopedias reflect the generic expectations of what there is to know about different kinds of things (people have careers, countries have governments, animals have habitats etc.). A *question template* is a representation of a question which is applicable to an entire class of concepts. For example, the question "What was PERSON's childhood like?" is a general question which might be asked about any person. When a specific concept is specified for the variable slot (e.g., George Wythe for the PERSON slot) the result is an instantiated question template (e.g., "What was GEORGE WYTHE's childhood like?").

Question template based indexing thus provides an explicit model of desired links for ASK System construction. The model has three components:

- The subjects which can be explored in the ASK System

- The questions which can be asked about these subjects

- When and where these questions will be made available for browsing

The concepts in the concept hierarchy represent the subjects which can be explored in the ASK System. The set of question templates represent the questions which can be asked about these subjects. Together, they imply a virtual space of questions which might be used to create ASK System links. Specifically, this virtual space circumscribes the potential relevance one text might have for other texts.

What remains is a notion of when and where these questions should be made available for browsing. Given the current state of the art in NLP technology computer software cannot automatically identify texts which answer specific questions in a scalable fashion, nor can it model the subtle conversational rules which make certain follow-up questions coherent and others bizarre. The task of selecting which questions are actually raised and answered by a text must therefore be left to a content analyst. However, software can be used to support the process by explicitly noting which concepts are *referenced* by a text and using this as a basis for suggesting possible questions raised and answered.

The most obvious concepts referenced by a text correspond loosely to the words used. String-based searching of databases leverages off this correspondence to provide a cheap mechanism for approximating concepts referenced by a text. In addition to these direct references to concepts, there are also *implicit* references which derive from conceptual associations between concepts (e.g., a text which explicitly mentions "the Boston Tea Party" implicitly references the concepts AMERICAN REVOLUTION and POLITICAL-PROTEST). Once these concepts are identified for each text software can suggest questions which might be raised or answered. A content analyst can then select from these questions those which are in fact raised and answered to create a standard ASK System with static links between texts. Alternatively, the content analyst can simply identify the questions answered and the dynamic suggestion of questions raised can be offered to the end-user for immediate browsing.

4   The Tapestry Tool Set

Tapestry is a set of software tools to help content analysts create ASK Systems using question templates. Using question templates the representation of an ASK System node is distributed across two stages: domain analysis and indexing [see Figure 3].

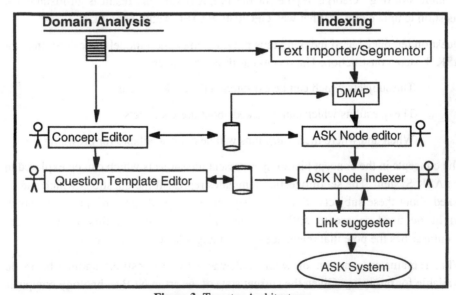

Figure 3: Tapestry Architecture

During the domain analysis stage, master content analysts build the question templates and the hierarchy of concepts which will be used later to index the texts of the ASK System. During the indexing stage, the concepts and question templates are used to represent particular questions answered and raised by each individual text segment.

4.1   Domain Analysis Using Tapestry

During the domain analysis stage the concept hierarchy and question templates are created. Tapestry provides syntactic support for this analysis in the form of the Concept Editor and Question Template Editor, and semantic support in the form of a pre-built conceptual memory and library of question templates.

Using the Concept Editor a content analyst creates concepts; attaches a set of text phrases; represents the associations between concepts and finally locates each concept in the abstraction hierarchy. The pre-built conceptual memory contains several hundred abstractions and over 5000 instances appropriate for indexing encyclopedic texts. During the indexing stage concepts can be added to the hierarchy as they are encountered in the individual text segments.

The Question Template Editor is used to build a set of question templates for the abstractions in the concept hierarchy (e.g., question templates are created for PERSON, SCENE, HISTORIC EVENT, etc.). A question template consists of a text template, a specification of its applicability, and a set of concept sets to indicate where the question is appropriate to suggest as a question answered or raised (e.g., the question "What was PERSON's childhood like?" applies to any instance of the PERSON concept and is appropriate to suggest as answered whenever a PERSON and CHILDHOOD are referenced). The current library of question templates contains 303 templates attached to 138 different abstractions.

4.2   Indexing Using Tapestry

The indexing stage begins when a source text is imported into the system. Initially a single ASK System node is created for each paragraph of text. Later, a content analyst may choose to override the automatic segmentation by joining or further splitting the text manually.

Each paragraph is then processed by the Direct Memory Access Parser (DMAP) to identify an initial set of concept references. This initial set is then filtered and augmented manually by the content analysts who can browse to associated concepts in order to identify implicitly referenced concepts using the ASK Node Editor

The final stage of indexing occurs when the content analyst identifies the concrete questions answered and raised by a text. Tapestry can suggest many possible questions answered for each text segment corresponding to each of the concepts which is referenced by the segment — even those which are only tangentially referenced and thus not a valid basis for suggesting questions answered. In order to simplify the process of question identification, Tapestry suggests questions only when the content analyst specifies a particular concept as the focus of the question. For example, a content analyst indexing the text in Figure 2, would first specify THE BOSTON TEA PARTY as the focus of a question answered and then receive the suggestion "What was the BOSTON TEA PARTY?" (among others) as a possible suggestion.

After the questions which a text segment answers have been identified the content analyst proceeds to identify the questions which the text segment raises. By default Tapestry suggests all possible questions raised for every concept which is focused on by a text segment (e.g., since the text in Figure 2 answers a question about THE BOSTON TEA PARTY Tapestry suggests all possible questions raised about THE BOSTON TEA PARTY). For other concepts (e.g., NATIVE AMERICAN for the text in Figure 2) Tapestry uses the filter sets to decide which associated questions to suggest.

Once a suggestion for a question raised (or answered) is accepted by the content analyst, Tapestry automatically searches for texts which can be linked through the question. These texts are then suggested as potential links to be used in the ASK System. In most case Tapestry suggests creating a link when one text raises a specific concrete question and another text answers exactly this question. For example, whenever a text raises the question "What was the BOSTON TEA PARTY?" a link would simply be suggested to the text in Figure 2. However, when more general questions are raised, Tapestry will often find a number of possible links. The question "What did JOHN ADAMS do?" is a general question and so has a number of possible answers describing his activities in different roles and during different stages of his life (e.g., his role in the Continental Congress, his presidency, etc.). Each of the link suggestions can be accepted by the content analyst as long as the labels used to identify the links differentiates them to the end user of the ASK System.

4.3   Indexing with Tapestry Compared to Manual Indexing

Question template based indexing differs methodologically from manual indexing in that an explicit representation of the kinds of links which the ASK system will contain is created. This representations allows for the increased software support of the indexing process which Tapestry offers. In addition, the explicit representation helps to insure consistency across time and across content analysts in large indexing projects.

The two major advantages of the question template based methodology which enable it to scale to large numbers of texts are:

1. Content analysts are presented with a consistent set of suggestions from the software tool set at each stage of the indexing process.

2. Linking is accomplished automatically using the canonical representations of questions raised and answered.

Indexing with Tapestry thus preserves most of the positive features of the manual indexing methodology while removing the reliance on the human analyst to remember the content of each text [see Figure 4].

Manual Indexing	
+	• Concrete question-based indices
+	• No constraints on linking model
+	• Linking model is dynamically extensible
–	• Linking model is implicit/unstable
–	• All texts must be indexed before linking
Question template based indexing	
+	• Concrete question-based indices
+	• Independent indexing of texts
+	• Explicit linking model
+	• Automatic linking
+/–	• Linking model is constrained
–	• Linking model is only partially extensible

Figure 4: Comparison of manual and question template based indexing

5   Evaluation

Question templates were used to index 760 paragraphs of text taken from Compton's Online encyclopedia. The individual sections of text were taken from 17 articles (people, cities, events, and general activities — abstractions which account for approximately 75% of the articles of Compton's encyclopedia). A total of 15,630 question based indices were created for the texts resulting in 5670 links. There were 9116 questions raised and 439 questions answered which remained unlinked pending the addition of other texts. When texts which raise or answer the appropriately matched questions are later indexed software will automatically suggest links to these texts independent of whether the human content analyst is aware of their existence, relying instead on the explicitly represented questions.

Using the manual indexing methodologies it requires roughly 5 person weeks to index 100 texts [Cleary & Bareiss 96]. The 760 paragraphs from Compton's were indexed by the author over a period of 6 person weeks — a six-fold increase over the manual rate of indexing. Since the indexing of each text with question templates is independent of the indexing of other texts, indexing time remained roughly constant as more texts were entered into the system.

6 Other Models of Indexing and Linking Hypertexts

Question-template based indexing differs from previous methods for automatically creating typed links along several dimensions including the skill required of the indexer, and the precision and recall of the methods. The most similar models are *concept-based linking* and *rule-based linking*.

Concept Based linking

Concept-based linkers [Cleary & Bareiss 1996] represent a text by the set of concepts which the text references; links are then proposed between texts which reference the same concepts.[4] Variations on this general approach include marking certain concepts as *elaborated* by a text and some as merely referenced. Texts which elaborate a concept can thus be linked to with greater precision.

In question-template based indexing, concepts do not directly lead to links. Instead, concept references indicate the potential for question-based *indices* which themselves lead to links.[5] This indirection adds to the complexity of the indexing task, but increases the precision with which links can be proposed between texts.

Rule Based linking

Rule-based linkers [Nanard & Nanard 1993, Osgood 1994, Cleary& Bareiss 1996] employ a representation of a text's content and a library of rules which act on this representation to infer where to create links between texts. .

The advantage of conventional rule-based linkers occurs when many links can be inferred from a relatively simple representation. However, in practice either the number of links which can be inferred is small, the precision with which links can be inferred is low, or the representation is not simple.

In question-template based indexing the representation of a text *is* precisely the questions which it raises and answers (its potential for links), exhaustively specified; and the linking rules are either identity or simple abstraction. The representation is thus extremely simple (in terms of the skill required of the content analyst) and the precision with which a link can be inferred is extremely high (the only reason that a text which raises a question might not be linked to a text which answers it is that a better answer exists).

---

[4]Same might refer to identity, or it might be broadened to mean membership in a synonym set, or sharing a key common abstraction.
[5]The notion of concept reference used in concept-based linkers is also slightly different from that used in Tapestry. Concept-based linkers represent texts by the concepts which are directly referenced by the text, ignoring indirect references derivable from conceptual associations.

7 Summary

Question-template based indexing takes advantage of the generic nature of questions which are answered in encyclopedic texts to create an indexing methodology which is both relatively simple and sound.

Using a taxonomy of concepts and a set of question templates, software is used to suggest question-based indices for each text. These indices represent the potential use of each text to the content analyst involved in creating ASK System links, and ultimately to the user browsing through the ASK System in search of information.

The index suggestions made by software are presented to the indexer as concrete English questions with an easily understandable semantics. Thus, once the library of question templates has been created the indexing process can be accomplished with little training. Question-based indices enable software to make link suggestions with a high degree of precision ASK System since the representations are derived directly from an explicit model of desired links. Question template-based indexing thus strikes a balance between fully automated (but generally imprecise) methods of linking and skill-intensive manual indexing methods.

References

Ashley, K. D., *Modeling Legal Argument: Reasoning with Cases and Hypotheticals*. (Revision of Ph.D. thesis.) Cambridge, MA: MIT Press. 1990.

Bareiss, R., *Exemplar-based Knowledge Acquisition: Unified Approach to Concept Representation, Classification, and Learning*, Academic Press. San Diego. 1989.

Bareiss, R., & Beckwith, R. *The Evaluation of Trans-ASK* (Unpublished Technical Report), The Institute of the Learning Sciences. Northwestern University. 1994.

Bareiss, R. and Osgood, R. "Applying AI models to the design of exploratory hypermedia systems." *Hypertext '93*, 1993.

Bareiss, R. and Slator, B., *From PROTOS to ORCA: Reflections on a Unified Approach to Knowledge Representation, Categorization, and Learning*. Technical Report 20, Institute for the Learning Sciences, Northwestern University, Evanston Illinois, 1992.

Cleary, C., & Bareiss, R., Practical Methods for Automatically Generating Typed Links. In *The Proceedings of the Seventh ACM Conference on Hypertext*. Washington, DC: 1996.

Comptons on "Revolution, American." Compton's MultiMedia Encyclopedia: Compton's Learning Company, Britannica Software, Inc. San Francisco, California, 1991.

Conklin, E. "Hypertext: An introduction and survey." *IEEE Computer* 2 (1987): 17-41.

Ferguson, W., R. Bareiss, L. Birnbaum and R. Osgood. "ASK Systems: An approach to the realization of story-based teachers." *The Journal of the Learning Sciences* 1 (2 1992): 95–134.

Lenat, D. B. and Guha, R.V. *Building Large Knowledge-Based Systems: Representation and Inference in the CYC Project*. Reading, Massachusetts: Addison-Wesley, 1990.

Martin, C. E. "Case-Based Parsing" and "Micro DMAP." *Inside Case-Based Reasoning*, ed. Christopher K. Riesbeck and Roger C. Schank. Hillsdale, N.J.: Lawrence Erlbaum Associates, 1989.

Nanard, J., & Nanard, M., "Should anchors be typed too? An experiment with MacWeb." In*The Proceedings of the Fifth ACM Conference on Hypertext*, (pp. 51-62). Seattle, WA: ACM Press.1993.

Osgood, R. and Bareiss, R. "Automated index generation for constructing large-scale conversational hypermedia systems." *Eleventh National Conference on Artificial Intelligence*, 1993, 309-314.

Osgood, R. "The conceptual indexing of conversational hypertext" Ph.D., Northwestern University.1994.

Riesbeck, C. K. and C. E. Martin. "Direct Memory Access Parsing." In *Experience, Memory and Reasoning,* eds. J. Kolodner and C. K. Riesbeck. Hillsdale, N.J.: Lawrence Erlbaum Associates, 1986.

Schank, R. C. "Rules and topics in conversation." *Cognitive Science* 1 (1977): 421-441.

Spiro, R. J. and Jehng, J. "Cognitive flexibility and hypertext: Theory and technology for the nonlinear and multidimensional traversal of complex subject matter." *Cognition, Education and Multimedia: Exploring Ideas in High Technology*, ed. Don Nix and Rand Spiro. Hillsdale, NJ: Lawrence Erlbaum Associates, 1990.

An Explicit Representation of Reasoning Failures

Michael T. Cox

Computer Science Department. Carnegie Mellon University

Pittsburgh, PA 15213-3891

mcox@cs.cmu.edu

Abstract. This paper focuses upon the content and the level of granularity at which representations for the mental world should be placed in case-based explainers that employ introspective reasoning. That is, for a case-based reasoning system to represent thinking about the self, about the states and processes of reasoning, at what level of detail should one attempt to declaratively capture the contents of thought? Some claim that a mere set of two mental primitives are sufficient to represent the utterances of humans concerning verbs of thought such as "I forgot his birthday." Alternatively, many in the CBR community have built systems that record elaborate traces of reasoning, keep track of knowledge dependencies or inference, or encode much metaknowledge concerning the structure of internal rules and defaults. The position here is that a system should be able instead to capture enough details to represent causally a common set of reasoning failure symptoms. I propose a simple model of expectation-driven reasoning, derive a taxonomy of reasoning failures from the model, and present a declarative representation of the failure symptoms that have been implemented in a CBR simulation. Such representations enable a system to explain reasoning failures by mapping from symptoms of the failures to causal factors involved.

1 Introduction

An early tenet of artificial intelligence is that reasoning about the world is facilitated by declarative knowledge structures that represent salient aspects of the world. An intelligent system can better understand and operate in such a represented world as opposed to one in which knowledge is encoded procedurally or implicitly. The system may inspect and manipulate such structures, the system can be more easily modified and maintained, and such representations provide computational uniformity. Likewise, if a system is to reason about itself and its own knowledge (for instance, when reasoning about its mistakes as a precondition to learning), explicit representations of its reasoning can facilitate the process. The goal of this paper, therefore, is to outline a declarative representation of reasoning failure and to posit a level of granularity for such representations. A case-based explainer can thus reason about its own memory system when it forgets and can reason about its knowledge and inferences when it draws faulty conclusions. A case-based learner can then use such explanations as it attempts to repair its knowledge in memory.

To represent reasoning failures declaratively is to create a second order representation. That is, the representation is not about the world; rather, it is a representation about the reasoner who reasons about the world. For example, a case-based explainer such as AQUA (Ram, 1994) uses abstract patterns of causality (i.e., abstract cases) to explain and understand events in the world of an input story. The explanation it generates about why a character in the story performs a particular action is a first-order representation. However, given the fact that AQUA's case-base is not complete (or necessarily consistent), such explanations may fail to predict the future actions of the character. When the expectation generated by an explanation then fails, the task of the learner is to examine a trace of the reasoning that generated the explanation and to explain the failure. The Meta-AQUA system (Cox, 1996) uses second-order representations to explain how and why its story-understanding component generates faulty explanations. In this sense, these cases are explanations of explanation failure. Hence, such representations are called meta-explanations.

The choice of story understanding as the reasoning task is somewhat arbitrary. The representations could be applied equally as well to learning from failures of planning or design instead. This is possible because we derive the classes of reasoning failure from a simple and task-independent model of expectation-driven reasoning. However, because the aim of this paper is to explain and to catalog the kinds of failure representations used by the system, we do not explain either the story-understanding process that generates reasoning failures nor the learning process that uses these representations to learn from such failures. Instead a companion paper in this volume (Cox, 1997) sketches the performance and learning tasks, and moreover, it empirically evaluates the usefulness of these representations to the learning system. Further details of the implementation can be found in Cox (1996) and Cox and Ram (1995).

The focus of this paper is upon the representations that allow a system to explain a reasoning failure as a precursor to learning. Section 2 begins by discussing the alternatives when representing forgetting, a variant of an impasse failure. Section 3 then proposes a simple model of expectation-driven reasoning, derives a taxonomy of failure symptoms from the model, and then presents a representation for each class. Five types of reasoning failure symptoms are presented including contradiction, unexpected success, impasse, surprise, and false expectation. Section 4 concludes with a brief discussion.

2 Representing Forgetting: An Example

In order to use representations of mental terms effectively, a system should consider the structure and semantics of the representation. For instance, it is not useful to simply possess a predicate such as "forget" or "remember" when trying to understand retrieval failure of memory item M.

$$\text{Forget (John, M)} \equiv$$
$$\neg \text{Remember (John, M)}$$

The non-occurrence of a mental event is not well represented by the simple negation of a predicate representing an event which did occur. Because the predicates involve memory, it is helpful to propose instead the existence of two contrasting sets of axioms: the background knowledge (BK) of the person, P, and the foreground knowledge (FK) representing the currently active propositions of the person. A logical interpretation of forget is then expressed in (1).

(1) $\exists M \mid (M \in BK_p) \wedge (M \notin FK_p)$

With such a representation, one can also express the proposition that the person P knows that he has forgotten something; that is, the memory item, M, is on the tip of person P's tongue. P knows that M is in his background knowledge, but cannot retrieve it into his foreground knowledge:

(2) $\exists M \mid (M \in BK_p) \in FK_p \wedge (M \notin FK_p)$

To add these interpretations is to add content to the representation, rather than simply semantics. It is part of the representation that determines an ontological category (i.e., what ought to be represented), and it begins to provide epistemological commitments (e.g., that the sets BK and FK are necessary representational distinctions). However, meaning is also determined by the inferences a system can draw from a representation. But as it stands, the forget predicate provides little assistance to a reasoning system when trying to understand or explain what happens when it forgets some memory item. This is not to say that logic cannot represent such a mental "non-event," rather, this simply illustrates the difficulty of constructing an adequate representation of forgetting.

An alternative approach was undertaken by Schank, Goldman, Rieger and Riesbeck (1972) in order to specify the representations for all verbs of thought in support of natural language understanding. They wish to represent what people say about the mental world, rather than represent all facets of a complex memory and reasoning model. They therefore use only two mental ACTS, MTRANS (mental transfer of information from one location to another) and MBUILD (mental building of conceptualizations), and a few support structures such as MLOC (mental locations, e.g., working memory, central processor and long term memory).[1] As a consequence, the representation by Schank et al. of forgetting is as depicted in Figure 1.

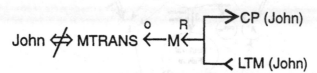

Fig. 1. CD representation of forgetting

o=mental object or conceptualization; R=Recipient; CP=Central Processor; LTM=Long Term Memory

John does not mentally transfer a copy of the mental object, M, from the recipient case of John's long term memory to his central processor. Such a representation does provide more structure than the predicate forms above, and it supports inference (e.g., if M was an intention to do some action, as opposed to a fact, then the result of such an action was not obtained; Schank, 1975, p. 60), but the CD formalism cannot distinguish between the case during which John forgot due to M not being in his long-term memory[2] and a case

---

1. Schank et al. (1972) actually referred to working memory as immediate memory and the central processor as a conceptual processor. I have used some license to keep terms in a contemporary language. Moreover, Schank et al. used a third primitive ACT, CONC, which was to conceptualize or think about without building a new conceptualization, but Schank (1975) dropped it. For the purposes of this paper, however, the differences do not matter.

2. I am ignoring the issue of whether human memory is ever really lost. But, a computer can certainly delete memories.

of forgetting due to missing associations between cues in the environment and the indexes with which M was encoded in memory. It does not provide enough information to explain the failure fully.

An alternative representation exists for such mental phenomena based upon Explanation Pattern (XP) theory (Cox & Ram, 1995; Ram, 1993; Schank, 1986; Schank, Kass, & Riesbeck; 1994). A *Meta-Explanation Pattern* (Meta-XP) is a directed graph whose nodes represent mental states and processes (see Figure 2). Enables links connect states with the processes for which they are preconditions, results links connect a process with a result, and initiate links connect two states. Numbers on the links indicate relative temporal sequence. Furthermore, attributes and relations are represented explicitly in these graphs. For instance, the Truth attribute of the expectation E in Figure 2 has the value out_{FK} (the interpretation of the value will be explained presently). This relation is represented explicitly by the node marked Truth having domain E and co-domain out_{FK}.[3]

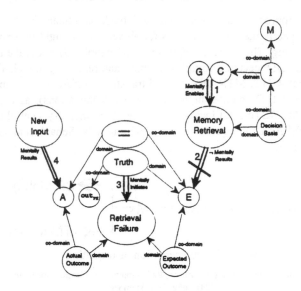

Fig. 2. Meta-XP representation of forgetting

A=actual; E=expected; G=goal; C=cues; M=memory item;
I=memory index.

The Meta-XP structure of Figure 2 shows that memory retrieval could *not* produce an expected outcome (hence the strike bar at 2); whereas, further input reveals the actual outcome (at 4). More formally, the structure represents a memory retrieval attempt enabled by goal, G, and cues, C, that tried to retrieve some memory object, M, given an index, I, that did not result in an expectation (or interpretation), E, that should have been equal to some

---

3. This is isomorphic to mathematical functions that have a *domain* and a *range*.

215

actual item, A. The fact that E is *out* of the set of beliefs with respect to the reasoner's foreground knowledge (i.e., is not present in working memory) initiates the knowledge that a retrieval failure had occurred.

This representation captures an entire class of memory failures: failure due to a missing index, I; failure due to a missing object, M; failure because of a missing retrieval goal, G;[4] or failure due to not attending to the proper cues, C, in the environment. Such a representation allows the system to reason about these various causes of forgetting; it can inspect the structural representation for a memory failure and pose hypotheses about the reasons behind the failure. Such an ability facilitates explanation because it allows a system to map the failure symptoms to the faults that caused such failure during self-diagnosis and then to generate a learning goal. For example, if the explanation of forgetting is that the item M is missing, then the goal to acquire a new case is licensed. If the explanation is that I is missing, then a memory reorganization goal is appropriate instead (see Cox & Ram, 1995).

However, to represent reflective thoughts about reasoning, complete representations for all inferences and memory processes that generate such inferences, along with a complete enumeration of all knowledge dependencies, are not required. Humans certainly cannot maintain a logically complete and consistent knowledge base, nor can they perform full dependency-directed backtracking (Stallman & Sussman, 1977) or reason maintenance for belief revision (Doyle, 1979); rather, they depend on failures of reasoning and memory of past errors to indicate where inconsistencies in their knowledge lie. That is, as knowledge is locally updated, memory will often become globally inconsistent and partially obsolete. It is at the point in which a system (either human or machine) attempts to reuse obsolete information that inconsistency becomes most apparent.[5] People often do know when they err if their conclusions contradict known facts, if plans go wrong, or if they forget (even if they cannot remember the forgotten item). Representations should support such types of self-knowledge, and it is at this level of granularity that an adequate content theory of mental representations can be built.

For the above reasons, capturing the full level of details concerning mental activity is not necessary, and CD's two primitives mental ACTS are not sufficient to comprise an adequate representational system that can express states and mechanisms of the mental world. Rather, a vocabulary needs to be delivered that can minimally express qualitative causal relationships involved in reasoning, but concurrently support the explanation of failure in sufficient detail that it can decide what to learn. That is, representational granularity is determined functionally.

---

4. The agent never attempted to remember. For instance, the reasoner may have wanted to ask a question after a lecture was complete, but failed to do so because he never generated a goal to remember. Alternatively the agent may know at the end of the lecture that he needs to ask something, but cannot remember what it was. This second example is the case of a missing index.

5. Glenberg, Wilkinson and Epstein (1982/1992) have shown that self-comprehension of text can be an illusion (i.e., people often do not accurately monitor their own level of text comprehension), and they speculate that it is at the point where reading comprehension fails that humans are alerted to the need for improvement.

3 Representing Reasoning Failure

So as to support introspective reasoning, a representation should have a level of detail that reflects the causal structure and content of reasoning failures. One of the most basic mental functions is to compare one's expectations with environmental feedback (or, alternatively, a "mental check" of conclusions) to detect when the potential for improvement exists. The reasoner calculates some expected outcome (E) and compares it with the actual outcome (A) that constitutes the feedback. When reasoning is successful, E is equal to A.

A reasoning failure is defined as an outcome other than what is expected (or a lack of some outcome or appropriate expectation). Given the simple comparison model above, a logical matrix can be drawn depending on the values of the expected and actual outcomes (see Table 1). The expected outcome may or may not have been produced; thus, the expected outcome node, E, either exists or does not exist. Likewise, the actual outcome node, A, may be present or it may not.

Table 1: Taxonomy of failure symptoms

	$\exists E$ expectation exists	$\not\exists E$ expectation does not exist
$\exists A$ actual exists	Contradiction - - - - - - - - Unexpected Success	Impasse - - - - - - - - Surprise
$\not\exists A$ actual does not exist	False Expectation	Degenerate (N/A)

Given a mismatch between the expected outcome and the actual outcome when both exist, two types of failure can result. A *contradiction* occurs when a positive expectation conflicts with the actual result of either reasoning or action in the world. An *unexpected success* occurs when the reasoner did not believe that reasoning would be successful, yet it was nonetheless. Alternatively, failure may happen when no expectation is generated prior to some outcome. That is, an *impasse* occurs when the reasoner cannot produce a solution or understanding prior to being given it; whereas, a *surprise* occurs when an actual outcome demonstrates that the reasoner should have attempted a solution or prediction, but did not. Finally, a *false expectation* is the case where a reasoner expects some positive event, but none occurs (or when a solution is attempted for a problem having no solution). The *degenerate* case represents the condition such that no expectation was generated and no outcome presents itself. This paper presents a declarative representation for each of these first five classes of reasoning failure.

In our ontology, mental processes are nodes labeled Cognize, and can be refined to either an inference process, a memory retrieval process, or an I/O process.[6] Expected outcomes come from one of these three basic processes. That is, an intelligent agent can form an expectation by remembering, by inferential reasoning (logical or otherwise), or by another agent's communication.

The state terms used to identify reasoning failure constructions represent the vocabulary labels that compose meta-explanations. I propose two types of commission error labels. *Inferential expectation failures* typify errors of projection. They occur when the reasoner expects an event to happen in a certain way, but the actual event is different or missing. *Incorporation failures* result from an object or event having some attribute that contradicts a restriction on its values. In addition, I propose four omission error labels. *Belated prediction* occurs after the fact. Some prediction that should have occurred did not, but only in hindsight is this observation made. *Retrieval failures* occur when a reasoner cannot remember an appropriate piece of knowledge; in effect, it represents a memory failure. *Construction failure* is similar, but occurs when a reasoner cannot infer or construct a solution to a problem. *Input failure* is error due to lack of some input information. *Successful prediction* represent the condition whereby expectations agree with actual outcomes. This often labels a state that should have occurred, but did not. Combinations of these are used to represent each reasoning failure type listed in Table 1.

3.1 Contradiction

Figure 3 illustrates the representation for contradiction. Some goal, G, and context or cues, C, enables some cognitive process to produce an expected outcome, E. A subsequent cognitive mechanism produces an actual outcome, A, which when compared to E, fails to meet the expectation. This inequality of actual outcome with expected outcome initiates the knowledge of contradiction. If the right-most Cognize node was some inferential process, then the failure becomes an expectation failure and the node C represents the context, whereas if the process was a memory function, the contradiction is labelled an incorporation failure and C represents memory cues.

An incorporation failure occurs when an input concept does not meet a conceptual category. For example, an agent may be told that a deceased individual came back to life (which is false) or a novice student may have a conceptual memory-failure when told that the infinite series $.999\overline{9}$ is equivalent to 1.0 (which is true). These examples contradict the agent's concept of mortal and the naïve concept of numbers respectively. Both inferential expectation failure and incorporation failure are errors of commission. Some explicit expectation was violated by later processing or input.

3.2 Unexpected Success

Figure 4 contains a Meta-XP representation of an unexpected success, a failure similar to contradiction. However, instead of E being violated by A, the expectation is that the violation will occur, yet does not. That is, the agent expects not to be able to perform some computation (e.g., create a solution to a given problem), yet succeeds nonetheless. In such cases the right-most Cognize node will be an inferential process. If it is a memory pro-

---

6. This is in keeping with Schwanenflugel, Fabricius, Noyes, Bigler and Alexander (1994) who analyzed folk theories of knowing. Subject responses during a similarity judgement task decomposed into inference, memory, and I/O clusters through factor analysis. In the scope of this paper, however, I will ignore I/O processes.

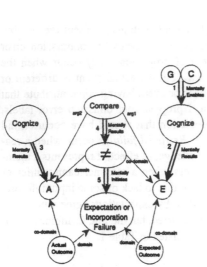

Fig. 3. Meta-XP representation of
contradiction

A=actual; E=expected; G=goal; C=context or cues

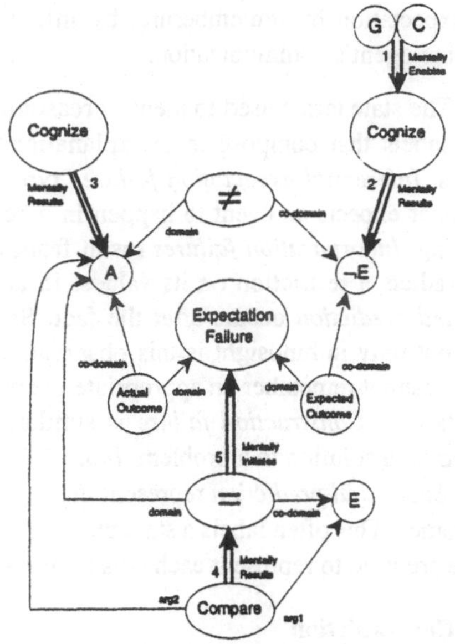

Fig. 4. Meta-XP representation of
unexpected success

A=actual; E=expected; G=goal; C=context or cues

cess instead, the failure represents an agent that does not expect to be able to remember some fact, for example, during a memory test. Yet at test time or upon further mental elaboration of the cues the agent remembers it. See the experimental studies of feelings-of-knowing, i.e., judgements of future recognition of an item that was not recalled during some memory test (e.g., Krinsky & Nelson, 1985) and judgements-of-learning, i.e, judgements at rehearsal time as to future memory performance (e.g., Nelson & Dunlosky, 1991). Like the representation of contradiction, the agent expects one outcome (failure), yet another occurs (success) during unexpected successes.

3.3 Impasse

Figure 5 represents a class of omission failures that include forgetting as discussed earlier. If the right-most Cognize is a memory retrieval process, then the Meta-XP indeed represents forgetting. The impasse is a memory process that fails to retrieve anything. If the node is an inferential process, however, then the impasse failure is equivalent to the failures as recognized by Soar (Newell, 1990) —a blocked attempt to generate the solution to a goal. Thus, a construction failure is when no plan or solution is constructed by the inference process. In either case, the node E is not in the set of beliefs with respect to the foreground knowledge of the system (i.e., was not brought into or created within working memory).

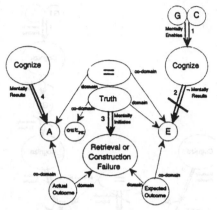

Fig. 5. Meta-XP representation of impasse

A=actual; E=expected; G=goal; C=context or cues

3.4 Surprise

Figure 6 represents a class of failures rarely treated in any AI system. A surprise is an omission error instantiated when a hindsight process reveals that some expectation was never generated. The explanation is that there was never a goal, G2, to create the expectation, either through remembering or inferring. Some earlier process with goal, G1, failed to generate the subsequent goal. When the node A is generated, however, the system realizes that it is missing. This error, by definition, is a missing expectation discovered after the fact. Both false expectation and surprise are quite related in structure. As is apparent in the figures, they both share the incorrectly anticipated Successful Prediction node and also the node labeled Belated Prediction. Semantically, they both have a passive element (i.e., non-occurrences for A and E, respectively).

3.5 False Expectation

A false expectation is an erroneously generated expectation or one that proved false. For example, a spectator may expect to see the launch of a space shuttle while at Cape Canaveral, but engineers abort the launch. The spectator experiences a false expectation when the launch time comes and goes with no takeoff. A novice theoretical computer scientist might expect that she has a solution to the Halting Problem, not knowing that Turing proved many years ago that no such solution is possible. Note that, unlike the second example, the first is out of the reasoners control.

As seen in Figure 7, the representation of false expectation anticipates an actual event (A_1) which never occurs or cannot be calculated. Instead, another event (A_2) causes the reasoner to realize the error through hindsight. It is not always evident what this second event may be, however. Sometimes it is a very subtle event associated with just the passage of time, so there is no claim here that the second event is a conscious one. In this sequence, the reasoner realizes that the anticipated event is out of the set of beliefs with respect to the FK, and will remain so.

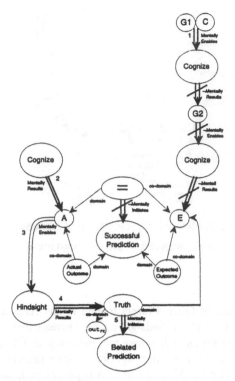

Fig. 6. Meta-XP representation of surprise

A=actual; E=expected; G1,G2=goals; C=context or cues

4 Conclusion

If a case-based explanation system is to reason about its reasoning failures effectively, it needs to represent the kind of mental symptoms and faults it is likely to encounter so that these can be manipulated explicitly. Yet, only enough representational detail need be provided so that the system can explain its own failures and thereby learn from them. That is, the representations must have causal and relational components that identify those factors that explain how and why a failure occurred. A knowledge structure called a Meta-Explanation Pattern is used to provide these attributes.

The Meta-XP representations presented here fall into a taxonomy of five failure symptoms. These include contradiction, unexpected success, impasse, surprise, and false expectation. The types of failure are derived from the simple assumption that reasoning involves the comparison of expected outcomes to actual outcomes.

Despite the difficulty of formulating a complete representation of mental events, the effort promises to aid a system when reasoning about itself or other agents, especially when trying to explain why its own or another's reasoning goes astray. Furthermore, even though the CD representation of mental terms leaves much detail unrepresented, the origi-

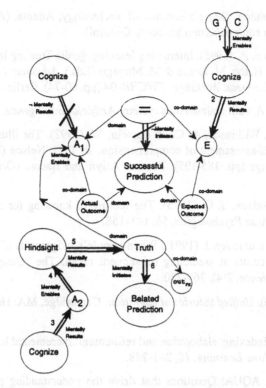

Fig. 7. Meta-XP representation of false expectation

A=actual; E=expected; G=goal; C=context or cues

nal goal of Schank and his colleagues some twenty-five years ago to represent the mental domain is still an ambitious and crucial one. If future research can more fully specify a representational vocabulary for the representation, then these domain independent terms can help many different intelligent systems reason in complex situations where errors occur.

Acknowledgments

The Air Force Office of Scientific Research supported this research under grant number F49620-94-1-0092. I also thank the anonymous reviewers for their insights.

References

1. Cox, M. T. (1997). *Loose Coupling of Failure Explanation and Repair: Using learning goals to sequence learning methods*. This volume.

2. Cox, M. T. (1996). Introspective multistrategy learning: Constructing a learning strategy under reasoning failure. Doctoral dissertation, Technical Report, GIT-CC-96-06,

College of Computing, Georgia Institute of Technology, Atlanta. (Available at URL ftp://ftp.cc.gatech.edu/pub/ai/ram/git-cc-96-06.html)

3. Cox, M. T., & Ram, A. (1995). Interacting learning-goals: Treating learning as a planning task. In J.-P. Haton, M. Keane & M. Manago (Eds.), *Advances in case-based reasoning: Second European Workshop, EWCBR-94* (pp. 60-74). Berlin: Springer-Verlag.

4. Doyle, J. (1979). A truth maintenance system, *Artificial Intelligence, 12*, 231-272.

5. Glenberg, A. M., Wilkinson, A. C., & Epstein, W. (1992). The illusion of knowing: Failure in the self-assessment of comprehension. In T. O. Nelson (Ed.), *Metacognition: Core readings* (pp. 185-195). Boston: Allyn and Bacon. (Original work published in 1982)

6. Krinsky, R., & Nelson, T. O. (1985). The feeling of knowing for different types of retrieval failure. *Acta Psychologica, 58*, 141-158.

7. Nelson, T. O., & Dunlosky, J. (1991). When people's Judgements of Learning (JOLs) are extremely accurate at predicting subsequent recall: The "Delayed-JOL Effect." *Psychological Science, 2*(4), 267-270.

8. Newell, A. (1990). *Unified theories of cognition.* Cambridge, MA: Harvard University Press.

9. Ram, A. (1993). Indexing, elaboration and refinement: Incremental learning of explanatory cases. *Machine Learning, 10*, 201-248.

10. Ram, A. (1994). AQUA: Questions that drive the understanding process. In R. C. Schank, A. Kass, & C. K. Riesbeck (Eds.), *Inside case-based explanation* (pp. 207-261). Hillsdale, NJ: Lawrence Erlbaum Associates

11. Schank, R. C. (1975). *Conceptual information processing.* Amsterdam: North-Holland Publishing.

12. Schank, R. C. (1986). *Explanation patterns.* Hillsdale: LEA.

13. Schank, R. C., Goldman, N., Rieger, C. K., & Riesbeck, C. (1972). *Primitive concepts underlying verbs of thought* (Stanford Artificial Intelligence Project Memo No. 162). Stanford, CA: Stanford Univ., Computer Science Dept. (NTIS No. AD744634)

14. Schank, R. C., Kass, A., & Riesbeck, C. K. (1994). *Inside case-based explanation.* Hillsdale, NJ: LEA.

15. Schwanenflugel, P. J., Fabricius, W. V., Noyes, C. R., Bigler, K., D., & Alexander, J. M. (1994). The organization of mental verbs and folk theories of knowing. *Journal of Memory and Language, 33*, 376-395.

16. Stallman, R. M., & Sussman, G. J. (1977). Forward reasoning and dependency-directed backtracking in a system for computer-aided circuit analysis. *Artificial Intelligence, 9*, 135-196.

On the Admissibility of Concrete Domains for CBR Based on Description Logics

Gerd Kamp

Universität Hamburg, Vogt-Kölln-Str.30, 22527 Hamburg
kamp@informatik.uni-hamburg.de

Abstract. In order to use descriptions logics for case-based reasoning it must be possible to use primitive datatypes such as numbers and strings within the representation and inference mechanisms of the logic. The best way to do so is via so called admissible concrete domains. In this paper we address the general problem of the admissibility of concrete domains, using the application area of the retrieval of bibliographic data as an example. We investigate the theoretical limitations on admissible concrete domains over numbers and strings imposed by decidability results known from mathematical logic and automata theory, as well as the prospects of potential implementations in our description logic CTL.

1 Introduction

Recently, description logics caught a lot of interest within the case-based reasoning community. In order to use descriptions logics as a powerful object-oriented representation scheme for case-based reasoning, it must be possible to use primitive datatypes such as numbers and strings within the representation and inference mechanisms of the logic. In [9] we presented a general framework for using description logics with concrete domains for knowledge-intensive CBR. [12,10] showed how the application of this framework to the domain of diagnosis of technical devices. In this paper we study the feasibility of this framework in another application area: retrieval of bibliographic data, putting our focus on the concrete domains that are required to answer questions that integrate pure bibliographic data with knowledge about the contents of the paper. As an example we use a real retrieval problem that occurred to us. We tried to find a certain scientific paper, and the only things we could remember were:

"It was a paper from an Information Retrieval conference around 1995 that had something to do with logic and information retrieval and had a figure with Allens interval relations in the upper left hand of a page"

Therefore, at least the following datatypes are necessary

1. *Numbers*, e.g. for expressing the fact that it is a publication from 1995.
2. *Strings*, e.g. to search for "SIGIR" within the publications booktitle.
3. *Spatial Objects* e.g. for expressing the relation "in the upper left corner of a page".

In the remainder of this paper we first study how numerical domains can be employed in the area of bibliographic data. We then present a number of admissible concrete domains over strings and texts and finally show how in this scenario qualitative spatial relations can be reduced to numerical concrete domains.

2 CTL

CTL is a description logic system that implements the ideas of admissible concrete domains presented in [1,6] in order to properly incorporate primitive datatypes into the reasoning services of a description logic. As we have shown in [9] such a description Logic can be used for knowledge-intensive case-based reasoning. As all description logics using tableaux-calculus techniques for checking the satisfiability of an ABox, CTL implements sound and complete algorithms for a variety of inferences including concept and object classification as well as retrieval and is based on a model-theoretic semantics. Since the CTL framework is described in detail in [9,11,12] we will only briefly recap the syntax and semantics of the TBox and ABox constructs and some of the inferences. Because this paper focuses on admissible concrete domains, we will also present the criteria for admissible concrete domains.

2.1 Syntax and Semantics

CTL is based on the description language $\mathcal{ALCF}(\mathbf{D})$ [6]. As usual in description logics, complex constructs are built up inductively from sets of atomic terms: concept names N_C, role names N_R and attribute names N_f by use of various constructors. The different description languages differ in the set of concept, role and attribute constructors they support. $\mathcal{ALCF}(\mathbf{D})$ and hence the language of CTL consist of the operators shown in Table 1.

The model theoretic semantics is also given inductively by extending the interpretation function $^{\mathcal{I}}$ on the atomic terms to the complex terms as shown by the defining equalities shown in Table 1. The interpretation domain consists of the abstract domain Δ_a and the concrete domain $\Delta_{\mathbf{D}}$ ($\Delta_a \cap \Delta_{\mathbf{D}} = \emptyset$). Concept terms C are interpreted a unary relations $C \subseteq \Delta_a$, whereas roles R are binary relations $R \subseteq \Delta_a \times (\Delta_a \cup \Delta_{\mathbf{D}})$ and attributes f are partial functions $f : \Delta_a \mapsto (\Delta_a \cup \Delta_{\mathbf{D}})$.

Syntax	Semantics
top	Δ_a
bottom	$\emptyset$
(and $C_1 \ldots C_n$)	$C_1{}^{\mathcal{I}} \cap \ldots \cap C_n{}^{\mathcal{I}}$
(or $C_1 \ldots C_n$)	$C_1{}^{\mathcal{I}} \cup \ldots \cup C_n{}^{\mathcal{I}}$
(not C)	$\Delta_a \setminus C^{\mathcal{I}}$
(some R C)	$\{d \in \Delta_a \mid \exists e.(d, e) \in R^{\mathcal{I}} \wedge e \in C^{\mathcal{I}}\}$
(all R C)	$\{d \in \Delta_a \mid \forall e.(d, e) \in R^{\mathcal{I}} \Rightarrow e \in C^{\mathcal{I}}\}$
(constrain $R_1 \ldots R_n$ P)	$\{d \in \Delta_a \mid \exists e_1, \ldots, e_n . (d, e1) \in R_1{}^{\mathcal{I}} \ldots$
	$\ldots \wedge (d, e_n) \in R_n{}^{\mathcal{I}} \wedge (e_1, \ldots, e_n) \in P^{\mathbf{D}}\}$
(compose $R_1 \ldots R_n$)	$\{(d, e) \in \Delta_a \times (\Delta_a \cup \Delta_{\mathbf{D}}) \mid$
	$\exists d_1, \ldots, d_{n-1}.(d, d_1) \in R_1 \wedge \ldots \wedge (d_{n-1}, e) \in R_n\}$
(define-concept CN C)	$CN^{\mathcal{I}} = C^{\mathcal{I}}$
(define-primitive-concept CN C)	$CN^{\mathcal{I}} \subseteq C^{\mathcal{I}}$
(define-primitive-role RN toprole)	$RN^{\mathcal{I}} \subseteq \Delta_a \times (\Delta_a \cup \Delta_{\mathbf{D}})$
(define-primitive-attribute A topattr)	$A^{\mathcal{I}} \subseteq \Delta_a \times (\Delta_a \cup \Delta_{\mathbf{D}})$

Table 1. Syntax and Semantics of CTL

Terminological axioms are used to assign symbolic names to concept, role and attribute names. One distinguishes defined vs. primitive concepts (roles, attributes). Whereas defined concepts are completely determined via necessary and sufficient conditions, primitive concepts are only partially described via necessary conditions.

Concrete objects are realized as instances of concepts. New instances o can be introduced into the ABox , and assertions concerning the membership of an instance to a concept C, or about existing relations r between two objects o_1 and o_2 can be made. The set of assertions finally constitutes the *ABox* $\mathcal{A}$. We don't need ABox instances in the remainder of this paper we omit the exact syntax and semantics and refer the reader to [9] for details.

2.2 Admissible concrete domains

In order to ask the query from the introduction, the description logic must provide some means to incorporate primitive datatypes such as numbers, strings etc. Baader and Hanschke [1,6] developed a *general scheme* for integrating concrete domains into description languages rather than describing an ad hoc extension by some specific concrete domain, as it is done in most current description logic systems. In the following we give a brief overview over the main concepts and results of this scheme:

Definition 1. A *concrete domain* **D** is a relational structure $\mathbf{D}=\langle \Delta_\mathbf{D}, \{p_j \mid j \in J_D\} \rangle$, with $\Delta_\mathbf{D}$ being the domain and $N_D = \{p_j \mid j \in J\}$ a set of predicate names. Each $p \in N_D$ is associated with an arity n_p and an n_p-ary predicate $P^\mathbf{D} \subseteq (\Delta_\mathbf{D})^{n_p}$.

In order to be useful a concrete domain must be *admissible* [1].

Definition 2. A concrete domain **D** is *admissible* iff.

1. it is closed under negation, i.e. $\forall p \in N_D.\exists q \in N_D.q = (\Delta_\mathbf{D})^{n_p} \setminus p$,
2. it contains a name $\top$ for $\Delta_\mathbf{D}$, i.e. $\exists \top \in N_D.\forall d \in \Delta_\mathbf{D}.(d \in \top^\mathbf{D})$,
3. the satisfiability problem of finite conjunctions $K = \bigwedge_{i=1}^{k} p_i(\mathbf{x}_i)$ is decidable. The finite conjunction is *satisfiable*, iff. there exists an assignment of the variables such that K becomes true.

Theorem 3. *Let $\mathcal{D}$ be an admissible concrete domain. Then there exists a sound and complete algorithm which is able to decide the consistency problem of an ABox for $\mathcal{ALCF}(\mathbf{D})$.*

This general scheme for admissible concrete domains has to be filled with concrete instances in order to be successfully applied. In CTL admissible concrete domains are realized by interfacing to existing decision procedures via a generic interface, resulting in a modular system that can be customized to the actual application.

2.3 Inferences

Based on the model-theoretic semantics a number of basic inferences can be defined and sound and complete algorithms for this inferences can be given.In [9] we showed how the basic inferences of *retrieval, concept and object classification* are the base for a broad range of similarity-based retrieval techniques. In this paper we focus on the admissibility of concrete domains. Hence we cannot go into detail concerning the various similarity-based retrieval techniques.

For the purpose of the paper it is sufficient to know that concept and object classification are very powerful indexing mechanisms for classes and instances. Input to retrieval inference is an *arbitrary query concept term* C_q and the result of the inference are the instances of the ABox a_j *subsumed* by the query, i.e. $a_j{}^{\mathcal{I}} \subseteq C_q{}^{\mathcal{I}}$. In other words, retrieval returns the instances that fulfill the restrictions imposed by the query for sure. In our case we use the retrieval inference to find the publications that meet a number of criteria.

Since the inferences are sound and complete, the represented knowledge and all of its implications are taken into account. Hence the retrieval is very flexible and powerful. In a number of domains (see e.g. [10]) pure classification and retrieval are already sufficient. But they can also be used as the base for more conventional CBR techniques (e.g. as a first step in a two-step retrieval scheme that in the second step computes a similarity value for the instances retrieved in the first).

In the remainder of this paper we present the theoretical limitations and practical realizations for a number of admissible concrete domains that are viable in the area the retrieval of bibliographic data as described in the introduction. As we have seen there we need concrete domains over the numbers, strings and a means allowing to express qualitative spatial relations over objects. We'll start with the numerical domains

3 Numerical domains

Numerical domains are needed in nearly every application. Actually, they were the starting point for the development of CTL. In the introduction we have seen that we need numerical domains in order to handle the "1995" part of the query. Clearly this is not the only use of numerical data within the area of bibliographic retrieval. In the following we address the topic, of choosing the appropriate expressiveness for this application area, by presenting a hierarchy of admissible numerical domains and present typical queries from bibliographic retrieval that can be handled with the respective domain.

3.1 Comparisons with constants

The smallest admissible concrete domain for whichever domain consists only of $\top$ and its negation, i.e.

$$\mathbf{D_0} = \langle \Delta_{\mathbf{D}}, \top, \bot \rangle$$

Apparently this domain is of no actual use. In order to be useful, a concrete domain must at least contain some unary predicates that allow us to relate attributes to constants of the domain. Therefore the most simple useful admissible numerical concrete domains are

$$\mathbf{N_1} = \langle \Delta_{\mathbf{N}}, \top, \bot, =_n, \neq_n, n \in \Delta_{\mathbf{N}} \rangle, \Delta_{\mathbf{N}} \in \{\mathbb{N}, \mathbb{Z}, \mathbb{Q}, \mathbb{R}, \mathbb{C}\}.$$

Already this minimal domain is sufficient for describing *"A publication is something with a year of publication"* with the following terminology:

```
(define-primitive-attribute year)
(define-primitive-concept publication (and (constrain year top)))
```

Then the following part of our example query *"All publications in 1995"* translates to the query concept term:

```
(retrieve (and publication (constrain year (number (?x) (=1995 ?x)))))
```

If the data type is totally ordered – as are all numerical ones except $\mathbb{C}$– one would rather use a concrete domain that allows arbitrary comparisons between variables and constants, i.e. a domain

$$N_2 = \langle \Delta_N, \top, \bot, =_n, \neq_n, <_n, \leq_n, >_n, \geq_n, n \in \Delta_N \rangle, \Delta_N \in \{\mathbb{N}, \mathbb{Z}, \mathbb{Q}, \mathbb{R}\}$$

It is easy to show that it is admissible. With N_2 we can refine our definition of a publication by adding an attribute number-of-pages and define a specialization of publication describing publications in proceedings of conferences. Note that we are able to constrain the admissible page ranges.

```
(define-primitive-attribute year)         (define-primitive-attribute start-page)
(define-primitive-attribute pages)        (define-primitive-attribute end-page)
(define-constraint >=1                     (define-concept inproceedings
   (number (?x) (>=1 ?x)))                    (and publication
                                                 (constrain start-page x>=1)
(define-primitive-concept publication         (constrain end-page x>=1)))
   (and
      (constrain year top)
      (constrain pages >=1)))
```

Using this concrete domain it is possible to describe queries like: *"All publications between 1994 and 1996"* or *"All publications longer than 20 pages"* with the following query concept terms:

```
(retrieve (and publication (constrain year (number (?x) (>=1992 ?x)))
(constrain year (number (?x) (<=1994 ?x))))))
```

```
(retrieve (and publication (constrain pages (number (?x) (> ?x 20)))))
```

The same domain can be used for example to describe queries concerning other numerical attributes like volume number etc. So this concrete domain has already a number of uses. Therefore it is the one that is implemented in some description logics systems, e.g. CLASSIC.

If one wants to express and use available background knowledge more expressive concrete domains are needed, for retrieval as well as for the description of the concepts. Note that for example we are not able to express the facts: *"The page number of the last page of a publication is greater or equal to the page number of the first page"* or *" The number of pages of an publication is the difference between the page numbers of the last and the first page plus 1"*. In the remainder of this section we present a number of more expressive admissible concrete domains, including one that allows us to express the first fact and another that in addition copes with the second.

3.2 Systems of Polynomials

Instead of gradually increasing the complexity of the admissible concrete domains to cope with this requirements, we take the opposite approach. We first recall some fundamental decidability and undecidability results for arithmetic first-order theories. These results more or less define the maximal admissible numerical concrete domains over the different base number types. Let in the following $\langle\langle \Delta_{\mathbf{N}}, c_1, \ldots, c_n \rangle\rangle$ denote the first-order theory with domain $\Delta_{\mathbf{N}}$ and the non-logical constants $c_1, \ldots, c_n$.

Theorem 4. *Then the following results hold (see [14,15,2,8] for the various proofs):*

(i) *Number theory, i.e.* $\langle\langle \mathbb{N}, +, \cdot, =, <, 0, 1 \rangle\rangle$ *is undecidable.*
   Moreover, even $\langle\langle \mathbb{N}, +, \cdot, =, 1 \rangle\rangle$ *is undecidable.*
(ii) *The theory of rings, i.e.* $\langle\langle \mathbb{Z}, +, \cdot, =, 1 \rangle\rangle$ *is undecidable.*
(iii) *The Presburger arithmetic, i.e.* $\langle\langle \mathbb{Z}, +, =, <, 0, 1 \rangle\rangle$ *is decidable.*
(iv) *The theory of fields, i.e.* $\langle\langle \mathbb{Q}, +, \cdot, =, 1 \rangle\rangle$ *is undecidable.*
(v) $\langle\langle \mathbb{Q}, +, =, <, 0, 1 \rangle\rangle$ *is decidable.*
(vi) *The theory of real closed fields, i.e.* $\langle\langle \mathbb{R}, +, \cdot, =, <, 0, 1 \rangle\rangle$ *is decidable.*
(vii) *The theory of algebraically closed fields, i.e.* $\langle\langle \mathbb{C}, +, \cdot, =, <, 0, 1 \rangle\rangle$ *is decidable.*

We further recall that the terms of the above theories are the multivariate polynomials over the respective domain (linear multivariate polynomials in the cases where $\cdot$ is missing). Hence the respective theories consist of sentences over (in)equations between multivariate polynomials. Tarskis proof for $\langle\langle \mathbb{R}, +, \cdot, =, <, 0, 1 \rangle\rangle$ was constructive, but unfortunately its complexity was hyperexponential[1] More recently, algorithms that are doubly exponential in the number of variables [3] have been found and implemented [7]. There exist also algorithms that are singly exponential in the number of variables and doubly exponential in the number of quantifier alternations were described. But for any reasonable input they perform worse than the doubly exponential. The complexity for $\langle\langle \mathbb{Z}, +, =, <, 0, 1 \rangle\rangle$ is also doubly exponential [8].

However, most often one is only interested in algorithms that decide admissible fragments of the general theory. Since the general theory is admissible, a fragment is admissible as long as it contains $\top$ and it is closed under negation. These fragments of the theory could be constructed by either restricting:

1. the allowed *function symbols* $+, \cdot$,
2. the allowed *comparison operators* $=, \neq, <, \leq, >, \geq$,
3. the allowed *logical operators* $\vee, \wedge, \neg$,
4. the allowed *quantifiers* $\forall, \exists$,
5. the *degree* $\deg(p)$ of the polynomials,
6. the *number of variables* $x, y, \ldots$ *(of a polynomial)*, or
7. *number of quantifier alternations* $\forall\exists\forall$.

The restrictions along different dimensions in the above enumeration can be combined, resulting in concrete domains of different expressiveness. The domains $\mathbf{N_1}$ and $\mathbf{N_2}$ from above are just extremely restricted fragments of the theory of the elementary algebra. $\mathbf{N_2}$ is the fragment that has no function symbols, logical operators and quantifiers.

---

[1] I.e. it could not be bounded by a finite tower of exponentiations.

Since no function symbols are available all polynomials are univariate. Moreover, only applications of the the comparison operators in the form $\circ(x, n)$ are allowed, i.e. the second subterm must be a constant. N_1 is the restriction of N_2 to the comparison operators $=$ and $\neq$.

The first step in relaxing the restrictions from N_2 is removing the restriction that the second subterm of a comparison operator must be ground. This results in an admissible concrete domain

$$N_3 = \langle\langle \Delta_N, < \rangle\rangle, \Delta_N \in \{\mathbb{N}, \mathbb{Z}, \mathbb{Q}, \mathbb{R}\}$$

This admissible concrete domain enables us to compare two attributes and stating that they must be equal etc. For example it allows us to express the fact: *"The page number of the last page of a publication is greater or equal to the page number of the first page"* from above:

```
(define-constraint x>=y                  (define-concept inproceedings
  (number (?x ?y) (>= ?x ?y)))             (and publication
(define-primitive-attribute start-page)    (constrain start-page x>=1)
(define-primitive-attribute end-page)      (constrain end-page x>=1)
                                           (constrain end-page start-page x>=y)))
```

This ensures that all publications in the knowledge base have correct page ranges and can also be used to detect the faulty ones.

It is this numerical domain, that is implemented in the description logic systems KRIS and TAXON and therefore the most expressive numerical concrete domain found in a description logic other than CTL. On the other hand $N_3' = \langle\langle \mathbb{Q}, < \rangle\rangle$ is the least expressive concrete domain implemented in CTL[2].

Despite its usefulness, N_3 is not expressive enough to represent the relation between the number of pages and the page numbers of the start and the end page, since only univariate linear polynomials are admissible terms and we need a linear multivariate polynomial $x - y + 1$. The following domain provides arbitrary sentences over linear multivariate polynomials and hence is expressive enough to represent this constraint.

$$N_4 = \langle\langle \Delta_N, +, =, <, 0, 1 \rangle\rangle, \Delta_N \in \{\mathbb{N}, \mathbb{Z}, \mathbb{Q}, \mathbb{R}\}$$
$$= \langle\langle \Delta_N, +, \cdot, =, <, 0, 1 \rangle\rangle, \deg(p) \le 1$$

We provide a domain $N_4' = \langle\langle \mathbb{R}, +, \cdot, =, <, 0, 1 \rangle\rangle, \deg(p) \le 1$ by interfacing to a CLP(R)-system. Therefore it is possible to describe the relation between the number of pages and the start and end page:

```
(define-constraint x>=y                      (define-concept inproceedings
(number (?x ?y) (>= ?x ?y)))                   (and publication
(define-constraint x=y-z+1                      (constrain start-page x>=1)
  (number (?x ?y ?z) (= ?x (+ (- ?y ?z) 1))))  (constrain end-page x>=1)
(define-primitive-attribute start-page)        (constrain end-page start-page x>=y)
(define-primitive-attribute end-page)          (constrain pages end-page start-page x=y-z+1)))
```

Whereas nonlinear systems are needed in technical domains, e.g. for describing laws of physics like $M = f \times r$ (see for example [12]), we see no apparent need for them in the retrieval of bibliographic data. However we provide a domain N_5 capable

---

[2] Of course we could easily implement N_1 or N_2.

of handling quadratic polynomials by interfacing to a computer algebra system [4][3] :

$$\mathbf{N_5} = \langle \langle \mathbb{R}, +, \cdot, =, <, 0, 1 \rangle \rangle, \deg(p) \leq 2.$$

4 String Domains

In this section we will briefly discuss the possibilities to realize admissible concrete domains over strings.

4.1 Domains based on comparison

Strings $\omega \in \Sigma^*$ together with the lexicographic ordering $\prec$ are an totally ordered datatype. Thus it is clear that the concrete domains $\mathbf{N_1}$, $\mathbf{N_2}$ and $\mathbf{N_3}$ that we presented in the previous section can be directly translated into concrete domains $\mathbf{S_1}$, $\mathbf{S_2}$ and $\mathbf{S_3}$ by replacing $\Delta_\mathbf{N}$ with the domain Σ^*, the usual set of all words over an alphabet Σ. I.e.

$$\mathbf{S_1} = \langle \Sigma^*, \top, \bot, =_\omega, \neq_\omega, \omega \in \Sigma^* \rangle$$
$$\mathbf{S_2} = \langle \Sigma^*, \top, \bot, =_\omega, \neq_\omega, \prec_\omega, \preceq_\omega, \succ_\omega, \succeq_\omega, \omega \in \Sigma^* \rangle$$
$$\mathbf{S_3} = \langle \langle \Sigma^*, \prec \rangle \rangle$$

In $\mathbf{S_1}$ it is therefore to formulate queries like: *"All publications in conference proceedings titled 'SIGIR' "* with:

> (retrieve (and inproceedings (constrain booktitle (string (?x) (=SIGIR ?x)))))

$\mathbf{S_2}$ allows us to use prefixes[4] in our queries, like *"All publications in proceedings having a title starting with 'SIGIR' "* with

> (retrieve (and inproceedings
> (constrain booktitle (string (?x) (>=SIGIR ?x))) (constrain booktitle (string (?x) (<SIGIS ?x)))))

4.2 Regular languages

One possibility to provide more expressive concrete domains are regular expressions.

Definition 5. *Regular expressions* are terms over the signature $\cup$ (union), $\cdot$ (concatenation), * (Kleene-star), δ (Empty word) and the letters a $(\forall a \in \Sigma)$.

The *language* $L(r)$ represented by a regular expression r is defined inductively over the structure of regular expressions, that is:

---

[3] It is easy to realize additional numeric domains, e.g. $\mathbf{N_6} = \langle \langle \mathbb{R}, +, \cdot, =, <, 0, 1 \rangle \rangle, \deg(p) \leq$ 3 or the full theory of real closed fields when appropriate implementations of the decision procedures are freely available.

[4] But no postfixes.

(i) $L(\delta) := \emptyset, L(a) := \{a\}$,

(ii) $L(r \cdot s) := L(r) \cdot L(s), L(r \cup s) := L(r) \cup L(s), L(r^\star) := (L(r))^\star$.

Generalized regular expressions are regular expressions, but with the additional operation symbols $\cap$ (intersection), $\setminus$ (set difference), $\sim$ (complement wrt. $\Sigma^\star$).

The following results from the area of formal languages hold (see [8] and [13]):

Theorem 6. *The class of regular languages is closed under complement.*

Theorem 7. *Let r and s be two (generalized) regular expressions. Then the intersection problem, i.e. deciding if the intersection of the accepted languages is empty, that is* $\mathcal{L}(r) \cap \mathcal{L}(s) = \emptyset$ *is decidable.*

The proof of the above theorem is constructive and proceeds by using (non)deterministic finite state automata. Hence regular expressions with complement and generalized expressions define admissible concrete domains over strings ($T(\Sigma^\star, c_1, \ldots, c_n)$ denotes the set of terms over the signature $c_1, \ldots, c_n$.):

$$S_4 = T(\Sigma^\star, \cdot, ^\star, \sim, \delta, a \in \Sigma)$$
$$S_5 = T(\Sigma^\star, \cdot, ^\star, \sim, \cup, \cap, \setminus, \delta, a \in \Sigma)$$

Therefore we can for example describe the query: *"All publications containing 'SIGIR' in its booktitle"* by[5]

(retrieve (and inproceedings (constrain booktitle (string (?x) (regexp ?x "*SIGIR*")))))

Other, more complex queries can be constructed using more complex regular expressions making use of the other regular expression operators. This can be taken even further, as additional operators can be introduced. This is due to the following results [13]:

Theorem 8. *The class of regular languages is closed under reversion, prefix, suffix, minimum, maximum, left and right quotient:*

(i) $\text{reverse}(L) = \{a_1 \ldots a_n \mid n \in \mathbb{N}, a_n \ldots a_1 \in L\}$

(ii) $\text{prefix}(L) = \{\omega \in \Sigma^\star \mid \exists \upsilon \in \Sigma^\star : \omega\upsilon \in L\}$

(iii) $\text{suffix}(L) = \{\omega \in \Sigma^\star \mid \exists \upsilon \in \Sigma^\star : \upsilon\omega \in L\}$

(iv) $\min(L) = \{\omega \in L \mid \forall \upsilon \in \text{prefix}(\{\omega\}) \setminus \{\omega\} : \upsilon \notin L\}$

(v) $\max(L) = \{\omega \in L \mid \forall \upsilon \in \Sigma^+ : \omega\upsilon \notin L\}$

(vi) $\text{lquotient}(L_1, L_2) = \{\omega \in \Sigma^\star \mid \exists \upsilon \in L_1 : \upsilon\omega \in L_2\}$

(vii) $\text{rquotient}(L_1, L_2) = \{\omega \in \Sigma^\star \mid \exists \upsilon \in L_1 : \omega\upsilon \in L_2\}$

Hence the domain S_6 that extends S_5 with all these operations is admissible. Currently we implement the S_6 by interfacing to the AMoRE system [13]. Obviously, the most complex relations between strings can be described in S_6.

---

[5] Using the well known notation for regular expressions, using *, ? etc. as metacharacters.

5 Spatial Relations

We now turn our focus to the part of our example query that is concerned with qualitative spatial relations, i.e. *"that has a figure ... in the upper left hand corner"*.

The first thing we have to do is to extend our concepts for publications with means for the description of the layout. We recall, that in terminological systems as soon as a text-frame and a float are asserted with an actual publication this publication is classified as a publication-with-layout. There is no need to actually declare the publication as such.

We then have to decide how to represent spatial objects. The first solution that becomes to mind is to represent the x and y coordinates of the objects as attributes and then use the numerical domains of the previous section. But this solution tends to be cumbersome for complex objects. A more natural solution is to represent the area of the spatial object as one attribute over $\mathbb{R}^2$ instead of two attributes over $\mathbb{R}$. This is possible, due to the following result of Tarski [15]:

Theorem 9. *The decision method for the theory real closed fields, i.e.* $\langle\langle \mathbb{R}, +, \cdot, =, <, 0, 1\rangle\rangle$ *can be extended to various algebraic systems built upon real numbers, including that of n-dimensional vectors.* $\langle\langle \mathbb{R}^n, +, \cdot, =, <, 0, 1\rangle\rangle$.

With this representation we are able to represent the text-frame of a publication and the bounding-boxes of the floats within a publication:

```
(define-primitive-attribute area)
(define-concept 2d-object (constrain area (top (number 2))))
(define-primitive-attribute topleft)
(define-primitive-attribute botright)
(define-concept ortho-rect
  (and 2d-object
    (constrain topleft ((number 2) ((?x ?y)) (and (>= ?x 0) (>= ?y 0))))
    (constrain botright ((number 2) ((?x ?y)) (and (>= ?x 0) (>= ?y 0))))
    (constrain topleft botright ((number 2) ((?x1 ?y1)(?x2 ?y2)) (and (<= ?x1 ?x2) (<= ?y1 ?y2))))
    (constrain area topleft botright
      ((number 2) ((?x1 ?y1)(?x2 ?y2) (?x3 ?y3))
        (and (>= ?x1 ?x2)(<= ?x1 ?x3) (>= ?y1 ?y2)(<= ?y1 ?y3))))))
(define-primitive-attribute text-frame)
(define-primitive-attribute bounding-box)
(define-primitive-role floats)
(define-primitive-concept float (some bounding-box ortho-rect))
(define-concept publication-with-layout
  (and publication (some text-frame ortho-rect)(all floats float)))
```

In order to represent *"topleft"* we use a well known method from qualitative spatial reasoning based on Allens relational algebra over the 13 interval relations[6]. In this approach qualitative spatial relations are defined by using Allen relations between the intervals that result from projecting against the axis of the coordinate system (see e.g. [5]). Although there is a general understanding in qualitative spatial reasoning, that this technique is not sufficient for more complex situations, it is sufficient for our purposes, because we only have to deal with paraxial rectangles (see Figure 1).

A formulation of *"topleft"* is shown in the following terminology:

---

[6] We are not able to go into all the diverse results concerned with Allen's algebra.

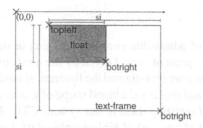

Fig. 1. The bounding box and the associated spatial relations

```
(define-constraint is-topleft
  ((number 2) ((?xmin1 ?ymin1) (?xmax1 ?ymax1) (?xmin2 ?ymin2) (?xmax2 ?ymax2))
  (and ; si in the x dimension
    (= ?xmin1 ?xmin2)(< ?xmax1 ?xmax2) (< ?xmin1 ?xmax2)(> ?xmax1 ?xmin2)
    ; si in the y dimension
    (= ?ymin1 ?ymin2)(< ?ymax1 ?ymax2) (< ?ymin1 ?ymax2)(> ?ymax1 ?ymin2))))
```

Unfortunately the following attempt to formalize *"that has a figure . . . in the upper left hand corner"* does not work as expected:

```
(retrieve (and publication
  (constrain (compose text-frame topleft)(compose text-frame botright)
  (compose floats bounding-box topleft)(compose floats bounding-box botright) is-topleft))
```

This is not due to an error in our formalization, but to the fact that our semantics of constrain allows for different role fillers, e.g. different floats to be used as the third and forth argument of is-topleft. A general way to fix this problem would require additional constructs in the description logic core that allow to fix a role filler for nested constraints. In our case a more special solution is possible. Since we are only dealing with paraxial rectangles we represent these rectangles as quadruples of numbers instead of two binary tuples:

```
(define-constraint is-bounding-box
  ((number 4) (?xmin ?ymin ?xmax ?ymax?)
  (and (>= ?xmin 0)(>= ?ymin 0)
    (>= ?xmax 0) (>= ?ymax 0)
    (<= ?xmin ?xmax) (<= ?ymin ?ymax))))

(define-primitive-attribute text-frame)
(define-primitive-role floats)
(define-primitive-attribute bounding-box)
(define-primitive-concept float
  (constrain bounding-box is-bounding-box))
(define-concept publication-with-layout
  (and publication
    (constrain text-frame bounding-box))
    (all floats float)))
```

```
(define-constraint is-topleft
  ((number 4)
  ((?xmin1 ?ymin1 ?xmax1 ?ymax1)
   (?xmin2 ?ymin2 ?xmax2 ?ymax2))
  (and
    ; si in the x dimension
    (= ?xmin1 ?xmin2)(< ?xmax1 ?xmax2)
    (< ?xmin1 ?xmax2)(> ?xmax1 ?xmin2)
    ; si in the y dimension
    (= ?ymin1 ?ymin2)(< ?ymax1 ?ymax2)
    (< ?ymin1 ?ymax2)(> ?ymax1 ?ymin2))))
```

Using this representation we are able to handle the query: *"that has a figure in the upper left hand corner"* by:

```
(retrieve (and publication (constrain text-frame (compose floats  bounding-box)) is-topleft))
```

6 Summary

We discussed the topic of admissible concrete domains in description logics from a theoretical and a practical point of view. Driven by the needs of the application area retrieval of bibliographic data we investigated the theoretical borders concerning domains over number and strings and presented a broad scope of practically feasible domains together with the means of realizing them in our system CTL. This research is not only interesting in the context of retrieval of bibliographic data, but for the applicability of description logics in CBR in general.

References

1. F. Baader and P. Hanschke. A Scheme for Integrating Concrete Domains into Concept Languages. Research Report RR-91-10, DFKI, Kaiserslautern, Germany, April 1991.
2. Stanley Burris and H.P. Sankappanavar. *A Course in Universal Algebra.* Springer Verlag, New York, 1981.
3. G. E. Collins and Hoon Hong. Partial cylindrical algebraic decomposition. *Journal of Symbolic Computation,* 12:299–328, 1991.
4. Andreas Dolzmann and Thomas Sturm. REDLOG – Computer Algebra Meets Computer Logic. Technical Report MIP-9603, Universität Passau, Passau, Germany, February 1996.
5. H. W. Güsgen. Spatial reasoning based on Allen's temporal logic. Technical Report TR-89-049, ICSI, August 1989.
6. P. Hanschke. *A Declarative Integration of Terminological, Constraint-Based, Data-driven, and Goal-directed Reasoning.* Dissertation, Universität Kaiserslautern, 1993.
7. H. Hong. RISC-CLP(Real): Constraint Logic Programming over the real numbers. In *Constraint Logic Programming: Selected Research.* MIT Press, Cambridge, MA, 1993.
8. John E. Hopcroft and Jeffrey Ullman. *Introduction to automata theory, languages and computation.* Addison-Wesley, 1979.
9. Gerd Kamp. Using Description Logics for Knowledge Intensive Case-based Reasoning. In I. Smith and B. Faltings, editors, *Advances in Case-Based Reasoning,* pages 204–218, Lausanne, Switzerland, November 1996. Springer Verlag.
10. Gerd Kamp and Bernd Neumann. Knowledge-based Inference Methods for Modeling Technical Systems. In *Proc. 30th Hawaiian International Conference on System Sciences,* Wailea, HA, 1997. Computer Science Press.
11. Gerd Kamp and Holger Wache. CTL – a description logic with expressive concrete domains. Technical report, LKI, 1996.
12. Gerd Kamp and Holger Wache. Using Description Logics for Consistency-based Diagnosis. In *International Description Logics – Collected Papers from the 1996 Workshop –,* number WS-96-05, pages 136–140, Boston, MA, November 1996. AAAI Press.
13. O. Matz, A. Miller, A. Potthoff, W. Thomas, and E. Valkema. Report on the Program AMoRE. Technical Report 9507, Universität Kiel, Germany, October 1995.
14. Alfred Tarski. *A Decision Method for Elementary Algebra and Geometry.* University of California Press, Berkeley and Los Angeles, CA, 1951.
15. Alfred Tarski, Andrzej Mostowski, and Raphael M. Robinson. *Undecidable Theories.* Studies in Logic and the Foundations of Mathematics. North-Holland, Amsterdam, Netherlands, 1971.

Similarity Metrics: A Formal Unification of Cardinal and Non-Cardinal Similarity Measures

Hugh Osborne and Derek Bridge

University of York
U.K.

Abstract. In [9] we introduced a formal framework for constructing ordinal similarity measures, and suggested how this might also be applied to cardinal measures. In this paper we will place this approach in a more general framework, called similarity metrics. In this framework, ordinal similarity metrics (where comparison returns a boolean value) can be combined with cardinal metrics (returning a numeric value) and, indeed, with metrics returning values of other types, to produce new metrics.

1   Introduction

In this paper we present a formal framework for the construction of *similarity metrics*, which subsume a number of ways of measuring similarity. In particular similarity measures that return boolean values, numeric values and structured data can all be modelled by similarity metrics.

1.1   An Example Case Base

We shall use the small example case base in Fig. 1 throughout this paper. Each case represents a holiday and has three attributes — the destination, the price and the activities available. In practice, a case could be a more complex structure than the simple tuples of the example. Our framework anticipates this, and we explain, in Sect. 3.2, how more complex case representations are accommodated. We use tuples in the example only because it makes for an easier exposition.

Dest	Price	Act
And (Andalucia)	500	{*golf,swimming*}
Ben (Benidorm)	350	{*swimming*}
Cre (Crete)	750	{*swimming,golf,windsurfing*}
Cre (Crete)	500	{*swimming,windsurfing*}
Dor (Dordogne)	400	{*golf*}

Fig. 1. An example case base.

Our presentation assumes that the similarity metric is applied to the whole case base. In those case-based systems where case base interrogation is a two-stage process [1, 7] (a retrieval step and then a case selection step that applies a similarity measure only to the subset of the case base that has been retrieved) our framework can be used in the second of the two stages.

1.2 Similarity Measures Returning Booleans

In [9], to complement numeric-valued similarity measures, we introduced a formal framework for constructing ordinal (boolean-valued) similarity measures, which can be used in situations where cardinal information [13] is not available or is likely to be misleading.

A retrieval request was presented as a pair, comprising a similarity measure and a 'seed'. The values in the seed were the values against which elements of cases in the case base were compared by the similarity measure.

Most typically, constructing a retrieval request in our previous framework would begin by defining orders on the domains of each of the relevant attributes of the cases. Some domains might have an existing order (e.g. **Price**, being numeric, has the existing total order $\leq$); for other domains (e.g. ones with symbolic values) we showed ways in which orders could be defined (e.g. a user-defined order would be the most suitable way to rank values in **Dest** — see e.g. Fig. 2).

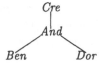

Fig. 2. A possible partial order — $\sqsubseteq_{\textbf{Dest}}$ — for destinations.

We provided a set of operators for producing new orders from these 'underlying' orders. Orders on the domains of individual attributes could be extended to orders on whole tuples. A number of different orders on tuples, e.g. one per relevant attribute, would be combined using one of a number of connectives we defined (conjunction, disjunction and prioritisation), to give a new single order, and it would be this order that would be applied to the case base and the maxima taken.

Our new approach, using similarity metrics in place of orders, is similar in construction. Metrics on the domains of individual attributes can be imputed to whole tuples, and may be combined in various ways to give new metrics. These metrics can be applied to the case base and the maxima taken.

1.3 Similarity Measures Returning Other Types

The ordinal (boolean-valued) measures we introduced in [9] were never intended to supplant, but merely to complement cardinal measures. In recognition of this, in [9] we defined numeric-valued similarity measures in a manner analogous to the way we had defined boolean-valued ones. The operators were redefined for the numeric case and different connectives were used (e.g. weighted addition and multiplication); there were no straightforward correspondences to the connectives of the ordinal framework (because cardinal and ordinal measures were not instances of a single framework). There were no connectives allowing cardinal and ordinal measures to be combined (not least since the result of such a combination would not have fallen within either the ordinal or the cardinal framework). Recent work [6, 11, 12] has proposed the use of similarity measures that are neither boolean- nor numeric-valued. It is desirable that these measures also be part of a common framework. This is also achieved by our framework. See [10] for details.

1.4 Similarity Metrics: A Single Framework

The work reported in this paper has three inter-related advantages. It proposes a framework in which different types of similarity metrics (returning boolean values, numeric values or values of some other type) are all instances of a single framework. Secondly, the connectives we define for combining metrics to produce new metrics not only allow us to combine metrics that return values of the same type, e.g. two or more boolean-valued metrics, but also allow combination of metrics that return values of different types, e.g. a boolean-valued metric with a numeric-valued metric. In contrast to our earlier framework, our new framework can combine such measures without the need to inter-convert. And finally, the framework provides a richer set of connectives than we had in [9].

As explained in detail in the remainder of the paper, a metric is a function that returns values from some *lattice*. Appropriate lattices include those defined on booleans, on numbers, on structured data values, on pairs of booleans, on pairs of booleans and numbers, and so on. This generalises many definitions of similarity. We do not need special definitions of operators for, e.g., numeric-valued metrics: a single set of definitions applies to all metrics, irrespective of the result lattice. And a metric of any type may be combined, using connectives we define, with a metric of any other type, and the result will still be a metric.

Proofs of the work reported in this paper can be found in [10]. Since metrics are lattice-valued functions, we begin our detailed explanation by reminding the reader of some lattice definitions.

2 Lattices

Recall that a partial order is a reflexive, transitive, anti-symmetric relation.

Definition 1 *A lattice is a partially ordered set* $(S, \sqsubseteq)$ *with the property that for all elements* $x, y \in S$, *x and y have a* least upper bound, $x \sqcup y$, *and a* greatest lower bound $x \sqcap y$. *The least upper bound and greatest lower bound are both unique[1].*

---

[1] In [10] we take the definitions of the binary operators $\sqcup$ and $\sqcap$ to be basic, and then derive the definition of the partial order: $x \sqsubseteq y \equiv x = x \sqcap y$. This explains why, in the rest of this paper, lattices are defined in terms of $\sqcup$ and $\sqcap$.

A complete *lattice is a lattice where all subsets have a least upper bound and a greatest lower bound*[2].

Figure 3 contains some examples of standard (complete) lattices. This figure also introduces some notation that we will use throughout, e.g. $\mathcal{L}(\textbf{Bool})$ for the Boolean lattice. There are several ways of generating new lattices from lattices. These are summarised in Sect. 2.1.

$\mathcal{L}(\textbf{Bool})$	$\mathcal{L}(\mathcal{P}(\{a,b,c\}))$			$\mathcal{L}(\Re^\infty_{-\infty})$	$\mathcal{L}([n,m])$
		$\{a,b,c\}$		∞	m
		↗ ↑ ↖		⋮	⋮
True	$\{a,b\}$	$\{a,c\}$	$\{b,c\}$	↑	↑
↑	⤬		⤬	0	0
False	$\{a\}$	$\{b\}$	$\{c\}$	↑	↑
	↖	↑	↗	⋮	⋮
		$\emptyset$		$-\infty$	n
⊔ ⊓ ⊑ ⊤ ⊥	∨ ∧ ⇒ *True* *False*	∪ ∩ ⊆ $\{a,b,c\}$ $\emptyset$		max min ≤ ∞ $-\infty$	max min ≤ m n

Fig. 3. The lattices $\mathcal{L}(\textbf{Bool})$, $\mathcal{L}(\mathcal{P}(\{a,b,c\}))$, $\mathcal{L}(\Re^\infty_{-\infty})$ and $\mathcal{L}([n,m])$.

2.1 Generating Lattices from Lattices

Inverses. If $\mathcal{L} = (\mathcal{C}, \sqcup, \sqcap)$ is a lattice, then the inverse $\mathcal{L}^{-1}$, defined as $(\mathcal{C}, \sqcap, \sqcup)$ is also a lattice. The ordering for $\mathcal{L}^{-1}$ can be derived, and satisfies $\sqsubseteq^{-1}=\sqsupseteq$ (and also $\sqsupseteq^{-1}=\sqsubseteq$, etc.). If $\mathcal{L}$ is a complete lattice then $\top^{-1} = \bot$ and $\bot^{-1} = \top$. To see the inverses of the lattices in Fig. 3, stand on your head!

Homomorphisms. If $\mathcal{L}_1 = (\mathcal{C}_1, \sqcup_1, \sqcap_1)$ and $\mathcal{L}_2 = (\mathcal{C}_2, \sqcup_2, \sqcap_2)$ are two lattices, a lattice-homomorphism from $\mathcal{L}_1$ to $\mathcal{L}_2$ is a function $\circledh$ from $\mathcal{C}_1$ to $\mathcal{C}_2$ that preserves least upper bounds and greatest lower bounds — i.e. $x \sqcup_1 y = z \Rightarrow \circledh(x) \sqcup_2 \circledh(y) = \circledh(z)$ and $x \sqcap_1 y = z \Rightarrow \circledh(x) \sqcap_2 \circledh(y) = \circledh(z)$. A lattice-homomorphism is written $\circledh(\mathcal{L})$, so that, in this case, $\circledh(\mathcal{L}_1) = \mathcal{L}_2$. Some lattice homomorphisms are illustrated in Fig. 4. The third and fourth homomorphisms in Fig. 4 are examples of homomorphisms from product lattices, which will be introduced below.

---

[2] See [3] for a more detailed introduction to lattice theory.

Homomorphism	Type	Definition
$\circledR$	$\mathbf{Bool} \to \Re^{\infty}_{-\infty}$	$\circledR(\mathit{True}) = 1$ $\circledR(\mathit{False}) = 0$
$\circledB$	$\Re^{\infty}_{-\infty} \to \mathbf{Bool}$	$\circledB(n) = (n \geq 0)$
$\circledwedge$	$(\mathbf{Bool}, \mathbf{Bool}) \to \mathbf{Bool}$	$\circledwedge(x, y) = x \wedge y$
$\circledvee$	$(\mathbf{Bool}, \mathbf{Bool}) \to \mathbf{Bool}$	$\circledvee(x, y) = x \vee y$

Fig. 4. Some lattice homomorphisms.

Products. If $\mathcal{L}_1 = (\mathcal{C}_1, \sqcup_1, \sqcap_1)$ and $\mathcal{L}_2 = (\mathcal{C}_2, \sqcup_2, \sqcap_2)$ are both lattices, then their product, $\mathcal{L}_1 \times \mathcal{L}_2$ is also a lattice $(\mathcal{C}_1 \times \mathcal{C}_2, \sqcup_\times, \sqcap_\times)$ with $(x_1, x_2) \sqsubseteq_\times (y_1, y_2)$ defined to be $x_1 \sqsubseteq_1 y_1 \wedge x_2 \sqsubseteq_2 y_2$. If $\mathcal{L}_1$ and $\mathcal{L}_2$ are both complete lattices, then $\mathcal{L}_1 \times \mathcal{L}_2$ is also a complete lattice, with $\top = (\top_1, \top_2)$ and $\bot = (\bot_1, \bot_2)$.

An Example. The product of the power set lattice and the boolean lattice — $\mathcal{L}(\mathcal{P}(\{a, b, c\}))$ and $\mathcal{L}(\mathbf{Bool})$ — is the lattice $(\mathcal{P}(\{a, b, c\}) \times \mathbf{Bool}, (\cup, \vee), (\cap, \wedge))$ (or, conventionally, $\mathcal{L}(\mathcal{P}(\{a, b, c\}) \times \mathbf{Bool}))$.

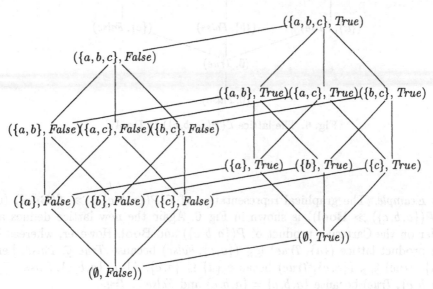

Fig. 5. The lattice $\mathcal{L}(\mathcal{P}(\{a, b, c\}) \times \mathbf{Bool})$.

This lattice is shown graphically in Fig. 5, and defines an order on the Cartesian product of $\mathcal{P}(\{a, b, c\})$ and $\mathbf{Bool}$ in which, for example, $(\{a, b, c\}, \mathit{False}) \sqsubseteq_\times (\{a, b, c\}, \mathit{True})$ because $\{a, b, c\} \sqsubseteq \{a, b, c\}$ and $\mathit{False} \sqsubseteq \mathit{True}$.

Prioritisations. Lattice inverses, homomorphisms and products are standard lattice operations. Prioritisation is an operation that we have defined for its usefulness to our framework.

If $\mathcal{L}_1 = (C_1, \sqcup_1, \sqcap_1, \top_1, \bot_1)$ and $\mathcal{L}_2(C_2, \sqcup_2, \sqcap_2, \top_2, \bot_2)$ are both *complete* lattices, then the *prioritisation* of $\mathcal{L}_1$ over $\mathcal{L}_2$, notation $\mathcal{L}_1 \gg \mathcal{L}_2$, is the complete lattice $(C_1 \times C_2, \sqcup_\gg, \sqcap_\gg, (\top, \top), (\bot, \bot))$ where $(x_1, x_2) \sqsubseteq_\gg (y_1, y_2)$ is defined to be $x_1 \sqsubset_1 y_1 \vee (x_1 = y_1 \wedge x_2 \sqsubseteq_2 y_2)$. This is an ordinary lexicographic ordering extended to lattices.

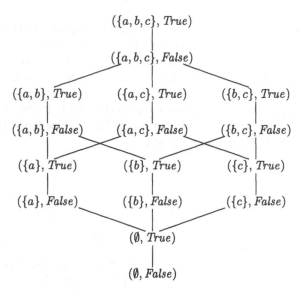

Fig. 6. The lattice $\mathcal{L}(\mathcal{P}(\{a,b,c\}) \gg \textbf{Bool})$.

An Example. The graphical representation of $\mathcal{L}(\mathcal{P}(\{a,b,c\})) \gg \mathcal{L}(\textbf{Bool})$ (or $\mathcal{L}(\mathcal{P}(\{a,b,c\}) \gg \textbf{Bool}))$ is shown in Fig. 6. Again the new lattice defines an order on the Cartesian product of $\mathcal{P}(\{a,b,c\})$ and **Bool**. However, whereas in the product lattice $(\{a\}, \textit{True}) \not\sqsubseteq_\times (\{a,c\}, \textit{False})$ because $\textit{True} \not\sqsubseteq \textit{False}$, here $(\{a\}, \textit{True}) \sqsubseteq_\gg (\{a,c\}, \textit{True})$ because $\{a\} \sqsubset \{a,c\}$. Also $(\{a,b,c\}, \textit{False}) \sqsubseteq_\gg (\{a,b,c\}, \textit{True})$ because $\{a,b,c\} = \{a,b,c\}$ and $\textit{False} \sqsubseteq \textit{True}$.

3   Similarity Metrics

A *similarity metric* is a generalisation of a transitive relation. For some set α an $(\alpha, \mathcal{L})$ metric is a pair $(\unlhd, \mathcal{L})$, where $\mathcal{L}$ is a complete lattice, with $\unlhd :: \alpha \to \alpha \to \mathcal{L}$, such that

$$((x \unlhd y) \sqcap_\mathcal{L} (y \unlhd z)) \sqsubseteq_\mathcal{L} (x \unlhd z) . \tag{1}$$

The expression $x \trianglelefteq y = v$ is pronounced "y exceeds x by v". The value of v is also called the "excess of y over x". Similarity metrics are inspired by the definition of *distance* in metric spaces [4], (1) being similar to a triangle inequality. In a metric space, however, the distance function is symmetric, and distances have a total order defined on them. In similarity metrics the order may be partial, and the distance function need not be symmetric. This partial ordering means that not all excesses need be comparable. The definition of maxima for similarity metrics must take account of this possible incomparability.

An element x of a set S is a maximum if, whenever the excess of x over y is comparable to the excess of y over x, then the excess of x over y is greater than or equal to the excess of y over x. An equivalent formulation is: if the excess of x over y is less than or equal to the excess of y over x, then the two excesses are equal. I.e. the maxima of a metric are given by:

$$\max S = \{x \in S | \forall y \in S : ((y \trianglelefteq x) \sqsubseteq_{\mathcal{L}} (x \trianglelefteq y)) \Rightarrow ((y \trianglelefteq x) = (x \trianglelefteq y))\} . \quad (2)$$

3.1 Some Examples

Similarity measures that return boolean values, numeric values, or values of other types can all be modelled as metrics, which shows that our framework subsumes many other approaches to similarity measurement. We demonstrate this with examples relating to the holiday case base given in Fig. 1.

Destinations. In Fig. 2 we showed a partial order, $\sqsubseteq_{\mathbf{Dest}}$, on holiday destinations. This order (boolean-valued function) can be modelled by a metric $(\sqsubseteq_{\mathbf{Dest}}, \mathcal{L}(\mathbf{Bool}))$. Its result type is the lattice $\mathcal{L}(\mathbf{Bool})$. By this metric $Ben \sqsubseteq Cre = True$ — i.e. *Crete* exceeds *Benidorm* by *True* — and $And \sqsubseteq Dor = False$ — *Dordogne* exceeds *Andalucia* by *False*[3]. In fact, for any transitive relation $\sqsubseteq$ on α (i.e. a boolean valued function $\alpha \to \alpha \to \mathbf{Bool}$), the pair $(\sqsubseteq, \mathcal{L}(\mathbf{Bool}))$ is an $(\alpha, \mathcal{L}(\mathbf{Bool}))$ metric. It is easy to show that the maxima given by substituting in (2) are the usual maxima of a transitive relation.

Price. The most obvious metric for real numbers is the metric $\mathcal{M}_{\Re^{\infty}_{-\infty}}$ defined by $\mathcal{M}_{\Re^{\infty}_{-\infty}} = (\dot{-}^{-1}, \mathcal{L}(\Re^{\infty}_{-\infty}))$, where $\dot{-}$ is the operator $x \dot{-} y = \max(x-y, 0)$. This is a $(\Re^{\infty}_{-\infty}, \mathcal{L}(\Re^{\infty}_{-\infty}))$ metric. By this metric $500 \dot{-}^{-1} 750 = 250$ and $750 \dot{-}^{-1} 500 = 0$ — i.e. 750 exceeds 500 by 250, and 500 exceeds 750 by 0. The metric $(\dot{-}^{-1}, \mathcal{L}(\Re^{\infty}_{-\infty}))$ may be suitable for many numeric domains, and we can again show, by substituting in (2), that (2) would compute the maxima we would expect. Since this metric reflects the usual ordering ($\leq$) on real numbers, it will rank larger numbers higher than smaller ones. Unless one is an elitist member of the super rich jet set, this is probably not the criterium one would apply to prices. A more sensible metric for prices would be $\mathcal{M}_{\mathbf{Price}} = (\dot{-}, \Re^{\infty}_{-\infty})$.

---

[3] For metrics defined on $\mathcal{L}(\mathbf{Bool})$, simpler paraphrases are possible, and clearer: we can say that *Crete* exceeds *Benidorm*, and *Dordogne* does not exceed *Andalucia*.

Activities. Using w, s, and g as abbreviations for *windsurfing*, *swimming* and *golf*, a possible metric for holiday activities — $\mathcal{M}_{\mathbf{Act}}$ — would be the similarity metric $(\backslash^{-1}, \mathcal{L}(\mathcal{P}(\{g, s, w\})))$, where $\backslash^{-1}$ is the inverse of set difference — so that $\{g\} \backslash^{-1} \{g, s\} = \{s\}$, i.e. *golf* and *swimming* exceeds *golf* by *swimming*. Again (2) gives suitable maxima.

We see it as a strength of the framework that not only can boolean-valued and numeric-valued metrics be defined, but metrics of other types (e.g. set-valued as above, and feature-structure-valued as described in [10]) are also instances of the framework. That these different metrics can all be combined is another strength.

3.2 Generating Metrics from Metrics

Inverses. If $\mathcal{M} = (\trianglelefteq, \mathcal{L})$ is a metric, then its inverse, $\mathcal{M}^{-1} = (\trianglelefteq^{-1}, \mathcal{L})$ is also a metric. For example, $\mathcal{M}_{\mathbf{Price}} = \mathcal{M}_{\Re_{-\infty}^{\infty}}^{-1}$. Note that while it is certainly not the case that $(\trianglelefteq^{-1}, \mathcal{L}) = (\trianglelefteq, \mathcal{L}^{-1})$, it is the case that $\mathsf{max}_{(\trianglelefteq^{-1}, \mathcal{L})} = \mathsf{max}_{(\trianglelefteq, \mathcal{L}^{-1})}$.

Compositions.

Left Composition. If $\mathcal{M} = (\trianglelefteq, \mathcal{L})$ is an $(\alpha, \mathcal{L})$ metric and f is a function of type $\beta \to \alpha$, then the left composition of the metric and f, notation $\mathcal{M} \circ f$, defined as $(\trianglelefteq \circ f, \mathcal{L})$, where $x \, (\trianglelefteq \circ f) \, y = f(x) \trianglelefteq f(y)$, is a $(\beta, \mathcal{L})$ metric.

Obvious candidates for left composition are *projection functions*. For example, π_1 will select the first element of a tuple. Then the left composition $\mathcal{M}_{\mathbf{Dest}} \circ \pi_1$ is a metric that applies to whole tuples. Specifically, since $\mathcal{M}_{\mathbf{Dest}} = (\sqsubseteq_{\mathbf{Dest}}, \mathcal{L}(\mathbf{Bool}))$ is a $(\mathbf{Dest}, \mathcal{L}(\mathbf{Bool}))$ metric, $\mathcal{M}_{\mathbf{Dest}} \circ \pi_1$ is a $(\mathbf{Holiday}, \mathcal{L}(\mathbf{Bool}))$ metric, in which, for cases c_1 and c_2, $c_1 \trianglelefteq c_2 = \pi_1(c_1) \sqsubseteq_{\mathbf{Dest}} \pi_1(c_2)$ — i.e. c_2 exceeds c_1 in the new metric if c_2's destination exceeds c_1's.

Although we are here using simple projection from a tuple, more complex case representations may require more complex projection functions. Projection functions might even implement inferencing [5, 8], perhaps to obtain "deep" features [2] from "surface" features.

Right Composition. If $\mathcal{M} = (\trianglelefteq, \mathcal{L})$ is an $(\alpha, \mathcal{L})$ metric, and $\textcircled{h}$ is a lattice homomorphism, then the right composition of these,. $\textcircled{h} \circ \mathcal{M}$, defined as $(\textcircled{h} \circ \trianglelefteq, \textcircled{h}(\mathcal{L}))$, where $x \, (\textcircled{h} \circ \trianglelefteq) \, y = \textcircled{h}(x \trianglelefteq y)$, is an $(\alpha, \textcircled{h}(\mathcal{L}))$ metric. An example of a right composition could be the metric that simply compares prices — $\textcircled{B} \circ \mathcal{M}_{\mathbf{Price}}$, so that, for example, $750 \trianglelefteq 500 = True$, rather than 250.

Products. If $\mathcal{M}_1 = (\trianglelefteq_1, \mathcal{L}_1)$ and $\mathcal{M}_2 = (\trianglelefteq_2, \mathcal{L}_2)$ are two metrics, then their product, $\mathcal{M}_1 \times \mathcal{M}_2$, is the metric $(\trianglelefteq_1 \times \trianglelefteq_2, \mathcal{L}_1 \times \mathcal{L}_2)$, with $\trianglelefteq_1 \times \trianglelefteq_2$ defined by $(x_1, x_2) \, (\trianglelefteq_1 \times \trianglelefteq_2) \, (y_1, y_2) = (x_1 \trianglelefteq_1 y_1, x_2 \trianglelefteq_2 y_2)$. A metric that will compare both destination and price is the metric $\mathcal{M}_{\mathbf{Dest}} \times \mathcal{M}_{\mathbf{Price}}$. In this metric, for example, $(Ben, 350) \trianglelefteq (Cre, 750) = (True, 0)$ because $Ben \sqsubseteq_{\mathbf{Dest}} Cre$, and $350 \dot{-} 750 = 0$. This is a new metric whose result type is the product of $\mathcal{L}(\mathbf{Bool})$

and $\mathcal{L}(\Re^{\infty}_{-\infty})$. Crucially, the combination of an ordinal and a cardinal metric results in a new metric, which could be applied to a case base, and the maxima taken. If this is done it will select not only the cheaper Cretan holiday (being the cheaper of the two in the preferred location), but also the cheapest holiday — i.e. the one in Benidorm. Our goal of combining different types of metric has been achieved.

It is also possible to take the **(Price, Bool)** metric defined above, i.e. $\circledB \circ \mathcal{M}_{\mathbf{Price}}$, and take its product with $\mathcal{M}_{\mathbf{Dest}}$ — a **(Dest, Bool)** metric. The resulting metric will be a **((Dest, Price), (Bool, Bool))** metric, $\mathcal{M}_{\mathbf{Dest}} \times (\circledB \circ \mathcal{M}_{\mathbf{Price}})$ This metric is one whose result is a lattice defined on pairs of truth values, e.g. $(Ben, 350) \trianglelefteq (Cre, 750) = (True, False)$. The disjunctive homomorphism can now be applied. This will result in a **((Dest, Price), Bool)** metric — $\circledV \circ (\mathcal{M}_{\mathbf{Dest}} \times (\circledB \circ \mathcal{M}_{\mathbf{Price}}))$, in which, for example, $(Ben, 350) \trianglelefteq (Cre, 750) = True$. Note also that — in contrast to the **((Dest, Price), (Bool, Bool))** metric above, where $(Cre, 750) \trianglelefteq (Cre, 500)$ and $(Cre, 500) \trianglelefteq (Cre, 750)$ are not equal, since $(Cre, 750) \trianglelefteq (Cre, 500) = (True, True)$, while $(Cre, 500) \trianglelefteq (Cre, 750) = (True, False)$ — in this new metric $(Cre, 750) \trianglelefteq (Cre, 500)$ and $(Cre, 500) \trianglelefteq (Cre, 750)$ *are* equal (both being *True*). As a consequence, the maxima according to this metric will be both the Cretan holidays and the holiday in Benidorm (and the mutual excesses between all three cases will be comparable).

Prioritisations. If $\mathcal{M}_1 = (\trianglelefteq_1, \mathcal{L}_1)$ and $\mathcal{M}_2 = (\trianglelefteq_2, \mathcal{L}_2)$ are two metrics, then the prioritisation of $\mathcal{M}_1$ over $\mathcal{M}_2$, notation $\mathcal{M}_1 \gg \mathcal{M}_2$, is the metric $(\trianglelefteq_1 \times \trianglelefteq_2, \mathcal{L}_1 \gg \mathcal{L}_2)$. If the destination is more important than the price, this can be reflected in the metric — e.g. $\mathcal{M}_{\mathbf{Dest}} \gg \mathcal{M}_{\mathbf{Price}}$. In contrast to the product metric, this metric will prefer the cheaper Cretan holiday to the Benidorm holiday — the excesses are the same, but the lattice is different. I.e. in both $\mathcal{M}_{\mathbf{Dest}} \times \mathcal{M}_{\mathbf{Price}}$ and $\mathcal{M}_{\mathbf{Dest}} \gg \mathcal{M}_{\mathbf{Price}}$, the two excesses between these two holidays are:

$$(Ben, 350) \trianglelefteq (Cre, 500) = (True, 0)$$
$$(Cre, 500) \trianglelefteq (Ben, 350) = (False, 150)$$

but in $\mathcal{M}_{\mathbf{Dest}} \times \mathcal{M}_{\mathbf{Price}}$ it is not the case that $(False, 150) \sqsubseteq (True, 0)$ (since $False \sqsubseteq True$, but $150 \not\sqsubseteq 0$), while this relation does hold in $\mathcal{M}_{\mathbf{Dest}} \gg \mathcal{M}_{\mathbf{Price}}$.

To consider a more complex example, if the activities available are less important than the destination and price, the following metric can be used:

$$(\circledV \circ (\mathcal{M}_{\mathbf{Dest}} \times (\circledB \circ \mathcal{M}_{\mathbf{Price}}))) \gg \mathcal{M}_{\mathbf{Act}} .$$

The first part of this metric will, as shown above, select the two Cretan holidays and the Benidorm holiday. The second part will then maximise the activities available, and therefore recommend the more expensive Cretan holiday.

4 Conclusions

We have presented a formal framework for the specification of similarity measures — ordinal or cardinal, and also similarity measures returning other types, such as sets or feature structures. We can not only define individual similarity measures, but also combine similarity measures, possibly returning values of different types, to produce new similarity measures. This, in combination with the large set of connectives available within the formalism, gives a powerful formalism for the construction of a wide range of similarity measures applicable to many problem domains.

References

1. A. Aamodt and E. Plaza. Case based reasoning: Foundational issues, methodological variations and system approaches. *AI Communications*, 7(1):39–59, 1994.
2. K.D. Ashley and E.L. Rissland. A case-based approach to modeling legal expertise. *IEEE Expert*, 3(3):70–77, 1988.
3. G. Birkhoff. *Lattice Theory*. American Mathematical Society, 1967.
4. M. Fréchet. Sur quelques points du calcul fonctionel. *Rendiconti del Circolo Matematico di Palermo*, 22:1–74, 1906.
5. T.R. Hinrichs. *Problem Solving in Open Worlds: A Case Study in Design*. Lawrence Erlbaum, 1992.
6. K.P. Jantke. Nonstandard concepts of similarity in case-based reasoning. In H.H. Bock, W. Lenski, and M.M. Richter, editors, *Proceedings der Jahrestagung der Gesellschaft für Klassifikation*, Information Systems and Data Analysis: Prospects, Foundations, Applications, pages 29–44. Springer Verlag, 1994.
7. J.L. Kolodner. *Case Based Reasoning*. Morgan Kaufmann, 1993.
8. P. Koton. Reasoning about evidence in causal explanations. In *Proceedings of AAAI-88*, pages 256–261, 1988.
9. Hugh Osborne and Derek Bridge. A case base similarity framework. In Ian Smith and Boi Faltings, editors, *Advances in Case-Based Reasoning*, Proceedings of EWCBR'96, pages 309–323, 1996.
10. Hugh Osborne and Derek Bridge. Similarity metrics: A formal approach to case base retrieval using general similarity metrics. Technical report, Department of Computer Science, University of York, 1997. In preparation.
11. E. Plaza. Cases as terms: A feature term approach to the structured representation of cases. In *Proceedings of the First International Conference on Case-Based Reasoning*. Springer Verlag, 1995.
12. E. Plaza. On the importance of similitude: An entropy-based assessment. In Ian Smith and Boi Faltings, editors, *Advances in Case-Based Reasoning*, Proceedings of EWCBR'96, pages 324–338, 1996.
13. M.M. Richter. Classification and learning of similarity measures. In *Proceedings der Jahrestagung der Gesellschaft für Klassifikation*, Studies in Classification, Data Analysis and Knowledge Organisation. Springer Verlag, 1992.

The Case for Graph-Structured Representations*

Kathryn E. Sanders[1] and Brian P. Kettler[2] and James A. Hendler[3]

[1] Computing and Information Services, Brown University, Providence, RI 02912,
Kathryn_Sanders@brown.edu
[2] ISX Corporation, 2000 N. 15th St., Suite 1000, Arlington, VA 22201,
bkettler@isx.com
[3] Dept. of Computer Science, University of Maryland, College Park, MD 20742,
hendler@cs.umd.edu

Abstract. Case-based reasoning involves reasoning from *cases*: specific pieces of experience, the reasoner's or another's, that can be used to solve problems. We use the term "graph-structured" for representations that (1) are capable of expressing the relations between any two objects in a case, (2) allow the set of relations used to vary from case to case, and (3) allow the set of possible relations to be expanded as necessary to describe new cases. Such representations can be implemented as, for example, semantic networks or lists of concrete propositions in some logic.

We believe that graph-structured representations offer significant advantages, and thus we are investigating ways to implement such representations efficiently. We make a "case-based argument" using examples from two systems, CHIRON and CAPER, to show how a graph-structured representation supports two different kinds of case-based planning in two different domains. We discuss the costs associated with graph-structured representations and describe an approach to reducing those costs, implemented in CAPER.

1 Introduction

Case-based reasoning (CBR) involves reasoning from *cases*: specific pieces of experience, the reasoner's or another's, that can be used to solve problems. As a result, case representation is critical. A system's case representation must support its operations: indexing, retrieval, and comparison or adaptation. An incomplete case representation limits the system's reasoning power.

Efficiency pushes systems in the direction of simpler representations. An extreme example of this is found in information-retrieval (IR) systems. Like CBR systems, IR systems index and retrieve information, but without adaptation

* This work has benefited from the comments of Bill Anderson, Karl Branting, Janet Kolodner, Sean Luke, and Robert McCartney. Research was supported in part by grants to J. Hendler and T. Dean from NSF (IRI-8907890, IRI-8905436, IRI-8957601, IRI-8801253), ONR (N00014-J-91-1451, N00014-91-J-4052), AFOSR (F49620-93-1-0065), ARPA/ARPI (F30602-93-C-0039, F30602-91-C-0041), and IBM (17290066, 17291066, 17292066, 17293066).

or further processing. Most IR systems have used very simple representations: essentially, each document is represented by the set of words it contains. Representing a document as a list of words is not necessarily trivial; but it is relatively easy to automate, an important factor given that commercial IR systems such as Dialog, Lexis, and Nexis incorporate hundreds of thousands of documents.

In this paper, we adopt the term "feature-based," used to describe these simple IR representations [5], and use it to denote any representation that expresses facts about individual objects in a case without relating them to each other. Such representations may be implemented using a set of attribute-value pairs, a feature vector, or frames with atomic slot-fillers.

We use the term "graph-structured" for representations that (1) are capable of expressing the relations between any two objects in a case, (2) allow the set of relations used to vary from case to case, and (3) allow the set of possible relations to be expanded as necessary to describe new cases. Such representations can be implemented, for example, as semantic networks or lists of concrete propositions in some logic. Whether the representation is implemented as a list of propositions or as a graph is immaterial, since there is a simple translation from propositional to graph representation [21].

Balancing the need for an expressive representation with efficiency considerations, most CBR systems have used representations that fall between feature-based and graph-structured. For example, several systems include some relational information but use the same structure for each case (e.g., [4, 8]). Graph-structured representations are more expressive, but at a significant computational cost.

We believe that graph-structured representations offer significant advantages, and thus we are investigating ways to implement such representations efficiently. We make a "case-based argument" using examples from two systems, CHIRON and CAPER, to show how a graph-structured representation supports two different kinds of case-based planning in two different domains. We discuss the costs associated with graph-structured representations and describe an approach to reducing those costs, implemented in CAPER.

2   Overview of CAPER and CHIRON

This section gives a brief overview of CHIRON and CAPER. Details can be found in [22] and [15].

CHIRON is a hybrid rule-based and case-based system in the domain of tax planning. It uses rules and structured cases to solve a cluster of problems having to do with buying, selling, renting, and owning residential housing.

CHIRON's knowledge base includes representations of part of the United States Internal Revenue Code and approximately twenty-four cases under various provisions of that statute. It also includes safe harbor plans, or prototypes, that satisfy the rules; a representation of the relationship between the rules, prototypes, and cases; and finally, a representation of the input description of the taxpayer's goals and current situation. The facts of both previous cases and the current situation are represented as lists of propositions in a temporal modal logic.

CHIRON's case-based reasoner takes partial plans generated by the hierarchical planner, refines them, and generates arguments in support of the resulting plan. Given a partial plan, the case-based planner first retrieves a prototype for that plan and adapts it along directions suggested by previous cases, to the extent necessary to fit the current situation. It then retrieves all the previous cases that share any fact with the resulting plan. Next, it computes a mapping between the facts of each case and the facts of the current situation, in order to determine the overlap between the two, and sorts the cases by inserting them into a HYPO-style case lattice [3]. It uses the case lattice to determine whether there is sufficient support for the plan being considered (generally, whether the plan falls between the prototype and previous successful cases of a given strategy), and if so, also uses the lattice to generate HYPO-style arguments for and against the success of a plan.

CAPER is a case-based planning system that makes use of massive parallelism to access a large casebase (currently several hundred cases) [16, 15]. CAPER uses graph-structured representations for cases and conceptual knowledge, implemented as a single semantic network. Given the availability of fast parallel case retrieval methods, memory does not have to be pre-indexed for efficiency and thus can be accessed flexibly and often.[4] Retrieval is flexible because any feature of the target problem description can be included in the retrieval probe, a graph to be matched against the subgraphs of the semantic net. A case can be retrieved via any of its constituent nodes. Domain knowledge and planning techniques are used to form probes at case retrieval time. Multiple plans (or subplans) can be retrieved and merged into a target plan using stored plan rationale (validations) and methods based on those used in the PRIAR system [14]. CAPER is being tested in our (artificial) transport logistics planning domain.

CAPER's semantic network memory is implemented using Parka, a high, performance frame-based knowledge representation system.[9].[5] A case includes the goals, initial situation, and plan/subplan hierarchy, and plan validation structures for a planning problem. during plan adaptation and plan merging.

3 Benefits of Graph-Structured Representations

Graph-structured representations allow a system to capture a reasonably complete description of a case. By "reasonably complete," we mean a representation that includes all the information about a case that is likely to be useful. As argued in [20], in order to maximize their usefulness, case representations should be

---

[4] We use "indexing" to mean the use of pointers for case retrieval, rather than a more recent, broader interpretation of "indexing" that includes any domain knowledge used in the retrieval of cases (e.g., [17]).

[5] Parka runs on parallel platforms (Thinking Machines' CM-2 and CM-5, IBM SP2, and others) and provides very fast inferencing mechanisms. A serial version of Parka has also been developed.

Fig. 1. Part of CHIRON's representation of *Hughston v. Commissioner.*

as complete as possible. Complete representations increase a system's reasoning power: a system cannot reason with information that it does not have.

In particular, a graph-structured representation makes it possible to express the relations between objects. Consider the graph shown in Figure 1. This graph corresponds to part of the representation of *Hughston v. Commissioner*, one of the cases in CHIRON's casebase. The nodes in the graph correspond to objects in CHIRON's logical representation; edges correspond to binary predicates; and the endpoints of an edge correspond to the predicate's parameters. For simplicity, the node labels are not shown in Figure 1, but every node has one or more such labels. Node labels correspond to unary predicates on a given object. For example, Hughston is a lawyer; house1 is both a house and real property; Shell-Oil-Company is a corporation; and so forth. For the actual representation and the original text of the case, see [22].

In this case, the taxpayer, Hughston, was a lawyer for Shell Oil, in Texas. When he was transferred to a new location in Texas, he sold his old house (which had a bathroom with a tile floor) and bought another, closer to his new place of work. He had three children, of whom the oldest was ten years old. At issue was the question of whether he would have to pay taxes on the profit made on the first house. The relations between the objects in this case are important: the fact that the taxpayer is selling one house and buying another, for example; the facts (represented in the case, but not shown here), that the two houses are far apart, but the second one is close to the taxpayer's new place of employment; and so forth. These could not be expressed in a simple feature vector.

In CAPER, graph-structured representations provide the required expressivity to represent relations between objects and relations between plan actions. In our transport logistics domain the configuration of packages with respect to vehicles in a problem's initial situation is important in retrieving a case to adapt to the target problem. Consider the graph based on a piece of a case from CA-PER's transport logistics domain, shown in Figure 2. This case involves a plan to deliver a package, Pkg99, starting at 3 p.m. on March 15, 1994, in a truck (Truck22) whose original location is Boston. To represent information such as the fact that Truck22 and Pkg99 have the same origin, graph-structured representations are required. To match cases on such relations, "structure" queries

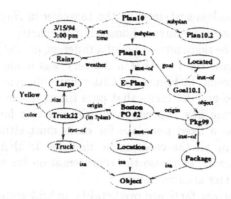

Fig. 2. Sample Piece of CAPER's Memory for Transportation Logistics Domain. ("inst-of" links are "Instance Of" (∈). "isa" links are ⊂ relations.)

that contain two or more variables are needed: e.g., "find all plans in whose initial situation `inst-of`(t,`Truck`) ∧ `inst-of`(p,`Package`) ∧ `origin`(t, x) ∧ `origin`(p, x)."

CAPER also needs to represent and match on plan validations, relations among plan actions that capture which effects (postconditions) of actions (or the initial situation/context) contribute to which preconditions of actions. They capture plan rationale which is then used to determine which actions can be reused from a previous case's plan and what modifications are necessary to adapt the previous case to the current situation and goals.

CHIRON's graph-structured representation permits the system to capture the detailed facts of its cases, and the system's algorithms for indexing, adapting, comparing, and contrasting cases exploit this rich representation. For example, every case is indexed under each of the predicates used in its case representation; thus, the system can identify as many partial matches as its rich representation language can express. Every fact can form the basis for an argument. A fact shared with a previous successful case supports an argument that the taxpayer in the current situation should succeed; a fact shared with a previous unsuccessful case suggests a possible problem. Similarly, unshared facts suggest possible distinctions between the current situation and previous cases. Finally, any fact in one of the previous cases can potentially be added to the prototype to make a new plan. Similarly, facts can be subtracted from the prototype, and their parameters can be varied.

In general, a complete case description is desirable for several reasons. First, it is not always possible at case-representation time to be sure of the future use of a case. A legal case may be used as the basis for analyzing a future situation, a plan, or a prediction of issues that might arise as the result of execution of a plan. A plan for transporting a package may be used for constructing a new transport plan or for recognizing the plan of another agent.

Second, even if a case is reused for the same purpose, it is not always clear which facts of the original case were relevant to the result. For example, a taxpayer trying to avoid the loss sustained by the taxpayer in *Hughston* might succeed if he is not a lawyer; if he buys a house that is exactly comparable to the house sold; or simply if he takes advantage of a different provision of the statute. In CAPER, we can express the fact that a delivery was made to or through a particular city (e.g., Boston, in Figure 2). Cities have idiosyncratic restrictions on the types of packages and deliveries that pass through them.

Finally, each new case has unpredictable idiosyncratic facts. Designers of hybrid systems that use a fixed template for cases must either decide on the template after examining all the cases to be included in their casebase, omit information from new cases, or revise the representation for all previous cases whenever a new useful fact is encountered.

Even if all the important facts are predictable, hybrid systems using a fixed structure for cases must choose between completeness and economy of representation. The important facts may vary widely from one case to the next. If a critical fact occurs in one case out of a thousand in the casebase, it would be wasteful to provide a slot for it in every single case representation.

4 Overcoming the costs

The benefits of graph-structured representations described in the previous section come at the cost of increased computational complexity of matching and increased case acquisition effort.

4.1 Matching

The matching operation puts two cases in correspondence and is used for case retrieval and comparison. For feature-based representations (feature vectors and frames with atomic slot-fillers), this operation is linear in the number of features. For hybrid representations with fixed structures, it is also linear.

Using a graph-structured representation increases the computational cost of matching. If cases were represented as unlabelled graphs, matching would be the subgraph isomorphism problem, which is NP-complete [11]. If the graphs had node labels and no node label ever occurred more than once in a given case, matching would be linear in the sum of the number of nodes and the number of edges. In practice, the complexity of matching cases with a graph-structured representation lies somewhere between these two extremes.

In CHIRON, for example, the matching algorithm works as follows. First, the system retrieves each case that shares any predicate (or in graph terms, any node or edge label) with the current plan. Then, for each node in the description of the current situation, the system identifies the nodes in the previous case that could match that node. In the case shown in Figure 1, for example, there are two houses; so if the current situation involves a house, the current house could match either of these. Finally, the system considers each of the possible mappings permitted by that list and returns the one that causes the most edges to match.

In practice, the average case has forty-four facts, and there are often a couple of "sellings," or two or three "objects," or a couple of "houses." There are between zero and three mappings for each node. Altogether, there are probably no more than fifteen possible mappings for any case, and the search could be pruned so that not all of these are examined (as done in GREBE [6]). For a small casebase, in a domain where instantaneous response time is not required, CHIRON's response times (typically three to five minutes per problem) are tolerable. Still, the time required for matching is significant, and increases linearly with the size of the casebase.

Some serial systems with graph-structured representations have used indexing to reduce the cost of matching. Indexing restricts the search for relevant cases to a subset of the casebase. Feature-based techniques are often employed such as the construction of a discrimination network using selected case features (attributes). For example, CHEF indexes cooking plans under their main ingredients and cooking failures under sets of causally relevant features [12]. Similarly, CHASER indexes tort cases under features such as the harm caused and possible legal defenses [7]. The main disadvantage of indexing is that it hinders flexibility at case retrieval time. Cases that share unindexed features with the target problem will not be retrieved. (See discussion in [20, 16, 15]).

A few systems have used parallel techniques to reduce the cost of matching. PARADYME, for example, is a massively parallel frame system that has been used to implement a memory for a CBR system [18].[6] In CAPER, the massively parallel mechanisms of the Parka Structure Matcher are used to match a probe graph to CAPER's semantic network memory [2].[7]

To evaluate the average-case behavior of matching a (labelled) probe graph to a subgraph of CAPER's (labelled) memory graph, we have done some preliminary experiments. We generated representative retrieval probes for a transport logistics domain and recorded the time taken to process them by the Parka Structure Matcher. The purpose of these experiments was to assess the absolute parallel retrieval times and the scalability of the parallel methods used, for a variety of representative retrieval probes (generated by hand) and casebase sizes. The probes were matched to non-pre-indexed casebases of varying sizes. Details can be found in [15]. Probes (structure-matching queries) were run on a 1, 8, and 16 processor configuration of an IBM SP2 parallel processing computer on a 200 case casebase (8130 component plans represented by 116728 Parka frames and 1746060 Parka assertions). The scalability of the parallel retrieval mechanisms is indicated by the probe matching times in Figure 3. The complexity of the underlying subgraph-matching algorithm on actual casebases is much less than the worst case complexity (exponential in the number of binary constraints). For a detailed analysis of the algorithm, see [2].

As the size of the casebases grow, additional processors result in subsecond retrieval times. Small retrieval times for complex structure-matching queries are required because CAPER spends a lot of time doing them. For example, in solving

---

[6] For a comparison of PARADYME to Parka, see [9] and [15].

[7] A sample memory graph is shown in Figure 2. The probe graph contains nodes that are constants or variables and links that are constants (predicates).

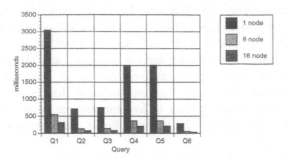

Fig. 3. Timings for sample structure-matching queries on a 200 case transport logistics casebase (116728 frames and 1746060 assertions) using 1, 8, and 16 parallel processors on an IBM SP2

a simple transport logistics planning problem, CAPER spent 51% of its query time (and 27% of its total running time) – 36 seconds on an unoptimized serial version of Parka - processing 15 structure-matching queries (with an average of 7.5 conjuncts). [8]

4.2   Case Acquisition

The cost of case acquisition can be high, particularly if a CBR system uses many cases. Case acquisition includes the costs of representing and indexing individual cases. The time cost of acquiring cases can be lower in systems using feature-based representations. In IR systems, for example, a document is represented and indexed by the words it contains and does not have to be hand-encoded nor hand-indexed: thus case acquisition can be fully automated.

In most CBR systems, the initial cases are derived from the experience of the system designer or some other expert, rather than from a document. As a result, a simple automated translation is not possible. The need to encode a case by hand makes case acquisition more costly.

Some hybrid systems solve this problem by using the same structure for each case. For example, for each case a person might fill a frame with fixed slots or create a feature vector for predesignated features. Representing cases using a fixed template is harder than translating a document into a set of words, but it is still fairly easy: having chosen a frame representation, the system designer can use the representation as a checklist when entering cases. There is no need to analyze each case separately, and different cases are likely to be treated consistently.

In systems that use pure graph-structured representations, a structure needs to be created for each case during case representation. For example, in CHIRON,

---

[8] Timings on the (preliminary) serial version of Parka-DB, which uses an RDBMS for persistent storage to process queries Q2 and Q3 on the 200 case casebase were 1051 and 1776 milliseconds, respectively on an IBM RS6000 workstation.[23]

the facts of a case are hand-encoded into a graph representation. Since the facts can vary widely from case to case, representing a case is more complicated than merely filling in fixed slots in a frame.

Automated methods can be used to create graph-structured representations. CAPER uses a generative planner, UM Nonlin, to seed the initial casebase. Plans created by UM Nonlin on randomly generated problems are automatically converted to cases in CAPER's semantic net representation. As cases are not indexed, the initial casebase acquisition process is completely automated.

5 Related Work and Conclusions

Other CBR and analogical reasoning systems that have used graph-structured representations include PLEXUS, GREBE, and COOKIE, ARCS, ACME and SME.[1, 6, 19, 24, 13, 10] Space limitations prohibit detailed discussion of these systems here (see [15]).

In this paper we have argued for *graph-structured* case representations, which express arbitrary relations among objects in a flexible way, over more limited or inflexible methods, illustrating the distinction between these kinds of representations with examples of information retrieval systems, CBR systems, and computational models of human analogical reasoning. Graph-structured representations provide the benefits of greater expressivity and economy. We have given examples of these benefits from two case-based planning systems, CAPER and CHIRON, and demonstrated how the case matching and case acquisition costs can be reduced through the use of high performance retrieval techniques such as the use of massively parallelism.

References

1. R. Alterman. Adaptive planning. *Cognitive Science*, 12:393–421, 1988.
2. W. A. Andersen, J. A. Hendler, M. P. Evett, and B. P. Kettler. Massively parallel matching of knowledge structures. In H. Kitano and J. Hendler, editors, *Massively Parallel Artificial Intelligence*, pages 52–73. AAAI Press/The MIT Press, Menlo Park, California, 1994.
3. K. D. Ashley. Modelling legal argument: reasoning with cases and hypotheticals. Technical Report 88-01, University of Massachusetts, Amherst, Department of Computer and Information Science, 1988. (PhD Thesis).
4. K. D. Ashley. *Modelling legal argument: reasoning with cases and hypotheticals*. MIT Press, 1991.
5. N. J. Belkin and W. B. Croft. Retrieval techniques. *Annual Review of Information Science and Technology*, 22:109–145, 1987.
6. L. K. Branting. Integrating rules and precedents for classification and explanation: automating legal analysis. Technical Report AI90-146, Artificial Intelligence Laboratory, Department of Computer Sciences, University of Texas at Austin, 1990. (PhD Thesis).
7. B. Cuthill and R. McCartney. Issue spotting in legal cases. In *Proceedings of the Fourth International Conference on Artificial Intelligence and Law*, Amsterdam, pages 245–253, 1993.

8. E. Domeshek. What Abby cares about. In *Proceedings of the Workshop on Case-Based Reasoning*, pages 13–24, 1991.

9. M. P. Evett, J. A. Hendler, and L. Spector. Parallel knowledge representation on the Connection Machine. *Journal of Parallel and Distributed Computing*, 22:168–184, 1994.

10. B. Falkenhainer, K. D. Forbus, and D. Gentner. The structure-mapping engine: Algorithm and examples. *Artificial Intelligence*, 41:1–63, 1990.

11. M. R. Garey and D. S. Johnson. *Computers and intractability*. W. H. Freeman and Company, New York, 1979.

12. K. J. Hammond. Case-based planning: A framework for planning from experience. *Cognitive Science*, 14:384–443, 1990.

13. K. J. Holyoak and P. R. Thagard. Analogical mapping by constraint satisfaction. *Cognitive Science*, pages 295–355, 1989.

14. S. Kambhampati and J. A. Hendler. A validation-structure-based theory of plan modification and reuse. *Artificial Intelligence*, 55:193–258, 1992.

15. B. P. Kettler. *Case-based Planning with a High Performance Parallel Memory*. Doctoral dissertation, University of Maryland at College Park, Dept. of Computer Science, November 1995. Technical Report CS-TR-3561.

16. B. P. Kettler, J. A. Hendler, W. A. Andersen, and M. P. Evett. Massively parallel support for case-based planning. *IEEE Expert*, pages 8–14, Feb. 1994.

17. J. L. Kolodner. *Case-Based Reasoning*. Morgan Kaufmann Publishers, San Mateo, California, 1993.

18. J. L. Kolodner and R. Thau. Design and implementation of a case memory. Technical Report RL88-1, Thinking Machines Corporation, Cambridge, Mass., Aug. 1988.

19. R. McCartney. Episodic cases and real-time performance in a case-based planning system. *Expert Systems with Applications*, 6:9–22, 1993.

20. R. McCartney and K. E. Sanders. The case for cases: a call for purity in case-based reasoning. In *Proceedings of the AAAI Symposium on Case-based Reasoning*, pages 12–16, 1990.

21. N. J. Nilsson. *Principles of Artificial Intelligence*. Morgan Kaufman, San Mateo, California, 1980.

22. K. E. Sanders. Chiron: planning in an open-textured domain. Technical Report 94-38, Computer Science Department, Brown University, 1994. (PhD Thesis).

23. K. Stoffel, M. G. Taylor, and J. A. Hendler. Efficient management for very large ontologies. In *Fifteenth National Conference on Artificial Intelligence (AAAI 97)*, page (submitted), 1997.

24. P. R. Thagard, K. J. Holyoak, C. Nelson, and D. Gochfeld. Analog retrieval by constraint satisfaction. *Artificial Intelligence*, 46:259–310, 1990.

The Evaluation of a Hierarchical Case Representation Using Context Guided Retrieval

Ian Watson[†] & Srinath Perera[*]

[†]AI-CBR, Bridgewater Building, University of Salford, Salford, M5 4WT, UK

[*]Department of Building Economics, University of Moratua, Moratua, Sri Lanka

{i.d.watson | r.s.perera}@surveying.salford.ac.uk

Abstract. This paper presents the results of the comparison of the performance of a hierarchical case representation using a context guided retrieval method against that of a simpler flat file representation using standard nearest neighbour retrieval. The estimation of the construction costs of light industrial warehouse buildings is used as the test domain. Each case comprises approximately 400 features. These are structured into a hierarchical case representation that holds more general contextual features at its top and specific building elements at its leaves. A modified nearest neighbour retrieval algorithm is used that is guided by contextual similarity. Problems are decomposed into sub-problems and solutions recomposed into a final solution. The comparative results show that the context guided retrieval method using the hierarchical case representation out performs the simple flat file representation and standard nearest neighbour retrieval.

Keywords Context Guided Retrieval, Hierarchical Case-Representation

1. Introduction

Representing cases as a set of constituent pieces [Barletta & Mark, 1988, Macedo et al., 1996], snippets [Kolodner, 1988; Redmond, 1990; Sycara & Navinchandra, 1991] or footprints [Veloso, 1992; Bento et al., 1994], instead of as a single large entity, has long been proposed as a way of improving the effectiveness of a CBR system. These parts, when represented as separate structured cases, can be represented, retrieved and recomposed separately to create new solutions [Flemming, 1994; Maher & Balchandran, 1994; Bartsch-Sporl, 1995; Hunt & Miles, 1995]. Some systems, for example, CADSYN, explicitly take into account the context of a snippet or sub-problem to reduced constraint problems when recomposing solutions [Maher & Zhang, 1991].

Many successful CBR systems use relatively simple case representations of attribute-value pairs stored in flat files or record structures similar to those of a conventional database. There are good reasons for this. A primary one is, that for many commercial applications, the knowledge engineering effort required to create case-bases must be kept to a minimum. These case representations may be characterised as being *knowledge-poor*. That is they do not contain many (or any) structures that describe the relationships or constraints between case features. However, these case representations usually describe relatively simple cases with few indexed features, perhaps in the order of ten to twenty indexed features.

As the number of indexed case features increases (i.e., the number of features that are predictive of a case's solution or outcome) the utility of this knowledge-poor approach reduces. As the problem space increases, from say a 20 dimensional space to a 200 dimensional space it becomes statistically less likely that a close matching case will exist. Thus, a retrieve and propose CBR system (i.e., one without adaptation) may be proposing a relatively distant solution. If adaptation is used, the adaptation effort or distance will increase correspondingly, possibly reducing the accuracy or utility of the solution. This is illustrated in the two figures below, after Leake [p8, 1996]. Figure 1, shows, on the left, a relatively small problem space and assumes a similar sized solution space. Notice that the retrieval distance (the arrow labelled R) and the adaptation distance (the arrow labelled A) are both quite short. As the size of the problem space increases (shown on the right) the retrieval and adaptation distances may increase, as shown by the lengths of the arrows.

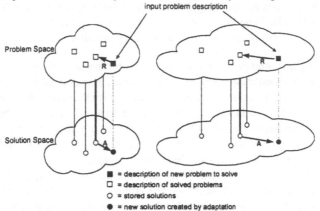

Figure 1. Small and Large Problem & Solution Spaces, after Leake [p.8, 1996]

Moreover, as has been reported by Maher et al. [1995] there is often an inverse relationship between the number of cases in a case-base and the number of indexed features in the cases. This is because it often harder to collect a few large cases than it is to collect hundreds of small cases. Thus, case coverage is often likely to be lower in a large problem space than in a small problem space. This may cause the case-base to return a mediocre match that will require considerable adaptation, resulting in poorer solutions. A potential solution to this problem is the *divide and conquer* approach. This suggests that, where suitable, a large problem is divided into several smaller sub-problems, each of which can be solved separately using CBR. The sub-solutions can then be combined to produce an accurate solution to the entire problem [Maher & Zhang, 1991]. A key assumption for this approach is that the sub-problems are not highly constrained one upon the other, so that they can be solved independently (i.e., that the problem can be sensibly decomposed and the solution recomposed). This approach may be visualised as in Figure 2.

The advantage of this approach is that each individual sub-problem is represented by a case-base that is significantly smaller (in terms of problem and solution space size) than if the whole problem were represented by a single case-base. Because each sub-problem space has fewer case features, the theory predicts, that each individual sub-case retrieval distance will be shorter than for the un-decomposed problem. Therefore, the adaptation distance will be shorter and a better sub-solution will be generated. Assuming there are no conflicting constraints, the recomposition of sub-solutions will produce a better solution than would have been obtained by using a single large case-base. One way that has been suggested to reduce constraint problems with solution recomposition is to use contextual information to guide retrieval [Hammond, 1986; Hennessy & Hinkle, 1992; Kolodner, 1993; Maher et al., 1995; Marir & Watson, 1995; Ram & Francis, 1996]. The argument being, that if cases share similar contexts, this will reduce constraint problems during solution recomposition.

The purpose of the study presented in this paper was to quantitatively assess the accuracy of a CBR system that uses a hierarchical case representation and context-guided retrieval to decompose a complex problem and recompose a solution. The accuracy of this complex case representation and retrieval technique is compared to that of a simple flat record of attribute-value pairs using a standard nearest neighbour retrieval algorithm. The evaluation will show that the more complex representation and retrieval method out performs the simpler representation, thereby justifying the knowledge engineering and programming effort put into it.

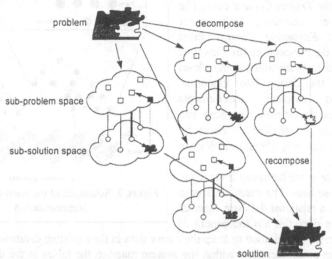

Figure 2. Problem Decomposition and Solution Recomposition

2. The Problem Domain

For this study we selected the estimation of the construction costs of light industrial warehousing as a suitable domain. These buildings are used as storage and distribution warehouses, as low cost retail buildings, and as light industrial factory units. They were suitable for this study for the following reasons:

- Warehouses are strictly functional buildings with aesthetic issues being very secondary (i.e., they rarely win design prizes). Consequently, cost is a more important issue than for most other building types.
- They are constructed using steel frames that are produced in standard sizes along with many other components (e.g., roofing sheets) that are also produced in standard sizes.
- The buildings are structurally fairly simple and consequently the constraints between different building elements are small. This therefore suggested that divided and conquer would be appropriate.
- The cost of a building is derived directly from the cost of its sub-assemblies. Thus, the problem decomposes naturally. This is supported by the way that cost estimators usually work. They calculate the cost of each sub-assembly and sum them to obtain a total cost.
- Finally, we had access to a cost estimating computer system for this building type. This has significant methodological importance and will be discussed later.

3. The Case Representation

The system, called NIRMANI, was implemented in ART*Enterprise, from BrightWare, on Windows 95 [Watson & Perera, 1995]. The environment provides an object-oriented knowledge-based development environment, that supports objects, rules (a forward chaining Rete algorithm), a procedural programming environment, case-based reasoning (nearest neighbour), a GUI builder, and an ODBC database interface [Watson, 1997]. Representing cases hierarchically is a popular approach to the use and reuse of sub-cases (e.g., Redmond, 1990; Goel, 1994; Aha & Branting, 1995). A building in NIRMANI is a meta-case, consisting of a hierarchy of cases and sub-cases. At the top of the hierarchy is the *Project Context* case. The second level contains *Architectural Context* and *Estimating Context* cases representing the perspectives (or views) of architects and cost estimators. A third level decomposes the design into functional spaces and aesthetic requirements hierarchies and the estimating problem into an industry standard elemental classification hierarchy [Perera & Watson 1996].

Each node in the hierarchy is stored in a separate case-base. The cases are stored as records in a relational database external to the system since this has the benefit of

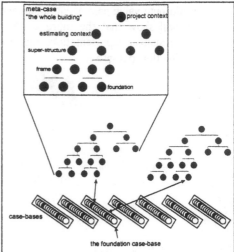

Figure 3. Schematic of the Hierarchical Case Representation

allowing a design organisation to keep their case data in their existing databases [Brown et al., 1995]. An object hierarchy within the system maps to the tables in the database and cases are presented (when required) as instances. Cases contain attribute-value pairs as case features.

A *Project Context* case describes the environment within which the project was carried out (features such as the type of building, its intended function, gross internal floor area (GIFA), the site conditions, and other features common to the project context). The second level cases (architectural and estimating) describe the context of the sub-problems. The system prefers to retrieve sub-cases with similar contexts (i.e., with similar parents in the hierarchy) in order to reduce problems of case adaptation and solution recomposition due to contextual dissimilarity.

	Attribute	Value(s)	Data Type
1.	Case_No	Value per project	cat-nir:capitols
2.	Number-key	Unique integer value per case per case-base	cat:integer-or-nil
3.	Source_cases	List of cases	default
4.	Name_of_Project	Text	default
5.	Site_Address	Text	default
6.	Client	Text	default
7.	Client_Address	Text	default
8.	Type_of_warehouse	Storage Distribution Retail	catnl:wh-type
9.	Type_of_occupier	Owner occupier Tenant occupier Developer	catnl:occupier
...	...	...	...
66.	Structural_Engineer	Text	default
67.	Services_Engineer	Text	default
68.	Other_Consultants	Text	default
69.	Contractor	Text	default
70.	Contractor_Address	Text	default

Table 1. A Selection of Attributes from the Project Context Case Definition

The interface of NIRMANI allows cases to be viewed as attribute-value pairs along with CAD drawings and other multimedia elements. It supports case comparison using a tabulated form (similar to a spreadsheet).

4. Retrieval

NIRMANI provides a variety of retrieval methods, of which only two are compared in this paper. Full details of these retrieval methods can be found in Perera & Watson [1996]. ART*Enterprise uses a nearest neighbour algorithm with weighted features. Its programming environment gives the developer considerable control of the algorithm making it a good environment to explore different retrieval strategies. The two strategies compared in this paper are described below.

4.1 Default Retrieval

This is essentially standard nearest neighbour retrieval. The user is allowed to select which features are indexed. These will usually be the majority of the features in the Project Context case (except the construction cost) plus some other significant features from other aspects of the building. For example, the user may want a glazed curtain wall on the front elevation of the building but have no definite views or wishes as to the roofing type. The user may set weights on features reflecting their relative importance to them. In default retrieval an index is prepared dynamically at run-time for those case features entered by the user. Feature comparison is carried out as in normal nearest neighbour retrieval. A normalised match score for each entire meta-case is calculated and the highest ranking cases are then presented to the user. Only an entire meta-case can then be selected for adaptation.

4.2 Context Guided Retrieval

Context guided retrieval proceeds in series of recursive steps down the hierarchy of the case representation. In the first step, the features of the *Project Context* case (at the top of the hierarchy) are used to retrieve similar *Project Context* cases from the *Project Context* case-base. This is done using ART*E's standard nearest neighbour algorithm. In the second step, retrieval

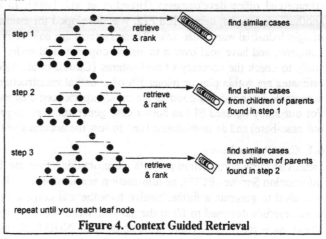

Figure 4. Context Guided Retrieval

of cases from the *estimating* or *architectural* case-bases (the next nodes down the hierarchy) is restricted to those cases that are the children of the cases found similar in the first retrieval step. That is, retrieval is limited to those sub-cases that share similar project contexts (i.e., similar parents). This process is repeated all the way down the hierarchy. Retrieval at each level is restricted to those cases in a case-base that have similar parents.

This process reduces the search space by enforcing contextual similarity. However, if a close enough match cannot be found at any level (this is more likely to occur at leaf nodes since the number of cases included in the search may reduce at each level) then the contextual guiding can be relaxed. This relaxation is achieved by back tracking up the hierarchy and reducing the threshold at which similarity is judged acceptable for the parent case. This will increase the number of cases allowed into the children's retrieval process. This relaxation can proceed all the way to zero, if necessary, allowing retrieval from all cases in a child's case-base, thus removing the context guidance completely.

5. Adaptation

Cases are ranked and presented to the user. Users are allowed to select cases and case features for adaptation. Note that using the default retrieval method only sub-cases from one meta-case can be used for adaptation. Whereas, for context guided retrieval, sub-cases from different meta-cases with a similar context can be used. Moreover, using context guided retrieval adaptation can occur at the elemental unit level of detail, whereas for the default retrieval adaptation occurs at the level of the project context case (i.e., only the total estimated construction cost is adapted). A modification knowledge-base, containing a set of rules, functions and procedures provides the adaptation. In general, adaptation is in the form of parameter adjustment through interpolation. For example, if a retrieved case has the feature *"floor finishes"* at a cost of *"£12,000"* with a GIFA of *"2000m^2"*, then the adaptation function will calculate a *rate* for floor finishes of *"£6 per m^2"*. This rate can then be applied to a new case with a different GIFA but a similar specification for floor finishes.

6. Methodology

In the 1980s and early 1990s Salford University, in collaboration with the Royal Institution of Chartered Surveyors (the RICS is the professional institution for cost estimators in the UK), developed several knowledge-based construction cost estimation systems. The first of these, a rule-based system called ELSIE, could estimate the construction costs of commercial office developments [Brandon et al., 1988]. In a subsequent development another rule-based system, called ELI, was developed for estimating the construction costs of light industrial warehouse units. These systems are sold commercially, by a joint venture company, and have sold over a thousand copies world-wide. The RICS commissioned a study to check the accuracy of the systems [Castell et al., 1992], which found that their estimates are within plus or minus 5% of eventual construction costs. This is well within acceptable error and is a good as the most experienced cost estimators [Skitmore, 1990]. For our study we used ELI as both a case generator (i.e., to produce projects to populate our case-base) and as an evaluator (i.e., to test the accuracy of the CBR systems).

6.1 Case Acquisition

Details of thirty construction projects were obtained from the Building Construction Cost Information Service (BCIS), an information service for the UK construction industry. ELI was used to generate a further twelve hypothetical construction projects. These projects were carefully designed to fill in the gaps between the thirty real projects from the BCIS. These were then entered into a database that NIRMANI used for its case data. The projects generated by ELI were carefully designed so as to create a case-base with an even case distribution. Thus, projects were created which had a variety of functions (e.g., dry goods distribution warehouses, cold storage warehouses, flammable goods storage and distribution, retail warehouses, etc.). The projects varied in size consistently in graduations of approximately 100 m^2, from 1,500 m^2 to 3,500 m^2. In addition, a range of construction complexity with additional features, such as office space, were included. We recognise that this case-base is artificial. We felt that a well distributed case-base should be analysed before attempting a randomly distributed one.

6.2 Evaluation

Evaluation of the accuracy of NIRMANI using the two retrieval techniques described above was done in three ways.

1. Cases with a known construction cost that were in NIRMANI's case-base were removed and used as target cases (i.e., as a new problem to solve). This would remove a known case from the well-distributed case-base and force NIRMANI to solve the problem using neighbouring cases. This test was performed five times.

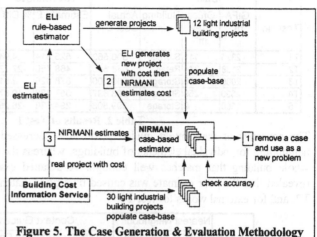

Figure 5. The Case Generation & Evaluation Methodology

2. New projects (i.e., ones that NIRMANI had never seen) were developed by ELI and hence we new ELI's estimation of their construction cost. These were then presented to NIRMANI as new problems for it to estimate. This test was performed ten times.

3. Finally, as a test of both ELI's and NIRMANI's accuracy, real projects (with known costs) were obtained from the Building Cost Information Service and given to ELI and NIRMANI to solve. This acted as an independent check on the accuracy of both systems.

These evaluation methods are shown schematically in Figure 5. The results from the evaluation tests were statistically analysed using the coefficient of variation method. This technique is widely used as the most common criteria for the determination of the accuracy of an estimating method or model [McCaffer, 1975]. CV is defined as:

$$CV = \frac{\text{Standard Deviation of Residuals } (S_r)}{\text{Mean Cost of All Schemes - Actual } (M_a)}$$

Thus, CV can be termed as the estimating error where: *accuracy = 1 - % estimating error* and therefore: *accuracy = 100 - CV*

7. Results

A summary of the tests is given below and shown in Figure 6. Exactly the same feature weightings were used for both the NN retrieval and the context guided retrieval.

7.1 Test 1

For test 1 a case was removed from NIRMANI's case-base and used a target case. The results of the five tests are summarised in Table 2. Two major studies on the accuracy of estimation in the construction industry revealed that an accuracy ranging from ± 15% to ± 20% [Ashworth & Skitmore, 1983] and ± 8% to ± 15% [Skitmore et. al., 1990] are acceptable for early stage estimating of construction costs. Therefore, all the estimates using context guided retrieval were well within acceptable error. However, the flat representation using standard nearest neighbour failed in tests T2 and T5 (with context guided retrieval the percentage difference was also considerably greater for these two).

This was because the cases in these two tests do not have close nearest neighbours within NIRMANI's case-base.

Test No	Data				NN Retrieval		Context Guided NN	
	GIFA m^2	Office Area m^2	Building Use	Actual Cost £	Estimate £	% Diff.	Estimate £	% Diff
T1	2325	111	Storage	500,562	525,314	4.94	499,539	-0.20
T2	2138	244	Retail	648,500	468,750	-27.72	603,825	-6.89
T3	2000	100	Storage	660,100	678,628	2.81	663,129	0.46
T4	2590	250	Storage	593,697	657,029	10.67	592,075	-0.27
T5	1500	0	Storage	399,506	294,636	-26.25	421,566	5.52

Table 2. Results of Test 1

The accuracy of the context guided retrieval is increased because it can find nearest neighbours for individual elements of buildings, whereas the other technique cannot find a whole building that matches well enough. A detailed examination of these two tests revealed that the poor estimate was caused by a poor match for the substructure, for test T2, and for external works for test T5.

Test No	Nearest Neighbour		Context Guided NN	
	% Diff.	Contributor	% Diff.	Contributing Cases
T1	4.94	WHS_A3	-0.20	*WHS_A2*3*, WHS_A3*2
T2	-27.72	WHS_A3	-6.89	*WHS_T1*, WHD_GG1, WHS_A4, WHS_A1*2, WHS_A2
T3	2.81	WHS_T2	0.46	*WHS_T2*5*
T4	10.67	WHS_C2	-0.27	*WHS_C2*3*, WHS_C3*2
T5	-26.25	WHS_A4	5.52	*WHS_E1*, WHS_A4, WHS_A2, WHS_T2, WHS_G1, WHD_K1,

Table 3. Cases Contributing to a Solution for Test 1

For the standard nearest neighbour retrieval only one entire meta-case can contribute to the solution. For context guided retrieval parts of different meta-cases can contribute. In Table 3, the underlined italic case reference number contributed most to the solution.

7.2 Test 2

For test 2, ELI was used to generate ten new projects and to estimate their construction costs. NIRMANI was then given the same projects to estimate.

Test No.	Data			ELI	Nearest Neighbour		Context Guided NN	
	GIFA m^2	Office Area m^2	Building Use	Estimate £s	Estimate £s	% Diff.	Estimate £s	% Diff.
CS1	1,500	75	Storage	329,600	320,773	-2.68	322,177	-2.25
CS2	1,750	100	Storage	388,500	430,783	10.88	391,598	0.80
CS3	2,000	125	Storage	486,600	477,114	-1.95	488,709	0.43
CS4	2,000	200	Retail	575,600	614,457	6.75	581,639	1.05
CS5	2,250	175	Storage	607,400	474,812	-21.83	606,749	-0.11
CS6	2,500	200	Storage	663,200	602,832	-9.10	661,294	-0.29
CS7	2,750	200	Storage	1,221,100	809,090	-33.74	1,233,125	0.98
CS8	3,000	250	Retail	825,100	903,321	9.48	809,475	-1.89
CS9	3,250	300	Retail	898,400	970,686	8.05	910,048	1.30
CS10	1,250	50	Distribution	363,700	326,330	-10.27	369,652	1.64

Table 4 Results of Test 2

This test gave consistently similar estimates with a maximum percentage difference of -2.25% for context guided retrieval. However, the standard nearest neighbour retrieval was more inconsistent, ranging from 10.88% to -33.74%.

Test No.	Nearest Neighbour		Context Guided NN	
	% Diff.	Contributor	% Diff.	Contributors
CS1	-2.68	WHS_A4	-2.25	*WHS_A4*5*, WHS_F1, WHS_W1
CS2	10.88	WHS_T2	0.80	*WHS_A4*4*, WHS_T2*3, WHS_D1*2
CS3	-1.95	WHS_T1	0.43	*WHS_T1*3*, WHS_T2, WHR_B1, WHS_A3*2, WHR_BB1*2
CS4	6.75	WHR_BB1	1.05	*WHR_BB1*4*, WHR_M1, WHS_A4, WHS_A3
CS5	-21.83	WHS_A3	-0.11	*WHS_X1*3*, WHS_A1, WHS_A3, WHS_T3
CS6	-9.10	WHS_T4	-0.29	*WHS_T4*3*, WHS_C1, WHS_C5, WHS_D1
CS7	-33.74	WHS_C2	0.98	*WHS_AA1*2*, WHS_C2*4, WHR_BB1, WHS_W1
CS8	9.48	WHR_N1	-1.89	*WHR_N1*3*, WHR_Q1*2, WHR_FF1, WHR_V1
CS9	8.05	WHR_N1	1.30	*WHR_N1*2*, WHR_Z1, WHR_M1, WHS_AA1, WHS_W1
CS10	-10.27	WHD_HH1	1.64	*WHD_HH1*3*, WHR_V1, WHS_W1*2, WHS_T2*2

Table 5. Cases Contributing to a Solution For Test 2

7.3 Statistical Analysis

The results from test 1 and 2 were combined (i.e., n = 15)and are summarised in Table 6.

Statistic	BCIS or ELI	Nearest Neighbour				Context Guided NN		
	$Cost/m^2$	$Cost/m^2$	Diff. Absolute	% Diff. Absolute		$Cost/m^2$	Diff. Absolute	% Diff. Absolute
Mean	275.92	256.51	37.58	12.47		276.02	4.53	1.61
Stan Dev	55.09806	40.93379	37.559007	10.008		56.080815	7.192149	1.993
Coefficient of Variation (CV)			14.090187				2.095961	
T Test		0.282962				0.9958138		
Co-relation coefficient		0.502196				0.9917861		
Estimating Accuracy			85.909813				97.904034	

Table 6. Summary of Results from Tests 1 & 2

Since the sample size was less than 30 (i.e., n = 15), the Students' *t* Test was used for statistical analysis. Three tests were carried out. All were carried out initially for 95% confidence limits, which is accepted as providing statistically significant results.

1. *Hypothesis Test 1 (HT 1)* The context guided retrieval achieves a mean accuracy of 98% (i.e. 2% error in estimating). In statistical terms this means hypothesising a population mean of 2% (μ = 2 null hypothesis. The statistical aim of the test is to prove that μ = 2 is not possible. H_O has to be accepted, because the hypothesis μ = 2, or estimating accuracy EA_N = 98%, cannot be disapproved at a 95% level of confidence.

2. *Hypothesis Test 2 (HT 2)* The same test as HT 1 was carried out to check if the standard nearest neighbour retrieval could achieve a mean accuracy of 86% (i.e. 14% error in estimating). The test hypothesis was, H_O: μ = 14 Null hypothesis. H_O has to be accepted, because the hypothesis μ = 14 or estimating accuracy EA_F = 86% cannot be disapproved at a 95% level of confidence.

3. *Hypothesis Test 3 (HT 3)* The aim of this test is to determine whether the results obtained for the standard nearest neighbour and context guided retrieval represent significantly different approaches. In statistical terms this involve testing whether the test samples could be from the same population. In order to achieve these results a "Paired Sample Student' *t* Test" was carried out. The test hypothesis was as follows: H_0: $\mu = 0$ (The mean of the difference between the two techniques is zero). The test was repeated for the differences in estimated values (absolute) obtained from Table 6. T-Tests were carried out as for HT 1 for a 95% level of confidence. This found that H_0 could not be rejected at 95% confidence levels. However, at 90% confidence levels H_0 could be rejected.

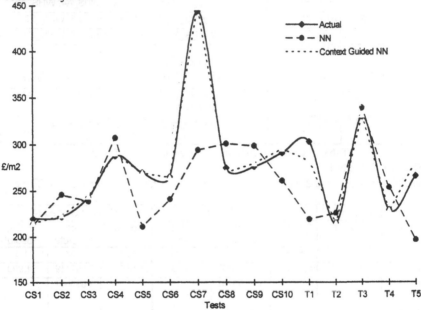

Figure 6. Summary of Test Results

8. Conclusion

The systematic evaluation of a CBR system is very difficult because such systems are typically very complex with many interacting components [Santamaria & Ram, 1996]. Consequently, this study has simplified the performance of our system down to a single quantifiable measure - estimating accuracy. We accept that this measure is a simplification of the performance of our system. Nonetheless, the evaluation demonstrates that the context guided retrieval method out performs that of the simpler flat-file nearest neighbour method. The only times that the simpler technique performed acceptably were when a problem happened to find a close near neighbour within the case-base. When the simpler technique performed badly it was because it was unable to find a complete matching case and was forced to use the closest case that matched on a subset of features. Conversely, when the context guided retrieval method significantly out performs the simpler technique it is because it has composed a solution from many cases. Thus, when a close near neighbour cannot be found the divide and conquer approach, using context guided retrieval, performs better as the theory predicts. It is interesting to note that that the simpler technique usually recognises which case can contribute most to solution, but, by being unable to use snippets from other cases as well, its accuracy is reduced.

We recognise that this has been a fairly limited study, with a small sample size. We have shown that for our tests the context guided retrieval (HT 1) was accurate. However, there was only a 90% confidence that this technique was statistically different from standard nearest neighbour retrieval (HT 3). Because of the size of each meta-case (i.e., approx. 400 case features) each single evaluation test took one day to perform. Consequently, the number of tests was limited and therefore it would be unwise to rely too heavily on the simple statistical analysis performed here. However, the results are indicative and support the view that divide and conquer, through problem decomposition and solution recomposition, is an effective method of solving problems with large complex cases. The context guided retrieval method evaluated here may also be a useful way of reducing the problems of conflicting constraints between parts of the solution.

The fact that the case-base was populated with an evenly distributed set of cases may have skewed our results. Although from the results it would appear that this should skew the results in favour of the simpler method. Since it performs better when a close good match can be found, one would expect it to perform more erratically with a more unevenly distributed case-base. Finally, it was interesting to see that the case-based estimator performed as well as the rule-based estimation system, with a mean error of 2%. The rule-based estimator took over three person years to implement, whilst the case-based estimator took less than half that time. This further supports the many findings that show that CBR systems can be implemented quicker than their rule-based counterparts [Simoudis & Miller, 1991; Mark et al., 1996].

9. References

Aha, D., & Branting, K. (1995). Stratified Case-Based Reasoning: Reusing Hierarchical Problem Solving Episodes. In, *Proceedings of the 13th International Joint Conference on Artificial Intelligence, IJCAI-95*, pp.384-390. IJCAI, Menlo Park, Calif., US.

Ashworth, A., & Skitmore, R.M. (1982), Accuracy in Estimating. *The Chartered Institute of Building*, Occasional Paper No. 27.

Barletta, R., & Mark, W. (1988). Breaking Cases into Pieces. In, *Proceedings of the DARPA Case-Based Reasoning Workshop*, Kolodner, J.L., (Ed.), Morgan Kaufmann, Calif., US.

Bartsch-Sporl, B. (1995), Towards the Integration of Case-Based, Schema-Based and Model-Based Reasoning for Supporting Complex Design Tasks. In, *Case-Based Reasoning Research & Development - ICCBR '95*, Veloso, M., & Aamodt, A. (Eds.), pp. 145 - 156, Springer-Verlag, Berlin.

Bento, C., Macedo, L., & Costa, E. (1994). RECIDE - Reasoning with Cases Imperfectly Described and Explained. In, Proceeding of the 2nd European Workshop on Case-Based Reasoning.

Brandon, P., Basden, A., Hamilton, I., & Stockley, J. (1988). *The Strategic Planning of Construction Projects*, RICS Publications, London, UK.

Brown, M., Watson, I., & Filer, N. (1995). Separating the cases from the data: Towards more flexible case-based reasoning. In, *Case-Based Reasoning Research and Development*, Veloso, M., & Aamodt, A. (Eds.), Lecture Notes in Artificial Intelligence 1010, Springer-Verlag, Berlin.

Castell, A.M., Basden, A., Erdos, G., Barrows, P., & Brandon, P.S. (1992). Knowledge Based Systems In Use: A Case Study. In, *Proceedings of the 12th. Annual Conference of the British Computer Society Specialist Group on Expert Systems*. Cambridge University Press, Cambridge, UK.

Flemming, U., (1994). Case-based design in the SEED system,. *Automation in Construction*, 3: pp.123-133, Elsevier Science B.V.

Goel, A., Ali, K., Donnellan, M., Garza, A., & Callantine, T. (1994). Multistrategy Adaptive Navigational Path Planning. *IEEE Expert*, 9(6): pp.57-65

Hammond, K.J. (1986), CHEF: A model of case-based planning. In, *Proc. American Association for Artificial Intelligence, AAAI-86*, Philadelphia, PA, US.

Hennessy, D., & Hinkle, D. (1992), Applying Case-Based Reasoning to Autoclave Loading, *IEEE Exper,t* 7(5): pp.21-26.

Hunt, J., & Miles, R. (1995), Towards an Intelligent Architectural Design Aid. *Expert Systems*, 12(3): pp.209-218.

Kolodner, J.L. (1988). Retrieving events from a case memory: A parallel implementation. In, *Proceedings of the DARPA Case-Based Reasoning Workshop*, Kolodner, J.L. (Ed.), Morgan Kaufmann, Calif., US.

Kolodner, J.L. (1993), *Case-Based Reasoning*. Morgan Kaufmann Publishers Inc., CA, US.

Leake, D.B., (1996). CBR in Context: The Present and Future. In, *Case-Based Reasoning: Experiences, Lessons, & Future Directions*, Leake, D.B. (Ed.). AAAI Press / The MIT Press, Menlo Park, Calif., US.

Macedo, L., Pereira, F.C., Grilo, C., & Cardoso, A. (1996). Plans as Structured Networks of Hierarchically and Temporally Related Case Pieces. In, *Advances in Case-Based Reasoning*, Smith, I., & Faltings, B. (Eds.), Lecture Notes in Artificial Intelligence 1168, Springer-Verlag, Berlin.

Maher, M.L., & Balachandran, B. (1994). Flexible Retrieval Strategies for Case-Based Design. In, *Artificial Intelligence in Design '94*, Gero, J.S., & Sudweeks, F. (Eds.), pp.163-180, Kluwer Academic Publishers, Netherlands.

Maher, M.L., Balachandran, M.B., & Zhang, D.M. (1995). *Case-Based Reasoning in Design*. Lawrence Erlbaum Associates, US.

Maher, M.L. & Zhang, D.M. (1991). CADSYN: using case and decomposition knowledge for design synthesis. In, *Artificial Intelligence in Design*, Gero, J.S. (Ed.), Butterworth-Heinmann. Oxford. UK.

Marir, F., & Watson, I. (1995), Representing and Indexing Building Refurbishment Cases for Multiple Retrieval of Adaptable Pieces of Cases. In, *Case-Based Reasoning Research & Development - ICCBR '95*, Veloso, M., and Aamodt, A. (Eds.), pp.55 - 66, Springer-Verlag, Berlin.

Mark, W., Simoudis, E., & Hinkle, D. (1996). Case-Based Reasoning: Expectations and Results. In, *Case-Based Reasoning: Experiences, Lessons, & Future Directions*, Leake, D.B. (Ed.). AAAI Press / The MIT Press, Menlo Park, Calif., US.

Perera, R.S., and Watson, I.D. (1996). Multi-Agent Collaborative Case-Based Estimating and Design in NIRMANI: Organising a Multi-Perspective Case Memory. In, *Information Processing in Civil and Structural Engineering Design*, pp.53-64, Kumar, B. (Ed.), Civil-Comp Press, Scotland.

Ram, A., & Francis, A.G. (1996). Multi-plan Retrieval and Adaptation in an Experience-Based Agent. In, *Case-Based Reasoning: Experiences, Lessons, & Future Directions*, Leake, D.B. (Ed.). AAAI Press / The MIT Press, Menlo Park, Calif., US.

Redmond, M. (1990). Distributed Cases for Case-Based Reasoning: Facilitating Use of Multiple Cases. In, *Proceedings of AAAI*.

Santamaria, J.C., & Ram, A. (1996). Systematic Evaluation of Design Decisions in Case-Based Reasoning Systems. In, *Case-Based Reasoning: Experiences, Lessons, & Future Directions*, Leake, D.B. (Ed.). AAAI Press / The MIT Press, Menlo Park, Calif., US.

Simoudis, E. & Miller, J.S. (1991). The Application of CBR to Help Desk Applications. In, *Proceedings of the DARPA Workshop on Case-Based Reasoning*, Bareiss R. (Ed.). Morgan Kaufmann, San Francisco, Calif., US.

Sycara, K.P. & Navinchandra D. (1991). Influences: A Thematic Abstraction for Creative Use of Multiple Cases . In, *Proceedings of the DARPA Case-Based Reasoning Workshop*, Bareiss, E.R., Morgan Kaufmann, Calif., US.

Veloso, M.M. (1992). *Learning by analogical reasoning in general problem solving*. Carnegie Mellon University, School of Computer Science Technical Report no. CMU-CS-92-174.

Watson, I. (1997). *Applying Case-Based Reasoning*. Morgan Kaufmann, CA, USA (forthcoming).

Watson, I., and Perera, R.S. (1995). NIRMANI: A Case-Based Expert System for Integrated Design & Estimating. In, *Applications and Innovations in Expert Systems III*, pp.335-348, Macintosh, A. and Cooper, C. (Eds.). SGES Publications, UK.

10. Acknowledgements

The authors would like to acknowledge the Association of Commonwealth Universities, the University of Moratuwa, Sri Lanka, and EPSRC, whose grants: GR/J42496, GR/J43660 and GR/L16330, helped support this work.

Refining Conversational Case Libraries

David W. Aha and Leonard A. Breslow

Navy Center for Applied Research in Artificial Intelligence
Naval Research Laboratory, Washington, DC 20375 USA
{aha,breslow}@aic.nrl.navy.mil

Abstract. Conversational case-based reasoning (CBR) shells (e.g., Inference's *CBR Express*) are commercially successful tools for supporting the development of help desk and related applications. In contrast to rule-based expert systems, they capture knowledge as cases rather than more problematic rules, and they can be incrementally extended. However, rather than eliminate the knowledge engineering bottleneck, they refocus it on *case engineering*, the task of carefully authoring cases according to library design guidelines to ensure good performance. Designing complex libraries according to these guidelines is difficult; software is needed to assist users with case authoring. We describe an approach for revising case libraries according to design guidelines, its implementation in CLIRE, and empirical results showing that, under some conditions, this approach can improve conversational CBR performance.

1 Introduction

Now that CBR shells have attained commercial viability, some researchers have begun addressing the practical problem of assisting case authors with the daunting task of constructing complex libraries (e.g., Kitano et al., 1993; Heider et al., 1997). Contrary to some claims, CBR systems do not, in fact, eliminate the need for knowledge engineering required by expert systems. Instead, they refocus knowledge extraction efforts from abstracting expertise to specifying cases. This *case engineering* process requires skill, and is responsible for the growing business of CBR consultancy; ambitious clients, given guidelines for designing case libraries, often eventually find that the complexity of their large libraries prevents them from applying these guidelines.

This is especially true for a specific popular breed of commercial CBR shells that we refer to as *conversational CBR* (CCBR) systems. These systems, exemplified by Inference's CBR EXPRESS, have grabbed a large share of the market for automated help desk support tools. Their popularity stems, in part, from their ability to incrementally and interactively acquire *queries* (i.e., unsolved case descriptions) describing customer problems while imposing few a priori restrictions on the query's information content and internal sequencing. Furthermore, they provide an enormous benefit; system users (e.g., help desk and call center personnel) need only guide customers through a dynamically determined set of questions, but need not be experts on the problem solving task itself.

This approach allows potential solutions, stored in cases whose descriptions are highly similar to the query, to be offered at any time during a customer-user *conversation*.[1]

Unfortunately, this same flexibility also complicates the case engineering task; it introduces the problem of deciding which questions and cases to present to the user at each point during a conversation. Poor choices for questions will prevent useful further diagnosis of the customer's problem, while poor choices for cases will prevent a good solution from being retrieved. In this context, good guidelines for designing cases are crucial for the library engineer, but they can be large in number (e.g., Inference (1995) lists 46 guidelines for building CCBR libraries using CBR EXPRESS) and require substantial expertise to apply correctly. Novice case engineers building client libraries frequently incur high costs in either time (i.e., a long learning curve) or capital (i.e., consultant fees).

We advocate an alternative solution: software that assists case authors by revising case libraries to improve their conformance with design guidelines. If effective, this should reduce the time required to generate high-performance case libraries. Towards this goal, this paper describes an example of this approach, implemented in a system named CLIRE (Case LIbrary REvisor), and its evaluation on three case libraries. Our evidence suggests that CLIRE, which uses simple machine learning techniques to revise case libraries, can improve the performance (i.e., precision and efficiency) of conversational case libraries.

Section 2 describes the CCBR context in more detail, including our performance measures. Section 3 then outlines our approach for revising cases and its implementation in CLIRE. We describe its evaluation in Section 4, discuss the implications of these results in Section 5, and summarize related and future research issues in Section 6.

2 Conversational Case-Based Reasoning

Conversational CBR systems iteratively interact with a user in a *conversation* to solve a *query*, defined as the set of questions selected and answered by the user during a conversation. During each iteration, the user is prompted with two displays and selects an element from one of them. The first display shows a ranked list of questions. The user can select and answer any question from this display. The second display shows a ranked list of cases ordered by nonincreasing similarity to the user's query. The user can select any case from this list for retrieval. For purposes of measuring performance (as explained below), we assume that a conversation ends when the user directs the system to retrieve a case.

Each answered question updates the query and the rankings in both displays. The CCBR engine's similarity function determines the new case ranking, where the number of cases displayed might be either the most similar K cases or the set of cases above a predetermined similarity threshold. These cases are assumed to be among the most relevant to the user's query. Therefore, the displayed

---

[1] In some applications, the customer interacts with the system directly (e.g., Nguyen et al., 1993).

questions are taken from these cases (i.e., those questions not already answered during the current conversation). They are ordered according to their potential for distinguishing the best case to retrieve. Questions can be ranked in many ways, such as by frequency of occurrence in the ranked cases, or by their rank in these cases (i.e., the highest ranked questions are those in the first case, etc). The number of ranked questions can be pre-determined, limited to those above a preset frequency, or limited by some other means.

CCBR case descriptions can be arbitrarily complex, but in this paper we limit the representation of questions and answers to (feature,value) pairs, although questions can be internally disjunctive (i.e., having multiple answers). A case solution is a sequence of *actions*. For example, when diagnosing printer failures, questions might refer to the printer's display panel or the status of the paper tray, while an action might be to fill the tray, clear a jam, or give up all hope. Cases are assumed to be implicitly grouped into topics, which can be distinguished by a few key *context* questions. Cases should be designed so that their context questions are displayed first, and their low-level *detail* questions displayed later. This ranking encourages users to follow this ordering during conversations.

We will focus on two measures to evaluate the performance of a CCBR library for solving a set of queries. The first is *precision*, defined as whether the retrieved case's actions solves a user's query. The second is *efficiency*, defined as the number of questions asked before retrieval takes place (i.e., lower values correspond to higher efficiency). Good CCBR libraries permit both high precision and efficiency.

Case engineering is the art of designing good libraries. Sample CCBR design guidelines are:

1. reuse questions when possible,
2. order context questions before detail questions,
3. eliminate questions that do not distinguish cases,
4. ask for only one thing in a question, and
5. use a similar, short number of questions per case.

When analyzed separately, each guideline appears sensible, and contributes to good CCBR performance. For example, Guideline 1 encourages similar cases to be distinguished by a *shared* question, while Guideline 4 encourages a distinct focus per question. However, it is unclear, to most novices, how to resolve conflicts between multiple guidelines. For example, Guidelines 1 and 5 can conflict; while reusing questions is important, cases should not be described by large sets of answered questions (i.e., this could yield inefficient CCBR retrieval behavior). Furthermore, when a library contains thousands of questions and cases, or the CCBR system allows novice users to modify the case library, or several users jointly extend and maintain a library, design flaws can mount quickly and degrade performance. Novice users can consult experts for help, but this is a costly alternative. We instead advocate the use of software to assist novices with the case authoring process.

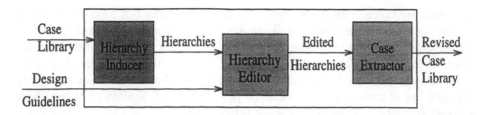

Fig. 1. The Case Library Revision Process

3 Revising Conversational Case Libraries

Figure 1 summarizes the three phases of our approach. The first phase creates a representation of the library that is more amenable to both assessing the library's structure and applying revision operators to its cases. A suitable representation for use in CLIRE is a set of hierarchies, one per topic, that identify common questions among related cases and distinguish their context from their detail questions. Revisions to this representation are performed in the second phase, according to the available design guidelines. The final phase extracts the revised cases from this representation. This revision process is transparent to users; they interact with the revised library only, and not with its intermediate representation.

We implemented this approach in a simple first version of CLIRE, which uses a top-down algorithm to induce a decision tree (TDIDT) (e.g., Quinlan, 1986; Breslow & Aha, 1997) from the cases. Although a bottom-up or other search algorithm could also be used, TDIDT approaches are conceptually simple and easy to implement. Standard TDIDT algorithms require that cases have class labels, which ours do not possess. Therefore, we instead focussed on generating a separate leaf for each case.

TDIDT algorithms recursively apply a selection criterion to choose an *index* question for partitioning a node's cases. Most selection criteria assume that cases are defined by the same set of questions, although several methods exist for tolerating missing values (Quinlan, 1989). They also assume that cases have been clustered (e.g., by class). These assumptions are violated here. CCBR libraries typically have few, if any, questions answered in all of its cases, and each case's solution (i.e., action sequence) can be unique. Therefore, we used an alternative selection criterion that chooses a most frequently answered question among a node's cases. Cases that do not contain an answer for the selected question are grouped into a separate node and recursively partitioned.

Figure 3 summarizes CLIRE's induction algorithm. Its inputs are a set of *active* cases, a set of *inactive* cases, and a list Q of used questions. A leaf is returned for the given cases if none of the questions answered in the active cases can further distinguish them from each other or from the inactives. Otherwise (steps 3–8), a question $q \notin Q$ is selected for recursive partitioning, and a subtree is generated for each answer a of q that appears in at least one of the actives.

```
Key: L: Set of cases in the case library
     Actives: Set of cases to be distinguished from each other
     Inactives: Set of cases to be distinguished from Actives
     Q: Questions used in ancestors of this node (initially ∅)
     N: A new internal node (N_q is its selected question)
Top level call: induce_tree(L,∅,∅)
induce_tree(Actives,Inactives,Q) =
1.  IF stop_splitting(Actives,Inactives,Q)
2.  THEN RETURN make_leaf(Actives ∪ Inactives)
3.  ELSE N_q = select_question(Q,Actives)        // N_q ∉ Q
4.       FOREACH a ∈ answers(N_q)
5.            Actives_a = {c|c ∈ Actives, c_q = a}
6.            IF Actives_a ≠ ∅
7.            THEN Inactives_a = {c|c ∈ Inactives, c_q = a}
8.                 N_a = induce_tree(Actives_a,Inactives_a, Q∪{N_q})
9.       Actives_? = {c|c ∈ Actives, c_q = ?}
10.      IF Actives_? = ∅
11.      THEN Inactives_? = {c|c ∈ Inactives, c_q = ?}
12.      ELSE Inactives_? = Actives ∪ Inactives − Actives_?
13.      IF Actives_? ≠ ∅ ∨ Inactives_? ≠ ∅
14.      THEN N_? = induce_tree(Actives_?,Inactives_?,Q∪{N_q})
15.      RETURN N
```

Fig. 2. CLIRE's Top-Level Pseudocode

The recursive call constrains the lists of active and inactive cases to those cases c where $c_q = a$, adds q to Q, and annotates N as partitioning its cases using q (i.e., with N_q). Steps 9–14 generate a subtree for N containing its cases c where c_q is unknown. However, if some active cases have no answer for q, then Inactives_? is set to the complement of Actives_? within the union of the Actives and Inactives. At this point, the answered questions in the Actives_? set of cases are a proper subset of the answered questions in Inactives_?. Thus, cases in these two sets are not easily distinguished in CCBR conversations. Whenever possible, this algorithm forces recursive splits until the active and inactive cases are distinguishable.

The function induce_tree yields a decision tree that indexes a library's cases. In this first version of CLIRE, the editing phase is simple: it performs case-specific feature selection, removing all questions of a case c that do not appear on any path from the root to leaves containing c. The assumption here is that the deleted ⟨question,answer⟩ pairs are not needed because they do not assist in distinguishing their case. Finally, the case extraction phase records, for each case c, the order in which ⟨question,answer⟩ pairs appear on paths to c.

This implementation of CLIRE addresses the first three guidelines listed in Section 2 (i.e., reuse questions, order context before detail questions, eliminate non-distinguishing questions). Extracting cases from a tree reuses answered ques-

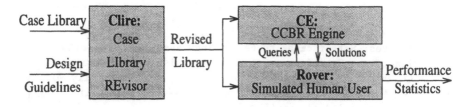

Fig. 3. Evaluating Revised Case Libraries

tions on overlapping multiple paths, thus encouraging question reuse. Frequently answered questions are assumed to be context questions. They are identified as those on the higher nodes of paths, and this question ordering is preserved in the revised cases. Non-distinguishing questions are removed during case-specific feature selection.

Our approach for revising conversational case libraries is knowledge poor; we do not anticipate that domains experts are available to supply detailed information on how to revise a library. This limits the types of revisions that can be made. For the moment, we use an approach that is fully automated, but recognize that more interactive approaches might better demonstrate the utility of library revision.

Section 4 empirically examines whether the strategy implemented in CLIRE will improve the CCBR performance of case libraries.

4   Empirical Evaluation

Our evaluation focuses on determining whether CLIRE can improve the CCBR performance of CCBR libraries and, if so, why. This section reports the results; we postpone their discussion until Section 5.

4.1   Methodology

Figure 3 summarizes our methodology for evaluating CLIRE's performance. This required implementing both CE, a CCBR Engine that attempts to mimic CBR EXPRESS, and ROVER, which simulates a human user interacting with CE. Both are highly parameterized.

CE is used by ROVER to conduct conversations. The questions in the libraries we obtained for our experiments have only boolean or symbolic values. We defined CE to use a simple case similarity measure: the number of matching minus mismatching answers between a query and a case, normalized by the case's number of answered questions. CE displays a ranked list of the most similar K cases to the user. CE also displays the top Q ranked questions not answered in the query, where question ratings are determined by a simple function that biases rankings in favor of their ordering within the K ranked cases. CE does not yet simulate CBR EXPRESS's ability to input text from the user to initialize the

Table 1. Case Libraries Used in the Experiments

Name	#Cases	#Actions	Original		After CLIRE Revision	
			#Questions	#Answers	#Questions	#Answers
Printing	25	28	27	70	16	55
VMLS	114	227	597	710	83	395
ACDEV	3334	1670	2011	28200	1266	26827

question and case rankings. Instead, CE initializes its query with the answers of the top n questions from the target case (recall that the questions in each case are ordered). We call this process *query seeding*. When $n = 0$ (i.e., no query seeding), question ranking is initialized based on frequency of use in the library.

ROVER cycles through a library's cases in turn, using a process we call *leave-one-in*. That is, it selects a *target* case c, with replacement, and the query is initialized with c's top n questions' answers. During conversations, it ignores questions that are not answered in c. A successful retrieval is one where the retrieved case's action sequence is identical with the target case's. In each iteration of a conversation, ROVER either selects one of the ranked questions answered in c with probability p_q or terminates the conversation by selecting a case. ROVER also selects a case when none of c's answered questions is ranked, or if one of the ranked cases exceeds a similarity threshold. In our experiments, we set ROVER's parameters so that its selections yield either a highest ranking (answerable) question from the ranked questions or a most similar case from the ranked cases. Because ranking ties in these lists are randomly broken, all reported results are averages from running ROVER on CE ten times.

4.2 Libraries

We experimented with the three case libraries summarized in Table 1. The first, named *Printing*, is a simple example library provided with Inference's products; it is used to diagnose and recommend solutions for printer failures. VMLS, obtained from NSWC Port Hueneme personnel, provides technical assistance for maintaining a vertical missile launch system. ACDEV, from Circuit City's Answer City product, was designed to support branch store personnel. The first library is fairly well designed, while the latter two are known to be problematic. ACDEV's size prevents us from using all cases as queries (i.e., as done in leave-one-in). Instead, we randomly selected 100 cases from for querying according to a uniform distribution with replacement. ROVER used only these cases as queries during experiments with ACDEV.

Table 1 shows that CLIRE reduced the total number of questions by between 37% and 86%, and the total number of answers in cases by between 5% and 44%. It is plausible that this should increase CE's efficiency on these libraries as determined by evaluating its interaction with ROVER. However, it is not clear whether CLIRE simultaneously sacrifices precision.

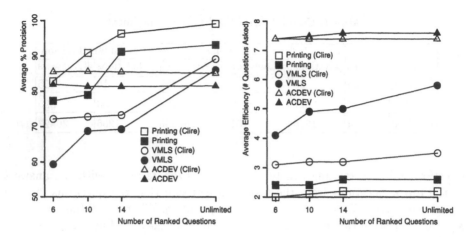

Fig. 4. CLIRE Improves CCBR Performance in a Baseline Study

4.3 Experiments

In our initial experiment, we fixed $K = 4$ and varied Q, the size of the ranked list of questions. Figure 4 summarizes the results for these three case libraries.[2] As shown, CLIRE slightly increased precision and efficiency for these libraries across the conditions tested. In this experiment, we did not use query seeding (i.e., $n = 0$). The same relative results occurred when setting $n = 1$, although absolute precisions increased while the number of questions asked decreased (i.e., by about 1). Similar relative results also occurred when we varied K, the number of ranked cases.

However, modifying p_q, the probability that ROVER continues to ask unanswered questions from the target case instead of selecting a case, does affect relative performance. We observed this by setting $K = 4$, $Q =$ unlimited (i.e., all unanswered questions among the top K cases were included in the display of ranked questions), and varying p_q in $\{70\%, 80\%, 90\%, 100\%\}$. For VMLS and ACDEV, performance benefits with the CLIRE-revised libraries did not occur for smaller settings of p_q. Thus, CLIRE's benefits accrue primarily when conversations are not terminated prematurely.

Although our initial experiments establish that revision by CLIRE can improve CCBR performance for these libraries, it is not clear why. Therefore, we evaluated CLIRE in an ablation study to answer this question. Our implementation of CLIRE makes two modifications to case libraries:

1. case-specific question selection and
2. reordering questions in each case.

Our ablation study applies only one of these modifications to the libraries at a time, which allows us to isolate their effects. Question selection is eliminated by

---

[2] Standard deviations for efficiency were very small throughout our experiments, and were always below 5% for precision.

Table 2. Ablation Study Results ($K = 4, Q = 6, n = 0, p_q = 100$)

Revisions	Libraries					
	Printing		VMLS		ACDEV	
	Precision	Efficiency	Precision	Efficiency	Precision	Efficiency
Neither	78.8%	2.4	59.3%	4.1	80.5%	7.6
Reorder	75.6%	2.4	68.7%	5.0	83.7%	7.6
Selection	82.8%	2.0	72.5%	3.2	85.8%	7.4
Both	82.8%	1.8	72.1%	3.1	85.8%	7.4

reinstating the "deleted" ⟨question,answer⟩ pairs of each case c, placing them after the CLIRE-selected pairs in c's question ordering. Question re-ordering is eliminated by retaining each revised case's original question ordering, but without deleted questions.

Table 2 summarizes some typical results we found in this ablation study. Reading downwards, its four rows correspond to testing with the original libraries, testing using only question reordering, testing using only question selection, and testing using both (i.e., as in the previous experiment). Invariably, we found that CLIRE's power emanates primarily from its question selection capability. While using only question selection yields behavior similar to using both revision operators, using only question reordering yields smaller gains, and sometimes even decreases the performance measures. This behavior occurred independently of the parameter settings given to CE and ROVER and for alternative question-ranking strategies in CE. We discuss possible causes of this behavior in Section 5, including reasons why we cannot yet test our hypotheses.

5 Discussion

The challenge of designing high-performance CCBR libraries has huge ramifications for companies interested in deploying this technology. Although commercial vendors supply guidelines for designing cases to ensure good CCBR performance, they are difficult to implement for complex libraries. This has caused several companies to abandon their own case authoring efforts in exchange for either costly consulting services or alternative technologies. Software assistants for case authoring, including more mature versions of CLIRE, can potentially meet this challenge.

The results of the ablation study indicate that question selection during library revision improves CCBR performance. However, question reordering had no consistent positive effect, and occasional adverse affects. Perhaps no objective relationship exists between question ordering and performance. However, ordering questions might still be a good design guideline for case authors; a consistent question ordering makes it easier to locate similar cases and, thus, encourages question reuse. Alternatively, our implementations of CE and ROVER might not adequately assess the relationship between ordering and performance. An adequate test must permit different question orderings in cases to yield different question selections during conversations. For example, ROVER might select questions other than those answered in the target case, and introduce answer noise. This would more realistically simulate CCBR conversations, and cause less similar cases to become ranked. If the question ranking function prefers the top-ranking questions among the K cases and questions in cases are carefully ordered, then the ranked questions would probably include some answered in the target case. Random question orderings would decrease this probability. However, this method is difficult to test because it requires a domain model that dictates how to answer questions that are not answered in cases, and a model of answer noise. Because we do not have these models, we cannot yet test this conjecture. We plan to build case libraries in our areas of expertise, which will allow us to investigate how to usefully provide task-specific knowledge to ROVER.

Like ROVER, CLIRE should be revised to exploit domain knowledge, which is needed for ROVER to more realistically simulate user behavior. For example, CLIRE deletes questions from cases because they are not selected in the tree. But the question selection function is knowledge poor, and might delete important questions. Also, CLIRE does not implement the design guideline that every case's descriptions should contain a similar number of questions because it does not know how to *add* answered questions to a case. Finally, we are considering replacing CE with a CBR EXPRESS API so that we can evaluate CLIRE's ability in the context of a mature CCBR engine.

6 Related and Future Research

We are not aware of any extensive research on conversational case-based reasoning. Nor is there much research yet on automated support for case authoring. However, some researchers have investigated methods for improving the manual case authoring process. Heider et al. (1997) describe problems due to poorly designed cases (i.e., incomplete or noisy), and a methodology for improving their quality by imposing more structure on the authoring process. Kitano et al. (1993) also describe a general methodology for building case bases. However, these publications do not target conversational CBR systems, nor describe computational approaches for revising case libraries.

Some previous research investigates case-based tasks in which queries are derived incrementally. For example, CS-IBL (Tan & Schlimmer, 1990) incrementally evaluates features that have non-zero evaluation cost; it selects features to evaluate that maximize the ratio of expected match success to cost. Smyth and Cunningham (1994) instead focus on tasks where features have either zero or a fixed nonzero evaluation cost. Their algorithm uses the zero cost features to retrieve a subset C of matching cases, and then dynamically induces a decision tree that selects, at each step, the feature which maximizes the information gain for distinguishing cases in C. Unlike CCBR, these question-answering processes are not user-driven, and they do not use trees to revise case indices. CLIRE would require extension for tasks where feature evaluation has nonzero cost.

ROBBIE (Fox & Leake, 1995) is a failure-driven CBR system that re-indexes cases by selecting alternative indices for cases in a planning task. It uses introspective analysis to encourage the retrieval of more easily adaptable cases. Efficiency is measured in the context of a traditional rather than a conversational CBR context. In contrast, our approach works on the entire library simultaneously, without knowledge of specific retrieval failures. CLIRE could benefit from using a failure-driven process to modify case indices.

Many CBR systems use decision trees to index and retrieve cases. For example, this includes IBPRS (Ku & Suh, 1996), which uses K-trees, and INRECA (Auriol et al., 1995), which integrates decision trees and k-d trees. Manago et al. (1993) describe how INRECA incrementally processes unknown values. Questions are automatically selected by reading the decision tree, induced from the cases, in a top-down manner. This process defaults to a CBR approach when a selected question's answer is unknown. Whereas INRECA uses decision trees to guide conversations, CLIRE instead uses trees to revise case indices, and conversations in our CCBR engine are user-driven. We are not aware of other research where trees, or related data structures, are used to revise rather than index cases.

CLIRE's current implementation edits each case c_j using a tree-based feature selection process similar to Cardie's (1993), but operates on a case-specific basis. Specifically, CLIRE deletes questions in c_j that do not appear on paths leading to leaves containing c_j. Although case-specific feature selection algorithms exist (e.g., Domingos, 1997), they assume that cases are all described by the same questions, which is not true for CCBR libraries.

This research is limited in that we have no models of expected retrieval behavior for these libraries. We plan to build libraries with corresponding models of expected retrieval behavior, which will allow us to more accurately examine whether question ordering relates to performance, and how other library characteristics impact CLIRE's performance. We also plan to address some of the implementations' limitations. For example, CLIRE can be extended to *interactively* revise cases, to incrementally accept edits to the set of design guidelines, and to incrementally revise libraries as new cases are acquired. CE's similarity function needs to be extended so that question weights can be applied, which might shed insight on when question ordering can affect performance.

7 Conclusion

This paper described an approach for revising conversational case libraries, its implementation in CLIRE, and an empirical evaluation. The library revision approach consists of three stages: induce editable hierarchical data structures, edit them according to a set of library design guidelines, and extract the revised cases. We showed that, on three case libraries, CLIRE improved retrieval performance (i.e., precision and efficiency) as tested by a simulated human user on a simple CCBR engine. Two of the libraries tested are serious applications; VMLS is undergoing extensive and prolonged manual revision, while ACDEV has been abandonded due to the complexity of the library design and maintenance process. Software for assisting the case authoring process (e.g., CLIRE) holds promise for improving the design of complex case libraries.

Acknowledgements

Thanks to Ralph Barletta, John Grahovac, Kirt Pulaski, Scott Sackin, and Gene Scampone for providing the libraries used in our experiments and feedback on our results. Thanks also to Margaret Drake for proofreading edits. This research was supported by the Office of Naval Research.

References

Auriol, E., Wess. S., Manago, M., Althoff, K. -D., & Traphöner, R. (1995). INRECA: A seamlessly integrated system based on inductive inference and case-based reasoning. *Proceedings of the First ICCBR* (pp. 371–380). Sesimbra, Portugal: Springer.

Breslow, L., & Aha, D. W. (1997). Simplifying decision trees: A survey. To appear in *Knowledge Engineering Review*.

Cardie, C. (1993). Using decision trees to improve case-based learning. *Proceedings of the Tenth ICML* (pp. 25–32). Amherst, MA: Morgan Kaufmann.

Domingos, P. (1997). Context-sensitive feature selection for lazy learners. *Artificial Intelligence Review, 11*, 227–253.

Fox, S., & Leake, D. L. (1995). Using introspective reasoning to refine indexing. *Proceedings of the Fourteenth IJCAI* (pp. 391–397). Montreal: Morgan Kaufmann.

Heider, R., Auriol, E., Tartarin, E., & Manago, M. (1997). Improving the quality of case bases for building better decision support systems. In R. Bergmann & W. Wilke (Eds.) *Fifth German Workshop on CBR: Foundations, Systems, and Applications* (Technical Report LSA-97-01E). University of Kaiserslautern, Department of Computer Science.

Inference Corporation (1995). *CBR2: Designing CBR Express Case Bases*. Unpublished.

Kitano H., Shimazu H., & Shibata A. (1993). Case-method: A methodology for building large-scale case-based systems. *Proceedings of the Eleventh NCAI* (pp. 303–308). Washington, DC: AAAI Press.

Ku, S., & Suh, Y.-H. (1996). An investigation of the K-tree search algorithm for efficient case representation and retrieval. *Expert Systems with Applications, 11*, 571–581.

Manago, M., Althoff, K.-D., Auriol, E., Traphoner, R., Wess, S., Conruyt, N., & Maurer, F. (1993). Induction and reasoning from cases. *Proceedings of the First EWCBR* (pp. 313–318). Kaiserslautern, Germany: Springer-Verlag.

Nguyen, T., Czerwinsksi, M., & Lee, D. (1993). COMPAQ QuickSource: Providing the consumer with the power of artificial intelligence. *Proceedings of the Fifth IAAI* (pp. 142–150). Washington, DC: AAAI Press.

Quinlan, J. R. (1986). Induction of decision trees. *Machine Learning, 1*, 81–106.

Quinlan, J. R. (1989). Unknown attribute values in induction. *Proceedings of the Sixth IWML* (pp. 164–168). Ithaca, NY: Morgan Kaufmann.

Smyth, B., & Cunningham, P. (1994). A comparison of incremental CBR and inductive learning. In M. Keane, J. P. Haton, & M. Manago (Eds.) *Working Papers of the Second EWCBR*. Chantilly, France: Unpublished.

Tan, M., & Schlimmer, J. C. (1990). Two case studies in cost-sensitive concept acquisition. *Proceedings of the Eighth NCAI* (pp. 854–860). Boston, MA: AAAI Press.

Perspectives: A Declarative Bias Mechanism for Case Retrieval *

Josep Lluís Arcos and Ramon López de Mántaras

IIIA, Artificial Intelligence Research Institute
CSIC, Spanish Council for Scientific Research
Campus UAB, 08193 Bellaterra, Catalonia, Spain.
{arcos,mantaras}@iiia.csic.es

Abstract. The aim of this paper is to present a mechanism, called *perspectives*, to describe declarative biases for case retrieval in structured representations of cases. Our approach is based on the observation that, in complex tasks, the identification of the relevant aspects for retrieval in a given situation may involve the use of knowledge intensive methods. This identification process requires dynamical decisions about the relevant aspects of a problem and usually forces to consider non predefined retrieval indexes in the memory of cases. Declarative biases provide a flexible way of constructing dynamical perspectives for retrieval in the memory of cases. We have implemented the notion of perspectives in a reflective object-centered representation language, called Noos, based on feature terms. Finally, we have used perspectives as declarative biases for retrieval in the *Saxex* application, a complex real-world case-based reasoning system for generating expressive performances of melodies based on examples of human performances that are represented as structured cases.

1 Introduction

The research on complex representations of cases is motivated by the construction of CBR systems in complex real-world domains. Structured representations of cases based on the notion of objects and relations among them, usually implemented as graph structures, allow a flexible and higher expressive power than attribute-value representations.

Structured representations of cases offer the capability of treating subparts of cases as full-fledged cases: a new problem can be solved using subparts of multiple cases retrieved from the system's memory. On the other hand, structured representations of cases increase the complexity of retrieval mechanisms and requires the development of new retrieval techniques supporting the complex representations of cases.

* The research reported on this paper has been supported by the Spanish project *SMASH* TIC96-1038-C04-01. Research by J.L. Arcos was also supported by a CSIC fellowship. This work has benefited from the comments and discussions with Enric Plaza.

In our research work we have described *feature terms* as a formalization of structured representation of complex cases [7,17]. We have developed Noos, a reflective object-centered representation language designed to support knowledge modeling of problem solving and learning based on feature terms [5,6]. In [17] a similitude measure based on a preference ordering among cases was presented. The use of inductive learning techniques using feature term representations is also investigated in [8].

The aim of this paper is to present a mechanism, called *perspectives*, to describe declarative biases for case retrieval in structured representations of cases. Our approach is based on the observation that, in complex tasks, the identification of the relevant aspects for retrieval in a given situation may involve the use of knowledge intensive methods. This identification process requires dynamical decisions about the relevant aspects of a problem and usually forces to consider non predefined retrieval indexes in the memory of cases. Declarative biases provide a flexible way of constructing dynamical perspectives for retrieval in the memory of cases. We have implemented the notion of perspectives in Noos.

We use perspectives as declarative biases for retrieval in the *Saxex* application, a complex real-world case-based reasoning system for generating expressive performances of melodies based on examples of human performances that are represented as structured cases.

The organization of this paper is as follows. In Section 2 we present the notion of feature terms and their use in the Noos representation language. Section 3 describes *perspectives* as a declarative bias mechanism for retrieval. Section 4 shows the use of perspectives in the *Saxex* application. Section 5 discusses related work. Finally, in Section 6 we present the conclusions.

2 Feature Terms

Feature terms are record-like data structures embodying a collection of *features*. The difference between feature terms and first order terms is the following: a first order term, e. g. $f(x, g(x, y), z)$, can be formally described as a tree and a fixed tree traversal order—in other words, variables are identified by position. The intuition behind a feature term is that it can be described as a labeled graph—in other words, variables are identified by name (regardless of order or position). This difference allows to represent partial knowledge.

For instance, a sequence of two notes where the first one is a $C5$ with a quarter duration (noted as Q) followed by a $G4$ with an eighth duration (noted as E) is described using the feature term representation as follows:

$$
X : Note \begin{bmatrix} pitch & \doteq X_1 : C5 \\ duration \doteq X_2 : Q \\ \\ next & \doteq Y : Note \begin{bmatrix} pitch & \doteq Y_1 : G4 \\ duration \doteq Y_2 : E \\ previous \doteq X \end{bmatrix} \end{bmatrix}
$$

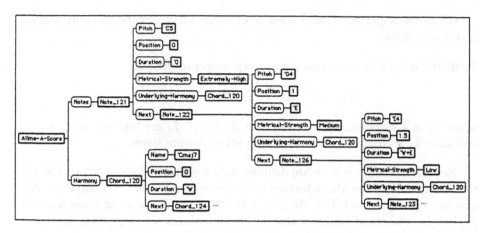

Fig. 1. Partial browse of the score for the 'All of me' ballad. Features are represented as thin boxes, dots indicate not expanded terms, and gray boxes express references to existing terms.

We use the common dot notation for field selection (for instance $X.pitch = X_1 : C5$).

Feature terms have a correspondence to labeled graphs representation. For instance, Figure 1 shows the description of a musical score containing two main interlaced sequences: the melody as a sequence of notes and the harmonization as a sequence of chords.

Our approach to formalize feature terms is related to the research based on ψ-terms [2,10] that proposes formalisms to model object-oriented programming constructs. We describe the signature Σ of feature terms as the tuple $\langle \mathcal{S}, \mathcal{F}, \leq \rangle$ such that:

- $\mathcal{S}$ is a set of *sort symbols* including $\perp, \top$;
- $\mathcal{F}$ is a set of *feature symbols*;
- $\leq$ is a decidable partial order on $\mathcal{S}$ such that $\perp$ is the least element and $\top$ is the greatest element.

We define an interpretation $\mathcal{I}$ over the signature $\langle \mathcal{S}, \mathcal{F}, \leq \rangle$ as the structure

$$\mathcal{I} = \langle \mathcal{D}^{\mathcal{I}}, (s^{\mathcal{I}})_{s \in \mathcal{S}}, (f^{\mathcal{I}})_{f \in \mathcal{F}} \rangle$$

such that:

- $\mathcal{D}^{\mathcal{I}}$ is a non-empty set, called *domain* of $\mathcal{I}$ (or, universe);
- for each symbol s in $\mathcal{S}$, $s^{\mathcal{I}}$ is a subset of the domain; in particular, $\top^{\mathcal{I}} = \mathcal{D}^{\mathcal{I}}$ and $\perp^{\mathcal{I}} = \emptyset$;
- for each feature f in $\mathcal{F}$, $f^{\mathcal{I}}$ is a total unary function $f^{\mathcal{I}} : \mathcal{D}^{\mathcal{I}} \mapsto \mathcal{P}(\mathcal{D}^{\mathcal{I}})$. When the mapping is not defined it is assumed to have value $\top$.

Given the signature Σ and a set $\mathcal{V}$ of variables, we define formally *feature terms* as follows:

Definition 1. A feature term ψ is an expression of the form:

$$\psi \quad ::= \quad X : s\,[f_1 \doteq \Psi_1 \cdots f_n \doteq \Psi_n]$$

where X is a variable in $\mathcal{V}$, s is a sort in $\mathcal{S}$, $f_1, \cdots, f_n$ are features in $\mathcal{F}$, $n \geq 0$, and each Ψ_i is either a feature term or a set of feature terms.

Note that when $n = 0$ we are defining only a sorted variable $(X : s)$. We call the variable X in the above feature term the *root* of ψ (noted $Root(\psi) = X$), and say that X is *sorted* by the sort s (noted $Sort(X) = s$) and has features $f_1, \cdots, f_n$. The set of variables and the set of features occurring in ψ are noted respectively as $\mathcal{V}_\psi$ and $\mathcal{F}_\psi$.

A feature term is a syntactic expression that denotes sets of elements in some appropriate domain of interpretation $(\llbracket \psi \rrbracket^{\mathcal{I}} \subset \mathcal{D}^{\mathcal{I}})$. Thus, given the previously defined interpretation $\mathcal{I}$, the denotation $\llbracket \psi \rrbracket^{\mathcal{I}}$ of a feature term ψ, under a valuation $\alpha : \mathcal{V} \mapsto \mathcal{D}^{\mathcal{I}}$ is given inductively by:

$$\llbracket \psi \rrbracket^{\mathcal{I}} = \llbracket X : s[f_1 \doteq \psi_1 \cdots f_n \doteq \psi_n] \rrbracket^{\mathcal{I}} = \{\alpha(X)\} \cap s^{\mathcal{I}} \bigcap_{1 \leq i \leq n} (f_i^{\mathcal{I}})^{-1}(\llbracket \psi_i \rrbracket^{\mathcal{I}})$$

where $f^{-1}(S)$, when f is a function and S is a set, stands for $\{x | \exists s \in S$ such that $f(x) = s\}$; i.e., denotes the set of all elements whose images by f are in S.

Using this semantical interpretation of feature terms, it is legitimate to establish an order relation between terms. Given two terms ψ and ψ', we will be interested in determine when $\llbracket \psi \rrbracket^{\mathcal{I}} \subset \llbracket \psi' \rrbracket^{\mathcal{I}}$.

2.1 Subsumption

We have just seen that the semantical interpretation of feature terms allows to define an ordering relation among feature descriptions. We call this ordering relation *subsumption*. The intuitive meaning of subsumption is that of *informational ordering*. We say that a feature term ψ_1 subsumes another feature term ψ_2 $(\psi_1 \sqsubseteq \psi_2)$ when all information in ψ_1 is also contained in ψ_2. Formally,

Definition 2. (Subsumption)

Given two feature terms ψ and ψ', ψ subsumes ψ', $\psi \sqsubseteq \psi'$, if there is a total mapping function $\upsilon : \mathcal{V}_\psi \to \mathcal{V}_{\psi'}$ such that :

1. $\upsilon(Root(\psi)) = Root(\psi')$,
   and $\forall x \in \mathcal{V}_\psi$
2. $Sort(x) \leq Sort(\upsilon(x))$,
3. for every $f_i \in \mathcal{F}$ such that $x.f_i \doteq \Psi_i$ is defined, we have that $\upsilon(x).f_i \doteq \Psi_i'$ is also defined,
4. $\forall \psi_k \in \Psi_i \; \exists \psi_k' \in \Psi_i'$ such that $\upsilon(Root(\psi_k)) = Root(\psi_k')$, and

5. $v(Root(\psi_k)) \neq v(Root(\psi_j))$ when $k \neq j$.

For instance, the following feature term is a partial description of a sequence of two notes that subsumes all the sequences of two notes where the first one is a $C5$ and the following a $G4$ (specifically subsumes the previous showed example):

$$
X : Note \begin{bmatrix} pitch \doteq X_1 : C5 \\ next \doteq Y : Note \begin{bmatrix} pitch & \doteq Y_1 : G4 \\ previous \doteq X \end{bmatrix} \end{bmatrix}
$$

This notion of subsumption is the basis of the retrieval mechanism in our approach. Specifically, the set of retrieval methods provided in Noos is based on the lattice generated by the subsumption ordering.

2.2 The Noos Language

Noos is a reflective object-centered representation language designed to support knowledge modeling of problem solving and learning based on feature terms. Noos is based on the task/method decomposition principle and the analysis of knowledge requirements for methods —and it is related to knowledge modeling frameworks like KADS [22] or ComMet [20].

Problem solving in Noos is considered as the construction of an *episodic model*. The view of "problem solving as modeling" is that problem solving is the construction of an episodic model from problem data and problem solving knowledge. A clear and explicit separation between tasks, methods, and domain knowledge permits a dynamical link between a given problem, tasks, and methods as well as a dynamical choice of a suitable method to achieve a task in a given resolution context : a 'task' applies a 'method' on a 'episode' (described using domain knowledge and problem data). Thus, an episodic model gathers the knowledge pieces used for solving a specific problem. Once a problem is solved, Noos automatically memorizes (stores and indexes) the episodic model that has been built. *Episodic memory* is the (accessible and retrievable) collection of episodic models of the problems that a system has solved. The memorization of episodic models is the basic building block for integrating learning, and specifically CBR, in Noos.

Noos incorporates *preferences* to model decision making about sets of alternatives present in domain knowledge and problem solving knowledge. For instance, preference knowledge can be used to model criteria for ranking some precedent cases over other precedent cases for a task in a specific situation.

3 Perspectives

The goal of the retrieval task in CBR is to search for similar precedents from the memory of cases. Our goal is to retrieve structured cases using domain specific knowledge expressed as complex relations among objects. The identification of the relevant aspects in complex situations requires the use of knowledge-intensive

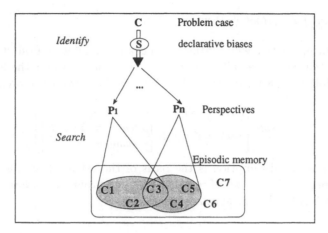

Fig. 2. Using perspectives in the Retrieval task. First, given a problem case C and using syntactic patterns S as declarative biases, the identification phase determines the relevant aspects building perspectives $P_1 \cdots P_n$. Then, perspectives are used to search precedent cases in the episodic memory.

methods. These relevant aspects constitute the base for the search in the memory of cases. We claim that the use of declarative biases in the identification phase provides a clear and flexible way to express retrieval mechanisms in complex-real applications.

The view of feature terms as partial descriptions allows the representation of declarative biases also as feature terms in a natural way. The declarative biases are interpreted as syntactic patterns. *Perspectives* are the way to construct, from these syntactic patterns, partial descriptions of the current problem embodying the aspects considered as relevant. These partial descriptions are used as retrieval patterns for searching similar cases in the lattice of feature terms. The intuition behind perspectives is shown in Figure 2.

There are two possibilities for constructing perspectives. The first option is via a syntactic pattern using unsorted variables in some feature values. For instance, in order to declare as relevant aspects of a note its duration and its metrical strength on the melody, we will use the following syntactic pattern,

$$X : Note \begin{bmatrix} duration & \doteq Y \\ metrical\text{-}strength \doteq Z \end{bmatrix}$$

Then, the application of this bias to note *note_121* illustrated in Figure 1 (the theme 'All of me'), for instance, will construct the following perspective,

$$X : Note \begin{bmatrix} duration & \doteq Y : Q \\ metrical\text{-}strength \doteq Z : extremely\text{-}high \end{bmatrix}$$

that in turn will be used for retrieval obtaining, as a result, the set of note precedents from the memory of cases with duration Q (quarter duration) and a *extremely-high* metrical strength.

The second way to build a perspective is to use a syntactic pattern where the relevance of some features is declared using variables of features. This alternative allows to identify the roles of features and terms in the structure. For instance, in order to declare as relevant the role that a given note X plays in the structure of the cognition model of musical understanding of Narmour's theory (see Section 4 for more details) we will use the following syntactic pattern where feature variables are noted with the $ symbol,

$$X : Note\left[belongs\text{-}to \doteq Y : N\text{-}structure\left[\$f \doteq X\right]\right]$$

Specifically, in our example where the note *note_121* is the *first-note* of a melodic process structure, according to Narmour's theory, the following perspective will be constructed,

$$X : Note\left[belongs\text{-}to \doteq Y : Process\left[first\text{-}note \doteq X\right]\right]$$

Finally, using this perspective for retrieval we obtain all the notes playing the same role that the note problem from the memory of cases (i.e. first notes of melodic process structures).

Formally, the signature of syntactic patterns is an extension of the signature Σ of feature terms that incorporates a set of feature variables $\mathcal{L}\left(\langle \mathcal{S}, \mathcal{F} \cup \mathcal{L}, \leq \rangle\right)$. Thus, syntactic patterns are expressed as second order feature terms as follows:

Definition 3. A syntactic pattern ω is an expression of the form:

$$\omega \quad ::= \quad X : s\left[f_1 \doteq \Omega_1 \cdots f_n \doteq \Omega_n\right]$$

where X is a variable in $\mathcal{V}$, s is a sort in $\mathcal{S}$, $f_1, \cdots, f_n$ are features in $\mathcal{F} \cup \mathcal{L}$, $n \geq 0$, and each Ω_i is either a syntactic pattern or a set of syntactic patterns.

Given the previous definition of syntactic patterns, we define formally a perspective P as follows,

Definition 4. (Perspective)
Given a problem case C and a declarative bias defined by means of a syntactic pattern S, a *perspective* of C is defined as a feature term P such that there is a total bijective function $\beta : \mathcal{V}_P \to \mathcal{V}_S$, a total mapping function $\delta : \mathcal{V}_S \to \mathcal{V}_C$, and an instantiation function $\rho : \mathcal{F}_S \to \mathcal{F}_P$ satisfying:

1. $\rho(f) = f \quad \forall f \in \mathcal{F}$
2. $\beta(Root(P)) = Root(S)$, $\delta(Root(S)) = Root(C)$
   and $\forall x \in \mathcal{V}_P$
3. $Sort(\beta(x)) \leq Sort(\delta(\beta(x)))$,
4. $Sort(x) = Sort(\delta(\beta(x)))$,
5. for every $f_i \in \mathcal{F}$ such that $x.f_i \doteq \Psi_i$ is defined, we have that
   (a) $\exists f_j : \rho(f_j) = f_i$,
   (b) both $\beta(x).f_j \doteq \Psi_i'$ and $\delta(\beta(x)).f_i \doteq \Psi_i''$ have to be defined,
       and $\forall \psi_k \in \Psi_i :$

(c) $\exists \psi'_k \in \Psi'_i$ such that $\beta(Root(\psi_k)) = Root(\psi'_k)$

(d) $\exists \psi''_k \in \Psi''_i$ such that $\delta(\beta(Root(\psi_k))) = Root(\psi''_k)$.

Remark that a perspective P is constructed as a partial description of a problem case C. In other words, this implies that $P \sqsubseteq C$. Another important remark is that several perspectives satisfying the definition can be obtained. This implies that the implementation of the perspectives mechanism has to provide a way to obtain all of them (for instance, by providing a backtracking mechanism).

4 Using perspectives for generating expressive performances of melodies

Saxex [3,4] is a case-based reasoning system for generating expressive performances of melodies based on examples of human performances. Saxex incorporates background musical knowledge based on Narmour's implication/realization model [16] and Lerdahl and Jackendoff's generative theory of tonal music (GTTM) [13]. These theories of musical perception and musical understanding are the basis of the computational model of musical knowledge of the system.

We study the issue of musical expression in the context of tenor saxophone interpretations. We have done several recordings of a tenor sax performer playing several Jazz standard ballads with different degrees of expressiveness, including an (almost) inexpressive interpretation of each piece. These recordings are analyzed, using SMS spectral modeling techniques [19], in order to extract basic information related to the expressive parameters. The set of extracted parameters together with the scores of the pieces constitute the set of structured cases of the case-based system. From this set of cases and using similarity criteria based on background musical knowledge, expressed as biases upon which the perspectives are built, the system infers a set of possible expressive transformations for a given piece. Finally, using the SMS synthesis procedure and the set of inferred transformations, Saxex generates new expressive interpretations of the same jazz ballads as well as of other similar melodies.

The problem solving method developed in Saxex follows the usual subtask decomposition of CBR methods described in [1]: retrieve, reuse, and retain (see Figure 3). The overall picture of the subtask decomposition is the following:

- Retrieve: The goal of the retrieve task is to choose the set of notes (cases) most similar to the current problem. This task is decomposed in three subtasks:

  - Identify: The goal of this task is to build retrieval perspectives using two alternative biases. The first bias uses Narmour's implication/realization structures. The second bias uses Lerdahl and Jackendoff's generative theory.

  - Search: The goal of this second task is to search cases in the case memory using Noos retrieval methods and previously constructed perspectives.

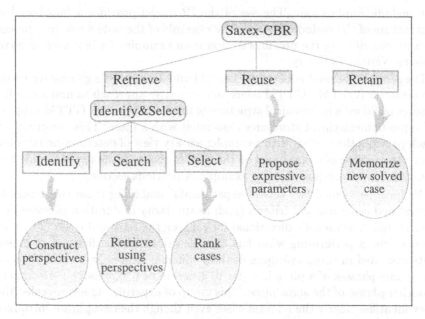

Fig. 3. Task decomposition of the *Saxex* CBR method.

- *Select*: The goal of the select task is to rank the retrieved cases using **Noos** preference methods. The preference methods use criteria such as similarity in duration of notes, harmonic stability, or melodic directions.
- *Reuse*: the goal of the reuse task is to choose a set of expressive transformations to be applied in the current problem from the set of more similar cases. The first criterion used is to adapt the transformations of the most similar case. When several cases are considered equally similar, the majority rule is used. Finally, when previous criteria are not sufficient, all the cases are considered equally possible alternatives and one of them is selected randomly.
- *Retain*: the incorporation of the new solved problem to the memory of cases is performed automatically in **Noos**. All solved problems will be available for the reasoning process in future problems.

Once we have described the overall picture of the CBR method, let us now explain in more detail the role of perspectives in the retrieval subtask in *Saxex*. The background musical knowledge incorporated in the system is the basis for the construction of perspectives for retrieval.

The first bias applied is based on the Implication/Realization (IR) theory of Narmour. IR propose a theory of cognition of melodies based on eight basic structures. These structures characterize patterns of melodic implications that constitute the basic units of the listener perception. Other parameters such as metric, duration, and rhythmic patterns emphasize or inhibit the perception of these melodic implications. The use of the IR model provides a bias based on the structure of the melodic surface. The example of the note's role in a process structure described in the previous section is an example of a bias used in *Saxex* following Narmour's theory.

The second bias used is based on Lerdahl and Jackendoff's generative theory of tonal music (GTTM). GTTM offers an alternative approach to understanding melodies based on a hierarchical structure of musical cognition. GTTM proposes four types of hierarchical structures associated with a piece. This structural approach provides the system with a complementary view of determining relevance biases. An example of a bias based on the GTTM theory is the use of the metrical importance of a note (see the first example in previous section).

We have performed two sets of experiments combining these two biases for retrieval and using musical criteria (such as similarity in duration of notes, harmonic stability, or melodic directions) for ranking the retrieved cases. The reuse task consists in performing what has been described above. first set of experiments consisted in using examples of three different expressive performances of twenty note phrases of a piece in order to generate new expressive performances of another phrase of the same piece. This group of experiments has revealed that *Saxex* identifies clearly the relevant cases even though the new phrase introduces small variations of phrases existing in the memory of cases.

The second set of experiments consisted in using examples of expressive performances of some pieces in order to generate expressive performances of other pieces. More concretely, we have worked with three different expressive performances of pieces having about fifty notes in order to generate expressive performances of new twenty note phrases. This second group of experiments has revealed that the use of perspectives allows to identify situations such as long notes, ascending or descending melodic lines, etc. Such situations are also usually identified by a human performer.

As a final remark, we want to emphasize that the final output of *Saxex* are sound files containing the new expressive performances resulting from applying adequate expressive transformations to the situations identified and retrieved by the use of perspectives. This capability offers a simple way to test the solutions proposed by the system by just listening to the output sound files and the results obtained are very promising[1].

5 Related work

Other works on structure-based representations are CAPLAN [15], focusing on case-based planning; the research around the FABEL project [11], and the use of parallel techniques in CAPER [12,18]. There is a growing interest on structured representation due to the higher representation power that is required in complex real-world applications.

---

[1] see <http://www.iiia.csic.es/Projects/music/Saxex> for a sample of sound example.

Another related work is the stratified case-based reasoning technique presented in [9]. Their approach is to use a hierarchical representation of cases in order to reduce the complexity associated to rich case representations.

The use of CBR techniques in music applications has also been explored in Macedo et al work [14] applying CBR techniques to music composition using a tree-like structured representation of cases. Previous work addressing the issue of learning to generate expressive performances based on examples is that of Widmer [21], who uses explanation-based techniques to learn rules for dynamics and rubato in the context of a MIDI electronic piano. Both, our approach and Widmer's approach take individual notes as training examples and therefore the learning takes place mainly at the note level. However, the structure level in our approach is used for guiding the retrieval and in Widmer's approach for guiding the abstraction process. Another difference concerns the set of expressive parameters that we use. Widmer's approach uses two expressive parameters whereas we use four (dynamics, rubato, vibrato, and articulation) because a saxophone is "richer" than a MIDI electronic piano, from the point of view of expressiveness.

6 Conclusions

We have shown that declarative biases provide flexible ways of constructing dynamical perspectives to guide the retrieval process in a memory of structured phrases. The notion of perspectives has been implemented in the object-centered representation language **Noos** based on feature terms. The practical feasibility of our approach has been shown in the context of a complex real-world CBR system for successfully generating expressive performances of melodies. The evaluation of the output sound files gives compelling evidence for the validity of our approach.

References

1. Agnar Aamodt and Enric Plaza. Case-based reasoning: Foundational issues, methodological variations, and system approaches. *Artificial Intelligence Communications*, 7(1):39–59, 1994.
2. Hassan Aït-Kaci and Andreas Podelski. Towards a meaning of LIFE. *J. Logic Programming*, 16:195–234, 1993.
3. Josep Lluís Arcos. Saxex: un sistema de raonament basat en casos per a l'expressivitat musical. Master's thesis, Institut Universitari de l'Audiovisual. Universitat Pompeu Fabra, 1996.
4. Josep Lluís Arcos, Ramon López de Mántaras, and Xavier Serra. Saxex : a case-based reasoning system for generating expressive performances. In *International Computer Music Conference (ICMC'97)*, 1997.
5. Josep Lluís Arcos and Enric Plaza. Integration of learning into a knowledge modelling framework. In Luc Steels, Guss Schreiber, and Walter Van de Velde, editors, *A Future for Knowledge Acquisition*, number 867 in Lecture Notes in Artificial Intelligence, pages 355–373. Springer-Verlag, 1994.

6. Josep Lluís Arcos and Enric Plaza. Inference and reflection in the object-centered representation language Noos. *Journal of Future Generation Computer Systems*, 12:173–188, 1996.

7. Josep Lluís Arcos and Enric Plaza. Noos: an integrated framework for problem solving and learning. In *Knowledge Engineering: Methods and Languages*, 1997.

8. Eva Armengol and Enric Plaza. Induction of feature terms with INDIE. In M. van Someren and G. Widmer, editors, *Machine Learning: ECML-97*, Lecture Notes in Artificial Intelligence. Springer-Verlag, 1997.

9. L. Karl Branting and David W. Aha. Stratified case-based reasoning: Reusing hierarchical problem solving episodes. In *IJCAI-95*, pages 384–390, 1995.

10. B. Carpenter. *The Logic of typed Feature Structures*. Tracts in theoretical Computer Science. Cambridge University Press, Cambridge, UK, 1992.

11. Friedrich Gebhardt. Methods and systems for case retrieval exploiting the case structure. Technical report, GMD, 1995. FABEL-Report N.39.

12. B.P. Kettler, J.A. Hendler, W.A. Andersen, and M.P. Evett. Massively parallel support for case-based planning. *IEEE Expert*, 9:8–14, 1994.

13. Fred Lerdahl and Ray Jackendoff. An overview of hierarchical structure in music. In Stephan M. Schwanaver and David A. Levitt, editors, *Machine Models of Music*. 1993. Reproduced from Music Perception.

14. Luís Macedo, Francisco C. Pereira, Carlos Grilo, and Amílcar Cardoso. Plans as structured networks of hierarchically and temporally related case pieces. In *Third European Workshop on Case-Based Reasoning EWCBR-96*, Lecture Notes in Artificial Intelligence, pages 234–248. Springer Verlag, 1996.

15. Héctor Muñoz-Avila and Jochem Huellen. Retrieving cases in structured domains by using goal dependences. In Manuela Veloso and Agnar Aamodt, editors, *Case-Based Reasoning, ICCBR-95*, number 1010 in Lecture Notes in Artificial Intelligence, pages 241–252. Springer-Verlag, 1995.

16. Eugene Narmour. *The Analysis and cognition of basic melodic structures : the implication-realization model*. University of Chicago Press, 1990.

17. Enric Plaza. Cases as terms: A feature term approach to the structured representation of cases. In Manuela Veloso and Agnar Aamodt, editors, *Case-Based Reasoning, ICCBR-95*, number 1010 in Lecture Notes in Artificial Intelligence, pages 265–276. Springer-Verlag, 1995.

18. K.E. Sanders, B.P. Kettler, and J.A. Hendler. The case for structured-based representations. Technical report, University of Maryland, 1995.

19. Xavier Serra. Musical sound modelling with sinusoids plus noise. In G. De Poli, A. Picialli, S. T. Pope, and C. Roads, editors, *Musical Signal Processing*. Swets and Zeitlinger Publishers, 1996. (in Press).

20. Luc Steels. Components of expertise. *AI Magazine*, 11(2):28–49, 1990.

21. Gerhard Widmer. Learning expressive performance: The structure-level approach. *Journal of New Music Research*, 25 (2):179–205, 1996.

22. Bob Wielinga, Walter van de Velde, Guss Schreiber, and H. Akkermans. Towards a unification of knowledge modelling approaches. In J. M. David, J. P. Krivine, and R. Simmons, editors, *Second generation Expert Systems*, pages 299–335. Springer Verlag, 1993.

Using Introspective Learning to Improve Retrieval in CBR: A Case Study in Air Traffic Control *

Andrea Bonzano[1], Pádraig Cunningham[1] and Barry Smyth[2]

[1]Artificial Intelligence Group, Trinity College Dublin, Ireland
[2]University College Dublin, Ireland

{Andrea.Bonzano,Padraig.Cunningham}@tcd.ie, bsmyth@cslan.ucd.ie

Abstract. We can learn a lot about what features are important for retrieval by comparing similar cases in a case-base. We can determine which features are important in predicting outcomes and we can assign weights to features accordingly. In the same manner we can discover which features are important in specific contexts and determine localised feature weights that are specific to individual cases. In this paper we describe a comprehensive set of techniques for learning local feature weights and we evaluate these techniques on a case-base for conflict resolution in air traffic control. We show how introspective learning of feature weights improves retrieval and how it can be used to determine context sensitive local weights. We also show that introspective learning does not work well in case-bases containing only pivotal cases because there is no redundancy to be exploited.

1. Introduction

It is standard for CBR tools to support case retrieval using Induction of Decision Trees or using a k-Nearest Neighbour (k-NN) technique (Watson, 1996). In machine learning terms, Induction is probably the more powerful technique, however it cannot be used when cases do not have simple atomic solutions as simple solution categories are required to drive the induction process. k-NN is commonly used in this circumstance but it has the disadvantage that it is very sensitive to the weights allocated to features. Determining a suitable set of weights is a significant knowledge engineering task for the case-base designer. However, there has been some research on automatically learning feature weights (see Wettschereck, Aha & Mohri, 1997 for a comprehensive review).

In this paper we describe the effectiveness of learning local feature weights in ISAC a CBR system for Air Traffic Control (Bonzano & Cunningham, 1996). The objective for ISAC is to help the controller select a manoeuvre so as to resolve

---

* This research is funded by Eurocontrol Experimental Centre, Bretigny-sur-Orge, France.

conflicts between aircraft. A conflict occurs when aircraft are on flight paths that cause them to pass too close. Developing the k-NN retrieval system used in ISAC has been problematic because the important features have been difficult to determine and the relative importance of features has been difficult to gauge. This problem has been confounded by the fact that the features are highly context sensitive; features that are very predictive in some conflicts are not relevant in others.

Introspective learning refers to an approach to learning problem solving knowledge by monitoring the run-time progress of a particular problem solver (Fox & Leake, 1995; Leake et al., 1995; Oehlmann et al., 1995). In particular, we have investigated the problem of learning local, case-specific feature weights by monitoring the retrieval performance of ISAC, work that is related to, and inspired by, similar research by the machine learning community (Saltzburg, 1991; Wettschereck & Aha, 1995; Wettschereck et al., 1997)

In this paper we will present our experiences with introspective learning and describe the lessons learned. We present three central findings:-

- How weights should be adjusted

- The context sensitivity of the weights

- We show that introspective learning doesn't work well with pivotal cases.

We begin with a general review of introspective learning in the next section and we present the findings of our case-study in section 3. We conclude with an assessment of the generality of these findings and some proposals for future work.

2   Introspective Learning

Traditionally, Artificial Intelligence research has focused on the acquisition of domain knowledge in order to provide basic problem solving competence and performance. However, even when a reasoner has a correct set of knowledge it may still experience reasoning failures. This can be explained as an inability of the reasoner to properly access and apply its knowledge. For this reason researchers have looked at how monitoring problem solving performance might lead to new learning opportunities that can improve the way in which available knowledge is used. This form of introspective reasoning and learning has become more and more important in recent years as AI systems have begun to address real-world problem domains, characterized by a high degree of complexity and uncertainty. In such domains, where determining the necessary world knowledge is difficult, it is also be difficult to determine the correct reasoning approach to manipulate this knowledge effectively. Hence the need for introspective learning, and its increasing popularity across a range of AI problem solving paradigms, from planning to case-based reasoning.

Meta-planning was an early model of introspective reasoning found in the MOLGEN planning system (Stefik, 1981). MOLGEN could, to some extent, reason about its own reasoning processes. Meta-planning provided a framework for partitioning knowledge into layers, separating planning knowledge (domain knowledge and planning operators) from meta-knowledge (planning strategies). Introspective reasoning is implemented as planning within the meta-knowledge layer.

SOAR (Laird, Rosenbloom & Newell, 1986; Laird, Newell & Rosenbloom, 1987) also employs a form of introspective reasoning by learning 'meta-rules' which describe how to apply rules about domain tasks and acquire knowledge. SOAR's meta-rules are created by chunking together existing rules and learning is triggered by sub-optimal problem solving results rather than failures.

Case-based reasoning researchers have also begun to understand the importance of introspective reasoning. Fox & Leake (1995) describe a case-based system called ROBBIE which uses introspective reasoning to model, explain, and recover from reasoning failures. Building on ideas first put forward by Birnbaum et al. (1990), Fox and Leake take a model-based approach to recognising and repairing reasoning failures. Their particular form of introspective reasoning focuses on retrieval failures and case index refinement. Work by Oehlmann, Edwards and Sleeman (1995) addresses on the related topic of re-indexing cases, through introspective questioning, to facilitate multiple viewpoints during reasoning. Leake, Kinley, and Wilson (1995) describe how introspective reasoning can also be used to learn adaptation knowledge in the form of adaptation cases.

Many case-based reasoning systems use the k-nearest neighbour (k-NN) classifier (or a derivative) to retrieve cases. One of the problems with this approach is that the standard k-NN similarity function is extremely sensitive to irrelevant, interacting, and noisy features. The typical solution has been to parameterise the similarity function with feature weights so that, for example, the influence of irrelevant features can be de-emphasised through a low weight assignment. However, suitable weight vectors are not always readily available. This has lead to a number of feature-weight learning algorithms which attempt to introspectively refine feature weights on the basis of problem solving successes or failures.

2.1 Introspective Learning of Feature Weights

The basic idea behind the introspective learning of feature weights is to increase or decrease the weights of selected case features on the basis of problem solving performance. For example, from a retrieval perspective, a problem solving failure can be blamed on a poor model of similarity, and in particular on an incorrect weighting of features. Feature weighting methods differ in terms of their learning criteria as well as in terms of their update models.

Two basic learning criteria are used, failure-driven and success-driven. Failure-driven methods only update feature weights as a result of a retrieval failure, and conform to the "if it's not broken don't fix it" school of thought. Success-driven approaches seek to update feature weights as a result of a retrieval success. For each approach the weights of matching and unmatching features are increased or decreased accordingly. Four distinct *learning policies* are possible:

1. There has been a retrieval *success* and the weights of *matching* features are *increased*.

2. There has been a retrieval *success* and the weights of *unmatching* features are *decreased*.

3. There has been a retrieval *failure* and the weights of *unmatching* features are *increased*.

4. There has been a retrieval *failure* and the weights of *matching* features are *decreased*.

Different feature learning algorithms employ different combinations of these techniques. By far the most common strategy is to use all four update policies (e.g., Salzberg, 1991, Wettschereck & Aha, 1995). However, more focused strategies have also been adopted. For example, Munoz-Avila & Hullen (1996) use policies 1 and 3 above to increase or decrease the weights of unmatched features after a retrieval failure or success respectively.

The way in which a feature's weight value is changed during learning, the *update policy*, is also critical. One of the simplest approaches is to increase or decrease feature weights by a fixed amount. For example, Salzberg (1991) uses this method in EACH where all four of the above policies are used to increase or decrease feature weights by some fixed amount Δ_f. Salzberg reported that the benefits associated with the weight learning depended on the value of Δ_f, and that different values of Δ_f worked better on different data-sets. Munoz-Avila & Hullen (1996) use a decaying update policy so that the magnitude of weight changes decreases over time.

In general, the relationship between the learning policy, the update policy, and the application domain is not at all clear and requires further work (this point is emphasised in Wettschereck, Aha & Mohri, 1997). In particular, different policies have been reported to give very different performance results. Moreover, the sensitivity of the learning algorithm to noise and feature interactions needs to be further studied.

3 Introspective Learning in ISAC

For efficiency, similarity in ISAC is calculated using a spreading activation mechanism. The parameters that describe a case can be either symbolic or continuous. When a parameter is symbolic, the activation is increased by w if the values are matching, decreased by w if the values are non-matching and left as it is if one of the two values is unknown: where w is the weight of that feature. The activation increase for continuous features is proportionate to the proximity of the feature values - very different values get a negative activation while similar values get a positive activation. The actual activation is calculated as follows:-

$$ w \times \left(2 \left(1 - \frac{|v_t - v_b|}{v_{max} - v_{min}} \right) - 1 \right) $$

where v_b and v_t are the base and target values and v_{max} and v_{min} are the maximum and minimum values for that parameter in the case base. This gives an activation that can vary from $-w$ to $+w$ as before. The objective for introspective learning is to determine local values for these weights for each feature in each case in the case-base.

3.1 Weight Updating Policies

As discussed in section 2.1, it is possible to update the weight of a parameter according to four different learning policies that depend on whether the retrieved case has the same solution as the target and whether the parameter is matching.

Let us imagine that in a solution space we have a target T and two cases A and B belonging to the case-base each with the same highest activation with respect to T (see Figure 1). A has a correct solution and B is incorrect. So A and B will be retrieved but we only want A to be retrieved. Introspective learning tries to "push" B away from T (i.e. to reduce its activation) and to "pull" A closer to T (i.e. to increase A's activation).

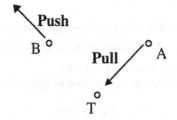

Fig. 1. Pushing and Pulling cases

The four learning policies in terms of this push-pull perspective are as follows:

- GM↑ (Good Matching Up): the case A has the same solution as the target (good retrieval) and we increase (up) the weights of the parameters that have the same value as the target (matching values). By doing this the activation is increased, i.e. we "pull" the case towards the target.

- GU↓ (Good Unmatching Down): the case has the same solution as the target (good retrieval) and the weights of the parameters that have a different value from the target (unmatching values) are decreased (down). The non-matching parameters decrease the case activation so we decrease their weights. By doing this we again "pull" the case towards the target.

- BU↑ (Bad Unmatching Up): the case has a different solution to the target (bad retrieval) and the weights of the parameters that have a different value from the target (unmatching values) are increased (up). By doing this we "push" the case away from the target because the activation in decreased.

- BM↓ (Bad Matching Down): the case has a different solution to the target (bad retrieval) and the weights of the parameters that have the same value as the target (matching values) are decreased (down). So we are again "pushing" the case away from the target.

We evaluated different combinations of these alternatives (see section 4).

The weight can be updated by an update policy which either modifies the existing weight by adding or multiplying by a constant. This weight change itself can be constant or it can decay as the learning proceeds (Munoz-Avila & Hüllen, 1996). We use a decay policy. We evaluated both the alternatives of adding and multiplying and found little difference between them - adding proved slightly better. The formulae are as follows:-

Addition, increase:- $\quad w_i(t+1) = w_i(t) + \Delta i \dfrac{F_c}{K_c}$

Addition, decrease:- $\quad w_i(t+1) = w_i(t) - \Delta i \dfrac{F_c}{K_c}$.

K_c indicates the number of times that a case has been correctly retrieved and F_c reports the number of times that a case has been incorrectly retrieved. The ratio F_c/K_c reduces the influence of the weight update as the number of successful retrievals increases.

The value Δ_i determines the initial weight change. We tested values between 0.1 and 2 and settled on $\Delta_i = 1.0$. There was little to choose between values from 0.5 to 2 because the weight change decreases anyway.

The multiplication alternative was to multiply or divide by the following value:-

$$1 + \Delta i \cdot \frac{F_c}{K_c}$$

When all the weights in a case have been updated they are normalized so that the maximum activation remains the same for all cases in the case-base. This is important to prevent popular cases becoming dominant attractors in the case-base.

3.2 Training the case-base

In the evaluation we present here we use three sets of cases: a **case-base** where the cases will have their local weights adjusted during the introspective learning, a **training set** for training the weights in the case base and a **test set** for testing the performance of the case-base. The steps to train and verify the effectiveness of introspective learning are as follows (see also Figure 2):-

- We test the initial performance of the case-base on the test set and on the training set with all the weights in the case-base set to 1: we call these performance figures P_{ts} and P_{tr}.

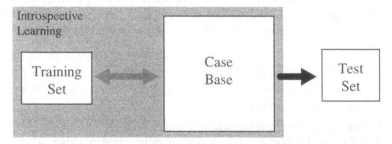

Fig. 2. The components in the introspective learning process.

- We train the case-base by retrieving the k-Nearest Neighbours for each case in the training set. The weights of the k cases are adjusted based on the various learning and update policies. The values for K_c and F_c are also updated for these cases.

- This training step is repeated several times and P_{tr} is calculated after each step.

In Figure 3 it can be seen that P_{tr} increases, but not monotonically, for all learning policy alternatives (see section 4.1 for details). In all evaluations the best figure for P_{tr} was found within 30 iterations. As might be expected the weights start to over-fit the training data by the time this best performance is reached and the performance on the test data disimproves. For this reason we stop the training after 20 iterations and select the weight set corresponding to the best value for P_{tr}.

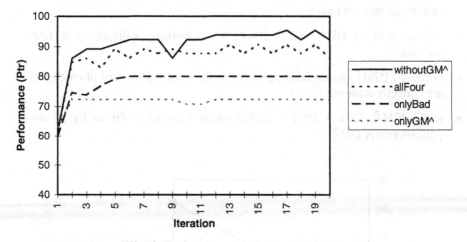

Fig. 3. Performance on the *Training* Set

A better policy would be to use a validation set to determine when to stop training but at present there are not sufficient cases in ISAC for that.

4 Evaluation

In our evaluation we focused on three different aspects:

- Did introspective learning improve retrieval?

- Will introspective learning work with pivotal cases?

- Does introspective learning produce much local variation in feature weights?

For all the experiments we used a case-base of 126 cases, carefully selected to maximise coverage, a training set of 40 cases and a test set of 27 cases. The training and test data are taken from real traffic samples. Each case has 23 parameters, of which 19 are symbolic and 4 numeric.

4.1 Improving Retrieval

The objective in using introspective learning is to improve the quality of retrieval. We found that additive update with decay worked best with the ISAC case-base so that was used throughout the following evaluations.

As explained in section 2.1 and 3.1 there are four learning policies that can be used to control the modification of weights, and there are several combinations of these that may be most effective. Initial evaluation showed that adjustments based on bad retrievals (failure driven) produced much greater improvements that those based on good retrievals.

The overall picture is best illustrated by the four combinations of alternatives graphed in Figure 4. The four combinations are as follows:-

- *onlyBad* (BU↑ + BM↓) where the weight update is driven only by the incorrectly retrieved cases.

- *allFour* (GM↑ + GU↓+ BU↑+ BM↓) where learning is driven by all four policies.

- *onlyGM↑* (GM↑) where learning works on the matched features of cases that are correctly retrieved.

- *withoutGM↑* (GU↓ + BU↑ + BM↓) where learning is driven by all the policies except GM↑.

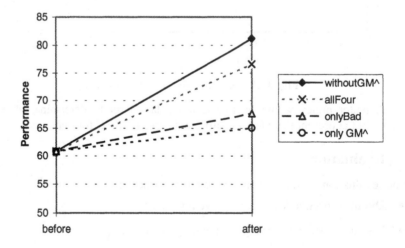

Fig. 4. Improvements in P_{ts}, the performance on the *Test* Set.

The additive update increment used for these tests was $\Delta_i = 1$. The graph shows improvements on P_{ts}, the performance on the test set. All the four learning policy combinations showed a performance increase. The best increase of performance was recorded with the method *withoutGM↑* where correct retrievals increased from 61%

to 81%. In general, it seems that the most effective policies are the ones that are driven by the bad retrievals. It is clear that the effect of increasing weights of features that match on correct retrievals (GM↑) results in very little improvement.

4.2 Introspective Learning with Pivotal Cases

Smyth and Keane (1995) show that a case-base can be reduced in size without losing competence provided pivotal cases are not removed. A pivotal case is one that provides coverage not provided by other cases in the case-base. This is related to the idea of having a case-base of 'clean' cases where cases are hand picked to be of good quality and to cover particular areas of the problem domain.

It might be expected that a case-base composed of pivotal or 'clean' cases will not benefit much from introspective learning of feature weights. Introspective learning depends on having adjacent cases so that the relevance of features can be determined. However, this redundancy will not exist in a pivotal case-base.

To verify this hypothesis we ran two experiments: one with a toy case-base where cases could be verified to be pivotal and one with the ISAC cases. Tests on the toy case-base supported the hypothesis. The 126 cases available in ISAC are specially prepared clean cases so our hypothesis suggests that introspective learning will not work with these. From this 126 we prepared a case-base of 86 cases and a training set of 40 pivotal cases. For comparison we also prepared a training set of 40 cases taken from real traffic samples. After training the case-base with each of these training sets in turn we tested it with a test set also taken from real traffic samples. This experiment was repeated 22 times with different training sets. The results showed that training with pivotal (or clean) cases only produced an improvement of just 7% while training with random cases produced an improvement of 18% (see Table 1). This supports our hypothesis that introspective learning of feature weights exploits redundancy in the case-base and there is little redundancy in a case-base of pivotal or clean cases.

Table 1. Pivotal versus non-pivotal Training Set

Training Set	P_{ts}(before)	P_{ts}(after)
pivotal	61%	68%
real	61%	79%

4.3 Analysis of Context Sensitivity

Initial development on ISAC suggested that the features were quite context sensitive and an examination of the learned weights shows that this is the case. The histograms in Figures 5 and 6 show distributions of weight values in the trained case-base for two specific features, 'Levels Available' and 'Close to Boundaries'. In each case the range of weights has been divided into 10 intervals and the frequencies of weights in each interval are shown. (Weights that remained unchanged at 1 have been removed).

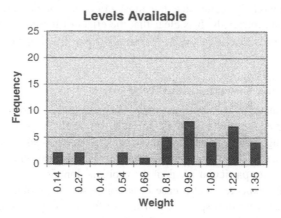

Fig. 5. The distribution of learned weights for the LevelsAvailable feature.

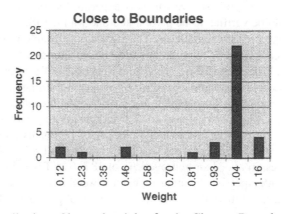

Fig. 6. The distribution of learned weights for the Close to Boundaries feature.

The situation for the Levels Available feature shown in Figure 5 is the most typical, showing quite a spread in its weight values across the case-base. Thus the relative important of this feature clearly changes from case to case and hence the feature is of local importance across the case-base. This accords with the meaning of this feature because it indicates whether other altitude levels are free and is only important when an altitude manoeuvre is being considered. By comparison the Close to Boundaries feature shown in Figure 6 is evidently more global and again this makes sense in the problem domain. If an aircraft is close to the boundary of the controller's sector then this is always an important consideration.

5   Conclusions and Future Work

We have shown that the *withoutGM*↑ learning policy improves retrieval in ISAC from 61% to 81%. It appears that failure driven rather than success driven learning contributes most to this improvement. This effect is not reported elsewhere so we need to determine why this is the case with ISAC. This is important because learning from good retrievals is required if we need to further improve on this figure. This is because most of the observations in training will be good retrievals when starting from a success rate already in the 80s.

We have also verified that introspective learning of feature weights does not work well when the cases used for training are pivotal. This is predicted by our understanding of the need for redundancy in the case-base in introspective learning. So this finding should be true in general.

Finally we have shown that, for many features in ISAC, the learned local weights vary considerably. This is predicted by our understanding that the importance of many features in this domain is context sensitive. Presumably this varies from problem to problem, however using local rather than global weights has definitely been helpful here.

In the future we propose to apply these techniques in other domains to see if the advantages of failure driven learning are true in general or are a quirk of the ISAC domain. We also need to evaluate other combinations of learning policies and to directly compare local and global learning strategies.

References

Birnbaum, L., Collins, G., Brand, M., Freed, M., Krulwich, B., and Prior, L. (1991) A Model-Based Approach to the Construction of Adaptive Case-Based Planning Systems. *Proceedings of the Case-Based Reasoning Workshop*, pp. 215-224. Washington D.C., USA.

Bonzano A., & Cuningham P., (1996) ISAC: A CBR System for Decision support in Air Traffic Control in Proceedings of EWCBR '96, Advances in Case-Based Reasoning, Ian Smith & Boi Faltings eds. Springer Verlag Lecture Notes in AI, pp44-57.

Fox, S. & Leake, D. B. (1995) Using Introspective Reasoning to Refine Indexing. *Proceedings of the 14th International Joint Conference on Artificial Intelligence*, pp. 391-397.

Laird, J. E, Rosenbloom, P. S., and Newell, A. (1986) Chucking in Soar: The Anatomy of a General Learning Mechanism. *Machine Learning.* 1(1).

Laird, J. E., Newell, A., and Rosenbloom, P. S. (1987) Soar: An Architecture for General Intelligence. *Artificial Intelligence.* 33(1).

Leake, D. B., Kinley, A., and Wilson, D. (1995) Learning to Improve Case Adaptation by Introspective Reasoning and CBR. Case-Based Reasoning Research and Development (Ed.s M. Veloso & A. Aamodt), Proceedings of the 1st International Conference on Case-Based Reasoning, pp. 229-240, Springer-Verlag.

Munoz-Avila, H., Hüllen, J. (1996) Feature Weighting by ExplainingCase-Based Planning Episodes. Advances in Case-Based Reasoning (Ed.s I. Smith & B. Faltings), Proceedings of the Third European Workshop on Case-Based Reasoning, pp. 280-294, Springer-Verlag.

Oehlmann, R., Edwards, P., & Sleeman, D. (1995) Changing the Viewpoint: Re-Indexing by Introspective Question. *Proceedings of the 16th Annual Conference of the Cognitive Science Society*, pp. 381-386. Lawrence-Erlbaum and Associates.

Saltzburg, S. L. (1991) A Nearest Hyperrectangle Learning Method. *Machine Learning,* **1**.

Stefik, M. (1981) Planning and Meta-Planning. Artificial Intelligence, **16**, pp. 141-170.

Smyth, B. & Keane, M. T. (1995) Remembering to Forget: A Competence Preserving Case Deletion Policy for CBR Systems. *Proceedings of the 14th International Joint Conference on artificial Intelligence (IJCAI-95),* pp. 377-382. Montreal, Canada.

Veloso, M. (1992) Learning by Analogical Reasoning in General Problem Solving. *Ph.D. Thesis,* (CMU-CS-92-174), School of Computer Science, Carnegie Mellon University, Pittsburgh, USA.

Watson I. D., (1996)   Case-Based Reasoning Tools: An Overview, In Proceedings of 2nd. UK CBR Workshop, Progress in Case-Based Reasoning, Watson. I.D. (Ed.) pp.71-88. University of Salford. (also available on the Web at http://146.87.176.38/ai-cbr/Papers/cbrtools.doc)

Wetterschereck, D., & Aha, D. W. (1995) Weighting Features. Case-Based Reasoning Research and Development (Ed.s M. Veloso & A. Aamodt), Proceedings of *The 1st International Conference on Case-Based Reasoning,* pp. 347-358, Springer-Verlag.

Wettschereck, D., Aha, D. W., & Mohri, T. (1997). A review and empirical evaluation of feature weighting methods for a class of lazy learning algorithms. To appear in Artificial Intelligence Review. (also available on the Web from http://www.aic.nrl.navy.mil/~aha/)

Using Machine Learning for Assigning Indices to Textual Cases*

Stefanie Brüninghaus and Kevin D. Ashley

University of Pittsburgh
Learning Research and Development Center, Intelligent Systems Program, and School of Law
3939 O'Hara Street, Pittsburgh, PA 15260
steffi+@pitt.edu, ashley+@pitt.edu

Abstract. *This paper reports preliminary work on developing methods automatically to index cases described in text so that a case-based reasoning system can reason with them. We are employing machine learning algorithms to classify full-text legal opinions in terms of a set of predefined concepts. These factors, representing factual strengths and weaknesses in the case, are used in the case-based argumentation module of our instructional environment CATO. We first show empirical evidence for the conncetion between the factor model and the vector representation of texts developed in information retrieval. In a set of hypotheses we sketch how including knowledge about the meaning of the factors, their relations and their use in the case-based reasoning system can improve learning, and discuss in what ways background knowledge about the domain can be beneficial. The paper presents initial experiments that show the limitations of purely inductive algorithms for the task.*

1 Introduction

In domains where human professionals reason with cases, the cases frequently are represented as texts. This is true of applications involving reasoning with legal or ethical cases, medical diagnostic and treatment records, customer service help desk reports, and even descriptions of software or production schedules which may guide adaptation and reuse. If CBR methods are to be applied, formal representations must be developed for capturing knowledge of a case's important features as described in the text so that a computer program can reason with the cases.

A common need in automating case-based reasoning in such domains is to map relatively unstructured textual descriptions onto highly structured representations. Unfortunately, to date this mapping has been largely a manual effort. Someone needs to read the text and fill out the structure for representing the case to a computer. In building a legal CBR system, candidate cases for the case base have to be identified and read, the most important cases selected, and then represented with some combination of frames and factors which capture relevant factual strengths and weaknesses (see, e.g., HYPO (Ashley 1990), BANKXX (Rissland & Daniels 1995), and CATO (Aleven & Ashley 1996). Likewise, GREBE (Branting 1991) required that cases be coded by hand, as semantic networks. This need manually to represent cases described as texts has been one

---

* We would like to thank Vincent Aleven for his support and numerous contributions to this research, in particular for making accessible CATO's Factor Hierarchy and Case Database.

of the chief disadvantages of CBR approaches as compared to information retrieval (IR) techniques, where large collections of full-text documents are processed automatically.

We describe preliminary work on an approach to classifying texts automatically, in which we are using domain knowledge associated with structured CBR case representations to guide training of inductive machine learning programs to classify texts. The project builds upon CATO (Aleven & Ashley 1996), an intelligent learning environment for teaching case-based argumentation to law students. In CATO, cases are represented in terms of 26 *factors*, stereotypical fact patterns which tend to strengthen or weaken a legal claim. More abstract domain knowledge is captured in the *Factor Hierarchy*, a multi-level hierarchical knowledge structure that relates factors to normative concerns of a particular body of law (*legal issues*) via a specific support relation. The Factor Hierarchy enables CATO to interpret and reason about the significance of partially-matched cases and to organize multi-case arguments according to issues (Aleven & Ashley 1997). CATO's Case Database contains 147 cases involving a claim for trade secret misappropriation. Trade secret law protects confidential corporate information from unfair use by competitors. These cases are represented manually in terms of the applicable factors, a "squib" or brief textual description of the case's facts and decision, and, for this work, the full-text opinions in which judges recorded in detail their decisions and rationales. In contrast to other legal CBR systems, the model of case-based argumentation in CATO includes a representation of abstract domain knowledge for interpreting cases, which, we believe, can be used to help induction programs classify texts.

In this paper we (1) report an experiment demonstrating the empirical basis of our intuition that the factor model can be useful in guiding machine learning programs to classify opinion texts according to the factors and issues that apply, (2) discuss seven hypotheses we will test to discover specific ways to integrate knowledge about the meaning and interrelations of factors and domain-specific information about the document structure into the text classification process, (3) report preliminary results from applying inductive machine learning algorithms to classify texts which will serve as a baseline for assessing any contributions from the knowledge-based methods, and (4) argue that our approach has significance for domains other than legal reasoning.

2 Approaches for Analyzing Text Documents

Finding a way to extract and represent the contents of textual documents so that one can reason with them symbolically has been recognized as a research problem in many fields within AI. Information Extraction (IE) (Cowie & Lehnert 1996), a subfield of natural language processing, is concerned with identifying specific pieces of information within documents for filling in predefined frames with a relatively simple object/relation structure. The underlying texts are generally rather simple. Despite good performance in limited domains, IE systems are often not appropriate for bridging the gap between a case-based reasoning system and textual cases, since they require large numbers of manually annotated texts (typically on the order of 1000 or even more documents).

In order to facilitate the representation of textual cases in a way suitable for a case-based reasoning system, another possible solution could be to help the user to identify the section of the text in which the information related to the indexing term is given, like in SPIRE (Rissland & Daniels 1995). SPIRE is a hybrid CBR/IR system aiming at overcoming the current bottleneck in deriving a frame-based representation of legal opinion texts. Cases are manually annotated to include textual segments that contain the information needed to fill in the slots of its case representation. These annotations are used by the relevance feedback module of the INQUERY retrieval system (Callan, Croft, & Harding 1992) to retrieve and present the most similar text sections in a new case. Daniels attempts to automate indexing by focusing the human user on pertinent sentences in a text to reduce the time and effort needed for finding important features. We intend to develop a system that classifies a new case under more abstract factual patterns and to make use of the information about relations among factors contained in the Factor Hierarchy, which could probably be applied very beneficially in conjunction with locating relevant information in a case.

The assignment of abstract indexing terms may also be seen as a classification task, as performed in IR and Machine Learning (ML). In IR, the task is to retrieve, categorize, route or filter documents, and IR systems can be seen as classifiers deciding to which category (e.g., relevant or irrelevant to a query) a document belongs, or how strongly it belongs to a class (i.e., ranking) (Lewis et al. 1996). The methods used are domain-independent, and aimed at very large document collections, which makes them not directly applicable for indexing textual documents for case-based reasoning, where numbers of training instances in the case base typically are rather small. The use of ML algorithms for deriving text classifiers has been explored in recent work (Lewis et al. 1996; Papka, Callan, & Barto 1996). In ML research, the main focus in text learning has been on filtering relevant documents, in particular Web pages, email messages and usenet news messages. These approaches do not consider any domain specific knowledge or semantic structure, and represent documents as highly-dimensional word-vectors.

From a CBR perspective, the main focus in the research on automatic indexing has been on refining and modifying the representation of cases in problem-solving CBR systems if a critic component detects failed plans and identifies a repair strategy (Fox & Leake 1995). This requires a strong model of the domain to detect failure, as well as the ability to assign blame for it (Cox 1994), which are both missing in our application. In case-based story-retrieval systems, less knowledge-intensive, frame-based methods for supporting human indexers and facilitating automatic cross-referencing of episodes have been developed (Osgood & Bareiss 1993), similar to the approach in SPIRE.

3 From Texts To Factors

We regard the task of assigning factors to opinion texts as one of learning to classify instances from examples. The cases in which factor f applies form a class of instances under the concept $\mathcal{F}$. Using the cases in CATO's Case Database as training instances, we are going to use ML algorithms together with knowledge-based techniques to find a weighted set of features that enable deciding whether a new trade secret opinion belongs to concept $\mathcal{F}$. More formally, we can describe the learning task as follows:

Given: (1) the full-text opinions of the cases in the CATO database as training examples, labeled by the set of factors f_i that apply (according to a manual indexer), (2) a set of relations that hold over CATO's factors (the Factor Hierarchy), and (3) additional background knowledge about opinion texts,

Learn: to assign a set of factors f_j to a new case j presented as a full-text opinion.

In order to provide the textual cases in a form compatible with the ML approach defined above, our project employs document representation and matching methods based on the vector space model developed in IR research. The three main elements in that model are *Lexical Analysis, Term Weighting* and *Document Matching* (Frankes & Baeza-Yates 1992). In the process of generating a document representation, texts are first split into single words by a *Lexical Analyzer*. In the next step, stop-words (like "the", "a", or "to") are filtered out and word endings (like "ing", "ly" or "ed") are removed using Porter's algorithm (Frankes & Baeza-Yates 1992). In addition, we decided to use bigrams as tokens, i.e., pairs of adjacent words that are not stop-words. The frequency vector is a set of feature/value pairs consisting of the tokens and the respective terms' frequency count. A sentence like "The secret recipe is considered to be a trade secret" will be translated into the frequency vector tf = (consid 1, recip 1, secret 2, trad 1, tradscret 1, secretrecip 1). *Term Weighting* assigns weights to the terms in a document vector based on the assumption that the more often a term occurs within a document, the more important the term is for that document, and the more documents contain that term, the less important it is for any single document. The weight for a word in a document is calculated as the frequency of the word within the document multiplied by the logarithm of the proportion of documents containing that word. In the *Document Matching* process, the similarity of a pair of documents is calculated as the cosine of the angle between their weight vectors, taking the inner product of the normalized document vectors.

An important assumption underlying our research project is that a connection exists between the representation of a legal case in the factor model, and its representation in the vector-space model. However, the representation of textual documents in the vector space model is fundamentally different from the representation in CATO's factor model, and likewise the document matching using the cosine measure appears to have little in common with the symbolical case comparison in CATO.

In the factor model, cases are compared symbolically, and sets of factors shared between cases are an indicator of similarity. Cases are considered *relevantly similar* to a problem situation under HYPO's definition (Ashley 1990) if they have at least one factor in common. For the experiments, we defined the *top-tier* cases as those that either share all factors or a maximally inclusive subset of factors with the problem situation. They can be found in the root node and the first layer of HYPO's claim lattice.

For each case in CATO's Case Database, we calculated the average similarity to the *top-tier* cases by taking the mean of the cosines between the the cases and document vectors of the *top-tier* cases. Accordingly, we calculated the average similarity of each case to the *relevantly similar* cases and to *all cases*. For many cases, the average similarity to *all cases* was smaller than to *relevantly similar* and *top-tier* cases, but we also found a number of cases where this did not hold. We used statistical inference methods to confirm the hypothesis that overall the *top-tier* cases are more similar to a problem situation than the *relevantly similar* cases, which are more similar than *all cases*.[2] For each of the 147 cases, we calculated the difference of the average-similarity $\Delta_{top-tier,all-cases}$. If all variance in the difference between *all-cases* and *top-tier* cases

---

[2] The following description will focus on the test between *top-tier* and *all cases*, the other two relations were established in the same way.

is due to chance, the frequency distribution of Δ will be a Bell curve with mean 0.

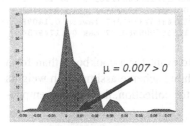

$\mu = 0.007 > 0$

Fig. 1 Freq. Distribution of Δ

However, when we plot the frequency distribution of $\Delta_{top-tier,all-cases}$ (see Fig. 1), the curve "leans to the right" (is skewed), and the mean $\mu \approx 0.007$ is greater than 0. Using a matched-pair t-test, we found the results of the t-test to be statistically significant (p = 0.00). In other words, we found empirical evidence that the more similar cases are in the factor model, the more similar they are in the vector-space model.

4 Adding Background Knowledge to Automatic Indexing Methods

Inductive learning methods for text classification and IE have been successful in domains where large training sets are available, where the concepts are relatively simple, and where only one concept is assigned to a case. In our project, however, the multiple abstract concepts are more complex, strongly interrelated, and the number of training instances is small, which makes the task much harder and limits the utility of purely inductive learning methods (as shown in Section 5). We believe that combining inductive learning with analytical learning techniques (Mitchell 1997) or enhancing them with background knowledge to guide the learning process can help more effectively to deduce classifiers for opinion texts under abstract index categories. The sources of domain knowledge are the factors and their interrelations in CATO's model, information about the general structure and content of opinions, as well as domain knowledge captured in a dictionary.

We have developed a set of hypotheses which explain in more detail in what ways this knowledge can be used. To illustrate our ideas, we will focus on an example from CATO's case database. In *Peggy Lawton v. T.M. Hogan*, an employee of a food company resigned after he managed to gain access to the secret ingredient for chocolate chip cookies. Afterward, he sold cookies baked with an identical recipe under his own name, and was sued by his former employer for trade secret misappropriation. In CATO's Case Database, *Peggy Lawton* is represented by factors F6 (Security-Measures), F15 (Unique-Product) and F18 (Identical-Products).

> HYPOTHESIS I *A knowledge-rich representation of the meaning of terms used in documents will improve the learning process and enhance the effectiveness of a classifier.*

Typically, documents are represented in IR and ML by splitting the text into words, and taking those as tokens. However, this approach neglects the specialized language used in an area of discourse, and the meaning inherently assigned with technical terms. We believe that identifying domain specific concepts in the document text, e.g., using a concept dictionary, can help more reliably to determine what the document is about by focusing ML, matching and ranking algorithms on the more relevant input tokens. First experiments confirming this hypothesis are reported at the end of Sec. 5. The limitations of traditional document representations can be illustrated with the initial part of the (normalized) vector representing the *Peggy Lawton* opinion.

```
peggy-lawton kitchen 0.469961365319674 cooki 0.265727788994812 chocolatchip 0
.265727788994812 chocolat 0.265727788994812 hogan 0.245080291589835 hogie 0.2
3915501009533 hogiebear 0.23915501009533 recip 0.204872439324538 chip 0.20423
3576324863 cookie 0.18798454612787 chipcooki 0.159436673396887 lawton 0.14098
8409595902 wolf 0.130196867068915 ingredient 0.119556905660277 bak 0.11749034
```

The vector contains more terms that would be relevant for a cookbook than for a legal application. The domain-independent IR weighting scheme assigns high weights to terms that allow identifying this document within the collection, thereby overemphasizing words not useful for assigning factors.

HYPOTHESIS II *Decomposing the problem by first determining which broader index applies to a case, and then refining the indexing decreases the complexity of the learning task.*

Another technique potentially useful is to decompose the problem into less complex subproblems by assigning issues first, and then use this as input to subsequent classifiers which identify more specific factors presented in the text. We suspect that (1) deciding which general issues a case involves is easier than assigning the more detailed factors, and (2) once issues have been identified, the Factor Hierarchy's relations of issues to factors can be used to focus learning on particular factors and reduce their hypothesis space.

HYPOTHESIS III *Relations among factors and issues in the Factor Hierarchy can enhance performance by supporting predictions of the likelihood that a factor applies in situations where training instances are scarce.*

In the CATO database, six of the factors apply to as few as ten or fewer cases. These numbers are too small for learning algorithms to generalize well. In order to compensate for the small number of instances, we intend to employ heuristics based on the meaning of factors and on their relationships expressed in the Factor Hierarchy. Based on either semantic or empirical grounds, one may infer that certain factors naturally occur together (or not). The Factor Hierarchy expresses semantic relations among factors via more abstract parent concepts (i.e., issues and other high-level factors), which can provide confirming evidence for a factor in a text and to test the credibility of an assignment of factors.

Consider, for instance, F23, Waiver-Of-Confidentiality, which applies to only six cases in the database. The concept is very hard to find, since it can involve diverse fact situations. It would be much easier to train a classifier to identify factors F1, Disclosure-In-Negotiations, or F21, Knew-Info-Confidential, which apply in many more cases. F23 has some useful relationships with these easier-to-learn factors. There would rarely be a waiver of confidentiality without a disclosure in negotiations. It would also be unlikely to find a waiver of confidentiality in a case where there is a non-disclosure agreement (represented by F4) or knowledge that information is confidential. Our expectations about these relationships can be expressed probabilistically, and then used with Bayes' Law to help assess whether F23 is in fact present:

$$E(F1|F23) \mapsto high, E(F4|F23) \mapsto low, E(F21|F23) \mapsto low$$

The knowledge about the relations among factors represented in CATO's Factor Hierarchy can also be used to check the factors assigned by the system for consistency and detect incorrect classifications. Moreover, if it is possible to determine from an (IE-like) analysis of the text which side won, plaintiff or defendant, a system can also reason about whether the assigned factors are consistent with the result. If only pro-defendant factors were found, but plaintiff won, the factor assignment is suspect.

HYPOTHESIS IV *Identifying quotations of statutory texts in an opinion text should help identify applicable issues.*

In legal opinion texts, the courts refer to the relevant statutes or restatement commentaries to provide a justification for their decision. Spotting these quotations is evidence for the issue raised. The following quote of the (First) Restatement of Torts § 757 can be found in *Motorola*:

"(A) substantial element of secrecy must exist, so that, except by the use of improper means, there would be difficulty in acquiring the information. ... Matters of public knowledge or of general knowledge in an industry cannot be appropriated by one as his secret."

This code section is related to high-level factor F120 (Info-Legitimately-Obtained-Or-Obtainable), in CATO's Factor Hierarchy. Supporting evidence for F120 is high-level factor F105 Info-Is-Known-Or-Available ("general knowledge"), while Questionable-Means (F111), referred to as "improper" above, blocks this conclusion. From the quote in *Motorola* one may expect that these abstract factors are related to the issues discussed in the text of the opinion.

HYPOTHESIS V *Accounting for document structure can help identify relevant text segments, thus focussing the classifier on predictive input.*

Information about the structure of the text of an opinion can be employed beneficially in identifying important and less relevant sections. While not following a rigid format, legal opinions do have a basic structure: first the facts of the case are described, then the applicable law is stated and applied to the facts, and finally, the legal consequences are drawn. If a system can detect this structure, the information contained in the different parts can be used more specifically. The applicable law is usually a good indicator for the issues raised, while the factors themselves are mainly determined by the facts of the case. Paragraphs discussing the amount of damages payable to plaintiff are not related to factors, and should be ignored, since they introduce irrelevant information, or noise.

HYPOTHESIS VI *Identifying cases cited in an opinion text where it is known which factors apply to the cited case can support inferences about the issues and factors of the opinion.*

This hypothesis is fairly specific for the legal domain, and illustrates how one can employ a model of reasoning with cases in this domain. Knowing which factors apply to the cases cited in an opinion is evidence for which issues are dealt with in the citing case, since citations are made to support the court's decision related to an issue by comparing the case to precedents. The information derived from cases cited would not allow us

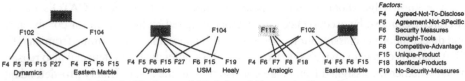

Fig. 2. Citations and High-Level Factors in *Peggy Lawton*

directly to ascertain which factors apply, but it effects our beliefs about the case, as we will illustrate with the *Peggy Lawton* case.

In three separate paragraphs, shown in Fig. 2, *Peggy Lawton* cites ten cases, for five of which we have a factor representation. The factors in the cases cited can be related to abstract factors in the Factor Hierarchy. For example, the factors in *Dynamics* and *Eastern Marble* are related to F101 via F102 and F104.

To show this in detail, we focus on the third paragraph. The court cites *Eastern Marble*, in which F4, F5, F6, and F15 apply, and *Analogic*, in which F4, F6, F7, F8, and F18 apply. Both cases share abstract factors F102 Info-Valuable and F104 Efforts-To-Maintain-Secrecy. The strategy is to treat the most inclusive shared abstract factors (in Fig. 2 shaded in dark grey) as likely issues. From the *Peggy Lawton's* court's selection of cases to cite, for example, we thus expect it was held that plaintiff's information was a trade secret (F101), that plaintiff took measures to maintain the secrecy of the information (F102) and that the information was valuable (F104). We also expect that the factors of the case would relate to those abstract factors. We can conjecture that the factors in *Peggy Lawton* are the same as those shared in the cited cases, which would be F6 and (incorrectly) F4 for the efforts to keep the information secret, and F15 for the worth of the information.

> HYPOTHESIS VII *An appropriate combination of some or all of the knowledge-based methods for learning to assign factors to opinion texts (items I through VI) and some of the known inductive learning algorithms can improve performance.*

We think that the task of assigning factors to opinions texts is so complicated and involves so many different aspects that some combination of several or all of the techniques described above is most appropriate. Combining these techniques may help in overcoming the limitations inherent in each of them.

5 Initial Experimental Results

In an initial experiment with the cases in CATO's Case Database we tried to find out how well purely inductive methods can do for the given problem. Some of the algorithms we implemented are directly based on the vector space model and had been successfully used in IR and IF experiments (Rocchio and TFIDF-Prototype (Joachims 1996)). In theoretical investigations and in experiments for text filtering, Winnow (Golding & Roth 1996), Widrow-Hoff and Exponentiated-Gradient (Lewis *et al.* 1996) were found to be particularly suitable for learning problems where the input consists of a large number of tokens, many of which are irrelevant for the classification task. We also used Libbow[3] to test the performance of a naive bayesian classifier and a probabilistic version of TFIDF-prototype.

---

[3] Libbow is a code package developed by Andrew McCallum for text classification experiments. For a description of the algorithms see (Mitchell 1997) and (Joachims 1996). It is available from http://www.cs.cmu.edu/afs/cs/project/theo-11/www/naive-bayes.html.

The opinions were converted into feature/value vectors which could be used as an input to the algorithms, as described in Sec. 3. The case collection was split into test and training data during 5-fold cross-validation. As an evaluation measure, we used the accuracy of the algorithms, which is defined as the percentage of test instances classified correctly. This measure favors labeling cases as negative when positive instances in the training set are scarce. Precision (percentage of instances labeled as positive where a factor applies) and recall (percentage of instances where a factor applies that were recognized as positive) are the common measures in IR, but only focus on retrieving the relevant documents in a collection, which is not the primary goal in classification. Thus, we use accuracy as the main criterion, but also to interpret the results in the light of precision and recall.

To find a baseline for the algorithms' performance, we used a *random strategy*. Without any prior knowledge, cases are classified by chance, and with a probability of 0.5 labeled as positive instances of the factor. This strategy did actually achieve pretty respectable values for recall - since even for the most difficult factors, it retrieved about half of the relevant cases. We also included another *default strategy*, which labels all cases presented to the system as "factor does not apply". Although this strategy achieved excellent accuracy on factors with only few cases, recall is zero, and precision undefined. For practical use, however, both strategies would be unacceptable.

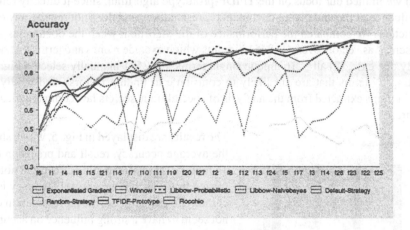

Fig. 3. Results of the experiments

The results of our experiments are summarized in Fig. 3. The accuracy of the algorithms is plotted over the factors, which are arranged by decreasing number of cases in which they apply; the leftmost factor F6 applies to 79 cases in the case-base, while the rightmost factor, F25 applies to only 5 cases. Fig. 3 shows that the inductive machine learning algorithms we tested do not provide a good solution. No algorithm achieves a consistently high accuracy and at the same time desirable precision and recall. We did not observe a trade-off between precision and recall, as one would expect from IR. Instead, algorithms either performed reasonably on precision and recall, with low accuracy, or had high accuracy, with weak performance on precision and recall. When we tried to find how well the algorithms can perform when the parameters are optimized manually, and post-tuned the threshold for Rocchio, both precision and recall increased with only minor decrease in accuracy (see Fig. 4).

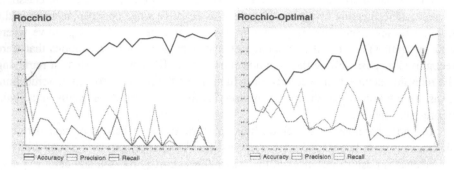

Fig. 4. Precision and recall Rocchio with automatically and manually set threshold

Since most algorithms inherently aim at maximizing accuracy (and not precision or recall), one expects them to generalize by classifying too many examples as negative, especially for factors with only very few positive examples.

We also did a first set of experiments in which we tried to confirm HYPOTHESIS I, in which we limited our focus on the TFIDF-prototype algorithm, since it directly reflects the influence of the underlying document representation, and does not require any other parameters. We compared the performance of the algorithm when the documents were represented as vectors over: (1) 8451 bigrams which exclude names and terms that occur in only one case, (2) all 5216 unique single terms, (3) 2531 manually selected bigrams (deleting all terms that are not likely to contribute to finding factors), and finally, (4) 1553 bigrams extracted from the analysis of special trade secrets law commentaries and keyphrases.

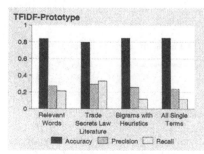

Fig. 5 Performance on different representations

The results are displayed in Fig. 5, which shows the average accuracy, recall and precision over all factors. (Many interesting effects get not displayed this way, but the general tendency is accurate.) To our surprise, the representation does not seem to have a strong influence on accuracy. The more domain-specific representations lead to a moderate increase in precision, and recall was about doubled, which suggests that an improved representation can increase performance for this classification task.

6 Conclusion

In this paper, we have presented evidence (a) of an empirical correspondence between case similarity as measured by our CBR factor model and the IR vector space model. When cases were selected as more similar to a problem represented with the factor model, the associated texts turned out also to be more similar when represented with the vector space model. We have also shown evidence that (b) machine learning techniques alone do not successfully classify texts according to the factors that apply.

We will test hypotheses how to use the CBR domain model to improve machine learning text classification performance by: (1) enriching the representation of texts using a domain ontology and information about the document structure, (2) integrating into the inductive learning algorithms knowledge from our (incomplete) domain model of document contents, specifically what factors mean and how they are interrelated, and (3) combining different learning techniques using the domain model.

These ideas should be important in other domains, as well. While the details of the model, document structure, enriched representations and decompositions will differ across domains, documents from other domains evidence their own models, structures, and possibilities for enriching representations and clever decompositions. In a number of domains where case-based reasoning is performed or could be very beneficial, a model of the use of documents can be constructed, and the cases are available in the form of partially structured textual descriptions. In these domains, highly structured representations and relatively unstructured textual descriptions need to be mapped to each other. Using small sets of existing examples, available background knowledge, and some information about document structure could serve to reduce the costs of mapping. For instance, large medical databases record patients' circumstances, diagnoses, pre-scribed treatments and outcomes in a somewhat structured form. Reuse and adaptation of this information is being attempted in (Portinale & Torasso 1995). Reuse and adap-tation of software is a potential application for CBR, but there is a need to match the software to the specification documents, and the handbooks or other documents created to describe the code. General descriptions of production plans and constraints result in detailed production plans and schedules. These plans can be adapted to new situations and reused, but again, it would be important to match text descriptions to plan specifics. Similarly, help desk systems require free-text descriptions of customer service problems and solutions to be mapped to and compared with other problems and solutions.

Even the factor model of the use of legal cases is of more general importance than may at first appear, since it addresses a problem similar to one faced by the development of CBR and IR/information filtering techniques in domains other than the law. With the proliferation of databases of on-line documents, information filtering needs to do more than label subject matter. It needs to address how interesting or important a document is likely to be in light of a more detailed model of a reader's interests and of what use the reader can make of the document. The most important information in a text may be the strengths and weaknesses, costs and benefits, or pluses and minuses of the subject matter it describes. This kind of information, which factors are intended to capture, enables a reader to compare the subject matter described to other cases known by or available to the reader. It relates low level factual circumstances described in the text to more specific conclusions about the text's usefulness in light of the reader's purpose. If an automatic filter is to work realistically, it will need to implement a model of factors representing the kinds of circumstances which are important to the reader, the conclusions to which they are relevant, and how the circumstances affect the conclusions in terms of relative benefits and costs, strengths and weaknesses, pluses and minuses.

References

Aleven, V., and Ashley, K. 1996. How Different is Different? Arguing about the Significance of Similarities and Differences. In *Proc. of the 4th European Workshop on Case-Based Reasoning*, 1–15.

Aleven, V., and Ashley, K. 1997. An Empirical Evaluation of an Intelligent Learning Environment for Case-Based Argumentation. In *AIED-97*. to appear.

Ashley, K. 1990. *Modeling Legal Argument, Reasoning with Cases and Hypotheticals*. MIT-Press.

Branting, L. 1991. Building explanations from rules and structured cases. *Internation Journal on Man-Machine Studies* 34(6).

Callan, J.; Croft, W.; and Harding, S. 1992. The INQUERY Retrieval System. In *Proc. of the 3rd Internat. Conference on Database and Expert Systems Applications*, 78–83.

Callan, J. 1996. Document Filtering with Inference Networks. In *Proc. of the 19th Annual International ACM SIGIR Conference*.

Cowie, J., and Lehnert, W. 1996. Information extraction. *Comm. ACM* 39(1):80–91.

Cox, M. 1994. Machines that Forget: Learning from retrieval failure of mis-indexed explanations. In *Proc. of the 16th Conf. of the Cognitive Science Society*, 225–230.

Fox, S., and Leake, D. 1995. Learning to Refine Indexing by Introspective Reasoning. In *Proceedings of the 1st International Conference on Case-Based Reasoning*.

Frankes, W., and Baeza-Yates, R. 1992. *Information Retrieval - Data Structures & Algorithms*. Prentice-Hall.

Golding, A., and Roth, D. 1996. Applying winnow to context-sensitive spelling correction. In *Proceedings of the 13th International Conference on Machine Learning*.

Joachims, T. 1996. A Probabilistic Analysis of the Rochio Algorithm with TFIDF for Text Categorization. Technical report, Carnegie Mellon University. CMU-CS-96-118.

Lewis, D.; Shapire, R.; Callan, J.; and Papka, R. 1996. Training Algorithms for Linear Text Classifiers. In *Proc. of the 19th Annual International ACM SIGIR Conference*.

Mitchell, T. 1997. *Machine Learning*. Mc Graw Hill.

Osgood, R., and Bareiss, R. 1993. Automated Index Generation for Constructing Large-scale Conversational Hypermedia Systems. In *Proc. of the 11th National Conference on Aritificial Intelligence*, 309–314.

Papka, R.; Callan, J.; and Barto, A. 1996. Text-Based Information Retrieval Using Exponentiated Gradient Descent. In *Neural Information Processing Systems*. To appear.

Portinale, L., and Torasso, P. 1995. ADAPtER: An Integrated Diagnostic System Combining Case-Based and Abductive Reasoning. In *Proc. of the 1st Int. Conf. on Case-Based Reasoning*, 277–288.

Rissland, E., and Daniels, J. 1995. Using CBR to drive IR. In *Proc. of the 14th International Joint Conference on Artificial Intelligence*, 400–407.

How Case-Based Reasoning and Cooperative Query Answering Techniques Support RICAD?

Jirapun Daengdej and Dickson Lukose

Department of Mathematics, Statistics and Computing Science
The University of New England
Armidale, NSW 2351, Australia
E-mail: {jirapun, lukose}@neumann.une.edu.au

Abstract. Many Case-Based Reasoning (CBR) systems are built using the conventional database systems as their case memory. Even though these Database Management Systems (DBMSs) provide a large number of advantages, CBR systems developers face one major draw back. That is, *partial-match* retrieval is not supported by most of the conventional DBMSs. To overcome this limitation, we investigated contemporary research in CBR and Cooperative Query Answering (CQA). Our finding indicates that there are a number of issues in CQA that can be solved by applying some of the innovative techniques developed by the CBR community, on the other hand, the CQA provide a number of *new* features which enable easy development of CBR systems. The main contribution of this paper is in explicating how CBR can benefit from the CQA research, and how CQA techniques can enhance the CBR systems. Further, it describes the CQA features in RICAD (Risk Cost Advisor, our experimental CBR system), and how these features enhance its performance.

1 Introduction

The ability to adapt previously solved cases to match with a case at hand before proposing a solution is a unique capability that has distinguished Case-Based Reasoning (CBR) from other reasoning approaches [19]. Recently, a number of approaches have been developed to efficiently acquire *adaptation knowledge*. Among them are *learning adaptation- rules from cases* [13], and improving the systems adaptation capability by *storing traces* of how the new adaptation is derived [20], for future use.

However, most of the CBR systems built to date *do not* have such a capability (e.g., [14][23]) (see also [12] for the result of a survey). Basically, these retrieve-only CBR systems are only able to find similar cases from the case base, or find only the best matched cases. One of the major difficulties in acquiring the adaptation-knowledge is that, the CBR systems are usually applied in domains where clearly defined knowledge is not available [20]. In addition, in some domains it is more appropriate to leave the task that a computer does best (i.e., searching for similar cases in a large case library) to the computer, and leave the part that humans perform better (i.e., adaptation and evaluation) to the humans [21]. As a result, most CBR systems only retrieve and reuse the historical cases. They interact with knowledge engineers when adaptation or evaluation of retrieved cases are required [26]. The other difficulty arises from the use of Database Management Systems (DBMSs) by the CBR systems as their case memory. Even though the DBMSs facilitate *scalability*, preserve sensitivity of historical cases, provide security to these cases, and avoid maintenance of duplicate cases (i.e., case integrity) [24][5], they do not provide the most sort after feature, that is, *partial-match retrieval*.

In view of this type of retrieve-only CBR systems, one begins to ponder the following question: *What is the difference between a conventional relational DBMS and a retrieve-only CBR system?* The answer lies in the following two advantages provided by this type of CBR systems in comparison to the conventional relational DBMSs: *more flexible query can be asked*; and *partial match between query and the records in the database*. However, the database community proposed and have widely investigated the *Cooperative Query Answering* (CQA) (or sometimes called *Intelligent Query Answering*), [2][10][22]. The issues and problems addressed by these researchers have a lot in common to their counterpart in the CBR community (i.e., retrieval of similar cases and dealing with incomplete "case" query). Kolodner [16] pointed out that there is a need for additional features added to the current DBMSs to support the CBR requirements, also evident in our investigation [5]. However, little attention has been given to how the database can be effectively applied in building a CBR system. The main contribution of this paper is to demonstrate how CQA can be used to support CBR, and vice versa. Further, we show how some of the features of CQA are incorporated into RICAD [5] to enhance its performance.

The outline of this paper is as follows: Section 2 of the paper describes in details the CQA. Section 3 discusses all the features resulting from CQA research that can be used to support CBR. Then, from an opposite point of view, Section 4 discusses how CBR can be used to enhance the capabilities of the CQA. Section 5 outlines the features of CQA that are incorporated in RICAD to enhance its performance. Finally, Section 6 attempts to conclude this paper by summarizing the main points and discussing future developments of RICAD.

2 Cooperative Query Answering (CQA)

In querying a conventional relational database, users must know details of their database schema and what they want to ask. This is usually very difficult for inexperienced users. For example, a new secretary of a computer company may *not* be able to remember all the hardware dealers located around a particular suburb. With the conventional relational DBMSs and its associated SQL, she *must* know all the suburb names before she can query the database to find all the dealer names.

Another major drawback of using the conventional database is that it can only perform *exact* matching between user queries and the records in its database. For example, if the same secretary wants to identify a particular brand of disk within the company's inventory and assuming that none of these types of disks are in stock, the conventional DBMSs would respond *negatively* to her query, rather than suggesting alternative brands (i.e., which has similar functionality and capacity) which may be in stock.

CQA techniques are developed to overcome these drawbacks (i.e., by providing additional features). There are three main components which are used by the CQA based systems when intelligently constructing queries for the users. They are: *domain knowledge, new SQL operators*, and *query relaxation techniques*. Note that in addition to the traditional SQL operators such as: SELECT, FROM, WHERE, AND, and IN, the CQA based systems also employ a number of new SQL operators that will take advantage of domain knowledge during query processing. Further, the CQA based systems also employ various techniques to find *all relevant* answers to a user query. Consider the following user query in the domain of computer maintenance where the user wants to find *"All computer dealers which are located near a particular suburb called* St.James":

SELECT DealerName, PhoneNumber FROM DealerDatabase
WHERE Suburb = AROUND('St.James');

Let us assume that the domain knowledge made available to the CQA based systems states that there are 3 main suburbs which are located near St. James: Wynyard, Townhall, and Central. Based on this domain knowledge, the system will use appropriate relaxation rules to translate the above query to the following SQL statement.

SELECT DealerName, PhoneNumber FROM DealerDatabase
WHERE Suburb = IN('Wynyard', 'Townhall', 'Central');

From this example, we can see that the users do not need to know the names of the suburbs surrounding (or near) the suburb specified in the query (i.e., St. James), but they are able to retrieve the names and phone numbers of *all* companies located near their specified suburb.

A typical example dealing with numerical values follows: *"Find a list of all* DealerName *that sell 1 MB of RAM at around $5.00"*. The CQA query follows:

SELECT DealerName FROM MemoryDatabase
WHERE RAMCost = APPROXIMATE(5);

Again, the domain knowledge is used to *relax* the attribute RAMCost and the system constructs the following SQL statement:

SELECT DealerName FROM MemoryDatabase
WHERE RAMCost $\geq$ 3 AND RAMCost $\leq$ 7;

Similar to the previous query, the users can find all DealerName who sells computer memory at the *approximate* specified price. The following sub-sections will discuss how CQA uses domain knowledge, the new SQL operators, and query relaxation techniques to enhance the capabilities of conventional DBMSs.

2.1 Using Domain Knowledge

Humans use various types of knowledge when solving their problems [1]. This knowledge can be represented in a computer by using many different knowledge representation schemes. In most cases, the domain knowledge used by CQA based systems are contained in hierarchical structure. Different names have been used to refer to the hierarchies (e.g., Concept Hierarchy [11] and Type Abstraction Hierarchy [3]). CQA based systems generally use a number of concept hierarchies to represent different types of domain knowledge. Each one of them contains relationships between concepts at different levels of the hierarchy. Figure 1 shows an example of a concept hierarchy that may be used by RICAD. This concept hierarchy represents the fact that the car type *Ford Falcon* is much more similar to *4 Runner RV6* and *Mazda 929* than to *Toyota Starlet*. The similarity measure is based on the *semantic distance* algorithm proposed by Sowa [25].

2.2 Additional SQL Operators

In order for the DBMSs to support CQA requirements, researchers have introduced a number of additional SQL operators. Among them are: AROUND, ∧ (APPROXIMATE), RELAXATION-ORDER, and BASED-ON, as used in CoBase [3]. These operators enable CoBase to perform *partial-match retrieval*. These operators are usually applied to either of the following two situations: *when the system cannot find records that matches exactly to the user's query*, or *when the system wants to carry out comparison activities*.

2.3 Query Relaxation

CQA based systems, use *heuristics, semantic-network,* and/or *past user queries* [8] for retrieving similar cases. However, most of them rely heavily on using the concept hierarchy when relaxing the values of an attribute (e.g., [9][10]). The following example describes how this form of relaxation is performed. Consider the domain knowledge shown in Figure 1. Let us assume that the attribute CarModel represents all possible car models. If one would like to find all cars which are similar to *Ford XR-6*, the value of CarModel can then be relaxed to include all cars which are classified in the same group (i.e., *High Performance Cars* such as *Holden HSV* and *BMW M5* in this case).

Query relaxation can also be performed by using *generalization* and *summarization* techniques [4]. In addition to the method of relaxation as shown above, generalized information are also used to answer user queries. Consider the previous example of finding the names of all cars that are similar to *Ford XR-6*. By using the generalization technique, rather than just listing all cars for the users, the system can also provide summarized information such as: *There are two other* CarTypes *which are categorized under* 4DoorsSedan (i.e., Family Cars and Small Cars). This type of generalized information are highly valuable to the inexperienced users, in addition to helping users who may have forgotten that there are other CarTypes which are similar to the one the user wants. Even though CQA needs extra heuristics and domain knowledge to provide additional information (i.e., such as the generalized information described in the above example), the availability of the new SQL operators allow efficient implementation of the necessary functions.

3 Using CQA in CBR Implementation

Constructing a CBR system is much more sophisticated than just using constraints entered by the users and retrieving similar cases from the database. Typically, a number of tasks have to be done before a CBR system can propose answers (see *task-oriented* view from [1] for details, also [5], [6] and [7]). The task usually involves *interpreting* the entered problem (i.e., query case), *identifying indices* that should be used for retrieving similar cases, *calculating similarity* between the query case and the retrieved cases, and finally *proposing solutions* to the users (or perhaps if the new solved case seems to identify a new experience (situation) to the system, it may also be integrated into the case base for future use). From the DBMSs' perspective, what CQA can offer to the CBR are those new SQL operators that allow the CBR systems to be *rapidly* implemented when using the DBMSs as their case memories.

In general, an *exact match* is achieved when the values of the attributes of the case at hand and some of the historical cases are *identical*. Unfortunately, in most situations, it is almost impossible to find such a perfect match. Usually, the process of finding similar cases consist of two main steps: *initial matching* and *ranking the retrieved cases*. For example, in SQUAD [24], rather than allowing the system to retrieve all similar cases then ranking them in order to find best matched cases, each generated SQL queries are associated with a similarity value.

Irrespective of the technique used in finding similar cases, it is obvious that the only way to find similar cases when using SQL is to relax the constraints in the original query [5]. One approach is to use the AROUND operator which enables the system to find partially matched concepts by relaxing the values of a particular attribute. The relaxation process is performed by referring to the concept hierarchy. In addition to the AROUND operator, the BASED-ON operator can also be used to add more constraint(s) to the search. Consider the following SQL statement which uses these two operators.

```
SELECT DealerName, PhoneNumber FROM DealerDatabase
WHERE Suburb = AROUND('St.James') BASED-ON (RAMCost);
```

The above query states that we want to find all DealerName and PhoneNumber which is located near St.James, but they *must* also sell their RAM at a similar price. On the other hand, for the numeric fields, an operator such as APPROXIMATE can be used to find cases within a certain range of values.

Since the closest matched cases are those that have the least number of differences with the query case, the system must try to keep the number of attributes whose values have to be adjusted as low as possible. Furthermore, in order to find the closest matched cases, the system must also try to adjust the value of attributes which are considered least important [5]. The use of an operator like RELAXATION-ORDER can allow the developers to easily specify the order of attributes' adjustments.

4 Using CBR to Support CQA

Even though the CQA process can automatically use domain knowledge that was provided by users, a number of important issues still remain as major problems for non-expert users. The main problem results from the fact that the level of *significance* (i.e., value of importance) of a specific attribute used in the user queries are context dependent [15][17]. For example, the size of a computer's main memory is important if one wants to purchase new software for it. However, the "VDO card" may become more significant if one wants to purchase a new monitor. Thus, knowing what attributes should be used to retrieve records will result in better answers.

Although CQA researchers have identified a number of very useful SQL operators, the users still have to examine the query case themselves (manually), to rate the attributes in the query case according to its significance within the situated context. In order to solve this problem, there are at least two important tasks that occur in the CBR reasoning process that can be used to enhance the performance of the CQA. These two *related* tasks are: *situation assessment* and *identifying suitable indices*, which are explained in the following sub-sections, respectively.

4.1 Situation Assessment

Typically, in a CQA based system, when a new query is entered, the system will simply use *all* the user specified constraints to retrieve records from the database. In other words, they *do not* analyze their problems before querying the database. Consider the following example: if a customer wants to purchase a new monitor for his computer, the constraint on *"the amount of available RAM in his computer"* may *not* be relevant, and therefore can be ignored.

The importance of a specific attribute depends on the context or situation at that moment. One has to understand the situation before one can correctly solve it [18]. The situation assessment allows the system to better understand the problem it is facing. In fact, without properly interpreting or assessing the query case, there is a very high chance that the system will miss important cases [17]. As a result, a correct set of indices can be identified and used to retrieve relevant cases from the case base.

So, in a nutshell, even though CQA provides a number of useful operators which allow it to constrain the search (e.g., BASED-ON), it should also carry out an "intelligent" analysis of the query to further increase its efficiency. Most CBR systems incorporate this form of "intelligent" analysis of the query case. This type of processing is highly necessary to further enhance CQA based systems.

4.2 Identifying Suitable Indices

Identifying suitable indices may be an easy task for domain experts or someone who clearly understands the domain, however, it is a *very* difficult task for novel users especially if there are a large number of possible values in each attribute.

From our experience in developing RICAD, understanding and manually analyzing the query case each time it is entered is not an easy task. So, we have developed "statistically" based techniques into RICAD to enable it to automatically determine which attributes (i.e., indices) to use for retrieving similar cases [6][7]. These types of techniques should be incorporated into CQA based systems to free the users from these very difficult tasks. In the following section, we will explain RICAD in more detail, and how it utilizes CQA based techniques to enhance its performance.

5   Application of CQA Techniques in RICAD

RICAD is a CBR system designed to determine the *risk cost* of an insurance client. Details on the architecture of RICAD is found in [5]. The problem domain of RICAD consists of approximately two million cases, which have been supplied by an insurance company. Each case is a policy record from the personal automobile insurance line, and consists of a number of descriptive attributes, and the total cost of claims for that policy for a set period. Claims in this context are generally the result of accidents and theft. The risk cost is defined as the average cost of claims incurred for each set of descriptive attributes, **including** the cases for which no claims were incurred. It is the probabilistic cost of each policy, taking into account both the magnitude of costs when claims occur and the frequency with which claims occur. Of these two million records, only approximately ten percent of them have a non-zero claims cost. This means that if one enters a new case into the system, the system may find hundreds of cases that are applicable, but only approximately ten percent of them have a non-zero answer. The problem is magnified when those cases contain largely different values of claims cost due to the unpredictiveness of accidents and theft.

To dynamically calculate search indices, a number of different domain knowledge have to be provided to RICAD. They are represented using a number of knowledge representation schemes (e.g., *hierarchical* or *spatial* structures). Figure 1 shows an example of the domain knowledge in RICAD. In the spatial structure in Figure 1, the area with post code *2010* is much 'closer' (therefore similar) to areas *2016, 2021, 2033, 2011*, and *2000* than areas *2041, 2044*, and *2034*. Since all cases are stored in the database, RICAD has to generate a set of SQL statements to retrieve similar cases. However, since some attributes contain up to 2,000 different values, RICAD has to refer to this domain knowledge when generating these indices. Implementation of the *Dynamically Indices Generation* mechanism in RICAD has been the most costly activity.

The CQA capabilities of RICAD is *hard coded* (as in most conventional CBR systems). Typically, when RICAD encounters a new case, it goes through a series of iterations to obtain a sufficient number of historical cases to computer the risk cost. For example, if the new case is as follows: *A person aged* **26** *living in area with post code* **2010** *driving a* **Ford Falcon**, then in the first iteration, the SQL query will be as follows:

```
SELECT AVG(ClainCost FROM CustomerTable
WHERE CarModel = 'Ford Falcon' AND Postcode = 2010;
```

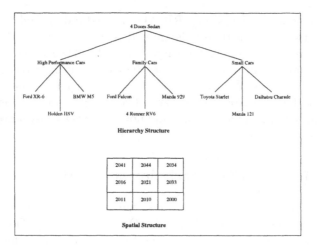

Fig. 1. Example of the Taxonomic and Spatially Structure knowledge used in RICAD

But, if RICAD is unable to find a sufficient number of cases from its case base to provide an answer at the "required" level of confidence, then RICAD will begin to utilize its domain knowledge to relax its query. Details of these relaxation rules are found in [5]. In fact, what RICAD is trying to achieve is the following query: "*Find the average Claim Cost of all customers around 26 years old, drive a Ford Falcon, and live in area 2010*". This may be represented in CQA query (using the new SQL operators) as follows:

```
SELECT AVG(ClaimCost) FROM CustomerTable
WHERE CarModel = SIMILAR('Ford Falcon')
AND Postcode = AROUND(2010) AND Age = APPROXIMATE(26);
```

RICAD will continue with its iterations (expending a single attribute at a time) until it is able to retrieve a sufficient number of 'similar' cases from its case base. The final SQL statement that RICAD may end up executing for our example may look similar to the following:

```
SELECT AVG(ClaimCost) FROM CustomerTable
WHERE CarModel = IN('Ford Falcon', 'Mitsubishi Magna', 'Toyota Camry')
AND Postcode = IN(2010, 2016, 2021, 2033, 2011, 2000)
AND Age ≥ 25 AND Age ≤ 27;
```

Even though, the size of the final SQL query generated by RICAD can be very large (e.g., in our previous experiments, some of the queries were as long as an *A4* page), it does not affect the users at all, since all this is done automatically, and it does not require any form of intervention from the domain user.

6 Conclusion

Even though there are several major advantages in using DBMSs as case memories in CBR systems, there are a number of limitations in the contemporary

DBMSs that hinder its liberal exploitation in CBR systems. The main problem is the lack of *partial matching* capabilities between constraints in a query and records in the database, which is a necessary feature for a CBR system.

This paper investigated the methods developed by the CQA researchers to enhance the capabilities of conventional DBMSs to handle *partial matching*. The result of this investigation clearly indicates that both the CBR and the CQA communities are addressing many similar issues, but from different perspectives. This paper further demonstrated how features of CQA can be used by CBR systems to enhance its performance, and how CQA could incorporate some of the novel techniques developed by the CBR community to further enhance the performance of the CQA based systems. Finally, we reviewed the CQA features that are incorporated in RICAD to enhance its performance. These features are currently hard-coded into RICAD. Currently we are working on several improvements to RICAD to fully utilize the techniques developed by the CQA community.

References

1. Aamodt, A. and Plaza, E. Case-Based Reasoning: Foundational Issues, Methodological Variations, and System Approaches, *AICom-Artificial Intelligence Communications*, Vol. 7, No. 1, 1994.

2. Bosc, P. and Pivert, O. Some Approaches for Relational Database Flexible Querying, *Journal of Intelligent Information Systems*, 1:323-354, 1992.

3. Chu, W. W., Merzbacher, M. A., and Berkovich, L. The Design and Implemention of CoBase, *In Proceedings of ACM SIGMOD'93*, Washington D. C., 1993.

4. Chu, W. W., Yang, H., and Chow, G. A Cooperative Database System (CoBase) for Query Relaxation, *In Proceedings of the Third International Conference on Artificial Intelligence* Planning Systems. Edinburgh, May 1996.

5. Daengdej, J., Lukose, D., Tsui, E., Beinat, P., and Prophet, L. Dynamically Creating Indices for 2 Million Cases: A Real World Problem. *In Proceedings of the Second European Workshop in Case-Based Reasoning*, Switzerland, Springer Verlag, 1996.

6. Daengdej, J., Lukose, D., Tsui, E., Beinat, P., and Prophet, L. Combining Case-Based Reasoning and Statistical Method for Proposing Solution in RICAD, *In Proceedings of Knowledge-Based Computer System (KBCS-96)*, Mumbai, 1996.

7. Daengdej, J. and Lukose, D. Identifying Similarity Between Cases Using Values of Their Solutions, *In Proceedings of the International Conference on Applied Informatics (IASTED)*, Austria, 1997.

8. Gaasterland, T., Godfrey, P., and Minker, J. Relaxation as a Platform for Cooperative Answering, *Journal of Intelligent Information Systems*, Vol. 1, No. 3/4, 293-321, December 1992.

9. Gaasterland, T. Restricting Query Relaxation Through User Constraints, *International Conference on Cooperative and Intelligent Information Systems*, Rotterdam, The Netherlands, May 1993.

10. Han, J., Fu, Y., and Ng, R. T. Cooperative Query Answering Using Multiple Layered Database, *In Proceedings of the 2nd International Conference on Cooperative Information Systems (COOPIS'94)*, Toronto, Cannada, 1994.

11. Han, J., Huang, Y., Cercone, N., and Fu, Y. Intelligent Query Answering by Knowledge Discovery Techniques, *IEEE Transactions on Knowledge and Data Engineering*, Vol. 8, No. 3, pp. 373-390, 1996.
12. Hanney, K., Keane, M. T., Smyth, B. and Cunningham, P. What Kind of Adaptation do CBR Systems Need?: A Review of Current Practice, In Aha D. and Ram A. (Eds.) *Adaptation of Knowledge for Reuse: Proceedings of the 1995 AAAI Fall Symposium*, Technical Report FS-95-02. Menlo Park, CA: AAAI Press. 1995.
13. Hanney, K. and Keane, M. T. Learning Adaptation Rules from Case-Base, *In Proceedings of the Second European Workshop in Case-Based Reasoning*, Switzerland, Springer Verlag, 1996.
14. Jones, E. K., and Roydhouse, A. Iterative Design of Case Retrieval Systems, In Aha, D. W. (eds.), *In Proceedings of AAAI Workshop on Case-Based Reasoning*, AAAI Press, 1994.
15. Jurisica, I. How to Retrieve Relevant Information?, *In Proceedings of the AAAI Fall Symposium Series on Relevance*, New Orleans, Louisiana, 1994.
16. Kolodner, J., *Case-Based Reasoning*, Morgan Kaufmann, 1993.
17. Kolodner, J., Making the Implicit Explicit: Clarifying the Principles of Case-Based Reasoning, *Case-Based Reasoning: Experiences, Lessons, and Future Directions*, David B. Leake, editor. AAAI Press/MIT Press, Menlo Park, CA, 1996.
18. Kolodner, J. and Leake, D. B. A Tutorial Introduction to Case-Based Reasoning, *Case-Based Reasoning: Experiences, Lessons, and Future Directions*, David B. Leake, editor. AAAI Press/MIT Press, Menlo Park, CA, 1996.
19. Leake, D. B. CBR in Context: The Present and Future. *Case-Based Reasoning: Experiences, Lessons, and Future Directions*, David B. Leake, editor. AAAI Press/MIT Press, Menlo Park, CA, 1996.
20. Leake, D. B., Kinley, A., and Wilson, D. Linking Adaptation and Similarity Learning, *In Proceedings of the 18th Annual Conference of the Cognitive Science Society*, 1996.
21. Mark, W., Simoudis, E., and Hinkle, D. Case-Based Reasoning: Expectations and Results, *Case-Based Reasoning: Experiences, Lessons, and Future Directions*, David B. Leake, editor. AAAI Press/MIT Press, Menlo Park, CA, 1996.
22. Minock, M. J. and Chu, W. W. Explanation for Cooperative Information Systems, *In Proceedings of 9th International Symposium on Methodologies for Intelligent Systems*, June 1996.
23. Rissland, E. L., Skalak, D. B., and Friedman, M. T. Evaluating BankXX: Heuristic Harvesting of Information for Case-Based Argument, In Aha, D. W. (eds.), *In Proceedings of AAAI Workshop on Case-Based Reasoning*, AAAI Press, 1994.
24. Shimazu, H., Kitano, H., and Shibata, A. Retrieving Cases from Relational Databases: Another Stride Towards Corporate-Wide Case-Base Systems, *International Joint Conference in Artificial Intelligence*, Morgan Kaufmann, 1993.
25. Sowa, J. *Conceptual Structures: Information Processing in Mind and Machine*, Addison Wesley, Reading, Mass., USA, 1984.
26. Watson, I. The Case for Case-Based Reasoning. Available on the World Wide Web at http://146.87.176.38/ai-cbr/Papers/ita01.htm.

What You Saw Is What You Want: Using Cases to Seed Information Retrieval *

Jody J. Daniels and Edwina L. Rissland

Department of Computer Science
University of Massachusetts
Amherst, MA 01003 USA

Abstract. This paper presents a hybrid case-based reasoning (CBR) and information retrieval (IR) system, called SPIRE, that both retrieves documents from a full-text document corpus and from within individual documents, and locates passages likely to contain information about important problem-solving features of cases. SPIRE uses two case-bases, one containing past precedents, and one containing excerpts from past case texts. Both are used by SPIRE to automatically generate queries, which are then run by the INQUERY full-text retrieval engine on a large text collection in the case of document retrieval and on individual text documents for passage retrieval.

1 Introduction

A good indication of what to look for in a new problem situation is often given by examples of what has worked in the past. This idea—the fundamental tenet of case-based reasoning—is applicable in information retrieval (IR) as well. We have employed this idea at two levels in a hybrid CBR-IR approach:

1. within a corpus of documents, to find documents relevant to a new problem situation, retrieve documents similar to those that are already known to be relevant;
2. within an individual document, to find passages that address a particular aspect of a situation, retrieve passages that are similar to those that illustrate past discussions of the topic.

We call these two levels of retrieval the *corpus* and *document* levels. At both levels, exemplars of relevant text—documents or excerpts—from past problem solving experiences provide good clues of what to look for in a new situations.

In this paper, we describe our system called SPIRE (Selection of Passages for Information REduction) that performs retrieval at both the document and passage levels. Given a new problem situation input as a case frame, SPIRE retrieves relevant documents from a full-text document corpus, and, within each of these, highlights the passages most likely to discuss important problem-solving

* This research was supported by NSF Grant no. EEC-9209623, State/Industry/-University Cooperative Research on Intelligent Information Retrieval.

features. In this paper, we emphasize retrieval at the passage level; other papers have detailed retrieval at the document level [DR95, RD96].

After problem entry, SPIRE performs all of its processing, including the generation of needed queries, without *any* intervention on the part of the user. Thus, the only representational or processing burden on the user is the specification of the problem case, which is done in a manner that is standard practice in CBR systems (without natural language front-ends) [Kol93]. Thus SPIRE locates relevant textual regions within documents without imposing on the user the burden of reading entire documents.

SPIRE uses two case-bases:

1. A case-base of past, resolved problem situations (precedents) represented as case-frames of features for use by a HYPO-style CBR module.

2. For each case feature in the case-frame, a case-base of actual text excerpts, culled from past cases, that contain useful information about the value of the feature.

Both case-bases are used by SPIRE to generate queries, which are then acted upon by the INQUERY retrieval engine in its usual manner [CCH92].

The first case-base is the standard type of case-base used by many generations of our own HYPO-style CBR systems with their concomitant mechanisms of dimension-based analysis, sorting into a claim lattice, etc. [Ash90]. The second is simply a collection of textual fragments partitioned into sub-case-bases, one for each problem feature of interest. Indexing and selection are minimal in the second case-base at this point; the feature (name) serves as the index and all fragments are selected. We note that in the future, as these collections grow, more highly attenuated indexing and selection will most likely be needed. However, even now, the question of what cases, that is, text fragments, to include is an interesting one. In Section 5.3 we discuss the impact of the composition of the excerpt case-base on the performance of the system.

Although SPIRE does not actually extract the information contained in the passages it retrieves, we believe SPIRE could play a key role in the text extraction process by focusing an extractor's (human or machine) attention on those passages that are worth the effort of careful "reading." Currently, it is not feasible nor reasonable to apply an extraction effort across a long text, especially when there are only a few small portions that are relevant. Thus, we can use the passages highlighted by SPIRE as input to an extraction process. The output of the extraction effort can then be plowed back into a knowledge base, used by our system or some other symbolic reasoner. SPIRE can thus aid in executing the full loop of case-based reasoning by assisting in the acquisition of new, symbolically represented cases. This is particularly important in domains where a large volume of data already exists in textual form.

2 System Description

SPIRE works in two stages (as shown in Figure 1):

1. from a large text collection, SPIRE retrieves documents that are relevant to the presented problem case, and

2. within those retrieved documents, SPIRE highlights passages that contain information relevant to specific case features.

In the first stage, SPIRE is given a new problem situation. It uses its HYPO-style CBR module to analyze it and select a small number of most relevant cases from its own case-base consisting of symbolically represented texts. In the usual CBR fashion, SPIRE determines the similarity of each known case to the new problem and represents the results of this analysis in a standard claim lattice [Ash90].

The most relevant cases from this analysis—typically the cases in the top two layers of the claim lattice—are then used to "prime the pump" of INQUERY's relevance feedback module. This set of cases is called the *relevance feedback case-knowledge-base* or RF-CKB [RD95, RD96]. (These are labeled as "Best Case Texts" in Figure 1.) The original texts of the cases in the RF-CKB are passed to the INQUERY IR engine, which then treats them as though they had been marked relevant by a user. INQUERY automatically generates a query by selecting and weighting terms or pairs of terms from within this set. This query is then run against the larger corpus of texts, with the result that new documents are retrieved and ranked according to INQUERY's belief as to their relevance to the posed query. (A detailed description of this first stage can be found in [DR95, RD96].)

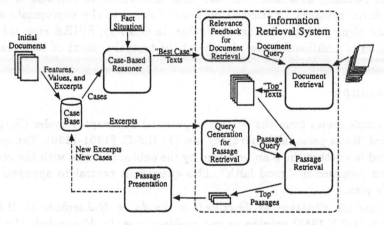

Fig. 1. Overview of SPIRE.

In the second stage, SPIRE locates germane passages within each of the texts retrieved in stage one. In this stage SPIRE locates passages within a single document rather than documents within a collection. Again SPIRE uses a hybrid CBR-IR approach. This was motivated by our belief that past discussions of a topic would provide good clues to the location of new discussions.

To locate passages, SPIRE generates queries by using excerpts from past discussions of a feature. Each excerpt is an actual fragment of text containing relevant information about a case feature and comes from an episode of information location/extraction performed on a past case. Example excerpts are given in Section 3.

There are numerous techniques for transforming the excerpts into passage retrieval queries. (A fuller discussion of this can be found in [Dan97].) SPIRE presents the query along with a specified document to the IR engine, which, in turn, retrieves the top ranked passages for presentation to the user or possibly to an information extraction system. Thus, excerpts are used analogously to the RF-CKB's of stage one: their terms are used to generate queries.

We created these case-bases of excerpts by asking an individual familiar with the representation of the problem domain to read a small number of opinions corresponding to cases in SPIRE's case-base and to highlight any portion of text—whether it be just a few terms, a phrase, or several sentences or more— that was useful for determining the feature's value. It was common for pieces from different locations throughout the text to be highlighted. Normally, this step would be done in conjunction with the creation of the case-base for the domain and the encoding of the first few cases and thus would not require a full review of the textual sources. However, since we were re-using a portion of the bankruptcy case-base used in the BankXX project [RSF96], this highlighting of textual examples was done *post hoc*.

As each document and feature is addressed in stage two, the user (or information extraction program) can examine the presented passages, determine (if possible) the actual value of the feature, and add it to the representation for the text, for instance, as a case. The user may also decide to add one or more of the retrieved passages, or selected portions of them, to the appropriate excerpt case-base along with the feature and value. In this way, SPIRE may aid in the acquisition of additional knowledge about the textual context of each feature.

3 Example

Our example comes from the domain of personal bankruptcy under Chapter 13 of United States personal bankruptcy law (11 U.S.C. §1301-1330). The question presented is whether the plan proposed by the debtor to settle with the creditors has been proposed in "good faith". This question is central to approval of the debtor's plan.

We use the situation as described in the *In re Makarchuk*, 76 B.R. 919 (Bankr.N.D.N.Y.1987) opinion as our problem case. In *Makarchuk*, the debtor proposed a plan whose dominant purpose was to discharge two student loans. The debtor had recently unsuccessfully attempted to discharge these same loans under Chapter 7 of the code.

We submit this case to SPIRE, which compares it to those situations found in its own case-base. The full-text documents associated with the most similar cases—the RF-CKB—are passed to the IR system. The IR system creates a document-level query, poses it, and retrieves a set of documents. The ten top-rated documents for the *Makarchuk* situation are listed in Table 1. We note that *Ali, Akin,* and *Hawkins*, as well as *Makarchuk* were already known to SPIRE (i.e., represented in its case-base of documents,) while only *Ali* has text fragments in the excerpt case-base. Thus, the other six of the top ten cases must be "read" in order for their facts to be ascertained in preparation for any use in a legal analysis for *Makarchuk*. This completes SPIRE's stage one.

Rank	Doc-Id	Case Name	Belief Score
1	877	In re Stewart	(0.518380)
2	178	In re Ali	(0.508805)
3	565	In re Makarchuk	(0.504300)
4	353	Matter of Akin	(0.503330)
5	427	In re Gathright	(0.500740)
6	177	Matter of Hawkins	(0.498640)
7	693	In re Ellenburg	(0.496048)
8	915	In re Carpico	(0.493452)
9	733	In re Newberry	(0.492010)
10	764	In re Porter	(0.491779)

Table 1. The most highly ranked documents for the *Makarchuk* problem.

We would like to examine specific facts in these newly retrieved cases, such as, finding out whether the court found the debtors to be sincere when proposing their plans. (Other features of bankruptcy cases are discussed in Section 4.1.) To do this, we direct SPIRE in stage two to locate passages within the top case texts that concern the feature called *sincerity*. SPIRE uses excerpts from its case-base of excerpts on *sincerity* to form a query to retrieve passages. Sample excerpts from this case-base are:

- "represents an earnest effort to repay his unsecured creditors"
- "sincerity is tempered by her desire to avoid returning to Maine."
- "The Court believes the debtors' motivation and sincerity are genuine."
- "The Chapter 13 petition was intended to wipe out BNY's claims rather than to repay them."
- "this couple makes a concerted effort to live sensibly and substantially within their means."

To illustrate passage retrieval, we use the *In re Stewart* case, the top rated document for the *Makarchuk* problem. INQUERY, the IR engine, divides the *Stewart* opinion into overlapping windows of 20 words each, approximating the length of a sentence. Since the windows overlap, each word in the opinion will appear in two windows (except for the first 10 words). The retrieved passages are ranked by INQUERY according to its belief that each is relevant to the query.

For this example, we allow SPIRE to use two simple methods to generate queries. The first combines the terms from all the excerpts about a feature into a single "natural language" query. Each word in each excerpt provides a possible match against the words in the window. Regardless of whether two words were in different excerpts, each contributes to the total belief. We refer to this type of query as a *bag of words* query. The second type of query places a restriction so that terms from within an excerpt need to be found co-occurring in the passage. We refer to this type of query as the *sum* query because it is formed by wrapping an INQUERY #Sum operator around each excerpt. Part of both queries are shown below:

```
#Passage20(
 represents an earnest effort to repay his unsecured creditors
 sincerity is tempered by her desire to avoid returning to Maine. ...)

#Passage20(
 #Sum( represents an earnest effort to repay his unsecured creditors)
 #Sum( sincerity is tempered by her desire to avoid returning to Maine.)
 ...);
```

Posing these two queries over the *Stewart* opinion causes INQUERY to retrieve passages. In this particular example, both the *bag of words* and *sum* queries retrieve the same top five passages, although with differing belief values. Below are the top five passages for the *bag of words* query, annotated with whether or not each is relevant:

	Bag of Words	
Rank Psg	Strt Belief	
1	3390	(0.410120) Rel
2	3400	(0.409335) Rel
3	2580	(0.405726)
4	2570	(0.405726)
5	2160	(0.404761)

The following is the text of the 3390 and 3400 passages, top-ranked by both retrievals. We boldface content terms that match those found in the excerpts and show word counts along with the text.

```
      ...(9) the frequency with which the debtor
3390| has sought relief under the Bankruptcy Reform Act; (10) the
3400‖ motivation and sincerity of the debtor in seeking Chapter 13
3410| relief; *1004 (11) the burden which the plan's administration would
      place upon the trustee.
```

From these passages we cannot determine whether the court found the debtor to be *sincere*, however the text is highly on-point to the topic. The next few passages are not relevant to *sincerity*, but because most of them discuss the debtor's effort to make an "earnest" or "substantial" effort to repay creditors, they are are highly ranked.

The next cluster of relevant passages are ranked 8 through 14. Passages 4030, 4040, and 4050, which received ranks 11, 10, and 13, respectively, by the *bag of words* query, and 14, 8, and 12, respectively, for the *sum* query, are given below.

```
      ...not a requirement for confirmation of every Chapter
4030| 13 plan, was one intended purpose of Chapter 13's enactment.
4040‖ Failure to provide substantial repayment is certainly evidence that a
4050‖ debtor is attempting to manipulate the statute rather than attempting
4060| to honestly repay his debts....[sic]
```

In stage two, SPIRE has thus located passages relevant to the *sincerity* feature without requiring a user to pose a query. Unlike other approaches, which merely retrieve entire documents, SPIRE is able to retrieve documents and then present a significantly reduced amount of text about features contained within the document. This greatly decreases the amount of text a user must inspect.

By comparison, if we had intervened after SPIRE's first stage, and manually generated a query for *sincerity*, we might have posed the following query:

```
#Passage20( motivation sincerity genuine sensible earnest );
```

On the *Stewart* opinion, this query yields:

```
Rank Psg Strt Belief
  1    3400  (0.443848) Rel
  2    3390  (0.443848) Rel
```

The text of both of these passages is given above. While they are relevant to the feature, unfortunately, they are the *only* relevant passages that are retrieved by the manual query. In fact, they are the only passages that this query retrieved at all.

4   Domain Knowledge

We now describe the various types of features we examined, the case-bases of textual excerpts, generation of answer keys, and the evaluation metric.

4.1   Features examined

We selected ten features from a bankruptcy good faith case representation. There were five types of values that these features could have: Boolean, date, category, set, or numeric. For our set of ten features, we included two of each type. They were: *sincerity* (was the debtor sincere in proposing the plan), *special-circumstances* (were there any extenuating conditions affecting the debtor), *loan-due-date*, *plan-filing-date*, *procedural-status* (such as appeal or affirmation), *future-income* (the likelihood that the debtor will experience an increase in income), *debt-type* (such as educational or consumer), *profession*, *monthly-income*, and *duration* (of the proposed plan in months).

4.2   Excerpt case-bases

For the above set of ten features we gathered excerpts from 13 case opinions. Once SPIRE stemmed and removed non-content terms, the average number of remaining unique content terms for the ten features was 46.7, although two of the features only have 18 content terms. (See Table 2.)

In the previous section, we included example excerpts for *sincerity*. The following are examples for the feature of *future income*:

Future income – this is text that discusses whether the debtor's income is projected to increase in the future. The text might be negative or positive on this matter.

- "the Court cannot see any likelihood of future increases"
- "the prospect of a regular job with substantially increased income is not great. "

Feature	Num Excerpts	Total Words	Num Unique Terms	Num Unique Content Terms
Plan Duration	14	212	92	59
Monthly Income	13	110	52	34
Sincerity of the Debtor	9	123	89	52
Special Circumstances	8	188	117	71
Loan Due Date	4	47	32	18
Plan Filed Date	10	145	66	45
Debt Type	10	164	102	63
Profession	3	36	29	18
Future Income	8	88	68	36
Procedural Status	13	194	100	71

Table 2. Number of terms contained in the excerpts.

- "her health brings into question her future ability to work."
- "no evidence that raises are likely."

Examples of excerpts for the feature of *special circumstances*, which include unusual events (e.g. pending divorce, being in prison) that can affect the debtor's ability to repay debts, include:

- "The Court believes the debtors' medical expenses will increase as time goes on and believes this is a 'special circumstance' under factor 8."
- "This debtor has not been the victim of extraordinary 'outside' forces."
- "The debtor is now in treatment for the condition that may have contributed to the debtor's need for Chapter 13 relief."
- "Debtor was incarcerated in the New Mexico State Penitentiary for fraudulent practices"

4.3 Answer keys

In order to evaluate SPIRE's ability to locate relevant passages, we needed to create answer keys specifying where within our test documents there was text discussing each of the features. These answer keys were created by outside readers.

We hired two undergraduates to read case opinions and underline any text that they perceived as being about a given feature. They were given a set of written instructions that described each feature and samples of the sort of text they should mark.

4.4 Evaluation metric

Most retrieval systems are judged on the basis of precision and recall. These measure what percentage of the retrieved items are relevant (coverage) and what percentage of the relevant items are retrieved (accuracy), respectively.

We are not concerned with locating *every* relevant item, so recall is not a concern. If we only look at precision, by examining the passages retrieved at certain cutoff depths, we will lose information about the ordering of the relevant and non-relevant passages. We are concerned with how much effort will be wasted by users as they examine retrieved passages. This can be measured by *expected search length* (esl)[Coo68], which measures the number of non-relevant items encountered before finding a specified number of relevant ones. In this work we use esl_1, esl_3, and esl_5, which are esl values when 1, 3, or 5 passages are specified.

5 Experiment results

We ran SPIRE using three problem cases and collected the top documents for each. Removing duplicates and documents that had been used to derive the excerpt case-bases, we made a test collection from among the top 10 retrievals for each problem to make a test set of 20 documents. Using various methods for passage query generation, we tested SPIRE on these 20 documents with 10 different case features.

5.1 Query types

In the experiments reported here, we are concerned primarily with the two previously mentioned query formation methods: *bag of words* and *sum*. These are the two *base* methods that performed the best. The others in this set were: *bag of words plus phrases*, *sum plus phrases*, and *set of words*. Formation and results for these queries is discussed in more detail in [Dan97].

We had SPIRE build two other sets of queries. The first is based on a term weighting scheme suggested by Kwok [Kwo96] and the second set is what we called *semi-random*. The latter incorporated only one-half or one-third of the available query terms from the excerpt case-base. Neither of these sets performed better than the two base queries. (See [Dan97] for details.)

To provide another point of comparison, we also had a human expert, familiar with both the domain and INQUERY query operators, create queries. These manual queries are highly refined expert queries and provide a very high baseline. We used the best manual query for each feature as a point of comparison and refer to this set as the *manual* queries.

5.2 Results

Comparison of the *bag of words* and *sum* queries revealed that they performed about equally well as measured by esl scores. Across all 20 documents and 10 features, the *sum* queries performed slightly better when requesting one or five relevant passages, and the *bag of words* queries performed slightly better when requesting three passages. Overall, SPIRE-generate queries performed just about equally to the expert manual queries. (See Table 3, which provides a comparison between the manual and SPIRE-generated queries on half of the test document collection; results on the other half are similar.)

When we look at the results broken down by feature, there are noticeable differences. There were two features where the manual queries did better: *procedural status* and *plan filed date*, and two features where the SPIRE-based queries

334

Doc-ID	Debt Type	Duration	Future Income	Loan Due	Mthly income	Plan Filed	Proc. Status	Profession	Sincere	Special Circ
001	=	M	=	=	=	SP	M	SP	M	s
180	M	SP	=	M	=	M	M	=	=	s
188	s	M	M	SP	SP	M	M	=	SP	s
204	SP	SP	=	SP	SP	M	SP	M	SP	SP
206	M	M	M	=	SP	SP	=	SP	SP	=
260	M	SP	SP	=	SP	M	M	=	=	b
289	=	M	=	=	=	M	M	M	SP	SP
353	=	M	=	SP	=	=	s	SP	=	=
407	SP	=	=	=	s	M	b	b	=	SP
427	=	M	M	=	SP	SP	M	=	=	s

Table 3. Comparison between the esl_3 of manual and SPIRE-generated queries. An "SP" indicates that both SPIRE queries performed better than the manual. An "M" indicates that the manual query performed better. If the manual fell between the two, the SPIRE query performing the best is given: "b" for *bag of words* and "s" for *sum*. If all three queries performed equally well, an "=" is shown.

did distinctly better: *sincerity* and *loan due date*. With the other features, the results were closer.

For *procedural status* this difference is easily explained: discussion about this feature normally includes at least one of a small set of easily enumerated keywords, such as "confirmation" and "appeal". Not all of these terms were present in SPIRE's excerpt case-base, but all were included in the manual query. For example, "affirmation" and "convert" were never given as the status of any of the cases found in our small corpus. This is an instance where knowledge of a domain-specific vocabulary, particularly a small set of technical terms, is easily enumerated and should be used to form the query.

The difficulty SPIRE had in finding the *plan filed date* is partially due to the way in which the opinions express the date. For example:
- "At the time of filing the Chapter 13 proceeding," [case opinion 289]
- "LeMaire signed a promissory note evidencing a debt to his parents of $12,722 only one day prior to filing his bankruptcy petition. Prior to this filing, LeMaire had ..." [case opinion 860]

In neither is a calendar date given. Additionally, the first text fragment is the only relevant passage within that text. We note that pattern matching techniques or concept recognizers, would also be unable to locate these passages.

5.3 Reexamining the excerpt case-base

In the course of examining the retrieved passages for *plan filed date* we noticed that they often included specific names of debtors in a prior case. In our excerpt case-base, such names had sometimes been included, for instance, "Debtors-Appellants, Mr. and Mrs. Okoreeh-Baah, filed for bankruptcy on November 19, 1985." Since the case name, "Okoreeh-Baah", was included in the excerpt, it caused SPIRE to rate passages that included it very highly, even though the presence of this specific name does not make a passage relevant to the issue of *plan filed date.*

Based on this realization, we reexamined SPIRE's excerpt case-base. Within the excerpts for several features, proper names were frequently included. Additionally, there were instances where excerpts contained text that had no real bearing on discussion of the feature. Where reasonable (i.e., at the beginning or end of an excerpt), we subsequently removed any proper names or superfluous text from the excerpt case-base to create a second excerpt case-base. A second case-base of excerpts was created for the features of *debt type, duration, future income, monthly income, plan filed date,* and *procedural status.* We then recreated and reran the *bag of words* and *sum* queries.

For all of the features, the queries from the new case-base showed improvement over the original one. *Plan filed date* had the largest improvement. For this feature it was not uncommon for the relevant passages to move up in the ranking by as many as ten to twenty, or even forty positions. Besides proper names, deleted text included several instances of "under Chapter 7;" these have no bearing on this feature. Table 4 shows the average number of non-relevant passages that were no longer required to be read before reaching the requested number of relevant passages.

Average reduction in esl		
ESL level	Bag of Words	Sum
1	2.30	3.95
3	9.85	9.70
5	10.53	10.94

Table 4. Difference in esl between the two excerpt sets for *plan filed date.*

The results were similar for the other features. For instance, the *monthly income* results benefited from the deletion of a reference to the *In re Flygare* opinion, and *future income* results improved with the deletion of a fragment: "Mr. Severs testified that".

From this experience with the modified case-bases, we conclude that one must be a bit more careful when creating the excerpt case-base. This is particularly true regarding the inclusion of proper names. On the other hand one cannot simply use a few generic keywords to form a good query, since the excerpts did better than the manual queries for many of the topics.

6 Conclusion

We have presented the SPIRE system, which incorporates a two-stage approach to first, retrieve documents relevant to a given problem situation and second, locate passages within them that discuss particular aspects of the case. SPIRE automatically generates the queries needed for both of these stages in a case-based manner. SPIRE minimizes the amount of effort expended—by human or machine—in locating important pieces of information without sacrifice in performance. We found that SPIRE does as well or better than manually crafted passage queries for many of the case features we tested.

SPIRE is a hybrid CBR-IR system. Its CBR processing makes use of two case-bases: a traditional HYPO-style case-base of precedents, and a case-base of specific text excerpts. While the question of case indexing in SPIRE's current excerpt case-base is not particularly interesting (at this point), the question of what excerpts to include, or alternatively, the level of generality needed in such excerpts, is indeed interesting. We discussed how the content of the excerpt case-base can affect performance, and noted that overly specific excerpts that contain specific names, dates, and dollar amounts, can hurt performance. In our comparison of SPIRE against manually created queries of generic keywords, we also demonstrated that an overly general approach is not optimal either.

References

[Ash90] Kevin D. Ashley. *Modeling Legal Argument: Reasoning with Cases and Hypotheticals*. M.I.T. Press, Cambridge, MA, 1990.

[CCH92] James P. Callan, W. Bruce Croft, and Stephen M. Harding. The INQUERY Retrieval System. In A. M. Tjoa and I. Ramos, editors, *Database and Expert Systems Applications: Proceedings of the International Conference in Valencia, Spain*, pages 78–83, Valencia, Spain, 1992. Springer Verlag, NY.

[Coo68] William S. Cooper. Expected Search Length: A Single Measure of Retrieval Effectiveness Based on the Weak Ordering Action of Retrieval Systems. *American Documentation*, 19:30–41, 1968.

[Dan97] Jody J. Daniels. *Retrieval of Passages for Information Reduction*. PhD thesis, University of Massachusetts, Amherst, Amherst, MA, May 1997.

[DR95] Jody J. Daniels and Edwina L. Rissland. A Case-Based Approach to Intelligent Information Retrieval. In *Proceedings of the 18th Annual International ACM/SIGIR Conference on Research and Development in Information Retrieval*, pages 238–245, Seattle, WA, July 1995. ACM.

[Kol93] Janet L. Kolodner. *Case-Based Reasoning*. Morgan Kaufmann, 1993.

[Kwo96] K. L. Kwok. A New Method of Weighting Query Terms for Ad-Hoc Retrieval. In *Proceedings of the 19th Annual International ACM/SIGIR Conference on Research and Development in Information Retrieval*, pages 187–195, Zurich, Switzerland, August 1996. ACM.

[RD95] Edwina L. Rissland and Jody J. Daniels. Using CBR to Drive IR. In *Proceedings, 14th International Joint Conference on Artificial Intelligence*, pages 400–407, Montreal, Canada, August 1995. AAAI.

[RD96] Edwina L. Rissland and Jody J. Daniels. The Synergistic Application of CBR to IR. *Artificial Intelligence Review*, 10:441–475, 1996.

[RSF96] Edwina L. Rissland, D. B. Skalak, and M. Timur Friedman. *BankXX: Supporting Legal Arguments through Heuristic Retrieval*. *Artificial Intelligence Review*, 10(1-71), 1996.

On the Relation between the Context of a Feature and the Domain Theory in Case-Based Planning

Héctor Muñoz-Avila & Frank Weberskirch &
Thomas Roth-Berghofer

Centre for Learning Systems and Applications (LSA)
University of Kaiserslautern, Dept. of Computer Science
P.O. Box 3049, D-67653 Kaiserslautern, Germany
E-mail: {munioz|weberski|roth}@informatik.uni-kl.de

Abstract. Determining the context of a feature (i.e., the factors affecting the ranking of a feature within a case) has been subject of several studies in analysis tasks, particularly for classification but not in synthesis tasks like planning. In this paper we will address this problem and explain how the domain theory plays a key role in determining the context of a feature. We provide a characterization of the domain theory and show that in domains meeting this characterization, the context can be simplified. We also use explanation-based learning techniques to determine the context in domains not meeting the characterization. Our work relates for the first time CBR, machine learning and planning theory to determine the context of a feature.

1 Introduction

Determining the context of a feature (i.e., the factors affecting the ranking of a feature within a case) is important because cases usually match new problems only partially. Thus, whereas the absence of a certain feature in the case in one context may not be very important for reusing the case, the absence of the same feature in another context may fundamentally make it difficult to reuse the case. Related to the question of the context of a feature is the question of its relevance. [1] pointed out that the relevance of the feature is a context-specific property. Traditional approaches for classification tasks, e.g. [14], have defined the relevance and context of a feature in terms of statistical information such as the distribution of their values relative to the values of other features.

In contrast to classification tasks, in synthesis tasks such as planning, other elements affect the context and relevance of a feature: first, the same problem may have several solutions, and second, there is a domain theory available that partially models the world. The first factor was already observed in [15], where the particular solution is used to classify the features as relevant or non relevant. In this work we are interested in studying how the domain theory affects the context of a feature.

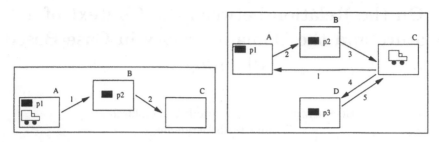

Fig. 1. Initial situation of (a) the case and (b) the new problem

In Section 2 we will motivate that the domain theory has an influence on the context of a feature. Section 3 will give an overview of planning theory that will be used to characterize the context of a feature in case-based planning. Then, Section 4 summarizes a feature weighting approach for case-based planning. In the next two sections a characterization of the context of a feature and a weakened form are presented. Section 6 explains how explanation-based learning techniques can be used to handle domains not meeting any of the two characterizations. In the next section the claims of this paper are validated and the last section makes concluding remarks.

2 Motivation

Consider the initial situation in the logistics transportation domain [15] illustrated in Figure 1 (a). In this situation there are three post offices A, B and C. In post office A there is a package $p1$ and a truck. In post office B there is a package $p2$. In the final situation both packages, $p1$ and $p2$, must be located at C. There are basic restrictions that any solution must meet: (1) only trucks can move between post offices, (2) to load a package in a truck, both have to be located at the same post office, and (3) to unload a package from a truck in a certain office, the truck must be located at that post office. A possible solution is to load package $p1$ at A, move the truck from A to B, load package $p2$ in the truck, move the truck from B to C and unload both packages (the arcs show the path followed by the truck, the numbers indicate the order). Suppose that this problem and solution are stored as a case.

Consider a new problem with the initial situation illustrated in Figure 1 (b). In the final situation the three packages must be located at C. If the case is used to solve the new problem, the truck follows the path illustrated by the arcs, collecting at each post office the corresponding package, leaving the packages $p1$ and $p2$ in C as indicated in the case. Finally, package $p3$ is loaded and moved to C. In this situation, the retrieval of the case is considered to be *successful* because steps taken from the case (2 and 3 in the new problem) could be extended to solve the new problem [10,4]. The problem solved in the case was not totally contained in the new problem: in the case, the truck is located in the same post office as a package whereas in the new problem, the truck is located in a post office with no packages. Technically, this means that some initial features (i.e., the features describing the initial situation), were unmatched by the initial features of the new problem. If we take the unmatched and matched features of the case as input for a weighting model, the weight of the unmatched features is decreased relative to the weight of the other features in the case because their absence did not affect the reusability of the case. Only initial features are in consideration for updating the weights.

Now consider the same case and problem as before, but suppose that additional restrictions have been added: (4) trucks must not be moved into the same post office more than once and (5) problem-specific restrictions such as not allowing the truck to move from D to A in Figure 1 (b). These restrictions are made to improve the quality of the plan. Clearly, the path illustrated in Figure 1 (b) violates restriction (4) because the truck is moved to post office C twice (arcs 3 and 5). This means that the solution of the case must be revised. In particular, moving the truck from B to C is revised and instead it must be moved from B to D, where package $p3$ is loaded. Finally, the truck is moved from D to C, where the three packages are unloaded. In this situation, the retrieval of the case is considered to be a *failure* and the weight of the unmatched features is increased relative to the weight of the other features in the case. However, this does not reflect the real reasons for the failure: even if the truck is located at A, the plan must still be revised. The real reason is that in solving the additional goal, to locate $p3$ in C, a conflict with the solution of the case occurs. This means that *there are factors that affect the effectiveness of reusing cases different than the initial features*. As a result, the strategy of updating the weights of the features based solely on the matched and unmatched features of the case becomes questionable. We will now see that depending on the characteristics of the domain theory, we can decide whether this strategy is adequate or not.

3 Planning Theory

We will now recall a planning theory developed in recent years [5,2]. Initially, this theory was conceived to explain the advantages of partial-order planners such as SNLP [7], over state-space planners such as TOCL [2].

A plan P achieving a set of goals G is *serially extensible* with respect to an additional goal g if P can be extended to a plan achieving $G \cup \{g\}$. For example, in the case and problem illustrated in Figure 1, the plan locating the two packages $p1$ and $p2$ in C is serially extensible with respect to the goal locating $p3$ in C if restrictions (4) and (5) are not considered. In contrast, this plan is not serially extensible with respect to this goal if they are considered because moving the truck from B to C needs to be revised (i.e., the arc 3 in the new problem).

If any plan achieving a goal $g1$ is serially extensible with respect to a second goal $g2$, then the order $g1$, $g2$ is called a *serialization order*. This definition is extended to sets of goals of any size in a natural way. Serial extensibility is not a commutative property: $g1$, $g2$ might be a serialization order but not $g2$, $g1$. If any permutation of a set of goals is a serialization order, the goals are said to be *trivially serializable*. For example, the three goals of the problem depicted in

Figure 1 (b) are trivially serializable if condition (4) is not taken into account and not trivially serializable if condition (4) is considered.

Trivial serializability of goals in a domain depends on the particular planner being used; [2] give examples of domains where goals are trivially serializable for SNLP but not for TOCL. Trivial serializability does not imply that planning in the domain is "easy". Finding the adequate extension might require a significant search effort. However, having this property says that the work performed to achieve a set of goals will not be undone when planning for an additional goal.

4 Feature Weighting in Case-based Planning

In [10] an algorithm is presented that analyzes the contribution of the initial features of the case during a reuse episode and updates the weights of these features accordingly. The similarity metric used is an extension of the foot-printed similarity metric [15], called the weighted foot-printed similarity metric. Similarity is meassured according to feature weights, which are case-specific. Thus, a local similarity [12] for each case is defined. Feature weights are updated following a reinforcement/punishment algorithm.

The adaptation strategy followed [3] is known as *eager replay*. Eager replay is done in two phases: in the first phase, each plan step contained in the retrieved cases is replayed in the new situation if replaying the step does not introduce any inconsistency in the new solution. Once this phase is finished, a partial solution is obtained. In the second phase, the partial solution is completed by first-principles planning. Decisions replayed from the case are only revised if no completion is possible. If decisions from the case are revised, the retrieval is considered to be a failure, otherwise it is considered to be a success.[1]

As stated before, a problem may have several solutions. This can make a feature weighting approach particularly difficult to apply because a solution obtained in a reuse episode may never occur again. However, because of the definition of success and failure, feature weights are increased if *any* completion of the partial solution is found or decresed if *no* completion is found. Thus, reinforcement or punishment does not depend on the particular solution found.

5 Feature Context and Trivial Serializability

As we saw before, different factors may affect the effectiveness of its reuse. In the feature weighting approach presented in [10] (see the last section) emphasis is given to the initial features. In another approach presented in [4], explanation-based learning techniques are used to generate rules explaining retrieval failures. These rules play the role of censors to the case. They are conceived to detect goals occuring in the problem but not in the case that interact negatively with the goals of the case. Thus, emphasis is given to the additional goals in the case.

---

[1] The definition of failure and success in [10] is a variation of this, but we omit details for the sake of simplicity.

Goals in Domain are	Context
trivially serializable	$Sol^{Ca} + I^{Ca} + I^{Pb} + (G^{Ca} \cap G^{Pb})$
not trivially serialiable	$Sol^{Ca} + I^{Ca} + I^{Pb} + G^{Ca} + G^{Pb}$

Table 1. Context according to the characteristics of the goal interactions in the domain.

For example, in Figure 1 (b), the goal to locate $p3$ in C interacts negatively with the goals of the case when restriction (4) and (5) are considered. Even as these are two different approaches towards improving retrieval in case-based planning, both report positive results when tested in experiments with different domains. In particular, in [10] the original version of the logistics transportation domain is used (i.e., as defined in [15]) whereas in [4] the restriction (4) is added. Goals in the logistics transport domain are trivially serializable for SNLP.[2] However, as we saw, when condition (4) is added, goals might not be trivially serializable. This motivates the following claim which is the main result of this paper:

Claim 1. In domains where goals are trivially serializable, the factors influencing the effectiveness of the reusability are the initial features of the problem and of the case, the goals common to the problem and the case, and the solution of the case.

This claim essentially says that the additional goals do not affect the effectiveness of the reuse. As a result, weighting models on initial features can be used. To show this, let G^{Ca}, G^{Pb} denote the goals of the case and of the problem respectively, then the subplan achieving $G^{Ca} \cap G^{Pb}$ in the case is taken and extended relative to the initial situation of the new problem (in the example, this extension corresponds to moving the truck from C to A, i.e., arc 1). Once the plan achieving $G^{Ca} \cap G^{Pb}$ has been generated, it can be extended to a plan achieving G^{Pb} because the goals are trivially serializable (i.e., arcs 4 and 5). Of course, retrieval failures will still occur if the subplan achieving $G^{Ca} \cap G^{Pb}$ in the case cannot be extended to solve these goals relative to the initial situation of the new problem. But the point is that such a failure is due to the initial features and not the additional goals.

Table 1 summarizes these results (Sol^{Ca} represents the solution of Ca). If goals are trivially serializable, only goals that are common to the problem and the case need to be considered. However, if goals are not trivially serializable, additional goals in the problem and the case might affect the effectiveness of the reusability of the case. This result establishes a direct relation between the concept of trivial serializability and feature context and shows the feasibility of previous research on feature weighting in case-based planning [10]. Notice

---

[2] This affirmation has never been reported in the literature. Intuitively, plans in the transportation domain can always be extended. For example, if a plan locates an object at a certain post office, this plan can always be extended to relocate the object in another office provided that the transportation means are available.

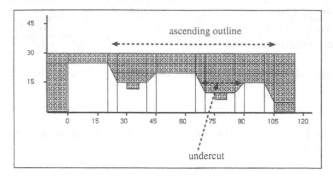

Fig. 2. Half display of a mechanical workpiece.

that the claim is independent of the particular kind of planner being used; all it requires are the goals to be trivially serializable for that particular kind of planner.

6 Weakening the Conditions

In [9], it has been shown that there are domains for which ordering restrictions, called *dependencies*, to achieve the goals in the plan can be determined previous to the problem solving process. For example, in the domain of process planning for manufacturing mechanical workpieces such as the one shown in Figure 2, the ordering constraints are the result of geometrical considerations. To manufacture a workpiece, the workpiece is clamped from a certain position using a certain kind of clamping mechanism. Once clamped, a cutting tool is used to remove layers of material. There are different clamping operations and cutting tools depending on the particular geometry of the area being *machined*. Typically, there are several areas conforming a workpiece. For this reason, the cutting tool and the clamping operation must be changed several times during the manufacturing process. In the representation being used, each area corresponds to a different goal [11]. From the geometry of the workpiece, it is clear that some areas cannot be machined before other areas have been removed. For example, in Figure 2, the area called *undercut* cannot be machined until the area called *ascending outline* has been removed because only after the ascending outline has been removed the undercut can be reached. This ordering restriction can be predetermined because it is independent of the particular solution [9].

The ordering restrictions are used in [9] to add additional conditions for a case to be retrieved: the case and the new problem should not only be similar modulo the footprinted similarity metric [15], but also the order for achieving the goals in the case should not violate the ordering restrictions of the goals in the new problem. Recent work shows that, for the particular domain specification used, when the goals are ordered in permutations extending these ordering restrictions, these permutations are serially extensible. In addition, the resulting plans are near optimal as they minimize the application of certain costly operations [11].

To see the implications of these results to our claim, consider a problem consisting of three goals, $g1$, $g2$, $g3$. Suppose that any solution must meet the ordering restriction $g1 \rightarrow g3$. Then, it is clear that any case retrieved in which $g1$ and $g3$ are achieved, $g1$ must be achieved before $g3$ because otherwise a retrieval failure will occur. In addition, suppose that any permutation on the goals $g1$, $g2$, $g3$ is a serialization order if $g1$ is ordered before $g3$ in the permutation.[3] Then, if a case is retrieved and $g3$ is achieved in the case, $g1$ must also be achieved in the case. If this is not the situation, for example, if the case achieves only $g3$, then it is clear that planning for achieving the goals is done in the order $g3$, $g2$, $g1$ or $g3$, $g1$, $g2$. In either case $g3$ is ordered before $g1$. Thus, the order might not be a serialization order and hence a retrieval failure might occur. The following definition formalizes these restrictions:

Definition 1 (Consistency of Retrieval). Let G^C, G^P denote the goals of the case C and of the problem P respectively. Suppose that ordering restrictions, $\rightarrow$, are given for G^P. Then, the retrieval of C is consistent if and only if the following holds:

1. If g', g are in $G^C \cap G^P$ and $g' \rightarrow g$, then g' is achieved before g in C.
2. If g is in $G^C \cap G^P$, then for every g' in G^P with $g' \rightarrow g$, g' is in $G^C \cap G^P$.

We say that a permutation on the goals *extends* the ordering restrictions $\rightarrow$, if for any two goals g', g such that $g' \rightarrow g$, then g' is ordered before g' in the permutation. We can now formulate the weakened form of our claim:

Claim 2. Suppose that a domain is given where ordering restrictions of the goals can be predetermined and the permutations on the goals extending these restrictions are known to be serially extensible. Then, the factors influencing the effectiveness of the reuse are the initial features of the problem and of the case, the goals common to the problem and the case, and the solution of the case provided that only consistent cases are retrieved.

As before, retrieval failures still occur if the subplan achieving $G^C \cap G^P$ in the case cannot be extended to solve these goals relative to the initial situation of the new problem. But this claim says that if the subplan can be extended to achieve $G^C \cap G^P$, no failure will occur when extending it further to achieve the additional goals in the new problem (i.e., $G^P - G^C$). Finally, this claim is also independent of the particular kind of planner being used.

7 Handling Arbitrary Planning Domains

There are several domains that are known to meet the condition regarding trivial serializability or serial extensibility of the claims 1 and 2 [2,11]. However, not

---

[3] For example, $g2$, $g1$, $g3$ is a serialization order but not $g2$, $g3$, $g1$.

for every domain it can be supposed that the goals are trivially serializable or at least that ordering restrictions can be predetermined such that the resulting permutations on the goals are serially extensible. A typical example is the logistics transportation domain if restrictions (4) and (5) are considered (see Section 2). Notice that even with these restrictions, there are several situations in which the retrieval is successful. For example, suppose that we have the same case as before and that the initial situation of the problem corresponds to a slight modification of the situation given in Figure 1 (b): $p3$ is located at C and in the final situation, $p1$, $p2$ must be located at C and $p3$ at D. In this situation, the retrieval of the case is successful because the extended subplan achieving the first two goals can be extended to a plan achieving these two goals relative to the new problem by moving the truck from C to A (i.e., arc 1). In addition, this subplan can be extended by loading $p3$ in the truck, moving the truck from C to D and unloading the package (i.e., arc 4). In this situation, the weights of the features can be updated because the additional goals do not interfere with the success of the retrieval. We will now show how explanation-based learning methods can be used dynamically to detect the situations in which the failure was caused by the additional goals.

Explanation-based Learning (EBL) has been used to guide the search process in planning [8]. The current state is viewed as a node in the so-called search tree.[4] If the node representing the current state has more than one successor node (i.e., there is more than one alternative to transform the current state), the planner has to chose one. If the decision was wrong (i.e., there is no node representing a solution in the subtree whose root is the chosen node), another neighbouring node has to be chosen. If all alternatives have been exhausted, the planner will have to go back to the predecessor of the node representing the current state and make another decision. This backtracking process is very expensive. For this reason, the search path can be analyzed to generate search control rules that explain the failure. When the same situation is encountered the planner will avoid making the choice known to be wrong.

We will not provide a detailed description of EBL (in our work we implemented [13] an extension of the mechanism presented in [6]), but, rather, we will illustrate with an example how EBL is used to detect if the failure was caused by an additional goal. Figure 3 sketches the search tree of the situation illustrated in Figure 1 if condition (4) is taken into account. The root of the tree is the leftmost node. The search three grows from left to right. Nodes labelled with Bn indicate that backtracking has taken place. Nodes always show the goal being solved and the operator selected to achieve that node (e.g., in the root node the goal is $at(p1,C)$ and the operator $unload(truck,p1,C)$). The nodes explored first are the ones taken from the case. As explained in Section 2, the subplan in the case achieving the first two goals can be extended relative to the initial situation of the new problem. However, the extended subplan cannot be extended to achieve the third goal because of condition (4). From a technical point of view, a

---

[4] The meaning of the term "state" depends on the particular planning paradigm: for [8] "state" is a world state whereas for [6] it is a plan state.

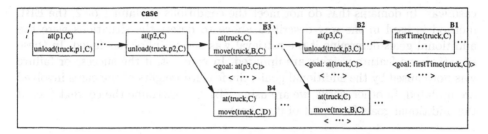

Fig. 3. Example of the regression of explanations over a search tree.

node will be reached that does not represent a solution and that either represents an inconsistent state or has no successors (not shown in Figure 3). At this node, EBL generates a so-called *initial explanation* that describes the inconsistency or the fact that the node cannot be further transformed. This initial explanation is *propagated* to the predecessor of the node. This propagation, called regression, results in an explanation of the failure in terms of the conditions that were valid at the predecessor node. If a node has more than one successor node its failure explanation is the conjunction of the regressed explanations of each successor node together with the goal being achieved. The obtained explanation can further be regressed when backtracking occurs using the same principle. In Figure 3, four of the backtracking nodes are shown and their corresponding regressed explanations are sketched between <>. Two observations can be made here:

1. To have a retrieval failure is equivalent to backtracking on nodes that were taken directly from the cases [4]. For example the node *B3* was taken from the case and backtracking on this node occurs. This means that the case could not be extended.
2. *If additional goals caused backtracking on nodes that were taken directly from the case, these goals are present in the regressed explanation of the backtracking nodes.* This fact is illustrated at the explanation < *goal : at(p3, C)* > illustrated in the node *B3*.

The second observation is very important because it clearly states how to identify if the revision of a decision taken from the case was due to an additional goal, g. Then the goal appears in the regressed explanation at the corresponding node. We will illustrate why this affirmation is valid: notice that g will be included in the explanation of the backtracking at the node representing the state were g was pursued to be achieved (node *B2* in Figure 3). Because g is an original goal in the problem, there was no other node that added g. That is, every regression of an explanation containing g will contain g again. This shows why the explanation of *B3* includes the additional goal *at(p3,C)*.

In our case-based planning system, CAPLAN/CBC, a similarity metric is used based on feature weighting [10]. The feature weights are updated based on the performance of the retrieved cases in solving the new problem: feature weights are increased or decreased depending on how effective the guidance of a case was. In domains that do not meet the conditions of claim 1 or 2, the EBL method is used in the way described above to detect the situations were the additional goals determine if the retrieval was successful or has failed. In these situations no feature weights are updated. In contrast, if the success or failure was not caused by the additional goals, the feature weights of the cases involved are updated. In other words, we are using EBL to determine the context (i.e., if the additional goals form part of it or not).

8 Validation

This work provides a theoretical framework explaining two different but related works [4,10]. As explained in Section 5, [4] learns EBL rules that basically indicate the conditions for which *additional goals* will cause a retrieval failure in a case. Interestingly each of the three domains used to test this approach is *not trivially serializable*: the logistics transportation domain with restriction (4), the domain of process planning (for a proof of the non trivially serializability of this domain see [11]), and the artificial domain $\theta_2 D^m S^1$ [2]. We can explain these results by observing that because in these domains neither the conditions given in claim 1 nor in claim 2 are valid, the additional goals form part of the context.

In [10] experiments with domains meeting the conditions in claim 1 or 2 are given. One of the domains used to test this approach is the logistics transportation domain which as we saw is trivially serializable. Thus, according to claim 1 the additional goals do not form part of the context. The second is the domain of process planning, which in CAPLAN/CBC always has associated the dependencies [9]. Permutations on the goals extending the dependencies are serially extensible [11]. Thus, according to claim 2 the additional goals do not form part of the context, so in these domains concentrating on the initial goals was the right approach to follow.

We perform an experiment to study the improvements of using the EBL regression technique as a censor to the updating process of the feature weights. We perform experiments in the logistics transportation domain including restrictions (4) and (5). At each experimental setup a case was fixed and features in the case were selected. A collection of problems was formed by changing the selected features and/or adding new goals. Changing a feature means relocating it. For example, if a selected feature is a truck, changing the truck means relocating it in a different place as it was in the case. Notice that when new goals are added, retrieval failures due to the additional goals might occur. The collections of problems were ordered in a way that the changes of features were equally distributed through the collection. In this way, we ensure that all the selected features have the same chance to affect the learning process. Finally, each ordered collection was divided in two subcollections. The first subcollection was used as training examples for updating the feature weights and the second one was used to meassure the effectiveness of the learning method.

Each case was trained in two modes: the *noEBL-mode* and the *EBL-mode*. In both modes feature weights are updated using the algorithms described in [10],

	Static	Weighting	
		noEBL	EBL
% Cases Retrieved	100	78	67
% Retrieval Failures	57	43	28
% Incorrect Non Retrieval	0	21	4

Table 2. Measuring the effectiveness of the retrieval.

in which essentially the weights of certain features are increased if the retrieval failed and decreased if the retrieval is successful. In the EBL-mode and if the retrieval failed, it is tested if the failure was caused by the additional goals in the way explained in the last section. If this is the situation the weights are not updated. In contrast, in the noEBL-mode feature weights are updated always.

The results are shown in table 2. The first column shows the results when weights were not considered for retrieval (i.e., all features of the cases are supposed to have the same relevance). The second column shows the results when feature weights were updated in noEBL-mode. The last column shows the results when feature weights were updated in EBL-mode. The first row shows ther percentage of cases retrieved. The second row the percentage of retrieval failures. The third column shows the percentage of times the case was not retrieved although retrieving it would be adequate. We called these *incorrect non retrieval episodes* and they result from the feature weighting process. In a sence, cases become "specialized" to certain context.

Notice that the best results are obtained with the EBL-mode, where the percentage of retrieval failures was reduced from 57% (with the static mode) to 28% and the percentage of incorrect non retrieval episodes is just 4%. With the noEBL the percentage of retrieval failures also decreases from 57% to 43% although not as significant as with the EBL-mode. A clear negative effect is that the percentage of incorrect non retrieval episodes increases in a significant way (i.e., 21%). The difference in results between the noEBL and the EBL modes shows the importance of censoring the learning method.

9 Conclusion

We have seen that the domain theory is an important factor determining how goals may affect the success of a retrieval episode. We have seen that there is a large collection of domains, those containing goals that are trivially serializable, for which the context can be simplified in that additional goals not occuring in the cases do not affect the success of a retrieval episode. We have shown that the explanation regression technique of EBL can be effectively used to determine dynamically situations in which the context can be simplified for domains not falling in the collection. Our work relates for the first time CBR, machine learning and planning theory to determine the context of a feature.

Acknowledgements

The authors want to thank David W. Aha for the helpful discussions and comments on earlier versions of this paper as well as the reviewers.

References

1. D. W. Aha and R. L. Goldstone. Learning attribute relevance in context in instance-based learning algorithms. In *Proceedings of the Twelfth Annual Conference of the Cognitive Science Society*, pages pp 141–148, Cambridge, IN: Lawrence Erlbaum, 1990.
2. A. Barrett and D.S. Weld. Partial-order planning: Evaluating possible efficiency gains. *Artificial Intelligence*, 67(1):71–112, 1994.
3. L. Ihrig and S. Kambhampati. Derivational replay for partial-order planning. In *Proceedings of AAAI-94*, pages 116–125, 1994.
4. L. Ihrig and S. Kambhampati. Design and implementation of a replay framework based on a partial order planner. In D. Weld, editor, *Proceedings of AAAI-96*. IOS Press, 1996.
5. S. Kambhampati, L. Ihrig, and B. Srivastava. A candidate set based analysis of subgoal interactions in conjunctive goal planning. In *Proceedings of the 3rd International Conference on AI Planning Systems (AIPS-96)*, pages 125–133, 1996.
6. S. Kambhampati, S. Katukam, and Y. Qu. Failure driven dynamic search control for partial order planners: An explanation-based approach. *Artificial Intelligence*, 88(1-2):253–315, 1996.
7. D. McAllester and D. Rosenblitt. Systematic nonlinear planning. In *Proceedings of AAAI-91*, pages 634–639, 1991.
8. S. Minton. *Learning Search Control Knowledge: An Explanation-Based Approach*. Kluwer Academic Publishers, Boston, 1988.
9. H. Muñoz-Avila and J. Hüllen. Retrieving relevant cases by using goal dependencies. In M. Veloso and A. Aamodt, editors, *Proceedings of the 1st International Conference on Case-Based Reasoning (ICCBR-95)*, number 1010 in Lecture Notes in Artificial Intelligence. Springer, 1995.
10. H. Muñoz-Avila and J. Hüllen. Feature weighting by explaining case-based planning episodes. In *Third European Workshop (EWCBR-96)*, number 1168 in Lecture Notes in Artificial Intelligence. Springer, 1996.
11. H. Muñoz-Avila and F. Weberskirch. A specification of the domain of process planning: Properties, problems and solutions. Technical Report LSA-96-10E, Centre for Learning Systems and Applications, University of Kaiserslautern, Germany, 1996.
12. F. Ricci and P. Avesani. Learning a local similarity metric for case-based reasoning. In *Case-Based Reasoning Research and Development, Proceedings of the 1st International Conference (ICCBR-95)*, Sesimbra, Portugal, 1995. Springer Verlag.
13. T. Roth-Berghofer. Explanation-based learning of control information of failures in planning. Masters thesis (in german), University of Kaiserslautern, 1996.
14. P. D. Turney. The identification of context-sensitive features: A formal definition of context for concept learning. In *Proceedings of the ECML-96 Workshop on Learning in Context-Sensitive Domains*, 1996.
15. M. Veloso. *Planning and learning by analogical reasoning*. Number 886 in Lecture Notes in Artificial Intelligence. Springer Verlag, 1994.

Theoretical Analysis of Case Retrieval Method Based on Neighborhood of a New Problem

Seishi Okamoto   and   Nobuhiro Yugami

Fujitsu Laboratories Limited.
2-2-1 Momochihama, Sawara-ku, Fukuoka 814, Japan
{seishi, yugami}@flab.fujitsu.co.jp

Abstract. The retrieval of similar cases is often performed by using the neighborhood of a new problem. The neighborhood is usually defined by a certain fixed number of most similar cases (k nearest neighbors) to the problem. This paper deals with an alternative definition of neighborhood that comprises the cases within a certain distance, d, from the problem. We present an average-case analysis of a classifier, the d-nearest neighborhood method (d-NNh), that retrieves cases in this neighborhood and predicts their majority class as the class of the problem. Our analysis deals with m-of-n/l target concepts, and handles three types of noise. We formally compute the expected classification accuracy of d-NNh, then we explore the predicted behavior of d-NNh. By combining this exploration for d-NNh and one for k-nearest neighbor method (k-NN) in our previous study, we compare the predicted behavior of each in noisy domains. Our formal analysis is supported with Monte Carlo simulations.

1 Introduction

The retrieval of similar case plays an important role in case-based reasoning. This is because the retrieval of more similar cases to a new problem reduces the load of adaptation and leads to a more precise solution. Case retrieval is often performed by using the neighborhood of the problem. That is, the cases in the neighborhood are retrieved, then these are used to produce a solution for the problem. The most common definition of neighborhood is based on a certain fixed number of most similar cases (*i.e.*, k nearest neighbors) to the problem. Actually, the k-nearest neighbor method (k-NN) or its variants are used in many case retrieval algorithms (*e.g.*, [1, 4, 13]). In contrast, there is an alternative definition of neighborhood as a region bounded by the distance from the problem [8]. This paper deals with a neighborhood comprising the cases within a certain fixed distance, d, from the problem (see Fig.1). The goal of this paper is to present a formal comparison of the case retrieval methods based on these definitions of neighborhood in the classification domain including noise.

There have been several theoretical analyses of k-NN. By comparisons with a Bayesian Classifier, Cover and Hart [3] showed the bound for the error rate (risk) of k-NN for an infinite training set, and the new bounds of 1-NN risk was given for a finite training set [5]. Aha *et al.* [1] analyzed 1-NN with a similar model to PAC (Probably Approximately Correct) learning, and this analysis was

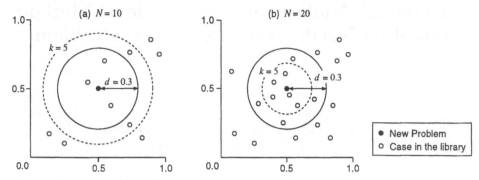

Fig. 1. Neighborhoods based on a fixed number ($k = 5$) of the nearest cases and a fixed distance ($d = 0.3$) from a new problem in the normalized 2D space. N represents the number of cases in the case library.

generalized to k-NN [2]. Although these theoretical results give some insights into the behavior of k-NN, all of these studies assume noise-free instances.

An average-case analysis is a useful theoretical framework to understand the behavior of learning algorithms [12]. This framework is based on the formal computation of the expected accuracy of the learning algorithm for a certain fixed class of concepts. Using the result of this computation, we can explore the predicted behavior of the algorithm that directly relates to the empirical results. There have been some average-case analyses of k-NN. Langley and Iba [6] analyzed 1-NN for conjunctive target concepts, and we [9] analyzed k-NN for m-of-n concepts without irrelevant attribute. However, these studies assumed noise-free cases. For noisy domains, we presented an average-case analyses of 1-NN for m-of-$n$concepts with irrelevant attribute [10], and this study was recently generalized to k-NN [11].

This paper presents an average-case analysis of a classifier that retrieves cases within a certain fixed distance, d, from the problem and predicts their majority class as the class of the problem. We refer to this classifier as the d-nearest neighborhood method (d-NNh). Our analysis deals with m-of-n target concepts with l irrelevant attributes, and handles three types of noise: relevant attribute noise, irrelevant attribute noise, and class noise. We formally compute the expected classification accuracy (*i.e.*, predictive accuracy) of d-NNh after N cases are stored in the case library. We represent this accuracy as a function of the domain characteristics: d, N, m, n, l, the probabilities of occurrence for relevant and irrelevant attributes, and noise rates. Using the accuracy function, we explore the predicted behavior of d-NNh in noisy domains. By combining this exploration for d-NNh and one for k-NN in our recent study [11], we compare the predicted behavior of each. We describe the predictive accuracy of d-NNh against the value of d, and present the theoretical learning curves of d-NNh and k-NN. Also, we show the optimal values of d and k against the size of case library. Our formal analysis is supported with Monte Carlo simulations.

2 Characteristics of the Domain

We represent a new problem as an instance comprising Boolean attribute/value pairs, and each case in the case library as the instance with a class label. In the following discussions, we refer to a new problem as the test instance, and refer to each case in the case library as the training instance.

Our analysis deals with m-of-n/l target concepts defined over the threshold m, n relevant and l irrelevant Boolean attributes [7]. These concepts classify an instance as positive if and only if at least m out of n relevant attributes occur (*i.e.*, take the value 1) in its instance.

Our analysis handles three types of noise. Each type of noise is introduced by the following common definition. Relevant attribute noise flips an arbitrary relevant attribute value in each instance with a certain probability σ_r, and irrelevant attribute noise flips an arbitrary irrelevant attribute value with a probability σ_i. Class noise replaces the class label for each instance with its negation with a certain probability σ_c.

This paper deals with a d-nearest neighborhood method using hamming distance (*i.e.*, the number of attributes on which two instances differ) as a distance measure. Our analysis assumes every relevant and irrelevant attribute independently occurs with a certain probability p and q. Each training instance is independently drawn from the instance space with respect to these probabilities. After the effects of each type of noise, all training instances are stored into the case library to allow for duplication. When a test instance is given, d-NNh retrieves training instances within a certain fixed distance d from the test instance (the d-nearest neighborhood of the test instance), and then predicts their majority class (positive or negative) as the class of the test instance. If there is no training instance or there are the same number of positive and negative training instances in the d-nearest neighborhood, then d-NNh randomly determines the class of the test instance.

3 Predictive Accuracy

We formally compute the predictive accuracy of d-NNh for m-of-n/l target concepts after N training instances are given. The predictive accuracy is represented as a function of the domain characteristics: d, N, m, n, l, p, q, σ_r, σ_i, and σ_c. However, to avoid complicated notation, we will not explicitly express these characteristics as parameters of the accuracy function with the exception of d.

We compute the predictive accuracy in the case where each type of noise affects only training instances. After this computation, we also give the accuracy function in the case where noise affects both test and training instances.

To compute the predictive accuracy, we use a set of instances in which x relevant attributes and y irrelevant attributes simultaneously occur (we denote this set with $I(x, y)$). Let $P_{occ}(x, y)$ be the probability that an arbitrary noise-free instance belongs to $I(x, y)$. This probability is given by

$$P_{occ}(x, y) = \binom{n}{x}\binom{l}{y}p^x(1-p)^{n-x}q^y(1-q)^{l-y}.$$

Under the assumptions given in Section 2, d-NNh has the same expected probability of correct classification for an arbitrary test instance in $I(x, y)$. Hence, we can represent the predictive accuracy of d-NNh after N training instances as

$$A(d) = \sum_{y=0}^{l}\left\{\sum_{x=0}^{m-1} P_{occ}(x, y)\left(1 - P_{pos}(d, x, y)\right) + \sum_{x=m}^{n} P_{occ}(x, y)P_{pos}(d, x, y)\right\},$$

where $P_{pos}(d, x, y)$ represents the probability that d-NNh classifies an arbitrary test instance in $I(x, y)$ as positive.

Let $t(x, y)$ be an arbitrary test instance in $I(x, y)$. To represent $P_{pos}(d, x, y)$, we compute the appearance probability for an arbitrary training instance with distance $e(0 \le e \le n + l)$ from $t(x, y)$. Let $P_{dp}(x, y, e)$ be this probability for an arbitrary training instance with the positive class label, and $P_{dn}(x, y, e)$ be that for the negative class label. $P_{dp}(x, y, e)$ and $P_{dn}(x, y, e)$ were computed using Eq.(14) and Eq.(15) in our previous paper [10]. Hence, we simply state the computation of these probabilities here.

$P_{dp}(x, y, e)$ and $P_{dn}(x, y, e)$ are given by

$$P_{dp}(x, y, e) = \sum_{X=0}^{n}\sum_{Y=0}^{l} P_p(X, Y)P_{dis}(x, y, X, Y, e),$$

$$P_{dn}(x, y, e) = \sum_{X=0}^{n}\sum_{Y=0}^{l} P_n(X, Y)P_{dis}(x, y, X, Y, e).$$

In these equations, $P_p(X, Y)$ represents the probability that an arbitrary training instance belongs to $I(X, Y)$ and has the positive class label. $P_n(X, Y)$ does the same for the negative class label. Moreover, $P_{dis}(x, y, X, Y, e)$ denotes the probability that an arbitrary training instance in $I(X, Y)$ has distance e from $t(x, y)$.

First, we represent $P_p(X, Y)$ and $P_n(X, Y)$ by considering the effects of each type of noise on the training instances. These probabilities are represented as

$$P_p(X, Y) = (1 - \sigma_c)P_{p0}(X, Y) + \sigma_c P_{n0}(X, Y),$$
$$P_n(X, Y) = \sigma_c P_{p0}(X, Y) + (1 - \sigma_c)P_{n0}(X, Y),$$

where $P_{p0}(X, Y)$ denotes the appearance probability for an arbitrary positive training instance in $I(X, Y)$, and $P_{n0}(X, Y)$ denotes that for an arbitrary negative one, before the effect of class noise. $P_{p0}(X, Y)$ and $P_{n0}(X, Y)$ are given by

$$P_{p0}(X, Y) = \sum_{X_0=m}^{n}\sum_{X_0=0}^{l} P_{occ}(X_0, Y_0)P_{nr}(X_0, X)P_{ni}(Y_0, Y),$$

$$P_{n_0}(X, Y) = \sum_{X_0=0}^{m-1} \sum_{Y_0=0}^{l} P_{occ}(X_0, Y_0) P_{nr}(X_0, X) P_{ni}(Y_0, Y),$$

where $P_{nr}(X_0, X)$ represents the probability that the number of relevant attributes occurring in an arbitrary training instance is changed from X_0 to X by the effect of relevant attribute noise, and $P_{ni}(Y_0, Y)$ represents the probability that the corresponding number for irrelevant attributes is changed from Y_0 to Y by irrelevant attribute noise. These probabilities are represented as

$$P_{nr}(X_0, X) = \sum_{s=\max(0,X_0-X)}^{\min(X_0,n-X)} \binom{X_0}{s} \binom{n-X_0}{X-X_0+s} (1-\sigma_r)^n \left(\frac{\sigma_r}{1-\sigma_r}\right)^{X-X_0+2s},$$

$$P_{ni}(Y_0, Y) = \sum_{t=\max(0,Y_0-Y)}^{\min(Y_0,l-Y)} \binom{Y_0}{t} \binom{l-Y_0}{Y-Y_0+t} (1-\sigma_i)^l \left(\frac{\sigma_i}{1-\sigma_i}\right)^{Y-Y_0+2t}.$$

Next, we represent $P_{dis}(x, y, X, Y, e)$. Let z_r be the number of relevant attributes which occur in both $t(x, y)$ and an arbitrary training instance in $I(X, Y)$, and z_i be that for irrelevant attributes. Then, $P_{dis}(x, y, X, Y, e)$ is given by

$$P_{dis}(x, y, X, Y, e) = \sum_{(z_r, z_i) \in S} \frac{\binom{x}{z_r}\binom{n-x}{X-z_r}}{\binom{n}{X}} \frac{\binom{y}{z_i}\binom{l-y}{Y-z_i}}{\binom{l}{Y}},$$

where S is a set of a pair of z_r and z_i, that satisfies all conditions of

$$\max(0, x + X - n) \le z_r \le \min(x, X),$$
$$\max(0, y + Y - l) \le z_i \le \min(y, Y),$$
$$z_r + z_i = \frac{x + y + X + Y - e}{2}.$$

We have represented $P_{dp}(x, y, e)$ and $P_{dn}(x, y, e)$. Using these probabilities, we compute $P_{pos}(d, x, y)$ in the accuracy function. For this computation, we consider the situation that exactly n_d out of N training instances appear within distance d from $t(x, y)$, and exactly n_p out of these n_d instances have the positive class label. Let $P_{num}(x, y, d, n_d, n_p)$ be the probability that this situation occurs. Under this situation, if $n_p > n_d/2$, then d-NNh classifies $t(x, y)$ as positive, and if $n_p < n_d/2$, then d-NNh classifies $t(x, y)$ as negative. Moreover, if $n_p = n_n/2$, then d-NNh classifies $t(x, y)$ as positive with a probability of $1/2$. Hence, we can represent $P_{pos}(d, x, y)$ as

$$P_{pos}(d, x, y) = \sum_{n_d=0}^{N} \left\{ \frac{1}{2} P_{num}(x, y, d, n_d, \frac{n_d}{2}) + \sum_{n_p=\lfloor \frac{n_d}{2} \rfloor+1}^{n_d} P_{num}(x, y, d, n_d, n_p) \right\},$$

where the first term in the outer summation is zero when n_d is an odd number. We can represent $P_{\text{num}}(x, y, d, n_d, n_p)$ as

$$P_{\text{num}}(x, y, d, n_d, n_p) = \binom{N}{n_p} \binom{N - n_p}{n_d - n_p} P_{\text{wp}}(x, y, d)^{n_p} P_{\text{wn}}(x, y, d)^{n_d - n_p}$$
$$\times (1 - P_{\text{wp}}(x, y, d) - P_{\text{wn}}(x, y, d))^{N - n_d},$$

where $P_{\text{wp}}(x, y, d)$ denotes the probability that an arbitrary training instance occurs within distance d from $t(x, y)$ and has the positive class label, and $P_{\text{wn}}(x, y, d)$ does the same for the negative class label. These probabilities are given by

$$P_{\text{wp}}(x, y, d) = \sum_{e=0}^{d} \{P_{\text{dp}}(x, y, e) + P_{\text{dn}}(x, y, e)\},$$

$$P_{\text{wn}}(x, y, d) = \sum_{e=0}^{d} \{P_{\text{dp}}(x, y, e) + P_{\text{dn}}(x, y, e)\}.$$

We have computed the predictive accuracy of d-NNh in the case where each type of noise affects only the training instances. When noise affects both test and training instances, the predictive accuracy of d-NNh after N training instances can be represented as

$$A(d) = \sum_{x=0}^{n} \sum_{y=0}^{l} \{P_{\text{n}}(x, y)(1 - P_{\text{pos}}(d, x, y)) + P_{\text{p}}(x, y)P_{\text{pos}}(d, x, y)\}.$$

4   Predicted Behavior

Using the accuracy function given in Section 3, we explore the predicted behavior of d-NNh for m-of-n/l concepts. Although we defined the accuracy function for both noise-free and noisy test instances, our exploration deals with only noise-free test instances for lack of space. Moreover, we investigate the effects of each individual noise type on the predicted behavior of d-NNh. By combining this exploration for d-NNh and one for k-NN in our recent study [11], we compare the predicted behavior of each. The version of k-NN in [11] uses hamming distance as a distance measure, and randomly determines the class of test instance if there are same number of positive and negative training instances among its k nearest neighbors. Throughout our exploration, we set both probabilities of occurrence for both relevant and irrelevant attributes to $1/2$.

For irrelevant attribute noise, we can formally prove the following claim from the accuracy function (the proof is omitted here due to space limitations).

Claim 1
If the probability of occurrence for irrelevant attribute is $1/2$, then the predictive accuracy of d-NNh for m-of-n/l concepts is entirely independent of the noise rate for the irrelevant attributes.

From this claim, we can expect that irrelevant attribute noise does *not* greatly

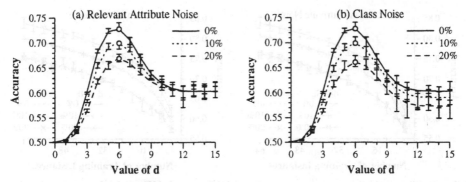

Fig. 2. Predictive accuracy of d-NNh against the value of d for a 5-of-10/5 concept. Each curve comes from the theoretical result, and the error bars indicate the result of Monte Carlo simulations. Each circle denotes the predictive accuracy with the optimal value of d. The number of training instances is fixed at 32.

affect the classification accuracy of d-NNh. This independence of irrelevant attribute noise on the accuracy also holds for k-NN [11]. Therefore, the following discussions focus on the effects of relevant attribute noise and class noise.

In addition to the theoretical results from the accuracy function, we give the results of Monte Carlo simulations to confirm our analysis. For each case, 100 training sets are randomly generated in accordance with each noise rate. Then the data is collected as the classification accuracy measured over the entire space of noise-free instances. We report a 95% confidence interval of the mean accuracy of 100 data items for each case. In the following figures, the error bar indicates this confidence interval.

4.1 Accuracy against Value of d

First, we report the predictive accuracy of d-NNh against the value of d for several noise levels, as shown in Fig.2. In this figure, the target is a 5-of-10/5 concept, and the number of training instances is fixed at 32. Each curve represents the theoretical result from the accuracy function, and the error bars indicate the empirical results of Monte Carlo simulations. Moreover, each circle denotes the highest accuracy at the corresponding noise level (*i.e.*, the corresponding value of d is optimal). The theoretical results agree well with the empirical ones for both relevant attribute noise and class noise.

Fig.2 shows that the predictive accuracy of d-NNh strongly depends on the value of d. As d increases, the predictive accuracy of d-NNh significantly improves, then reaches a maximum before starting to deteriorate. Due to this sensitivity to the value of d, a choice of the value of d is very important to get a high classification accuracy. However, the optimal value of d seems to be easily chosen for a certain fixed number of training instances. This is because the predictive accuracy of d-NNh has one peak against the value d. In contrast, the

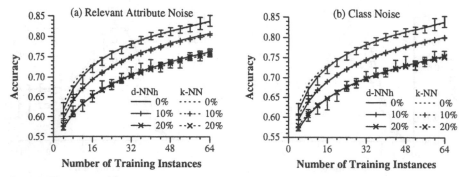

Fig. 3. Theoretical learning curves for d-NNh and k-NN with the optimal value of d and k for a 3-of-5/2 concept. Each solid curve corresponds with the predictive accuracy of d-NNh, and dotted curve corresponds with that of k-NN. The error bars indicate the results of Monte Carlo simulations for d-NNh.

accuracy of k-NN has two peaks against the value of k for small levels of relevant attribute noise and class noise [11]. Therefore, these observations suggest that it is easier to choose an optimal d for d-NNh than an optimal k for k-NN for a fixed number of training instances. Fig.2 also shows that the optimal value of d does *not* entirely change against each level of relevant attribute noise and class noise. This observation suggests that the optimal value of d is mostly independent of the noise level.

4.2 Learning Curves

Next, we describe the learning curves for d-NNh for a 3-of-5/2 target concept in comparison with that for k-NN, as shown in Fig.3. In this figure, each solid curve represents the theoretical learning curve for d-NNh with the optimal value of d, and each dotted curve denotes that for k-NN with the optimal k. The error bars come from the results of Monte Carlo simulations for d-NNh (that for a 10% noise level is omitted for simplicity). The theoretical results agree well with the empirical ones.

In Fig.3, both predictive accuracies of d-NNh and k-NN significantly improve as the number of training instances increases at each noise level. In other words, both d-NNh and k-NN require a large number of training instances to achieve a high accuracy. Fig.3 also shows that there are no significant differences between the predictive accuracy of d-NNh and k-NN at each level of relevant attribute noise and class noise. That is, the optimal d-NNh is comparable to the optimal k-NN with respect to the classification accuracy.

4.3 Optimal Value of d

Finally, we give the optimal value of d to achieve the highest accuracy of d-NNh against the number of training instances in comparison with the optimal

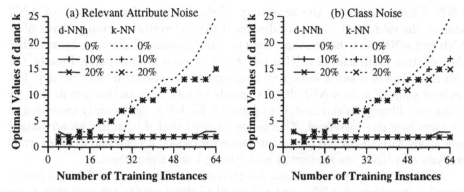

Fig. 4. The optimal value of d for d-NNh and that of k for k-NN for a 3-of-5/2 concept.

k for k-NN, as shown in Fig.4. In this figure, the optimal values of d and k come from the theoretical results, and the target is a 3-of-5/2 concept.

Fig.4 shows the most remarkable difference between d-NNh and k-NN. The optimal value of d for d-NNh does mostly *not* change as the number of training instances increases. This observation suggests that the optimal value of d is mostly independent of the size of case library. In contrast, the optimal k for k-NN significantly changes with an increase in the size of training set. This change in the optimal values of d and k against the number of training instances is a very important issue in terms of maintenance for the values of d and k. That is, k-NN requires an increase in the value of k to get a high accuracy as the size of the case library increases. In contrast, d-NNh does mostly *not* require the maintenance of the value of d with an increase in the case library size, after we choose the optimal value of d once for a certain size of the case library. This seems to be the remarkable advantage of d-NNh over k-NN. for our problem descriptions.

5 Conclusion

We have presented a formal comparison of two types of case retrieval method based on the neighborhood of a new problem in the classification domain. One was the d-nearest neighborhood method (d-NNh) that predicts the class of the problem as a majority class among cases within a fixed distance, d, from the problem, and other was k-nearest neighbor method (k-NN).

We presented an average-case analysis of d-NNh for m-of-n/l target concepts in noisy domains. Our analysis dealt with three types of noise: relevant attribute noise, irrelevant attribute noise, and class noise. We formally defined the predictive accuracy of d-NNh as a function of the domain characteristics. Using the accuracy function, we explored the predicted behavior of d-NNh in noisy domains. By combining this exploration for d-NNh with one for k-NN in our previous work, we compared the predicted behavior of d-NNh with that of

k-NN. First, we showed the sensitivity of the classification accuracy of d-NN against the value of d. Next, we described the theoretical learning curves of d-NNh and k-NN, and showed that there are no significant differences between the classification accuracies of d-NNh and k-NN at each level of noise. Finally, the optimal values of d and k were presented against the size of the case library. The optimal value of d for d-NNh did not mostly change with an increase in the size of the case library. In contrast, the optimal k for k-NN significantly increased as the case base size increased. That is, we showed that d-NNh has an advantage over k-NN with respect to the maintenance for the values of d and k. Our formal analysis of d-NNh was supported with Monte Carlo simulations.

Although this paper described the predictive bahavior of d-NNh and gave a formal comparison of d-NNh and k-NN, all of these results are true only when our many assumptions hold. In the future, we will confirm these results by the empirical evaluations.

References

1. Aha, D., Kibler, D., and Albert, M. Instance-Based Learning Algorithms. *Machine Learning*, **6**, (1991) 37–66.
2. Albert, M. and Aha, D. Analyses of Instance-Based Learning Algorithms. In *Proceedings of AAAI-91*, (1991) 553–558. AAAI Press/MIT Press.
3. Cover, T. and Hart, P. Nearest Neighbor Pattern Classification. *IEEE Transactions on Information Theory*, **13**(1), (1967) 21–27.
4. Creecy, H., Masand, M., Smith, J., and Waltz, D. Trading Mips and Memory for Knowledge Engineering. *Communications of the ACM*, **35**(8), (1992) 48–63.
5. Drakopoulos, J. Bounds on the Classification Error of the Nearest Neighbor Rule. In *Proceedings of ICML-95*, (1995) 203–208. Morgan Kaufmann.
6. Langley, P. and Iba, W. Average-Case Analysis of a Nearest Neighbor Algorithm. In *Proceedings of IJCAI-93*, (1993) 889–894. Morgan Kaufmann.
7. Murphy, P. and Pazzani, M. ID2-of-3: Constructive Induction of M-of-N Concepts for Discriminators in Decision Trees. In *Proceedings of IWML-91*, (1991) 183–187. Morgan Kaufmann.
8. O'Callaghan, J. F. An Alternative Definition for Neighborhood of a Point, IEEE Transactions on Computers, **24**(11), (1975) 1121–1125.
9. Okamoto, S. and Satoh, K. An Average-Case Analysis of k-Nearest Neighbor Classifier. In *Proceedings of ICCBR-95* (Veloso, M. and Aamodt, A. Eds., *LNAI*, **1010**), (1995) 243–264. Springer-Verlag.
10. Okamoto, S. and Yugami, N. Theoretical Analysis of the Nearest Neighbor Classifier in Noisy Domains. In *Proceedings of ICML-96* (1996) 355–363. Morgan Kaufmann.
11. Okamoto, S. and Yugami, N. An Average-Case Analysis of the k-Nearest Neighbor Classifier for Noisy Domains. In *Proceedings of IJCAI-97*, (1997) to appear. Morgan Kaufmann.
12. Pazzani, M. and Sarrett, W. A Framework for Average Case Analysis of Conjunctive Learning Algorithms. *Machine Learning*, **9** (1992) 349–372.
13. Wettschereck, D. and Aha, D. Weighting Features. In *Proceedings of ICCBR-95* (Veloso, M. and Aamodt, A. Eds., *LNAI*, **1010**), (1995) 347–358. Springer-Verlag.

The Adaptation Knowledge Bottleneck: How to Ease it by Learning from Cases

Kathleen Hanney and Mark T. Keane

Dept. of Computer Science, Trinity College, Dublin, Ireland
E-mail: kathleen.hanney, mark.keane@cs.tcd.ie

Abstract. Assuming that adaptation knowledge will continue to be an important part of CBR systems, a major challenge for the area is to overcome the knowledge-engineering problems that arise in its acquisition. This paper describes an approach to automating the acquisition of adaptation knowledge overcoming many of the associated knowledge-engineering costs. This approach makes use of inductive techniques, which learn adaptation knowledge from case comparison. We also show how this adaptation knowledge can be usefully applied and report on how available domain knowledge might be exploited in such an adaptation-rule learning-system.

1   Introduction

Case-based reasoning systems solve problems by reusing the solutions to previously solved problems. Typically, there are differences between a new problem and the previous case so the success of a CBR system often critically depends on its ability to adapt the solution of a previous case to suit a new situation. Up to the time of writing, the adaptation stage has been the least well-developed aspect of CBR, largely because of the lack of a methodology for acquiring and applying adaptation rules. At present, most CBR systems make use of hand-coded adaptation rules, which incur all the knowledge acquisition problems that plague expert system design. The simplest and most widely-used form of adaptation knowledge acts to resolve feature differences between a target problem and a retrieved case [3] . For example, in the Déja Vu system, which deals with the design of plant control programs for steel mills [9], many feature differences can arise between problem specifications and retrieved cases. A problem specification could require a two-speed buggy to pick up a load from one location and deliver it to another location, whereas the best retrieved case might only describe how a one-speed buggy carries out these actions. Déja Vu has a specific adaptation rule to deal with this buggy-speed feature-difference; this rule notes that two-speed buggies have to be slowed before they stop, whereas one-speed buggies do not and modifies the solution of the one-speed buggy case to reflect this difference. This speed-difference rule is typical of CBR adaptation rules; it is domain-specific and must be handcoded by the system developer. Hence, the knowledge-engineering effort expended in one domain tends not to be re-usable in other domains (although see [10, 12] for some exceptions). The knowledge engineer has to predict the feature-differences that are likely to arise between known cases and all possible future problems and then determine the solution changes produced by these differences. This knowledge engineering task will often require a deep understanding of the problem domain. If CBR is to deliver on the promise it clearly shows, then solutions to this knowledge engineering problem must be found. The obvious solution to this problem is to somehow learn adaptation knowledge. Hanney and Keane [4] have pointed out that there are three main ways this can be done: to exploit other domain knowledge, to rely on an expert user or, their preferred method, to learn adaptation knowledge from the case-base. Adaptation knowledge can be learned using other domain knowledge if a system is given general adaptation knowledge rules which when applied result in specific adaptation cases, that can be stored for future use [7, 2]. The main advantage of this method is that the domain knowledge used could already be available in an existing knowledge-based system. However, its main disadvantage lies in its reliance on a large amount of such domain knowledge. Adaptation knowledge could also be acquired directly from the expert, by presenting a target problem and a retrieved (but unadapted case) together. This interactive approach is attractive but would have to be used in a restrained fashion, to avoid overburdening the user. The final possibility, which has received less attention, is to acquire adaptation rules automatically from case knowledge (although for related ideas in data-mining see [1]). A case-base contains a lot of implicit domain knowledge and it makes sense to try to avail of this knowledge in learning adaptation rules. Hanney and Keane [4] have argued that it should be feasible to compute all feature-differences that exist between cases in the case-base and examine how these differences relate to differences in case solutions. From this analysis, they argued it should be possible to automatically learn a set of adaptation rules. The implicit assumption here is that the differences that occur between cases in the case-base are representative of the differences that will occur between future problems and the case-base (see [11] for more on this assumption). Hanney and Keane [4] have already reported some experiments which demonstrate the feasibility of this idea. In this paper, new results are reported along with a broader analysis of the system dependencies that underlie the success of the technique. In the next section (section 2), we describe the method used in more detail and discuss the main issues that arise in learning adaptation rules from cases (see section 3). Then, some experimental evidence supporting the technique is reported (section 4) before we assess the relationship between the present and other machine learning techniques

2 Overview of the Adaptation Rule Learning Algorithm

Our algorithm for learning adaptation rules from cases has two major components that are closely interrelated: adaptation-rule generation and rule application. Adaptation rule generation takes a case-base and performs pair-wise comparisons of its cases. The feature differences of each pair of cases are noted and become the antecedent part of an adaptation rule, with the consequent part of the adaptation rule being the differences between the solutions in the compared cases. The rule set is then generalised to average the consequents of rules with matching antecedents. We also assign to each rule a certainty factor based on the number of times it occurred (i.e., the more often an association is found the higher its certainty factor). Rule application concerns the application of these adaptation rules to deal with featural differences that are found between a target problem and a retrieved case. Using these differences the adaptation rule-base is searched and all rules that handle at least one of the differences between the target and retrieved cases are found. Then, all possible adaptation solutions are found by combining these rules. The 'best' adaptation solution is chosen using a set of heuristics and applied to give the solution to the target case.

feature	value		feature	value
case_id	caseA		case_id	caseB
location	loc8		location	loc8
nr-bed-rms	2-bed-rms		nr-bed-rms	2-bed-rms
nr-rec-rms	1-rec-rm		nr-rec-rms	2-rec-rms
kitchen	good-kitchen		kitchen	excellent-kitchen
structure	terraced		structure	terraced
nr-floors	1-floor		nr-floors	1-floor
condition	bad-condition		condition	bad-condition
age	young-age		age	young-age
facilities	facilities-very-near		facilities	facilities-very-near
price	20500		price	25000

feature	value		feature	value
case_id	caseC		case_id	caseD
location	loc5		location	loc5
nr-bed-rms	1-bed-rm		nr-bed-rms	1-bed-rm
nr-rec-rms	2-rec-rms		nr-rec-rms	2-rec-rms
kitchen	bad-kitchen		kitchen	bad-kitchen
structure	semi		structure	terraced
nr-floors	2-floors		nr-floors	2-floors
condition	good-condition		condition	good-condition
age	young-age		age	young-age
facilities	facilities-very-near		facilities	facilities-very-near
price	48500		price	41500

Fig. 1. Property Evaluation Domain Cases

Consider how the system operates in one domain, a property evaluation one, that we have used to test it. Suppose we have a case-base containing the cases A, B, C and D (See Figure 1). Comparison of caseA with caseB gives rule R1 while CaseC when compared with caseD the rule R2 is created (see Table 1).

At this point the adaptation rule-base contains the rules R1 and R2. Let us suppose that we are given the target case T for which the retriever returns the best match case BM (Figure 2). Now the feature differences that the adapter must resolve are those involving the features number of reception rooms, kitchen and structure. More precisely the differences between the target and best match

Table 1. Property Evaluation Domain Adaptation Rules

R1: if the value of the kitchen changes from excellent to good and the value of the nr-rec-rooms changes from 2-rec-rooms to 1-rec-room then decrease the house price by 4500

R2: if the value of the structure changes from terraced to semi then increase the house price by 7000

---

case are 1-rec-rooms compared with 2-rec-rooms, good-kitchen compared with excellent kitchen and semi-structure compared with terraced structure. The next step is to find adaptation rules applicable to these differences. The differences may be resolved by applying the rules R1 and R2 above. Application of these rules to the retrieved case causes the retrieved case solution to be increased by 2500 to give a target solution of 63000.

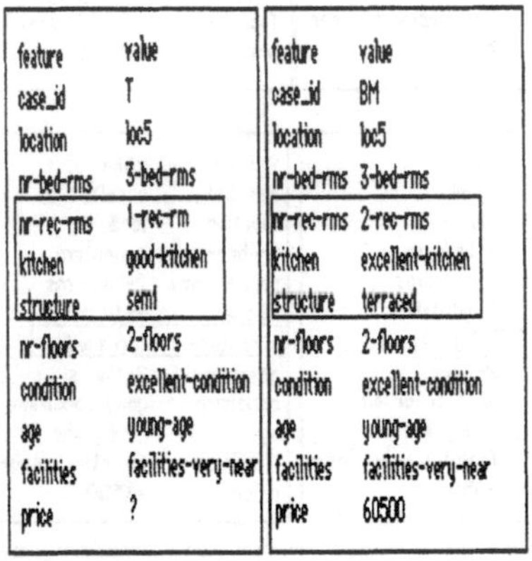

Fig. 2. Property Domain Problem

This example, gives a quick flavour of the rule-learning algorithm (see [5] for details). Along with this algorithm come a whole slue of issues about how to optimise such an algorithm, to make it effective and efficient. For example, it should be immediately clear that all case comparisons may not give rise to worthwhile rules. So, it makes sense to constrain the rule generation process. But, what is the best way to do this? In the next section, we turn our attention to this and other related issues.

Table 2. Challenges in adaptation rule learning from cases

How to identify candidates for comparison? Which cases are worth comparing?
How does the method of adaptation rule learning interact with the retrieval process?
How can adaptation rules extracted from cases be refined?
How can domain knowledge be exploited to aid adaptation rule learning
How to choose the best adaptation path
How can learned adaptation rules be successfully applied?

---

3 Issues in Adaptation Rule Learning from Cases

The above algorithm for learning adaptation rules from cases gives rise to a whole new set of issues which have not been considered before including how to identify cases for comparison, how to maximise co-operation between retrieval and adaptation, how to refine the large rule sets extracted from cases, how to use domain knowledge to guide adaptation rule learning, how to choose the best adaptation when there are several possibilities and how to apply adaptation rules (Table 2). For instance, when identifying suitable cases for rule generation the baseline situation involves simply comparing every case in the case-base with every other. However, this strategy soon gives rise to an unmanageable, prolixity in rule generation. It makes more sense to minimise the generation process by only considering some cases for comparison. We propose that the system only needs those rules that bridge the gap between case pairs judged to be similar enough by the retriever; a strategy that suggests that the retrieval mechanism may have a special role to play in identifying cases for comparison. This and other important issues are detailed in the following sections.

3.1 Which Cases are Worth Comparing ?

Any effective adaptation-rule learning algorithm will have to limit the number of rules generated. Thus, the problem arises of how to find ways to constrain case comparison without compromising the adequacy of the rule set generated. We have identified and applied three methods for constraining case comparison. They are presented in order of the degree to which they integrate the retrieval and adaptation stages of the CBR cycle. Again, we should reiterate that the success of these three methods hinges on our basic assumption: that cases in the case-base are representative of future target problems. The first method for finding cases to compare uses a syntactic measure of the distance between cases. This solution lets the retriever determine candidates for case comparison. A threshold number of differences between case pairs is determined, below which cases will be compared. Since the identification of candidates for comparison is solely syntactic (counting featural differences) it is important to consider only relevant features. This syntactic measure of similarity may be sufficient for some domains but more often a measure of semantic similarity is required. For example, some features may be irrelevant and some may be more important in assessing similarity than others. The basic idea behind the second method is that since we only need adaptation rules that bridge the gap between similar cases, we should only generate rules from those cases judged to be similar. Clearly, in order to use this method a similarity metric must be available and if the retriever is using a similarity metric it is best to use the same one during case-comparison for reasons that will become clearer below. The basic method is to examine each case-pair in the case-base and compare only those that exceed a minimum similarity. It should be noted that it is not necessary to have a perfect similarity metric because the coverage of the generated adaptation rules depends on the strictness of the similarity metric (i.e., the adaptation rules are tailored to the similarity metric). While some retrieval algorithms provide a set of cases similar to the target others provide a list of similar cases in order of decreasing similarity (i.e. the retriever identifies the top n best matches for a given target). The final method of selecting pairs for comparison involves comparing each case in the case-base with only its top n best match cases found by the retriever. This method leads to a significant reduction in the number of rules produced; e.g. for n=1 the number of rules generated will always be half the number of cases in the case-base or less.

The first method above can be used in conjunction with a retrieval algorithm and does not require a similarity metric or an ordered list of retrieved cases. For example, this method may be used when a cluster of similar cases are retrieved; that is, where there is no best matching case, only similar cases. The second method requires a similarity metric but as mentioned above this metric need not be perfect since the coverage of the adaptation rule set depends on the metric and will be adapted to fit a less than perfect metric. Method three may be used only when the retriever returns a list of similar cases in order of their usefulness for the current problem. In our test domains, we noted a progressive reduction in the number of rules produced from method one to method three but clearly this may not be true of all domains.

3.2 How Can the Adaptation Rule Set be Refined?

Before the rules generated by case comparison can be applied they must be refined so that each set of feature differences is associated with only one solution change. There are two stages in rule refinement. The first handles duplicate rules and assigns a confidence value to each rule based on its frequency. The second is concerned with widening the scope of the adaptation rules beyond what can be inferred by comparison by using various generalisation techniques. The rule set generated by case comparison may contain duplicate rules. The definition of duplicates varies according to the domain type but for illustration purposes we consider a domain with a numeric solution. In such a domain, two rules are duplicates if they associate the same featural differences with solution changes that are similar enough (where the notion of similar enough is precisely defined).

The knowledge expressed by a set of duplicated rules can be expressed by a single rule which characterises the deleted duplicates and the prescribed solution change entry is some average of the solutions in the individual rules (clearly, what constitutes an "average" solution will change from one domain to another). In this way, the system can generalise over multiple similar rule consequents. At this stage, each rule also receives a certainty factor that reflects the number of duplicates it captures (the higher the rating the more duplicates it captures). This step can be accounted for by the basic rule of thumb of induction that dictates that the more frequently an association is observed, the more likely it is to be generally true. Generalisation has an important role to play in filling gaps in the rule-set; it allows a general pattern to be induced from a set of specific rules, producing a wider coverage of possible differences. The main problem with generalisation is the huge size of the generalisation space. This problem may be avoided by postponing generalisation until the target and retrieved cases are identified and generalising only those rules that are potentially useful for resolving differences. That is, the system only generalises on demand when applying its adaptation rules. One of the generalisation heuristics used for generalising rule antecedents is Michalski's closing interval rule [8]. This rule states that if two descriptors of the same class differ in the values of only one linear descriptor, then the descriptions can be replaced by a single description whose reference is the interval between the two values. Application of this generalisation rule results in rule antecedents like:
if the no-of-bedrooms changes by 2 in the range of 2-bed-rooms to 6-bed-rooms

This rule is the result of a generalisation of the rules with antecedents

if the no-of bedrooms changes from 2-bed-rooms to 4-bed-rooms and if the no-of-bedrooms changes from 4-bed- rooms to 6-bed-rooms

The application scope of the generalised rule is greater than that of the two specific rules alone because it can handle the change from 3-bed-rooms to 5-bed-rooms.

3.3 How Can Adaptation Rules be Applied

The rule generation process described above provides many specific rules associating case differences with solution changes but these rules are useless without adequate methods for their application. Apart from learning adaptation rules, we have devised mechanisms for applying these rules when given a target problem. When a case has been retrieved for a target problem and the differences between the two noted, an attempt is made to find adaptation rules that can modify the retrieved case solution. The basic process involves a search for all rules that handle at least one difference followed by a combination process in which complete adaptation solutions are built. Given a target case, the system finds a best match case then finds the differences between the two. Initially, the system searches for the full list of differences occurring together in a single rule.

If no single rule can resolve all the differences it looks for a set of rules. The set of differences is reduced by looking at all possible ways of dropping a difference from the list of original differences. Then a search is made for all possible shorter antecedents. Reduction of the differences continues by dropping one difference from the list of differences and finishes with a search for rules handling one difference only. This search method gives all the rules that could potentially resolve one or more differences between the base and target cases. Generalisation is then applied to this set of rules. These rules are the building blocks to be used in solution construction. These building blocks are combined to give the set of all possible adaptation solution paths. Some paths are partial in that they only resolve some of the differences between the retrieved case and the target. There may also be complete paths (i.e. paths that handle all the differences). When more than one rule is applicable, we need some way to select a path from the set of applicable paths. Where the differences between the target and best case are only partially resolved, the set of rules which handle the most differences is chosen. Where all the differences between target and best match case have been resolved this decision is based on a set of preference heuristics. If the best match case cannot be fully adapted the user can choose to try the next best match until a satisfactory solution is found. There is a trade-off here between a full adaptation of a similar previous case and a partial adaptation of a case more similar to the target problem. In the next section, the adaptation rule learning algorithm is tested empirically.

4   Some Experimental Results

The fundamental test of these ideas requires a system equipped with adaptation rules acquired by this method to outperform a version of this system lacking such rules (a so-called retrieval-only system). We have carried out this fundamental test using a relatively simple CBR system, the property-evaluation system introduced earlier. In Hanney et al's [3] taxonomy of CBR systems, the simplest CBR system performing adaptation has an atomic solution (i.e., a single value, numeric or symbolic) and solves problems using a single adapted case. Therefore, the chosen system had these characteristics with the added constraint that feature changes in a case had local, non-interacting effects on the solution value. This type of system is representative of many simple systems currently used in CBR industrial applications. The CBR system was created from an expert system for property evaluation; the expert system was used to populate the case-base and to determine correct answers to problems. The CBR version of this system had 1000 cases in its case-base and used a standard, spreading-activation retrieval algorithm. The 1000 cases were generated randomly; that is, features values were selected for each possible slot of a case and then the expert system was used to provide the solution answer for this set of features.

4.1 Experiment 1: The Fundamental Test

The fundamental test of the adaptation-rule system versus the retrieval-only system was carried out using 3 randomly chosen test sets of 60 problems (called T1, T2 and T3). The error-rate of both systems was measured while the case-base size was varied in the range of 50 to 1000 cases. The formula used to measure this error is

$$E = \frac{\sum_{i=1}^{N} \frac{|estimate(i)-rbs(i)|}{rbs(i)}}{N} \tag{1}$$

where N is the number of test cases, rbs(i) is the expert system's solution and estimate(i) is the CBR system's solution. For each case-base a new set of adaptation rules was generated. Figure 3 shows the error-rate of the retriever alone and the retriever with adaptation knowledge for each of the three trial sets. On the whole the three test sets show very similar performance, although there is clearly more variability between them in the retrieval-only versions of the system. On the whole, beyond a case-base of around 150 cases, the systems with adaptation rules fare much better than the retrieval-only systems, although their rate of improvement beings to flatten in case-bases beyond 600 (see [5] for more details). A crucial factor in the success of our rule-learning method is whether or not the solution changes caused by feature value changes are context independent. In the experiment here, only those features of a case-pair with non-matching values contributed to rules (i.e. rules are context-independent). Before using this technique, it is important to know if context-independent rules are sufficient. If not, divergence between the contexts of the target and retrieved cases will lead to incorrect adaptations. In the next section we show how domain knowledge may be exploited to produce context-dependent adaptation rules.

4.2 Experiment 2: The Influence of Domain Knowledge

The basic rule acquisition algorithm encounters difficulties in domains where the same feature value change causes variable solution change; that is, where there is interaction between features. This problem can be solved by exploiting the different types of domain knowledge that might be available in such systems. Hanney and Keane [4] elaborated four main types of domain knowledge that were often present in CBR systems: known adaptation rules, knowledge of feature relevance, knowledge of contextual constraints and knowledge of interactions between adaptation rules. They also showed how these different forms of domain knowledge could be used to constrain adaptation-rule learning. For example, a new adaptation rule need not be generated by case comparison if a predefined adaptation rule exactly matches the potential antecedents of that rule (see [4] for further details). The use of domain knowledge may result in rules which specify the contexts in which the rule can be applied; i.e. domain knowledge can constrain rule applicability.

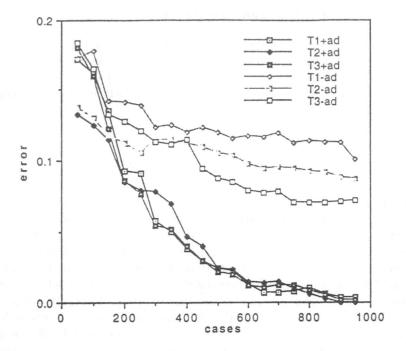

Fig. 3. Case-base size and adaptation performance

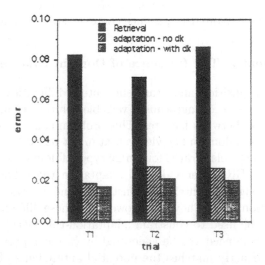

Fig. 4. Generating adaptation rules using domain knowledge

Figure 4 shows the results of tests using three different versions of the property evaluation system (with 1000 cases): a retrieval-only system, a system with learned adaptation rules that does not exploit domain knowledge and a similar adaptation system that exploits such domain knowledge. As in Experiment 1, three test sets of problems were used and the error measure determined in the same way. On the whole, the dominance of the adaptation systems over the retrieval-only system is readily apparent. However, there is also some improvement for the version of the adaptation system that exploits available domain knowledge. However, this graph underestimates the real improvements that such a system delivers. For, on average, the system using domain knowledge was a lot more accurate than the other systems, as it produced 14% more exactly correct solutions than its no-domain-knowledge companion across the three sample test sets (see [5] for a breakdown on the individual contributions of different specific forms of domain knowledge).

5 Adaptation Rule Learning and Machine Learning

The adaptation rule learning algorithm combined with a basic CBR system unites methods from the instance-based learning and rule-induction paradigms [6]. There are several reasons why this hybrid approach to classification/prediction has advantages over either technique used separately. A combination of instance-based learning and rule-induction is better than instance-based learning alone because:

- The closest case or k-cases found by the matcher may not be similar enough to the target. This happens if there is no case similar enough to the problem or if the retriever does not find the best case.
- A good similarity metric is crucial for instance-based learning but is not a requirement for our system with adaptation since the learned rules can be fitted to the retriever's needs.
- If cases are at a premium, adaptation knowledge can compensate since it allows more target problems to be solved than instances alone (i.e., targets involving the resolution of differences for which associated solution differences have been obtained by case comparison)

A combination of instance-based learning and rule-induction is better than rule-induction alone because:

- The "ballpark" solution (i.e. the solution of the retrieved case) is grounded in experience making the solution path more transparent, i.e. the user can refer to the best match case to understand a solution.
- Other domain knowledge may be exploited to guide rule generation from cases
- Over-generalisation by rule-induction algorithms may lead to loss of information whereas cases hold information about specific problem-solving instances.

6 Conclusions

A solution to the adaptation knowledge acquisition bottleneck has been described. The technique manipulates cases alone or a combination of cases and domain knowledge. Our results show that case-comparison can improve the performance of a CBR system without costly knowledge engineering. We provide a fully integrated solution to the adaptation problem by using the retriever to guide adaptation rule learning. The main limitation of the current work is that it handles only flat vector case representations. It is not yet clear if this method may be extended to structured cases but this is an important future research direction.

References

1. Agrawal R., Mannila H., Srikant R., Toivonen H., Verkamo A.: Fast Discovery of Association Rules. In Fayyad U., Piatetsky-Shapiro G., Smyth P., Uthurusamy R. (Ed.) Advances in Knowledge Discovery and Data Mining. *AAAI Press / The MIT Press* (1996)
2. Hammond K.:Case-Based Planning: Viewing Planning as a Memory Task. *Boston: Academic Press* (1989)
3. Hanney K., Keane M.T., Smyth B., Cunningham P.: Systems, Tasks and Adaptation Knowledge: Revealing some Revealing dependencies. In Proceedings of the First International Conference on Case-based Reasoning (1995) 461–470.
4. Hanney K.and Keane M.T.: Learning Adaptation Rules from a Case-Base. In Proceedings of the Third European Workshop on Case-based Reasoning (1996) 179–192.
5. Hanney K.: Learning Adaptation Rules from Cases. MSc Thesis, Computer Science Department, Trinity College Dublin
6. Langley, P.: Elements of Machine Learning. *Morgan Kaufmann* (1996)
7. Leake D., Kinley A., Wilson D.: Learning to Improve Case Adaptation by Introspective Reasoning and CBR. In Proceedings of the First International Conference on Case-based Reasoning (1995) 229–240.
8. Michalski R.: A Theory and Methodology of Inductive Learning. In R. Michalski, J. Carbonell, T. Mitchell (Ed.) Machine Learning: An Artificial Intelligence Approach Vol. 1. *Morgan Kaufmann* (1983)
9. Smyth B. 1996. Case-based Design. Ph.D. Dissertation, Computer Science Department, Trinity College Dublin.
10. Smyth B., Keane M.T.: Retrieving Adaptable Cases: The Role of Adaptation Knowledge in Case Retrieval. In Topics in Case-Based Reasoning: Lecture Notes in Artifical Intelligence 837. *Springer Verlag* (1994) 209–220
11. Smyth B., Keane M.T.: Remembering to Forget: A Competence-Preserving Deletion Policy in Case-Based Systems. In Proceedings International Joint Conference on Artificial Intelligence, Montreal. (1995)
12. Sycara E.P.: Using Case-Based Reasoning for Plan Adaptation and Repair. In Proceedings: Case-Based Reasoning Workshop (1988) 425-434.

A Case Study of Case-Based CBR*

David B. Leake, Andrew Kinley, and David Wilson

Computer Science Department
Lindley Hall 215, Indiana University
Bloomington, IN 47405, U.S.A.
{leake,akinley,davwils}@cs.indiana.edu

Abstract. Case-based reasoning depends on multiple knowledge sources beyond the case library, including knowledge about case adaptation and criteria for similarity assessment. Because hand coding this knowledge accounts for a large part of the knowledge acquisition burden for developing CBR systems, it is appealing to acquire it by learning, and CBR is a promising learning method to apply. This observation suggests developing *case-based* CBR systems, CBR systems whose components themselves use CBR. However, despite early interest in case-based approaches to CBR, this method has received comparatively little attention. Open questions include how case-based components of a CBR system should be designed, the amount of knowledge acquisition effort they require, and their effectiveness. This paper investigates these questions through a case study of issues addressed, methods used, and results achieved by a case-based planning system that uses CBR to guide its case adaptation and similarity assessment. The paper discusses design considerations and presents empirical results that support the usefulness of case-based CBR, that point to potential problems and tradeoffs, and that directly demonstrate the overlapping roles of different CBR knowledge sources. The paper closes with general lessons about case-based CBR and areas for future research.

1 Introduction

The role and relationship of multiple knowledge sources in case-based reasoning is receiving increasing attention from the CBR community. As pointed out by Richter (1995), the fact that CBR provides multiple overlapping "knowledge containers"—such as cases, similarity criteria, and case adaptation information—facilitates the development of CBR systems by enabling system developers to place knowledge in whichever container is most convenient. In addition, these multiple knowledge sources provide many opportunities for learning (e.g., Aha & Wettschereck, 1997).

Investigators have studied a range of analytic and inductive learning methods for refining the knowledge sources within CBR. For example, Hammond's (1989)

* This work was supported in part by the National Science Foundation under Grant No. IRI-9409348.

CHEF uses explanation-based methods to learn *ingredient critics* for use in adaptation, while Hanney and Keane (1997) and Wilke *et al.* (1997) propose inductive generalization to learn adaptation rules; Veloso's (1994) Prodigy/Analogy uses explanation-based methods to learn similarity criteria, while Ricci and Avesani (1995) advocate reinforcement learning. However, despite early work on using CBR within CBR systems, such as Sycara's (1988) study of case-based case adaptation, there has been little recent attention to such approaches. Yet CBR's advantages for top-level reasoning—ease of knowledge acquisition, ability to perform successfully despite imperfect domain theories, and simple learning—also suggest its potential benefit within CBR systems.

We refer to CBR performed by case-based components as "case-based CBR." This paper examines case-based CBR through a case study of the CBR system DIAL (Leake *et al.*, 1996), which uses CBR for both case adaptation and similarity assessment. DIAL's case-based adaptation was developed to address the classic knowledge acquisition problem for case adaptation. Preliminary studies showed that learning adaptation cases improved adaptation performance (Leake *et al.*, 1996), but the method also raised questions about how to refine similarity assessment as adaptation cases are acquired. The difficulty is that useful similarity judgments must reflect "adaptability" (Birnbaum *et al.*, 1991; Smyth and Keane, 1996). In a case-based adaptation system, adaptability is not static—it changes as adaptation cases are learned. Consequently, similarity judgments much change as well. This led us to investigate extending our system's internal case-based methods to use adaptation cases for similarity assessment as well, tying similarity judgments directly to the system's adaptation knowledge.

Case-based CBR raises a number of questions about the practicality of using case-based components in a CBR system:

1. **System design:** How should the components' knowledge be represented and organized?
2. **Knowledge acquisition:** How much specialized knowledge must be provided to support component CBR processes, and how does this effort compare to hand coding rules for these processes?
3. **Net efficiency:** How will use of case-based components affect the overall efficiency of the top-level CBR system?
4. **Learning interactions:** How do the effects of learning in the main case library and by the case-based components contribute individually to overall performance of a CBR system, and how do the multiple forms of learning interact?
5. **Coverage:** How does external feedback to the component CBR processes (e.g., during case adaptation) affect the range of problems that the top-level CBR system can solve?
6. **Utility of learning:** How does the proliferation of stored cases for the component CBR processes affect overall performance?

This paper examines these questions, discussing strategies, lessons, and issues arising from experience developing the case-based CBR system DIAL (Leake *et al.* 1996; 1997b). It begins with a synopsis of how basic CBR issues are addressed within DIAL's component CBR processes. It then highlights aspects of their performance and it discusses key lessons about the role and potential of case-based CBR.

2 Synopsis of DIAL

DIAL is a case-based planner in the disaster response planning domain. The system's task is to generate plans to guide damage assessment, evacuations, etc., in response to natural and man-made disasters such as earthquakes and chemical spills. DIAL's top-level planning component is based in a straightforward way on traditional case-based planning systems such as CHEF (Hammond, 1989). Given a new disaster, the response plan for a similar disaster is retrieved. The applicability of that plan to new circumstances is then evaluated by a simple evaluation component using the stereotype-based problem-detection process described in (Leake, 1992), with backup evaluation by a human user, in order to identify problems requiring adaptation. When problems are found, the plan and a description of the problem in a pre-defined problem vocabulary (either generated by the system or input by the user) are provided to the adaptation component. DIAL uses CBR both for similarity assessment during plan retrieval and for adaptation of the plans it retrieves. We describe these processes below.

3 A case-based framework for adaptation learning

DIAL's adaptation component begins with general domain-independent adaptation knowledge. It uses this knowledge to build up a library of adaptation cases to facilitate future adaptation of similar problems. DIAL's initial adaptation knowledge is a small set of abstract transformation rules and a library of "weak methods" for memory search, such as the "local search" strategy to find related concepts by considering nearby nodes in memory (Kolodner, 1993). Its adaptation rules are indexed under elements of a problem-description vocabulary. For example, the problem type FILLER-PROBLEM:UNAVAILABLE-FILLER indexes the transformation to substitute a role-filler. When presented with a new adaptation problem, DIAL first retrieves a transformation rule associated with the problem type. Each association between a problem type and transformation has associated information about how to determine—from the problem type—the parts of the plan to be transformed. The association also contains information about how to determine the information needed to apply the transformation. For substitutions within a schema, the system extracts from the schema constraints on the role whose filler is being substituted. After constraints have been identified and used to generate a knowledge goal (Hunter, 1990; Ram, 1987) for the information needed, it searches memory for that information.

The goal of adaptation learning is to learn the memory search strategies that apply to particular types of problems, in order to reuse them. Initially, however, the system has no memory search cases and must rely on weak methods such as local search. As a simple example, if part of a retrieved disaster response plan is to have the Red Cross deliver supplies, but there is no Red Cross in the country where a new disaster occured, a possible memory search path for a substitution would start at the memory node for Red Cross, move to its abstraction *relief organization*, and then move to specifications of that node (e.g., the Red Crescent). The memory search process is continued until it yields an acceptable result or reaches a limit on memory search effort. When DIAL is unable to generate an acceptable adaptation, an interactive interface allows a human user to guide it along the steps leading to a successful adaptation.

Once a successful adaptation has been generated, either by DIAL or by a human user, the system saves a trace of the steps used in its memory search process, packaged with the transformation rule used, as an *adaptation case* for future reuse. Learned adaptation cases make useful memory search paths explicitly available and may enable the system to solve adaptation problems that would otherwise have been impossible to solve within system resource limits.

4 Design choices and motivations

Designing a case-based component for a CBR system, like designing any case-based reasoning system, requires determining the type of CBR process to use (transformational or derivational), the case representation, the case organization scheme, and how to perform case adaptation. DIAL's case-based adaptation process reflects the following design decisions:

Transformational vs. derivational CBR: A key question for case-based case adaptation is the type of information that adaptation cases should store. Previous case-based adaptation systems store the solution of a prior adaptation—the change that was selected—and reapply it by transformational analogy (e.g., (Sycara, 1988)). This is appropriate when the derivation of the prior adaptation is not available. However, when derivations are available, derivational CBR is a natural means for providing flexible reuse (Veloso, 1994). Because DIAL's adaptation component has the trace of each new adaptation, it can use derivational analogy for case adaptation, even though DIAL must use transformational analogy for its top-level planning task, due to the lack of derivational information for the disaster response plans in its case library.

Case representation: DIAL's adaptation cases characterize adaptations by two types of information: general domain-independent transformations (e.g., substitute, add, delete) and the memory search information needed to apply them. This division is modeled on Kass's *adaptation strategies* (Kass, 1990), which have been shown capable of capturing a wide range of adaptations. However, the memory search procedures used by adaptation strategies are hand coded; DIAL's approach builds up memory search strategies from experience.

Case organization: DIAL's adaptation cases are organized by the problems they address, using a vocabulary of problem types similar to those that guide adaptation in numerous other CBR systems (e.g., Hammond, 1989; Leake, 1992). For example, if a candidate response plan is inappropriate because a role-filler is unavailable (e.g., a police commissioner may be out of town and unable to be reached in an emergency situation), the problem is described by the problem type FILLER-PROBLEM:UNAVAILABLE-FILLER, and that description is used as an index to retrieve adaptation cases for similar problems.

Adaptation: Using CBR to guide case adaptation prompts concerns about where the process will "bottom out." The need to adapt adaptation cases presents a new adaptation problem, and there is no reason to expect that developing adaptation rules for adaptation cases will be any easier than developing adaptation rules for the top-level system. DIAL's response is to strongly restrict adaptation of adaptation cases, by relying on a single domain-independent adaptation method. When following the memory search path in an adaptation case fails to identify a usable solution, DIAL seeks similar solutions by local search, starting from the end of the path. If that fails, it backtracks along the replayed memory search path, using local search from the points along that path. This gradually relaxes restrictions in the search path to find alternatives.

5 A case-based framework for similarity learning

Previous work on refining similarity criteria to match adaptation abilities focuses primarily on adjusting a set of similarity criteria (that approximate adaptability) rather than judging adaptability directly from adaptation knowledge (Birnbaum et al., 1991). Research by Smyth and Keane (1996) takes a valuable step in replacing semantic similarity with adaptability, but does not address learning: Their method assumes adaptation knowledge is static and depends on adaptation rules being annotated with estimated costs by the system designer. In addition, their method uses a single estimate for an entire problem class. Tests show that this may not be sufficiently fine-grained (Leake et al., 1997a).

A natural alternative is to use CBR for adaptability: To predict the adaptability of a problem from experience adapting similar problems. This approach enables similarity judgments to keep pace with learned adaptation experience and to provide fine-grained estimates of adaptation costs. Given a new disaster situation and a candidate response plan with applicability problems, DIAL's similarity assessment component retrieves the adaptation cases DIAL would apply to adapt each problem in the plan, and estimates the total cost of applying all the adaptation cases. Retrieved adaptation cases for the best plan are passed on to the adaptation component, in the spirit of Smyth and Keane (1996).

Ideally, in similar future contexts, replaying the same adaptation derivation will lead to a result that applies to the new context, so the length of the stored derivation is a good predictor of the re-application cost. However, differences between the old and new problems may prevent the prior derivation from being directly applicable, increasing the cost of adaptation. Consequently, DIAL multiplies the prior cost by a "dissimilarity" factor based on the semantic similarity of the old and new situations. This factor is simply the sum of distances between memory nodes for corresponding role-fillers in the problem descriptions, in the system's memory hierarchy. The rationale for this approach is that the guidance from an adaptation case is most useful when reapplied to closely-matching adaptation problems. Leake et al. (1997a) show that for a set of test problems in DIAL's domain, this method retrieves more adaptable cases than either standard similarity assessment methods or methods based on average adaptation costs for classes of problem types.

6 Design choices and motivations

A central question for developing a case-based similarity assessment component is what constitutes "similarity." Other key issues are the case representation, indexing, and adaptation.

Relating similarity to adaptability: Traditional similarity assessment uses semantic similarity as a proxy for adaptability; more recent approaches, led by Smyth and Keane's adaptation-guided retrieval, call for replacing semantic similarity with adaptability. DIAL's approach to similarity assessment emphasizes the importance of adaptability, but its approach to assessing adaptability is tempered by the principle that *minimizing total solution generation time takes precedence over minimizing adaptation time.* This principle was examined for the top-level CBR process by Veloso and Carbonell (1991), and is crucial to internal CBR as well.

To perform a low-cost initial filtering of candidate response plan cases, DIAL uses semantic similarity between the current and prior situations. After initial filtering, finer-grained filtering is based on the seriousness of differences (adaptability), rather than the level of semantic similarity. We are now investigating the tradeoffs resulting from different levels of effort in judging adaptability.

Other key issues: Because DIAL's case-based similarity component relies on the same case library as its case-based adaptation, its approach to other design issues closely follows the design choices for case-based adaptation. The case representation required for adaptation cases to support similarity assessment is virtually unchanged from that required for adaptation: The only added information is a count of the number of steps performed in the adaptation, which is stored for efficiency but could be re-calculated from the derivational trace. The indexing criteria used to retrieve adaptation cases when estimating adaptation costs are the same ones initially developed to retrieve adaptation cases when performing adaptation after similarity-based plan retrieval. Adaptation of adaptation cases during similarity assessment is simple: When adaptation cases are used to estimate the adaptation cost of new problems, the new cost is estimated by multiplying the old cost by the dissimilarity factor.

7 Lessons Learned

The previous sections describe DIAL's case-based adaptation and similarity assessment. Tests of DIAL's performance with these methods provide a first set of data points illuminating our general questions about the practicality and performance of using case-based CBR. We will address each question in turn, first discussing knowledge acquisition and efficiency issues, then examining how learning from the component CBR processes affects the range of problems the system can solve, and finally considering the potential utility problems accompanying case-based CBR. We view the primary interest of these results not as being specific to DIAL, but as a demonstration that case-based CBR can be practical and as an illustration of issues to address.

Knowledge acquisition: The knowledge requirements for DIAL's case-based adaptation fall between those for knowledge-intensive explanation-based methods and pure inductive approaches. DIAL does not require the detailed knowledge usually coded into adaptation rules, but does rely on three other forms of knowledge in order to learn and reapply its adaptations. The first is a semantic network of known domain concepts. This is a standard part of many CBR systems, and is routinely used for domain-independent adaptation methods (e.g., to find substitutions by local search (Kolodner, 1993)). Although this network must obviously include the concepts important for a CBR system's task, DIAL's case-based adaptation process can learn to use it effectively even if the most relevant connections are not pre-coded. The second type of knowledge enabling DIAL's case-based adaptation is a categorization of types of abstract transformations. A number of researchers have argued that considerable coverage can be achieved by a small set of such transformations (Carbonell, 1983; Hinrichs, 1992). The third type of knowledge is a vocabulary of problem types requiring adaptation. Such vocabularies are widely used by CBR systems to organize adaptation knowledge, so they are a prerequisite not only to DIAL's case-based methods, but also to effective use of hand-coded adaptation rules. In addition, they appear to have a wide range of applicability, minimizing the need to develop multiple vocabularies for different tasks. Thus DIAL's case-based adaptation approach facilitates knowledge acquisition compared to rule-based approaches, by avoiding manual coding of rules and requiring only standard supporting knowledge. In addition, unlike pure inductive approaches, the case-based approach can learn new adaptations from single examples.

Net efficiency: As discussed in detail in Leake, Kinley, and Wilson (1997b), we examined efficiency in a set of trials generating response plans for 18 disasters, starting from a case library of 5 response plans and performing 118 adaptations. Conditions were no learning (NL), plan case learning (CL), adaptation case learning (AL), combined adaptation learning and plan case learning (using semantic similarity to retrieve plan cases) (AL+CL), and the combination of adaptation, plan, and similarity learning (AL+CL+SL).

Figure 1 shows the average total execution time per problem solved, separated into two parts, (1) time spent in retrieval and similarity assessment, and (2) time spent in adaptation. One surprising result was the large speedup provided by adaptation learning alone, compared to case learning alone. Even more surprising was that the addition of case learning, in the AL+CL condition, degraded performance compared to adaptation learning alone. Adding similarity learning (AL+CL+SL) restored the efficiency to equal that of AL. The significance of these results will be discussed in the next section. Retrieval times increase from

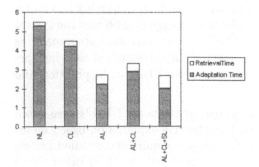

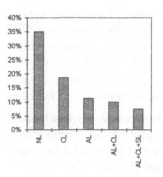

Fig. 1. Average retrieval/similarity assessment and adaptation time.

Fig. 2. Failure rates.

NL to CL (as expected from searching a larger plan case library), to AL (because the adaptation library to search through grows faster than the case library for CL, requiring more search effort for adaptations), and to AL+CL. The drop in retrieval time for AL+CL+SL is unexpected and merits investigation.

Learning interactions and efficiency: Given that CL and AL are each effective individually, we expected AL+CL to have better performance than either alone. However, adaptation cost with AL+CL increases compared to AL. Our explanation is that the cases that appear most relevant, according to static similarity criteria, may not be the easiest to adapt. The mismatch between static similarity criteria and learned adaptation abilities did not appear to cause significant problems with AL, however. Our explanation was that for AL, adaptations were being learned to apply to a small fixed library of plan cases, making it likely (after enough problems were processed) that any plan case chosen had been applied to a similar prior disaster, so the adaptations selected by similarity were generally appropriate. However, when novel plan cases are added to the case base by case learning (as in AL+CL), the newly-learned plans must initially be adapted with adaptation cases that were developed in other contexts and are not as directly applicable, increasing adaptation cost. AL+CL+SL increases retrieval cost but selects more adaptable cases, decreasing adaptation cost and resulting in similar total time.

Coverage and quality: In addition to efficiency, an important measure of the performance of a CBR system is the range of problems it can solve. DIAL's initial domain theory is incomplete, but its ability to store and reuse user-provided solutions (both disaster response plans and adaptations) allows it to augment its knowledge. In addition, the ability to reuse memory search paths from learned adaptation cases enables it to explore regions of memory that might otherwise have been too expensive to explore. Figure 2 shows the percentage of the trial problems the system could not find a satisfactory solution, for each of the learning conditions. Again, adaptation learning alone performed better than case learning alone, but the interference effect between adaptation and case learning

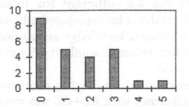

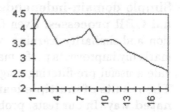

Fig. 3. Number of adaptation cases generated at each level of reuse.

Fig. 4. Number of novel adaptations per plan as a function of number of plans processed.

(AL+CL) that degraded efficiency compared to AL alone did not affect coverage. AL+CL+SL provided slightly better coverage than the other methods in these tests.

Utility of learning: Because the previous tests were performed on a comparatively small set of problems, we have no specific data on how performance is affected as many cases are learned. However, retrieval costs are a potential problem as the library of internal cases grows. One possible response would be to reduce case library size through selective "forgetting" of adaptation cases (Smyth and Keane, 1995). In DIAL's domain, precise analysis of which cases to delete is not possible, and efficiency—which may be furthered by retaining some cases not necessary for competence—is important as well. However, simple forgetting strategies may be useful. Figure 3 shows the number of times each learned adaptation case is reused in a sample run; the x-axis is the level of reuse (e.g., "1" for cases reused only once), and the y-axis is the number of cases at that level of reuse (e.g., five learned adaptation cases were reused only once). On this set of trials, roughly 20% of the cases were never reused. Adaptation cases that are not reused, or are not reused sufficiently frequently, could be deleted.

Figure 4 graphs the average number of new adaptation cases created per response plan, processed as a function of the number of response plans generated. It shows a rapid decrease in the number of adaptation problems that require reasoning from scratch from processing a comparatively small number of adaptations. Thus it might also be possible, for example, to control the utility problem by simply stopping adaptation learning after establishing a set of adaptation cases expected to produce adequate coverage.

8 Lessons about case-based CBR

Our previously-described research led to the following observations about case-based CBR:

- **Adaptation learning can be as important as case learning:** Our sample runs showed that for a given set of problems, the efficiency and coverage improvements from learning new adaptation cases with a fixed case library can surpass those of case learning with fixed adaptation knowledge.

- **Simple domain-independent methods can be sufficient for internal CBR processes:** Even DIAL's simple methods for case-based adaptation and similarity learning, which require minimal knowledge acquisition, markedly improve its performance. For example, semantic similarity can provide a useful pre-filtering stage during retrieval.
- **The results of multiple learning processes must be used in a coordinated way:** In our tests, problem-solving efficiency with AL+CL was worse than with AL alone, apparently because case selection did not take learned adaptation knowledge into account, preventing the system from making the best possible use of new cases it had learned. Learned similarity assessment criteria in AL+CL+SL coordinated selection of learned cases to fit learned adaptations, enabling the system to choose the most adaptable learned case given its learned adaptation knowledge.
- **Sharing a single case library between case-based components is a convenient way to coordinate learning:** Cases storing traces of adaptations already provide sufficient information to estimate adaptability, enabling a single case library to serve for both adaptation and similarity assessment. This assures that knowledge for both processes is synchronized.
- **Proliferation of internal cases is a potential problem:** Cases for the component processes of a CBR system may be learned at a much higher rate than cases for the top-level CBR system, and the usefulness of additional learned cases may drop rapidly.

9 Future directions

The previous results show that case-based components within a CBR system can improve performance compared to case learning alone. However, since our observations are based on limited tests in a single domain, a pressing future need is to extend the study to multiple domains and larger problem sets.

Our research so far has focused on case-based methods for adaptation and similarity assessment. Another rich research area is control of the case retrieval process. It is appealing for a case memory to learn which types of queries it tends to receive, which classes of cases are relevant to them, and which strategies are appropriate to retrieve these cases. Case-based reasoning appears to be a promising method for this task. For example, if the case retrieval process is modeled as strategic memory search (e.g., following Kolodner 1984), it will be possible to apply results from existing research on case-based and introspective analogy for learning memory search (e.g., as in DIAL's adaptation cases and Kennedy, 1995). CBR for retrieval provides another opportunity for sharing case bases between multiple component CBR processes: both the memory search paths followed during adaptation and those followed during case retrieval can form a single case library of memory search paths for future use.

Using case-based methods for learning retrieval information also has ramifications for case-based case storage. Cases that describe where to find relevant information in memory also describe where related new information should be stored; conversely, cases describing where information has been stored also describe where related information should be found. By using a single case library of search paths to guide both case retrieval and storage, learned storage and retrieval knowledge can be coordinated. This example shows that key lessons from applying case-based methods to the similarity and adaptation components of a CBR system may be useful for other components as well.

10 Conclusion

This paper identifies central questions about case-based CBR and presents a case study demonstrating that it can be a practical method, in terms of knowledge acquisition, processing efficiency, and quality of solutions. The key result is to show that simple CBR methods can be practical for guiding components of a CBR system, for refining their knowledge sources, and for making coordinated use of the results of their learning. Our tests also support the value of adaptation learning: In some situations, learning only adaptations has even greater benefit than learning new problem cases. This provides—to our knowledge—the first empirical demonstration of the overlapping contributions of case and adaptation knowledge within CBR. Overall, a combination of adaptation, case, and similarity learning provided comparable efficiency and slightly better problem coverage than any of the other methods. These results emphasize the potential of case-based CBR, the complex interactions between different types of learning, and the need for further study of multiple learning processes within CBR systems.

References

[Aha and Wettschereck, 1997] D. Aha and D. Wettschereck. Case-based learning: Beyond classification of feature vectors. Call for papers of ECML-97 workshop, 1997.

[Birnbaum et al., 1991] L. Birnbaum, G. Collins, M. Brand, M. Freed, B. Krulwich, and L. Pryor. A model-based approach to the construction of adaptive case-based planning systems. In R. Bareiss, editor, Proceedings of the DARPA Case-Based Reasoning Workshop, pages 215–224, San Mateo, 1991. Morgan Kaufmann.

[Carbonell, 1983] J. Carbonell. Learning by analogy: Formulating and generalizing plans from past experience. In R. Michalski, J. Carbonell, and T. Mitchell, editors, Machine Learning: An Artificial Intelligence Approach, pages 137–162. Tioga, Cambridge, MA, 1983.

[Hammond, 1989] K. Hammond. Case-Based Planning: Viewing Planning as a Memory Task. Academic Press, San Diego, 1989.

[Hanney and Keane, 1997] K. Hanney and M. Keane. The adaptation knowledge bottleneck: How to ease it by learning from cases. In Proceedings of the Second International Conference on Case-Based Reasoning, Berlin, 1997. Springer Verlag.

[Hinrichs, 1992] T. Hinrichs. Problem Solving in Open Worlds: A Case Study in Design. Lawrence Erlbaum, Hillsdale, NJ, 1992.

[Hunter, 1990] L. Hunter. Planning to learn. In Proceedings of the Twelfth Annual Conference of the Cognitive Science Society, pages 261–268, Cambridge, MA, July 1990. Cognitive Science Society.

382

[Kass, 1990] A. Kass. *Developing Creative Hypotheses by Adapting Explanations.* PhD thesis, Yale University, 1990. Northwestern University Institute for the Learning Sciences, Technical Report 6.

[Kennedy, 1995] A. Kennedy. Using a domain-independent introspection mechanism to improve memory search. In *Proceedings of the 1995 AAAI Spring Symposium on Representing Mental States and Mechanisms*, pages 72–78, Stanford, CA, March 1995. AAAI Press. Technical Report WS-95-05.

[Kolodner, 1984] J. Kolodner. *Retrieval and Organizational Strategies in Conceptual Memory.* Lawrence Erlbaum, Hillsdale, NJ, 1984.

[Kolodner, 1993] J. Kolodner. *Case-Based Reasoning.* Morgan Kaufmann, San Mateo, CA, 1993.

[Leake et al., 1996] D. Leake, A. Kinley, and D. Wilson. Acquiring case adaptation knowledge: A hybrid approach. In *Proceedings of the Thirteenth National Conference on Artificial Intelligence*, pages 684–689, Menlo Park, CA, 1996. AAAI Press.

[Leake et al., 1997a] D. Leake, A. Kinley, and D. Wilson. Case-based similarity assessment: Estimating adaptability from experience. In *Proceedings of the Fourteenth National Conference on Artificial Intelligence.* AAAI Press, 1997.

[Leake et al., 1997b] D. Leake, A. Kinley, and D. Wilson. Learning to integrate multiple knowledge sources for case-based reasoning. In *Proceedings of the Fourteenth International Joint Conference on Artificial Intelligence.* Morgan Kaufmann, 1997. In press.

[Leake, 1992] D. Leake. *Evaluating Explanations: A Content Theory.* Lawrence Erlbaum, Hillsdale, NJ, 1992.

[Ram, 1987] Ashwin Ram. AQUA: Asking questions and understanding answers. In *Proceedings of the Sixth Annual National Conference on Artificial Intelligence*, pages 312–316, Seattle, WA, July 1987. Morgan Kaufmann.

[Ricci and Avesani, 1995] F. Ricci and P. Avesani. Learning a local similarity metric for case-based reasoning. In *Proceedings of the First International Conference on Case-Based Reasoning*, pages 301–312, Berlin, October 1995. Springer Verlag.

[Richter, 1995] Michael Richter. The knowledge contained in similarity measures. Invited talk, the First International Conference on Case-Based Reasoning, Sesimbra, Portugal., October 1995.

[Smyth and Keane, 1995] B. Smyth and M. Keane. Remembering to forget: A competence-preserving case deletion policy for case-based reasoning systems. In *Proceedings of the Thirteenth International Joint Conference on Artificial Intelligence*, pages 377–382, Montreal, August 1995. IJCAI.

[Smyth and Keane, 1996] B. Smyth and M. Keane. Design à la Déjà Vu: Reducing the adaptation overhead. In D. Leake, editor, *Case-Based Reasoning: Experiences, Lessons, and Future Directions.* AAAI Press, Menlo Park, CA, 1996.

[Sycara, 1988] K. Sycara. Using case-based reasoning for plan adaptation and repair. In J. Kolodner, editor, *Proceedings of the DARPA Case-Based Reasoning Workshop*, pages 425–434, San Mateo, CA, 1988. Morgan Kaufmann.

[Veloso and Carbonell, 1991] M. Veloso and J. Carbonell. Variable-precision case retrieval in analogical problem solving. In R. Bareiss, editor, *Proceedings of the DARPA Case-Based Reasoning Workshop*, pages 93–106, San Mateo, 1991. Morgan Kaufmann.

[Veloso, 1994] M. Veloso. *Planning and Learning by Analogical Reasoning.* Springer Verlag, Berlin, 1994.

[Wilke et al., 1997] W. Wilke, I. Vollrath, K.-D. Althoff, and R. Bergmann. A framework for learning adaptation knowedge based on knowledge light approaches. In *Proceedings of the Fifth German Workshop on Case-Based Reasoning*, 1997.

Solution-Relevant Abstractions Constrain Retrieval and Adaptation

Erica Melis*

Universität des Saarlandes, FB Informatik
D-66041 Saarbrücken, Germany. melis@cs.uni-sb.de

Abstract. Two major problems in case-based reasoning are the efficient and justified retrieval of source cases and the adaptation of retrieved solutions to the conditions of the target. For analogical theorem proving by induction, we describe how a solution-relevant abstraction can restrict the retrieval of source cases and the mapping from the source problem to the target problem and how it can determine reformulations that further adapt the source solution.

1 Introduction

Case-based reasoning retrieves one or more source problems and their solutions in order to transfer and adapt the source solution to the needs of a given target problem. The efficient retrieval of similar source problems from a large case-base has been a major issue in the case-based reasoning research which has employed efficient inductive techniques for learning indices, with similarity measures, with the retrieval from a case-base of abstracted problems, and with analytically extracting relevant features of problems for a specific solution to solve the retrieval problem. Problem indices, learned by inductive techniques, reliably characterize an appropriate source solution to the extend of the correctness of the learning result only. In particular, for complex solutions, indexing by object-level problem features may not suffice to produce correct results by analogical replay.

However, most techniques lack strong justifications for the retrieval, i.e., they do not guarantee the retrieved source problem to provide a solution useful for the target problem. This is due to the fact, that in order to retrieve a source problem that has a solution which is potentially useful for the solution of the target problem, a criterion for the **a priori** similarity of problems has to predict an **a posteriori** similarity of the solutions, as discussed e.g. in [15]. This problem was also addressed by Hesse who stated the problem to justify analogical reasoning [6] and Russell [4] who introduced formulae, called determinations, into domain theories in order to represent how certain predicates of the problem determine certain predicates of the solution. Russell's determinations, however, require to know logical implication at the object-level that logically express the dependency of a feature X on a feature Y in all objects which is a very strong requirement.

---

* The author was supported by the SFB 3782

A second problem in analogical reasoning, addressed for instance by Holyoak [7] and Gentner [5], is to choose from a variety of possible analogical mappings. As we shall show, solution-relevant abstractions can be exploited for this task as well.

A third non-trivial job in the analogy procedure is to determine the reformulations (adaptations) of problems and solutions. To some extent the proof-relevant abstractions can also be employed to trigger reformulations.

In this paper, we shall present semantic, solution-relevant abstractions in inductive theorem proving that can be found automatically and the preservation of which guarantees a successful transfer of large parts of the proofs. We shall not go into details of the implemented analogy, but the paper focuses on the use of the abstractions for restricting the retrieval and the problem mapping. As we shall see, these abstractions can also serve to determine certain reformulations of the source solution that go beyond an adaptation by symbol mapping.

2 Proof Planning for Proofs by Induction

A proof plan is an abstract representation of a proof that consists of trees of method nodes which are connected by sequents, called goals. The proof planner $CLAM$ [3] has been applied successfully to inductive theorem proving because it knows patterns of inductive proofs consisting of base-cases and step-case and it employs a strong search heuristic, called rippling.

The major aim of the step-case proof is to rewrite the induction conclusion until the induction hypothesis is applicable, i.e., to reduce the differences between the induction conclusion and the induction hypothesis. To that end, rippling involves annotating the induction conclusion with *wave fronts* and *wave holes*: *Wave fronts* mark the differences between induction hypothesis and conclusion. *Waves* annotate the smallest terms containing wave-fronts. *Wave holes* represent the parts of waves that also appear in the induction hypothesis. For example, in planning the theorem lenapp:

$$\forall a, b.\ length(app(a, b)) = length(app(b, a)) \tag{1}$$

the induction hypothesis is

$$length(app(a, b)) = length(app(b, a)) \tag{2}$$

and the annotated induction conclusion is

$$length(app(\boxed{cons(h, \underline{a})}, b)) = length(app(b, \boxed{cons(h, \underline{a})})) \tag{3}$$

where $cons, app$ are the usual functions on lists. The boxes denote the waves. Wave holes are underlined and wave fronts are the non-underlined parts within the boxes. The *skeleton* of an annotated term is constructed from wave holes and the parts of the term that do not belong to a wave.

385

Rippling also annotates[2] rewrite rules such that the skeleton of the LHS equals the skeleton of the RHS. The resulting skeleton preserving rules are called *wave-rules*. E.g., a wave-rule for the function *app*, computed from defining rules of *app*, is

$$app(\boxed{(cons(X,\underline{Y}))},Z) \Rightarrow \boxed{cons(X,(app(Y,Z)))}. \tag{4}$$

The skeleton on each side of the implication is $app(Y,Z)$. Rippling works by systematically applying wave-rules to the induction conclusion and to subgoals in the plan. By applying wave-rules to successive goals in the planning process, wave fronts can be moved or removed. In this way, rippling works towards its goal of moving or removing those parts of the induction conclusion which are marked by the wave fronts, so that the induction hypothesis, represented by the skeleton, can be used. You can imagine that the wave fronts move through the term tree of the theorem when a wave-rule is applied. For instance, if (4) and another rule are applied to the goal (3) the following subgoal is obtained:

$$\boxed{s(length(app(a,b)))} = length(app(b,\boxed{cons(h,\underline{a})})) \tag{5}$$

For a visualization of rippling see Figure 1. Note how the wave front on the LHS has been moved outwards from the term tree of (3) to the term tree of (5).

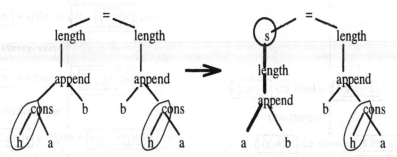

Fig. 1. Term tree of (3) changes to term tree of (5), rippling path in bold

3   Abstractions that Guide the Transfer of Proofs

Remember that one of the main problems for analogical reasoning is to recognize features of *problems* which ensure the similarity of their respective solutions in order to be able to retrieve useful sources and which allow for the choice of appropriate mappings from a possibly large set of (second-order[3])-mappings between source and target problems. We present a solution for this problem in analogy-driven proof plan construction for inductive theorem proving that employs proof-relevant abstractions. vspace-3mm

---

[2] The annotations being the wave fronts and wave holes
[3] second-order mapping means that function symbols are mapped to function terms.

3.1 Analogy-driven Proof Plan Construction

The analogy-driven proof plan construction introduced in [11] is a control strategy of a proof planner that suggests methods and instantiations rather than searching for them. This analogy comprises retrieval, mapping, reformulation, and replay. The reformulations that yield changes of the theorem and proof assumptions that are accompanied by certain changes of the proof plan. The analogy-driven proof plan construction has been implemented on top of the proof planner $CL^{A}M$. The resulting analogical transfer for the example step-case of the lenapp proof to a proof of halfplus is shown in Figure 2, where *length* is abbreviated by *len*, *app* by infix $<>$, *cons* by ::.

The retrieval based on proof-relevant abstractions is explained in section 4.

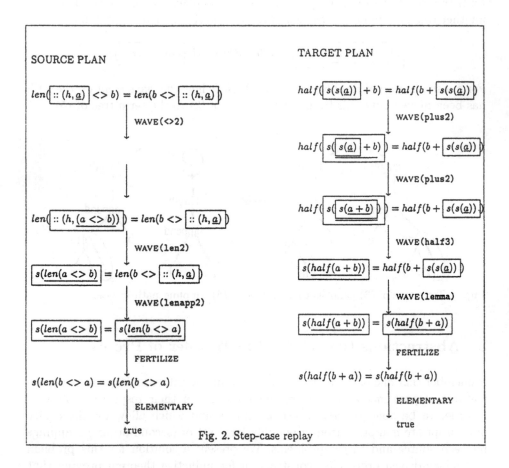

Fig. 2. Step-case replay

Before the actual analogical replay, second-order mappings from the source theorem and wave-rules to the target theorem and wave-rules are found guided by proof-relevant abstractions as explained in section 5. An analysis of these mappings and of their result w.r.t. changing proof-relevant abstractions decides which reformulations to be applied. This is described in section 6.

Note that the abstraction is used at a *meta-level*. This means that rather than taking the proof/plan of an abstracted problem as the source solution to be replayed and adapted, we use abstract features of the source and target problems to restrict the retrieval, mapping, and to trigger reformulations.

3.2 The Labelled Fragment Abstraction

Labelled fragments(LFs), introduced in [8], are an abstraction of wave-rules obtained by removing the structure of the wave-fronts and those parts of the skeleton not affected by wave-fronts. For each function/relation symbol occurring in the source and target theorem we automatically compute labelled fragments corresponding to wave-rules that belong to the source and target problem, respectively. Take, for instance, the wave-rule app2

$$app(\boxed{cons(X,\underline{Y})},Z) \Rightarrow \boxed{cons(X,(\underline{app(Y,Z)}))}.$$

Note that in the lhs of app2 the wave-front is situated at the left(first) argument of *app* and how it moves to the top of *app* in the rhs of app2. This situation is reflected in the most right labelled fragment of *app* as shown in Figure 3. The wave-rule len2 $length(\boxed{cons(X,\underline{Y})}) \Rightarrow \boxed{s(length(Y))}$ is abstractly encoded into the labelled fragment of *length*.

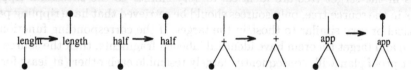

Fig. 3. Labelled fragments

As we shall see, the labelled fragment abstractions are semantically motivated by the course of inductive theorem proving that employs rippling, rather than purely syntactically motivated by symbol matching. In the following, we substantiate why labelled fragments are proof-relevant abstractions and explain how they are used by our analogy procedure.

4 How the Retrieval Employs Labelled Fragments

The term tree of a theorem is called the *theorem tree*. The *rippling paths*, as shown in Figure 4, are the paths in the theorem tree on which the wave-fronts are moved successfully by rippling.

The LFs of functions/relations in a theorem tree determine the rippling paths through the theorem tree. This can be seen in Figure 4, where the bold rippling paths start at the induction variables and are combined from LFs of Figure 3. Note how the rippling paths of lenapp and halfplus agree because the LFs of *app* and + and of *length* and *half* agree.

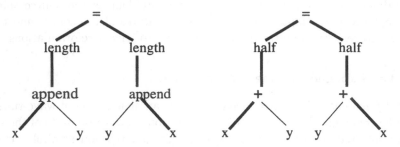

Fig. 4. Term trees of lenapp and halfplus with rippling paths in bold

The rippling paths in a theorem tree abstractly encode the step-case proof, in particular, the consecutive application of the WAVE method in proof plans. You can recognize how the WAVE methods in Figure 2 apply wave-rules, such as app2, that move the wave-fronts as abstractly shown in Figure 3. E.g., in Figure 2, first WAVE(app2) is applied and then WAVE(len2) which corresponds to the (abstract) rippling path of lenapp in Figure 4 which, in turn, is determined by the labelled fragments in Figure 3. Therefore, labelled fragments provide a proof-relevant abstraction of problems to be proved by induction. Since the step-case subplan of the source plan can likely be transferred successfully to the target if the rippling paths in the target tree are identical or very similar to the successful rippling paths in the source tree, only sources should be retrieved that have rippling paths identical or very similar to those in the target. If the corresponding functions in source and target theorem have identical labelled fragments, then the source and target proof plan will, consequently, largely resemble each other (at least for the step-case subplan). For a given target problem, the retrieval of a source should, thus, be restricted to those problems whose theorems have the same abstractions in terms of LFs.[4]

With the help of labelled fragments, the case base can be pre-structured into classes of cases with with the same LF-abstracted theorems. The elements of a class can be further distinguished by their rewrite rules (definitions, axioms). This makes the retrieval a **two-stage** process with a first cheap step that retrieves the source class and a second step more expensive that tries to second-order match the rewrites of each element of that class.

A class of source cases contains all stored cases with identical rippling paths. A class is represented by a theorem tree whose nodes on rippling paths are annotated with the LFs common to all its cases. The nodes occurring outside of rippling paths in any of the cases are abstracted to meta-variables in the class representation because they are irrelevant for the abstraction. The first stage tries to match the target theorem with one of the class representatives

---

[4] or differ in a controlled way - see below.

and checks the LFs in this process as well. It chooses the class with the fewest predefined deviations (that can be handled by reformulations later). Classes that have equal representatives except for these deviations can be linked in the memory in order to reduce the in the first stage. Only one of a set of linked representatives has to be matched with the target theorem tree.

The second stage chooses the best case from the retrieved class by trying to second-order match the target-rules (lemmata) with the rules of the cases in the retrieved class. Second-order match is decidable but can be expensive, in particular with many rules involved, and it has to be supported by heuristics to choose reasonable matches. The heuristics are not explained here, but see [16].

5 How Labelled Fragments Restrict the Mapping

In parallel to the retrieval the analogical mappings are computed. First, a basic second-order mapping m_b from source theorem to target theorem and then an extended mapping m_e from the source rewrites to the target rewrites (wave-rules). m_b maps the source theorem tree to the target theorem tree and thereby it maps the rippling-paths of the source theorem tree to rippling-paths of the target theorem tree. Similar to the previous section, we require the mapping m_b from source theorem to target theorem to **preserve the labelled fragments** or to change LFs in a controlled way such that the source rippling paths are mapped to similar successful target rippling paths.

According to [8], labelled fragments are rather insensitive to missing lemmas. This means that if a function f has a labelled fragment, constructed from f's definition or other wave-rules, that contributes to an (abstract) rippling path in the theorem tree, and if a particular lemma is missing for the *concrete* rippling at a node N, then very likely a lemma can be proven that can be used for rippling at N of the theorem tree. This situation is highly desirable for analogies because analogy should work despite missing wave-rules. We benefit from this situation in that – as a (re)action to a failed justification – our analogy procedure suggests target wave-rule based on m_b and some other information if no appropriate image of a source rewrite is given in the target problem. Space precludes us from decribing how m_e is computed. This mapping does not depend on LFs.

6 How Labelled Fragments Trigger Reformulations

Now we define reformulations that are devised for certain deviations from LF-preservation. Each reformulation is triggered by frequently occurring peculiarities in the mapping from source to target theorem or rules. The examples are presented for illustrating the situations in which reformulations are triggered.

shrink If m_b maps $f_i \mapsto \lambda w.w$, then the WAVE method for f_i becomes redundant and can be removed from the proof plan.
   Example:
   source: $sum(x) + sum(y) = sum(app(x, y))$

target: $+(x, s(y)) = s(+(x, y))$

For the first occurrence of sum[5] maps to the identity function. If the induction in the source is on x, a rule is needed to rewrite $sum(cons(v0, x))$ but this is redundant in the target.

blow If m_b maps a source function symbol f to a function $\lambda \overline{x}.g_1(g_2(\overline{x})$ that has the same (combined) labelled fragment as f, then m_e suggests a corresponding target rewrite with $m_b(f)$ in its skeleton.

An alternative not considered yet, is to introduce two WAVE methods (for g_1 and g_2) instead of one source WAVE method for f.

Example:

source: $+(x, s(y)) = s(+(x, y))$

target: $double(+(x, s(y))) = s(double(+(x, y)))$

condt If the source theorem is Th_s and the target theorem is $C_t \rightarrow Th_t$, and if the basic mapping m_b preserves labelled fragments and $m_b(Th_s) = Th_t$, then a *condt* reformulation of the proof plan replaces (weak) FERTILIZE by VERY (WEAK) FERTILIZE.[6] *condt* introduces into the target planning the instantiated antecedents C_{tj} of the target base-cases j as additional subgoals. *condt* transfers the source base-case if C_{tj} can be proven, and it terminates a target base-case if C_{tj} is disproved. An example is the reformulation used for

source: $half(double(x)) = n$

target: $even(x) \rightarrow double(half(x)) = x$.

case [7] Suppose a casesplit produces n subgoals in the source plan. Each of these subgoals will be associated with a conditional wave-rule Suppose the subgoals of the casesplit in the source are $cs_1, ..., cs_n$ and in the target the subgoals are $ct_1, ..., ct_n$. Then cs_i is mapped to ct_j if the labelled fragment of the wave-rule associated with cs_i is identical to that associated with ct_j. In this way, casesplit branches are permuted in a way such that an analogy is made between branches with similar rippling paths.

7 Conclusion and Related Work

We described a particular type of proof-relevant abstraction for proofs by induction. The abstraction of problems is based on labelled fragments. This abstraction provides a basis for theorem proving by analogy as implemented in the system ABALONE that works on top of the proof planner $CI^A M$. The preservation of the abstraction between source and target problems guarantees the step-cases of the corresponding source and target proof plans to be identical. Certain slight deviations from the strict preservation lead to forseeable changes of the proof plan that can be realized by reformulations.

---

[5] sum is a function on lists that returns the sum of the list members.

[6] VERY (WEAK) FERTILIZE produces the additional lemma $C_t' \rightarrow C_t$ to be proved, where C_t' is the antecedents of the induction conclusion and C_t is the antecedents of the induction hypothesis.

[7] This reformulation is due to Jon Whittle.

Evaluation The main goal of using analogy on top of $CIAM$ was to automatically provide proof plans for theorems that could not be proved automatically without analogy. That is, the primary goal was not to reduce the problem solving time because $CIAM$ plans very efficiently. Space precludes us from giving a list of theorems that have been proved with analogy and could not be proved without analogy, see [10, 16]. Even without automated retrieval of a source case the analogy would be useful because more theorems can be proved.

The results rely on the use of the LF-abstraction that guarantees success of the target step-case. Without these abstractions, full second-order problem matches had to be considered, as done in [9]. This is quite restricting. Our results do not depend of the size of the proof because only the size of the theorem tree and number of rules effect the retrieval, mapping, and reformulation. (The replay takes longer with complex plans to replay, of course.) That is, complicated theorems can be replayed.

For mathematical theorems, the retrieval (and mapping) is a very difficult task. Thus, any contribution is valuable. Since our technique applies to the whole class of theorems proved by induction, it provides progress. The presented abstraction is specific for proofs by induction. The general idea to look for proof-relevant abstractions is not specific, though.

Related Work Most attempts that make use of abstraction in the context of analogy, retrieve, transfer, and adapt solutions of an abstracted source problem, for instance the approaches in [9, 1, 14]. Instead, our approach retrieves, transfers, and adapts the object-level source proof plan and utilizes abstract features of the problem as a filter for the retrieval and the mapping. Börner [2] constructs prototypes by abduction. She abstracts a class of problems considered similar to each other to a prototype of the class by anti-unification. This abstract prototype is refined for the target. This suggests that a target problem that unifes with the prototype will have the same abstract solution but this largely depends on the sample set used for computing the prototypes.

Somewhat similar to our use of abstraction in analogical theorem proving is Veloso's footprint mechanism [13] that identifies solution-relevant features at the *object-level* and that works as a filter in the retrieval of source cases. The object-level features computed by the footprint contrast, however, with our abstract labelled fragment features and cannot be used to contrain the mapping or even trigger reformulations.

The idea of adaptation-guided retrieval in [12] is similar to our possibility of predefined deviations from the LF-preservation in the retrieval that triggers reformulatons. The mapping problem has been tackled syntactically, for instance, the Analogical Constraint Mapping Engine (ACME) [7]. Gentner's SME [5] is based on the systematicity principle that emphasizes syntactic structural constraints. Holyoak and Thagard's ACME [7] focuses on syntactic similarity constraints and manually predefined pragmatic constraint. Also purely syntactically, Kolbe and Walther [9] perform a second-order matching from a generalized source.

References

1. R. Bergmann and W. Wilke. On the role of abstraction in case-based reasoning. In B. Faltings and I. Smith, editors, *Fourth European Workshop on Case-Based Reasoning (EWCBR-96)*, Lausanne, 1996.
2. K. Börner. Structural similarity as guidance in case-based design. In *First European Workshop on Case-Based Reasoning 1993*, volume LNAI, Berlin, 1994. Springer Verlag.
3. A. Bundy, F. van Harmelen, J. Hesketh, and A. Smaill. Experiments with proof plans for induction. *Journal of Automated Reasoning*, 7:303–324, 1991.
4. T.R. Davis and S.J. Russell. A logical approach to reasoning by analogy. In *Proceedings of the 10th International Joint Conference on Artificial Intelligence*, pages 264–270, Milan Italy, 1987. Morgan Kaufmann.
5. D. Gentner. Structure mapping: A theoretical framework for analogy. *Cognitive Science*, 7(2):155–170, 1983.
6. M. Hesse. *Models and Analogies in Science*. Indiana: University of Notre Dame Press, Notre Dame, 1966.
7. K.J. Holyoak and P. Thagard. Analogical mapping by constraint satisfaction. *Cognitive Science*, 13:295–355, 1989.
8. D. Hutter. Synthesis of induction orderings for existence proofs. In A. Bundy, editor, *Proceedings of 12th International Conference on Automated Deduction (CADE-12)*, Lecture Notes in Artificial Intelligence 814, pages 29–41. Springer, 1994.
9. Th. Kolbe and Ch. Walther. Reusing proofs. In *Proceedings of 11th European Conference on Artificial Intelligence (ECAI-94)*, Amsterdam, 1994. http://kirmes.inferenzsysteme.informatik.th-darmstadt.de/ kolbe/.
10. E. Melis. Analogy in CLAM. Technical Report DAI Research Paper No 766, University of Edinburgh, AI Dept, Dept. of Artificial Intelligence, Edinburgh, 1995. available from http://jswww.cs.uni-sb.de/~melis/.
11. E. Melis. A model of analogy-driven proof-plan construction. In *Proceedings of the 14th International Joint Conference on Artificial Intelligence*, pages 182–189, Montreal, 1995.
12. B. Smyth and M.T. Keane. Retrieving adaptable cases. In *Topics in Case-Based Reasoning*, pages 209–220, Berlin, 1994. Springer.
13. M.M. Veloso. *Planning and Learning by Analogical Reasoning*. Springer, Berlin, New York, 1994.
14. A. Villafiorita and F. Giunchiglia. Inductive theorem proving via abstraction. In *Proceedings of the Fourth International Symposium on Artificial Intelligence and Mathematics, AI/MATH96*, pages 150–153, Fort Lauderdale, Florida, 1996.
15. S. Wess. *Fallbasiertes Problemlösen in wissensbasierten Systemen zur Entscheidungsunterstützung und Diagnostik*. PhD thesis, FB Informatik, Univ.Kaiserslautern, January 1995.
16. J. Whittle. Analogy in Cl^AM. Technical Report MSc.thesis, University of Edinburgh, Dept. of AI, Edinburgh, 1995.

Selecting Most Adaptable Diagnostic Solutions through Pivoting-Based Retrieval

Luigi Portinale, Pietro Torasso and Diego Magro

Dipartimento di Informatica - Universita' di Torino
C.so Svizzera 185 - 10149 Torino (ITALY)
e-mail: {portinal,torasso}@di.unito.it

Abstract. The aim of the present paper is to investigate a retrieval strategy for case-based diagnosis called *Pivoting Based Retrieval* (PBR), based on a tight integration between retrieval and adaptation estimation. It exploits a heuristic estimate of the adaptability of a solution; during retrieval, lower and upper bounds for such an estimate are computed for relevant cases and a pivot case is selected, determining which cases have to be considered and which have not. Such a technique has been evaluated on three different domain models and very satisfactory results have been obtained both in terms of accuracy, space and retrieval time

1 Introduction

Classical approaches to retrieval in Case-Based Reasoning (CBR) aim at returning cases having the highest similarity (often expressed in terms of surface features) with respect to the case representing the current problem to be solved [3]. These approaches assume that a measure of similarity is a good parameter for estimating the adaptation overhead needed to apply the solution(s) of the retrieved case(s) to the input problem. Recent studies have shown that this claim is not always supported in applications like design [11], planning [6, 9] and diagnosis [8], leading to the development of a class of approaches identified as *Adaptation Guided Retrieval* (AGR) [11] or *Constructive Similarity* [4]. In particular both in planning [6] and diagnosis [8], even very similar problems can give rise to hard adaptability problems in terms of computational complexity. The notion of similarity as simple weighted distance metrics (e.g. Nearest Neighbor matching) is no longer sufficient in such situations and aspects concerning adaptability must be taken into account before performing the actual selection of the "best case" [5, 7, 11]. However, a trade-off arises when considering the accuracy of *adaptation estimation* and the real *adaptation effort*; in some cases it is relatively simple to prune non-adaptable or hard to adapt cases [11], while in some other situations, having good estimate can be as hard as performing the actual adaptation and one has to sacrifice estimation accuracy [9].

The aim of the present paper is to investigate some aspects of the trade-off mentioned above in case-based diagnosis. In particular, we discuss an approach to adaptation-guided retrieval based on a tight integration between adaptation effort estimation and retrieval of past diagnostic solutions. The underlying memory model is assumed to be an *associative flat memory* with *shallow indexing* [3]. The main idea is to consider a heuristic estimate of the adaptation cost and then to exploit a technique called *Pivoting-Based Retrieval* (PBR), in order to determine which cases have to be considered or rejected on the basis of particular bounds on the computed adaptation cost. In section 2 we introduce the formal framework for diagnosis we refer to, in section 3 we discuss how an estimate of the adaptation effort can be computed and in section 4 we introduce the PBR technique based on such an estimation. Finally, in section 5 we discuss the results of a set of experiments we performed, in order to evaluate the PBR approach both with respect to a naive retrieval strategy and with respect to an E-MOP based retrieval [3].

2   On the Adaptation of Diagnoses

In a previous work [7] we discussed the architecture of *ADAPtER*, a diagnostic system integrating a formal theory of model-based diagnosis [2] with CBR. We pointed out how the selection of the best solutions retrieved by the CBR component had to be based on some estimation of the solution adaptation effort. This led us to the definition of a heuristic function aimed at estimating the cost of adapting a retrieved solution; the function strictly relies both on the formal diagnostic framework assumed by *ADAPtER* and on the different roles played by observable features in a given case. In particular, observable features may have different a-priori roles, depending on the partitioning into *contexts* and *manifestations*; while the latter set contains observable parameters that must be "explained" in the current problem, the former set contains parameters characterizing the problem to be solved that do not need explanation (they are contextual information such as the input to a device). The framework we refer to can be summarized as follows.

Definition 1. A diagnostic problem is a tuple $DP = \langle\langle T, H\rangle, CXT, \langle\Psi^+, \Psi^-\rangle\rangle$ where T is a set of logical formulae representing the behavioral model of the system to be diagnosed, H is a set of diagnostic hypotheses, CXT is the set of contextual information of the problem and Ψ^+, Ψ^- are the set of manifestations to be accounted for (covered) and conflicting with the observations respectively.

If OBS is the set of observed manifestations, then $\Psi^+ \subseteq OBS$ and $\Psi^- = \{m(a)|m(b) \in OBS, b \neq a\}$. A discussion about the right choice of the subset of OBS to be identified with Ψ^+ can be found in [2]. We will assume that the set of all ground manifestations present in the model is partitioned into the sets MAN^A of abnormal manifestations and MAN^N of normal manifestations; in particular we will deal with "fault models" (i.e. with models T describing the faulty behavior of a system) and we consider $\Psi^+ = OBS^A$ where $OBS^A = MAN^A \cap OBS$.

Definition 2. Given a diagnostic problem $DP = \langle\langle T, H\rangle, CXT, \langle\Psi^+, \Psi^-\rangle\rangle$, a diagnosis (i.e. a solution to DP) is a set $E \subseteq H$ such that

$$\forall m(a) \in \Psi^+ \ \ T \cup CXT \cup E \vdash m(a); \quad \forall m(a) \in \Psi^- \ \ T \cup CXT \cup E \nvdash m(a)$$

This kind of framework has a big impact on the adaptation process; indeed, as shown in [7], when comparing the set of features of a retrieved solution with that of the problem to be solved, different adaptation strategies must be employed depending on the content of sets Ψ^+ and Ψ^-. We will return on this aspect in the next sections.

3 Estimating Adaptation

In storing a case, we need to represent the set of observable features characterizing it (partitioned into contexts and manifestations) as well as the set of solutions (i.e. diagnoses) to the diagnostic problem represented by the case. Notice that it is possible that, according to definition 2, more than one solution exists for a given case; however, cases with a large set of possible solutions are usually underspecified in terms of observations (i.e. many observable features with significant discrimination power are just predicted by the solutions and have not been directly observed in the input case) and therefore, these cases are unsuitable candidates for storing. Another aspect concerns the fact that a contextual information can be *relevant* to only some of the stored solutions, meaning that for some diagnoses such a contextual information can be safely ignored without changing the properties of definitions 2. In general, a stored case is represented as the tuple $C = \langle CXT_{all}, CXT_{some}, OBS, SOL \rangle$ where:

- CXT_{all} is the set of contexts relevant to every solution of the case;
- CXT_{some} is the set of contexts relevant to some (but not all) solutions of the case;
- OBS is the set of manifestations observed in the case;
- $SOL = \langle \langle H_1, EXPL(H_1, CXT_1) \rangle, \ldots \langle H_n, EXPL(H_n, CXT_n) \rangle$ is a list of solutions where each H_j is a set of diagnostic hypotheses, CXT_j is the set of context relevant to the j-th solution and $EXPL(H_j, CXT_j)$ is the derivational trace from H_j and CXT_j to observable features, provided by the model T of the system.

Notice that in the derivational trace of a solution there can be manifestations that are not present in OBS (have not been observed in the input case) and they represent predictions of the solution.

An input case is represented by the pair $C_I = \langle CXT_I, OBS_I \rangle$ specifying observed contexts and manifestations respectively. Moreover, once the user has decided the subset of OBS_I to be covered, sets Ψ_I^+ and Ψ_I^- are determined for the input case. The estimate of the adaptation effort of a retrieved solution $S_j = \langle H_j, EXPL(H_j, CXT_j) \rangle$ is performed by comparing CXT_I with CXT_j and manifestations in OBS_I with those in $EXPL(H_j, CXT_j)$. In particular, a given instance of a context $c(a)$ can be defined as *slightly* or *totally incompatible* with another instance $c(b)$ of the same context[1]; if a contextual information present in the input case is totally incompatible with one present in a stored solution, then the solution is rejected for retrieval, while the case of slight incompatibility is suitably weighted in estimating adaptation.

Concerning the comparison of manifestations, the estimation has to consider two basic situations: 1) a manifestation $m(a)$ is present in the input case and the retrieved solutions has a different value $m(b)$ for it; 2) a manifestation $m(a)$ is present only in the input case. In the first situation we say that there is a *conflict* on manifestation m and a mechanism called *inconsistency removal* has to be activated, in order to remove in the derivational trace the support for $m(b)$, if $m(b)$ was actually

---

[1] For a given context, two different values are considered *totally incompatible* if, given the same set of diagnostic hypotheses, they give rise to significantly different evolutions.

supported; moreover, in case $m(a) \in \Psi_I^+$ an additional mechanism called *explanation construction* is invoked to build an explanatory support for $m(a)$ in the retrieved solutions. In the second situation, m is said to be a *new manifestation* and only the step of *explanation construction* is performed if $m(a) \in \Psi_I^+$. Let ρ be the estimated cost of *inconsistency removal* and γ that of *explanation construction*: we can identify the sets O_{CONFLICT} of conflicting manifestations and O_{NEW} of new manifestations and the following coefficients (see [7] for more details):

$$\alpha_{\text{CONFLICT}}(m(a)) = \begin{cases} \rho + \gamma & \text{if } m(a) \text{ to be covered and } m(b) \text{ supported} \\ \gamma & \text{if } m(a) \text{ to be covered and } m(b) \text{ not supported} \\ \rho & \text{if } m(a) \text{ not to be covered and } m(b) \text{ supported} \\ 0 & \text{otherwise} \end{cases}$$

$$\alpha_{\text{NEW}}(m(a)) = \begin{cases} \gamma & \text{if } m(a) \text{ to be covered} \\ 0 & \text{otherwise} \end{cases}$$

Moreover, let $SI(S_j)$ the set of contexts of solution S_j slightly incompatible with CXT_I and δ be the adaptation weight assigned to them, the heuristic estimate for the adaptation cost of S_j is computed as

$$h(S_j) = \sum_{m(a) \in O_{\text{CONFLICT}}} \alpha_{\text{CONFLICT}}(m(a)) + \sum_{m(a) \in O_{\text{NEW}}} \alpha_{\text{NEW}}(m(a)) + \delta \, |SI(S_j)|$$

Results of experiments concerning the accuracy of h are reported in [7]; they show that the heuristic function is a good estimate of the actual adaptation cost and we can then assume that S_i is more easily adaptable than S_j if $h(S_i) < h(S_j)$.

4 Pivoting-Based Retrieval

In this section we will present a novel retrieval mechanism based on a pivoting technique, able to iteratively prune cases on the basis of bounds on the estimate of the adaptation effort. The retrieval algorithm works on a *flat memory* with shallow indexing; every manifestation used in the behavioral model of the system to be diagnosed is considered with every possible value it can assume. In particular, with each instance $m_i(v_j)$ of a manifestation m_i, a list of indices is associated, each index pointing to a case containing $m_i(v_j)$ in its description. Notice that the indexed part of a stored case concerns only manifestations that are directly observed in the case, that is a given case $C = \langle CXT_{all}, CXT_{some}, OBS, SOL \rangle$ will be indexed only by manifestations instances present in OBS; predictions provided by its solutions in SOL will be considered only during adaptation.

The Pivoting-Based Retrieval (PBR) algorithm is composed of several steps and can be summarized as shown in figure 1. The filtering phase allows us to consider as candidates only cases having at least one feature in common with the input case; this is simply done by following indices for manifestations in the input case. A first pruning phase (context-based pruning) can then be performed at this point, by rejecting cases having in all their solutions contextual information conflicting with the input one (i.e. no one of their solutions survives to the check on contextual

Input: a case $C_I = \langle CXT_I, OBS_I \rangle$

Output: a set of solutions $S_j = \langle H_j, EXPL(H_j, CXT_j) \rangle$ with minimal $h(S_j)$.

Filtering. Construct a first set CC_1 of candidate cases by following indices $\forall m(a) \in OBS_I$.

Context-Based Pruning. Restrict the set CC_1 into the set CC_2 by removing each case C such that there is a context in CXT_{all} totally incompatible with a context in CXT_I.

Bound Computation. For every case $C \in CC_2$ compute a pair $[h_l^C, h_u^C]$ such that, for each solution $S_j \in SOL$, h_l^C is a lower bound of $h(S_j)$ and h_u^C is an upper bound (i.e. $\forall S_j \in SOL \; h_l^C \leq h(S_j) \leq h_u^C$).

Bound-Based Pruning. Restrict CC_2 to CC_3 by removing every case C such that $h_l^C > \alpha$ being $\alpha = \min_C h_u^C$.

Pivoting. Initialize BEST_SOL:=empty list.

For each case $C \in CC_3$, consider the midpoint $\mu^C = \frac{h_l^C + h_u^C}{2}$ of its bound interval and let $BEST_\mu = \min_C \mu_C$; consider now one case C for which $BEST_\mu = \mu_C$ (the *pivot case*) and compute $h(S_j)$ for each solution S_j of C such that in CXT_j there is no context totally incompatible with CXT_I (the other solutions of C are rejected). Select solutions having minimum computed estimation (i.e. SELECTED_SOL=$\{S_k | h(S_k) = \min_j h(S_j)\}$) and let $BEST = \min_j h(S_j)$.
Compare $BEST$ with the previous best match $BEST_P$ (initially assumed to be infinite).

If $BEST_P > BEST$

1. BEST_SOL:=SELECTED_SOL;
2. $BEST_P := BEST$;
3. remove from CC_3 every case C such that $h_l^C > BEST$.

If $BEST_P = BEST$ add SELECTED_SOL to BEST_SOL.

Remove the pivot case from CC_3 and repeat pivoting until CC_3 becomes empty.
Return BEST_SOL.

Fig. 1. The PBR Algorithm

---

information). The third phase concerns the computations of bounds on the adaptation estimates of solutions of cases and will be discussed in the section 4.1. Once such bounds are computed, a second pruning phase (bound-based pruning) allows us to reject cases which have definitively no solutions with minimal estimate. Such a kind of pruning is illustrated in figure 2(a) and is also iteratively applied in the subsequent phase of pivoting when a "point" estimate is available for the pivot case (figure 2(b)). Notice that in this phase, no deep investigations on the solutions of a case is performed, that is the only pieces of information considered for a stored case $C = \langle CXT_{all}, CXT_{some}, OBS, SOL \rangle$ are the ones contained into CXT_{all}, CXT_{some} (the latter in the bound computation phase as shown in the next subsection) and OBS. The pivoting phase is aimed at exploiting the intervals defined by computed bounds on cases survived to previous steps. We define as *pivot case* one of the cases for which the midpoint of the bound intervals is minimum. At this point, and only for the current pivot case, we consider stored solutions $S_j = \langle H_j, EXPL(H_j, CXT_j) \rangle$; solutions having relevant contexts CXT_j conflicting with CXT_I are pruned and the actual estimate $h(S_j)$ is computed for the remaining ones. Solutions S_k for which $h(S_k)$ is minimum are then selected as candidate best solutions and compared with previously selected best candidates, by possibly updating such a set and all the re-

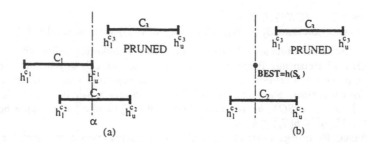

Fig. 2. Bound pruning

lated information. A new case is then selected as a pivot on the basis of the midpoint criterion and the analysis is repeated, until no case is left.

It should be clear that, under the assumption that the bounds are correct, the PBR algorithm is *admissible*, i.e. it returns all and only those solutions S having minimum $h(S)$. Let us now show how correct bounds on h can be computed.

4.1 Bound Computation

As mentioned in section 2, we will assume that only abnormal manifestations have to be covered[2]. Given the input case $C_I = \langle CXT_I, OBS_I \rangle$, let $OBS_I^A = OBS_I \cap MAN^A$ and $OBS_I^N = OBS_I \cap MAN^N$ be the set of abnormal and normal manifestations in the input case; as said above we will assume $\Psi_I^+ = OBS_I^A$.

The bound computation phase works on the set of candidate cases CC_2 determined by the filtering and context-based pruning phases. The first step consists in the computation of the lower bound h_l^C (initially considered equal to 0) for every case $C \in CC_2$; this is done by considering every manifestation $m(a) \in OBS_I$ and by retrieving (through indices) cases having $m(b)$ in their description for each admissible value $b \neq a$ of m. Among such cases, we consider those that are present into CC_2; let C' be one of such cases, the following situations are possible:

1. $m(a) \in OBS_I^N \wedge m(b) \in MAN^A$: this means that an inconsistency removal is needed and then the estimated cost ρ is added to $h_l^{C'}$;
2. $m(a) \in OBS_I^A \wedge m(b) \in MAN^N$: this means that an explanation construction is needed and then the estimated cost γ is added to $h_l^{C'}$;
3. $m(a) \in OBS_I^A \wedge m(b) \in MAN^A$: this means that both adaptation mechanisms are needed and then the estimated cost $\rho + \gamma$ is added to $h_l^{C'}$.

It should be clear that in case both $m(a)$ and $m(b)$ are in MAN^N no adaptation is needed and nothing has to be added to the lower bound. Moreover, the above considerations are valid for every solution of C' and the computed bound is clearly a lower bound since the following situations are not taken into account: 1) the comparison between OBS_I and the predictions of solutions of C'; 2) the fact that

---

[2] This reflects the current implementation status of *ADAPtER* which is dealing with fault models, however the approach described can be naturally extended to deal with models combining faulty and correct behavior of the system to be diagnosed.

cases in CC_2 not mentioning the feature m are not considered; 3) the fact that contexts in CXT_I slightly incompatible with relevant contexts of a solution are not considered. All the above situations may lead to an increment of the function h.

Concerning the computation of the upper bound, a suitable increment Δ to the previous computed lower bound can be determined in such a way that $h_u^{C'} = h_l^{C'} + \Delta$. In particular, the three situations discussed above have to be reconsidered in order to determine Δ (initially considered equal to 0). The first situation is dealt with by considering the maximum number of inconsistency removal steps due to situation 1; it can be computed as $MAX_1 = |OBS_I^N| - |COMM_{N,N}|$ where $COMM_{N,N}$ is the set of normal manifestations common to both the input case C_I and case C'. However, in computing the increment to the lower bound $h_l^{C'}$, we can subtract the part already considered in $h_l^{C'}$ by determining $MAX_1' = MAX_1 - |CONFL_{N,A}|$ where $CONFL_{N,A}$ is the set of manifestations having a normal value in C_I and an abnormal value in C'. The quantity $\rho\ MAX_1'$ is then added to Δ. The above computation takes into account the fact that inconsistency removal steps may be needed because of the discrepancy between the normal value observed for some manifestations in the input case and the abnormal value predicted (but not observed) for these manifestations by the set of solutions of C'.

The second and third situations are dealt with together by making the pessimistic hypothesis that the presence of an abnormal manifestation into C_I will give rise to both inconsistency removal and explanation construction. We consider then the quantity $MAX_2 = |OBS_I^A| - |COMM_{A,A}|$ being $COMM_{A,A}$ the set of abnormal manifestations common to both the input case C_I and case C'. As before, from this quantity we can subtract what has already been taken into account in computing $h_l^{C'}$, by obtaining $MAX_2' = MAX_2 - |CONFL_{A,N}| - |CONFL_{A,A}|$ where $CONFL_{A,N}$ is the set of manifestations having an abnormal value in C_I and a normal value in C' and similarly, $CONFL_{A,A}$ the set of those manifestations having two different abnormal values in C_I and C' respectively. The quantity Δ is then incremented by $(\rho + \gamma)MAX_2'$. What is still left from the computation of the upper bound are contexts having slight incompatibility. We can determine the maximum number of such contexts as follows. Let $C' = \langle CXT_{all}, CXT_{some}, OBS, SOL \rangle$ be the case for which the bounds have to be computed, we observe that, because of the context-based pruning phase, in CXT_{all} there is no context totally incompatible with a context in C_I. This is however possible for contexts in CXT_{some}; let CXT_{some}' be the set CXT_{some} pruned of contextual information totally incompatible with some context in CXT_I, we can compute the quantity $MAX_3 = |CXT_{all} - (CXT_{all} \cap CXT_I)| + |CXT_{some}' - (CXT_{some}' \cap CXT_I)|$. The parameter Δ is finally incremented by the quantity $\delta\ MAX_3$, so $h_u^{C'} = h_l^{C'} + \rho MAX_1' + (\rho + \gamma)MAX_2' + \delta MAX_3$.

5 Experimental Results and Conclusions

In order to evaluate the PBR approach we performed some experiments on three different domain models for diagnosis: a model in a mechanical domain (MECH) involving the diagnosis of car engine faults, a model in a medical domain (LEPR) for the diagnosis of the *leprosy* disease and a model derived from an industrial

application of model-based diagnosis (IND)[3]. The first set of experiments concerns
a comparison, in terms of retrieval time, between PBR and a *naive* retrieval strategy
computing the exact adaptation estimate for every solution of the case obtained after
the *filtering* and *context-based pruning* steps. Results are summarized in figure 3 in
terms of average retrieval time and sample standard deviation. In particular, for

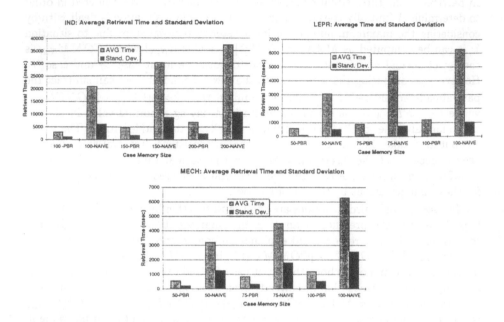

Fig. 3. Comparison between PBR and Naive Retrieval

each domain, we performed three bunchs of experiments with case memories of
different size (100, 150, 200 cases for IND and 50, 75, 100 cases for both MECH and
LEPR); both the training and the test set of cases used in the experiments have been
obtained by means of a *simulator* applied to each domain model, assuring that the
resulting training set is composed of different well specified cases (i.e. cases suitable
to storing). In all the experiments reported in the present paper, the size of the test
set has always been set to 100 (possibly repeated) cases. In particular the simulator
provided no duplicated cases for the test sets of MECH and IND and 3 duplicates
for LEPR. The size of 100 has been chosen since it allows to consider all the relevant
part of the domain knowledge for all considered domains. The average number of
features contained in both the training and test set was about 10 for MECH, 13 for
LEPR and 16 for IND. Notice that, while the accuracy of PBR and naive retrieval
is the same (they will return all and only those cases having minimal adaptation
estimate), retrieval time for PBR is significantly lower (it is about 1/5 of the time
for the naive strategy) in all the experiments we considered.

---

[3] The last model is covered by a nondisclosure agreement and no further details can be
provided.

A second kind of experiments concerns a comparison between PBR and an E-MOP based retrieval strategy [3]; in the latter, surface similarity is more heavily used to discriminate cases and the heuristic estimate is computed only on a restricted set of cases, the one obtained after following indices on the E-MOP discrimination net. These experiments have confirmed the space explosion problem of which the E-MOP case representation suffers [1], since for domains LEPR and IND it has not been possible to obtain reasonable case memories because of space overflow problems. As a consequence we obtained a comparison between PBR and E-MOP based retrieval only for the MECH domain (see figure 4). We first compared the retrieval time of

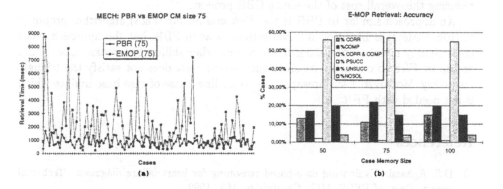

Fig. 4. Comparison between PBR and E-MOP Retrieval

both types of retrieval on the three case memories obtained for MECH (50,75 and 100 cases). The average retrieval time of PBR resulted significantly lower than in the other approach in all the considered experiments, however the very high standard deviation of the time in case of E-MOP based retrieval made not very significant an average time analysis. For this reason figure 4(a) shows the comparison on actual retrieval times in the situation concerning a case memory of 75 cases; the same kind of pattern, showing a better performance of PBR, has also been detected for the memories containing 50 and 100 cases respectively.

Another important aspect of the comparison concerns the accuracy obtained by E-MOP based retrieval (in terms of adaptation estimate) with respect to PBR. For this aim we define a retrieval to be *correct* iff the set of retrieved solutions $\mathcal{R}$ is a subset of the set $\mathcal{A}$ containing all the solutions with minimal estimate ($\mathcal{R} \subseteq \mathcal{A}$); a retrieval is *complete* iff $\mathcal{A} \subseteq \mathcal{R}$; a retrieval is *successful* iff $\mathcal{A} \cap \mathcal{R} \neq \emptyset$ (on the contrary it is said to be *unsuccessful*). Moreover, we define as *partially successful* a successful retrieval that is neither correct nor complete. Finally, since an empty retrieval is correct, it is interesting to consider it separately. Figure 4(b) shows the accuracy of the E-MOP based retrieval in terms of percentage of test cases resulting in correct (%CORR), complete (%COMP), correct and complete (%CORR&COMP), partially successful (%PSUCC), unsuccessful (%UNSUCC), and empty (%NOSOL) retrievals. While the overall accuracy of E-MOP retrieval can be considered relatively good (about 55% of retrievals is partially successful and about 20%, 15% are complete and correct respectively), the percentage of complete and correct retrievals (which are the kind of retrievals obtained using PBR) is significantly low, resulting again in a better performance, also in qualitative terms, of PBR.

In conclusion, the evaluation of the PBR approach results to be very satisfactory since: a) it exploits a very simple memory organization avoiding the space problems of more complex organizations like E-MOP; b) it allows one to obtain the best possible accuracy in terms of adaptation effort estimate; c) retrieval time is considerably reduced by the combination of pivoting and pruning techniques. Results on complex real-world domains (e.g. IND) show that the cost of retrieval can be very relevant; thus, any mechanism (like PBR) able to reduce retrieval time without giving up accuracy in the estimation of the adaptation effort is of primary importance for reducing the overall cost of the entire CBR process.

An approach similar to PBR is the *Fish and Shrink* (F&S) algorithm proposed in [10]; retrieval is based on interval estimates as in PBR, but the approach relies on similarity metrics not taking into account adaptability. For instance, we could not apply F&S to our estimate since such an estimate does not satisfy the triangle inequality. Moreover, F&S presupposes an off-line phase of case base update which is not needed with PBR.

References

1. D.S. Aghassi. Evaluating case-based reasoning for heart failure diagnosis. Technical report, Dept. of EECS, MIT, Cambridge, MA, 1990.
2. L. Console and P. Torasso. A spectrum of logical definitions of model-based diagnosis. *Computational Intelligence*, 7(3):133–141, 1991.
3. J.L. Kolodner. *Case-Based Reasoning*. Morgan Kaufmann, 1993.
4. D.B. Leake. Adaptive similarity assessment for case-based explanation. *International Journal of Expert Systems*, 8(2):165–194, 1995.
5. D.B. Leake, A. Kinley, and D. Wilson. Linking adaptation and similarity learning. In *Proc. 18th Int. Conf. of Cognitive Science Society*, San Diego, 1996.
6. B. Nebel and J. Koehler. Plan reuse versus plan generation: a theoretical and empirical analysis. *Artificial Intelligence*, 76:427–454, 1995.
7. L. Portinale and P. Torasso. ADAPtER: an integrated diagnostic system combining case-based and abductive reasoning. In *LNAI 1010*, pages 277–288. Springer Verlag, 1995.
8. L. Portinale and P. Torasso. On the usefulness of re-using diagnostic solutions. In *Proc. 12th European Conf. on AI - ECAI 96*, pages 137–141, Budapest, 1996.
9. J. Rousu and R.J. Aarts. Adapatation cost as a criterion for solution evaluation. In *LNAI 1168*, pages 354–361. Springer Verlag, 1996.
10. J.W. Schaaf. Fish and shrink. A next step towards efficient case retrieval in large scale case bases. In *LNAI 1168*, pages 362–376. Springer Verlag, 1996.
11. B. Smyth and M.T. Keane. Design a la Deja' Vu: reducing the adaptation overhead. In D.B. Leake, editor, *Case Based Reasoning: Experiences, Lessons and Future Directions*. AAAI Press, 1996.

Towards Improving Case Adaptability with a Genetic Algorithm

Lisa Purvis and Salil Athalye

Xerox Corporation, 800 Phillips Road, 128-51E
Webster, NY 14580
E-Mail: {lpurvis,athalye}@wrc.xerox.com

Abstract. Case combination is a difficult problem in Case Based Reasoning, as sub-cases often exhibit conflicts when merged together. In our previous work we formalized case combination by representing each case as a constraint satisfaction problem, and used the minimum conflicts algorithm to systematically synthesize the global solution. However, we also found instances of the problem in which the minimum conflicts algorithm does *not* perform case combination efficiently. In this paper we describe those situations in which initially retrieved cases are *not* easily adaptable, and propose a method by which to improve case adaptability with a genetic algorithm. We introduce a fitness function that maintains as much retrieved case information as possible, while also perturbing a sub-solution to allow subsequent case combination to proceed more efficiently.

1 Introduction

One of the more difficult problems in Case Based Reasoning (CBR) is how to adapt a case to fit the new situation requirements [2, 3, 11]. It is especially difficult in domains where it is necessary to *combine* several cases to find a new solution, as local inconsistencies among the sub-cases often prevent efficient synthesis of the global solution [7].

Our previous work on case combination via constraint satisfaction techniques [16, 17] provided a formalized methodology for combining cases. Each case was formulated as a constraint satisfaction problem (CSP), and the cases were then combined by applying the minimum conflicts algorithm [20]. The formalized methodology enables application of this adaptation process to any problem that can be formulated as a discrete, static or dynamic CSP. Our system COMPOSER implemented this adaptation methodology and tested it on assembly sequence and configuration design problems [16]. The results showed that starting with solutions from the case base provides better performance for the combination than does starting from scratch [16]. However, experiments performed with COMPOSER also showed that the existing case solutions did not *always* combine easily. In some situations, search performance towards the global solution was not improved by starting with solutions from the case base.

In order to improve case adaptability, we have begun to investigate the incorporation of a genetic algorithm (GA) into the adaptation process. We have formulated a fitness evaluation function that allows us to maintain the utility of retrieved cases while improving the ease of their combination.

In Section 2 of this paper, we first review related work on case combination, case adaptability, and the combination of genetic algorithms with CSPs. Section 3 describes our findings as to case adaptability, along with the motivation for choosing a GA to improve adaptability. In Section 4, we present the formulation of the CSP as a GA, describe our fitness function, and show how it can be used to improve initial case adaptability. Section 5 concludes the paper with a summary and discussion of future work.

2 Related Work

Other recent systems that have addressed the multi-case adaptation issue are EADOCS [15], PRODIGY [6], CAPlan [14], and IDIOM [9]. In EADOCS, each case addresses one feature of the new problem, and each case is used to adapt the corresponding solution feature. In PRODIGY, cases are replayed at specific choice points during the plan generation, and in CAPlan, the problem is analyzed into goals, the goals are used to retrieve cases, and each retrieved case replays its decisions. IDIOM uses a CSP during adaptation, with dimensionality reduction to eliminate constraint inconsistencies. In our work, the many matching cases are retrieved at one time from the case base during retrieval, and then these cases are all used simultaneously by the repair algorithm to find a solution to the new problem.

Case adaptability issues have been addressed in DEJA VU [19], where adaptability is assessed based on specially formulated adaptation knowledge, and is used to guide retrieval. Huang and Miles [8] calculate the conflict propagation potential of a case to assess ease of adaptation during retrieval. In KRITIK [5], candidate cases that satisfy certain functional specifications are preferred during retrieval, as those tend to have more easily adaptable matches. Birnbaum et al. [10] and Leake & Fox [12] index cases on the basis of their adaptability, avoiding cases with feature combinations that were difficult to adapt in previous problem-solving episodes. In our work, where several cases are being simultaneously combined, assessing adaptability of each individual case during retrieval is difficult, as the global case interaction cannot be measured until all sub-cases participating in the global solution have been retrieved. Therefore, our focus is on improving adaptability with a genetic algorithm *after* retrieval and matching.

Genetic Algorithms have been applied to solving the CSP [1, 21, 22], with a focus on the genetic representation and the reproduction mechanisms that enable efficient constraint optimization. Rojas [18] has investigated GAs in the CSP context, with a focus on a selection mechanism that uses information about the connectivity of the constraint network. Our work also considers the network topology, and additionally incorporates information about the sub-problem partitioning of the network. We incorporate the GA into our CSP-based adaptation process in order to perturb initially retrieved solutions to enable an easier case combination.

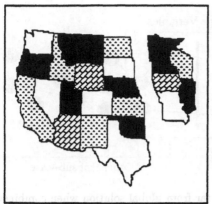

Fig. 1. Easy combination vs. Difficult combination

3 Adaptability of Initially Retrieved Sub-Solutions

The efficient combination of sub-solutions depends heavily on the solution values and the interactions between each sub-case. For example, consider a map coloring example, where we are trying to color a map of a portion of the United States using 4 colors so that no two neighboring states have the same color. Figure 1A depicts a scenario where the two sub-solutions can be combined with no required repairs. Figure 1B illustrates another scenario where a combination would require a recoloring of either the entire eastern map or the entire western map. Clearly, the combination effort for the two sub-solutions shown in Fig. 1A is much smaller than that for the sub-solutions shown in Fig. 1B.

Our experiments with assembly sequence generation and configuration design problems showed that the minimum conflicts algorithm cannot perform an efficient case combination when there are a large number of highly constrained, initially inconsistent edge variables [16]. This situation corresponds to that shown in Fig. 2, where two sub-solutions are combined. Each sub-solution is individually consistent, since it came from the case base, but the two solutions are inconsistent with one another. This inconsistency is caused by conflicts at the edge variables.

Since there are at most 3 pairs of nodes in conflict, this situation may seem promising: as it did to Minton in his initial experiments with the minimum conflicts algorithm [20]. However, to achieve a global solution, the boundary between the consistent sub-solutions must be pushed completely to the right or left during repair.

Pushing the boundary to the right or left causes new sub-problem conflicts, which in turn increases the total number of conflicts. The minimum conflicts heuristic attempts to reduce the total number of conflicts and therefore gets trapped in a local minimum around the initial boundary. Since there is no additional information available to direct the heuristic, the boundary tends to vacillate back and forth [20].

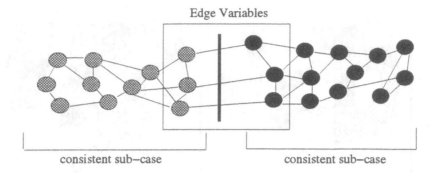

Fig. 2. Two sub-solutions that are far from global solution when combined

The situation, when considered from the perspective of case combination, is even less promising. As soon as values to the left *and* to the right of the boundary are changed, the retrieved case information is destroyed. The utility of knowledge is the cost of solving a problem with the knowledge item versus solving the problem without it [13]. The vacillation of the algorithm causes a loss of case utility, as the case can no longer efficiently guide the algorithm towards a solution. At the same time, it is impossible to determine case utility during retrieval and matching in multi-case combination. Inconsistencies and interactions between the sub-problems cannot be determined until all matched cases are retrieved from the case base. These cases must possess high utility, for we have expended significant effort in retrieving and matching them from the case base.

The utility of old solutions when used effectively during combination can be seen in Fig. 3. These results were obtained from our system COMPOSER, which combines sub-cases using the minimum conflicts algorithm. The assembly sequence problems used as experiments are described in detail in [16]. Figure 3 shows the empirical finding that the use of old solutions from the case base greatly reduces the number of backtracks necessary to find a solution (i.e., the cases maintain high utility in combination).

Figure 4 shows a situation where the case utility was lost [16], rendering the minimum conflicts algorithm ineffective for case combination. The difference between the examples shown in Fig. 3 and in Fig. 4 is that in Fig. 4, there were a large number of highly constrained, initially inconsistent edge variables, causing the minimum conflicts algorithm to vacillate and destroy the case utility.

The performance of the minimum conflicts heuristic when used for case combination must be improved for the situation shown in Fig. 4. Clearly, we need an approach for case combination that both preserves case utility and avoids vacillation around local minima. Our approach is to use a Genetic Algorithm (GA) in this situation. We have chosen a GA because of its ability to both operate with a progression towards an improved solution, and to examine multiple regions of the search space via crossover and mutation operators [21], thereby enabling an

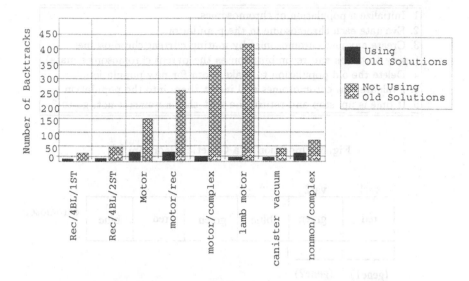

Fig. 3. The use of old solutions increases the efficiency of case combination

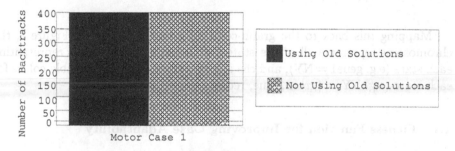

Fig. 4. Efficiency of case combination decreases as case utility decreases

escape from initial local minima. We intend to provide the GA with knowledge of the global constraint network topology and the sub-case partitioning of the network. Doing so ensures that only one sub-case is perturbed, leaving the rest of the cases' utilities intact. This in turn results in a network that is closer to the global solution with as much case information maintained as possible, allowing the minimum conflicts algorithm to proceed more effectively.

4   Formulation of the CSP as a Genetic Algorithm

A genetic algorithm operates by iterating through the steps shown in Fig. 5.

Mapping this to the constraint satisfaction domain, we can think of the variables as genes in the chromosome, and the values as the alleles. This representation is shown in Fig. 6.

1. Initialize a population of chromosomes.
2. Evaluate each chromosome in the population.
3. Create any new chromosomes by mating current chromosomes.
(apply mutation and recombination as the parent chromosomes mate).
4. Delete the old population to make room for new population.
5. Evaluate new chromosomes and insert them into the population.
6. If time is up, stop and return the best chromosome; if not, go to 3.

Fig. 5. Operation of a Genetic Algorithm [4]

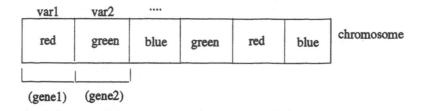

Fig. 6. Variable and Value Representation as a Chromosome

Mapping this back to the graph-coloring problems shown in Figure 1, the chromosome represents all of the states, with the genes/variables representing each state (e.g. gene1 = NY), and the alleles/values being the possible colors for each state (e.g. NY = {green, blue, red}).

4.1 Fitness Function for Improving Case Adaptability

The evaluation/fitness function that we propose for step 5 is based on the following principle: it is more important to satisfy those constraints that affect a larger number of variables. In these types of critical constraints, the effect of changing the value of one variable would be reflected in its other constraints (we will call this the variable's propagation potential). In Rojas [18], the evaluation function favors those chromosomes whose violated constraints have a low propagation potential. For example, in the network shown in Figure 7, the constraint C1 between V1 and V3 is more important to satisfy than the constraint C2 between V1 and V2. This is because V3 is connected to 3 other variables, while V2 is only connected to 2 other variables. Thus, the propagation potential of V3 is larger, and this potential can be eliminated by satisfying C1.

4.2 Formulation of Propagation Potential

We introduce a different propagation potential measurement that considers *inter-problem* constraint violations to be more important than *intra-problem* constraint

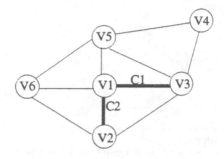

Fig. 7. Propagation Potential Example

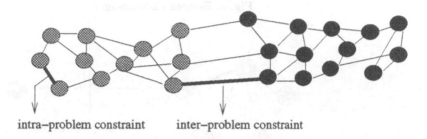

intra–problem constraint   inter–problem constraint

Fig. 8. Inter/Intra-problem Constraint Example

violations. An *inter-problem* constraint is one that crosses the sub-problem boundary, and an *intra-problem* constraint is one that connects only variables in the same sub-problem, as shown in Fig. 8. In effect, an inter-problem constraint is one that connects edge variables.

Each sub-solution should ideally satisfy two criteria: firstly, it should contain edge variables that are consistent, secondly, the intra-problem variables that are highly connected should also be consistent. These two criteria favor those sub-solutions that will not cause propagation into the neighboring sub-solution, and also favor those that promise to require little intra-problem repair. To accomplish this, we have developed a propagation potential measurement for each variable as follows:

Propagation Potential (v) = # Intra-problem constraint connections for v + ((# inter-problem constraint connections for v) *weightingFactor)

The Fitness function F then calculates the total fitness for the chromosome:

For all constraints c in the chromosome s.t. c is violated
    For each variable v connected to c
        totalFitness = Propagation Potential (v)+ totalFitness

Recall that the goal of this genetic algorithm is to minimize the evaluation/fitness function. Therefore, the chromosome shown in Fig. 9 would be fa-

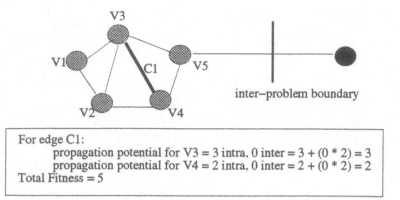

For edge C1:
    propagation potential for V3 = 3 intra, 0 inter = 3 + (0 * 2) = 3
    propagation potential for V4 = 2 intra, 0 inter = 2 + (0 * 2) = 2
Total Fitness = 5

Fig. 9. Favored Chromosome

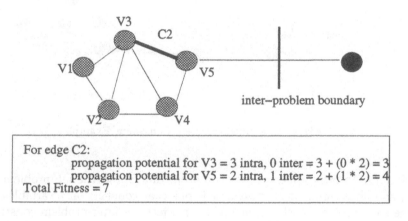

For edge C2:
    propagation potential for V3 = 3 intra, 0 inter = 3 + (0 * 2) = 3
    propagation potential for V5 = 2 intra, 1 inter = 2 + (1 * 2) = 4
Total Fitness = 7

Fig. 10. Unfavored Chromosome

vored over the chromosome shown in Fig. 10, since the evaluation function evaluates to a lower number. A dark edge indicates a constraint violation between
the connected variables.

Note that the chromosome shown in Fig. 9 is favored because violating C1
is considered less important than is violating C2. Intuitively, this is because a
violation of C2 has the direct potential to propagate across the inter-problem
boundary, destroying the other case's information.

By employing a fitness function that favors those chromosomes with little
propagation potential into the neighboring sub-cases, the case utility of all neighboring sub-problems is maintained. Favoring those chromosomes with little intra-
problem propagation potential means that it is less likely that a re-assignment
of the entire network will be required. If we think of the distance to the global
solution as being the number of variables that must be re-assigned, then we can
see that the chromosomes favored by our fitness function are those whose dis-

tance is small. Because the minimum conflicts algorithm works best when the distance is small, we can take the fittest chromosome, substitute its new values into the global network, and efficiently continue the combination process using the minimum conflicts heuristic.

5 Conclusion

We have presented a technique for case combination that is applicable when the cases initially retrieved from the case base are not easily adaptable. A genetic algorithm is used to allow a quick escape from the local minima while also moving towards a solution that is more easily combined with the other sub-cases. By employing a fitness function in our genetic algorithm that considers inter- and intra-problem connectivity, we keep as much case information intact as possible, while also moving towards a solution that has low propagation potential. That is, subsequent repair is not likely to require a complete re-labeling of all variables in the network.

Our future work will involve implementing this GA approach, and running experiments with graph-coloring problems to provide empirical evidence that shows the effectiveness of our fitness function in improving the performance of subsequent case combination via the minimum conflicts algorithm. We also intend to investigate techniques by which to determine which sub-case to perturb, and under what conditions it might be necessary to perturb more than one sub-case. We will also apply this methodology to the assembly sequence problems that we found difficult to adapt during earlier work with COMPOSER, and will investigate whether different mutation and crossover operators are more effective at moving quickly out of the initial local minimum.

References

1. P.E. Raue A. Eiben and Zs. Ruttkay. Solving constraint satisfaction problems using genetic algorithms. In *Proceedings of the IEEE World Conference on Computational Intelligence*, pages 543–547, 1994.
2. Dean Allemang. Review of the first european workshop on case based reasoning. *Case-Based Reasoning Newsletter*, 2, 1993.
3. Andrew Kinley David B. Leake and David Wilson. Learning to improve case adaptation by introspective reasoning and cbr. In *Proceedings of the First International Conference on Case Based Reasoning, Sesimbra, Portugal*, pages 229–240, 1995.
4. Lawrence Davis. *Handbook of Genetic Algorithms*. Van Nostrand Reinhold Publishers, 1991.
5. A. Goel. *Integration of Case-Based Reasoning and Model-Based Reasoning for Adaptive Design Problem Solving*. PhD thesis, Ohio State University, 1989.
6. K. Haigh and M. Veloso. Route planning by analogy. In *Proceedings of the First International Conference on Case Based Reasoning, Sesimbra, Portugal*, pages 169–180, 1995.
7. Kefeng Hua and Boi Faltings. Exploring case-based building design - cadre. In *Artificial Intelligence in Engineering Design, Analysis, and Manufacturing*, 1993.

8. Y. Huang and R. Miles. A case based method for solving relatively stable dynamic constraint satisfaction problems. In *Proceedings of the First International Conference on Case Based Reasoning, Sesimbra, Portugal*, pages 481–490, 1995.

9. C. Lottaz I. Smith and B. Faltings. Spatial composition using cases: Idiom. In *Proceedings of the First International Conference on Case Based Reasoning, Sesimbra, Portugal*, pages 88–97, 1995.

10. M. Brand et al. L. Birnbaum, G. Collins. A model-based approach to the construction of adaptive case-based planning systems. In *Proceedings of the Case Based Reasoning Workshop, Florida, USA*, 1989.

11. David Leake. Workshop report: The aaai'93 workshop on case based reasoning. *AI Magazine*, pages 63–64, 1994.

12. David Leake and S. Fox. Using introspective reasoning to guide index refinement. In *Proceedings of the Sixteenth International Conference of the Cognitive Science Society*, pages 313–318, 1992.

13. Kazuo Miyashita and Katia Sycara. Improving system performance in case-based iterative optimization through knowledge filtering. In *Proceedings of the International Joint Conference on Artificial Intelligence*, pages 371–376, 1995.

14. H. Munoz and J. Huellen. Retrieving cases in structured domains by using goal dependencies. In *Proceedings of the First International Conference on Case Based Reasoning, Sesimbra, Portugal*, pages 241–252, 1995.

15. B.D. Netten and R.A. Vingerhoeds. Adaptation for conceptual design in eadocs. In *Proceedings of the ECAI'96 Workshop on Case Adaptation, Budapest, Hungary*, 1996.

16. Lisa Purvis. *Intelligent Design Problem Solving Using Case-Based and Constraint-Based Techniques*. PhD thesis, The University of Connecticut, 1995.

17. Lisa Purvis and Pearl Pu. Adaptation using constraint satisfaction techniques. In *Proceedings of the First International Conference on Case-Based Reasoning, Sesimbra, Portugal*, pages 289–300, 1995.

18. Maria Cristina Riff Rojas. From quasi-solutions to solution: An evolutionary algorithm to solve csp. In *Proceedings of the Principles and Practice of Constraint Programming Conference (CP96)*, pages 367–381, 1996.

19. Barry Smyth and Mark T. Keane. Experiments on adaptation-guided retrieval in case-based design. In *Proceedings of the First International Conference on Case Based Reasoning, Sesimbra, Portugal*, pages 313–324, 1995.

20. A. Philips Steven Minton, M. Johnston and P. Laird. Minimizing conflicts: A heuristic repair method for constraint satisfaction and scheduling problems. *Artificial Intelligence*, pages 161–205, 1992.

21. E.P.K. Tsang and T. Warwick. Applying genetic algorithms to constraint satisfaction optimization problems. In *Proceedings of the European Conference on Artificial Intelligence, Stockholm, Sweden*, pages 649–654, 1990.

22. T. Warwick. *A GA Approach to Constraint Satisfaction Problems*. PhD thesis, University of Essex, Colchester, UK, 1995.

Merge Strategies for Multiple Case Plan Replay *

Manuela M. Veloso

Computer Science Department, Carnegie Mellon University
Pittsburgh, PA 15213-3891, U.S.A.
mmv@cs.cmu.edu, http://www.cs.cmu.edu/~mmv

Abstract. Planning by analogical reasoning is a learning method that consists of the storage, retrieval, and replay of planning episodes. Planning performance improves with the accumulation and reuse of a library of planning cases. Retrieval is driven by domain-dependent similarity metrics based on planning goals and scenarios. In complex situations with multiple goals, retrieval may find multiple past planning cases that are jointly similar to the new planning situation. This paper presents the issues and implications involved in the replay of multiple planning cases, as opposed to a single one. Multiple case plan replay involves the adaptation and merging of the annotated derivations of the planning cases. Several merge strategies for replay are introduced that can process with various forms of eagerness the differences between the past and new situations and the annotated justifications at the planning cases. In particular, we introduce an effective merging strategy that considers plan step choices especially appropriate for the interleaving of planning and plan execution. We illustrate and discuss the effectiveness of the merging strategies in specific domains.

1 Introduction, Related Work, and Motivation

Case-based planning and derivational analogy have been of interest to several re-searchers, who continue to investigate the singularities of using case-based reasoning in a planning framework. Many advances have been made in this context, building upon the pioneering CHEF [Hammond, 1986] and derivational analogy [Carbonell, 1986] work. CHEF showed how to explain plan failure and reason about failure for case indexing and retrieval. Derivational analogy introduced and showed the need to be reminded of the solution derivation rather than only of the final solution.

Several efforts have been following this line of research. Naming a few systems that address core planning problems helps to motivate this work and the interest in the area. PRIAR [Kambhampati and Hendler, 1992] notably formalizes and demonstrates the use of dependency links for plan reuse in hierarchical planning. Prodigy/Analogy [Veloso, 1994] develops the full derivational analogy approach and contributes an extensive analysis of the impact on planning efficiency of using the combination of case-based and state-space nonlinear planning. SPA [Hanks and Weld, 1995] is a simple and ele-gant interpretation of case-based plan adaptation, using SNLP as a plan-space planning approach. Using this same base-level planning approach and also building upon the

---

* This research is sponsored as part of the DARPA/RL Knowledge Based Planning and Scheduling Initiative under grant number F30602-95-1-0018. Thanks to Michael Cox and the anonymous reviewers for their comments on this paper.

Prodigy/Analogy approach, CAPLAN [Muñoz-Avila *et al.*, 1994] has been significantly extending the indexing and retrieval techniques and applying the paradigm to realistic domains, such as manufacturing. Similarly, DerSNLP [Ihrig and Kambhampati, 1994] is another successful implementation of derivational replay in SNLP. Several other systems, provide specific strong approaches to aspects of the case-based planning paradigm. For example, Dejà-vu [Smyth and Keane, 1995] shows how retrieval can use a prediction of the adaptation cost, PARKA [Kettler *et al.*, 1994] demonstrates massively parallel effective invocations to case memory during planning, and [López and Plaza, 1993] views medical diagnosis as a reactive planning task.

One of the interesting and less explored (or explained) aspects of the case-based planning paradigm is the use of multiple plans during the adaptation phase. In complex planning situations with multiple goals, a single past case that is similar to the complete new situation may not be found. However, several planning cases may be found that cover independent subparts of the new planning situation in a complementary way. Planning can then be viewed as the process of merging and adapting these multiple complementary planning cases. The effective use of multiple cases in planning is a challenging issue and is the focus of this work. This paper reports on our work in Prodigy/Analogy investigating and developing different plan merging strategies for analogical replay. A few other systems, such as [Redmond, 1990], and ASP-II [Alexander and Tsatsoulis, 1991] have addressed the use of multiple plans, although not necessarily in the replay or adaptation phase. An interesting recent effort in the Nicole system [Ram and Francis, 1996] explores the use of multiple *alternative* planning cases during reuse, as opposed to multiple *complementary* plans as carried out in Prodigy/Analogy.

This paper introduces several strategies to merge multiple planning cases during the adaptation phase (i.e., the replay phase in Prodigy/Analogy). These strategies are a refinement of the ones briefly discussed in [Veloso, 1994] within a re-implementation of Prodigy/Analogy integrated with the new Prodigy4.0 planner [Veloso *et al.*, 1995]. In analogical derivational replay, the merge algorithms are dependent on the underlying generative planning algorithm. In Section 2, we briefly introduce the Prodigy4.0 generative planner as the substrate planner of Prodigy/Analogy. We focus on explaining two main decision points of the planner and on showing the guidance that analogical replay can provide to improve planning efficiency. The remainder of the paper introduces different replay strategies for multiple plans. Section 3 sets the ground for the next sections by presenting serial replay as a simple strategy to replay a single case. Sections 4 and 5 present sequential replay and ordering-based interleaved replay, respectively. Section 6 introduces the novel choice-and-ordering-based interleaved replay. We illustrate our developed strategies in different domains. Finally, Section 7 concludes the paper with a summary of the contributions of the paper.

2   Improving Planning Efficiency: Replay of Planning Decisions

Planning is a complex task for which learning from past experience can improve planning performance along the three following dimensions: planning efficiency, task action model, and quality of plans generated [Veloso *et al.*, 1995]. Prodigy/Analogy is a case-based learning algorithm specifically designed to improve planning effi-

415

ciency. Therefore, it is important to understand what are the potential sources of planning inefficiency. Planning performance is dependent on the underlying planning algorithm and can vary with a great number of factors [Veloso and Blythe, 1994, Veloso and Stone, 1995]. Hence identifying universal causes of inefficiency for all domains and planning algorithms is not possible. We focus on explaining our planner's *decision points*, as opposed to its many other features, e.g., action representation, conditional planning, control knowledge, abstraction planning, or user interface.

2.1 Planning Decisions in Prodigy4.0

Prodigy4.0 combines state-space search corresponding to a simulation of plan execution of the plan and backward-chaining responsible for goal-directed reasoning. A formal description of Prodigy4.0 can be found in [Veloso *et al.*, 1995].

As opposed to the early state-space planners, such as Strips [Fikes and Nilsson, 1971] and Prodigy2.0 [Minton *et al.*, 1989], Prodigy4.0 performs a nonlinear state-space search by allowing the interleaving of subplans for different goals. At each point in its search, until the goal has been achieved, Prodigy4.0 faces both a set of goals that still need to be achieved and a set of plan steps (operators) already selected to achieve other goals. Some of these already selected plan steps may have all of its preconditions satisfied in the planner's state. When that is the case, Prodigy4.0 chooses between *applying* a plan step or continue planning for a pending goal, i.e., a goal that still needs to be planned for. Figure 1 shows these two main decisions.

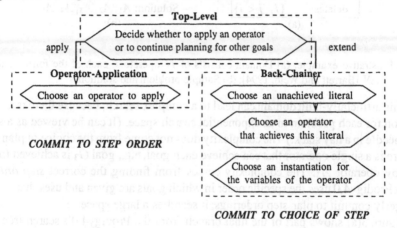

Fig. 1. Two Main Decisions while Planning: Step Order and Step Choice.

Applying an operator provides a new planning state. This decision is equivalent to a commitment in plan step order and therefore early simulation of plan execution while planning. Planning for a goal involves the selection of a specific step (instantiated operator) to achieve the goal. In some cases, selecting such a step can be easier, if updated state information can be taken into account. In a nutshell, we can view the planning search process depending on these two main choices, namely step ordering and choice of plan step. These two decisions are directly related to planning efficiency. For completeness, Prodigy4.0 can backtrack over all its choices, and eventually will generate a solution plan, if one exists. However, the *planning efficiency*, i.e., the performance of the algorithm in its search, depends on the choices made during the search process.

2.2 Analogical Replay as Guidance to Planning Decisions

Analogical reasoning in Prodigy/Analogy achieves the integration of case-based reasoning and generative planning. It provides guidance for the planning choices and can therefore improve Prodigy4.0's planning efficiency. Essentially, Prodigy/Analogy introspects into the Prodigy4.0's planning episode after the search process to generate a plan, and generates a planning case by capturing several justifications for why choices are made. Case indexing includes the goal and the solution-relevant initial state (footprint). Retrieval compares new and past goals and problem states and returns a set of planning cases to *cover* the new planning situation. Analogical replay involves validating and replaying the retrieved case [Veloso, 1994].

In this section, we illustrate through a simple example the reduction in search effort that can be provided by analogical reasoning. Consider the planning domain introduced by [Barrett and Weld, 1994] and shown in Figure 2(a). We show a sample illustrative planning problem in this domain and the corresponding solution in Figure 2(b).

Operator:	A_i
preconds:	I_i
adds:	G_i
deletes:	$\{I_j, j < i\}$

(a)

Problem:
- Initial state: I_1, I_2, I_3, I_4, I_5
- Goal: G_2, G_3, G_4, G_1, G_5
- Solution: A_1, A_2, A_3, A_4, A_5

(b)

Fig. 2. Illustrative example: (a) Domain consists of N operators, each of the form A_i shown, $i = 1, \ldots, N$ [Barrett and Weld, 1994]; (b) Sample problem and solution.

This artificially-built domain can lead to a complex search, because there is a unique solution for each problem in an exponential search space. (It can be viewed as a search for a needle in a hay stack.) The complexity does not come from the choice of plan steps, as there is a single operator that can achieve each goal, e.g., goal G_3 is achieved (added) only by operator A_3. The complexity comes from finding the correct *step ordering*. When Prodigy4.0 uses the specific order in which goals are given and uses that ordering to eagerly commit to plan step orderings, it searches a large space.

Figure 3(a) shows part of the final branch from the Prodigy4.0's search tree while generating a solution to the problem introduced above. The trace shows a sequence of numbered choices of goals (represented in parenthesis), operators (represented within angle brackets), and applied operators (represented in upper-case letters in angle brackets). The interested reader can work out the problem and confirm the generation of the solution. (The trace further shows the depth of each search node – the first number on the line – and the number of alternative goals not explored at that search level – the information within the square brackets at the end of the line.) A major fact to notice, however, is that 305 nodes can be searched in this simple problem.

Prodigy/Analogy can store a solution derivation into a planning case. Figure 3(b) shows the trace of the search guided by a planning case that solves the same problem.

```
  2  n2 (done)                      2  n2 (done)
  4  n4 <*finish*>                  4  n4 <*finish*>
  5    n5 (g2)    [g:4]             5    n5 (g2)    "c5" 5    -- goal     (g2)
  7    n7 <a2>                      7    n7 <a2>    "c5" 6    -- operator a2
  8    n289 (g1)  [g:1]             8    n8 (g1)    "c5" 289  -- goal     (g1)
 10    n291 <a1>                   10    n10 <a1>   "c5" 290  -- operator a1
 11    n292 <A1>    [g:3]          11    n11 <A1>   "c5" 292  -- apply "c5" 291
 12    n293 <A2>    [g:3]          12    n12 <A2>   "c5" 293  -- apply "c5" 7
 13    n294 (g3)    [g:2]          13    n13 (g3)   "c5" 294  -- goal     (g3)
 15    n296 <a3>                   15    n15 <a3>   "c5" 295  -- operator a3
 16    n297 <A3>    [g:2]          16    n16 <A3>   "c5" 297  -- apply "c5" 296
 17    n298 (g4)    [g:1]          17    n17 (g4)   "c5" 298  -- goal     (g4)
 19    n300 <a4>                   19    n19 <a4>   "c5" 299  -- operator a4
 20    n301 <A4>    [g:1]          20    n20 <A4>   "c5" 301  -- apply "c5" 300
 21    n302 (g5)                   21    n21 (g5)   "c5" 302  -- goal     (g5)
 23    n304 <a5>                   23    n23 <a5>   "c5" 303  -- operator a5
 24    n305 <A5>                   24    n24 <A5>   "c5" 305  -- apply "c5" 304
                                   End of current guiding case.
Achieved top-level goals.         Achieved top-level goals.
Solution:                         Solution:
        <a1>                              <a1> (case "c5" 291)
        <a2>                              <a2> (case "c5" 7)
        <a3>                              <a3> (case "c5" 296)
        <a4>                              <a4> (case "c5" 300)
        <a5>                              <a5> (case "c5" 304)
#<PRODIGY result: t, 1 sol,       #<PRODIGY result: t, 1 sol,
11.683 secs, 305 nodes>           0.75 secs, 24 nodes>

            (a)                                 (b)
```

Fig. 3. (a) Prodigy4.0 can search 305 nodes for a solution to the problem shown in Figure 2(b) (partial trace shown). This solution and its derivation is stored in a planning case,"c5"; (b) Analogical replay using "c5" guides planning for the same problem, finding immediately the solution with only 24 nodes searched. (The format of the traces was adapted for presentation.)

By replaying this planning case, all choices are revalidated successfully and search is completed avoided. This example illustrates the elementary case of search reduction provided by direct guidance. The search reduction is a result of the following two benefits provided by analogical replay:

- Proposal and validation of choices versus generation and search of possible alternatives operators and goal orderings.
- Reduction of the number of plausible alternatives – past failed alternatives are pruned by validating the failures recorded in the past cases.

In the most common and interesting situations of analogical replay, Prodigy/Analogy replays one or several cases in *similar* (and not the exact same) situation. We address next the complexity of the different replay strategies.

3 Serial Replay

The simplest replay situation involves using a single case and adapting it in a similar new situation. There are three kinds of possible differences between the new and the old situation, namely role (object), initial state, and goal differences.[2] Clearly, the most

---

[2] In [Wang and Veloso, 1994], we further consider situations in which the underlying available actions could be different between the past and the new situation. For the purpose of this paper, we assume a fixed set of actions.

common and challenging adaptation corresponds to the condition where we have a combination of different roles, initial states, and goals.

Consider the situation where the retrieval procedure returns a single case to cover the new planning roles, initial state, and goals. We introduce *serial replay* as the replay strategy with the following simple characteristics:

- A single case is retrieved.
- The past case is completely replayed before planning for any new goals.

This is clearly not a particularly involved replay technique to *merge* the past case into the new situation, as it postpones to the extreme reasoning about the differences between the case and the new situation. It represents a high degree of eagerness in terms of fully using the past case before considering the new situation. This technique has been implemented in a partial-order planner, DerSNLP [Ihrig and Kambhampati, 1994], as its replay strategy, where it showed to be appropriate.

Serial replay is potentially useful if the new goals correspond to minor changes to the retrieved case which can easily be performed *at the end* of the planning episode. The domain shown in Figure 4 illustrates this situation.

Operator:	A_i^1	A_i^2
preconds:	I_i	P_i
adds:	P_i	G_i
deletes:	$\{I_j, j < i\}$	$\{I_j, j \leq i\}$
		$\{P_j, j < i\}$

(a)

Problem:
- Initial state: $I_1, I_2, I_3, \ldots$
- Goal: $G_4, G_7, G_1, \ldots$

Solution: $A_1^1, A_2^1, A_3^1, \ldots, A_1^2, A_2^2, A_3^2, \ldots$

(b)

Fig. 4. Illustrative example: (a) Domain consists of $2N$ operators, N of the form A_i^1 and N of the form A_i^2 shown, $i = 1, \ldots, N$ [Barrett and Weld, 1994]; (b) Sample problem and solution.

We applied serial replay in this domain following the same experimental setup reported in [Ihrig and Kambhampati, 1994], namely, for each N-goal problem: (i) Solve and store an N-goal problem; (ii) Replay an N-goal case to solve a $N + 1$-goal problem using serial replay. We consistently achieved a large reduction in search space when comparing Prodigy4.0's eager step-ordering planning procedure against Prodigy/Analogy. An illustrative and representative sample of the results is shown in Table 1 for several 4-goal problems following different 3-goal case plans.

Serial replay backtracks in the case and returns to the case when the justifications (e.g. effects of the applied steps) are validated. The main advantage of replaying the $N - 1$ goal problem is the selection (with the inherent pruning of alternatives) of the right choices along all of the planning steps. Serial replay could be less efficient in situations that involve adaptation through the choices of plan steps instead of only step orderings and new step additions. In general, replay includes adding new steps, deleting old steps, and merging multiple planning cases.

Any 4-goal problem in Prodigy4.0 using eager step ordering (i.e., eager state changes) corresponds to searching > 10000 nodes; (Using completely delayed commitments to step orderings for a problem with n goals corresponds to a search of $4(2n + 1)$ nodes.)

Problem	Guiding Case	Serial Replay Nodes	Time (s)
p1-2-3-4	"case-p1-3-2"	58	1.95
p1-2-3-4	"case-p2-3-1"	58	1.98
p2-1-3-4	"case-p2-1-4"	65	2.3
p2-1-3-4	"case-p2-4-1"	65	2.3
p1-2-3-4	"case-p3-1-4"	75	2.566
p4-3-2-1	"case-p3-4-1"	75	2.666
p4-3-2-1	"case-p2-4-3"	85	2.933
p4-3-2-1	"case-p2-3-4"	85	2.867

Table 1. Sample table of results for solving 4-goal problems in the domain of Figure 4(a). The name of the problem and guiding case captures the goals in the problem and its order, e.g., p4-3-2-1 is a problem with goals G_4, G_3, G_2, G_1.

4 Sequential Replay

Adding new steps to a planning case is a common case adaptation found in analogical derivational replay. The reasons why steps need to be added to a planning case include the following two situations:

- New state misses precondition(s) of past applied step. For example, analogical replay finds a decision to apply a step with n preconditions; in the past case situation, there were $k < n$ preconditions true in the state; in the new state, there are m preconditions true, with $m < k < n$; extra planning is therefore needed to account for the extra $k - m$ unsatisfied preconditions.
- And the more interesting situation in which merging multiple plans requires adding new steps to combine individual cases.

Sequential replay is a technique that we developed to account for the situation where retrieval can provide information about the order in which multiple cases should be replayed. We developed this merge technique for the application of analogical replay to route planning [Haigh and Veloso, 1995, Haigh et al., 1997]. The geometric characteristics of the map used by the retrieval procedure allow for the specification of an ordering between multiple planning cases. Sequential replay has the following features:

- Guiding cases are *ordered* by the retrieval procedure.
- Each case is replayed *sequentially* in the retrieved order.
- Merging occurs by planning *to connect* the planning cases.

The sequential replay algorithm attempts to validate each step proposed by the cases. Usually case steps are viable in the current situation, but two situations exist when a choice may not be viable:

1. when a case step is not *valid*, i.e., when a choice made in the case is not applicable in the current situation, *e.g.* a route segment is closed for construction, and
2. when a step is *not reached yet*, i.e., the next step is not yet in the set of adjacent reachable states from the current step, *e.g.* when there is a gap between cases.

Empirical results using a real map of the city of Pittsburgh [Haigh *et al.*, 1997] showed that the sequential replay is effective due to its three main features: its combination of retrieval of ordered situational-dependent similar past routing cases; its revalidation of the availability of the case segments used; and its ability to do extra planning when needed.

5 Ordering-Based Interleaved Replay

We introduce interleaved replay as a merge strategy that reasons about the decisions in the multiple planning cases before committing to a particular merge ordering. Interleaved replay does not have a pre-defined merge ordering and it considers the different past cases and the new situation in equal standing while making merging decisions.

Ordering-based interleaved replay is a strategy to merge planning cases that reasons specifically about plan step ordering commitments in the past cases. Ordering-based interleaved replay has the following features:

- Guiding cases are not ordered in any predefined order.
- Each case is replayed until a step ordering commitment is found.
- Planning is done for new goals until step ordering commitments are needed.
- Merging occurs by reasoning about the ordering constraints among different steps.
- As usual, new steps are added and old steps are deleted when needed.

Cases and new plan steps for new goals are ordered using the ordering dependencies illustrated shown in Figure 5.

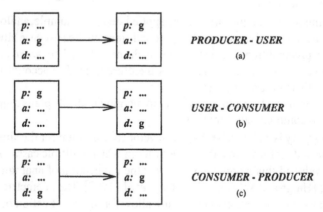

Fig. 5. Illustration of Plan Step Ordering Constraints. (p, a, and d represent the preconditions, adds and deletes of an operator, respectively.) For example, in (b) a step that needs a goal should precede a step that deletes that goal.

Deleting old steps occurs in the dual situations of the ones where new steps are found to be needed, namely:

- State provides precondition(s) of past applied step. For example, analogical replay finds a decision to apply a step with n preconditions; in the past case situation, there are $k < n$ preconditions true in the state; in the new state, there are m, preconditions true, with $k < m < n$; planning for for the $m - k$ unsatisfied preconditions in the past case are not needed; replay deletes all the planning done dependent on the $m - k$ goals no longer necessary, by removing all the steps introduced for these goals; the annotated justifications at the case decisions provide the necessary linking information for this adaptation.

- And the more interesting situation in which merging multiple plans may identify repetition of steps in the different cases; analogical replay skips the repetition.

Figure 6 shows an illustration of the ordering-based interleaved replay procedure in the one-way rocket domain [Veloso, 1994].

```
 2  n2  (done)
 4  n4  <*finish*>
 5  n5  (at obj1 locb)                      "case1"  5 -- goal (AT OBJ1 LOCB)
 7  n7  <unload-rocket obj1 locb r1>        "case1"  6 -- operator UNLOAD-ROCKET
                                           "case1"  7 -- bindings OBJ1,LOCB,R1
 8      n8  (inside obj1 r1) case           "case1"  8 -- goal  (INSIDE OBJ1 R1)
10      n10 <load-rocket obj1 r1 loca>      "case1"  9 -- operator LOAD-ROCKET
                                           "case1" 10 -- bindings OBJ1,LOCA,R1
11      n11 (at obj2 locb)                  "case2"  5 -- goal  (AT OBJ2 LOCB)
13      n13 <unload-rocket obj2 locb r1>    "case2"  6 -- operator UNLOAD-ROCKET
                                           "case2"  7 -- bindings OBJ2,LOCB,R1
14      n14 (inside obj2 r1)                "case2"  8 -- goal  (INSIDE OBJ2 R1)
16      n16 <load-rocket obj2 r1 loca>      "case2"  9 -- operator LOAD-ROCKET
                                           "case2" 10 -- bindings OBJ2,LOCA,R1
17      n17 (at obj3 locb) unguided goal #<AT OBJ3 LOCB>
19      n19 <unload-rocket obj3 locb r1>
20      n20 (inside obj3 r1) unguided goal #<INSIDE OBJ3 R1>
22      n22 <load-rocket obj3 r1 loca> [1]
23      n23 <LOAD-ROCKET OBJ2 R1 LOCA> "case2" 11 -- apply "case2" 10
24      n24 (at r1 locb) "case2" 12 -- goal  (AT R1 LOCB)
26      n26 <move-rocket r1> "case2" 14 -- operator MOVE-ROCKET
                                           "case2" 15 -- bindings R1
27      n27 <LOAD-ROCKET OBJ1 R1 LOCA> "case1" 11 -- apply "case1" 10
Goal (AT R1 LOCB): Goal causes a goal loop or is true in state.
Marking all dependent steps to be skipped. Advancing case.
28      n28 <LOAD-ROCKET OBJ3 R1 LOCA> apply unguided
29      n29 <MOVE-ROCKET R1> "case2" 16 -- apply "case2" 15
30      n30 <UNLOAD-ROCKET OBJ2 LOCB R1> "case2" 17 -- apply "case2" 7
End of current guiding case.
Switching to the last available case.
31      n31 <UNLOAD-ROCKET OBJ1 LOCB R1> "case1" 17 -- apply "case1" 7
End of current guiding case.
31      n32 <UNLOAD-ROCKET OBJ3 LOCB R1> apply unguided
Achieved top-level goals.
Solution:
        <load-rocket obj2 r1 loca> ("case2" 10)
        <load-rocket obj1 r1 loca> ("case1" 10)
        <load-rocket obj3 r1 loca>
        <move-rocket r1> ("case2" 15)
        <unload-rocket obj2 locb r1> ("case2" 7)
        <unload-rocket obj1 locb r1> ("case1" 7)
        <unload-rocket obj3 locb r1>
#<PRODIGY result: T, 0.467 secs, 32 nodes, 1 sol>
```

Fig. 6. Illustration of Ordering-based Interleaved Replay. (The format of the trace was adapted for presentation.)

In this domain, objects can be loaded into and unloaded to a rocket carrier, which can only move once from the initial to the goal location. Two goals of a new 3-goal problem are solved guided by two cases and the third goal is unguided. The trace representation is the same as used before. To note in the replay procedure are: the interleaved use of the two cases, case1 and case2, the deletion of repeated steps unnecessary steps after node n27, and the ordering-based switching points among the cases and the unguided goal (see nodes n11, n17, n23, n27, and n28).

6 Choice-and-Ordering-Based Interleaved Replay

Ordering-based interleaved replay reasons effectively about step-ordering commitments. As we noted earlier, however, step choice planning decisions may influence planning efficiency. Here we introduce choice-and-ordering-based interleaved replay, which goes beyond step orderings and reasons about the use of state information for step choices.

Figure 7 sketches the general reason why state information plays a role in step choices. Suppose an operator in the plan is applied and adds to the state some literal $p3$. (The effects of the operators, in particular if conditional or universal, are easily visible when an operator is applied.) Now the planner encounters a goal G for which there are 4 possible operators that can achieve it. If one of the operators needs the precondition $p3$, and the preconditions of the other operators are not satisfied in the state, then the planner may choose this operator because it does not need any further planning.

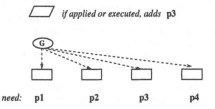

Fig. 7. State Information Guides Operator Choices

The choice of a plan step has been overlooked as a source of planning efficiency, but several concrete examples of its relevancy are introduced in [Veloso and Blythe, 1994]. Choice-and-ordering-based interleaved replay aims at using derivational analogy to provide guidance for this difficult planning decision.

We introduce a new dependency link to be annotated in a planning case: the *information-dependent step choice* link. This link is established if the choice of a plan step depends on the following condition: a previously applied or executed step adds (or deletes) information to the planning state that determines the choice of the plan step. This new kind of dependency link is in addition and contrasts to the ordering links based on interactions between preconditions and effects of planning operators (see Figure 5).

The choice-and-ordering-based interleaved replay merges cases by reasoning about the ordering and the information-dependent step choice constraints. The procedure that we are developing can perform the following functions:

- Consider effects of the result of operator application or execution and its impact in plan step choices.
- Use information-dependent and step ordering links to select merge order.
- Reconsider choices of plan steps, if justification for its selection is deleted.
- Use record of failed or untried alternatives as an opportunity for exploration.

This choice-and-ordering-based merge strategy is particularly appropriate for environments where planning and execution are interleaved and specifically in multi-agent environments where multiple plans need to be coordinated. Execution can act as a source of information for the planner [Pryor and Collins, 1992, Stone and Veloso, 1996]. Choice-and-ordering-based interleaved replay aims at making use of the record in a planning case of the consequences of execution information in planning decisions.

7 Conclusion

This paper reports on our work in case-based reasoning applied to planning, in particular on analogical replay as an integration of generative and case-based planning. We have pursued extensive research in this area within the Prodigy/Analogy system. In this paper, we focus specifically on the issues involved in *replaying* multiple planning cases.

We introduce why the use of planning cases can reduce planning search and provide an improvement in planning efficiency. The contributions of the paper build upon this analysis for the introduction of several strategies that merge multiple planning cases.

We first introduce serial replay, in which a single case is replayed before planning for any new goals in the new planning situation. Serial replay is shown to be appropriate when the new situation is an extension of the past case. We then introduce sequential replay where multiple cases are merged according to a predefined ordering. New steps may be added and parts of the cases may be deleted to provide a suitable connection between the cases. For the general case where multiple cases are presented unordered to the replay procedure, we introduce ordering-based and choice-and-ordering-based interleaved replay. For these two merge strategies, the replay algorithm reasons about step orderings and information-dependent step choice commitments and constraints. Choice-and-ordering-based interleaved replay is built upon new information-dependent links that capture the dependency between the choice of plan steps and state information gathered from simulation or real execution. We briefly discuss that choice-and-ordering-based may be appropriate to multi-agent planning and execution environments. An extensive empirical analysis of the domain-dependent tradeoffs and suitability of the different merge strategies is part of our research agenda.

References

[Alexander and Tsatsoulis, 1991] Perry Alexander and Costas Tsatsoulis. Using sub-cases for skeletal planning and partial case reuse. *International Journal of Expert Systems Research and Applications*, 4-2:221–247, 1991.

[Barrett and Weld, 1994] Anthony Barrett and Daniel S. Weld. Partial-order planning: Evaluating possible efficiency gains. *Artificial Intelligence*, 67:71–112, 1994.

[Carbonell, 1986] Jaime G. Carbonell. Derivational analogy: A theory of reconstructive problem solving and expertise acquisition. In R. S. Michalski, J. G. Carbonell, and T. M. Mitchell, editors, *Machine Learning, An Artificial Intelligence Approach, Volume II*, pages 371–392. Morgan Kaufman, 1986.

[Fikes and Nilsson, 1971] Richard E. Fikes and Nils J. Nilsson. Strips: A new approach to the application of theorem proving to problem solving. *Artificial Intelligence*, 2:189–208, 1971.

[Haigh and Veloso, 1995] Karen Zita Haigh and Manuela M. Veloso. Route planning by analogy. In *Case-Based Reasoning Research and Development, Proceedings of ICCBR-95*, pages 169–180. Springer-Verlag, October 1995.

[Haigh et al., 1997] Karen Z. Haigh, Jonathan Shewchuk, and Manuela M. Veloso. Exploring geometry in analogical route planning. *To appear in Journal of Experimental and Theoretical Artificial Intelligence*, 1997.

[Hammond, 1986] Kristian J. Hammond. *Case-based Planning: An Integrated Theory of Planning, Learning and Memory.* PhD thesis, Yale University, 1986.

[Hanks and Weld, 1995] Steve Hanks and Dan S. Weld. A domain-independent algorithm for plan adaptation. *Journal of Artificial Intelligence Research*, 2:319–360, 1995.

[Ihrig and Kambhampati, 1994] Laurie Ihrig and Subbarao Kambhampati. Derivational replay for partial-order planning. In *Proceedings of the Twelfth National Conference on Artificial Intelligence*, pages 992–997, 1994.

[Kambhampati and Hendler, 1992] Subbarao Kambhampati and James A. Hendler. A validation based theory of plan modification and reuse. *Artificial Intelligence*, 55(2-3):193–258, 1992.

[Kettler et al., 1994] B. P. Kettler, J. A. Hendler, A. W. Andersen, and M. P. Evett. Massively parallel support for case-based planning. *IEEE Expert*, 2:8–14, 1994.

[López and Plaza, 1993] B. López and E. Plaza. Case-based planning for medical diagnosis. In J. Romorowski and Z. W. Ras, editors, *Methodologies for Intelligent Systems (Proceedings of ISMIS'93)*. Springer Verlag, 1993.

[Minton et al., 1989] Steven Minton, Craig A. Knoblock, Dan R. Kuokka, Yolanda Gil, Robert L. Joseph, and Jaime G. Carbonell. PRODIGY 2.0: The manual and tutorial. Technical Report CMU-CS-89-146, School of Computer Science, Carnegie Mellon University, 1989.

[Muñoz-Avila et al., 1994] Héctor Muñoz-Avila, Juergen Paulokat, and Stefan Wess. Controlling a nonlinear hierarchical planner using case-based reasoning. In *Proceedings of the 1994 European Workshop on Case-Based Reasoning*, November 1994.

[Pryor and Collins, 1992] Louise Pryor and Gregg Collins. Cassandra: Planning for contingencies. Technical report, The Institute for the Learning Sciences, Northwestern University, 1992.

[Ram and Francis, 1996] Ashwin Ram and Anthony G. Francis. Multi-plan retrieval and adaptation in an experience-based agent. In David B. Leake, editor, *Case-Based Reasoning: experiences, lessons, and future directions*, pages 167–184. AAAI Press/The MIT Press, 1996.

[Redmond, 1990] Michael Redmond. Distributed cases for case-based reasoning; Facilitating the use of multiple cases. In *Proceedings of the Eighth National Conference on Artificial Intelligence*, pages 304–309, Cambridge, MA, 1990. AAAI Press/The MIT Press.

[Smyth and Keane, 1995] Barry Smyth and MArk T. Keane. Experiments on adaptation-guided retrieval in case-based design. In M. Veloso and Agnar Aamodt, editors, *Case-Based Reasoning Research and Development*, pages 313–324. Springer Verlag, October 1995.

[Stone and Veloso, 1996] Peter Stone and Manuela M. Veloso. User-guided interleaving of planning and execution. In *New Directions in AI Planning*, pages 103–112. IOS Press, 1996.

[Veloso and Blythe, 1994] Manuela M. Veloso and Jim Blythe. Linkability: Examining causal link commitments in partial-order planning. In *Proceedings of the Second International Conference on AI Planning Systems*, pages 170–175, June 1994.

[Veloso and Stone, 1995] Manuela M. Veloso and Peter Stone. FLECS: Planning with a flexible commitment strategy. *Journal of Artificial Intelligence Research*, 3:25–52, 1995.

[Veloso et al., 1995] Manuela M. Veloso, Jaime Carbonell, M. Alicia Pérez, Daniel Borrajo, Eugene Fink, and Jim Blythe. Integrating planning and learning: The PRODIGY architecture. *Journal of Experimental and Theoretical Artificial Intelligence*, 7(1):81–120, 1995.

[Veloso, 1994] Manuela M. Veloso. *Planning and Learning by Analogical Reasoning*. Springer Verlag, December 1994.

[Wang and Veloso, 1994] Xuemei Wang and Manuela M. Veloso. Learning planning knowledge by observation and practice. In *Proceedings of the ARPA Planning Workshop*, pages 285–294, Tucson, AZ, February 1994.

Loose Coupling of Failure Explanation and Repair: Using Learning Goals to Sequence Learning Methods

Michael T. Cox

Computer Science Department. Carnegie Mellon University
Pittsburgh, PA 15213-3891
mcox@cs.cmu.edu

Abstract. Because learning methods (i.e., knowledge repairs) can negatively interact, the arbitrary ordering of knowledge repairs can lead to worse system performance than no learning at all. Therefore, the problem of choosing appropriate learning methods given a performance failure is a significant problem for learning systems. Traditional case-based reasoners index learning or repair methods by specific failure characteristics so that once a failure is detected, a learning method can be brought to bear. Such *tight coupling* can be contrasted to a *loose coupling* in which the interaction between failure explanation and learning is mediated by the presence of learning goals generated by the learner. In an empirical study, the Meta-AQUA implementation performed significantly better under the guidance of learning goals (loose coupling) than under a condition in which learning goals were ablated (tight coupling). The conclusion is that unless repair interactions are known not to exist, a loose coupling is necessary for effective learning.

1 Introduction

Many case-based reasoning systems pursue a failure-driven approach to learning in order to guarantee that something worth learning exists. The systems use an analysis of typical failure situations to guide the learning and to focus it on those aspects of memory requiring change. The typical system uses some characterization of the failure as an index into memory in order to retrieve a repair method appropriate to fixing the fault that caused the failure. Given *multiple concurrent failures* each with an associated repair method, however, the learning methods may negatively interact if they are not sequenced carefully. In general, it is unreasonable to assume that all learning algorithms are functionally independent. For instance, if a memory decay function deletes any memory element at or below a given confidence threshold, and a reinforcement function increments the confidence values of particular memory elements, then clearly the second function call must precede the first; otherwise, any common elements at threshold will be "forgotten" and not strengthened. The problem is that, until now, very little research has been focussed on the effects of multiple concurrent failures. To address the negative interactions between repair methods that appear in such situations, this paper will argue that an intermediate mechanism must be inserted between failure analysis and knowledge repair.

Tight coupling involves a direct mapping of failure to repair method (Owens, 1990b); whereas, *loose coupling* involves a more indirect mechanism that not only selects a repair, but sequences repairs when more than one exists (Cox, 1996). Indexing implementations of tight coupling have been used in a number of well-known case-based reasoners. CHEF, a case-based planner, uses configurations of goal failures to directly map to strategies for plan repair (Hammond, 1989). The TWEAKER module of SWALE, a case-based explainer, uses a taxonomy of explanation pattern (XP) failure types that directly map to strategies for repair of XPs (Kass, 1990). Both systems use direct mapping (indexing) techniques to associate particular failure symptoms with specific repair methods. For instance, the SWALE program explains the unexpected death of a healthy thoroughbred using the "Jim Fixx" XP. Jim Fixx was a world-class athlete who died of a congestive heart failure while jogging. When applying the XP to the death of Swale, the XP fails because it expects Swale to be a human jogger. The failure type NORMATIVE-FILLER-VIOLATION directly points to a repair strategy that adapts the old explanation to fit the current situation and stores the new explanation for similar future situations (Kass, 1986).

Other CBR programs use a tight coupling approach from an explanation of failure (i.e., the failure cause) to repair, rather than from symptom of failure to repair. CELIA (Redmond, 1992), a case-based trouble-shooting apprentice, explains its failure to predict expert problem-solving behavior using a discrimination net. The resultant failure characterization indexes a repair method. The use of plan failure explanation patterns (PFXPs) by the Anon case-based planning system (Owens, 1990a) improves on this tactic by using the failure symptom to index to an abstract PFXP. The PFXP is then applied to the failure in order to generate an explanation of the failure (in much the same way that SWALE uses XPs to explain Fixx's death). The instantiated PFXP is also used as an index to retrieve the right plan repair method. But although the principle of tight coupling is useful to explain the failure, it presents problems for repair selection when multiple faults occur and negatively interacting repairs exist.

Analogous problems have been shown to exist with respect to intelligent planners. In Sussman's anomaly (Sussman, 1975), for instance, a negative interaction in planning occurs when the side-effect of one plan step removes a precondition of another step. Likewise, if a repair method specifies a change to the memory of the system, as opposed to a change in the state of the world, then repair methods can have similar interactions. For example, any change to a concept attribute during abstraction must occur before a separate indexing function uses the same attribute during memory reorganization, otherwise the new index can become obsolete after the abstraction (Cox & Ram, 1995).

A loose coupling solution to the problems above is to insert an additional process between failure explanation and failure repair in order to sequence the repair strategies and avoid interactions. This process takes an explanation of failure and generates a specific *learning goal*. A learning goal is an explicit specification of some change to the systems memory and is used to focus learning (Ram & Leake, 1995). Given a learning goal, the learner then needs to plan for the goal as it would for planning in the blocks world. A learning plan is created composed of a series of repairs that achieve the goals without negative side-effects. Therefore, the solution is to partition learning into three stages. First, failure is explained by mapping failure symptom to failure cause using case-based reasoning. Secondly, this explanation is used to generate a set of learning goals that specify specific changes to the systems memory. Finally, a nonlinear planner sequences a corresponding set of repair methods to achieve the learning goals while avoiding negative interactions. This paper will empirically compare and contrast such loose coupling to a more tightly coupled solution.

Section 2 briefly presents the Meta-AQUA system by describing the input generation module with which experimental trials are generated and by providing a brief explanation of the performance and learning tasks. Section 3 provides a computational experiment designed to compare learning under tight and loose coupling using data obtained from the Meta-AQUA system. Section 4 summarizes the results and concludes with a short discussion.

2 Meta-AQUA

Meta-AQUA is a learning system that chooses and combines multiple learning methods from a toolbox of algorithms in order to repair faulty components responsible for failures encountered during a story-understanding task. A problem generation module outputs a story to the performance system with the initial goal to understand the input. The performance module uses causal schemas from memory to interpret the story and to build a coherent representation for it using case-based explanation (Schank, Kass, & Riesbeck, 1994). If the performance task fails, then a trace of the reasoning preceding the failure is passed to the learning subsystem. A CBR component within the learner uses past cases of introspective reasoning to explain the comprehension failure and to generate a set of learning goals. These goals, along with the trace, are then passed to a nonlinear planner. The planner subsequently builds a learning strategy from its toolbox of learning methods. The learning plan is passed to an execution system that examines and changes memory items.

Although the algorithms used by Meta-AQUA have been reported elsewhere (e.g., Cox 1996; Cox & Ram 1995; Ram & Cox 1994), this section outlines the system in order to provide a context for understanding the evaluation. See also the companion paper in this volume (Cox, 1997) that describes the knowledge structures used by the system.

2.1 Story Understanding

To support large data collection, a story generation program provides a potentially infinite number of input variations that test Meta-AQUA's ability to learn from explanation failure. Given a main character and a problem, the generator simulates the actions that would be necessary for the character to achieve goals stemming from the problem. For example if a character is bored, it assigns the character an initial goal to remove the state of boredom. The character can achieve the goal by convincing a friend to play, finding a ball, going outside, and then batting the ball back and forth (see Figure 1). For each event in the story, the generator adds any associated causal results. These results change the world and enable further actions by characters in the story. For example, the act of getting the ball and going outside enables the hitting of the ball which results in the ball's movement between the characters. In turn, these actions remove the boredom. The story terminates when the goals and subgoals of the main character have been achieved or when all possible plans to achieve them have been exhausted.

To facilitate the performance task, we programmed the story-generation program so it generates explanations of key events in the stories. The resolution of all anomalies are thereby incorporated within each story. For example, the story generator includes a reason why Dad strikes the ball in the story above because it knows that Meta-AQUA will find the action anomalous and thus try to explain it.

```
Lynn was bored and asked Dad, "Do you want to play ball?" Then
Dad went to the garage and picked up a baseball, and they went
outside to play with it. He hit the ball hard so that it would
reach her in left field. Lynn threw the ball back. They con-
tinued like this all afternoon. Because of the game, Lynn was
no longer bored.
                       --- The End ---
```

Fig. 1. Sample input story

2.2 Explanation and Learning (Repair)

The Meta-AQUA system learns about drug-smuggling and sports activities, given a library of prior cases about terrorists and its general knowledge of physical causality. The systems' performance task is to "understand" stories by building causal explanations that link the individual events into a coherent whole. When an anomalous or otherwise interesting input is detected, the system builds an explanation of the event, incorporating it into the preexisting model of the story.

In the story from Figure 1 for example, Meta-AQUA finds it unusual for a person to strike a ball because its concept of "hit" constrains the object attribute to animate objects. It tries to explain the action by hypothesizing that Dad tried to hurt the ball (an abstract explanation pattern, or XP, retrieved from memory instantiates this explanation). However, the story specifies an alternate explanation (i.e., the hit action is intended to move the ball to the opposing person). This input causes an expectation failure (contradiction) because the system had expected one explanation to be true, but another proved true instead.

When Meta-AQUA detects an explanation failure, the performance module passes a trace of the reasoning to the learning subsystem. The learner is composed of a CBR module for self-diagnosis and learning-goal generation and a non-linear planner for learning-strategy selection or construction. At this time, the learner needs to explain why the failure occurred by applying an introspective explanation to the trace. A meta-explanation (Meta-XP) is retrieved using the failure symptom as a probe into memory (Cox, 1997). Meta-AQUA instantiates the retrieved meta-explanation and binds it to the trace of reasoning that preceded the failure. The resulting structure is then checked for applicability. If the Meta-XP does not apply correctly, then another probe is attempted. An accepted Meta-XP either provides a set of learning goals that are designed to modify the system's memory or generates additional questions to be posed about the failure. Once a set of learning goals is posted, the goals are passed to the nonlinear planner for building a learning plan.

Figure 2 lists the major state transitions that the learning processes produce. The learning plan is fully ordered to avoid interactions. For example, the abstraction step must precede the other steps. A knowledge dependency exists between the changes on the hit concept as a result of the abstraction and the use of this concept by both generalization and the indexing.[1] After the learning is executed and control returns to sentence processing,

---

1. During mutual re-indexing, the explanations are differentiated based on the object attribute-value of the hit. However, the abstraction repair changes this attribute. The generalization method applied to the new explanation also uses this attribute. See Cox (1996) for a more complete analysis.

Symptoms:
Contradiction between input and memory
Contradiction between expected explanation and actual explanation

Faults:
Incorrect domain knowledge
Novel situation
Erroneous association

Learning Goals:
Reconcile input with conceptual definition
Differentiate two explanations

Learning Plan:
Abstraction on concept of hit
Generalization on hit explanation
Index new explanation
Mutually re-index two explanations

Plan Execution Results:
Object of hit constrained to physical obj, not animate obj
New case of movement explanation acquired and indexed
Index of hurt-explan = animate obj; of move-explan = inanimate obj.

Fig. 2. Learning from Explanation Failure

subsequent sentences concerning the hit predicate causes no anomaly. Instead, Meta-AQUA predicts the proper explanation.

3 Computational Evaluation

This section presents the results of computational studies performed with Meta-AQUA to compare tight and loose coupling. We assert that the rate of improvement in story understanding with learning goals exceeds that of story understanding without learning goals holding all other factors constant. Our hypothesis is that when repair methods interact negatively, loose coupling is *necessary* for effective learning. Converging with the arguments and hand-coded examples from previous research that favor this position (e.g., Cox & Ram 1995), this paper presents quantitative evidence that supports the utility of this stage.

The independent variable is the presence and influence of learning goals. The first experimental condition is referred to as the learning goal (LG) condition, and represents Meta-AQUA as briefly described earlier in this article. Under the LG condition, the system builds a learning strategy. This construction is guided by the learning goals spawned by the Meta-XPs that explain the failure. Hence, this condition represents a loose coupling approach between fault (failure cause) and repair (learning).

The second condition is called the random learning (RL) condition. Given an explanation of the causes of failure, the system directly assigns calls to particular learning algorithms for each fault. The construction of the learning plan is then performed by a random ordering of these function calls, rather than by non-linear planning to achieve the learning goals. In the example from Section 2, the learning goals would not be generated as shown in Figure 2 and thus the order of the learning-plan steps are not determined by a planner. Instead, failure analysis is performed as usual to determine the three faults and then a lookup table maps the faults to corresponding repair strategies (i.e., abstraction, generalization, and index learning). The order of these repairs are then assigned on a random basis. The RL condition represents a tight coupling approach (i.e., direct mapping from fault, or failure cause, to repair) that forgoes the use of learning goals altogether.

The final condition is called the no learning (NL) condition in which Meta-AQUA performs story understanding, but if a failure exists, the system performs no failure analysis, generates no learning goals, and constructs no learning strategy. This condition represents the baseline performance from which both the LG and RL conditions can be compared. Holding all parameters constant except the independent variable, Meta-AQUA is given input from the story generator and the dependent variable is measured.

The dependent variable measures story understanding by rating the ability of the system to generate plausible explanations about key points in the story. The evaluation criterion in Meta-AQUA assigns credit as follows. For each anomalous or interesting input in a story, a point is given for posing a question, an additional point is given for providing any answer whatsoever, and a third point is assigned for answering what the researcher judges correct. The sum represents the dependent variable.

3.1 Experimental Data

To serve as experimental trials and to minimize order effects, the story generator outputs six random sequences of stories. During each of these experiments, Meta-AQUA processes a sequence three times, once for each experimental manipulation. The system begins all experiments with the same initial conditions. For a given experimental condition, it processes all of the stories in the sequence while maintaining the learned knowledge between stories. At the end of the sequence, the system resets memory to its original state. The input size for each experiment varies in length, but averages 27.67 stories per experiment. The corpus for the six experiments includes 166 stories, comprising a total of 4,884 sentences. The stories vary in size depending on the actions of the story and the generator's randomness parameters, but average 29.42 sentences.

Experiment number four is particularly interesting because the greatest number of learning interactions occur in this set. The input to experiment four consists of 24 stories that contain a total of 715 sentences. The average number of sentences per story is 29.8. Table 1 summarizes the totals. The dependent variable (column 5) shows that Meta-AQUA's performance under the LG condition is significantly greater than the performance under the RL condition. In turn, Meta-AQUA performance in the RL condition far exceeded the performance under the NL condition.

Table 1: Results from experiment four

Learning Condition	Questions Posed	Answered Questions	Correct Answers	Question Points	Learning Episodes
LG	38	28	25	91	8
RL	38	15	7	60	26
NL	32	13	1	46	0

Alternatively, if only absolute performance (column 4) is considered, the differential is even greater. By this measure, the LG condition is more than three times the value of the RL condition, whereas, the performance of the NL condition is insignificant. By looking at column three, however, the numbers of questions answered in some way (right or wrong), are roughly equivalent in the RL and NL conditions, whereas the ratio of the LG condition to either of the other two is 2:1. Finally, the number of questions posed are virtually equal across all three conditions.

In contrast to these differences, Meta-AQUA attempts to learn from failure more than three times as often under the RL condition as under the LG condition. That is, learning is more *effective* with learning goals than without. In the RL condition, learning does not increase performance as much as does the LG condition, while concurrently, it leads Meta-AQUA to expend more resources by increasing the amount of learning episodes. Thus, the system works harder and gains less under RL than under LG.

Figure 3 graphs the accumulation of question points across all 24 trials (i.e., stories) of experiment number four. The behavior of the system as measured by the dependent variable is greatest under the LG condition, next best under RL, and worst under the NL condition. But, the trend does not hold for each trial. The NL condition actually outperforms the RL condition on trial number 14 of experiment four. The reason for this effect is that under worse-case conditions, if the interactions present between learning methods are negative, the performance may actually degrade. As a result, randomly ordered learning may be worse than no learning at all.

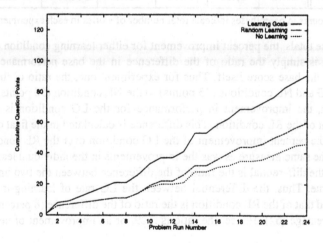

Fig. 3. Question points

The differences as a function of the independent variable are even more pronounced if only accuracy (the number of correct answers) is examined and partial credit ignored. Under the RL condition, Meta-AQUA did not answer a question correctly until trial number 10, whereas under the NL condition, it did not perform correctly until trial 21. On the other hand, because under the LG condition the system learned a new explanation early in trial number 1, it was able to answer a question by trial number two.

3.2 Overall Results

Table 2 summarizes the evaluation data from the six program experiments. As is evident across all runs, the LG condition consistently outperforms the RL condition in the total cumulative question points. In turn, the RL condition outperforms the NL condition, despite the occasional poor performance due to negative interactions. As indicated by the standard deviations, the amount of differences between and within conditions exhibit high variability across experiments.

Table 2: Summary of cumulative results

Experiment	Cumulative Question Points			% LG	% RL	% Differential
Number[a]	LG	RL	NL	Improved	Improved	Improvement
Run 1 (34)	85	81	50	70.00	62.00	12.90
Run 2 (30)	106	98	43	146.51	127.91	14.55
Run 3 (28)	120	102	60	100.00	70.00	42.86
Run 4 (24)	91	60	46	97.83	30.43	221.43
Run 5 (22)	57	49	27	111.11	81.48	36.36
Run 6 (28)	103	66	54	90.74	22.22	308.33
Averages	93.67	76.00	46.67	102.70	65.67	106.07
Std. Dev.	21.72	21.31	11.34	25.43	38.17	126.59

a. Amounts in parentheses indicate total number of stories in each experiment.

Given these totals, the percent improvement for either learning condition over the NL base condition is simply the ratio of the difference in the base performance score and either score to the base score itself. Thus for experiment one, the ratio of the difference between the LG and NL conditions (35 points) to the NL condition (50 points) is .7, or 70 percent. Again, the improvement in performance for the LG condition is consistently higher than that of the RL condition. This difference is calculated in the final column. The differential is the percent improvement of the LG condition over the RL condition and is computed by the same measure as was the improvements in the individual learning conditions. That is, the differential is the ratio of the difference between the two improvements to the lower rate. Thus, the differential between the LG rate of learning in experiment number one and that of the RL condition is the ratio of the difference (8 percentage points) to the RL percentage (62). Hence, the ratio is .129, or an improvement of nearly 13 percent.

Although the average differential between the two learning conditions (i.e., between loosely coupled and tightly coupled learning) is more than 106 percent with a large standard deviation, this figure still overstates the difference. The expected gain in learning is more conservative. The differential between the average LG improvement (102.70) and the average RL improvement (65.67) is a 56.38 percent difference. That is, across a number of input conditions, the use of learning goals to order and combine learning choices should show about 1.5 times the improvement in performance than will a straight mapping of faults to repairs when interactions are present.

4 Summary and Discussion

The experiments reported in this paper provide a number of results that support the hypothesis that loose coupling between failure explanation and repair is preferred over tight coupling when repair interactions exist. Meta-AQUA expended more learning resources and induced less performance improvement without learning goals than it did under a condition that included them. We have shown that because learning algorithms can negatively interact, the arbitrary ordering of learning methods (i.e., as under the RL condition) can actually lead to worse system performance than no learning at all. Thus, an explicit phase to decide exactly what to learn (i.e., to spawn learning goals or an equivalent mechanism) is *necessary* to avoid these interactions and to maintain effective learning in multistrategy environments.

Therefore, a tight coupling approach, such as that used by the Anon system, has distinct disadvantages when multiple faults occur simultaneously. Anon's plan failure explanation patterns must contain not only pointers to the repair strategies relevant to particular failures, but they must also contain information concerning how these strategies are interleaved. An additional issue also arises concerning what happens when two or more PFXPs both apply (e.g., how can Anon manage learning when PFXPs representing both *too many cooks spoil the broth* and *you can catch more flies with honey than you can with vinegar* apply to a given situation? cf. Owens, 1990a). If the interactions involved are captured in more complex PFXP types and if the researcher does not anticipate all of them, then the burden of acquiring these composite patterns is upon the learning system. Such interactions are managed naturally with a nonlinear planner when only the constituent failure types and the associated learning goals are specified by the researcher. Even if the tight coupling approach can acquire information about interactions, such a system must dynamically monitor its learning for goal violations (a process that is explicitly performed by standard planners).

Although the results reported in this paper challenge some of the assumptions contained in traditional indexing schemes for case-based learners, it must be emphasized that Meta-AQUA shares a greater intersection of technique and philosophy with the CBR systems reviewed here than with any learning system outside of CBR. Indeed, Meta-AQUA builds on their successes in defining a failure-driven approach to learning and an expectation-driven approach to performance. Moreover, the Meta-AQUA program is a direct descendant of an earlier case-based understanding system (AQUA. Ram, 1994) in this same generation of learners. Finally, the empirical results stem from a deliberate inclusion of repair methods that are known to interact. Given a suite of repair methods devoid of interactions, a tightly coupled approach represents a more straight-forward and efficient implementation. However, given a dynamic source of learning methods, a loose coupling represents the safer and more effective alternative.

Acknowledgments

This research was supported by AFOSR contract #F49620-94-1-0092 and by NSF contract IRI-9009710. I also thank the anonymous reviewers for their insights.

References

1. Cox, M. T. (1996). Introspective multistrategy learning: Constructing a learning strategy under reasoning failure. Doctoral dissertation, Tech. Rep. No. GIT-CC-96-06, Georgia Institute of Technology, College of Computing, Atlanta. (Available at URL ftp://ftp.cc.gatech.edu/pub/ai/ram/git-cc-96-06.html)

2. Cox, M. T. (1997). *An explicit representation of reasoning failures.* This volume.

3. Cox, M. T., & Ram, A. (1995). Interacting learning-goals: Treating learning as a planning task. In J.-P. Haton, M. Keane & M. Manago (Eds.), *Advances in case-based reasoning: Second European Workshop, EWCBR-94* (pp. 60-74). Berlin: Springer-Verlag.

4. Hammond, K. J. (1989). *Case-based planning: Viewing planning as a memory task. Vol. 1.* of *Perspectives in artificial intelligence.* San Diego, CA: Academic Press.

5. Kass, A. (1986). Modifying explanations to understand stories. In *Proceedings of Eighth Annual Conference of the Cognitive Science Society* (pp. 691-696). Hillsdale, NJ: Lawrence Erlbaum Associates.

6. Kass, A. (1990). *Developing creative hypotheses by adapting explanations.* Doctoral dissertation, Northwestern University, The Institute for the Learning Sciences, Evanston, IL.

7. Owens, C. (1990a). *Indexing and retrieving abstract planning knowledge.* Doctoral dissertation, Yale University, Department of Computer Science, New Haven, CT.

8. Owens, C. (1990b). Representing abstract plan failures. In *Proceedings of Twelfth Annual Conference of the Cognitive Science Society* (pp. 277-284). Hillsdale, NJ: Lawrence Erlbaum Associates.

9. Ram, A. (1994). AQUA: Questions that drive the understanding process. In R. C. Schank, A. Kass, & C. K. Riesbeck (Eds.), *Inside case-based explanation* (pp. 207-261). Hillsdale, NJ: Lawrence Erlbaum Associates

10. Ram, A., & Cox, M. T. (1994). Introspective reasoning using meta-explanations for multistrategy learning. In R. S. Michalski & G. Tecuci (Eds.), *Machine learning IV: A multistrategy approach* (pp. 349-377). San Francisco: Morgan Kaufmann.

11. Ram, A., & Leake, D. (1995). Learning, goals, and learning goals. In A. Ram & D. Leake (Eds.), *Goal-driven learning* (pp. 1-37). Cambridge, MA: MIT Press/Bradford Books.

12. Redmond, M. A. (1992). *Learning by observing and understanding expert problem solving* (Tech. Rep. No. GIT-CC-92/43). Doctoral dissertation, Georgia Institute of Technology, College of Computing, Atlanta.

13. Schank, R. C., Kass, A., & Riesbeck, C. K. (1994). *Inside case-based explanation.* Hillsdale, NJ: Lawrence Erlbaum Associates.

14. Sussman, G. J. (1975). *A computer model of skill acquisition.* New York: American Elsevier.

Using a Case Base of Surfaces to Speed-Up Reinforcement Learning

Chris Drummond

Department of Computer Science, University of Ottawa
Ottawa, Ontario, Canada, K1N 6N5
cdrummon@csi.uottawa.ca

Abstract. This paper demonstrates the exploitation of certain vision processing techniques to index into a case base of surfaces. The surfaces are the result of reinforcement learning and represent the optimum choice of actions to achieve some goal from anywhere in the state space. This paper shows how strong features that occur in the interaction of the system with its environment can be detected early in the learning process. Such features allow the system to identify when an identical, or very similar, task has been solved previously and to retrieve the relevant surface. This results in an orders of magnitude increase in learning rate.

1 Introduction

One important research issue for case based learning is its combination with other learning methods. As Aamodt and Plaza [1] point out, generally the machine learning community aims to produce "a coherent framework, where each learning method fulfills a specific and distinct role in the system." This paper discusses one such approach, combining case based and reinforcement learning. An advantage of the latter method is that it learns even when the information available is very limited. It requires only knowledge of its present state and infrequent real values of reward to learn the actions necessary to bring a system to some desired goal state. As often occurs in achieving this level of generality, the learning rate is slow. It is important then to exploit the results of prior learning and it would be a definite advantage to quickly recognise that the task, or a similar one, has been solved previously.

This paper explores the idea of storing the results of learning in a case base. A critical issue, as in most case based systems, is how to recognise and index these cases. The central intuition of this work is that there are strong features in an environment. Here "strong" means that the features are stable and easy to recognise accurately early in the learning process. The environment here includes the system. The features are not "in the world" but in the system's interaction with the world. This interaction can be represented by a surface, a multi-dimensional function. For the notion of strong features to be effective, they must largely dictate the shape of this surface. If the features differ by a small amount one would expect the surface to differ by a small amount. Research [9] has shown that a function can be accurately reconstructed from a record of its steep slopes. In this work, tasks producing similar features result in the same surfaces, at some qualitative abstraction.

This paper takes much of its insight from work done in vision and is closely related to Marr's early work [10]. The features are essentially Marr's zero crossing points. A popular technique in object recognition, the snake [14], will be used to locate and characterise these features. One important difference in this research, is that recognising the task is not an end in itself but is a means of initialising another learning process. Thus the recognition process need only be accurate enough to produce a significant speedup in the learning process, averaged over many learning episodes.

In the rest of the paper, Section 2 discusses the case base, giving a brief introduction to reinforcement learning and snakes. Section 3 presents experiments demonstrating feature extraction and how this leads to a substantial reduction of learning time. Following sections deal with limitations, future work and related research.

2 The Case Base

The case base consists of two parts: the cases and the indices. A *case* is a surface obtained using reinforcement learning on a particular task. An *index* is a curve associated with strong features of these surfaces extracted through the use of a snake. The rest of this section discusses how the cases and indices are produced.

2.1 Reinforcement Learning

A simulated robot environment of a main room and an inner room containing the goal is shown as the bold lines in figure 1 (the significance of the dashed lines will be made clear in Section 3). The robot's actions are small steps in any of eight directions. The learning task is to determine the shortest path to the goal from any start location. Here the location, or state, is simply the robot's x and y coordinates. The legal range of the coordinates, defined by the walls of the main room, is the state space. Under the simplifying assumption that the effect of an action is not dependent on previous actions, the task becomes one of learning the best action in any state. The best overall action would be one that takes the robot immediately to the goal. But this is only possible in states close to the goal. The problem is how to evaluate actions in other states, which may result in progress towards the goal without reaching it. This is often termed the credit assignment problem.

This problem has been the focus of much work in the reinforcement learning community. To address it an action is evaluated not by waiting until the final outcome of the task, but rather by correlating it to the evaluation of the best action in the next state [15]. For the robot learning task, at each state an estimate of the distance to the goal could be kept. This estimate would be the result of the best local action, one moving the robot to the new state with the smallest estimate of distance to goal. Early in the learning process only states close to the

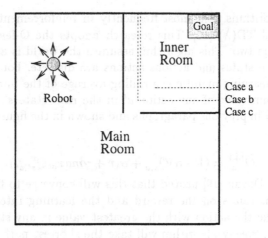

Goal

Inner
Room

Robot

Case a
Case b
Case c

Main
Room

Fig. 1. A Room Within a Room

goal are likely to have accurate estimates of true distance. Each time an action is taken, the estimate of the new state is used to update the estimate of the old state. Eventually this process will propagate back accurate estimates from the goal to all other states.

Rather than directly recording the distance to goal, this paper uses the more usual representation of reinforcement learning, the expected discounted reward for each state $E[\sum_{t=1}^{\infty} \gamma^t r_t]$. The influence of rewards, r_t, are reduced progressively the farther into the future they occur by using a γ less than one. In this work, the only reward is for reaching the goal. So the farther the state is from the goal the smaller the value. This forms a *surface* over the state space. Figure 2a shows such a surface produced by the learning process using the environment of figure 1.

The plot of figure 2b represents the magnitude of the gradient vector of this surface. Thus the absolute value of the state gradient (say direction) forms

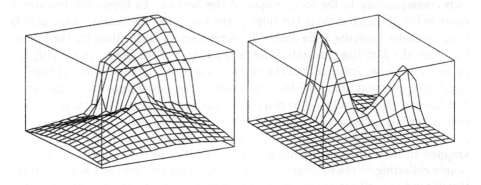

Fig. 2.   a) A Surface   b) Its Gradient Vector

The two algorithms used most frequently in reinforcement learning are Q-learning [19] and TD(λ) [16]. This research adopts the Q-learning algorithm, the simpler of the two. This algorithm assumes the world is a discrete Markov process thus both states and actions actions are discrete. For each action a in each state s, Q-learning maintains a rolling average of the immediate reward r plus the maximum value of any action a' in the next state s', equation 1. The surface discussed in previous paragraphs and shown in the figures represents this maximum value.

$$Q_{s,a}^{t+1} = (1 - \alpha)Q_{s,a}^t + \alpha(r + \gamma max_{a'}Q_{s',a'}^t) \qquad (1)$$

Watkins and Dayan [19] proved that this will converge to the optimal value with certain constraints on the reward and the learning rate α. The optimal solution is to take the action with the greatest value in any state. Thus in this robot problem, a greedy algorithm will take the shortest path to the goal. The extension to continuous spaces can be done using function approximation. The simplest method, and the one used here, is to divide both the state and action dimensions into intervals. Each resulting cell then represents the average of a range of actions taken from a region in the state space. In many applications this method is successful but there exists no general proof of its convergence.

2.2 Feature Extraction

In the plot of figure 2a, one can see two steep slopes separating a raised area from the rest of the plot. Comparing this to the environment shown in figure 1 it is apparent that these correspond to the walls of the inner room. These are the *strong features* discussed in this paper. They exist because the distance to goal is much less when the robot is at the side of the wall inside of the room than when it is outside the room. These features are visually readily apparent to a human, so it seems intuitive to use vision processing techniques to locate them.

The plot of figure 2b represents the magnitude of the gradient vector of this surface. This is the absolute value of the largest gradient in any direction, it forms hills corresponding to the steep slopes of the surface. To locate the features a curve is found that lies along the ridge of the two hills. The method used here is called a snake. In figure 3 the dashed lines represent contour lines for the hills of figure 2b, the dark lines the initial and final position of the snake. To simplify the exposition, we can imagine that the snake consists of a number of individual hill climbers spread out along the line representing the initial position of the snake. But instead of being allowed to climb independently their movement relative to each other is constrained. The main advantages of this approach is that the curve produced is relatively smooth and it tends to prevent individual points getting trapped in local minima. Additional characteristics of the process prevent the points collecting at the hills' apices. When the snake reaches the top of the ridge it will tend to oscillate around an equilibrium position, by limiting the step size the process can be brought into a stationary state. A more detailed mathematical treatment of this approach is given in [6].

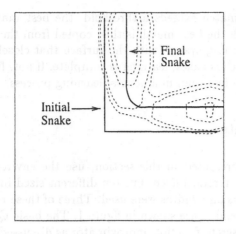

Fig. 3. Fitting the Snake

2.3 Constructing and Using the Case Base

As discussed at the beginning of this section, the case is exactly the surface produced by reinforcement learning. Multiple cases are produced by allowing the process to converge (when changes in the action values are less than some small amount) for different room configurations. Associated with each surface is a curve, the snake. The curve is positioned in the (x, y) plane, defining the bounds of the inner room. Of course, another critical aspect of the room is the position of the doorway. Looking at the gradient plot of figure 2b, the doorway is the valley separating the ends of the two hills. The width and position of the doorway can be determined from the magnitude of the gradient along the snake. The index consists of the (x, y) coordinates of sixty-four points along the snake and the surface gradient at these points.

When a new room configuration is being learnt, at fixed intervals the snake fitting procedure is repeated on the new surface. All snakes for the existing cases are retrieved. Their distances, $D(., ., .)$, from the new snake are determined using the weighted sum of two Euclidean norms, equation 2 where the superscript n is the new snake and c the case index. The actual magnitude of the differential was not used in the norm, as it varies considerably during the learning process. But the position of the snake and the position of the valley are largely static. To remove the effect of this variation, the magnitude values are thresholded, $Th()$, by the mean magnitude along the snake producing a vector of ones and zeros. The difference between thresholded magnitude values is much greater than that between location values. So the location norm is multiplied by a scaling factor of ten to normalise the sum.

$$D(s^n, s^c) = 10(\sum_i (x_i^n - x_i^c)^2 + (y_i^n - y_i^c)^2)^{1/2} + (\sum_i (Th(m_i^n) - Th(m_i^c))^2)^{1/2} \quad (2)$$

Providing this match exceeds a threshold, the best match is selected. The case associated with the best match is then copied from the case base and used to initialise the learning system with the surface that closely matches the task in hand. If the match is exact, learning is complete. If not, further refinement is necessary but much less than in a normal learning process.

3   Experiments

The experiments, presented in this section, use the environment discussed in Section 2. The goal remains fixed, but ten different sized inner rooms with different door positions and widths were used. Three of these room configurations, denoted cases a, b and c, are shown in figure 1. The basic Q-learning algorithm was used, with a discrete function approximator as discussed in Section 2.1. The function approximator divides the state space into a 17 by 17 array of discrete cells. The algorithm was run for each of the ten room configurations until there was no appreciable change in the surface. An initial position for the snake was established and then the method discussed in Section 2.2 used to locate the features. The snake's position and and gradient information was extracted to form the index, the surface the case. One of these room configurations (case b) was designated as the test case. The resultant surface and its gradient vector are shown in figure 4.

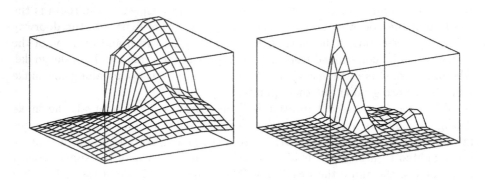

Fig. 4.   a) Test Case Surface   b) Its Gradient Vector

Each new learning episode started with a surface for the same goal but without an inner room, effectively the default case in the case base. The algorithm was then run in increments of 1000 actions up to 100000. To establish a base-line for comparison the algorithm was first run without using the case base. The algorithm was then rerun but this time, the snake was fitted to each of the resulting surfaces at each increment and the information extracted. If a good match to an existing case was found, the surface was reinitialised with the stored surface.

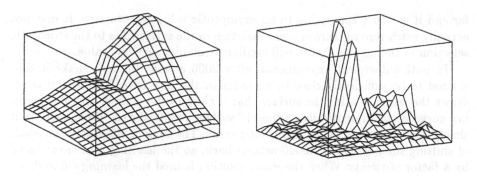

Fig. 5. a) Surface After 2000 Actions   b) Its Gradient Vector

In the first experiment the test surface was left out of the case base. The algorithm chose as the best match a slightly smaller room with a door in a similar position, case a in figure 1. In the second experiment the test surface was included in the case base and on repeating the procedure the actual surface was selected. In both experiments, a case was selected after 2000 actions, based on features extracted from the surface shown in figure 5. The gradient vector shows roughly the same form as the test case and this allowed the successful extraction of the features so early in the learning process.

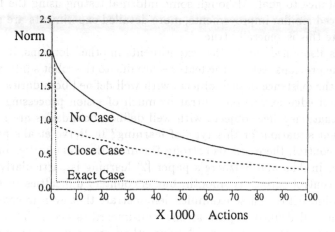

Fig. 6. The Learning Curves

Figure 6 shows learning curves from the experiments. These curves were produced by taking the Euclidean norm of the difference between the surface at each increment and the converged surface for the test case. The topmost curve shows the learning curve when not using the case base. As can be seen at the far end it is slowly converging to an asymptotic value close to zero. It may not actually reach zero as there is some variation in the surface due to the stochastic selection of the actions, but it will oscillate around a very low value.

In both subsequent experiments, after 2000 actions the new snake is considered to be sufficiently close to an index in the case base. The second curve shows the result of using the surface that is close to the desired one. The learning curve drops dramatically as the old surface is introduced. From then on it slowly decreases towards the asymptotic value. The curve is effectively the result of shifting the position at 40000 actions back, so the learning rate is increased by a factor of twenty. When the exact solution is used the learning curve drops to its minimum value. These experiments demonstrate that the features can be detected early in the learning process and are effective in indexing a case base. Even when there is not an exact match, using a surface from a close match results in a considerable increase in learning rate.

4   Limitations and Future Work

There are a number of limitations in the experimental validation of this approach. Firstly, the experiments used only a small case base representing ten room configurations, with a single fixed goal. More extensive experiments are needed with much larger case bases representing a variety of goals. Secondly, the learning curves represent the accuracy of the value surface rather than the average distance to goal. Although some informal testing using the latter measure produced similar improvements, more detailed experiments are required to demonstrate this is generally true.

There is also a need for further experiments in other domains. In the experiments of the previous section, the features are due to the robot's interaction with walls. It is the existence of such objects with well defined boundaries that makes the notion of edge extraction central to much of vision processing. But what of other situations where objects with well defined boundaries are not present, an important situation for this type of learning? In Herve et al's paper [5] on robot arm control, there are also strong features, the singularities in the arm's work space. In Aha and Salzberg's paper [2] learning is particularly successful where the control surface is smooth, but encounters difficulties in the area of strong non-linearities. These examples demonstrate that even in spaces that do not contain well defined objects strong non-linearities occur. This work aims to identify such features, not only because they are easy to recognise but also because they have such an impact on learning. But further experimentation is needed to determine whether or not they can be detected sufficiently early in the learning process to provide a significant increase in learning rate.

There are also a number of limitations in the present implementation of the ideas discussed in this paper. Firstly, a single snake is used and it will only locate features that are connected to the boundaries of the state space. In environments of a more complex collection of rooms and walls, it will be necessary to use multiple snakes. This should present no real technical problem but will somewhat complicate the matching algorithm. Secondly, surfaces that approximately match a new task are used without modification. Once detecting the position of the features, it should be possible to modify the case, as is typical in many case based systems, to better initialise the learning process.

Future work will involve solving these problems and investigating the combining of these ideas with a planning system. Each case would be a plan operator. The learning process would be initialised either from a single case or the composition, determined by the planner, of several cases. This would then be further refined through reinforcement learning, ultimately becoming itself a new case.

5 Related Work

The most closely connected work, to that presented in this paper, is the various forms of instance based or case based learning that have been used in conjunction with reinforcement learning. Their use has been to address a number of issues: the economical representation of the state space, prioritising states for updating and dealing with hidden state. The first issue is addressed by Peng [12] and Tadepalli [17] who use learnt instances combined with linear regression over a set of neighbouring points. Sheppard and Salzberg [13] also use learnt instances but they are carefully selected by a genetic algorithm. The second issue is addressed by Moore and Atkeson [11] who keep a queue of "interesting" instances. These are updated most frequently to improve the learning rate. The third issue is addressed by McCallum [7] who uses trees which expand the state representation to include prior states removing ambiguity due to hidden states. In further work [8] he uses a single representation to address both the hidden state problem and the general problem of representing a large state space by using a case base of state sequences associated with various trajectories. Unlike this other research, in the work presented here the case is not an example of the value function during learning. Instead, it is the result of a complete learning episode, so the method should be complementary to these other approaches.

This work is also related to case based planning [4, 18], through the general connection of reinforcement learning and planning. This connection will become stronger in future work, as discussed in the previous section, where the combination and modification of cases should have much in common with case based planning. Last but not least, is the connection with object recognition in vision research [14, 3]. In many ways model bases are similar to case bases. In this work, many of the methods if not the final application has come from such work.

6 Conclusions

This paper has shown how the use of a case base of surfaces can significantly improve the speed of reinforcement learning. It introduced the notion of using vision processing techniques to extract features from the evolving surface. The experiments demonstrated that the features are stable and can be extracted early in the learning process.

References

1. Agnar Aamodt and Enric Plaza (1994) *Case-Based Reasoning: Foundational Issues, Methodological Variations, and System Approaches.* AICom - Artificial Intelligence Communications V. 7 No. 1 pp 39-37

2. Aha, D. W., and Salzberg, S. L. (1993). *Learning to catch: Applying nearest neighbor algorithms to dynamic control tasks.* Proc. Fourth International Workshop on Artificial Intelligence and Statistics. pp 363-368

3. C. H. Chin and C. R. Dyer (1986) *Model-based recognition in Robot Vision.* Computing surveys V. 18 No 1 pp 67-108

4. Kristian J. Hammond (1990) *Case-Based Planning: A Framework for Planning from Experience.* The Journal of Cognitive Science V. 14 no. 3

5. Jean-Yves Herve and Rajeev Sharma And Peter Cucka (1991) *The Geometry of Visual Coordination.* Proc. Ninth National Conf. on Artificial Intelligence pp 732-737

6. Frederic Leymarie and Martin D. Levine. (1993) *Tracking Deformable Objects in the Plane Using an Active Contour Model.* IEEE Trans. Pattern Analysis And Machine Intelligence V. 15 No. 6 pp 617-634

7. R. A. McCallum, (1995). *Instance-based utile distinctions for reinforcement learning.* Proc. Twelfth International Conf. on Machine Learning. pp 387-395

8. R. A. McCallum (1995). *Instance-based state identification for reinforcement learning.* Advances in Neural Information Processing Systems 7. pp 377-384

9. Staphane Mallat and Sifen Zhong (1992). *Characterization of Signals from Multiscale Edges.* IEEE Trans. Pattern Analysis And Machine Intelligence V. 14 No. 7 pp 710-732

10. David Marr (1982) Vision : a computational investigation into the human representation and processing of visual information. W.H. Freeman

11. A. W. Moore and C. G. Atkeson (1993) *Prioritized Sweeping: Reinforcement Learning with Less Data and Less Real Time.* Machine Learning, V. 13 pp 103-130

12. Jing Peng (1995) *Efficient Memory-Based Dynamic Programming.* Proc. Twelfth International Conf. of Machine Learning pp 438-446

13. John W. Sheppard and Steven L. Salzberg (1996) *A teaching strategy for memory-based control.* To appear in AI Review, special issue on Lazy Learning.

14. P. Suetens and P. Fua and A. Hanson (1992) *Computational strategies for object recognition.* Computing surveys V. 24 No. 1 pp 5-61

15. R.S. Sutton (1988) *Learning to Predict by the Methods of Temporal Differences.* Machine Learning V. 3 pp 9-44

16. R.S. Sutton (1990) *Integrated architectures for learning, planning, and reacting based on approximating dynamic programming.* Proc. Seventh International Conf. on Machine Learning pp 216-224

17. P. Tadepalli and D. Ok (1996) *Scaling up Average Reward Reinforcement Learning by Approximating the Domain Models and the Value Function.* Proc. Thirteenth International Conf. of Machine Learning pp 471-479

18. Manuela M. Veloso and Jaime G. Carbonell (1993) *Derivational Analogy in PRODIGY: Automating Case Acquisition, storage and Utilization.* Machine Learning V. 10 No. 3 pp 249-278

19. Christopher J.C.H. Watkins and Peter Dayan (1992) *Technical Note:Q-Learning* Machine Learning V. 8 No 3-4 pp 279-292

PAC Analyses of a 'Similarity Learning' IBL Algorithm

A.D. Griffiths and D.G. Bridge

Department of Computer Science, University of York, York YO1 5DD, UK
Email: {tony|dgb}@minster.york.ac.uk

Abstract. *VS-CBR* [14] is a simple instance-based learning algorithm that adjusts a weighted similarity measure as well as collecting cases. This paper presents a 'PAC' analysis of *VS-CBR*, motivated by the PAC learning framework, which demonstrates two main ideas relevant to the study of instance-based learners. Firstly, the hypothesis spaces of a learner on different target concepts can be compared to predict the difficulty of the target concepts for the learner. Secondly, it is helpful to consider the 'constituent parts' of an instance-based learner: to explore separately how many examples are needed to infer a good similarity measure and how many examples are needed for the case base. Applying these approaches, we show that *VS-CBR* learns quickly if most of the variables in the representation are irrelevant to the target concept and more slowly if there are more relevant variables. The paper relates this overall behaviour to the behaviour of the constituent parts of *VS-CBR*.

1 Introduction

Instance-based learning (IBL) algorithms may learn by accumulating exemplars in a case base. However, empirical studies [1] [15] show that an instance-based learner that also tunes its similarity measure is generally more efficient than one that does not. More formal studies [8] [6] [7] indicate similar conclusions. For example, in [7] we show that an instance-based learner, which learns monomial target concepts (defined in Section 2) using a fixed but 'optimal' similarity measure, is less efficient than a learner with a simple rule for adjusting a weighted similarity measure. The ability to alter the similarity measure is therefore an important part of IBL.

This paper describes the formal analysis of a similarity-learning IBL algorithm within the PAC learning framework. Few publications describe analyses of this kind, and the most similar work to our own is that of Satoh and Okamoto [11]. These authors study the problem of similarity learning by defining a learning problem where the learner must infer a similarity measure from 'qualitative distance information'. In contrast, this paper analyses the problem of choosing, from positive and negative instances of the target concept, a case base and a similarity measure that together approximate the target concept. In other words, Satoh and Okamoto study instance-based learning only indirectly, via a model that abstracts the problem of learning weights for the similarity measure, while we make an actual instance-based learner the object of our study. In particular, our paper demonstrates two ideas that we suggest might be generally useful for the analysis of specific instance-based learners.

2 Definitions

For the purposes of this paper we assume that examples are represented by a number of binary (0 or 1) valued features. The *example space*, or space of possible problem descriptions, is therefore the space of N-bit binary vectors, referred to as D_N and defined $D_N \hat{=} \{0,1\}^N$.

The paper is concerned with a binary classification task, or the task of learning $\{0,1\}$-valued functions, or *concepts*, defined on D_N. The set of all such concepts is called B_N; $B_N \hat{=} D_N \rightarrow \{0,1\}$. In particular, this paper will study the behaviour of instance-based learning algorithms on *monomial* or conjunctive target concepts. A monomial concept can be represented in the propositional calculus by a simple conjunction of literals. The set of monomial concepts is referred to as M_N. Furthermore, $M_{N,k}$ is defined as the set of monomials with exactly k literals; u_1 represents a concept in $M_{N,1}$, while $u_1 \bar{u}_2 u_3 \bar{u}_4$ represents a concept in $M_{N,4}$. The i-th bit of the representation is said to be *relevant* to a monomial concept $t \in M_N$ if the literal u_i or $\bar{u}_i$ appears in the expression representing t, and *irrelevant* if not.

Simple IBL algorithms learn by adding cases to a case base CB and by adjusting a similarity measure σ. A case base CB is a set of *exemplars*, each of which is a pair $(d,n) \in (D_N \times \{0,1\})$. Normally, a case base is *compatible* with some target concept $t \in B_N$ such that for each exemplar $(d,n) \in D_N$, $t(d) = n$. This is written $CB \subseteq t$:

$$CB \subseteq t \hat{=} (\forall (d,n) \in CB \cdot t(d) = n)$$

The similarity measure σ is a total function in $D_N \times D_N \rightarrow [0,1]$ which returns a real value indicating the degree of similarity between its two arguments. The pair $\langle CB, \sigma \rangle$ is interpreted as the *representation* of a $\{0,1\}$-valued function defined on D_N as follows:

$$h_{\langle CB,\sigma \rangle}(d) = \begin{cases} 1 \ if \ \exists (d_{pos},1) \in CB \cdot \forall (d_{neg},0) \in CB \cdot \sigma(d,d_{pos}) > \sigma(d,d_{neg}) \\ 0 \ otherwise \end{cases}$$

(1)

In other words, a point $d \in D_N$ is positively classified by $h_{\langle CB,\sigma \rangle}$ if and only if there is a stored positive exemplar d_{pos} that is strictly more similar to d according to the similarity measure σ than any of the stored negative exemplars d_{neg}.

Like many other IBL algorithms (e.g. [12] [5] [1]), the learner studied here uses a *weighted* similarity measure; here, this measure is simply a sum of the weights of the bits of the representation on which two descriptions agree:

$$\sigma_{\overline{w}}(d_1, d_2) = \frac{1}{\sum_{i=1}^{N} w_i} \sum_{i=1}^{N} w_i \times (1 - |(d_1)_i - (d_2)_i|)$$

(2)

If the weight vector $\overline{w}$ has weight 1 in all elements then $\sigma_{\overline{w}}$ treats all dimensions of the representation equally and is analogous to the Hamming distance between the two descriptions. This special case will be written σ_H.

Finally, if $\overline{x} \in (D_N)^m$ is a sequence, or *sample*, of m descriptions from D_N, then let $\overline{x}_t$ stand for the sequence $\overline{x}_t = \langle(x_i, t(x_i))\rangle_{i=1}^m$ where x_i is the i-th element of $\overline{x}$. In other words, for each element x_i from $\overline{x}$, $\overline{x}_t$ contains both the element x_i and also $t(x_i)$, the value of the concept t on that example. $\overline{x}_t$ is called a *training sample* for t since it provides a partial definition of t through the labels $t(x_i)$. The *hypothesis* of a learner L on a training sample $\overline{x}_t$, written $L(\overline{x}_t)$, is the concept chosen from B_N by L to approximate the target concept t while the *hypothesis space* of L with respect to t, written H_t^L, is the set of hypotheses that might be output by L on some training sample for t:

$$H_t^L \hat{=} \{h \in B_N | \exists \overline{x} \in (D_N)^* \cdot L(\overline{x}_t) = h\} \tag{3}$$

The hypothesis space of a learner L with respect to a *set* of concepts or *concept space* $C \subseteq B_N$ is similarly written H_C^L and defined $H_C^L = \bigcup_{t \in C} H_t^L$.

3 Instance-Based Learning Algorithm $VS\text{-}CBR$

```
forall 1 ≤ i ≤ N, n ∈ {0, 1} set f[i, n] = 1
set CB = ∅
for i = 1 to m do
    if n_i = 1 then
        if ¬∃d ∈ D_N · (d, 1) ∈ CB then set CB = CB ∪ {(d_i, 1)}
        for j = 1 to N do
            set f[j, 1 − (d_i)_j] = 0
    else
        set CB = CB ∪ {(d_i, 0)}
forall 1 ≤ i ≤ N
    if f[i, 0] = 1 ∨ f[i, 1] = 1 then
        set w_i = 1
    else
        set w_i = 0
RETURN VS-CBR(s̄) = h_{⟨CB, σ_w̄⟩}
```

Fig. 1. $VS\text{-}CBR$ **Learning Algorithm for Concepts in** M_N **[14, Fig 4].** $\overline{s} = \langle(d_i, n_i)\rangle_{i=1}^m$ is a training sample from $(D_N \times \{0, 1\})^m$.

This paper studies $VS\text{-}CBR$, an IBL algorithm that has a simple rule for choosing weights for the weighted similarity measure $\sigma_{\overline{w}}$ (Figure 1). This algorithm learns only monomial target concepts and operates in the following fashion:

- Only the first positive example in the training sample is added to the case base. All other positive examples are discarded.
- All negative examples in the training sample are added to the case base.
- Only binary weights (0 or 1) are assigned to $\sigma_{\overline{w}}$.

- All weights are 1 initially. A weight changes to zero iff two *positive* examples are observed that disagree on that bit of the representation.

Wess and Globig [14] explain the workings of $VS\text{-}CBR$ with reference to Mitchell's Version Space algorithm [10]. In contrast, we find a closer analogy between the method used by $VS\text{-}CBR$ to calculate the weights for the similarity measure and the (non case-based) 'standard learning algorithm for monomials' [13] [3]. We call the standard algorithm M for convenience. On the first positive example in the training sample, M sets its hypothesis to the monomial expression representing the concept whose only positive instance is the positive example. On subsequent positive examples, M deduces that if bit j of the positive example is 1 then $\bar{u}_j$ cannot appear in the hypothesis and if bit j is 0 then u_j cannot appear. This rule correctly identifies whether a bit of the representation is relevant, as long as the target concept is a monomial. Literals judged irrelevant can then be deleted by the learner.

$VS\text{-}CBR$ operates in exactly the same way, using the array f to calculate which bits of the representation are irrelevant. After processing any sample $\bar{s}$, $f[i, n] = 1$ only if no positive exemple d_{pos} has been processed such that $(d_{pos})_i = (1 - n)$ and therefore all observed positive examples have value n on bit i of the representation. $VS\text{-}CBR$ must then convert f to the weight vector $\bar{w}$ to be used in the similarity measure. This is straightforward; a bit of the representation is irrelevant to the definition of the concept whenever both possible values have been seen in positive exemplars and hence $f[i, 0] = 0 \wedge f[i, 1] = 0$. In this case, the corresponding weight w_i is set to 0 so that bit i is ignored by $\sigma_{\bar{w}}$; otherwise, it is set to 1.

4 Direct Analysis of VS-CBR

The PAC Learning Framework [3] provides a means of evaluating learning algorithms and in particular defines a quantity called the *sample complexity* which serves as the measure of efficiency of a learning algorithm:

Definition 1. Sample Complexity [3]. The sample complexity $m_L(t, \delta, \epsilon)$ of a learning algorithm L with respect to a target concept t is the least value of m such that, for any degree of confidence and accuracy $0 < \delta, \epsilon < 1$, the hypothesis inferred by L from a training sample of size m will, with probability greater than $1 - \delta$, have an error less than ϵ with respect to the target concept t, using any underlying distribution.

Additionally the sample complexity $m_L(C, \delta, \epsilon)$ of a learner L with respect to a *concept space* C is defined $m_L(C, \delta, \epsilon) = \max_{t \in C} m_L(t, \delta, \epsilon)$ and stands for the minimum size of sample sufficient for *probably* (δ) *approximately* (ϵ) correct learning of *any* target concept in C.

An algorithm with a small sample complexity will therefore require fewer examples to choose a hypothesis that is probably approximately correct than an algorithm with a high sample complexity. Key results in the PAC framework [4] link the sample complexity of a learner to its hypothesis space. For example, an upper bound on sample complexity, in terms of the cardinality of the hypothesis space of the learner, is easily proven:

Theorem 2. [7, Prop 6.5.11] c.f. [4, Thm 2.2] *The sample complexity of any consistent learning algorithm L that learns a target concept $t \in B_N$ is bounded above by a quantity of the order of* $(\frac{1}{\epsilon} \log \frac{1}{\delta} + \frac{\log |H_t^L|}{\epsilon})$.

This result can also be expressed in terms of a concept space $C \subseteq B_N$, giving a bound on $m_L(C, \delta, \epsilon)$ in terms of $|H_C^L|$.

Our approach therefore is to explore the hypothesis space of VS-CBR to make predictions about the relative efficiency of the learner on different target concepts. Firstly, Proposition 3 shows that the discarded positive examples are redundant since they are equivalent, from the point of view of the weighted similarity measure, to the stored, 'prototypical' exemplar [14]. Hence the hypothesis space H_t^{VS-CBR} is simply the set of concepts with case based representation $\langle CB, \sigma_{\overline{w}_{CB}} \rangle$, where CB is a case base compatible with t and the similarity measure $\sigma_{\overline{w}_{CB}}$ has weights $\overline{w}_{CB} \in \{0, 1\}^N$ such that a bit of the representation has value 0 iff that bit can be proven to be irrelevant to the target concept from the positive exemplars in the case base:

$$(w_{CB})_i = \begin{cases} 1 \text{ if } \exists b \in \{0, 1\} \cdot \forall (d, 1) \in CB \cdot (d)_i = b \\ 0 \text{ otherwise} \end{cases} \tag{4}$$

Proposition 3. [7, Propn 6.3.2][1] *A concept f is a member of the hypothesis space of VS-CBR with respect to a target concept $t \in M_N$ if and only if there is a case base $CB \subseteq t$ such that $h_{\langle CB, \sigma_{\overline{w}_{CB}} \rangle} = f$, where $\sigma_{\overline{w}_{CB}}$ is defined as in equation (4):*

$$\forall t \in M_N \cdot \forall f \in B_N \cdot f \in H_t^{VS-CBR} \leftrightarrow \exists CB \subseteq t \cdot h_{\langle CB, \sigma_{\overline{w}_{CB}} \rangle} = f$$

While it is reassuring to know that the positive exemplars discarded by VS-CBR are redundant, the problem with Proposition 3 is that the hypothesis is represented using different similarity measures at different times. It is the constantly changing relationship between the case base and the similarity measure that makes the analysis of similarity learning IBL algorithms difficult. Fortunately, in the case of VS-CBR, changes in the similarity measure are unidirectional; weights can be changed from one to zero but not vice versa. The similarity measure therefore converges monotonically toward the ideal as more examples are read from the training sample. As a result, it is possible to express the hypothesis space H_t^{VS-CBR} as a set of concepts representable by a *single* similarity measure:

Proposition 4. [7, Propn 6.4.2] *The effective hypothesis space of VS-CBR w.r.t. any target concept $t \in M_N$ is the set of concepts $h_{\langle CB, \sigma_H \rangle}$ where CB is any*

---

[1] The proof of Proposition 3 and of all the other new results in this paper is ommitted but can be found in [7].

case base compatible with t and that in addition has no more than one positive exemplar:

$$\forall t \in M_N \cdot H_t^{VS-CBR} = \{h_{\langle CB, \sigma_H \rangle} | CB \subseteq t \wedge \#\{d_{pos} \in D_N | (d_{pos}, 1) \in CB\} \leq 1\}$$

A concept in H_t^{VS-CBR} can therefore be represented by σ_H and by a case base containing some subset of the negative instances of the target concept and no more than one positive instance. Since the concepts in $M_{N,1}$ are the most general monomial concepts, with the largest number of positive instances and therefore the smallest number of negative instances, there will be at least as many concepts in $H_{M_{N,N}}^{VS-CBR}$ as in $H_{M_{N,1}}^{VS-CBR}$. For example, the concepts in $H_{M_{N,1}}^{VS-CBR}$ are those concepts with a case-based representation where the negative exemplars are drawn from one half of the example space and the single positive exemplar lies in the opposite half. If, instead, a target concept that also has that positive exemplar as a positive instance is taken from $M_{N,2}$, then there will be an additional quarter of the example space whose descriptions can appear as negative exemplars in the representation of hypothesis concepts. In the limit, if the target concept is from some space $M_{N,N}$, then there is only one description in D_N that is a positive instance of the target concept, and all other descriptions can appear as negative exemplars. In addition, for each monomial concept $t \in M_{N,k}$, there will be more specific monomial target concepts that will have all the negative instances of t as negative instances and will still be positive on some single description. The result below therefore follows immediately as a corollary of Proposition 4:

Corollary 5. [7, Cor 6.4.3] *The hypothesis space* $H_{M_{N,k}}^{VS-CBR}$ *of VS-CBR w.r.t. the concept space* $M_{N,k}$ *is a subset of the hypothesis space* $H_{M_{N,k'}}^{VS-CBR}$ *w.r.t.* $M_{N,k'}$, *for all* $N \geq k' \geq k$.

$$\forall 1 \leq k \leq k' \leq N \cdot H_{M_{N,k}}^{VS-CBR} \subseteq H_{M_{N,k'}}^{VS-CBR}$$

This result shows that the size of the hypothesis space of $VS\text{-}CBR$ on the concept space $M_{N,k}$ increases in the value of k. We would therefore expect $VS\text{-}CBR$ to learn target concepts in $M_{N,1}$ most easily, since this is when it has the smallest hypothesis space, while target concepts in $M_{N,k}$ are learnt more slowly. Simple experiments reported in [7] confirm this. Corollary 5 therefore allows predictions to be made about the relative efficiency of $VS\text{-}CBR$ on different monomial target concepts and also gives some kind of explanation of why target concepts defined by the smallest monomial expressions are learnt more easily than target concepts represented by larger monomial expressions.

5 Constituent Analysis of VS-CBR

In Section 4, we showed that, in this instance, the size of the hypothesis space H_C^L correlates with the efficiency of the learner on target concepts $t \in C$. The link between hypothesis space and efficiency is only a heuristic one, however.

In particular, Theorem 2 is only an upper bound rather than an expression for the sample complexity itself. We therefore attempted to validate the results of the previous section by adopting a different line of analysis, and considering VS-CBR as two separate processes, or *constituents*, one of which tunes the similarity measure, while the other is responsible for populating the case-base.

1. We noted in our description of VS-CBR that the learner assigns a zero weight to a bit of the representation iff that bit is judged to be irrelevant by the monomial learner M; VS-CBR will choose the correct similarity measure on precisely those training samples where M correctly identifies the target concept. The convergence rate of the process by which VS-CBR chooses $\overline{w}$ can therefore be determined by considering the sample complexity of M.
2. On the other hand, the convergence rate of the process by which VS-CBR populates its case base can be studied through an IBL algorithm that does not have to learn a measure of similarity, but is given, *a priori*, a similarity measure whose weights are 1 iff that bit of the representation is relevant to the target concept. This new algorithm therefore *starts* learning with all the information needed for the similarity measure, and any subsequent learning is due to the exemplars added to the case base.

These two views are developed in the following subsections.

5.1 Learning the Similarity Measure for VS-CBR

We noted previously that VS-CBR chooses the correct similarity measure on precisely those training samples where M, the 'standard learning algorithm' for monomial target concepts [13], exactly identifies the target concept. M starts with a *specific* hypothesis corresponding to the first positive exemplar read from the training sample, and then generalises the hypothesis by deleting literals until the monomial expression that exactly represents the target concept is reached. For each target concept $t \in M_N$, each of the monomials more specific than t might have been chosen as an 'intermediate' hypothesis by M before t is correctly identified:

Proposition 6. [7, Propn 6.5.13] *The hypothesis space of M, the standard learning algorithm for monomial concepts, w.r.t. a k-literal monomial target concept $t \in M_{N,k}$, contains all concepts in M_N which specialise the target concept t along with the concept f_0 that has value 0 on all descriptions:*

$$H_t^M = \{h \in M_N | h \sqsubseteq t\} \cup \{f_0\}$$

where $h \sqsubseteq t$ is read 'h specialises t' $(\forall d \in D_N \cdot h(d) = 1 \rightarrow t(d) = 1)$ and f_0 is the concept such that $\forall d \in D_N \cdot f_0(d) = 0$.

[7, Propn 6.5.13] also argues that $|H_t^M| = 3^{N-k} + 1$, which agrees with what is already known about M. Langley and Iba claim in passing that the number of examples that M needs *in the average case* increases with the number of irrelevant attributes [9]. Proposition 6 and Theorem 2, correspondingly, show that the sample complexity of M (a *worst-case* measure of efficiency) can increase no more than linearly in $N - k$. The more irrelevant bits, the more examples will be needed by M, and therefore by VS-CBR before it chooses a good similarity measure. This contrasts with the overall picture of VS-CBR developed in Section 4, where target concepts with the most irrelevant variables appeared to be the easiest to learn. The reason for this difference must lie in the requirements of VS-CBR for examples to populate the case base.

5.2 Populating the case base for VS-CBR

```
set CB = ∅
for i = 1 to m do
     set CB = CB ∪ {(dᵢ, nᵢ)}
RETURN CB2(s̄) = h₍CB,σ_w̄ₜ₎
```

Fig. 2. CB2 Learning Algorithm for Concepts in M_N. $\bar{s} = \langle(d_i, n_i)\rangle_{i=1}^m$ is a training sample from $(D_N \times \{0,1\})^m$ and weight vector $\overline{w}_t$ has value 1 iff that bit of the representation is relevant to t.

Figure 2 shows the instance-based learning algorithm $CB2$. $CB2$ collects all the examples from the training sample into the case base CB and outputs the hypothesis represented by $\langle CB, \sigma_{\overline{w}_t}\rangle$, where $\sigma_{\overline{w}_t}$ is the instance of $\sigma_{\overline{w}}$ that is ideally weighted according to whether or not a bit of the representation is relevant to the target concept t ($(w_t)_i = 1$ iff bit i is relevant to t).

Whereas $CB2$ uses the ideal measure $\sigma_{\overline{w}_t}$ (as if this was known in advance), VS-CBR infers a similarity measure $\sigma_{\overline{w}_{CB}}$ from the available exemplars that *approximates* $\sigma_{\overline{w}_t}$ and will eventually converge to the 'ideal' weighting if sufficient positive exemplars are available. In this way, $CB2$ can be seen as a limiting approximation of VS-CBR that illustrates the maximum contribution that can be made by the best possible choice of similarity measure from the class defined by binary weight vectors $\overline{w} \in \{0,1\}^N$.

The fact that $CB2$ *starts off* with the correctly weighted similarity measure $\sigma_{\overline{w}_t}$ means that it has only to populate the 2^k classes of descriptions which are treated as equivalent by $\sigma_{\overline{w}_t}$ [14]. The sample complexity of $CB2$ therefore can be established to be a function of k and not of N. For example, by using a straightforward simplification of the analysis of Aha *et al* [2], the following upper bound can be established:

Proposition 7. [7, Cor 6.5.9] *The sample complexity of $CB2$ with respect to a target concept represented by a k-literal monomial expression, $t \in M_{N,k}$, is no more than $\frac{2^k}{\epsilon} \log_e \frac{2^k}{\delta}$, independent of the value of N.*

$$m_{CB2}(t, \delta, \epsilon) \le \frac{2^k}{\epsilon} \log_e \frac{2^k}{\delta}$$

Having established that the sample complexity of $CB2$ must be independent of N, the following result, similar to Corollary 5, can also be proven which suggests that the sample complexity of $CB2$ increases in k:

Proposition 8. [7, Propn 6.5.4] *The effective hypothesis space* $H^{CB2}_{M_{N,k}}$ *of CB2 w.r.t. the concept space* $M_{N,k}$ *is a subset of the hypothesis space* $H^{CB2}_{M_{N,k'}}$ *w.r.t.* $M_{N,k'}$ *for any* $N \geq k' \geq k$.

$$\forall 1 \leq k \leq k' \leq N \cdot H^{CB2}_{M_{N,k}} \subseteq H^{CB2}_{M_{N,k'}}$$

In contrast to M (Section 5.1), $CB2$ has a sample complexity apparently increasing in the number of *relevant* bits of the representation and independent of the overall size N of the representation. (As with $VS\text{-}CBR$ in Section 4, these statements can also be demonstrated in the average-case by simple experiment [7].) The *order* of the sample complexity of $CB2$ is not known, unlike that of M which we could state to be $O(N - k)$. To obtain such a result, we would need to characterise and count the number of different hypotheses in H^{CB2}_t in order to apply Theorem 2. We have made partial progress towards this; [7] gives some necessary conditions on the representation of concepts in the propositional calculus in order for them to be members of H^{CB2}_t. Counting the number of such concepts for small values of k [7, Table 6.2] makes it clear that, although $\log|H^{CB2}_t|$ increases more than linearly in k, the upper bound indicated by Theorem 2 would be greatly less than the exponential bound indicated by Proposition 8. We can say no more than this, however, since we have no general expression for $|H^{CB2}_t|$.

6 Conclusions

Section 4 showed that it is possible to re-express the hypothesis space of $VS\text{-}CBR$, an IBL algorithm that tunes its similarity measure as part of learning, as a set of concepts representable w.r.t. a single similarity measure. This characterisation is sufficient to show that the hypothesis space of $VS\text{-}CBR$ is smallest w.r.t. the concept space $M_{N,1}$, and becomes larger for the concept space $M_{N,k}$ as k increases. From this we infer, using standard results in the PAC learning framework, an upper bound on the sample complexity of $VS\text{-}CBR$ that also increases in k.

Section 5 then described $VS\text{-}CBR$ as two processes that operate in tandem, each independently manipulating an element of the representation $\langle CB, \sigma_{\overline{w}} \rangle$. This 'constituent' analysis showed that increasing the number of relevant variables (the parameter k) makes it harder for $VS\text{-}CBR$ to get sufficient exemplars to cover the example space but easier to infer a good similarity measure. However, decreasing k makes the similarity measure harder to infer but reduces the sample complexity of building a suitable case base. Since a target concept $M_{N,1}$ is more easily learnt by $VS\text{-}CBR$ than a target concept in $M_{N,N}$, it seems that populating the case base is the harder task. In an experiment where the accuracy of $VS\text{-}CBR$ is measured on target concepts in $M_{N,k}$ for decreasing values of k, the extra cost of inferring a similarity measure that ignores *more* irrelevant features must be compensated for by a greater reduction in the sample complexity of building the case base. This suggests that the sample complexity of $CB2$ increases more than linearly in k and, conversely, agrees with the results of

[11], which also suggest that the problem of finding suitable weights may have a relatively low sample complexity.

Our work aims to develop ways of evaluating and comparing IBL algorithms. We believe that theoretical analyses are a valuable complement to empirical comparisons such as [15] because they can define the limits of the performance of a learner, and characterise when one instance-based learner outperforms another. However, more work is needed to refine the theoretical tools that are available so that directly usable results can be derived for realistic learning algorithms. The work we describe here has explored two different ideas which seem promising for investigating instance-based learners:

1. We have shown that it is useful to define the hypothesis space of a learning algorithm (w.r.t. different target concepts) in order to predict the relative efficiency of the learner on those target concepts.
2. We have also shown that it can be useful to think of IBL algorithms in terms of their constituent parts.

In this paper we have considered only the straightforward world of conjunctive (monomial) target concepts. Further work must explore whether these principles are also useful for more general instance-based learners.

References

1. D. W. Aha. Tolerating noisy, irrelevant and novel attributes in instance-based learning algorithms. *International Journal of Man-Machine Studies*, 36:267–287, 1992.
2. D. W. Aha, D. Kibler, and M. K. Albert. Instance-based learning algorithms. *Machine Learning*, 6:37–66, 1991.
3. M. Anthony and N. Biggs. *Computational Learning Theory*. Cambridge University Press, 1992.
4. A. Blumer, A. Ehrenfeucht, D. Haussler, and M. K. Warmuth. Learnability and the Vapnik-Chervonenkis dimension. *Journal of the ACM*, 36(4):929–965, Oct 1989.
5. J. P. Callan, T. E. Fawcett, and E. L. Rissland. CABOT: An adaptive approach to case-based search. In *Proceedings of IJCAI-91*, pp 803–808, Morgan Kaufmann, 1991.
6. C. Globig, K. P. Jantke, S. Lange, and Y. Sakakibara. On case-based learnability of languages. *New Generation Computing*, 15(1), 1997.
7. A. D. Griffiths. *Inductive Generalisation in Case-Based Reasoning Systems*. PhD thesis, Published as Technical Report YCST-97-02, Department of Computer Science, University of York, York YO1 5DD, UK, 1997.
8. K. P. Jantke. Case-based learning in inductive inference. In *Proceedings of COLT92*, pp 218–223. ACM Press, 1992.
9. P. Langley and W. Iba. Average-case analysis of a nearest neighbour algorithm. In R Bajcsy, editor, *Proceedings of IJCAI-93*, pp 889–894. Morgan Kaufmann, 1993.
10. T. M. Mitchell. Generalisation as search. *Artificial Intelligence*, 18(2):203–226, 1982.
11. K. Satoh and S. Okamoto. Towards PAC-learning of weights from qualitative distance information. In D W Aha, editor, *Case-based reasoning: Papers from the 1994 AAAI Workshop*, Technical Report WS-94-01. AAAI Press, 1994.
12. C. Stanfill and D. L. Waltz. Towards memory-based reasoning. *Communications of the ACM*, 29(12):1213–1228, 1986.
13. L. G. Valiant. Deductive learning. *Philosophical Transactions of the Royal Philosophical Society of London A*, 312:441–446, 1984.
14. S. Wess and C. Globig. Case-based and symbolic classification - A case study. In S Wess, K-D Althoff, and M M Richter, editors, *Topics in CBR: Selected Papers from EWCBR93*, LNCS 837, pp 77–91. Springer-Verlag, 1994.
15. D. Wettschereck, D. W. Aha, and T. Mohri. A review and comparative evaluation of feature weighting methods for lazy learning algorithms. Technical Report AIC-95-012, Navy Center for Applied Research in AI, Naval Research Laboratory, Washington, DC 20375-5337, USA, 1995.

Examining Locally Varying Weights for Nearest Neighbor Algorithms

Nicholas Howe and Claire Cardie

Department of Computer Science, Cornell University, Ithaca NY 14850.
E-mail: nihowe@cs.cornell.edu; cardie@cs.cornell.edu

Abstract. Previous work on feature weighting for case-based learning algorithms has tended to use either global weights or weights that vary over extremely local regions of the case space. This paper examines the use of coarsely local weighting schemes, where feature weights are allowed to vary but are identical for groups or clusters of cases. We present a new technique, called class distribution weighting (CDW), that allows weights to vary at the class level. We further extend CDW into a family of related techniques that exhibit varying degrees of locality, from global to local. The class distribution techniques are then applied to a set of eleven concept learning tasks. We find that one or more of the CDW variants significantly improves classification accuracy for nine of the eleven tasks. In addition, we find that the relative importance of classes, features, and feature values in a particular domain determines which variant is most successful.

1 Introduction

The k-nearest-neighbor (k-NN) algorithm is among the oldest of classification schemes for case-based learning. It lies at the heart of many case-based (or instance-based) learning algorithms. (See, for example, Aha et al. (1991)). Given a test case described as pairs of features and values, k-NN finds previously seen cases with the most similar feature values and uses them to predict the class of the new instance. The algorithm works well for some tasks, depending on the type and complexity of the concept to be learned. Researchers have proposed numerous variations of k-NN in an effort to improve its effectiveness on more difficult tasks. In particular, many proposed schemes employ *feature weighting:* the contribution of a feature in calculating the nearest neighbors is scaled according to the importance of the feature. The collection of weights, one per feature, forms a *weight vector*. See Wettschereck, et al. (1997) for a useful survey of feature weighting methods.

Many feature weighting methods apply weights globally: they use a single weight vector that remains constant throughout testing. However, some domains contain features that vary in importance across the instance space (Aha and Goldstone, 1992). *Local weighting* schemes, where feature weights can vary from instance to instance or feature value to feature value, may perform better for such applications. For example, Aha and Goldstone (1992) use a combination of local and global weights for each training instance, and Hastie and Tibshirani

(1994) use weights produced individually for each test instance. Stanfill and Waltz's (1986) value difference metric (VDM) takes a slightly different approach by weighting features according to the particular feature values of the test case and individual training cases. Potentially, local weighting schemes can take into account any combination of global, test-case, and training-case data. The locality of particular weighting algorithms can be visualised on a continuum, from global methods that compute a single weight vector for all cases to extremely local methods that compute a different weight vector for each pair of test and training cases. This paper uses the term "local weighting" to describe any scheme in which the computed weights may vary depending on the classes of the cases being compared, their feature values, or other variables. The number of locally varying parameters the metric depends on determines the "degree of locality."

In spite of the existing work on individualized local weighting, less attention has been paid to local weighting on a coarser scale. While using individualized feature weights for each training instance or each test instance is a powerful approach, it may not be the best for all tasks. For example, using individual weights is unnecessary if the important features are the same across larger groups of instances. Statistical properties of larger homogeneous groups may simplify the task of computing appropriate weights.

This paper presents a coarsely local feature weighting scheme, *class distribution weighting* (CDW), that allows weights to vary at the class level. Although classes are certainly not always homogeneous, it is plausible that for many domains the defining features of a class are the same for most or all of the instances belonging to it. Instead of a single global weight vector, CDW computes a different weight vector for each class in the set of training cases using statistical properties of that subset of the data. Furthermore, the CDW scheme can be easily modified to generate a family of related feature weighting methods. Thus we can choose to apply a single set of global weights or to allow finer scale localization that accounts for the importance of particular feature value combinations. Although the algorithms considered here apply only to features with discrete (i.e., symbolic) attribute values, they can potentially be generalized for continuous (i.e., numeric) attributes.

In this paper, we apply CDW and its variants to a collection of classification tasks, and present evidence that the optimal amount of locality for feature weighting varies between the different tasks. For nine of the eleven data sets used, at least one of the CDW weighting schemes significantly improved classification accuracy. (In the other two, none of the fluctuation in results was statistically significant.) With $k = 1$, the most local technique tested produced the most accurate results for seven of the nine tasks for which results varied significantly, but showed significantly lower accuracies for the remaining two tasks. Given the variability, we conclude that it is advantageous to have a family of related techniques (like the CDW family): the best method for each task can be selected via cross-validation on the training cases, or can be based in many cases on relatively simple properties of the task (e.g., the presence of irrelevant features).

The remainder of this paper describes the algorithms and their performance.

Section 2 describes CDW and its variants. Section 3 analyzes the results of applying the different algorithms to a set of classification tasks, and discusses why certain algorithms perform better than others in specific tasks. Finally, Sect. 4 discusses related work, including other coarsely local weighting algorithms, and Sect. 5 concludes with possible further extensions of CDW.

2 Class Distribution Weighting Algorithms

The class distribution weighting (CDW) algorithm and its variants start from the premise that the features that are important to match on are those that tend to have different values associated with different classes. An ideal feature would take on a unique set of values for each class. If it existed, that feature would provide all class information readily. In most applications, of course, ideal features are not available, but we can measure the degree to which each feature approximates the ideal. We then weight each feature proportionally to this measurement of the amount of information it provides.

We measure the usefulness of a feature for classification by comparing the distributions of the feature values across various subsets of the training cases. CDW computes a different set of weights for each class in the training set. The weights for a particular class on a given feature are based on a comparison between the distribution of feature values for the cases in that class and the distribution of values for cases in all other classes. If the distributions are highly similar, the feature is considered not useful for distinguishing that class from others, and it is assigned a low weight. If the distributions are highly dissimilar, the feature is considered useful, and it is assigned a high weight.

During classification, we use a variation of the standard weighted k-NN algorithm for symbolic features. Given a test case τ, the proximity to each training case t_k is calculated by

$$D(t_k, \tau) = \sum_{i=1}^{m} \delta_{f_i}(t_k, \tau) W_{f_i, \mathrm{Cl}(t_k)} \tag{1}$$

where $W_{f_i, \mathrm{Cl}(t_k)}$ refers to the weight of feature f_i as computed for the class of t_k, and

$$\delta_{f_i}(t_k, \tau) = \begin{cases} 1 \text{ if } \mathrm{Val}(f_i, t_k) = \mathrm{Val}(f_i, \tau) \\ 0 \text{ otherwise} \end{cases} \tag{2}$$

Training instances with higher scores are considered closer to the test instance.

For each class C_j there exists a separate vector $\langle W_{f_1 C_j}, ..., W_{f_m C_j} \rangle$ of weights for each feature. The weights $W_{f_i C_j}$ are calculated as follows. Let $T = \{t_1, ..., t_n\}$ be the set of training examples, and let $F = \{f_1, ..., f_m\}$ be the set of features describing cases in T. Suppose that feature f_i takes on the r_i different values $v_{f_i 1}, ..., v_{f_i r_i}$ across the entire training set. We then define the distribution of feature values for feature f_i over an arbitrary subset $S = \{t_{q_1}, ..., t_{q_s}\} \subseteq T$ as a vector $\Psi(f_i, S) = \langle a_1, ..., a_{r_i} \rangle$ of length r_i such that

$$a_h(f_i, S) = \frac{1}{|S|} \sum_{k=1}^{|S|} \delta_{hik} \tag{3}$$

where

$$\delta_{hik} = \begin{cases} 1 \text{ if } \mathrm{Val}(f_i, t_{q_k}) = v_h \\ 0 \text{ otherwise} \end{cases} . \tag{4}$$

In other words, a_h is the fraction of instances across S where f_i takes on the value v_h.

Let $C_1, ..., C_p$ be subsets of T grouped by class (i.e., C_1 consists of all training cases in class 1, etc.). To find the raw weight for feature f_i and class C_j, we compare the distribution of values for C_j to that of the rest of the training examples:

$$R_{f_i C_j} = \|\Psi(f_i, C_j) - \Psi(f_i, T - C_j)\|_1 = \sum_{h=1}^{r_i} |a_h(f_i, C_j) - a_h(f_i, T - C_j)| . \tag{5}$$

This yields a raw weight vector $\langle R_{f_1 C_j}, ..., R_{f_m C_j} \rangle$ for each class C_j.[1] The final weights $\langle W_{f_1 C_j}, ..., W_{f_m C_j} \rangle$ used are simply the raw weights normalized to sum to 1.

During classification, the k nearest neighbors are calculated using (1). In case of ties, more than k cases may be returned. (In fact, to account for floating point rounding errors, all cases with scores within a small ϵ of the kth closest case are returned.) The retrieved cases then vote on the classification, and ties are broken by taking the first instance returned.

2.1 CDW Variants

CDW weights locally by class level groupings. Thus it should perform well in domains with homogeneous classes that are distinguished by different features particular to each class. The same approach can be applied to compute weights for groups more finely or coarsely grained than individual classes. For example, if a particular class was defined by the disjunction of two distinct subconcepts, then one might wish to compute different weights for the two sets of instances belonging to each subconcept. Unfortunately, subclass groupings are generally not known a priori, and computing appropriate groupings is not a straightforward problem. Because of these difficulties, we have not pursued this particular approach further. Instead, we examined three variants of the CDW algorithm: one that eliminates locality by using global weights derived from the local CDW weights, another that uses finer-grained locality by associating different weights with each individual feature value, and a third that is a straightforward combination of the first two.

---

[1] In (5), we could use the 2-norm or any Minkowski p-norm. Our tests indicate that the resulting algorithm behaves similarly to standard CDW on most data sets. In all results presented in this paper we use the standard form given above.

Global Mean CDW To go from the local CDW weights to a global weight for all features, we average the feature weight vectors across all classes to get a single global weight vector. This variant can be expected to perform well in domains where the relevant features are the same for all classes (e.g., *LED-24* from the UCI repository (Merz and Murphy, 1996)). The global weights can be computed by taking a simple mean over all classes or by an average weighted by the class frequency in the training data. The latter approach gives comparable overall results, but tends to bias predictions toward the most common classes. Because recent work has emphasized the importance of minority class predictions (Fawcett, 1996), we present only results for the simple mean here. We call this method *global mean CDW* (GM-CDW).

In domains with only two possible classes, CDW and GM-CDW will calculate the same set of weight vectors because CDW itself produces identical weights for the two classes. An examination of (5) reveals the reason: $T - C_1 = C_2$ and $T - C_2 = C_1$ if C_1 and C_2 are the only classes. Thus (5) degenerates to equivalent expressions for each class.

Expanded Feature CDW For some classes, particular feature values may be more significant than other values of the same feature. For example, the target class in the *Monks-2* data set is defined by the concept "exactly two features have the value 1." Thus another potentially useful form of local feature weighting allows the weights to vary locally according to the values of the test instance. A simple transformation of the case base allows the CDW algorithm to exploit this form of locality. Specifically, the feature set is expanded so that each instance is described by a set of binary features corresponding to all the feature value possibilities in the original training set. If instances in the training set T are described by the set of features $F = \{f_1, ..., f_m\}$, and feature f_i takes on values $V_{f_i} = \{v_{f,1}, ..., v_{f,r_i}\}$ across the entire training set, then instances in the transformed training set T' are described by the feature set $F' = V_{f_1} \cup V_{f_2} \cup ... \cup V_{f_m}$.

Since the transformed data set has a separate feature for each original feature value in the training cases, the CDW algorithm applied to it generates weights that vary for individual feature values. This can be described as a new form of local distance metric on the original data set, where the distance contribution from each feature is weighted according to the class of the training instance, and the feature's value in the two cases being compared:

$$D(t_k, \tau) = \sum_{i=1}^{m} d_{f_i}(t_k, \tau) . \tag{6}$$

Here the separate weight and δ function from (1) have been subsumed into the single weighted distance term

$$d_{f_i}(t_k, \tau) = (\delta_{f_i}(t_k, \tau) - 1) \left(W_{\text{Val}(f_i, t_k)\text{Cl}(t_k)} + W_{\text{Val}(f_i, \tau)\text{Cl}(t_k)} \right) + \sum_{j=1}^{r_i} W_{v_{f,j}\text{Cl}(t_k)}$$

$$\tag{7}$$

where $W_{v_{f,j}\text{Cl}(t_k)}$ is the weight assigned to the binary expanded feature $v_{f,j}$ for the class of the training case t_k. In other words, $d_{f_i}(t_k, \tau)$ is the sum of all the value weights $W_{v_{f,j}\text{Cl}(t_k)}$ minus the value weights for the training and test case if their values differ. This method, which we call *expanded feature CDW* (EF-CDW) has finer locality than the standard CDW since it varies with individual feature values. It should perform best on tasks in which some but not all values of a feature are important, and where the importance of each value varies from class to class.

EF-CDW is identical to CDW for domains whose features all have binary values, e.g., *LED-7* and *LED-24*. This is because feature expansion on binary features makes two new features with similar distributions. (One is the mirror of the other.) The two expansion features are each assigned weights that are half the normal CDW weights, and the relative distances are unchanged. The relative ranks of unweighted k-NN distances are also unchanged by feature expansion.

Global Mean Expanded Feature CDW This variant is a straightforward combination of GM-CDW and EF-CDW. The instances are transformed to the expanded-features format, the standard CDW algorithm is applied, and the expanded-feature weights on the classes are averaged to get global weights for each expanded feature. This variant exhibits test case locality but not class locality. It should do especially well on tasks where only certain feature values are relevant, but the relevant values do not vary from class to class (e.g., *Monks-2*).

3 Results of Testing

We use a variety of classification tasks to test the different weighting algorithms. Because we hypothesize that different data sets will require differing degrees of locality for greatest accuracy, we include a range of artificial and real-world domains. The data sets used are shown in the leftmost column of Table 1. The first six of these (*LED-7*, *LED-24*, *Monks-2*, *Lymph*, *Promoters*, and *Soybean*)[2] are from the UCI machine learning repository (Merz and Murphy, 1996). The tasks selected are a subset of those proposed as a benchmark by Zheng (1993). Tasks

---

[2] *LED-7* is the task of identifying the digit on a standard 7-LED digital display, with approximately 10% of the features flipped (to simulate random noise). Due to the noise, the optimal probability of a correct classification is about 74%. *LED-24* is the same task with an additional 17 irrelevant features that serve as distractors. The data sets used for these tasks each have 250 instances. *Monks-2* is an artificial data set with 6 features, where the class description to be learned is "exactly two features have the value 1." It has 432 test instances, of which 169 are designated as training cases. *Lymph* is a set of 159 medical cases provided by Zwitter and Soklic. The task is to predict a medical diagnosis given 18 descriptive features. *Promoters* is a set of 106 *E. coli* DNA sequences, where the task is to predict whether the sequence will act as a promoter. *Soybean* is a collection of crop disease records. The task is to predict the disease given 35 features providing information about the growing conditions. This task has 307 designated training instances, and 376 designated test instances.

from the benchmark with continuous features were discarded. Also, *NetTalk* was not used because of its similarity to the NLP datasets described below, and *Mushroom* was found to be too easy.

We also include an artificial task constructed specifically to exhibit feature importance that varies locally at the class level, and several problems from natural language processing (NLP) (Cardie, 1993a; Cardie, 1993b). *Construct* is an artificially constructed 200-instance data set designed to showcase the strength of the CDW algorithm. It consists of ten features with random values from 0 to 9, with one feature set at random to 10. The class of an instance is the number of the feature that is set at ten. *POS*, *Gen-Sem*, *Spec-Sem*, and *Concept* are NLP data sets of unknown words and are described in detail in Cardie (1993a). Briefly, the learning task involves predicting the part of speech, general and specific semantic class, and concept activation respectively for unknown words drawn from the MUC business joint venture corpus (MUC-5, 1994). In addition to the class value, each case is described by 34 features that encode information about the local and global context of the unknown word (Cardie, 1993b).

In the experiments below, ten-fold cross-validation was used for all tasks, except for two domains with designated training and test sets (*Monks* and *Soybean*). For these tasks, the designated sets were used to provide consistency with previous work.

3.1 Discussion

The results of the tests performed are shown in Table 1. Parentheses around an entry indicate that a particular test is degenerate with one of the other variants, as noted above. Bold face type indicates significance of at least .10 with respect to k-NN in a chi-square test, and footnotes indicate greater significance where applicable. Italic type indicates a significant decrease in accuracy.

Except for two tasks for which no results are statistically distinguishable (*LED-7* and *Soybean*), at least one of the CDW variants significantly outperforms the k-NN baseline. While the results tend to favor increased locality in weighting, no single variant is clearly superior for all tasks. Although Schaffer has shown theoretically that no single learning algorithm is best for every task (Schaffer, 1994), our results show empirically the effects of local variation in the distance metric on typical tasks. For some of the tasks we use, locally varying metrics bring no significant improvement in accuracy. Because the methods we compare are all variants of a single technique, we suggest that the lack of improvement stems from the intrinsic nature of these domains.

In particular, the CDW algorithm should attain higher accuracies for tasks where feature importance varies according to the class. For example, CDW shows high accuracy on *Construct* which is designed to exhibit varying feature importance. Interestingly, CDW performs significantly worse on all the NLP tasks. We suspect that the important features for these tasks are unrelated to the class of the instance. CDW may be basing its weights on spurious patterns in the training data, lowering its accuracy.

Table 1. Accuracy of CDW Variants Compared to 1-NN and 10-NN

Data Set	NN	CDW	GM-CDW	EF-CDW	GMEF-CDW	k Value
LED-7	64.80	63.20	63.20	(63.20)	(63.20)	$k = 1$
	72.40	70.40	68.80	(70.40)	(68.80)	$k = 10$
LED-24	44.40	**64.00‡**	**64.40‡**	**(64.00)‡**	**(64.40)‡**	$k = 1$
	59.60	**73.60‡**	**77.20‡**	**(73.60)‡**	**(77.20)‡**	$k = 10$
Monks-2	70.83	68.52	(68.52)	**75.00†**	**(75.00)†**	$k = 1$
	66.90	65.97	(65.97)	*62.73†*	*(62.73)†*	$k = 10$
Lymph	81.43	84.29	83.57	**86.43**	**86.43**	$k = 1$
	82.86	83.57	81.43	83.57	83.57	$k = 10$
Promoters	85.00	**90.00**	(90.00)	**91.00**	(91.00)	$k = 1$
	78.00	**87.00†**	**(87.00)†**	**89.00‡**	**(89.00)‡**	$k = 10$
Soybean	88.03	88.83	88.56	87.50	89.89	$k = 1$
	80.59	80.32	81.91	78.72	83.24	$k = 10$
Construct	64.00	**98.00‡**	*58.00†*	**100.00‡**	**99.50‡**	$k = 1$
	85.50	**100.00‡**	*76.50‡*	**100.00‡**	**100.00‡**	$k = 10$
POS	89.45	*88.04†*	**91.00†**	**91.73‡**	**93.63‡**	$k = 1$
	88.67	*86.87‡*	**90.61‡**	**93.63‡**	**93.53‡**	$k = 10$
Gen-Sem	64.59	*61.72‡*	**67.46‡**	**71.25‡**	**75.63‡**	$k = 1$
	67.02	*62.40‡*	**69.36†**	**75.63‡**	**75.19‡**	$k = 10$
Spec-Sem	71.79	*69.36‡*	72.28	**81.81‡**	**78.70‡**	$k = 1$
	75.92	*72.91‡*	76.85	**78.70‡**	**80.64‡**	$k = 10$
Concept	91.39	*88.57‡*	91.44	**93.43‡**	92.17	$k = 1$
	92.95	*92.07*	93.24	*92.17*	93.39	$k = 10$

Key: Results in parentheses are duplicates of other tests. **Bold face type** indicates significance with respect to NN of at least .10. *Italic type* indicates a significant decrease with respect to NN. † Indicates significance with respect to NN of at least .05. ‡ Indicates significance with respect to NN of at least .01.

The GM-CDW algorithm should do best in domains where the important features are the same regardless of class. As expected, it performs well in *LED-24*, demonstrating its ability to discard globally irrelevant features. In tasks like *LED-7*, where all features are important, neither GM-CDW nor any of the other CDW variants should have any particular advantage over k-NN, and the results reflect this. The remarkable uniformity of the *Soybean* results may seem to indicate a similar uniformity in feature importance. More probably, however, the case space is densely populated enough for this task that k-NN does not suffer in comparison with more sophisticated techniques. Wettschereck et al. (1997) report unexpectedly high accuracy for k-NN on a different task due to this effect.

The majority of the domains show the most improvement for the two binarized variants (EF-CDW and GMEF-CDW), which yield the most locally-tailored feature weights. The *Monks-2* results favor EF-CDW, which is not surprising because its concept definition explicitly refers to specific feature values.

Promoters, Construct, Lymph, and the four NLP data sets also respond well to the expanded-feature variants. It is worth noting that GMEF-CDW tends to work well for precisely the same tasks as GM-CDW and EF-CDW. This suggests that the relationships of feature importance to class and to particular feature values are independent of each other.

It may seem likely that many real-world tasks, due to their complexity, will respond well to increased locality in feature weighting. Our results show that while this conjecture is often true, it does not hold in all cases. In the results for $k = 1$, the most localized algorithm (EF-CDW) yields the highest accuracies for seven of the data sets tested (*LED-7*, *Monks-2*, *Lymph*, *Promoters*, *Construct*, *Spec-Sem*, and *Concept*). Four other tasks (*LED-24*, *Soybean*, *POS*, and *Gen-Sem*) show the best results with other algorithms for $k = 1$, and the difference is significant for the two NLP tasks. Choosing k carefully may help, since the pattern for $k = 10$ is slightly different. Still, the LED and NLP tasks provide evidence that allowing for variation that does not exist in the data can decrease accuracy on some tasks. Naturally these results may not extend to other tasks and algorithms not tested. However, based upon our results, we recommend pre-testing via cross-validation with varying types of locally-dependent metrics in order to empirically determine the optimum for a particular task. Alternately, expert knowledge, if available, can be used to select the best approach to use.

Each of the CDW variants has several tasks at which it performs well. This lends support to the "family of algorithms" approach. Overall, we find that CDW and GM-CDW are good at tasks with irrelevant features, and EF-CDW and GMEF-CDW are particularly good at tasks with partially relevant or interacting features. Together, they can handle many types of classification problems.

4 Related Work

Several surveys consider locality in k-NN variants. Atkeson et al. (1997a) survey locally weighted learning algorithms for numeric (e.g., continuous-valued) functions, including k-NN variants. A companion paper examines the application of various locally weighted techniques to practical robotic control problems (Atkeson *et al.*, 1997b). Researchers have also examined local similarity metrics based upon domain-specific knowledge (Cain *et al.*, 1991; Skalak, 1992).

Wettschereck et al. (1997) survey lazy learning algorithms, which include k-NN algorithms. One of their dimensions for comparing algorithms is the generality of the weighting scheme. They cite several studies reporting good results for locally weighted techniques (see Hastie and Tibshirani (1994) and Friedman (1994)), and conclude that the subject merits more research. Although they compare algorithms along several of the dimensions they define, the test results they present do not focus on comparing algorithms with differing degrees of locality.

Several previously introduced classifiers share similarities with CDW and its variants. For example, Stanfill and Waltz's (1986) VDM computes the feature value distributions, but unlike CDW the weights it computes do not depend on the class of the training instance. VDM computes different distances between symbolic feature values, and also weights the features based on the feature value of the test case. This can be viewed as weighting features locally based on both the training and test cases, although the computed distance between any two given feature values is the same across the entire data set. Of the methods presented here, VDM is most similar to GMEF-CDW.

Several feature weighting classifiers have used weights that, like CDW, vary at the class level. Per-category feature importance (PCF) (Creecy et al., 1992) binarizes features in the manner we have been calling "feature expansion", and then computes weights according to the formula

$$W_{f_i c_j} = P(C_j | f_i) \; . \tag{8}$$

Thus it assigns high weight to features that are highly correlated with the class. Unlike CDW, PCF fails to distinguish between a feature that tends to take on a particular value across the entire data set and one which tends to be on only for a particular class. Mohri and Tanaka (1994) report that PCF is biased toward predicting the majority class for data sets with a skewed class distribution.

Aha's IB4 classifier also calculates a different weight vector for each class (Aha, 1992). It attempts to learn feature weights by cycling through the training instances and adjusting their values. Weights are strengthened if feature values match for instances of the same class, and weakened if the values match but the instances are of different classes. Unlike CDW, IB4 is sensitive to the presentation order of training instances, and it assumes that the irrelevant feature values are uniformly distributed (Kira and Rendell, 1992). Aha reports that IB4 outperforms 1-NN in some domains with irrelevant features, and the fact that weights are learned allows it to change its bias to match that required by a particular task (Wettschereck et al., 1997).

5 Conclusions

We have developed a family of feature weighting techniques that vary in the degree of locality with which the feature weights are calculated. We present results of tests showing that at least one of the CDW variants significantly improves classification accuracy for nine of eleven benchmark classification tasks. Because no single technique proved to be the best in every task, we conclude that different tasks require differing degrees of locality in feature weighting. This justifies the use of a family of techniques, and suggests that some pre-testing using cross-validation on a particular task is necessary in order to determine the amount of locality required.

We are considering a number of improvements and extensions to the CDW algorithms. First, the CDW weighting algorithm could be extended to process numeric features in addition to symbolic ones. The most straightforward way to do this is to partition numeric features into histogram buckets. However, this discards some of the information present in the numeric values. A better extension would take into account the continuous nature of numeric features while preserving the paradigm that the weight of a feature should be based directly on its usefulness in distinguishing classes.

In addition, researchers have noted the superior performance of adaptive weight learning techniques, which attempt to adjust their bias to match that of the task (Wettschereck et al., 1997). Cross-validation on the training data to find the optimal level of locality may be flexible enough for most purposes. However, other feedback systems could be developed based upon the wrapper model introduced by John et al. (1994).

Finally, we would like to take advantage of the flexibility of CDW by using criteria other than the instance class to divide the training set into regions. Different criteria may divide the case base into more homogeneous groups in terms of feature importance. Applying the techniques of CDW to appropriate groupings should yield further improvements in accuracy.

6 Acknowledgements

We thank David Skalak and the anonymous reviewers for their advice and suggestions on this work. This work was supported in part by NSF CAREER Award IRI-9624639 and NSF Grant GER-9454149.

References

(Aha and Goldstone, 1992) Aha, D. W. and Goldstone, R. L. 1992. Concept learning and flexible weighting. In *Proceedings of the Fourteenth Annual Conference of the Cognitive Science Society*, Bloomington, IN. The Cognitive Science Society, Lawrence Erlbaum Associates. 534–539.

(Aha et al., 1991) Aha, D. W.; Kibler, D.; and Goldstone, R.L. 1991. Instance-based learning algorithms. *Machine Learning* 6:37–66.

(Aha, 1992) Aha, D. W. 1992. Tolerating noisy, irrelevant, and novel attributes in instance-based learning algorithms. *International Journal of Man-Machine Studies* 36:267–287.

(Atkeson et al., 1997a) Atkeson, C. G.; Moore, A. W.; and Schaal, S. 1997a. Locally weighted learning. *Artificial Intelligence Review* Special Issue on Lazy Learning Algorithms.

(Atkeson et al., 1997b) Atkeson, C. G.; Moore, A. W.; and Schaal, S. 1997b. Locally weighted learning for control. *Artificial Intelligence Review* Special Issue on Lazy Learning Algorithms.

(Cain et al., 1991) Cain, T.; Pazzani, M. J.; and Silverstein, G. 1991. Using domain knowledge to influence similarity judgement. In *Proceedings of the Case-Based Reasoning Workshop*, Washington, DC. Morgan Kaufmann. 191–199.

(Cardie, 1993a) Cardie, C. 1993a. A Case-Based Approach to Knowledge Acquisition for Domain-Specific Sentence Analysis. In *Proceedings of the Eleventh National Conference on Artificial Intelligence*, Washington, DC. AAAI Press / MIT Press. 798–803.

(Cardie, 1993b) Cardie, C. 1993b. Using Decision Trees to Improve Case-Based Learning. In Utgoff, P., editor, *Proceedings of the Tenth International Conference on*

Machine Learning, University of Massachusetts, Amherst, MA. Morgan Kaufmann. 25–32.

(Creecy *et al.*, 1992) Creecy, R. H.; Masand, B. M.; Smith, S. J.; and Waltz, D. L. 1992. Trading mips and memory for knowledge engineering. *Communications of the ACM* 35:48–64.

(Fawcett, 1996) Fawcett, T. 1996. *Learning with Skewed Class Distributions — Summary of Responses.* Machine Learning List: Vol. 8, No. 20.

(Friedman, 1994) Friedman, J. H. 1994. Flexible metric nearest neighbor classification. Unpublished manuscript available by anonymous FTP from playfair.stanford.edu (see /pub/friedman/README).

(Hastie and Tibshirani, 1994) Hastie, T.J. and Tibshirani, R.J. 1994. Discriminant adaptive nearest neighbor classification. Unpublished manuscript available by anonymous FTP from playfair.stanford.edu as /pub/hastie/dann.ps.Z.

(John *et al.*, 1994) John, G. H.; Kohavi, R.; and Pfleger, K. 1994. Irrelevant features and the subset selection problem. In Cohen, W. and Hirsh, H., editors, *Proceedings of the Eleventh International Conference on Machine Learning*, Rutgers University, New Brunswick, NJ. Morgan Kaufmann. 121–129.

(Kira and Rendell, 1992) Kira, K. and Rendell, L. A. 1992. A practical approach to feature selection. In *Proceedings of the Ninth International Conference on Machine Learning*, Aberdeen, Scotland. Morgan Kaufmann. 249–256.

(Merz and Murphy, 1996) Merz, C. J. and Murphy, P. M. 1996. UCI repository of machine learning databases. [http://www.ics.uci.edu/ mlearn/MLRepository.html].

(Mohri and Tanaka, 1994) Mohri, T. and Tanaka, H. 1994. An optimal weighting criterion of case indexing for both numeric and symbolic attributes. In Aha, D. W., editor, *Case-Based Reasoning: Papers from the 1994 Workshop*. AAAI Press, Menlo Park, CA. Technical Report WS-94-01.

(MUC-5, 1994) *Proceedings of the Fifth Message Understanding Conference (MUC-5)*. Morgan Kaufmann, San Mateo, CA.

(Schaffer, 1994) Schaffer, C. 1994. A conservation law for generalization performance. In Cohen, W. and Hirsh, H., editors, *Proceedings of the Eleventh International Conference on Machine Learning*, Rutgers University, New Brunswick, NJ. Morgan Kaufmann. 259–265.

(Skalak, 1992) Skalak, D. B. 1992. Representing cases as knowledge sources that apply local similarity metrics. In *Proceedings of the Fourteenth Annual Conference of the Cognitive Science Society*, Bloomington, IN. Lawrence Erlbaum Associates. 352–330.

(Stanfill and Waltz, 1986) Stanfill, C. and Waltz, D. 1986. Toward Memory-Based Reasoning. *Communications of the ACM* 29:1213–1228.

(Wettschereck *et al.*, 1997) Wettschereck, D.; Aha, D. W.; and Mohri, T. 1997. A review and empirical evaluation of feature weighting methods for a class of lazy learning algorithms. *Artificial Intelligence Review* Special Issue on Lazy Learning Algorithms.

(Zheng, 1993) Zheng, Z. 1993. A benchmark for classifer learning. Technical Report 474, Basser Department of Computer Science, The University of Sydney, N.S.W. Australia 2006.

(Zwitter and Soklic, 1988) Zwitter, M. and Soklic, M. 1988. Lymphography domain. [http://www.ics.uci.edu/ mlearn/MLRepository.html]. Donated by I. Kononenko and B. Cestnik.

Case-Based Planning to Learn

J. William Murdock, Gordon Shippey, and Ashwin Ram

College of Computing
Georgia Institute of Technology
Atlanta, GA 30332-0280

Abstract. Learning can be viewed as a problem of planning a series of modifications to memory. We adopt this view of learning and propose the applicability of the case-based planning methodology to the task of planning to learn. We argue that relatively simple, fine-grained primitive inferential operators are needed to support flexible planning. We show that it is possible to obtain the benefits of case-based reasoning within a planning to learn framework.

1 Problem

A recent view of learning is one in which learning is modeled as an active, deliberative, goal-driven process involving the explicit identification and pursuit of learning goals [12, 13]. In this view, modifications to memory are treated as planning operations and learning is done by constructing a plan over these operations. The work that has been done in this area has largely focussed on search-based planning algorithms such as non-linear planning; examples of this sort of work include [1, 3, 10, 14]. Furthermore, past work in this area has generally made use of large, complex learning algorithms as the operators for the planning algorithm; for example, Meta-AQUA [1] has a library of strategies such as explanation-based generalization which it combines to form learning plans. We argue, however, that a system capable of a truly broad and flexible range of learning needs to be able to construct its own learning algorithms from more basic components.

One approach to such basic components can be found in [5] which describes a taxonomy of *knowledge transmutations* which can be thought of as basic operations over knowledge elements. An example of one of these transmutations is *generalize*. The generalize transmutation specifies that given a fact about a knowledge element one can infer that information about a more general element which that element is an instance of. Our implementation uses a set of operations which is roughly (but not exactly) a subset of those defined by Michalski; see [6] for further discussion of knowledge planning using transmutation operators. In this paper we are concerned with the algorithms that are used to plan using such operators.

Search-based methods for planning are powerful and broadly applicable. However, using very low level primitive operations such as Michalski's knowledge transmutations means that the plans themselves are substantially longer than those formed from larger building blocks and thus may be intractable in sufficiently complex domains. Furthermore, because these primitive building blocks are so general, it may not be possible to completely identify whether an operator is guaranteed to produce a correct result. Case-based planning provides an potential solution to these problems.

Traditional case-based planning programs such as [2] have focused on planning in domains of physical action rather than in mental domains. More recent work [4, 8, 9] which has addressed mental domains has focused largely on the specific issue of using a "meta-level" CBR process to develop new adaptation strategies on top of more traditional CBR. In contrast, we are interested in how case-based planning can be extended into the mental domain of learning. Of the many advantages which case-based planning provides, the two which are most relevant to this research are:

- In complex domains, case-based planning may be considerably faster than methods which do searching.
- In domains for which no complete and correct theory is available, case-based planning may provide plausible plans on the basis of similarity to past examples while search may not be able to provide any meaningful insight.

The combination of case-based reasoning and planning to learn raises a variety of challenging issues; such a synthesis involves complex issues relating to both representation and processing. We propose a case-based method for planning to learn which provides the above benefits.

2 Example

As an example, consider a relatively novice poker[1] player. This player knows the rules to a small variety of different poker games but is not particularly familiar with the key strategic differences between these games. However, there is one specific distinction between two specific games of which the novice player is aware: the fact that the game acepots is strongly positional[2] and the fact that baseball is weakly positional. The problem that the player now wants to solve is whether some other poker variant is strongly or weakly positional.

---

[1] The example developed in this and succeeding sections involves a specific analysis of some particular poker games. The rationale behind this analysis and the specific details of the different games are not particularly important; all of the information which our system has about these games is illustrated in figure 1. For a relatively complete treatment of poker in general, see [15].

[2] By strongly positional, we mean that the relative value of a hand is strongly affected by the position which the individual holding the hand is seated with respect to the dealer because of the additional knowledge that players have by seeing what other players have already bet before deciding on their own bet. Again, the precise nature of this characteristic is not important to this example; what is important is that knowing the positionality is important to effective play but is not directly stated in the game rules.

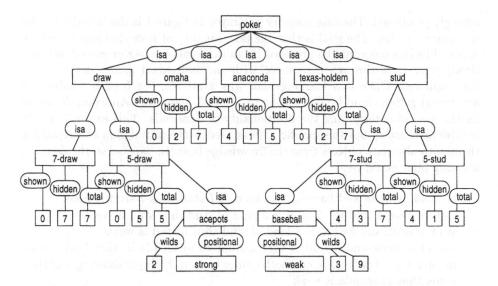

Fig. 1. This figure portrays a sample knowledge base in the domain of poker variants. Rectangular boxes indicate nodes in a semantic network. Rounded boxes indicate relationships between these nodes.

Figure 1 illustrates the sample knowledge base described in this example. A group of variants of poker are described along with a few specific characteristics of each variant.

If the player in this example had a deep understanding of what aspects of the rules of these two games affect whether the game is strongly positional then this player might be able to form generalizations for what constitutes a strongly positional poker game using a method such as EBG [7]. Similarly, if the player had a sufficiently large and diverse set of games for which this feature was known, then it would be possible to induce a decision tree mapping observable feature sets to the two positional classifications using a technique such as ID3 [11]. Lastly, a true expert at poker would probably already have in memory a precise normative characterization of what constitutes a strongly positional game and thus would be able to directly infer this feature from a description of the rules. The player in this example, however, has access to none of this information and thus cannot use any of these methods. In our example, the player does, however, have access to the following argument that texas-holdem is strongly positional:

- acepots is strong and acepots is a kind of 5-draw thus 5-draw is strong
- 5-draw is strong and 5-draw is a kind of draw thus draw is strong
- draw is strong and 7-draw is a kind of draw thus 7-draw is strong
- 7-draw is strong and 7-draw is very similar to texas-holdem in that both games involve a total of 7 cards *and* both games have each player showing none of their own cards thus texas-holdem is strong

This argument can be viewed as a plan for learning that texas-holdem is strongly positional. The case memory portrayed in figure 1 is the initial state for this *learning plan*. The goal is that the positionality of texas-holdem is known. A plan like this one could be provided by an external observer or even developed slowly over time through experience with the individual games described in the argument. Once this learning plan was available, the further analysis of additional games could be done using case-based reasoning. An example would be the goal of determining the positionality of anaconda. This example would involve abstracting out the specific objects used in the initial plan and replacing them with alternate objects from the knowledge base. In particular, the adapted learning plan would be:

- baseball is weak and baseball is a kind of 7-stud thus 7-stud is weak
- 7-stud is weak and the 7-stud is a kind of stud thus stud is weak
- stud is weak and 5-stud is a kind of stud thus 5-stud is weak
- 5-stud is weak and 5-stud is very similar to anaconda in that both games involve a total of 5 cards *and* both games have each player showing 4 of their cards thus anaconda is weak

Notice that this example requires a variety of different sorts of learning such as generalization, specialization, and analogy. Furthermore, in order to arrive at the desired conclusion, these different varieties of learning need to be combined dynamically (i.e. the particular pattern of interactions is specific to this problem and thus no single fixed strategy will solve this problem). We argue that case-based reasoning is the mechanism for accomplishing this dynamic combination of learning actions.

3 Representation

There are several general types of knowledge which must be represented in order to develop any sort of planning system. States correspond to arbitrary situations in the world; within the planning to learn framework a state encodes a complete set of memory contents. Goals characterize a set of states which a plan is intended to achieve; in our system this is done by specifying a particular feature which a goal state should have. The representation of operators requires information about when they are applicable and what their effects are. Finally the plans themselves need to encode the operations performed, the objects (i.e. memory items) which the operations affect, and the ordering constraints over these operations take place.

3.1 States and Goals

The states which our planning to learn system plans over are actually entire knowledge bases. The initial state of a plan corresponds to all of the knowledge available to the system at the start of the plan and the intermediate and final states correspond to the intermediate and final results of executing the plan. In our system, we have implemented this knowledge base as a semantic network, illustrated in figure 1. In this figure nodes represent concepts and links represent relationships; for example, baseball is a node which is part of a (positional baseball weak) relationship. Goals in our system are specified as conjunctive sets of variablized relationships. For example, the goal to determine the positionality of anaconda is described as {(positional anaconda ?x)}.

3.2 Operators

Learning actions are represented as operators over knowledge bases, i.e. knowledge transmutations. Four examples of transmutations are:

Generalize: Given that r holds for x and x is a y, assert that r holds for y.
Specialize: Given that r holds for x and y is an x, assert that r holds for y.
Weak Analogize: Given that r holds for x and y and that t holds for x, assert that t holds for y.
Strong Analogize: Given that r and s both hold for both x and y and that t holds for x, assert that t holds for y.

These four transmutations can be completely represented by preconditions and postconditions which are simply variablized relationships. As an example, the specialize transmutation is presented in table 1. The transmutation can apply when knowledge items exist which can bind to the variables (symbols starting with ?) in the precondition. It has the effect of asserting the relationship in the postcondition under those variable bindings. For example, to specialize the fact that draw is strongly positional to 7-draw, we use the preconditions to bind ?fr-2 to 7-draw, ?fr-1 to draw, ?rel-1 to positional, and ?val-1 to strong. The postcondition would then immediately require that (positional 7-draw strong) be asserted. A more complex transmutation, strong-analogize, is described in table 2.

Table 1: A simple example of a transmutation

transmutation	specialize
precondition	(isa ?fr-2 ?fr-1)
	(?rel-1 ?fr-1 ?val-1)
postcondition	(?rel-1 ?fr-2 ?val-1)

Table 2: A relatively complex transmutation

transmutation	strong-analogize
precondition	(?rel-1 ?fr-1 ?val-1)
	(?rel-2 ?fr-1 ?val-2)
	(?rel-3 ?fr-1 ?val-3)
	(?rel-1 ?fr-2 ?val-1)
	(?rel-2 ?fr-2 ?val-2)
postcondition	(?rel-3 ?fr-2 ?val-3)

Note that in general, the transmutations presented above are powerful enough to prove any possible statement. Since we do not have a theory here about which transmutations should be used under which circumstances, we simply cannot reason from first principles; case-based planning provides a partial solution to this dilemma. We may be able to adapt past cases to develop plausible learning plans.

3.3 Plans

A learning plan specifies a set of operations, a goal, and a set of bindings for the variables specified in the goal. A plan for the (positional anaconda ?x) goal would specify the final binding of ?x to weak as well as a series of steps in the form of transmutations and bindings for the variables in the transmutations. For example, the third and fourth steps in the initial plan described in section 2 are represented in tables 3 and 4; the variables are the same variables that appear in the description of the transmutations in tables 1 and 2.

The third and fourth steps in the positionality of texas-holdem plan

Table 3: The third step

step plan1-3	
of	specialize
has-bindings	(?fr-1 draw)
	(?fr-2 7-draw)
	(?rel-1 positional)
	(?val-1 strong)

Table 4: The fourth step

step plan1-4	
of	strong-analogize
has-bindings	(?fr-1 7-draw)
	(?fr-2 texas-holdem)
	(?rel-1 shown)
	(?val-1 0)
	(?rel-2 total)
	(?val-2 7)
	(?rel-3 positional)
	(?val-3 strong)

4 Algorithm

Our algorithm for case-based planning in the knowledge domain has four basic components: retrieval, adaptation, verification, and storage. Goals and plans correspond to the problems and cases in case-based reasoning respectively; the system begins with a goal, retrieves a plan from memory, adapts it to suit the new goal, stores the modified plan in memory, and returns the new learning plan as output.

4.1 Retrieval

The system we have developed does retrieval by conducting a linear search through a list of plans. The search returns only the first plan which accomplishes a goal similar the goal of the current problem. Our similarity metric requires that each postcondition for the goal of the plan in memory match the corresponding postcondition for the new goal being examined, with a match between postconditions requiring that they involve the same relation and have at least one of the arguments to the relation be equivalent (i.e. either they are the same node or they are both variables); this is similar to the similarity metric in [2, 16]. Thus, for example, (positional anaconda ?x) would match (positional texas-holdem ?y) but not (shown anaconda ?x) or (positional ?x strong). This algorithm is essentially based on the observation that such matches involve essentially demonstrating the same fact about a different data item; in the examples we have considered, it is far more plausible for such matches to use the same learning plan than it is for other sorts of matches (such as proving something different about the same data item).

4.2 Adaptation

The primary problem that we face in designing adaptation strategies for case-based planning to learn is one that runs throughout the field of case-based reasoning: the trade-offs between simple and complex strategies. Simple adaptation strategies are very limited in the breadth of modifications that they make and thus only work when a case in memory is extremely close to providing a solution to the new problem. Complex adaptation strategies require a great deal of complex reasoning. Consequently, they partially surrender both of the primary advantages of case-based reasoning that we outlined in section 1; they are less efficient than simpler adaptation mechanisms and they often provide weaker evidence for correctness based on similarity to an existing case (since the results are less similar to the existing cases). There is a spectrum of more and less powerful adaptation strategies and an ideal system would be able to draw from strategies all over the spectrum depending on the nature of the problem being addressed.

The most powerful and general adaptation mechanism which we have developed is to substitute the desired values for the nodes in the postconditions of the final step in the plan, then work backwards to construct preconditions which are consistent with those postconditions (using the relationships in the existing plan), and finally construct postconditions for the previous step that are consistent with those preconditions and so on.

Consider the problem described in section 2 of adapting the plan for learning that texas-holdem is strongly positional to the problem of learning that anaconda is weakly positional. We can describe this plan as pursuing the goal (positionality anaconda ?x). The last step of this plan is described in table 4. Our system begins by substituting the new problem's values for the variables in the postcondition of the strong-analogize transmutation; the postcondition of (?rel-3 ?fr-2 ?val-3) which was bound to (positional texas-holdem strong) requires that the value ?fr-2 now be bound to anaconda. Because this adaptation strategy involves holding the relations constant, the bindings for ?rel-1, ?rel-2, and ?rel-3 would be left unchanged. This would leave us with a partially adapted version of this step as shown in table 5.

The different stages which the adaptation of the fourth plan step goes through. Changes are from the previous stage are marked in **bold**.

Table 5: An early version of the last step of the plan; several values have not yet been filled in.

step plan1-4-modified-1	
of	strong-analogize
has-	(?fr-1 -)
bindings	(?fr-2 **anaconda**)
	(?rel-1 shown)
	(?val-1 -)
	(?rel-2 total)
	(?val-2 -)
	(?rel-3 positional)
	(?val-3 -)

Table 6: A prospective version of the last step of the adapted plan; only one value is still missing.

step plan1-4-modified-2	
of	strong-analogize
has-	(?fr-1 **5-stud**)
bindings	(?fr-2 anaconda)
	(?rel-1 shown)
	(?val-1 **4**)
	(?rel-2 total)
	(?val-2 **5**)
	(?rel-3 positional)
	(?val-3 -)

Table 7: The final version of the last step of the adapted plan; all values have been filled in.

step plan1-4-modified-3	
of	strong-analogize
has-	(?fr-1 5-stud)
bindings	(?fr-2 anaconda)
	(?rel-1 shown)
	(?val-1 4)
	(?rel-2 total)
	(?val-2 5)
	(?rel-3 positional)
	(?val-3 **weak**)

The strong-analogize transmutation has a precondition (?rel-1 ?fr-2 ?val-1); since ?rel-1 is bound to shown and ?fr-2 is bound to anaconda, we can directly retrieve from the knowledge base the value of 4 for ?val-1. Similarly, we can directly obtain the value of 5 for ?val-2. This leaves us with with ?fr-1 and ?val-3 still unaccounted for. Since we can't directly infer values for these variables, we can look in the knowledge base for nodes to fill these variables which are consistent with these values; since there are preconditions (?rel-1 ?fr-1 ?val-1) and (?rel-2 ?fr-2 ?val-2) we can deduce that ?fr-1 must be a node which has a value of 4 for shown and a value of 5 for total. The only values for which this is true are anaconda and 5-stud. We can create two different potential bindings to investigate and continue processing each of them. The system uses a heuristic which causes us to favor the new value 5-stud (since doing a strong-analogize from anaconda to itself is clearly not going to get us anywhere). Thus we first consider the possibility that ?fr-1 is bound to 5-stud. This presents us with a nearly complete adaptation of this plan step portrayed in table 6, leaving us with the goal of determining the value of ?val-3. We use this information to form a subgoal and apply this same mechanism to the previous step (table 3). This process continues backwards through the plan until we adapt the first step of the plan, and find that all of the bindings are filled (since we already have a value, weak, for the positionality of baseball). With all the values filled, we can then propagate this value forward fill the missing value slot in each of the other steps. Thus we get the last step of the final, adapted plan as shown in table 7.

4.3 Verification

One of the advantages of using case-based methods is that they may be able to provide plausible solutions in situations in which there is simply not enough information to provably identify a correct solution. For example, given the information in the poker example in figure 1 it is simply not possible to accurately verify whether the result of a plan execution is correct. In general, there may be a wide variety of characteristics which determine or correlate with correctness of a plan. We have worked primarily in domains in which potential verification is very limited because demonstrably correct solutions are not available; the general problem of verification is an important topic for future research.

4.4 Storage

The storage function for our system simply as appends the new case on to the front of the list of cases. However, it might be possible to make the retrieval function more efficient if a more complex store function involving hash tables or trees is used. Ultimately the resolution of this issue depends directly on the kind of retrieval operation being used; since our research has used very simple retrieval, our storage mechanism is also very simple.

5 Conclusion

We have developed an account of how case-based planning can be extended into the mental domain of learning. One major issue in this research is the question of what domains and problems are particularly amenable to case-based planning to learn. The domain of poker variants provides a concrete example of some features of domains in which case-based planning to learn is particularly applicable:

- Poker variants can often be classified into a relatively broad and deep "isa" hierarchy. This is essential to the usefulness of the particular transmutations (e.g. generalize) which we have implemented.
- Poker variants can also be completely specified as a (generally long) list of completely operationalized features as they are essentially mathematical constructs. This is an important feature of any domain for which we intend to apply concrete, parsimonious inferences such as those found in our knowledge transmutations.
- Most importantly, poker variants also have a great many interesting features (e.g. strategic properties) which are not directly observable and may often be unknown to a reasoner and impossible or intractable to derive from first principles. Often times these sorts of characteristics really are derived from analysis of the relationships of the variants to other variants in which the reasoner has access to a greater understanding. This feature is essential for there to be complex plans for learning. Such complex plans are essential for case-based planning to learn; in a domain in which all plans were extremely short and simple there would be no meaningful way to distinguish between plans in memory to adapt, no computational benefits to reusing plans, and no significant evidence that the new plans are particularly plausible.

476

While there are many useful approaches to planning which are based on a search through the state space, when there is a library of past planning cases available the technique of case-based planning may provide a variety of advantages over these techniques. Most notably, case-based planning may be considerably faster because it does not require a search through the entire space and may provide plausible solutions to problems where there is insufficient information to construct any solution from first principles. Our work has demonstrated the application of case-based planning to the planning-to-learn framework.

References

1. M. Cox, Introspective Multistrategy Learning: Constructing a Learning Strategy Under Reasoning Failure, Ph.D. Thesis, Technical Report GIT-CC-96/06, College of Computing, Georgia Institute of Technology, 1996.
2. K. Hammond, *Case-Based Planning: Viewing Planning as a Memory Task.* Academic Press, 1989.
3. L. Hunter, Planning to learn. *Proc. Twelfth Annual Conference of the Cognitive Science Society*, Hillsdale, NJ: Lawrence Erlbaum Associates, 1990.
4. D. Leake, Combining Rules and Cases to Learn Case Adaptation. *Proc. of the Seventeenth Annual Conference of the Cognitive Science Society*, 1995.
5. R. Michalski, Inferential Theory of Learning as a Conceptual Basis for Multistrategy Learning. *Machine Learning*, 11, 1993.
6. R. Michalski and A. Ram, Learning as goal-driven inference. In *Goal-Driven Learning*, A. Ram and D. Leake (eds.), MIT Press / Bradford Books, 1995.
7. T. Mitchell, R. Keller, S. Kedar-Cabelli, Explanation-Based Generalization: A Unifying View. *Machine Learning*, 1, 1986.
8. R. Oehlmann, Metacognitive adaptation: Regulating the plan transformation process. In *Proceedings of the AAAI-95 Fall Symposium on Adapation of Knowledge for Reuse*, D. Aha and A. Ram (eds.), pp. 73 - 79, San Mateo, CA: AAAI-Press.
9. R. Oehlmann, D. Sleeman, and P. Edwards, Learning plan transformations from self-questions: A memory-based approach. In *Proceedings of the 11th National Conference on Artificial Intelligence*, pp. 520-525, Cambridge, MA: AAAI-Press, 1993.
10. A. Quilici, Toward automatic acquisition of an advisory system's knowledge base. Applied Intelligence, In Press.
11. J. Quinlan, Induction of Decision Trees. *Machine Learning*, 1, 1986.
12. A. Ram and L. Hunter, The Use of Explicit Goals for Knowledge to Guide Inference and Learning. *Applied Intelligence*, 2(1), 1992.
13. A. Ram and D. Leake, Learning, Goals, and Learning Goals. In *Goal-Driven Learning*, A. Ram and D. Leake (eds.), MIT Press / Bradford Books, 1995.
14. Learning by Observing and Understanding Expert Problem Solving, Ph.D. Thesis, Technical Report GIT-CC-92/43, College of Computing, Georgia Institute of Technology, 1992.
15. J. Scarne, *Scarne's Guide to Modern Poker*, Simon & Schuster, 1984.
16. Case-Based Reasoning in PRODIGY. In *Machine Learning: A Multistrategy Approach Volume IV*, R. Michalski and G. Tecuci (eds.), Morgan Kaufmann Publishers, Inc., 1994.

A Utility-Based Approach to Learning in a Mixed Case-Based and Model-Based Reasoning Architecture

Maarten van Someren[1], Jerzy Surma[2] and Pietro Torasso[3]

[1] Universiteit van Amsterdam
Roetersstraat 15
1018 WB Amsterdam
The Netherlands
email: maarten@swi.psy.uva.nl

[2] Limburg University Centre
Universitaire Campus D
B-3590 Diepenbeek
Belgium
email: surma@rsftew.luc.ac.be

[3] Dipartimento di Informatica
Universita' di Torino
Corso Svizzera 185
Torino
Italia
email: torasso@di.unito.it

Abstract. Case-based reasoning (CBR) can be used as a form of "caching" solved problems to speedup later problem solving. Using "cached" cases brings additional costs with it due to retrieval time, case adaptation time and also storage space. Simply storing all cases will result in a situation in which retrieving and trying to adapt old cases will take more time (on average) than not caching at all. This means that caching must be applied selectively to build a case memory that is actually useful. This is a form of the utility problem [4, 2]. The approach taken here is to construct a "cost model" of a system that can be used to predict the effect of changes to the system. In this paper we describe the utility problem associated with "caching" cases and the construction of a "cost model". We present experimental results that demonstrate that the model can be used to predict the effect of certain changes to the case memory.

1 Introduction

Most current AI systems have an architecture with a single, uniform knowledge representation language and a single inference mechanism. Although this is a desirable situation from the viewpoint of designing, analysing and maintaining such a system, it is usually a compromise between different requirements. A system must be efficient, well structured to support verification and maintenance, reflecting natural representations used by people (e.g. experts) working in the domain involved, supporting interfaces with users and other software. Preferrably, it should even support automated refinement and adaptation. The choice of a representation and the corresponding architecture involves a trade-off between these dimensions. For example, a case-based reasoning architecture may not reflect explicit human knowledge about a domain and it may not be very efficient for implementing complex knowledge but its internal representation is similar to its input and output, which makes learning and analysis relatively easy (see e.g. [11]). It is possible, however, avoid trade-offs by using multiple representation forms in a single, hybrid architecture. Different components of the system can then be used for different purposes. Here, we shall consider an architecture that includes a *case memory* that can be used for *case based reasoning* and a *causal model* that can be used for *model-based reasoning* (MBR). MBR gives the advantages of comprehensible and maintainable knowledge and adding the CBR component is used to achieve efficiency.

Retrieving a solution to a new problem from a case base is likely to take less time than reasoning with a causal model. Caching problems (with their solutions) can reduce future solution time. However, this introduces a new problem. Retrieval time grows with the size of case memory. At some point the effect of "caching" on *average* solution time will begin to fall even if local problems can still be solved faster than without CBR. Within the CBR component, there is a similar problem. It is possible to include a *case adaptation* component which uses a limited form of reasoning to adapt an old case to the new problem. The adaptation component again may be costly in terms of solution time. At an even finer level of detail, we must consider the question which *cases* should be stored in memory. As with the whole CBR component and the adaptation component, adding a case may give a local reduction in solution time for some cases but the global effect on average solution time may be negative. These questions about extending a system with components that are aimed at reducing overall solution time is the *utility problem*.

In machine learning this problem received much attention in the context of explanation-based learning (EBL) or speedup learning. EBL systems derive shortcut rules from complex knowledge. These rules are redundant in the sense that they are derived directly from the knowledge that the system already had. However, these shortcut rules may reduce solution time. A "hybrid" architecture first tries to solve a problem with the shortcut rules and if that fails it uses the original knowledge base. As demonstrated by Keller [3] and Minton [4] the shortcut rules do not always lead to reduced solution time because the increase the branching factor of the search space. The negative effect of the increased branching rate can actually lead to a higher solution times. This raises the **utility problem**: when do new knowledge structures that achieve a "local" improvement (for a particular problem) also improve "global" performance (over all problems)? Although the utility problem has been studied mostly in the context of rule based architectures (including Horn clauses), it is in fact a very general problem. As discussed in [2] the utility problem also occurs in systems as sketched above, that "cache" cases to gain speed.

A simple approach to the utility problem is an empirical approach. The system could collect solution time data on its performance in different states (e.g. with and without a CBR component), compare the averages over some time and use this to decide about changes. The weakness of this empirical approach is that it will be slow and data intensive. The approach that we take to this problem is a mixed analytical and empirical approach, based on that followed by Subramanian [9] in the context of explanation-based learning, van Harmelen [10] in the context of metalevel control architectures. The idea is to predict the "global" performance of a system from performance characteristics of its components. In particular our ultimate goal is to predict the effect of changes to case memory on global performance. This can then be used to decide if a case should be added to (or dropped from) case memory. This means that we build a *cost model* of the system that expresses the expected solution time as a function of the solution times of components and the probability that these components will actually be used. A cost model is derived from a problem solving architecture and empirical performance data of components.

This paper addresses the question if the cost model gives accurate predictions of overall expected solution times and if this can be used to decide about the structure of the problem solving systems and the case memory. In this paper we first discuss the mixed CBR-MBR problem solving architecture (section 2) the general cost model for this architecture (section 3). In section 4 we show how the parameters of this model can be estimated from empirical (benchmarking) data and analytical arguments.

2 A mixed CBR-MBR architecture

The CBR-MBR architecture presented in this section is essentially the the one adopted in **ADAPtER** (**A**bductive **D**iagnosis through **A**daptation of **P**ast **E**pisodes for **R**e-use) [5], a diagnostic system which integrates a case-based component with a model-based component centered around the diagnostic inference engine AID. In general, model-based diagnosis is very expensive from a computational point of view since the search space is very large. In the following we just sketch the structure of the system and provide some more details on the modules which have been added in the revised version of the system. The architecture of ADAPtER involves the following basic components

MODEL-BASED REASONER (**MBR**): this is essentially the AID diagnostic engine [1], which uses of an abductive procedure for finding an explanation for the observations and uses consistency constraints for disregarding the tentative solutions which makes predictions on manifestations which are in conflict with observations. MBR uses a CAUSAL MODEL of the behaviour of the system to be diagnosed that includes initial causes for representing possible faults and malfunctions, internal states for representing influence of faults on the different subparts or components of the system, manifestations for representing observable consequences of the behaviour of the system and contexts for representing exogenous observable parameters. The main relation connecting different entities in the model is the causal relation which represents how a set of causes in a given context produces an effect. The CAUSAL MODEL has a precise semantics since it can be translated into a logical formalism (a more precise description of the formalism is reported in [5]).

CASE MEMORY MANAGER (**RETRIEVE**): stores and retrieves cases from the CASE MEMORY. This contains a set of diagnostic problems that were solved before. Each problem consists of two parts: the description in terms of pairs (*observable parameter - value*) and the solution. RETRIEVE evaluates the degree of match between the current case to be solved and the retrieved ones using a heuristic function which estimates the adaptation effort rather than just the similarity between the current case and the retrieved one. RETRIEVE finds the most promising case. It uses a threshold and thus can fail when there is no similar case in the *case memory*.

CHECK SOLUTION (**OK-SOLUTION**): replays the retrieved solution. The retrieved solution (initial causes and assumptions on incompleteness) is used together with the contextual data of the case under examination (potentially slightly different from the contextual data of the retrieved case) and the causal model to recompute all the possible consequences and therefore to recompute a causal evolution from initial causes to manifestations. This step is done to evaluate what the retrieved solution actually predicts in the contextual situation of the case under examination. It consists of two steps: *consistency check* and *covering check*. The first checks whether there is a conflict between the predicted values of the manifestations according to the replayed solutions and the observed values. If there is a conflict for at least one of the observations the replayed solution is not a solution for the case under examination and OK-SOLUTION fails. *Covering check* checks whether the replayed solution covers the manifestations that have to be covered. This means that we check whether the observed manifestations are actually predicted by the replayed solution. If all manifestations are covered, OK-SOLUTION succeeds and the replayed solution is a solution for the case under examination according to the definition of diagnosis, otherwise OK-SOLUTION fails. In this case the replayed solution is passed on to ADAPTATION.

ADAPTATION MODULE (**ADAPTATION**): adapts the solution of the retrieved case to be a solution of the current case by using the same domain knowledge (that is, the Causal Model) used by MBR. In particular, ADAPTATION tries to find an explanation in terms of initial causes for the manifestations which are not covered by the old solution. If an inconsistency is pointed out, then consistency must be re-established by the step of *inconsistency removal*; this mechanism disproves the explanation leading to the discovered inconsistency, by removing instances of states and/or manifestations.[4] *Explanation construction* builds abductive explanations for entities to be accounted for. The entities may

---

[4] Notice that, in general, there is more than one way for removing an inconsistency and *inconsistency removal* tries more than one possibilities, even if it does not consider all the possibilities.

be manifestations to be covered (for example, manifestations present just in the current case and not in the retrieved one) as well as internal states which are part of the retrieved solution, but, after the step of *inconsistency removal*, have no explanation. It is worth noting that *explanation construction* has to explore many alternatives since in general many causal relations have the same internal state for effect. The mechanisms of *inconsistency removal*, and *explanation construction* are quite complex from a computational point of view. As shown in [6], in the worst case ADAPTATION is as complex as MBR. ADAPTATION can fail because it is more restricted than the complete MBR component. In particular, *inconsistency removal* can involve disproving a conjunction of elements. In this case, ADAPTATION considers only scenarios where single elements of the conjunction and not all possible combinations are removed The top level problem solving architecture of ADAPtER is:

```
ADAPtER(new-case,Case-Memory,Causal-Model):

IF NOT RETRIEVE(new-case, Case-Memory, retrieve-solution)
   THEN MBR(new-case, Causal-Model)
   ELSE IF OK-SOLUTION(new-case, retrieve-solution, Causal-Model,
                       replayed-solution)
      THEN return replayed-solution
      ELSE IF ADAPTATION(new-case, replayed-solution,
                         Causal-Model, adapted-solution)
         THEN return adapted-solution
         ELSE MBR(new-case, Causal-Model)
```

Experiments with ADAPtER [6] have shown that it suffers from the utility problem in two ways. The first concerns the CBR component: storing more cases in CASE MEMORY leads to reduced solution times for problems that can be solved by RETRIEVE or by ADAPTATION but the **average** solution time reaches a minimum after which it begins to grow again. The second problem concerns the ADAPTATION component within the CBR component. ADAPTATION can take very much time. For some problems, the adaptation process can even be more expensive than solving the problem by MBR. This raises the question if ADAPTATION has a positive effect on the average solution time. A possible solution for both problems is selective storage of cases because the cases determine the average costs of CBR as a whole and ADAPTATION. The question is now: can overall solution time of a system be predicted from solutions times of components and of the probability of their application? The next section describes how a cost model is derived from the architecture.

3 A cost model

The purpose of the cost model is to express the expected costs of a computation as a function of the costs of elementary computations and the structure of the entire process. The cost model is derived from the control structure of the problem solving architecture. The expected costs (solution times) of components and the probability of their application are parameters of the cost model. The model is based on work by van Harmelen [10] and Straatman and Beys [8]. Their model was designed for rule based and "dynamic" logical languages that include control structures like "sequence" and "while loop".

A cost model is derived from a control structure as follows. The expected cost of a compound control expression is expressed in terms of its components by considering branches in the control flow. For example, a compound procedure of the form:

```
IF Proc1 THEN Proc2 ELSE Proc3
```

branches after executing `Proc1`. After `Proc1`, either `Proc2` or `Proc3` is executed, depending on the outcome of `Proc1`: success or failure. These occur with a certain probability. This gives the following expression for the expected cost of the compound procedure (`Ps` refers to probability of success and `Pf` to probability of failure):

```
cost(IF Proc1 THEN Proc2 ELSE Proc3) =
cost(Proc1) + (Ps(Proc1)* cost(Proc2)) + (Pf(Proc1) * cost(Proc3))
```

Analogous formulae can be derived for other control structures. The cost model in [8] gives formulae for *sequence, if-then-else* and *while-do*. Note that the model uses expected costs for a component procedure. If the costs of a procedure vary too much to obtain useful results then a model of finer grain size must be constructed.

Now we construct a model of the total costs of ADAPtER as a function of the costs of its components. This model will then be used to predict the effect of changes in the costs and probabilities of success that result from learning. This in turn will be used to control the learning process.

The cost model is derived from the problem solving architecture of ADAPtER given in section 2. We can express the expected costs of the entire system ADAPtER in terms of the costs of the basic procedures and the probabilities of success and failure as follows:

```
cost(ADAPtER) =
   cost(RETRIEVE) +
    Pf(RETRIEVE) * cost(MBR) +
    Ps(RETRIEVE) * [cost(OK-SOLUTION) +
              Pf(OK-SOLUTION) * (cost(ADAPTATION) +
              Pf(ADAPTATION) * cost(MBR))]
```

The probabilities and costs in this expression can be obtained empirically as follows. We use the following notation to indicate sets in the experiments: K refers to the test cases, R to the cases from K that were retrieved successfully, C to the cases from R that are solved by OK-SOLUTION and A to the cases from $R - C$ that were solved by adaptation. So the probabilities can then be estimated as follows:

Table 1. Estimators of parameters of the cost model

Probability	Estimator
Ps(RETRIEVE)	$Card(R)/Card(K)$
Pf(RETRIEVE)	$Card(K - R)/Card(K)$
Pf(OK-SOLUTION)	$Card(R - C/Card(R)$
Pf(ADAPTATION)	$Card(R - C - A)/Card(R - C)$

The (expected) costs are interpreted as an average time of performing the given task. For example, the expected cost of RETRIEVE is the average time of retrieval the test set (K) from Case-Memory and cost(MBR) is the average time of diagnostic problem solving by MBR on the set given by the union of the set $K - R$ with the set $R - C - A$ [5].

If the model is used to compare different versions of the architecture or to predict the effect of changes in components then it is enough to know the *difference* between the values before and after changes. These can often be estimated or reasonable assumptions can be made. For example, the effect of adding cases to memory on retrieval can be predicted if we know how retrieval time is a function of the number of cases in memory. If the Case Memory Manager performs a linear search, the retrieval costs with grow linearly with the size of the case memory.

In the next section we test if this model can indeed predict the overall performance of the system. First, will be shown if the CBR component is a useful addition in the ADAPtER architecture. Second, the potential application of the cost model in an incremental learning strategy will be discussed.

4 Empirical evaluation of the cost model

We can use the cost model to predict the effect of adding the CBR component of ADAPtER to the MBR component from the probabilities and costs of the basic components. In the experiment described below we obtained these values from measurements, assumptions and analytical arguments. We use these to evaluate the difference in performance of the two architectures.

To enable meaningful comparison we have developed a simulation module which automatically generates a case by taking into consideration a causal model and some parameters. In particular, important parameters are the maximum number of initial causes with abnormal values to be included in the case, the

---

[5] The choice of estimating cost(MBR) on such a set is not always justified since in many situations $Card(K - R)$ and $Card(R - C - A)$ are small and also Pf(RETRIEVE) and Pf(OK-SOLUTION) are small. In order to more accurate estimates, in the experiments we will describe below we have estimated cost(MBR) on the entire training set K.

probability that an assumption symbol is assumed true, etc. We can therefore generate cases with different characteristics. We have generated training set and test set by using the same values of parameters in both cases. However, there are constraints we have put just on the training set. All the cases in the training set are different (there is at least one observable parameter which is different from one case to another) so that the CASE MEMORY does not contain any redundant information. Whilst this requirement is quite obvious, the second requirement is less obvious. The cases in the training set are (almost) "complete" from the point of view of observations, that is, all relevant observable parameters have been actually observed and therefore no piece of information which could be used for discriminating among competing diagnostic solutions is missing. In this way we prevent as much as we can to have cases in the case memory with a lot a diagnostic solutions for each stored case. Experiments were done with causal models and cases from three domains, *car faults*, *leprosy*, a medical diagnosis domain and a technical diagnosis domain. The experiments were designed as follows. Case memory was filled with sets of cases of different sizes. The resulting system was run on a test set of 100 problems. If Case Memory is empty then all cases are solved by MBR.

4.1 The marginal utility of procedures

The ADAPtER architecture can be viewed as a basic MBR component that is extended with components that do not change the functionality but that improve solution time. This is the case for the CBR extension to MBR and also for, for example, the ADAPTATION extension to RETRIEVE and OK-SOLUTION. In fact, the decision to add cases to memory or to drop them depends on the same argument. Do the extensions indeed reduce the costs?

The utility threshold condition for adding or dropping the CBR component can be defined as `cost(ADAPtER) > cost(MBR)`. By substituting the cost models for the costs and some algebraic manipulation we get:

```
cost(RETRIEVE)/cost(MBR) +
   Pf(RETRIEVE) *
       [cost(OK-SOLUTION)/cost(MBR) +
       Pf(OK-SOLUTION) * (cost(ADAPTATION)/cost(MBR) +
       Pf(ADAPTATION))]
```

If this expression is bigger or equal to 1 than MBR alone is "cheaper" than ADAPtER. The experiments provide estimates of the parameters of the cost model for different sized Case Memories. The tables below give the average solution times of the procedures RETRIEVE, OK-SOLUTION, ADAPTATION and the compound procedure ADAPtER, which RETRIEVES a case, applies OK-SOLUTION and if that fails, applies ADAPTATION. The tables also give the probability that a procedure ends with success (**Ps**). Experiment 1, 2 and 3 involve *car faults*, experiment 4, 5 and 6 involve *leprosy* and experiment 7, 8 and 9 involve *technical diagnosis*. Measurements were done with 50 (experiment

1 and 4), 75 (experiment 2 and 5) and 100 cases in Case Memory (experiment 3 and 6). In the technical domain Memory sizes of 100, 150 and 200 were used.

Table 2. Experiment 1, 2 and 3: Faulty cars with 50, 75 and 100 cases in case memory

Component	Av. cost (SD)	Ps	Av. cost (SD)	Ps	Av. cost (SD)	Ps
RETRIEVE	551 (208)	1	873 (325)	1	1186 (527)	1
OK-SOLUTION	77 (12)	0.75	77 (12)	0.83	78 (13)	0.83
ADAPTATION	222 (71)	0.82	239 (73)	0.75	266 (92)	0.66
MBR	10679 (50346)	1	10679 (50346)	1	10679 (50346)	1
ADAPtER	814 (496)	1	1084 (553)	1	1518 (714)	1

Table 3. Experiment 4, 5 and 6: Leprosy: 50, 75 and 100 cases in case memory

Component	Av. cost (SD)	Ps	Av. cost (SD)	Ps	Av. cost (SD)	Ps
RETRIEVE	581 (102)	1	901 (165)	1	1212 (228)	1
OK-SOLUTION	88 (25)	0.86	92 (25)	0.88	93 (27)	0.92
ADAPTATION	213 (35)	1	212 (41)	1	205 (47)	1
MBR	19795 (112233)	1	19795 (112233)	1	19795 (112233)	1
ADAPtER	701 (152)	1	1050 (208)	1	1347 (262)	1

Table 4. Experiment 7, 8 and 9: Technical diagnosis with 100, 150 and 200 cases in case memory

Component	Av. cost (SD)	Ps	Av. cost (SD)	Ps	Av. cost (SD)	Ps
RETRIEVE	2982 (1118)	1	4746 (1692)	1	6890 (2337)	1
OK-SOLUTION	111 (18)	0.78	111 (18)	0.83	111 (18)	0.89
ADAPTATION	393 (96)	0.95	421 (118)	0.95	405 (81)	0.92
MBR	556 (825)	1	556 (825)	1	556 (825)	1
ADAPtER	3383 (1055)	1	5281 (1539)	1	7372 (2093)	1

We note that in Car Faults and Leprosy, even with 100 cases in Case Memory, complete ADAPtER is still much faster than only MBR. In these two domains it is quite apparent that the CBR component is a really useful addition to MBR.

However, as already pointed out in [6] the benefits are in average, since in many specific cases MBR could be better than ADAPtER because the cost of MBR is relatively small. It is worth noting the extremely large standard deviation of Cost(MBR) which makes clear that even in the same domain diagnostic problems can require very different amounts of time to be solved. This is not always the case. In the technical diagnosis domain, the costs of MBR are relatively low compared with CBR and we see that emprically, ADAPtER has higher costs (longer solution times) than MBR alone. This suggests that in this domain the entire CBR component can be dropped from the problem solving architecture.

For example in a technical domain we had the opportunity of making experiments, cost(MBR) is relatively constant and of the same magnitude than the cost(RETRIEVE). In such a domain the addition of a CBR component to MBR is questionable. On the other hand, increasing the size of the case memory is not always beneficial. In fact there is an increase in Ps(OK-SOLUTION) but this increase does not fully compensate the increase in cost(RETRIEVE). Therefore, the overall solution times of the entire system increase quite steeply, which shows that on average, caching makes the system slower rather than faster: the "marginal" effect of new cases in case memory becomes negative.

Next consider the marginal utility of subprocedures of the CBR component. In the Leprosy domain we see that ADAPTATION is very useful because it is always successful and has much smaller costs than MBR. In the Car Fault domain, ADAPTATION solves most of the cases it tries also at much smaller costs than they would generate if solved directly by MBR. In both cases ADAPTATION has a positive marginal utility.

4.2   The effect of the size of case memory

The benefit of the cost model must be that it enables analytical prediction of the costs. One question in connection with this is: how many cases should be stored? Here we address the question if it is possible to predict the effect of increasing the size of Case Memory. We note the following. RETRIEVAL times go up almost linearly with the number of cases in Case Memory. This is not surprising since memory is searched linearly. RETRIEVAL is always used and thus is a linear increasing factor in the costs. The cost of OK-SOLUTION is approximately constant with varying memory sizes. Its probability of success is increasing slowly when there are more cases in memory. This also allows good predictions of the costs of these two components by extrapolating a small amount of data. The times of ADAPTATION are less regular. The car fault example shows a slow increase and the leprosy data show a slow decrease with larger case memory. In the Leprosy domain, ADAPTATION is always succesful, which means that MBR is not used at all. In the car domain the probability that ADAPTATION is succesful is 0.72 for 50 cases in memory, 0.75 for 75 cases and 0.67 for 100 cases. We have no explanation for this.

Interesting enough, in the Technical diagnosis domain, the Ps of ADAPTA-TION seems to decrease slowly. It is possible that if there are more cases in case memory, less useful cases are retrieved, which creates problems for ADAPTA-TION.

Because most of these parameters appear to show regularity, the prospects for predicting the costs of various sized Case Memories are good. More data are needed in order to make more precise conclusions about all these issues.

5 Discussion

We showed how a model of the architecture of a hybrid problem solving system can be used to derive a cost model for the architecture. The model of the architecture can be more or less detailed, resulting in a more or less detailed cost model. The model specifies the relations between components and how these affect the computational costs of running the system. By making assumptions about some components and taking performance measurements of others, the model can be used to predict the computational costs of different problem solving architectures. This can then be used to control the learning process, in this case the problem of adding or deleting components in the architecture. For example, experiments showed that the effect of ADAPTATION is negative for some case memories and solution times are smaller if no ADAPTATION is attempted. At a finer level of granularity we intend to apply this approach to reasoning about the utility of individual cases for overall performance and to search for a case base that minimises computational costs. Preliminary data are presented to illustrate the use of the cost model and to show that it gives predictions with an acceptable accuracy.

The analysis makes the simplifying assumption that MBR has the same average cost both in isolation (that is when the MBR is used without the CBR component) and integrated within ADAPtER. Obviously MBR takes the same time of any specific case when is run in isolation or within ADAPtER. However, it could be the case that some criteria for selecting the cases to be stored in the case memory (for example just storing cases which take a very long time to be solved by MBR alone) have an impact on the kind of cases that MBR has to solve when it is integrated within ADAPtER.

There are several possible extensions of this work. One issue concerns controlling changes in the problem solving architecture and in case memory. The cost model supports the evaluation of possible changes to the architecture but automated learning also needs an algorithm for collecting data and for generating and evaluating possible changes. Experiments with analogous methods to achieve functionality (possibly combined with speedup) suggest that "forgetting" (deleting cases after some time) gives better results than "remembering" (deciding directly if a case should be stored or deleted) (e.g. [7]). A second issue concerns prediction of effects of adding or deleting individual cases. Our experiments sofar addressed larger components of the architecture but, as discussed, the same approach can in principle be applied to individual cases. A third issue concerns the nature of the costs. The cost model currently only addresses *solution time* as a cost factor but there can be other aspects of costs, for example memory space. If memory is "expensive" then memory costs can be modelled following the same approach as time costs.

Acknowledgement: The authors wish to thank Diego Magro (Univ. Torino) for running the experiments in section 4 and Remco Straatman and Pascal Beys for their comments on earlier drafts of this paper. This work was partially supported by European Science Foundation within the project Learning Humans and Machines.

References

[1] Console, L., Portinale, L., Theseider, D., and Torasso, P. (1993). *Combining Heuristic Reasoning with Causal Reasoning In Diagnostic Problem Solving*, pages 46–68. Springer Verlag.

[2] Francis, A. G. and Ram, A. (1995). A comparative utility analysis of case-based reasoning and controle-rule learning systems. In Lavrac, N. and Wrobel, S., editors, *Machine Learning: ECML-95*, pages 138–150. Springer Verlag.

[3] Keller, R. M. (1988). Defining operationality for explanation-based learning. *Artificial Intelligence*, 35:227–241.

[4] Minton, S. (1988). *Learning Effective Search Control Knowledge: An Explanation-Based Approach*. Kluwer.

[5] Portinale, L. and Torasso, P. (1995). Adapter: an integrated diagnostic system combining case-based and abductive reasoning. In Veloso, M. and Aamodt, A., editors, *Proceedings ICCBR-95*, pages 277–288. Springer Verlag.

[6] Portinale, L. and Torasso, P. (1996). On the usefulness of re-using diagnostic solutions. In Wahlster, W., editor, *Proceedings 12th European Conference on Artificial Intelligence ECAI-96*, pages 137–141. John Wiley and Sons.

[7] Smyth, B. and Keane, M. (1995). Remembering to forget. In Mellish, C., editor, *Proceedings IJCAI-95*, pages 377–382. Morgan Kaufmann.

[8] Straatman, R. and Beys, P. (1995). A performance model for knowledge-based systems. In Ayel, M. and Rousse, M. C., editors, *EUROVAV-95 European Symposium on the Validation and Verification of Knowledge Based Systems*, pages 253–263. ADEIRAS, Université de Savoie, Chambéry.

[9] Subramanian, D. and Hunter, S. (1992). Measuring utility and the design of provably good ebl algorithms. In Sleeman, D. and Edwards, P., editors, *Machine Learning: Proceedings of the Ninth International Workshop ML-95*, pages 426–435. Morgan Kaufmann.

[10] van Harmelen, F. (1994). A model of costs and benefits of meta-level computation. In *Proceedings of the Fourth Workshop on Meta-programming in Logic (META'94)*, volume 883 of *LNCS*, pages 248–261. Springer-Verlag.

[11] van Someren, M. W., Zheng, L. L., and Post, W. (1990). Cases, models or compiled knowledge? - a comparative analysis and proposed integration. In Wielinga, B. J., Boose, J., Gaines, B., Schreiber, G., and van Someren, M. W., editors, *Current trends in knowledge acquisition*, pages 339–355. IOS Press.

Qualitative Knowledge to Support Reasoning About Cases

Robert J. Aarts and Juho Rousu

VTT Biotechnology and Food Research
P.O. Box 1500, FIN–02044 VTT, Finland
{Robert.Aarts, Juho.Rousu}@vtt.fi

Abstract. Our recipe planner for bioprocesses, Sophist, uses a semi-qualitative model to reason about cases. The model represents qualitative knowledge about the possible effects of differences between cases and about the possible causes of observed problems. Hence, the model is a crucial resource of adaptation knowledge. The model representation has been developed specifically to support CBR tasks. The essential notion in this representation is that of an *influence*. Representation of domain knowledge in an influence graph and a mapping of case-features onto nodes of such a graph, enable a variety of interesting reasoning tasks. Examples of such task illustrate how qualitative reasoning and case-based reasoning support each other in complex planning tasks.

Keywords: qualitative reasoning, planning, domain knowledge.

1. Introduction

A feature of all learning systems is the information that is available *a priori*. The more knowledge is embedded into the system, the more effective the system is expected to be. In planning applications, domain knowledge typically includes representation of possible actions (operations) with e.g., preconditions and effects. Our bioprocess recipe planner Sophist (Aarts & Rousu, 1996) uses a qualitative model to represent a large amount of domain knowledge. This knowledge is used to analyse differences between cases, to construct adaptations, to evaluate suggested plan changes and to explain outcomes. This implementation of a module for Qualitative Modeling in a CBR system (QMC) rises a number of interesting issues and is the subject of this paper.

Of course, QMC is not the first attempt to integrate model knowledge effectively. CADET (Sycara *et al.*, 1992) and KRITIK (Batta *et al.*, 1994) use qualitative models to represent design cases whereas Sophist applications have one global QMC model. SME (Falkenhainer *et al.*, 1989) constructs analogies between two given qualitative models, but does not retrieve those models itself. Approaches based on explanation based reasoning such as CREEK (Aamodt 1994), SWALE (Schank & Leake, 1989) and CHEF (Hammond 1990) were influential to this work. The crucial difference is that QMC is intended for planning in continuous domains where the quantitative values of plan operations are important. CARMA (Hastings *et al.*, 1995) operates in a semi-continuous domain and uses a causal model to aid case retrieval but not for the adaptation *per se*. CASEY (Koton 1990) is another system that uses a qualitative model to compute case features for indexing purposes.

This paper describes the Qualitative Modeling framework for CBR (QMC). First the modeling language is introduced and illustrated with a simple model. Then the algorithms that support case-based reasoning are treated. Finally, the advantages and shortcomings of the current framework are discussed, also with respect to similar approaches.

2. Model Representation in QMC

In the next two sections QMC is introduced. The framework is designed to support planning in continuous domains, that is the planning problems are given in terms of continuous quantities. Throughout this paper a model of a very simple flight domain is used as an example (see Aarts & Rousu, 1996, for an example of a more realistic application). In this domain planes have to fly a required distance with a particular payload and a given amount of fuel. A single flight is a case with a given plane, payload and amount of fuel. The task of the case-based reasoner is to construct a flight path such that the requested distance is flown. A simple qualitative model of this domain was constructed (see Figure 1) and a handful of cases were conceived. These cases have flight paths consisting of three flight segments: an ascend, a period of level flight and a descend. A deterministic system of differential equations was used to simulate the plans.

2.1 Qualitative Modeling

QMC is loosely based on the Qualitative Process Theory (QPT) as developed by Forbus (1984). As in QPT, QMC represents *processes* and *variables*. A process is an activity that may *influences* the state of a variable. For instance the process `climbing` influences the variable `altitude`; the altitude of a plane will increase if the process is active (a `courier` typeface will be used to indicate a model node). *Influences* link processes to variables. Not only are variables influenced by processes, but processes may be influenced by variables. For instance, `fuel consumption` is influenced by the variable `friction`. In addition, QMC allows variables to be influenced by variables. For instance, `altitude` influences `friction`.

Influences are monotonic, an influence is either positive, or negative. Unlike in QPT, influences in QMC have weights that can be used to indicate the relative strength of an influence. For instance, `fuel consumption` is *strongly* influenced by `climbing` and *typically* influenced by `descending`, where *strongly* indicates a stronger link than *typically*. The information in weights can be used to infer that it is more effective to shorten an ascend than it is to quicken a descend when the fuel consumption should be reduced.

As in QPT, the activity of processes is conditional, i.e. a process is only active if its conditions are satisfied. In QMC complex conditions can be formed by *primitives* and *rules*. *Primitives* are evaluable expressions, i.e. the case-based reasoner should be able to compute the truth of each primitive used in a QMC model. An example of such a primitive (and a simple condition) is `climb rate > 0`, where the climb rate is not a variable of the model, but a case feature[1]. *Rules* simply combine primitives or other rules, through *support* links.

In essence then, a QMC model is a graph of process, variable and rule *nodes* linked by *influences*. It is a kind of spreading activation network, with different interpretations of activity for different types of nodes. For a rule the intuitive interpretation is "truth", for a process it is "rate", and for a variable it is "trend". These

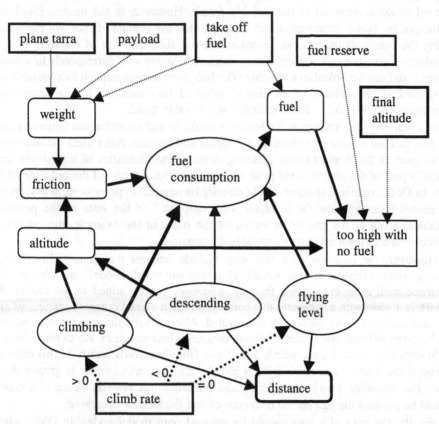

Figure 1. The influence graph of the simple flight domain. Ellipses denote *processes*, rounded rectangles are *variables* and rectangles indicate *primitives* and *rules*. Straight arrows are *influences*; dashed arrows are *support* links. Arrow print weights indicate the relative strength of link. **Bold** rectangles indicate nodes that are mapped onto case features.

concepts support the construction of rather comprehensive models in a variety of domains. Note that, although the links have associated weights, the models are primarily qualitative! Without cases, it is impossible to infer any quantitative information from such a model, for instance it is impossible to determine even a rough quantitative flight plan from the model presented in Figure 1.

---

[1] The climb rate is calculated from plan operations.

2.2 Mapping case features to a model

To effectively use a qualitative model in a CBR system, it is important to enable the mapping of case features to the appropriate nodes in the model. To this end, QMC offers several possibilities. First, variables may directly correspond to case features. However, such direct mapping is often inappropriate as variables represent a *changing* property, whereas a case feature is typically static. For instance, the amount of fuel at take-off could correspond to the variable `fuel`. However, in the model, `fuel` is influenced by `fuel consumption` to reflect that the amount of fuel will decrease during the course of the process. In order to avoid such dual use of variables QMC introduces *measurements* and *estimation links*. A *measurement* corresponds to a case property and can be linked to a variable. The link from a measurement to a variable is interpreted as an *estimate* of the (initial value of the) variable. For instance, the measurement `take-off fuel` estimates the variable `fuel`.

In a planning system such as Sophist, it is useful to make a difference between case features that are related to a *situation* (or input) and features that reflect the *outcome* of the case. In the Sophist recipe planning domain, characteristics of ingredients are typically part of the situation and product characteristics are part of the outcome of a case. In QMC, outcome features should directly be mapped to process variables; from the model point of view the outcome is a "snapshot" of the state of the process variables, taken at the end of execution of the plan. In the example, the outcome feature *distance flown* maps to the variable `distance`.

However, the outcome of a case may include features that cannot directly be mapped onto variables of the model. If is known which model variables *might* influence such indirect outcome features, a *remark* can be added to the model. A remark is a node with a statement that corresponds to a named outcome feature, when the case has this feature the remark is activated. Alternatively, the activity of a remark can be inferred from case features through measurements and rules. An example in the flight domain is `too high with no fuel` (in other words "crash"). This remark is true if the `fuel reserve` is zero and the `final altitude` is greater than zero. The variables `fuel` and `altitude` influence this remark, hence if a crash should be avoided the fuel should be increased and the altitude decreased.

Finally, the plan of a case should be mapped onto model nodes. In QMC, plan operations may affect particular processes by enabling or supporting particular conditions of processes. For instance, an ascending flight segment makes the primitive `climb rate > 0` true and enables `climbing`. This kind of mapping relies on the appropriate definition of operations. In Sophist operations are domain specific, e.g. *flight segments* have a climb rate, start and end altitude, etc. Now, if the activity of `climbing` has to be increased (extended), it may be possible to adapt an enabling flight segment.

In short, case features can be mapped to various nodes in the model graph provided that the representation of cases is in accordance with the model and with the QMC framework. To facilitate application development QMC is indeed a *framework* and is tightly integrated into Sophist, a framework for CBR. Note however, that QMC *supports* the mapping of cases to a model and a variety of reasoning tasks, but that it is the case-based reasoner that is responsible for the *control* of the reasoning processes.

3. Model-Based Reasoning About Cases

With the influence graph and a mapping of case features to graph nodes in place it is relatively straightforward to perform a number of reasoning tasks. In general, the case-based reasoner maps some features of a case to nodes in the graph, the influences are traversed and then relevant nodes return appropriate objects. Dependent on the task, particular features are mapped and different nodes should be traced. This is best illustrated with an example of plan construction. The example is based on the simple flight model shown in Figure 1. The task is to construct a plan for Flight 6 from the template case Flight 4 (see Table 1).

Table 1. A template case, Flight 4, and a target case, Flight 6. The task of the planner is to construct a flight path for Flight 6 on the basis of the flight path of Flight 4. The suggested plan and simulated outcome for Flight 6 are in *italic*.

	Flight 4	Flight 6
Distance to goal	500	600
Plane	Liner	Liner
Payload	20000 kg	25000 kg
Take-off fuel	15000 kg	10000 kg
Flight path	Ascend to 10000 in 20´ at 400	*Ascend to 10000 in 20´ at 400*
	Fly at 10000 for 20´ at 700	*Fly at 10000 for 21´ at 700*
	Descend to 0 in 15´ at 400	*Descend to 0 in 17´ at 400*
Distance flown	500 km	*533 km*
Fuel consumed	5743 kg	*6084 kg*
Final altitude	0 m	*0 m*

Sophist is a recipe planner, hence QMC offers strong support for plan adaptation. In Sophist, the plan of a new case is constructed by adaptation of the plan from a similar case. Finding such a template case is the task of the indexing system, but once a template case has been found it can be analysed with the aid of the model. Naturally, it is expected that the template case is similar to the target case, but it is important to analyse the differences. In addition, it may well be the case that the template was not very successful, hence it is important to check for and analyse potential pitfalls. Analyses of differences should include inferring what the effects of those differences might be and which of these effects require adaptations. The next step is to ask the model for adaptations that may achieve the desired (counter-)effects. Finally, *all* the expected effects, including side effects, of selected adaptations are retrieved. Knowledge of these effects allows for the combination of possible adaptations and for ranking adaptations according to benefit.

3.1 Analysis of differences and pitfalls

It is the task of the case-based reasoner (in Sophist this is done by the indexing system) to construct *case differences*. Case differences are structures that hold the values of both a template and a target case for a particular feature. In the flight example, one of the constructed case differences is "a greater requirement for distance"[2]. These case differences are now, one at a time, mapped to an appropriate model node. Finding such relevant nodes is done by searching for nodes that have a name, or quantity, that is associated with (or is identical to) the subject (feature) of the difference. For example, "a greater requirement for distance" maps to the distance variable in the model because the subject of the difference is a *minimum* (a kind of constraint) for the *quantity* named "distance". That quantity is shared with the model variable distance. (Figure 1).

Actual analysis of the difference starts by traversing the influence graph to processes that in principle could compensate for the difference. Such processes return an *adaptation goal*. According to the example model, a greater distance can be achieved by an increase in climbing, flying level or descending, as each of these processes influence distance. The model thus, returns three *adaptation goals*. An adaptation goal asks for an increase or decrease of the activity of a process in order to compensate for one or more differences. The case difference is a justification for the adaptation goal. The *importance* of an adaptation goal corresponds to the importance of its justifying differences[3]. Adaptation goals provide some invariance with respect to case feature values: for example, similar adaptation goals would result if the required distances of the two example cases were halved. Very similar reasoning is performed for pitfalls. The outcome of the template case (if it has any) is checked for violations of the specification (constraints) of the target. In the example, the distance flown in Flight 4, 500 km, does not meet the requirement of Flight 6, which requests a distance of 600 km. Sophist constructs a *deficit* (a kind of *specification violation*) for the distance requirement. This deficit maps to the same distance node and returns the same three adaptation goals. Sophist (not the model) recognises that these adaptation goals are identical to the ones obtained earlier except for their justifications. Hence, it adds the deficit to the justifications of the earlier goals and discards the other, similar, goals.

Finally, the template case is mapped onto the model to check for the activation of remark nodes in the model. This is done by means of spreading activation. Primitives, such as fuel reserve in the example, recalculate their activity from the template and propagate the obtained value. The case-based reasoner then simply checks for remark nodes that are active and indicate a problem. The next step is then to construct a *remark* for each such a node and analyse that in similar fashion as a case difference.

---

[2] More specifically this is an *aim increment*, one of the different supported subclasses of *case difference*. Others are *aim decrement*, *property increment* and *property decrement*. These are classes in the Sophist case-based reasoning framework.

[3] It is the task of the domain specific quantity to compute an importance for a difference, but such a quantity may rely solely on some of the domain-independent heuristics that may be based on minimum and maximum values or the reproducibility of the quantity.

3.2 Construction of adaptations for adaptation goals

The result of the analysis of the template is a number of adaptation goals. These goals may be contradicting and the planner first adjusts the importance of such contradicting goals; the importance of the less important goal is subtracted from the importance of the more important goal and the less important goal is discarded. Now the model is asked for adaptations of the template plan for each of the remaining goals. The model maps the adaptation goal to one or more appropriate nodes (as for case differences) and asks that node for relevant adaptations. Variables pass this request on along their influences, but processes also ask their conditions for adaptations. This recursion bottoms out at support links from measurement nodes to other nodes. The measurement checks if any of the template operations activates the link. Such an operation is then asked for an adaptation that meets the adaptation goal. For example, the adaptation returned for "an increase of flying" is "an increase in the length of the level flight segment" of Flight 4. Note that the actual adaptation is provided by the operation. This knowledge however, is not as domain specific as it seems. The example solution, increase the length of the operation, is valid for almost any step- or segment-like operation. Would no operation in the template enable flying, than an adaptation that adds such an operation would have been suggested.

3.3 Retrieval of expected effects

For each adaptation goal, one or more possible adaptations may have been obtained. These were suggested to satisfy one adaptation goal. However, each adaptation may have a number of possible effects, other than the requested effect. Some of these other effects may partly satisfy other adaptation goals, while others may be counter-productive with respect to other adaptation goals. Hence, it is very valuable to have an idea of *all* the effects of each adaptation. This again can be obtained easily from the influence graph. The adaptation is mapped to the node that constructed it, and its effect is propagated along influences. Visited nodes can add the effect of the proposed change to the list of effects of the adaptation.

For example, the effects of the proposed increment in the length of the level flight segment include an increase of fuel consumption and a decrease in fuel. These effects can now be compared to all the adaptation goals and the *expected benefit* of adaptations with positive side effects can be increased, and vice versa. For example, the benefit of a proposed "increase of length of the ascend segment" was reduced because of the strong effect on fuel consumption, where a goal for a reduction of fuel consumption had been constructed.

The adaptations can now be ranked according to expected benefit. Most beneficial adaptations are committed first, application of less beneficial adaptations stops as soon as the adaptation goals are expected to be satisfied. Therefore, the proposed increase of the ascend segment was not made (see Table 1).

4. Discussion

A framework for qualitative reasoning about cases was presented. The description of a few reasoning tasks that are enabled by a qualitative model indicates that such knowledge is a rich source of problem solving power. The availability of a model enhances the problem solving performance when the casebase is small. When a casebase grows, problem solving gets easier, as suitable template cases are found more frequently. However, in a complex domain the interesting problems are often those that are somewhat abnormal, and that are not encountered frequently. In addition, it is often not acceptable to wander through the solution space, suggested solutions should be of a high quality. Having a model to point out the correct direction of change does not guarantee that the outcome will be acceptable, but it certainly helps to make progress towards the goal, nevertheless. It would be very helpful if the appropriate *size* of an adaptation would be learned. This may be well possible by integration of case-based adaptation (Leake *et al.*, 1995).

Another important role of a qualitative model is to provide comprehensibility to the system. A very large obstacle in the deployment of knowledge-based systems into real-world situations is that people do not tend to trust a system that presents itself as a black box. In very simple domains, it is enough for a system to justify some action by just pointing out that some case is similar to the current problem, as judged by surface features. In more complex domains this clearly is not enough: the system should be able to provide explanations why adaptations are suggested, etc. QMC supports this very well indeed. Using the model, the system generates explanations of the adaptation process.

QMC models work as a universal knowledge source that can be utilised for retrieval, adaptation, evaluation, and explanation of outcomes alike. In this way, QMC is somewhat orthogonal to the idea of four knowledge containers by Richter (1995): we argue for using all the knowledge that is available. Neither replicating knowledge between containers nor excluding information in some container from another seems efficient. For example, embedding some domain knowledge in the distance metric hides it from an adaptation algorithm. During adaptation one would like to utilise any information that is available about to the importance of differences and pitfalls. A similar position was presented by Kamp (1996): integration of knowledge and reasoning tasks provides for more powerful systems than the approach of segregation.

The software engineering benefits of having a single location for knowledge are also obvious: consistency of the knowledge is far more easily ensured and, consequently, one can expect the system to be more robust. Another nice property is that the knowledge is far more accessible to the end user.

Naturally model construction is not trivial, although a qualitative model is often far easier to construct than a quantitative (mathematical) model or a set of adaptation rules. A crucial question is what information should be represented by the cases and what by the model. Several arguments suggest to represent quantitative information in cases. Quantitative aspects are likely to be very context-specific and are easily represented as case features, whereas identification of quantitative models is often impossible. On the other hand qualitative aspects are often better represented in a model. For example, it is space consuming to have a trajectory of fuel consumption as a case feature, and difficult to use such a feature. Also, the more qualitative the knowledge is, the more context-independent it seems to be. For example, the law of thermodynamics that depicts that energy flow is always from warm to cold is literally universal, but the exact amount of energy transferred in a heat exchanger can be very difficult to calculate[4].

QMC is intended for continuous domains, put perhaps some domains that seem discrete are somewhat continuous and can effectively be represented in QMC. For example, issues such as present in the Factor Hierarchy of CATO (Aleven & Ashley, 1996), a case-based legal argumentation system, are not unlike QMC variables. Such a factor hierarchy is almost identical to a QMC model. The main difference is that QMC considers variables and processes, whereas the factors and issues in a Factor Hierarchy are all variables. Hence, CATO like argumentation would be easily realised with the aid of QMC. In effect, during recipe adaptation contradicting adaptation goals are often constructed. These contradictions are resolved by comparing the justifications of the adaptation goals.

Explanation based reasoning as in SWALE (Schank & Leake, 1989) hints at possibilities to *learn* the model with the aid of expectation violations. The model could be asked to construct explanations for the observed outcome of the case, given the plan and the situation, that is. If the model can indeed explain all the observations, the model is valid. If however, the model cannot explain an observation, it obviously needs to be revised. Another reason to revise the model could be rejection of a proposed recipe by the user. Work by DeJong (1994) demonstrates how model learning might be achieved in continuous domains. Other research on model identification, i.e. determining the underlying "deep" variables from system behaviour, includes work by Say & Kuru (1996) and Nayak & Joskowicz (1996). The time-dimension inherent to planning problems expands the search space very much; for example, it seems one has to consider relationships of differential equation flavour, even if we only consider qualitative modeling. However, in more simple domains than dynamic systems, such as the flat domain presented in Hanney and Keane (1996), the idea of searching trough the space of possible relationships between the variables seems reasonable.

5. Conclusions

QMC, a framework for the representation of qualitative knowledge in CBR systems was presented and examples of some reasoning tasks associated with the adaptation of plans were given. The availability of qualitative knowledge enhances the robustness of a CBR system, it will be able to solve more problems and to provide better solutions. In addition, QMC enables the construction of explanations of system behaviour. Although QMC is intended for planning in continuous domains, it, or similar approaches, may be useful in other domains as well. A great step forward would be to learn or improve the model from cases, another to learn the appropriate size of adaptations.

---

[4] Such predictions can be made with numerical simulation of finite element models.

References

Aamodt, A. (1994). Explanation-driven case-based reasoning, In S. Wess, K. Althoff, M. Richter (Eds.): *Topics in Case-based reasoning*. Springer Verlag, pp. 274-288.

Aarts, R.J. & Rousu, J. (1996). Towards CBR for bioprocess planning. In Smith I., Faltings, B., (Eds.): Proceedings of EWCBR-96, Lausanne, *Lecture Notes in Artificial Intelligence*, **1186**: 16-27.

Ashley, K.D. & Aleven, V. (1996). How different is different? Arguing About the Significance of Similarities and Differences. In Smith I., Faltings, B., (Eds.): Proceedings of EWCBR-96, Lausanne, *Lecture Notes in Artificial Intelligence*, **1186**: 1-15.

Bhatta, S., Goel, A. & Prabhakar, S. (1994). Innovation in Analogical Design: A Model-Based Approach. *Proc. of the Third International Conference on AI in Design, Aug. 1994, Lausanne, Switzerland.*

DeJong, G. F. (1994). Learning to plan in continuous domains. *Artificial Intelligence* **65**: 71–141.

Falkenhainer, B., Forbus, K.D. & Gentner, D. (1989). The Structure-Mapping Engine: Algorithm and Examples. *Artificial Intelligence* **41**: 1-63.

Forbus. K.D. (1984). Qualitative Process Theory. *Artificial Intelligence* **24**: 85–168.

Hammond, K. (1990). Explaining and Repairing Plans That Fail. *Artificial Intelligence*, **45**:173–228.

Hanney, K. & Keane, M.T. (1996). Learning Adaptation Rules from a Case-Base. In Smith I., Faltings, B., (Eds). Proceedings of EWCBR-96, Lausanne, *Lecture Notes in Artificial Intelligence*, **1186**: 179-192.

Hastings, J.D., Branting, L.K. & Lockwood, J.A. (1995), Case Adaptation Using an Incomplete Causal Model. In: Veloso, M. & Aamodt, A. (Eds.): Proceedings ICCBR-95, Sesimbra, *Lecture Notes in Artificial Intelligence*, **1010**: 181–192.

Leake, D.B., Kinley, A. & Wilson, D. Learning to Improve Case Adaptation by Introspective Reasoning and CBR. In: Veloso, M. & Aamodt, A. (Eds.): Proceedings ICCBR-95, Sesimbra, *Lecture Notes in Artificial Intelligence*, **1010**: 229–240.

Kamp, G. (1996). Using Description Logics for Knowledge Intensive Case-Based Reasoning. In Smith I., Faltings, B., (Eds). Proceedings of EWCBR-96, Lausanne, *Lecture Notes in Artificial Intelligence*, **1186**: 204-218

Koton, P. (1989). *Using experience in learning and problem solving*. Massachusetts Institute of Technology, Laboratory of Computer Science (Ph.D. diss., October 1988), MIT/LCS/TR-441.

Nayak P. & Joskowicz, L. (1996). Efficient compositional modeling for generating causal explanations. *Artificial Intelligence* **83**: 193-227.

Richter, M. (1995). The similarity Issue in CBR : The knowledge contained in similarity measures, Invited talk at ICCBR -95, Sesimbra.

Say, A.C.C. & Kuru, S. (1996). Qualitative system identification: deriving structure from behavior. *Artificial Intelligence* **83**: 75-141.

Schank, R.C. & Leake, D.B. (1989). Creativity and Learning in a Case-Based Explainer. *Artificial Intelligence* **40**: 353-385.

Sycara, K., Guttal, R., Koning, J., Narasimhan, S. & Navinchandra, D. (1992) CADET: a Case-based Synthesis Tool for Engineering Design, *Intl. J. Expert Systems*, **4**:2.

Integrating Rule Induction and Case-Based Reasoning to Enhance Problem Solving

Aijun An, Nick Cercone and Christine Chan

University of Regina, Regina, Saskatchewan, Canada S4S 0A2

Abstract. We present a new method that integrates rule induction and case-based reasoning. The method is new in two aspects. First, it applies a novel feature weighting function for assessing similarities between cases. By using this weighting function, optimal case retrieval is achieved in that the most relevant cases can be retrieved from the case base. Second, the method handles both classification and numeric prediction tasks under a mixed paradigm of rule-based and case-based reasoning. Before problem solving, rule induction is performed to induce a set of decision rules from a set of training data. The rules are then employed to determine some parameters in the new weighting function. The induced rules are also used to detect possible noise in the training set so that noisy cases are not used in case-based reasoning. For classification tasks, rules are applied to make decisions; if there is a conflict between matched rules, case-based reasoning is performed. The method was implemented in ELEM2-CBR, a learning and problem solving system. We demonstrate the performance of ELEM2-CBR by comparing it with other methods on a number of designed and real-world problems.

1 Introduction

Case-based reasoning (CBR) is a learning and problem solving paradigm that solves new problems by recalling and reusing specific knowledge obtained from past experience. As a learning method, CBR has several advantages: computational cost of incremental learning is small; and it can learn non-linearly separable categories and continuous functions. CBR algorithms have been applied to various tasks such as planning, design, diagnosis and speech recognition. Despite its success in real world applications, CBR suffers from some limitations: it does not yield concise representations of concepts that can be easily understood and reasoned about by humans or machines; and CBR systems are highly sensitive to noise and irrelevant features. On the other hand, rule induction systems learn general domain-specific knowledge from a set of training data and represent the knowledge in comprehensible condition-action rules. In addition, rule induction systems often succeed in identifying small sets of highly predictive features, and can make effective use of statistical measures to combat noise [5]. However, rule induction systems have been blamed for only forming axis-parallel frontiers in the instance space and have trouble in recognising exceptions in small low-frequency sections of the space. Furthermore, rules are symbolic in nature and are not good at representing continuous functions.

Due to their complementary properties, CBR and rule induction techniques have been combined in some systems to solve problems to which only one technique fails to provide a satisfactory solution. Examples of these systems include INRECA [1], RISE [5] and FCLS [9]. These systems focus on employing hybrid techniques to learn classification rules and therefore solve only classification problems. We propose a new method, referred to as ELEM2-CBR, that integrates CBR and rule induction. ELEM2-CBR is new in two aspects. First, it employs a new weighting method, called *relevance weighting*, to assess similarities between cases. The relevance weighting method makes use of rule induction results to assign weights to attribute-value pairs of the query case. By using this method, cases in the case base can be ranked according to their probability of relevance to the new case. The produced weights are optimal in the sense that most possibly relevant cases can be retrieved. Second, ELEM2-CBR performs both classification and numeric prediction under a mixed paradigm of rule-based and case-based reasoning. Before case-based reasoning, rule induction is performed and the induced rules are applied in case retrieval to determine weight settings for features. The induced rules are also used to detect possible noise in the training set so that the noise can be removed before CBR is conducted. During classification, rules are applied first to make decisions; if there is a conflict between matched rules, CBR is performed to resolve the conflict.

The paper is organised as follows. We present the relevance weighting method in Section 2. In Section 3, a method for estimating parameters in the new weighting function is presented. In Section 4, we describe how to utilise the weighting function to compute similarities between cases. Problem solving procedures of ELEM2-CBR are given in Section 5. Empirical evaluations of ELEM2-CBR are provided in Section 6. We conclude the paper with a summary of ELEM2-CBR.

2 A New Weighting Method

Feature weighting is a key issue in case retrieval. Many case-based reasoning algorithms retrieve cases using the k-nearest neighbour (k-NN) method with different weighting methods, such as per-category feature importance (PCF) and cross-category feature importance (CCF) methods [4]. Most weighting methods are clearly calculatable methods. However, there is no explanation about whether they are optimal in any sense. Furthermore, although many weighting methods are case specific, they do not take into account the query case when assigning weights to features, i.e., the feature values used in calculating the weights belong to the case that the query case is compared to and not to the query case. We argue that the specifics of the query case should be considered in feature weighting because they have the best information about which region in the instance space the query belongs to, which is helpful in searching for its most relevant neighbours. In this section, we propose a new feature weighting method, referred to as *relevance weighting*. The relevance weighting method assigns weights to features based on the feature values of the query case. In addition, the weighting function is optimal according to a probability ranking principle.

2.1 Probability Ranking Principle for Optimal Retrieval

The idea of ranking cases to achieve optimal retrieval is inspired from the area of information retrieval. The goal of information retrieval is to find from a collection of documents a set of documents that satisfy the user. To achieve this goal, Cooper [3] proposed a probability ranking principle (PRP) which can briefly be stated as: *If a retrieval system's response to each request is a ranking of the documents in the collection in order of decreasing probability of usefulness to the user, then the overall effectiveness of the system to its users will be the best that is obtainable on the basis of that data.* Formal justifications of this principle were given by Robertson [8], who proved that the PRP leads to optimum performance in terms of measures of retrieval effectiveness and that PRP is the correct decision procedure to use according to the dictates of Bayesian decision theory.

The goal of case retrieval in the CBR process is to find a set of past cases from the case base that are useful for solving new problems. Since this goal is similar to that of information retrieval, it is natural to apply the probability ranking principle to case retrieval. We define a case in the case base is *relevant* to a new case if it is useful in solving the problem represented by the new case. For optimal case retrieval, we restate the probability ranking principle as follows:

> *The probability ranking principle for optimal case retrieval:* If a case retrieval system's response to a new case (query) is a ranking of the cases in the case base in order of decreasing probability of relevance to the query, where the probabilities are estimated as accurately as possible on the basis of whatever data has been made available to the system for the purpose of using the retrieval result to solve the problem represented in the query, then the overall effectiveness of the system in terms of the probability of relevant cases being retrieved will be the best that is obtainable on the basis of that data.

Briefly speaking, this principle claims that optimal case retrieval, in terms of maximising the probability of relevant cases being retrieved, can be achieved if the system ranks the retrieved cases in the decreasing order of their probability of relevance to the new case.

2.2 Weighting for Optimal Retrieval

Knowing that optimal retrieval can be obtained by ranking the cases in order of decreasing probability of relevance, our next step is to find a way to achieve this ranking. Let p denote the probability of a query term t occurring in a document, given that the document is relevant; and let q be the corresponding probability for a non-relevant document. Robertson and Spark Jones [7] show that assigning weights to query terms with values of

$$\log \frac{p(1-q)}{q(1-p)} \tag{1}$$

yields an optimal result, i.e, using this formula to assign weights to query terms results in the ranking that leads to optimal document retrieval.

Our objective is to find a weighting method to achieve optimal case retrieval in CBR. Suppose that a query case qc in CBR consists of a set of attribute-value pairs $\{av_1, av_2, \cdots, av_n\}$, where n is the number of attributes. Since the role of attribute-value pairs av_i $(i = 1, \cdots, n)$ in case retrieval is the same as the role of the query terms in document retrieval, we employ the same weighting funtion for optimal document retrieval to assign weights to attribute-value pairs of qc as follows:

$$w(av_i) = \log \frac{p_i(1 - q_i)}{q_i(1 - p_i)} \tag{2}$$

where p_i is the probability that av_i occurs in an old case in the case base given that the old case is relevant to the new case, while q_i is the probability that av_i occurs in an old case given that the old case is not relevant. It can be proved [2] that using this weighting method to assess the similarity between the query case and a case in the training set yields a ranking of training cases in order of decreasing probability of relevance to the query case. Thus, optimal case retrieval is achieved according to the probability ranking principle. A precondition of using this weighting function to achieve optimal case retrieval is that the attributes are symbolic. To handle continuous attributes, discretization is performed to transform the domain of a continuous attribute into numeric ranges.

If it is known which cases in the case base are relevant and which are not, the weight for av_i is calculated as follows. Suppose that there are N cases in the case base of which R cases are relevant, and the attribute-value pair av_i occurs in n cases, of which r cases are relevant. Using simple proportion estimations of the two probabilities, the formula becomes:

$$w(av_i) = \log \frac{r(N - n - R + r)}{(n - r)(R - r)} \tag{3}$$

3 Estimation of Parameters

As shown in equation 3, parameters N, R, n and r need to be determined before using the weighting formula. Obviously, N and n are easy to be obtained. However, R and r, i.e, the information about which or how many cases in the case base are relevant, are normally not available in advance. Therefore, a method for estimating R and r is needed in order to use the relevance weighting.

Suppose that every case in the case base belongs to a symbolic concept.[1] We assume that the cases that are relevant to the new case, i.e., useful for solving the problem represented by the new case, are those that belong to the concept the new case belongs to. Thus, if we can estimate which concept the new case belongs to, then the cases in the case base that belong to the concept are

---

[1] This assumption holds for classification problems. If the task is numeric prediction, discretization is performed to transform a continuous decision value into a symbolic concept.

considered relevant to the new case. Rule induction systems can analyse data and generate classification rules from the data. Moreover, rule induction systems can make effective use of statistical measures to deal with noise and irrelevant features. Therefore, we employ rule induction and deductive reasoning techniques to estimate the parameters R and r. ELEM2 [2] is chosen to perform the rule induction. ELEM2 is an inductive system that generates classification rules by selecting the most relevant attribute-value pairs. A salient feature of ELEM2 is that it uses several techniques, including post-pruning of generated rules and probabilistic classifications, to deal with possible noise in the training data.

The procedure of using ELEM2 to estimate R and r is as follows. Before case-based reasoning is performed, ELEM2 is applied to derive rules from the training cases. When a new case is presented, it is matched with the rules. If there is a single match, i.e., only one rule is matched with the new case, or if there are multiple matches but the matched rules predict the same concept, then the cases that belong to the concept indicated by the matched rule(s) are considered relevant to the new case. If there are multiple matches and the matched rules indicate different concepts, then the new case is in the boundary region between the indicated concepts. In this situation, all the cases that belong to the indicated concepts are considered relevant. In the case of no-match, i.e, no rules are matched with the new case, partial matching is performed in which some attribute-value pairs of a rule may match the values of corresponding attributes in the new case. A partial matching score between the new case and a partially matched rule is calculated. The concepts that are indicated by partially matched rules compete with each other based on their partial matching scores. The cases that belong to the concept that wins the competition are chosen as relevant cases. After the set S of relevant cases is determined, R is assigned as the number of cases in S and r is set to the number of cases in S that match the attribute-value pair av_i. In this way, estimation of the two parameters of R and r is achieved by using rule induction and rule-based reasoning.

4 Similarity Assessment Using the Weight Function

This section describes how to use the new weighting function to assign scores to training cases so that the cases can be ranked in order of probability of relevance. Suppose that all the features are symbolic. Given a new case q, weights for each attribute-value pair of q are calculated according to equation 3. For each case x in the case base, we assign a score to x as the sum of the weights of those attribute-value pairs in q that occur in x. It can be proved [2] that if the cases are ranked in order of decreasing value of this score, then the ranking is actually a ranking of cases in order of their decreasing probability of relevance to the new case. If the cases contain continuous attributes, we adjust the weight for a continuous attribute by multiplying the absolute difference between q's value for that attribute and x's value for the same attribute. Therefore, the function for calculating the score for a case x becomes a similarity measurement between x and q which can be stated as follows: $Similarity(x,q) = \sum_{i=1}^{n} w_i \times Simil(x_i, q_i)$, where n is the number of attributes, x_i is x's value for the ith attribute a_i, q_i is q's value for a_i, w_i is the weight for q's ith attribute-value pair calculated using the new relevance weighting method, and

$$Simil(x_i, q_i) = \begin{cases} 0 & \text{if } a_i \text{ is symbolic and } x_i \neq q_i; \\ 1 & \text{if } a_i \text{ is symbolic and } x_i = q_i; \\ 1 - |norm(x_i) - norm(q_i)| & \text{if } a_i \text{ is continuous.} \end{cases}$$

where $|norm(x_i) - norm(q_i)|$ denotes the absolute value of the difference between the normalised values of x_i and q_i.

5 Problem Solving in ELEM2-CBR

ELEM2-CBR employs the above weighting and case ranking methods and can perform both classification and numeric prediction. Given a set of training data, ELEM2-CBR performs rule induction using ELEM2 to generate a set of classification rules. Since ELEM2 employs several techniques to handle noise, we consider a training case that can not be classified into its associated class by using the induced rules to be noise. Therefore, ELEM2's classification is performed over the training set after rule induction and the misclassified cases, i.e., noise, are removed from the case base before CBR is performed.

5.1 Numeric Value Prediction

If the task is to predict numeric values, problem solving in ELEM2-CBR is basically a CBR process. Case retrieval is done by using the relevance weighting and case ranking methods described in the previous sections. Rules generated by ELEM2 are used to determine the parameters in the weighting function. After the cases in the case base are ranked according to their relevance to the new case, the next task is to select several most relevant cases and adapt the solutions for these selected cases to a solution for the new case. The adaptation procedure is as follows: (1) Select a set S of k most relevant cases to the new case q where k is a user-defined parameter. (2) For each case c_i in S, compute a partial contribution value of c_i as $PCV(c_i, q) = Similarity(c_i, q) \times F(c_i)$, where $F(c_i)$ is the real decision value of case c_i that is stored in the case base. (3) Let $Sum = \sum_{c_i \in S} Similarity(c_i, q)$. (4) Compute a numeric decision value for the new case q as: $Prediction(q) = \frac{\sum_{c_i \in S} PCV(c_i, q)}{Sum}$.

5.2 Classification

If the application task is to classify a new case into a category, ELEM2-CBR performs the classification by using both deductive reasoning and case-based reasoning as follows: (1) Match the new case with the rules generated by ELEM2. (2) If there is a single match, i.e., only one rule is matched with the new case, then the case is classified into the class that the rule indicates. (3) If there are multiple matches, but the matched rules indicate the same class C, then the new case is classified into C. (4) If there are multiple matches and the matched rules indicate different classes, or if there is no match, i.e, no rules are matched with the new case, but partial matches exist, then rank the cases in the case base by using the weighting method and the similarity measure described in the last section. The parameters in the weighting function are determined by considering as relevant cases those cases that belong to the classes that matched rules (or partially matched rules in the case of no match) indicate. Go to step 6. (5) If partial matches do not exist, then rank the cases in the case base using the weighting function with $R = r = 0$ and the similarity measure described in the last section. (6) Select a set S of k most relevant cases from the ranked cases where k is a user-defined parameter. (7) If all the cases in S predict class C, the new case in classified into C. (8) Otherwise, for each class Y_i that exists in S, compute a decision score (DS) of Y_i defined as: $DS(Y_i) = \sum_{j=1}^{m} Similarity(c_j, q)$, where c_j is one of the m cases in S that predict Y_i and q is the new case. (9) Classify the new case into the concept that has the highest decision score.

In the above procedure, Steps 1-3 perform deductive reasoning. If there are matches between rules and the new case and the matched rules provide a unanimous decision, the new case is classified by the matched rule(s). Otherwise, case-based reasoning is conducted to solve the conflicts between rules or to deal with partial matching. Steps 4-6 perform case retrieval in which rules are used to determine the set of relevant cases which is needed by the relevance weighting function. Steps 7-9 perform case adaptation to determine a class for the new case from the retrieved cases.

6 Empirical Evaluation

The objective of our experiments is to investigate whether ELEM2-CBR's expected benefits are observed in practice. To achieve this objective, we implemented ELEM2-CBR and three other case-based reasoning algorithms, referred to as CBR-NW, CBR-PC and CBR-CC. These three algorithms are similar to ELEM2-CBR except that no rule induction is performed in the three algorithms and different weighting methods are used. CBR-NW considers the attributes are equally important, so it assigns equal weights to every attribute. CBR-PC employs the PCF weighting method and CBR-CC uses the CCF method. In our experiments, the four algorithms run in an incremental learning mode.[2] We also compare ELEM2-CBR with C4.5 [6] and ELEM2 on classification problems. Performance of a tested algorithm on classification problems is measured by classification accuracy, i.e., the percentage of correct classifications made by the algorithm on a set of test examples. On numeric prediction problems, performance is measured by the average of relative errors over test examples.

---

[2] By incremental learning we mean the already tested examples in the testing set are used in case-based reasoning (not in rule induction) to solve problems represented by later test cases.

6.1 Experiments on Classification Problems

Five problems are designed to evaluate the performance of ELEM2-CBR on classification problems. Each problem contains a target concept, i.e., an example in a problem either belongs to the target concept or does not belong to it. *Problem 1* contains five nominal conditional attributes with four values each: 0, 1, 2, and 3. The target concept is "if and only if any two or more of the first three attributes of an example have value 0 or 1, then the example belongs to the concept". From the entire space of 1024 possible examples, 256 were randomly chosen as training examples and the remaining as the testing set. *Problem 2* and *Problem 3* are designed to test ELEM2-CBR's ability to learn concepts with non-linear boundaries. Each problem contains two continuous attributes representing two axes (x and y) in a two dimensional space. An irrelevant attribute is added to each problem to test the algorithms' ability to tolerate irrelevant features. The target concepts of *Problem 2* and *Problem 3* are "if $ax^2 + by^2 \leq c$, then the example belongs to the concept" and "if $y > ax^3 + bx^2 + cx + d$, then the example belongs to the concept", respectively, where a, b, c and d are constants. *Problem 4* is the same as *Problem 3* except that there is no irrelevant feature in the data. *Problem 5* is derived from *Problem 4* by randomly adding 5% classification noise into the training set. For each problem, a set of examples is chosen from the instance space, one-third of which are used as the training set and the reminder constitutes the testing set. The results of the experiments on each problem in terms of classification accuracy on testing sets are shown in Table 1. The best result for each problem is highlighted in boldface. From the results, we can see

Problems	CBR-NW	CBR-PC	CBR-CC	ELEM2-CBR	ELEM2	C4.5
Problem 1	85.55%	64.84%	84.64%	**100%**	**100%**	**100%**
Problem 2	93.40%	70.40%	96.00%	**98.60%**	96.60%	**98.60%**
Problem 3	92.86%	74.06%	86.09%	**95.86%**	95.13%	95.10%
Problem 4	**96.24%**	83.46%	87.22%	95.86%	95.50%	95.40%
Problem 5	95.12%	76.32%	76.70%	**95.16%**	94.00%	93.60%

Table 1. Performance Comparison on Designed Problems.

that ELEM2-CBR, ELEM2 and C4.5 perform perfectly on *Problem 1*, while the three pure CBR algorithms do not perform well. This is because the concept in *Problem 1* has "rectangular" boundary regions and rule induction algorithms are good at learning and representing this kind of concepts, while pure CBR algorithms are not . On the other four problems, ELEM2-CBR performs better than pure rule induction algorithms: ELEM2 and C4.5. This result is consistent with what we expected: rules are not good at representing concepts with non-linear boundaries. On *Problem 4*, CBR-NW performs the best among the algorithms. The reason for this is that there is no irrelevant feature or noise in this problem

Datasets	CBR-NW	CBR-PC	CBR-CC	ELEM2-CBR	C4.5
australian	85.07%	**86.67%**	80.43%	85.65%	83.20%
breast-cancer	**96.93%**	94.58%	96.78%	95.90%	95.00%
glass	71.96%	52.34%	51.87%	**74.77%**	65.40%
heart	81.48%	79.63%	80.37%	**82.22%**	78.90%
tic-tac-toe	67.43%	65.34%	75.26%	99.37%	**99.50%**
zoo	94.06%	58.42%	94.06%	**96.04%**	93.10%
AVERAGE	82.82%	72.83%	79.80%	**88.99%**	85.85%

Table 2. Performance Comparison on Real-World Classification Problems

and the two features are equally important. In addition to artificial domains, we have also experimented with 6 real-world datasets from the UCI repository, for which the underlying concepts are unknown. Table 2 reports the results of *leave-one-out* evaluation on the 6 datasets.

6.2 Experiments on Numeric Prediction Problems

To evaluate ELEM2-CBR's ability to predict numeric values, we have conducted experiments with CBR-CC, CBR-PC, CBR-CC and ELEM2-CBR on four designed numeric prediction problems and three real-world problems from the UCI repository. Definitions of the designed problems are as follows: *NP-1*: $f(x, y, z) = x^2 + y^2 + z^2$; *NP-2*: $f(x, y) = \log_e(x) + \log_e(y)$; and *NP-3*: $f(x, y) = sin^{-1}(x) + cos^{-1}(y)$. *NP-4* is derived from *NP-1* by randomly adding 5% prediction noise into the training set. For each problem, a set of examples are picked up from the domain. One-third of them are randomly selected as training examples and the remaining ones as test samples. For each problem, the average of the relative errors made by each tested algorithm over the testing examples is reported in Table 3. Boldface is used to indicate the best result on each problem. The results of *leave-one-out* evaluation on three selected real-world datasets, *housing*, *imports-85*, and *machine*, are also shown in Table 3.

7 Conclusions

We have presented ELEM2-CBR, a new method to integrate rule induction and case-based reasoning. A salient feature of ELEM-CBR is that it utilises a novel feature weighting function in case retrieval. The weighting method is optimal in the sense that the most probably relevant cases to the new case can be retrieved from the case base. Another salient feature of ELEM2-CBR is that it can perform both classification and numeric prediction under a mixed paradigm of rule-based and case-based reasoning. Before problem solving, rule induction

508

Problems	CBR-NW	CBR-PC	CBR-CC	ELEM2-CBR
NP-1	2.36%	8.18%	2.49%	**2.02%**
NP-2	1.74%	2.68%	**1.45%**	1.69%
NP-3	5.92%	26.00%	11.57%	**5.77%**
NP-4	2.50%	8.01%	2.65%	**1.84%**
housing	**12.55%**	19.82%	17.29%	12.81%
imports-85	12.06%	21.24%	15.18%	**11.72%**
machine	44.77%	66.11%	55.10%	**37.00%**

Table 3. Performance Comparison on Numeric Problems.

is conducted on a set of training cases. The results of rule induction are used to estimate parameters in the proposed weighting function. For classification tasks, rule-based reasoning and case-based reasoning are intertwined so that "typical" cases can be classified by rules and "boundary" cases are classified by CBR. Experimental results show that ELEM2-CBR performs better than PCF and CCF weighting methods on almost all the tested problems. Its classification ability is better than or comparable with C4.5 on the test problems. On problems with irregular boundary regions, ELEM2-CBR performs better than its ancestor ELEM2 which performs only rule-based reasoning in problem solving. A problem needs to be addressed in the future is to further clarify the bias of ELEM2-CBR, i.e., the relation between the algorithm and the nature of problems.

References

1. Althoff, K., Wess, S. and Traphoner, R. 1995. "INRECA - A Seamless Integration of Induction and Case-Based Reasoning for Decision Support Tasks". *Proceedings of the 8th Workshop of the German Special Interest Group on Machine Learning.*
2. An, A. 1997. *Integrated Analysis Tools for Enhanced Problem Solving.* Ph.D. Thesis, Dept. of Computer Science, University of Regina, Regina, Canada. To appear.
3. Cooper, W.S. 1973. "On Selecting a Measure of Retrieval Effectiveness." *Journal of the American Society for Information Science.* Vol.24, pp.87-100.
4. Creecy, R.H., Masand, B.M., Smith, S.J. and Waltz, D.L. 1992. "Trading MIPS and Memory for Knowledge Engineering". *Communications of the ACM*, 35, pp.48-64.
5. Domingos, P. 1995. "Rule Induction and Instance-Based Learning: A Unified Approach." *IJCAI-95.* Montreal, Canada. pp.1226-1232.
6. Quinlan, J.R. 1993. *C4.5: Programs for Machine Learning.* Morgan Kaufmann Publishers. San Mateo, CA.
7. Robertson, S.E. and Sparck Jones, K. 1976. "Relevance Weighting of Search Terms". *Journal of the American Society for Information Science.* Vol.27. pp.129-146.
8. Robertson, S.E. 1977. "The Probability Ranking Principle in IR". *Journal of Documentation.* Vol.33, No.4, pp.294-304.
9. Zhang, J. 1990. "A Method That Combines Inductive Learning with Exemplar-Based Learning", *Proceedings of the 2nd International IEEE Conference on Tools for Artificial Intelligence*, Herndon, VA. pp.31-37.

Using Software Process Modeling for Building a Case-Based Reasoning Methodology: Basic Approach and Case Study

Ralph Bergmann, Wolfgang Wilke, Jürgen Schumacher

University of Kaiserslautern
Centre for Learning Systems and Applications (LSA)
PO-Box 3049, D-67653 Kaiserslautern, Germany
{bergmann, wilke, jschuma}@informatik.uni-kl.de

Abstract. Building a methodology for developing and maintaining CBR applications is an important goal currently addressed by CBR researchers and practitioners. Since CBR application development is a special kind of software development, building a CBR methodology can certainly be viewed as a software engineering research and development activity. This paper presents a perspective of how software process modeling, which is a recent approach in software engineering, can be used for building a case-based reasoning methodology. Further we describe a case study to show the applicability of the proposed concepts.

1 Introduction

Recently, several activities have been initiated with the goal of establishing a *methodology* for developing case-based reasoning applications. A methodology usually combines a number of *methods* into a philosophy which addresses a number of phases of the software development life-cycle. A methodology should give guidelines about the activities that need to be performed in order to successfully develop a certain kind of product, e.g. any kind of software system, a knowledge-based system, or – as in our case – a CBR application. A methodology should make the development an engineering activity rather than an art known by a few experts [15]. Therfore a methodology must cover *project management*, *product development* and *maintenance*, the specification of the *products* and the *analysis* and *reorganisation of the environment* in which the CBR system should be introduced.

Contributions to the goal of developing a methodology for CBR can be found in books on CBR (e. g. [16]) and in papers collecting the experience of people who have successfully developed CBR applications (e. g. [10], [11]. [5], [7]). Most valuable contributions arose from projects where methodology development was explicitly included as one project task, like INRECA[1] [2], [9] or APPLICUS[2] [4].

---

[1] INRECA: Esprit Project P6322. Induction and Reasoning from Cases.
[2] APPLICUS: Esprit Trial Application P20824.

The main focus of the INRECA-II[3] Esprit project is the development of such a methodology for CBR applications in the area of diagnosis and decision support. As a first contribution to this task, the ingredients of a case-based reasoning methodology were discussed in [6].

The goal of this paper is to analyze whether software process modeling, which is a recent approach in software engineering, can be used as a basis for developing a CBR methodology. Therefore, we will first describe software process modeling in general and show what must be done in order to use it in the context of CBR. Then, we describe a case study in which we re-modeled a project plan in terms of a particular software process modeling approach.

2 Methodologies in Software Engineering

Software Engineering (SE) is concerned with aspects of software development and maintenance, planning of software developments projects, performing development and project management, including quality assurance [14]. Particularly, SE is concerned with principles, methods, techniques and tools that can support these activities. Since CBR application development is a special kind of software development, building a CBR methodology can certainly be viewed as a SE research and development activity.

2.1 Software Process Modeling

One area of SE that can provide such a philosophy also for a CBR methodology is *software process modeling* (SPM, [14]). In this area *product engineering process models* model the engineering of the product, i.e., the software that has to be produced. Unlike early approaches in SE, the software development is not considered to follow a single fixed process model with a closed set of predefined steps. A tailored process model particularly suited for the current project must be developed in advance. Product engineering process models include *technical SE processes* like requirements engineering, design of the system to be built, coding etc., *managerial SE processes* like management of product related documentation, project management, quality assurance etc. and *organizational processes*, covering those parts of the business process in which the software system will be embedded and that need to be changed in order to make best use of the new software system. From time to time, such a model must be refined or changed during the execution of the project if the real world software development process and the model do not match any longer.

Using SPM for managing a software project involves four related levels:

Experience-base level: At this level generic process models and product models are described that have a certain degree of generality. These models are collected in an experience-base for (re)use during the planning of a new software project.

---

[3] INRECA-II Esprit Project P22196. Information and Knowledge Reengineering for Reasoning from Cases.

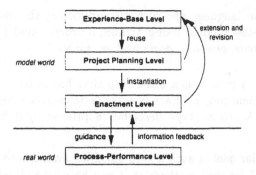

Fig. 1. Different levels in software process modeling

Project planning level: At this level, a project plan is constructed that combines a particular set of processes required for a certain project. Primarily, the models contained in the experience base are reused to construct a project plan. However, one cannot expect that the experience-base always contains process models that are completely appropriate or at a sufficient level of detail. If we do not find appropriate process models, the existing models must be extended or refined, or even new models must be constructed. Such new or revised models may enter the experience-base at some later point.

Enactment level: At this level, a project plan is instantiated and information about the current state of enactment of the processes is included.

Process-performance level: While the three previous levels deal with representations of the real world, the process-performance level *is* the real world in which agents are concerned with the development and maintenance of the software, performing the processes defined in the project plan. The project plan at the enactment level guides the real-world project by providing information about the project's state, next meaningful steps and expected qualities of products and processes. The process performance domain provides feedback about results, events or changes in order to allow updating the representation.

Managing a software project does not necessarily mean to follow these four levels in a sequence from the experience-base level to the process-performance level. Most likely, there will be changes at the project planning level during the enactment. Sometimes, certain detailed decisions in the project plan can only be drawn after some early parts of the project plan have already been enacted so that certain products (e.g. a requirements analysis document) are available as a basis for more detailed decisions.

2.2 Representing process models

Several representation formalisms and languages have been already developed for representing process models. Goal of the MILOS project [8] is the development of a representation language and of tools supporting the modeling, enactment and storing of process models. Using MILOS, a process model is defined in terms of *processes*, *methods*, *products*, *goals* and *resources*.

Process Types: A process is a basic step that has to be carried out in a software development project. Each process is defined as an instance of a certain *process type*. A process type describes a process by defining the following properties:

- A particular *goal* of such a step specifies *what* has to be achieved.
- A set of alternative *methods* that can be used to implement the step.
- *Input*, *output* and *modified products* that describe which products are required at the beginning, which products must be delivered at the end of the step, and which products are changed during enactment.
- A set of *resources* (agents or tools) that are required to perform the step. Here the necessary qualifications or specifications are defined that an agent or a tool respectively must have so that he or it can be assigned to the process.
- Additional attributes can be declared, e.g. for measuring the effort spent on the enactment of the process.

Methods: *Methods* contain a detailed specification of a particular way of reaching the goal of a process. A method can be either *atomic* or *complex*. While an atomic method provides only a description of "what to do" to reach the goal of the associated process, a complex method specifies a set of subprocesses, a set of intermediate products and the flow of products between the subprocesses. This is one of the most important features, because it allows the definition of very flexible process models in a hierarchical manner, since very different process refinements can be described by utilizing alternative subprocess models.

Product Types: The main goal of processes is to create or modify products. Products include the executable software system as well as the documentation like design documents or user manuals. Products are modeled by defining *product types*, which declare attributes a product of this type may have, e.g. the current state of the product. A product can be decomposed in subproducts so it is possible to pack products belonging together into a single complex product.

Resources: *Resources* are entities necessary to perform the tasks and are divided into agents and tools. Agents are models for humans or teams (e.g. designers or programmers), which can be designated to perform the real-world processes. The most relevant properties of agents are their qualifications. Tools (e.g. editors or modeling tools) are used to support the enactment of a process and can be described by a specification. Therefore, by using the required qualifications and specifications defined in the process type, it is possible to compute the set of agents and tools which can be assigned to a certain process.

3 A CBR Methodology Based on Software Process Modeling

Now, the question arises what the impact of using SPM for a CBR methodology is and what benefits can be expected.

3.1 Components of the Methodology

Using software process modeling for developing a CBR methodology basically means building an experience-base of generic process types, methods, product types, resources. So, *the core of the methodology is an experience base*, which contains CBR specific managerial, technical and organizational processes at different levels of abstraction organized in a hierarchical way. Such an experience-base should be based upon the experience of successfully enacted CBR projects. From such a CBR project a concrete project plan can be extracted and the processes involved can be identified. An experience-base can then be built by abstracting process types as well as the other required entities. In terms of SE, this approach can be described as building an *experience factory* [13] for CBR application development companies. A CBR methodology built using SPM should therefore consist of:

- a *set of process types*, each of which denotes a complex or elementary step required for
  - CBR application development (technical process) or
  - managing the CBR application development (managerial process) or
  - introducing the CBR application into the new environment (organizational process).

  Examples of such complex tasks can be: *define the scope of the CBR project, characterize the sources of information available in the organization, define the content of a case, case modeling* etc.
- a *description for each such process type* (input- and output products, resource consumption, methods). For example, the process *case modeling* may require as input a documentation describing the *content of a case* and the *user manual of the selected CBR tool* and it delivers as output a *descriptive model*, e.g. in CASUEL format.
- a *set of product types* that describe the products like *descriptive models, case-bases, CBR prototype, technical environment* (user-interfaces, hard- and software), *documentation*, etc.
- a set of *resource descriptions* that describe the required human resources like *domain expert, problem owner, software developer, CBR specialist*, etc. and tools like *descriptive model editor, case manager, validation tool*, etc.

3.2 Applying and Maintaining the Methodology

The methodology provides a set of basic components that can be reused or in order to plan and monitor a CBR project. Applying this methodology for a concrete CBR project means to:

1. select appropriate CBR processes and methods from the experience base,
2. extend or refine the selected processes,
3. combine the processes to a project plan,
4. enact and monitor the project plan,
5. review the project plan after execution to detect flaws and generalize new generic elements that should enter the experience base.

These five points can be seen as processes that implement an experience feedback cycle (at the level of CBR application development) which is similar to the general idea of CBR as captured in the CBR cycle in [1]. This issue is further discussed in [3].

3.3 Benefits of Process Modeling for a CBR Methodology

We expect that SPM leads to several benefits within the scope of a CBR methodology. First of all, they provide a clear philosophy and a particular notation for writing down a methodology. It supports communication within team members developing a CBR application (which is a general benefit of the methodology). It supports to control and monitor the CBR development. Because of its hierarchical nature, it allows one to first start with an abstract process model and to refine the important or difficult steps when the methodology grows, also based on the experience gained from its application. It also allows to have a general part of the methodology and several more specific parts each of which is suited for a particular kind of application. It allows one to share CBR development experience and workflow management techniques and tools [17] can be used to organize and coordinate technical and business processes.

4   A Case Study

In the APPLICUS project [4] a sample project plan for the development of a CBR-based customer support application is discussed. In the following we set up a process model based on this project plan to examine if it is possible to model the concepts and processes occurring in a real-world development project by means of a process representation language like proposed in the MILOS project. A second goal of this study is to test whether all concepts provided by MILOS are required for our purposes.

4.1   Building a process model based on a project plan

The development of the CBR system described in the APPLICUS report took place in two phases: First a prototype was developed to test the feasibility of the project and get feedback from the future users. In a second cycle the system was revised, tested, installed and introduced to the users. For the sake of visualisation we have built our model with the workflow management tool CoMo-Kit [12], which is one of the predecessors of MILOS and allows a graphical representation of the product flows. The following figures are screenshots from this system.

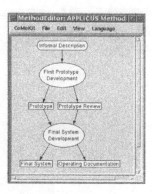

Fig. 2. Structure of the top-level method

The model starts with an initial process named *CBR Application Development*, which can be performed by using the method *APPLICUS Method*. In a more complex model there could be several alternative methods – chosen with respect to the application domain of the CBR system – to reach the goal of the process. The structure of *APPLICUS Method* is shown in fig. 2. In this view ellipses denote the subprocesses of the method, while rectangles denote the products which are produced and consumed by the processes. As stated above, two development phases are enacted. The first one produces a prototypical system along with a documentation of the test results and reviews which describe what is to be done in the second phase. In this phase all components of the system are revised, the final system is tested and installed, and the users are trained. Each phase is modeled as one process, the structures of these two processes are refined in the following.

Fig. 3 shows the subprocesses and the product flow in the method for the first (left) and the second phase (right). Note that some processes in both methods are very similar. For example in both methods a *System Integration* process has to be enacted to produce an executable system. In terms of our terminology these processes have the same process type, i.e. products of the same type are required and produces and the same methods are available for the enactment, but the process type has to be defined only once and can be used during the construction of a project plan.

Fig. 4 gives a more detailed model for the *Case Acquisition* process which is part of the first phase. There are two subprocesses, one of them describes the actual collection of cases. For this process the APPLICUS report proposes three alternative methods. During the enactment of the process the agent who works on this process can choose one of the methods that seems to be appropriate for the application domain or the available data. Note that this decision can be delayed until the process is actually to be executed and is not necessary to be made during the project planning. So it should be possible to set up very flexible project plans.

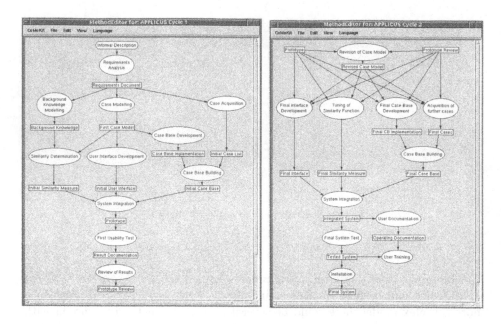

Fig. 3. The two development phases in detail

One feature we missed in MILOS was an explicit support for modeling process cycles. These would be useful when modeling processes like the *Tuning of Similarity Function* process in the second phase of our example, where two processes *Tuning* and *Reviewing* could have to be enacted alternating until the review gives a positive result.

Many of these features need explicit tool support to be fully usable: Decisions about chosen methods need to be propagated, subprocesses delegated, documents traced etc. A software tool like CoMo-Kit provides an agenda for every team member, showing him or her which processes are ready to be started, and updates the agenda according to decisions made by other members. Subprocesses can then be delegated to other agents. Decisions which method was

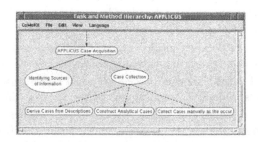

Fig. 4. Alternative methods for one process

chosen for a process are recorded and can be reviewed. Such decisions can even be retracted if parts of the project must be replanned. This leads to invalidating complete products, canceling processes in enactment and informing team members about the new processes which must be enacted now.

4.2 Results

Based on the experiences from this case study we conclude that a process representation language like MILOS is sufficient for our purposes. In particular the following points seem important to us: Process types are useful for two purposes: First, a project manager who is new to developing CBR systems can be given a set of sample process types and a guide to build project plans from them, so he should be able to set up reasonable project plans from the start. Second, experiences gained during the enactment of projects can be saved in process types for later reuse thus leading to better plans in future projects. The definition of different alternative methods for a single process leads to flexible project plans because the details of enactment can be decided at that point in the project when the process has to be started instead of specifying it during planning when parameters may be unknown which may lead to better decisions. Moreover, by providing alternative complex methods for one process we can model very different project plans in one model. This should guarantee the necessary flexibility to react to problems which could not be foreseen during the initial project planning. Tool support is essential for the enactment of project plans based on these concepts.

5 Future Work

To reach the goal of having a comprehensive CBR methodology, it is necessary to further generalize appropriate processes types, methods, product types, and resources out of existing plans of CBR projects and thereby build up a larger experience-base. Furthermore, already existing workflow management systems that show a high degree of flexibility must be enhanced to support the reuse of process models from the experience-base. For this purpose, CBR itself may become useful to support the retrieval of appropriate process models.

Acknowledgement Funding for this work has been provided by the Commission of the European Union (INRECA-II, Esprit contract no. P22196. Partners: Acknosoft (prime contractor, France), Daimler Benz (Germany), tecInno (Germany), Interactive Multimedia Systems (Ireland), University of Kaiserslautern (Germany)), to which the authors are greatly indebted.

References

1. A. Aamodt and E. Plaza. Case-Based Reasoning: Foundational Issues, Methodological Variations and System Approaches. *AI Com.*, 7(1):39–59, March 1994.

2. K.-D. Althoff, S. Wess, K.-H. Weis, E. Auriol, R. Bergmann, H. Holz, R. Johnston, M. Manago, C. Meissonnier, A.and Priebisch, Traphöner R., and Wilke W. An evaluation of the final integrated system. Technical report, Esprit Project INRECA Deliverable D6, 1995.

3. K.-D. Althoff and W. Wilke. Potential uses of case-based reasoning in the experience-based construction of software systems. In R. Bergmann and W. Wilke, editors, *Proceedings of the 5th German Workshop in Case-Based Reasoning.* Centre for Learning Systems and Applications, University of Kaiserslautern, 1997.

4. B. Bartsch-Spörl. How to introduce case-based reasoning in customer support. Technical report, Esprit Project APPLICUS Deliverable D3, 1996.

5. B. Bartsch-Spörl. Towards a methodology for how to make cbr systems work in practice. In H.-D. Burkhard and M. Lenz, editors, *Proceedings of the 4th German Workshop on Case-Based Reasoning - System Development and Evaluation,* Informatik-Bericht No. 55. Humboldt Universität Berlin, 1996.

6. R. Bergmann, W. Wilke, K.-D. Althoff, S. Breen, and R. Johnston. Ingredients for developing a case-based reasoning methodology. In R. Bergmann and W. Wilke, editors, *Proceedings of the 5th German Workshop in Case-Based Reasoning.* Centre for Learning Systems and Applications, University of Kaiserslautern, 1997.

7. O. Curet and M. Jackson. Towards a methodology for case-based systems. In *Expert Systems'96. Proceedings of the 16th annual workshop of the British Computer Society,* 1996.

8. B. Dellen, F. Maurer, J. Münch, and M. Verlage. Enriching software process support by knowledge-based techniques. Technical report, SFB 501 Internal Report No. 0/96, 1996.

9. R. Johnston, S. Breen, and M. Manago. Methodology for developing cbr applications. Technical report, Esprit Project INRECA Deliverable D30, 1996.

10. H. Kitano, H. Shimazu, and A. Shibata. Case-method: A methodology for building large-scale case-based systems. In *Proceedings of the National Conference on Artificial Intelligence, Washington D.C.* AAAI, 1993.

11. L. Lewis. *Managing computer networks: A case-based reasoning approach.* Artech House Publishers, London, 1995.

12. F. Maurer. Modeling the knowledge engineering process. Technical report, Bericht 1/96 of the SFB 501. University of Kaiserslautern, 1996.

13. Basili V. R., Caldiera G., and Rombach H. D. The experience factory. In J. J. Marciniak, editor, *Encyclopedia of Software Engineering,* volume 1, pages 469–476. Wiley, New York, 1994.

14. H. D. Rombach and M. Verlage. Directions in software process research. *Advances in Computers,* 41:1–61, 1995.

15. M. Shaw. Prospects for an engineering discipline of software. *IEEE Software 7,* pages 15–24, 1990.

16. S. Weß. *Fallbasiertes Problemlösen in wissensbasierten Systemen zur Entscheidungsunterstützung und Diagnostik.* PhD thesis, Universität Kaiserslautern, 1995.

17. Workflow Management Coalition. The workflow management coalition specification, June 1996. Doc. WFMC-TC-1011, http://www.aiai.ed.ac.uk/WfMC/DOCS/glossary/glossary.html.

Stratified Case-Based Reasoning in Non-Refinable Abstraction Hierarchies

L. Karl Branting

Department of Computer Science
University of Wyoming
P.O. Box 3682
Laramie, WY 82071
karl@index.uwyo.edu
(307) 766-4258 / FAX: -4036

Abstract. Stratified case-based reasoning (SCBR) is a technique in which case abstractions are used to assist case retrieval, matching, and adaptation. Previous work showed that SCBR can significantly decrease the computational expense required for retrieval, matching, and adaptation in a route-finding domain characterized by abstraction hierarchies with the downward refinement property. This work explores the effectiveness of SCBR in hierarchies without the downward refinement property. In an experimental evaluation using such hierarchies (1) SCBR significantly decreased search cost in hierarchies without the downward refinement property, although the speedup over ground-level A* was not as great as in refinable hierarchies, (2) little difference was observed in SCBR search costs between case libraries created top-down in the process of REFINE-MENT and those created bottom-up from a valid ground solution, and (3) the most important factor in determining speedup appeared to be *a priori* likelihood that a previous solution can be usefully applied to a new problem.

1 Stratified Case-Based Reasoning

Stratified Case-Based Reasoning is a technique under which case abstractions are used to assist case indexing, matching, and adaptation. This approach has been applied to case-based planning [BW95, KH92], design of control software [SK94, SC92], and route planning [BA95] (See [BW96] for a comparative analysis of previous approaches). Use of case abstractions has the following potential benefits:

- **Indexing and retrieval.** A more abstract solution to a problem can provide an accurate index to less abstract solutions to the problem because it consists of the most important aspects of the less abstract solutions.
- **Matching.** Retaining case abstractions permits cases to be compared in an abstract space in which matching may be much less expensive than at the ground level of abstraction.
- **Adaptation.** An abstraction of a stored case may be much easier to reuse than the ground-level case itself. Stratified cases can be reused at the most

specific level of abstraction at which they can be applied to the given problem without requiring adaptation of less abstract, non-matching facts.

A systematic analysis set forth in [BA95] compared the performance of heuristic search (A*), REFINEMENT (i.e., hierarchical problem solving), ground-level CBR, and SCBR as a function of (1) number of levels of abstraction, (2) the size of the case library, and (3) resemblance among cases. The comparison was in the context of a route-finding task restricted to fields for which a simple aggregation abstraction method produced hierarchies satisfying the downward refinement property [Kno94, BY94], i.e., every abstract solution can be refined to a concrete solution, if a concrete solution exists). Under these conditions, the SCBR algorithms outperformed ground-level CBR and ground-level A* under all conditions, and outperformed REFINEMENT given 3 or more levels of abstraction.

However, these results were restricted to domains for which there are abstraction methods that can create hierarchies with the downward refinement property. Unfortunately, many abstraction hierarchies lack this property [BY94]. Determining the range of applicability of SCBR requires establishing whether it can lead to improvement in hierarchies without the downward refinement property (henceforth, "nonrefinable hierarchies").

This paper describes an experimental evaluation of the relative performance of SCBR in refinable and nonrefinable hierarchies. The evaluation showed that in the route-finding domain SCBR leads to increases in search efficiency nearly as great in nonrefinable hierarchies as in refinable hierarchies.

2 The Route-Finding Task

Route-finding was originally chosen to evaluate the utility of stratified case-based reasoning because this task is an important area of activity in robotics and is amenable to hierarchical problem solving. This task involves finding an optimal or near-optimal path between a given pair of start and goal positions through a field containing obstacles. Fields consist of $N \times N$ arrays of positions, where N is a power of 2. Fields of this form are amenable to a simple abstraction hierarchy in which an abstract position at Level 1 position $\langle R, C \rangle$ (zero indexing) abstracts over the following four ground-level positions: $\langle 2 \times R, 2 \times C \rangle, \langle 2 \times R, 2 \times C + 1 \rangle, \langle 2 \times R + 1, 2 \times C \rangle, \langle 2 \times R + 1, 2 \times C + 1 \rangle$.

The goal of the route-finding task is to locate a route connecting the start and goal positions using a sequence of straight and curved track segments, or *traversal operators*, such that the start and goal positions lie at the ends of the connected track. Each position is associated with the set of operators that can be used to traverse it. Thus, each unblocked position at the ground level is associated with all possible operators, which are shown in Figure 1. Each blocked position is associated with the empty set of traversal operators since traversal through them is impossible. Determining the available operator set for each abstract position involves determining (1) what operators are available for each of the four positions it abstracts and (2) which of the six operators, if any, are still possible after joining these four lower-level positions.

A   B   C   D   E   F

Fig. 1. The Set of Possible Traversal Operators Per Position

3 Search Using Abstraction Hierarchies

3.1 REFINEMENT

REFINEMENT [HMZM96] is a form of hierarchical problem solving in which a solution at one level of abstraction is used to guide search at a lower level of abstraction. One approach to REFINEMENT is to use the length of the solution at a higher level of abstraction to estimate the path length at the lower level. In the abstraction method used in the route-finding task, this can be accomplished for positions that are in the abstraction path by multiplying the distance to the abstract goal along the abstract solution by 2 and adding the distance from the current position to the closest position that is a member of the next closer abstract position. The distance estimate can be used as the h* estimate in A* search. This process can be repeated at multiple levels of abstraction.

If the abstract solution is refinable into an optimal solution, then this estimate will be very accurate. If the abstract solution is not refinable, the estimate will still be admissible provided that the optimal solution is at least twice the length of the abstract solution plus 2. However, the treatment of positions off the abstract solution path is problematical. Ideally, one would like a heuristic for these points that is both admissible and also larger than the distance estimate for points on the abstract path (to focus search on position on the abstract path). However, for refinable abstract solutions the estimated distance for positions on the abstract solution path is very close to the actual distance, so it is not generally possible to find an admissible heuristic for points outside that is greater than the distance estimate for points on the path. In the experiments described below the distance estimate consisted of Manhattan distance times a large constant. This metric insures that the h* value of every point off of the abstract path is higher than the h* value of any point on the path but is still sensitive to the actual distance to the goal.

The experimental evaluation in [BA95] showed that REFINEMENT (called "hierarchical A*" in [BA95]) was significantly more efficient than ground-level A* given even a single abstraction level, and its performance improved with more levels of abstraction.

3.2 Stratified CBR Algorithms

Stratified CBR algorithms can reuse case solutions stored at any abstraction level. Each algorithm starts by retrieving from the case library the set of *most specific matching* cases (i.e., lowest-level cases whose solutions include abstract positions that abstract the given start and goal positions). This search begins at the root of the case library, recurses with its children (i.e., top-level abstractions of solved cases), and continues recursing until it reaches the ground level (in which case the segment of a solution connecting the new start and goal positions is returned) or cases that no longer cover both the start and goal positions.

The CLOSEST algorithm supports partial matching between new problems and previous solutions. Starting with the most specific matching cases (or the most abstract cases, if no cases match) CLOSEST finds the refinements of each case, adapts each refinement (i.e., uses A* to find the shortest adaptation paths from the start and goal positions to the solution path at that level of abstraction, restricting search to positions in the parent case's adaptation paths), and selects the refinements having the shortest adapted solution paths. CLOSEST recursively calls these three steps until the ground level is reached, at which time it randomly selects and returns an adapted case.

The THRESHOLD algorithm, attempts to recognize situations in which adapting an existing case will be more expensive than problem solving *ab initio*. THRESHOLD behaves identically to CLOSEST if there are matching cases. However, if there are no matching cases, then THRESHOLD uses A* to find the shortest path from the start to the goal position at the highest level of abstraction. If there are top-level cases whose adapted solution paths are no longer than the path length found by A*, then THRESHOLD treats these cases in the same manner as CLOSEST. If there are no such cases, then THRESHOLD uses REFINEMENT rather than CBR.

The process of adaptation is illustrated in Figures 2 and 3. Figure 2 shows a very simple new problem and a previous solution. Figure 3 shows an abstraction of the previous solution, an adaptation of this abstraction, and an adaptation of the previous solution at the ground level. Given an abstraction hierarchy for a particular field and start and goal positions, REFINEMENT generates a path connecting the start and goal positions at every level of abstraction. Each solution at a given level of abstraction is treated as a separate case.

Generation of abstract cases by REFINEMENT is *top-down* abstract case creation. An alternative is *bottom-up* abstraction: a ground-level case created by REFINEMENT or A* is successively abstracted as many times as there are levels in the case library. In refinable abstraction hierarchies, top-down and bottom-up approaches generate identical abstract cases.

Regardless of whether cases are generated top-down or bottom-up, distinct cases at a lower level may have identical parents because distinct positions at the ground level may be identical at more abstract levels. Cases can therefore be organized into a forest of taxonomic trees. A *case library* consists of a taxonomic forest of cases sharing a common abstraction.

4 Case Retrieval and Adaptation in Nonrefinable Hierarchies

The abstraction method described in the previous section is not guaranteed to lead to refinable abstract solutions. Figure 4 illustrates a solution path through a

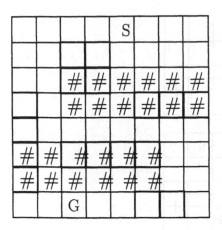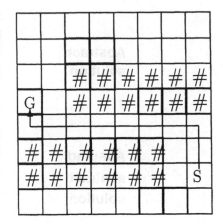

Fig. 2. A new problem and the solution to previous problem.

32×32 field. Figure 5 shows the abstract solutions found by REFINEMENT start-ing three levels of abstraction above the ground level.[1] The two most abstract solutions show, incorrectly, that there is a path almost directly down from the start position to the bottom quarter of the field. Moreover, the abstract solutions fail to show the deviation up the right side of the field necessary to reach the bottom row of the field.

Errors like these can arise whenever a series of adjacent obstacles are arranged in a row that (1) crosses a pair of a region which is abstracted into a single position and that (2) leaves unobstructed positions on either side. For example, the barrier in the upper-left corner of the field shown in Figure 4 crosses abstract positions with width 4 leaving a path on either side. Abstract positions crossed by such a barrier contain operators A, C, D, E, and F, but not B. REFINEMENT may construct a path across such a barrier because information about which side of the barrier the current position is on has been abstracted away. For example, in the most abstract solution shown in Figure 5 the path goes straight down from S because at this level it can't be determined which side of the barrier the starting position is on. The abstract solution at the next lower level of abstraction shows a horizontal path for one step followed by a downward path. This path was constructed from operators A and D because when operator D was applied no information was available about which side of the barrier the current position was on.

Nonrefinability can potential create problems for SCBR algorithms in two different ways. First, an abstract solution that appears to be reusable at an abstract level may turn out not to have useful children. For example, if the

---

[1] In this representation of solutions, the actual operators are not shown because there are insufficient typographic characters to represent all six. Instead, the direction of the path from each position is represented by $\lor$, $\land$, $<$, and $>$.

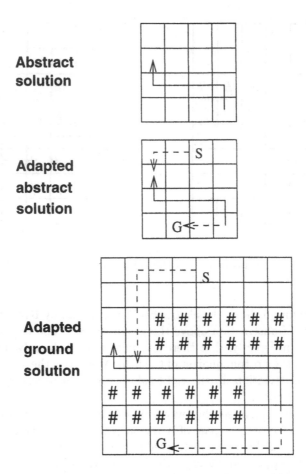

Fig. 3. Adaptation of an abstract solution leading to adaptation of the ground-level solution. Adaptation paths are shown as dotted lines.

start and goal positions in a new case were both along the left edge of the field shown in Figure 4, the most abstract case in Figure 5 would appear to be a good precedent, since its path appears to go the length of the left edge. However, the solution two abstraction levels lower goes down along the middle and right side of the field, but not the left side. Thus, reuse of this solution might be more expensive than simply generating a new path *ab initio*. Second, CLOSEST and THRESHOLD use REFINEMENT to find adaptation paths (e.g., the paths shown as dotted lines in Figure 3). The computational expense of this application of REFINEMENT will typically be greater in nonrefinable hierarchies. The cost of adaptation will therefore be higher as well.

The problems associated with nonrefinable hierarchies were not addressed in the experiments described in [BA95] because those experiments involved only fields satisfying the following conditions (referred to hereinafter as "field refinability conditions"): (1) all adjacent obstacles are arranged in rectilinear regions

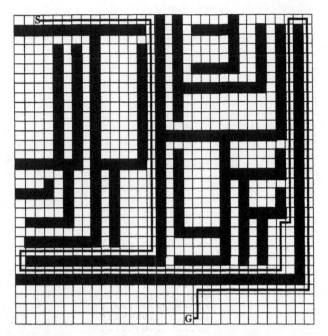

Fig. 4. A ground-level solution in a 32 × 32 field.

and (2) whenever the length of a sequence of adjacent obstacles is at least the size of an abstract region at some level of abstraction, then its width is at least the region size minus 1. These conditions preclude the errors described above.

5 Empirical Evaluation

Intuitively, it seems that SCBR algorithms should perform well even in nonrefinable hierarchies because these algorithms have access to previous successful solutions. This intuition suggests the following hypotheses:

1. SCBR can reduce search even in hierarchies without guaranteed refinability.
2. The performance of CLOSEST relative to that of REFINEMENT is better for nonrefinable than for refinable hierarchies.
3. When the field refinability conditions are not satisfied, abstraction hierarchies created bottom-up lead to better performance by SCBR and THRESHOLD than those created top-down.

These hypotheses were tested in experiment that compared the performance of ground-level A*, REFINEMENT, and the SCBR algorithms as a function of the nature of the abstraction hierarchy. The dependent variable was computational expense as measured by the number of nodes expanded by A* in the execution of each algorithm. The independent variables were:

1. Whether the abstraction hierarchy guarantees refinability.
2. For nonrefinable hierarchies, whether abstract cases were created top-down or bottom-up.

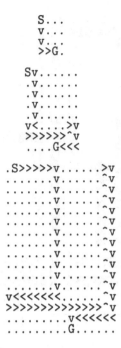

```
S...
v...
v...
>>G.

Sv......
.v......
.v......
.v......
.v......
v<....>v
>>>>>>^v
....G<<<

.S>>>>>v......>v
.......v......^v
.......v......^v
.......v......^v
.......v......^v
.......v......^v
.......v......^v
.......v......^v
.......v......^v
.......v......^v
.......v......^v
.......v......^v
v<<<<<<<......^v
>>>>>>>>>>>>>^v
.........v<<<<<<
.........G......
```

Fig. 5. Three abstract solutions created by REFINEMENT.

3. The number of cases in the case library (1, 5, 10, or 20).
4. Whether the start and goal positions are selected randomly or are constrained to be on opposite sides of the field. This affects the likelihood that a case will be useful for reuse (start/goal positions on opposite sides increase the likelihood that some segment of a previous solution can be reused in any given new problem).

Field size was fixed at 32×32, and the number of levels of abstraction was fixed at 3 (not counting the ground level). Refinable hierarchies were created by using fields that satisfy the "field refinability conditions" described above. Non-refinable hierarchies were created by using fields that violate these conditions, such as the field shown in Figure 4. Six trials with 10 test cases each were run for each combination of refinable vs. nonrefinable hierarchy, case library size, top-down vs. bottom-up abstract case creation, and random vs. opposite sides selection of start and goal positions.

Figure 6 shows the mean speedup of CLOSEST over ground-level A* on case libraries generated bottom-up as measured by the mean number of nodes expanded by ground-level A* divided by the mean number of nodes expanded by the CLOSEST. These results provide initial confirmation for the first hypothesis: SCBR can reduce search even in hierarchies without guaranteed refinability. For both the random and opposite ends conditions the speedup was greater for refinable hierarchies than for nonrefinable hierarchies. However, for both refinable and nonrefinable hierarchies the speedup was greater for the opposite sides condition than for random start and goal positions.

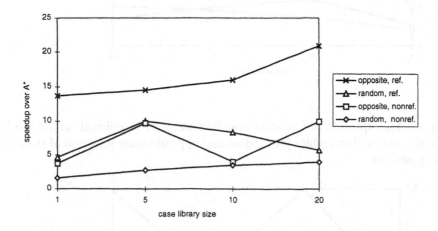

Fig. 6. Mean speedup of SCBR algorithms over ground-level A* (i.e., ratio of nodes expanded by ground-level A* to those expanded by COVER) for refinable vs. nonrefinable abstraction hierarchies and random vs. opposite sides selection of start and goal positions. All abstraction hierarchies were created bottom-up.

Figure 7 shows the ratio of the number of nodes expanded by REFINEMENT to the number of nodes expanded by CLOSEST as a function of case library size for refinable and nonrefinable hierarchies (with cases created bottom-up in the latter). Contrary to hypothesis 2, the speedup over REFINEMENT appeared to be greater for refinable than for nonrefinable hierarchies given opposite sides start/goal position selection. For random start/goal pairs, refinability had little effect on the relative performance of CLOSEST and REFINEMENT.

Figure 8 shows the ratio of nodes expanded by CLOSEST and THRESHOLD in abstraction hierarchies created top-down to nodes expanded in abstraction hierarchies created bottom-up in fields without the field refinability conditions (in field with the field refinability conditions, abstraction hierarchies created top-down and bottom-up are identical). Hypothesis 3 was confirmed only in THRESHOLD under the opposite sides condition, when bottom-up abstraction led to much higher performance. For CLOSEST and random start/goal positions bottom-up abstraction produced little improvement.

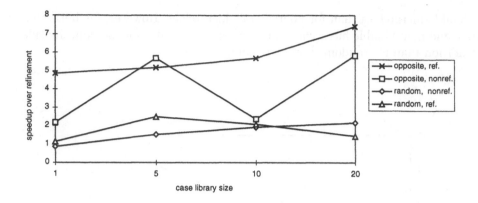

Fig. 7. Mean speedup of CLOSEST over REFINEMENT in refinable and nonrefinable abstraction hierarchies for random and opposite sides selection of start and goal positions.

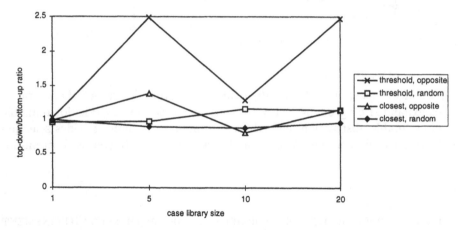

Fig. 8. Ratio of nodes expanded by CLOSEST and THRESHOLD in abstraction hierarchies created top-down to nodes expanded in abstraction hierarchies created bottom-up.

6   Discussion and Future Work

The empirical evaluation demonstrated that the range of applicability of SCBR algorithms extends to at least some domains lacking the downward refinement property. CLOSEST produces impressive speed-ups over both ground-level A* and REFINEMENT even for hierarchies that lack guaranteed refinability. Although the speed-ups were greater for refinable than for nonrefinable hierarchies, the variable with the greatest affect on the efficiency of SCBR appeared to be the distribution of start/goal positions. This variable determines the *a priori* likelihood that a previous solution can be usefully applied to a new problem.

Bottom-up abstraction had surprisingly little effect on the efficiency of CLOS-EST. The only pronounced benefit occurred for THRESHOLD under the opposite sides condition, evidently because bottom-up abstraction makes estimation of adaptation costs at a high level more accurate. This permits THRESHOLD to recognize more accurately abstraction cases whose adaptation cases are greater than *ab initio* problem solving. The observation that the speed-up of the SCBR algorithms over REFINEMENT is less for nonrefinable than for refinable hierarchies even when bottom-up abstraction is used suggests that nonrefinability diminishes the performance of SCBR algorithms by increasing adaptation costs rather than by diminishing retrieval accuracy.

The evaluation suggests a number of additional questions. The abstraction hierarchies generated from fields like that shown in Figure 4 lack the guarantee of refinability, but the abstract solutions are close enough to enable REFINEMENT to outperform ground-level A*. However, there are many abstraction hierarchies where lack of refinability makes REFINEMENT more expensive than ground-level search [BY94]. It is unclear from the empirical evaluation whether, or under what conditions, SCBR algorithms would outperform ground-level search in such domains.

To clarify the range of applicability of SCBR, additional experiments are needed to test the sensitivity of SCBR to the following independent variables:

(1) The degree of refinability. This will help to determine whether there are circumstances under which SCBR, but not REFINEMENT, outperforms ground-level search.

(2) The degree of intercase relevance. The apparent sensitivity of SCBR to the distribution of start/goal positions suggests that it would be desirable to develop a general metric for intercase relevance to help determine the conditions under which SCBR is appropriate.

We are currently investigating the utility of SCBR on other types of information-processing tasks, including a configuration task—constraint satisfaction—and an analytical task, analogical legal reasoning. In addition, we are attempting to apply SCBR to abstraction hierarchies created using the star abstraction method described in [HMZM96].

7 Conclusion

This paper has described the process of stratified CBR in the context of hierarchies without the downward refinement property. A source of nonrefinability was identified in route finding in fields that fail to satisfy two "field refinability conditions." An experimental evaluation using hierarchies derived from such fields showed that SCBR significantly decreased search cost in such hierarchies, although the speedup over ground-level A* was not as great as in refinable hierarchies. The evaluation showed that the ratio of the search costs for REFINEMENT to those of SCBR was highest for opposite sides start/goal position selection, indicating that *a priori* likelihood that a previous solution can be usefully applied to a new problem is a more important factor than refinability in determining the relative performance of REFINEMENT and SCBR. Finally, a difference in SCBR search costs between case libraries created top-down in the process of REFINE-MENT and those created bottom-up from a valid ground solution was observed only for THRESHOLD with opposite sides start/goal selection.

Acknowledgments

This research was supported by NSF Faculty Early Career Development Grant IRI-9502152. This work is an extension of collaborative research with David Aha.

References

[BA95]   K. Branting and D. Aha. Stratified case-based reasoning: Reusing hierarchical problem solving episodes. In *Proceedings of the Fourteenth International Joint Conference on Artificial Intelligence(IJCAI-95)*, Montreal, Canada, August 20–25 1995.

[BW95]   R. Bergmann and W. Wilke. Building and refining abstract planning cases by change of representation language. *Journal of Artificial Intelligence Research*, 3(53–118), 1995.

[BW96]   R. Bergmann and W. Wilke. On the role of abstraction in case-based reasoning. In *Proceedings of the Third European Workshop on Case-Based Reasoning (EWCR-96)*, pages 28–43, Lausanne, Switzerland, November 1996.

[BY94]   F. Bacchus and Q. Yang. Downward refinement and the efficiency of hierarchical problem solving. *Artificial Intelligence*, 71:43–100, 1994.

[HMZM96] R. Holte, T. Mkadmi, R. Zimmer, and A. MacDonald. Speeding up problem-solving by abstraction: A graph-oriented approach. *Artificial Intelligence*, 85(1–2):321–362, 1996.

[KH92]   S. Khambamppati and J. Hendler. A validation-structure-based theory of plan modification. *Artificial Intelligence*, 55:193–258, 1992.

[Kno94]   C. Knoblock. Automatically generating abstractions for planning. *Artificial Intelligence*, 64, 1994.

[SC92]   B. Smyth and P. Cunningham. Deja vu: A hierarchical case-based reasoning system for software design. In *Proceedings of the 10th European Conference on Artificial Intelligence*, pages 587–589, Vienna, Austria, 1992.

[SK94]   B. Smythe and M. Keane. Retrieving adaptable cases. In S. Wess, K. Althogg, and M. Richter, editors, *Topics in Case-Based Reasoning*, pages 209–220. Springer, 1994.

Supporting Combined Human and Machine Planning:
An Interface for Planning by Analogical Reasoning

Michael T. Cox and Manuela M. Veloso

Computer Science Department. Carnegie Mellon University

Pittsburgh, PA 15213-3891

{mcox;mmv}@cs.cmu.edu

Abstract. Realistic and complex planning situations require a mixed-initiative planning framework in which human and automated planners interact to mutually construct a desired plan. Ideally, this joint cooperation has the potential of achieving better plans than either the human or the machine can create alone. Human planners often take a case-based approach to planning, relying on their past experience and planning by retrieving and adapting past planning cases. Planning by analogical reasoning in which generative and case-based planning are combined, as in Prodigy/Analogy, provides a suitable framework to study this mixed-initiative integration. However, having a human user engaged in this planning loop creates a variety of new research questions. The challenges we found creating a mixed-initiative planning system fall into three categories: planning paradigms differ in human and machine planning; visualization of the plan and planning process is a complex, but necessary task; and human users range across a spectrum of experience, both with respect to the planning domain and the underlying planning technology. This paper presents our approach to these three problems when designing an interface to incorporate a human into the process of planning by analogical reasoning with Prodigy/Analogy. The interface allows the user to follow both generative and case-based planning, it supports visualization of both plan and the planning rationale, and it addresses the variance in the experience of the user by allowing the user to control the presentation of information.

1 Introduction

In mixed-initiative planning, automated and human planners need to interact in order to mutually construct a plan that satisfies a set of goals in a specific situation. Ideally, joint cooperation has the potential of achieving better plans than either the human or the machine can create alone [5, 9]. However, given the significant disparity between human and automated planning mechanisms, achievement of this potential is a difficult goal. The challenges of creating a successful mixed-initiative planning system fall into at least three categories: planning paradigms differ in human and machine planning; plan visualization is a complex, although necessary, task; and human users range across a spectrum of experience, both with respect to the planning domain and the planning technology. This paper describes the directions we are pursuing to address these problems when designing a mixed-initiative interface for the PRODIGY planning system.

One of the most significant problems facing the integration of human and automated planning is the cognitive metaphor shared between the participants. In general, AI planning assumes a model of actions in the world and generates new plans by searching the space of possible actions. Alternatively, the case-based metaphor of planning as a memory task [7] can be more accessible to the human user. Indeed, few humans plan as if they have never faced a problem like the current one before [10]. Instead, the solution is a matter of remembering concrete past experience to form a new plan similar to an old one previously performed [8, 11]. Yet, when gaps exist in experience, reasoning from first principles is equally as natural and necessary for deriving a successful plan. The Prodigy/Analogy planning system represents a hybrid metaphor that reflects planning in a more complete manner than is the case with traditional case-based planners. Within the same planning system, both generative and case-based algorithms have an equal role.

A related issue is the task of visualizing the plan itself. Although a plan can be conceptualized as a simple sequence of actions, the relationship of each action to the goals of the planner and the state of the world has complex structure. Plan steps often interact with each other depending on the conditions necessary for performing the action and the results of having carried out given actions. Instead of sequential action, a goal tree representation aids a planner when trying to discover or make concrete the structure of plans. Moreover, the *reasons* for why certain actions are chosen (that is, the planning justifications or rationale) are seldom represented, although beneficial for a user when trying to reason in complex domains either from a past case or from first principles. Therefore as presented in this paper, we have designed a mixed-initiative planning interface that supports the planning process through plan and rationale visualization. The inclusion of both facets of planning is aimed at supporting the metacognitive as well as the cognitive aspects of reasoning.

Finally, users of mixed-initiative planning systems differ in experience along at least two dimensions. Users differ in experience with respect to their knowledge and skills of the planning domain (e.g., military deployment planning), and they also differ with respect to their knowledge and skills of the underlying planning technology in the mixed-initiative system. Therefore, a tension exists when presenting information to the user. In some cases a user may wish to override or have access to information concerning the operation of the automated planner, while such information and decisions may bewilder other users. From the beginning, the PRODIGY philosophy has been one of a *glass-box* approach, allowing the user to exert control over all aspects of decision making in the planner [15]. Within a mixed-initiative framework, however, a *black-box* philosophy that shields some of the technological and implementational details from the user (especially the naïve user) can be appropriate as well [4]. A major goal of the interface reported here is to develop a *selective-control mechanism* to support the range of expertise from novice to expert in both dimensions. That is, the user should be able to examine and control any desired decision, while the remainder is abstracted or hidden from the user. This paper reports on the implementation of the interface that begins to support such a philosophy.[1]

The mixed-initiative interface contains a number of features that solve or mitigate the above problems. The user is able to switch between generative and analogical planning manually, or the interleaving of both modes can be left to automation. The interface provides mechanisms to save in the case library planning cases created generatively or analogically, to retrieve old cases that match current demands (either automatically or manually) and to choose various case interleaving strategies for adaptation and replay. The evolving plan is graphically presented to the user as a goal-tree structure and justifications for automated choices is displayed upon demand. Finally, the user can maintain a custom level of information display and user-control depending upon experience and interests.

---

1. The interface is publicly available at http://www.cs.cmu.edu/afs/cs/project/prodigy/Web

Section 2 describes the PRODIGY control algorithms, both in generative and analogical mode. Section 3 then introduces the mixed-initiative interface of PRODIGY, describing how both the plan and the planning decisions are displayed to the user. Section 4 briefly describes the current efforts to make the interface more responsive to the user's level of expertise. Finally, Section 5 concludes with a short discussion.

2 PRODIGY: A Hybrid of Generative and Case-Based Planning

PRODIGY is an automated planner that combines generative state-space planning and case-based planning. In a generative planning mode (Prodigy4.0), the system uses search through a space of operator choices. When under case-based planning mode (Prodigy/Analogy), it retrieves from a case library past plans that are most similar to a given new problem. These plans are reused (replayed) to create a solution for the current goals.

2.1 The Generative Planning Algorithm

The Prodigy4.0 system [15] employs a state-space nonlinear planner and follows a means-ends analysis backward-chaining search procedure that reasons about both multiple goals and multiple alternative operators from its domain theory appropriate for achieving such goals. A domain theory is composed of a hierarchy of object classes and a suite of operators and inference rules that change the state of the objects. A planning problem is represented by an initial state (objects and propositions about the objects) and a set of goal expressions to achieve. Planning decisions consist of choosing a goal from a set of pending goals, choosing an operator to achieve a particular goal, choosing a binding for a given operator, and deciding whether to commit to a possible plan ordering and to get a new planning state or to continue subgoaling for unachieved goals. Different choices give rise to different ways of exploring the search space. These choices are guided by either control rules, by past problem-solving episodes (cases), or by domain-independent heuristics.

1. Initialize.
2. Terminate if the goal statement has been satisfied.
3. Determine which goals are pending, i.e. still need to be achieved.
4. Determine if there are any selected operators that have their preconditions satisfied in the current state, and hence could be applied to the state as the next step in the plan.
5. Choose to subgoal on a goal or to apply an operator: (backtrack point)
   * To subgoal, go to step 6 * To apply, go to step 7
6. Select one of the pending goals (no backtrack point), an instantiated operator that can achieve it (backtrack point); go to step 3.
7. Change the state according to an applicable operator (backtrack point); go to step 2.

Fig. 1. A top-level view of Prodigy4.0's planning algorithm.

As shown in Figure 1, Prodigy4.0 follows a sequence of decision choices, selecting a goal, an operator, and an instantiation for the operator to achieve the goal. Prodigy4.0 has an additional decision point, namely where it decides whether to "apply" an operator to the current state or continue "subgoaling" on a pending goal. "Subgoaling" can be best understood as regressing one goal, or backward chaining, using means-ends analysis. It includes the choices of a goal to plan for and an operator to achieve this goal. "Applying" an operator to the state means a commitment (not necessarily definite since backtracking is possible) in the ordering of the final plan. On the other hand, updating the state through this possible commitment allows Prodigy4.0 to use its state to more informed and efficient future decisions. Hence, the planning algorithm is a combination of state-space search corresponding to a simulation of plan execution of the plan (the head plan; [6]) and backward-chaining responsible for goal-directed reasoning (the tail plan).

The reasons that these choices are made by the automated planner (or, if under user control, the user) are preserved in a plan derivation trace to improve planning efficiency in the future. When the user saves a planning episode, these decision justifications (i.e., the traces) are saved along with the solution in the case library. The case is indexed by the problem goals and a subset of the initial state responsible for the achievement of the goals.

2.2 The Derivational Analogy (CBR) Planning Algorithm

Under a case-based planning mode, Prodigy/Analogy [12] creates plans, interprets and stores planning episodes, and retrieves and reuses multiple past plans that are found similar to new problems. Stored plans are annotated with plan rationale so that, when the plans are retrieved in the future, new decisions can be guided and validated by the past rationale, hence avoiding inefficient search as can be the case in generative mode. The derivational-analogy strategy is to derive new solutions based on the *decision-making process* used in the past, rather than by adapting old *solutions* created in the past [3].

Figure 2 outlines the derivational analogy algorithm used by the system. When a new

1. Initialize.
2. Select a case to follow: follow the justifications and the selected strategy to merge the guidance from multiple past cases.
3. Get the relevant operators from the past cases.
4. Prune alternative failures from the current search path if the reasons for past failure hold.
5. Check syntactic operator-applicability by testing whether its left-hand side matches in the current state.
6. Check semantic applicability by determining whether the past reasons for their use still hold.
7. If choice not valid, choose a suitable action:
   Suspend the guiding case if extra planning work needed to make choice valid:
      Retrieve additional case
      Or replan using domain theory.
   Advance guiding case for past planning work that is not necessary.
   Change the focus of attention by selecting another guiding case.

Fig. 2. A top-level view of the case-based planning algorithm.

problem is proposed, Prodigy/Analogy retrieves from the case library one or more problem solving episodes that may partially cover the new problem solving situation. The system uses a similarity metric that weighs goal-relevant features [14]. Essentially, it selects a set of past cases that solved subsets of the new goal statement. The initial state is partially matched in the features that were relevant to solving these goals in the past. Each retrieved case provides guidance to a set of interacting goals from the new goal statement. At replay time, a guiding case is always considered as a source of guidance, until all the goals it covers are achieved.

The general replay mechanism involves a complete interpretation of the justification structures annotated in the past cases in the context of the new problem to be solved. Equivalent choices are made when the transformed justifications hold. When that is not the situation, Prodigy/Analogy plans for the new goals using its domain operators adding new steps to the solution or skipping unnecessary steps from the past cases.

Prodigy/Analogy constructs a new solution from a *set* of guiding cases, as opposed to a single past case. Complex problems may be solved by resolving minor interactions among simpler past cases. However, following several cases poses an additional decision making step of choosing which case to pursue. Prodigy/Analogy includes several strategies to merge the guidance from the set of similar cases [13].

3 Visualization of the Plan and the Planning Process

One of the main goals underlying the design of the graphical user interface for PRODIGY is to provide a clear animation of the planning algorithm [2]. Given the planning algorithm outlined in the previous section, we discuss several features in the user interface that enable the visualization of the running of algorithm.

The user interface (UI) is implemented in Tcl/Tk, a scripting language which includes a set of Motif widgets (see [2] for additional implementational details). The user interface runs in a separate process from the planner, and the two communicate through Tcl/Tk's IPC mechanism. The planner currently runs in a Common Lisp process that listens for commands from two sources: the terminal running lisp and a socket connected to the user interface. This allows problems to be loaded or planning to be initiated from either the terminal or the interface. The interface makes use of a publicly available preprocessor for drawing directed graphs that represent parts of the domain, plan, and goal structure.

The original interface to PRODIGY is a simple command line interface from Lisp. The user loads a planning domain and a problem to solve, retrieves and loads past cases, and then calls the planner by invoking the run command. The output is composed of print statements at selected decision points in the search tree with indentation indicating search depth. The plan is printed as a list of instantiated operators, and then a brief statement reports success, running time, the number of search nodes expanded, and the number of solutions obtained.

Figure 3 shows the graphical user interface for PRODIGY (in CBR mode). The main control and display window is at the top of the figure, while two cases for replay are shown below. As with the direct command-line interface in Lisp, the user can load a domain and problem with the "Load" button, control program parameters through the "Control Variables" pull-down menu, and execute the planner with the "Replay" button (called the "Run" button in generative mode) or incrementally step through the execution using the "Step" button. During planning, the user can "Break" the execution to pause and then "Restart" to continue or "Abort" to halt the execution after a break. During execution of either generative or case-based planning, the current state of the plan is maintained in two major graphical windows (Tk canvases). The UI generates a view of the tail plan in the Goal Tree Display on the left, and the head plan is printed as a list of committed plan-

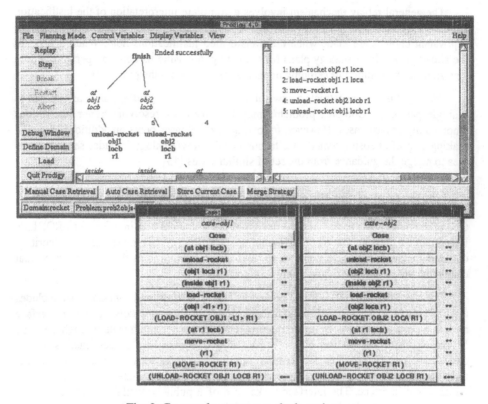

Fig. 3. Case replay, merge, and adaptation

ning steps in the Instantiated Operator Display on the right.

The segment of the goal tree displayed in Figure 3 shows that the user is finished with planning in the current problem in the one-way rocket domain if the two top goals are solved (i.e., objects 1 and 2 are at location locb). These goals can be solved if operator unload-rocket is executed twice while rocket r1 containing both objects is at locb. The two previous cases below the main window show a merge of separate parts of the plan. Stars mark reused plan steps, the arrows mark current locations in the old plans, and blank spaces indicate skipped steps. The Instantiated Operator Display enumerates the steps of final merged plan. Although simplified due to space limitations here, the UI provides full access to PRODIGY to help the user visualize arbitrarily complex planning examples.

Selecting from the "Planning Mode" pull-down menu, the user can alternate control to and from a generative and case-based planning mode.[2] In response, a number of mode-specific buttons are arranged along the bottom of the window. The Prodigy/Analogy but-

---

2. Alternatively, the user can switch to a conditional-planning version that can use analogy along with a generative mechanism [1].

tons allow for retrieval (either automated or manual), storage, and merge selection. The user can visualize the merging procedure as it interleaves multiple cases, marks the steps that are used after successful validation, and skips the ones that are no longer necessary or are invalid. Guiding cases are displayed as shown in the two additional windows at the bottom of Figure 3.

Figure 4 shows the interface window for manual retrieval. The user is able to override the cases Prodigy/Analogy believes to be most similar to the new problem and to select one or more cases in the library for a particular domain. Cases are clicked for selection (or chosen with the "Select Case" button) and they are loaded in to the system via a "Load Selected Cases" button. The loading procedure establishes variable substitution according to the new goals and initial state and maps these values to the operator variables in the old cases.

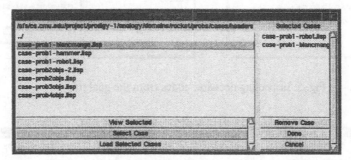

Fig. 4. Manual case retrieval

The UI attaches actions to the displayed graph nodes in the main window so that if the user clicks on them it will pass another message to the planner to display appropriate information. From the Goal Tree Display, the left mouse button causes the system to display the search tree node that relates justifications for the choice of that operator or goal (see Figure 5). Among other information, the sub-windows show that the choice of goal and operator bindings were made based on past experience linked to case-obj2. The middle (or right) mouse button causes the system to display the operator definition from the domain theory. From these opened windows the user can obtain the parent and children of a search tree node or information in the property lists of a given node.

The nodes also reveal other types of information about the rationale of the planner (whether human or automated). For example Figure 6 shows why some planning decisions fail.[3] Node number 25 fails dues to an attempt to re-establish a goal condition, while node 26 fails due to attempting to achieve a goal that is not possible (the rocket destination is not legal). Both of these failure justifications are saved to a case so that when following similar decisions in the future, the search path can be pruned *a priori*. In addition to these types of justifications, the cases represent decisions based on user selection, the application of control rules, failure due to state loops, and success due to goal achievement.

---

3. The failures shown are under generative mode and without control rules. Thus, variable bindings and goals are selected arbitrarily. Under case guidance this is less likely to occur given a good matching past case.

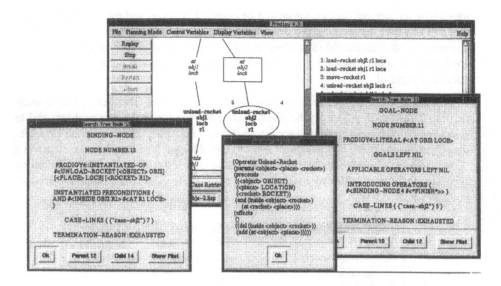

Fig. 5. Inspecting decision nodes from the goal tree

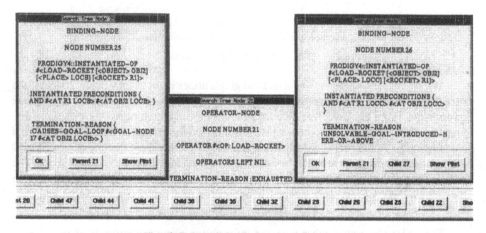

Fig. 6. Reasons for failed decisions.

4 Expertise in Planning Versus Expertise in Technology

At the current time, the interface to PRODIGY has been optimized for users who are familiar with the underlying planning system (e.g., the AI research community in planning). As such it provides a detailed level of access to the internal mechanisms, data representations, and plan structure. For example, the entire decision cycle described in Section 2 is open for inspection through the search-tree node windows. However, given that the development of the interface is still a work in progress, we have made substantial efforts to facilitate use by the more naïve user. A context sensitive help system is partially in place, the ease of execution of the planner has improved given menu selections to replace command-line switches, flags, and function calls, a substantial domain-specification subsystem exists, and the graphical display of the plan enhances plan visualization. Also, although not shown here (see [2] instead), the user can easily preempt automated planning decisions, making them manually instead. Finally, the system supports a concrete experiential basis for planning (i.e., planning is by cases, rather than strictly by first principles).

To further support the planner who is both a novice in the planning domain and knows little about planning formalisms, we have integrated Prodigy/Analogy with the ForMAT military-force deployment planner (see [16]). Using stored cases that match current planning problems, Prodigy/Analogy provides adaptation advice to the ForMAT user when modifying old deployment plans. In this mode, the user is remote across the internet and knows nothing about the manner in which Prodigy/Analogy works.

Finally, we are also working on a new *novice mode* that presents the output to the user in a more natural format. For example, instead of representing the predicates in prefix form in the goal tree display, infix is output so that is reads more like natural language. Likewise in this mode, we are substituting the technical data-structure terms in the justification windows with more intuitive language that describes their function.

5 Conclusion

This paper presents a case-based, mixed-initiative and extensible user interface built using Tcl/Tk that we developed for the PRODIGY architecture. Planning is a complex process and developing user planning interfaces is an important contribution for making implemented systems available to researchers, students, and practitioners. The user is able to switch between generative and analogical planning manually, or the interleaving of both modes can be left to automation. The interface provides mechanisms to save planning cases created generatively or analogically, to retrieve old cases that match current demands (either automatically or manually) and to choose various case interleaving strategies for adaptation and replay. The evolving plan is graphically presented to the user as a goal-tree structure, and justifications for automated choices is displayed upon demand.

The goals of the interface have been to facilitate the interaction between human and machine during the planning process by integrating both generative and case-based planning in the same framework, by providing plan visualization and plan rationale information, and by working toward a more flexible architecture that allows the user to settle to a personal level of equilibrium between too little information and too much. Because the user should not be arbitrarily subjected to the full technological details of the underlying planning technology, our ultimate aim is to develop a user view that abstracts the details of the underlying planner according to need. Our belief is that the immediate focus should be upon what the user sees (the interface), what the user wants (the goals), and what the user does (the task). Additional details should remain transparent to the user unless requested.

Acknowledgments

This research is sponsored as part of the DARPA/RL Knowledge Based Planning and

Scheduling Initiative under grant number F30602-95-1-0018. The authors thank Jason Reisman for programming the Tk code that invokes the manual case-retrieval function.

References

1. Blythe, J. & Veloso, M. M. (in press). Analogical Replay for Efficient Conditional Planning. To appear in the Proceedings of the Fourteenth National Conference on Artificial Intelligence. Menlo Park, CA: AAAI Press.

2. Blythe, J., Veloso, M. M., & de Souza, L. (1997). *The Prodigy user interface* (Tech. Rep. No. CMU-CS-97-114). Carnegie Mellon University, Computer Science Dept.

3. Carbonell, J. G. (1986). Derivational analogy: A theory of reconstructive problem solving and expertise acquisition. In R. Michalski, J. Carbonell & T. Mitchell (Eds.), *Machine learning: An artificial intelligence approach, Vol. 2* (pp. 371-392). San Mateo, CA: Morgan Kaufmann.

4. Cox, M. T., & Veloso, M. M. (1997). *Controlling for unexpected goals when planning in a mixed-initiative setting.* Submitted.

5. Ferguson, G., Allen, J. F., & Miller, B. (1996). TRAINS-95: Towards a mixed-initiative planning assistant. In *Proceedings of the Third International Conference on AI Planning Systems (AIPS-96)*, Edinburgh, Scotland, May 29-31, 1996.

6. Fink, E., & Veloso, M. M. (1996). Formalizing the Prodigy planning algorithm. In M. Gahllab & A. Milani (Eds.), *New Directions in AI Planning* (pp. 261-271). Amsterdam: IOS Press

7. Hammond, K. J. (1989). *Case-based planning: Viewing planning as a memory task. Vol. 1.* of *Perspectives in artificial intelligence.* San Diego, CA: Academic Press.

8. Kolodner, J. L. (1993). *Case-based reasoning.* San Mateo, CA: Morgan Kaufmann.

9. Oates, T. & Cohen, P. R. (1994). Toward a plan steering agent: Experiments with schedule maintenance. In *Proceedings of the Second International Conference on Planning Systems (AIPS-94) (pp. 134-139).* Menlo Park, CA: AAAI Press.

10. Riesbeck, C. K., & Schank, R. C. (1989). *Inside case-based reasoning* (pp. 1-24). Hillsdale, NJ: Lawrence Erlbaum Associates.

11. Seifert, C. M., Hammond, K. J., Johnson, H. M., Converse, T. M., McDougal, T. F., & Vanderstoep, S. W. (1994). Case-based learning: Predictive features in indexing. *Machine Learning, 16,* 37-56.

12. Veloso, M. (1994). *Planning and learning by analogical reasoning.* Springer-Verlag.

13. Veloso, M. (1997). *Merge strategies for multiple case plan replay.* This volume.

14. Veloso, M., & Carbonell, J. G. (1993). Towards scaling up machine learning: A case study with derivational analogy in PRODIGY (pp. 233-272). In S. Minton (Ed.), *Machine learning methods for planning.* Morgan Kaufmann.

15. Veloso, M., Carbonell, J. G., Perez, A., Borrajo, D., Fink, E., & Blythe, J. (1995). Integrating planning and learning: The PRODIGY architecture. *Journal of Theoretical and Experimental Artificial Intelligence, 7*(1), 81-120.

16. Veloso, M. M, Mulvehill, A., & Cox, M. T. (in press). Rationale-supported mixed-initiative case-based planning. To appear in *Proceedings of the Ninth Annual Conference on Innovative Applications of Artificial Intelligence.* Menlo, Park, CA: AAAI Press.

Using Case-Based Reasoning for Argumentation with Multiple Viewpoints

Nikos Karacapilidis*   Brigitte Trousse*   Dimitris Papadias**

* INRIA Sophia Antipolis, Action AID
2004 Route des Lucioles BP 93
06902 Sophia Antipolis Cedex, France
e-mail: {nikos, trousse}@sophia.inria.fr

** Dept. of Computer Science
The Hong Kong University of Science and Technology
Clear Water Bay, Kowloon, Hong Kong
e-mail: dimitris@cs.ust.hk

Abstract. The integration of classical case-based reasoning with other problem solving methods attracts increasing research interest in the broader area of information and decision support systems. This paper presents a framework where CBR and Argumentation Based Reasoning jointly aid agents to address various discourse instances in group decision making processes. The ability to comprehend and engage in arguments is essential for these environments, while use of precedent cases is well-suited. Cases in our model are not merely considered as representations of past data, but as flexible entities associated with the underlying *viewpoint* of an agent and the *evolution* of the corresponding discussion. The paper provides an object-oriented description of the elements involved, and illustrates their dependencies through a comprehensive example.

1 Introduction

Group decision making and planning environments are usually characterized by multiple goals and diverse interests, depending on the points of view of the agents involved. In order to reach understanding, negotiate and resolve conflicts, agents may use various types of knowledge to warrant their arguments towards the selection or rejection of a statement or action. In such domains, case-based reasoning and learning techniques have been particularly useful [14], due to their resemblance to the way people evaluate a potential future action by using past experience, the scarcity (or even absence) of explicitly stated rules, and the ill-structured definitions of the associated problems [1]. On the other hand, mainly stemming from legal reasoning procedures, argumentation has become an appropriate means of interaction in such environments, because it provides agents a means of handling incomplete, uncertain and inconsistent information and accommodating the different methods of expressing and evaluating knowledge they use [7], [18].

This paper deals with the integration of CBR with Argumentation Based Reasoning. The involvement of numerous participants from different contexts (e.g., resource managers, designers, politicians, citizen groups, etc.) in a discussion implies the presence of various selection criteria, preferences, goals etc. We address this issue by explicitly specifying the notion of *viewpoints*. According to our approach, agents involved in a discussion make their viewpoints transparent to the others. Argumentation is performed by various discourse acts aiming at challenging an opponent's opinion. Viewpoints are not static, but may evolve upon time, under the presence of new information or appropriate retrieved cases. Integration of CBR techniques aims at supporting agents involved in group decision making processes to retrieve, adapt and re-use old cases. We view cases not merely as representations of past data, but as flexible entities that can be filtered according to the viewpoint of an agent and the episode of the corresponding discussion (i.e., previous instances of the related argumentation graph), as it has evolved over time.

Previous research has (mostly implicitly) addressed only parts of our approach. For instance, focusing on the legal domain, BankXX system [16] retrieves previous cases and other domain knowledge in support of an argument. In this approach, an argument consists of a set of *argument pieces* representing appropriate fragments of legal knowledge, but as admitted, the corresponding "idealization" of arguments does not reflect the logical and rhetorical connections between the various pieces of an argument. The integration of case and rule based reasoning paradigms, in order to construct an argument to support a particular interpretation of an agent, is also addressed in CABARET system [15]. The concept of viewpoint is involved in the system in a narrow way: one uses cases in order to determine whether the new case is *in* or *out* of the category of the predicate (citing [15], the system supports only *pro* and *con* points of view).

The majority of CBR applications views cases as instances of a standardised template. This results to a considerable reduction of the computational cost involved for the indexing, matching and retrieval processes, but reduces the flexibility and efficiency of the system. Consideration of cases as *virtual views* of the underlying data is proposed in [6]. Actually, this approach involves population of a case base by *mappings* attached to a standardised case format; in such a way, cases are only indirectly linked to the data on which they are based. *Reinterpretation* and *adaptation* of cases in the presence of new input are jointly considered in [8], the distinction among them being at the level which a case description has to be modified. Re-interpretation of a case is meant to be a "look" from a new point of view, and is associated with a new high-level description of it, while keeping the same low-level one; on the other hand, adaptation of a case relates to the change of both its high-level and low-level descriptions. This can be translated to giving a case-based system the ability to create its own dimensions in response to an input problem. In our framework, agents are the ones that decide the dimensions of a case in order to force its retrieval. However, we also follow a similar approach concerning conceptualised representation of cases at different levels.

Addressing the needs of agents to integrate reasoning with cases, reasons and underlying argumentation principles, TRUTH-TELLER [4] compares pairs of cases (presenting ethical dilemmas about whether to tell the truth), and generates a comparison text contrasting the reasons in each case. Even if the program does not retrieve and select relevant precedent cases in order to analyze problematic instances (like in traditional and our approach), the approach is interesting and in line with our goals, in that it explicitly involves in a case the salient reasons for its overall assessment (for more on the role of the general knowledge in providing explanatory support to the case-based processes, see [2], [12]).

Sycara's PERSUADER functions as a mediator in hypothetical labor negotiations. Given such a dispute, the program suggests an appropriate settlement (compromise) to the disputants. If this is rejected, PERSUADER tries to modify either the settlement (by CBR and preference analysis methods) or the opposing party's view (through persuasive argumentation). Our approach addresses the wider area of argumentative discourses; all discourse acts are performed by the agents involved in a discussion.

Finally, the dynamic aspect of our approach in the consideration of cases has been addressed in [3], where case retrieval performance is shown to be improved when keeping a memory of answered questions. The suggested module "remembers" all the previously asked questions, together with the answers that were generated in response, and uses this information to improve the performance of the CBR retriever. Our model works similarly, in that it tracks the history of cases used (or not) at any point of the argumentative discourse. Accumulated information at parts of a discussion episode, about the usage of a certain (old) case, is usually helpful for speculations.

The rest of the paper proceeds as follows: Section 2 describes the argumentation and viewpoint elements of the system and their object-oriented modeling. Section 3 deals with the representation of cases, while Section 4 illustrates the integration of all the above with an example. Section 5 concludes the paper discussing future work plans.

2 Viewpoint-Based Argumentation

Our framework integrates previous work on the modeling and implementation of a Group Decision and Negotiation Support System for Argumentation Based Reasoning on the Web [9], [10] with studies on the argumentative process in cooperative design [19] and viewpoint modeling [20]. The platform system is implemented in Java and can be run using any standard Web browser. It maps a multi-agent decision making process to a discussion graph with a tree-like structure. Throughout the paper, we refer to a real example about the planning of cyclepaths in the city of Bonn (Figure 1). The agents involved represent two parties: the Cyclists Union and the City Hall Planning department. The discussion is about the selection of a plan among two alternatives.

2.1 Argumentation Elements

The argumentation elements of our framework are issues, alternatives, positions, arguments, and preferences (due to space limitations, we focus here on the CBR-related elements and features of the Argumentation System; for a more comprehensive description, see [10]). *Issues* correspond to decisions to be made, or goals to be achieved (e.g., "planning of cyclepaths for the city of Bonn"). They consist of a set of alternatives that correspond to potential choices (e.g., alternatives a_1 : "construct a ring around the city center", a_2 : "select the already planned cyclepath *in Oxfordstrasse*"). *Positions* are asserted in order to advocate the selection of an alternative, or avert the agents' interest from it. For instance, position $p_{1.1}$: "it is faster to move around the city using the ring" is asserted to support a_1, while position $p_{1.3}$: "two car lanes will be replaced by a single one in some streets" to express one's objection to a_1. Positions may also refer to some other position in order to provide additional information about it (e.g., positions $p_{1.1.3}$: "no traffic congestion with pedestrians (when using the ring)", and $p_{2.1.1}$: "there is enough space already available in Parking Houses (providing details about $p_{2.1}$)"). *Arguments* are tuples of either the form (*position, link, position*) or (*position, link, alternative*), where a link marked by + denotes a *supporting argument* and a link marked by − a *counterargument*. In other words, arguments link together a position with an alternative (e.g., $(p_{1.1},+,a_1)$ is a supporting argument for a_1) or another position (e.g., $(p_{2.1.1},-,p_{2.1})$ is a counterargument for $p_{2.1}$). As in real life instances, two or more conflicting arguments can be simultaneously applied.

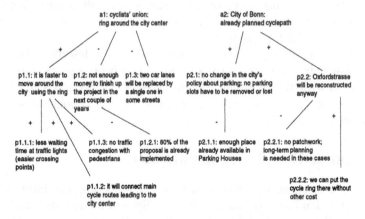

Fig. 1. An instance of the discussion.

Alternatives and positions may be *active* or *inactive*, depending on the related argumentation. The system involves numerous procedures for the propagation of the argumentation up in the discussion tree, such as *labelling* of the argumentation elements according to the different *proof standards* (they correspond to the type of evidence needed to decide if an element is active or not), aggregation of preferences, *consistency checking*, *scoring mechanisms* (in order to decide which is the best alternative), etc. The argumentation framework combines concepts from various well-established areas such as Decision Theory, Non-Monotonic Reasoning, Constraint Satisfaction and Cognitive Modeling. As a stand-alone module, it can act as an assistant and advisor, by recommending solutions and leaving the final enforcement of decisions and actions to the agents. It facilitates access to the current knowledge by making available all relevant data and documents (with URL links), and maintaining them in a well-structured way.

2.2 Viewpoint Elements

While the previous section focused on the argumentation elements *per se*, this one considers argumentation from the agents' perspective. Generally speaking, the *viewpoint* of an agent involved in a group decision making process consists of the (implicit or explicit) value system references which guide his action. The concept of viewpoint [20] is *agent-oriented*. It represents the general interests and - implicitly - goals of an agent, by maintaining lists of *predicates* and *inference schemata* adopted by him for the issue under discussion. In any case, an agent *represents* a viewpoint, while a viewpoint is *shared by* one or more agents. Except of an Id, viewpoint consists of the following parts:

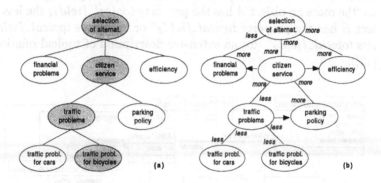

Fig. 2. Viewpoints involved in the discussion of Figure 1.

discussionContext: Describes the semantics of the discussion. More specifically:
    domain: The broader discussion domain (e.g., medicine, environment, etc.);
    type: The broader discussion type (e.g., group decision making, cooperative problem solving, etc.);
    dictionary: Consists of domain-dependent *topical fields* (i.e., predicates which have been previously used for the classification of cases and will be used in the future for retrieval purposes), organised in a hierarchical way, as illustrated in Figure 2a (shaded nodes denote topical fields that belong to both City Hall and Cyclists Union agent dictionaries). The notion of topical field relates to Aristotle's concept of *Topics* and corresponds to an (explicit or implicit) attribute. For instance, in the position *p1.1* the topical field can be *move-fast*.
inference schemata: They represent the various ways that agents relate topical fields with. Inference is the normative aspect of reasoning. Agents follow certain (logical) rules in order to defend their viewpoints or defeat those of their opponents. Such schemata can be (as positions and alternatives) *active* or *inactive*, depending on the argumentation underneath them. Moreover,

an inference schema can be *consistent* or *inconsistent*, depending on the other schemata attached to the discussion. Our model includes the following two types of schemata (we don't claim that the list is exhaustive; however other schemata, suitable to a particular type of discussion, can be easily incorporated):

preferences: they provide a qualitative way to weigh reasons for and against the selection of a certain course of action by weighing the predicates of two different positions. Preferences are tuples of the form $(topical\_field_1, relation, topical\_field_2)$, where the *relation* can be ">", "=" or "<". $(topical\_field_1, >, topical\_field_2)$ is interpreted as $topical\_field_1$ is more important than $topical\_field_2$. Preferences may attach various levels of importance to positions or alternatives in the discussion graph (preferences are denoted with arrows in Figure 2b).

topical relations: Topical relations [19] are tuples of the form $(sign_1, topical\_field_1, sign_2, topical\_field_2)$, where *sign* can be one of more, less (Figure 2b). (more, $topical\_field_1$, less, $topical\_field_2$) is interpreted as "the more an object A has the property $topical\_field_1$, the less an object B has the property $topical\_field_2$" or "the more $topical\_field_1$, the less $topical\_field_2$" (for an extensive description of topical relations, see [19]).

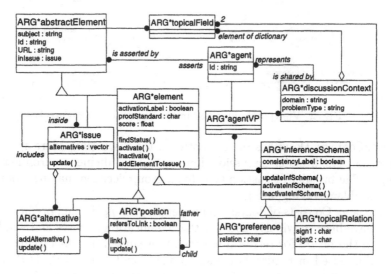

Fig. 3. OMT diagram of the argumentation and viewpoint elements.

2.3 O-O Model Representation

Following an object-oriented approach, we have integrated a part of the Viewpoint model suggested in [20] with the above model of argumentation, the aim being to have a viewpoint-based representation of cases in order to support argumentation in multi-agent settings.

Figure 3 illustrates the OMT diagram for the viewpoint and argumentation elements of our framework (Object Modeling Technique (OMT) [13] is one of the most well-tried analysis and design methods, able to illustrate object-oriented systems from three perspectives: *object diagrams* showing data structures and their relationships, *functional diagrams* showing data flow between processes, and *dynamic models* describing events, states and causal dependencies). Note that each abstractElement includes a list of *topicalFields* and a *url* corresponding to a http address where all the relevant documentation has been stored. Topical fields are currently denoted manually by the users; a semi-automatic field annotation is a future work direction. Furthermore, each element is now linked to a viewpoint through the agent that has asserted it. With such dependencies, we can retrieve the viewpoints that "speak" about a certain topical field by using the dictionary attached to each declared viewpoint.

3 Case Representation

The representation of a case should clearly reflect the purpose for which it will be used [5]. Aiming at providing the ability of extracting multiple views of cases representing the same data, we follow a hybrid approach based on the classical case representation [11] and the structure of the argumentation graph[1] (Figure 4). A case, in our framework, consists of a set of argumentation elements that directly depend on the current status of the discourse and the agents' viewpoints. Except of an Id, cases consist of the following parts:

situation: the relevant part of the discussion at the time the case has been stored; it is composed by:

target: represents the argumentation element to be argued by an agent. It can be an issue, alternative or position (see different instances of the example described in the next section).

discussion: the discussion which the case has been extracted from; it is related to *time* and includes: (i) initialIssue: the issue at the top of the discussion tree; (ii) discussionContext: information about the *domain* and the *problem type* the discussion refers to (e.g. cooperative planning); (iii) abstractElements (ordered list): refer to the corresponding discussion graph and describe the status of the dispute at the time the case has been involved. Cases have a link to the relevant part of the discussion tree they *refer to* (case situation). That is, whenever we store a case, we keep track of the related discussion graph (i.e., the issue it refers to, alternatives and constraints of the issue, agents in the discussion, discussion domain, etc.).

solution: it is the solution the system derives in order to argue about the target; the solution returned can be of the class *alternative* or *position*, depending on whether the case target above was an *issue* or *alternative*, respectively.

---

[1] The similarity of a case indexing tree structure and the argumentation graph of the model is rather straightforward.

evaluation: an indication of how well the case fits to the agents' agenda. It is calculated (using various formulas depending on the discussion domain and type) from the number of the current's case brotherCases (cases with the same target element) and childrenCases (cases that have as target the solution element of the current case).

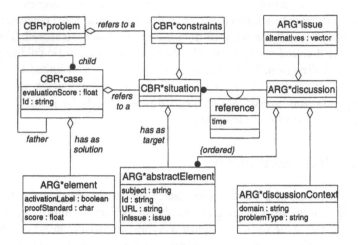

Fig. 4. OMT diagram for a case.

As shown in Figure 4, a problem is defined by a situation together with a constraints part, representing the conditions set by an agent. They may be different each time, depending on the agent's intensions, and are associated with *discussion* and *case filtering*. In addition, some of them (soft constraints) may be relaxed in order to retrieve more cases. They may include elements such as *caseType* (it can be *pro* or *con*, depending on whether the agent wants to advocate or express some objection for the target element, respectively), *problemType* of the discussion, and numerous other elements from the argumentation and viewpoint classes. For instance, the query "retrieve positions that speak against the selection of an alternative, and have been brought up by agents that don't represent public departments and hold inference schemata that incorporate the topical field(s) of the required positions" involves the following constraints: (i) `case.solution.link = "-"`, (ii) `agent.Discussion_Context` $\neq$ `"public_department"`, and (iii) $\exists$ `solution.topicalField` in `agent.inference.topicalFields`. Finally, *temporal constraints* describing various events in the argumentation graphs of the retrieved discussions can be also incorporated here.

4   CBR and Argumentation Based Reasoning

In the model proposed in this paper, control switches from CBR to argumentation-based reasoning and vice-versa, depending on the task to be performed. As mentioned, each agent "enters" a discussion by making clear his own

viewpoint to the others. For the example of the paper, the *cyclist_ union agent* is aware that interests and preferences of the *City_ Hall agent* focus on financial aspects, while he makes clear that his own interests are on the quality of the citizen service. Argumentation with CBR includes four phases: (i) *intension submission,* (ii) *case retrieval and selection,* (iii) *case adaptation,* and (iv) *argument assertion.*

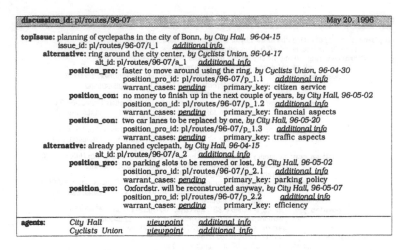

Fig. 5. CBR and Argumentation Based Reasoning: An early instance.

Agents first submit their intensions, by declaring the arguments they want to bring up in the discussion. This phase is considered to be a mapping of each agent's viewpoint to the current discussion. The explicit declaration of agents' intensions "drives" the argumentation process by motivating search for similar instances in the case base (search should be oriented towards similar argument structures). Agents' intensions implicitly specify the *CBR agenda,* i.e., actions to be performed through the case base (at the next phase). Figure 5 illustrates an early instance of the discussion (as of May 20, 1996), where the *City_ Hall agent* intends to argue against alternative a_1 using financial (position $p_{1.2}$) and traffic (position $p_{1.3}$) reasons, while he wants to support alternative a_2 for their advantages on parking policy and efficiency aspects (positions $p_{2.1}$ and $p_{2.2}$, respectively). Note that, at this point, the *cyclist_ union agent* only intends to support a_1 for citizen service reasons (position $p_{1.1}$); he has no desire to challenge a_2. An entry being at this phase is indicated by the slot warrant_cases:*pending* .

Case retrieval is performed with the use of topical fields from agents' dictionaries. The model initially checks the case base for precedent instances with the same field(s) at the target case element, taking into account the situation of the desired case as specified by the constraints (for the domains we address, when target is an alternative, the topical field used is *"selection of alternative").* A simple case base query related to the intended position $p_{1.2}$ can be of the form: "give me all cases where the selection of an alternative is argued via financial aspects". We can further restrict the query, asking for cases where the selection

of an alternative is objected due to financial reasons (as in the type of argument that the *City_ Hall agent* intends to assert using position $p_{1.2}$). However, with similar types of query relaxation, users may also retrieve *opposite cases*, possibly useful during the adaptation phase. During the case retrieval phase, agents may also alter their viewpoints, while observing similar precedent instances under the presence of certain participants in the corresponding discussions.

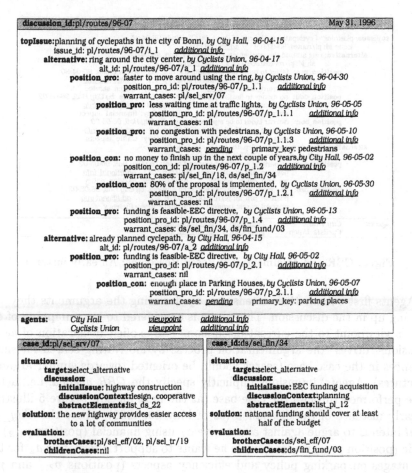

Fig. 6. CBR and Argumentation Based Reasoning: A second instance.

Case selection and *case adaptation* are based on agent viewpoints and the current status of argumentation. Assume that two cases have been retrieved for the above query, one with caseType:pro and another with caseType:con. *City_ Hall agent* intends to bring up an argument against the selection of alternative a_1 due to financial aspects, so he may use the first case. Similarly, *cyclist_ union agent* may use the second one to challenge the argument of the *City_ Hall agent*. In any case, before the final argument assertion, *case adaptation* should be performed. While case selection is automatic, case adaptation is semi-automatic, in that the system proposes potential matches and the user selects the cases he thinks

appropriate to adapt (according to the context of the current discussion) and use. Potential matches correspond to combinations of *caseType* with the *topical inferences* included in viewpoints. Shortly described here, *ranking* of best cases is performed according to the number of *brother* and *children cases* of the ones retrieved, the justification being that the more cases are related to them, the more robust they are (due to their potential challenge in previous disputes).

Using the retrieved (and possibly adapted) cases, agents provide warrants for their assertions. The *argument assertion* phase involves firing of the appropriate discourse acts for the propagation of the information in the discussion graph, and storage of the new case used. Figure 6 illustrates a later instance of the same discussion (as of May 31, 1996), where further argumentation has been provided. Samples of cases used at this instance appear at the lower two windows of the figure. Note that some of the initial intentions may have been completely discarded as the discussion evolves (see, for instance, the ones initiated by positions $p_{2.2}$ and $p_{1.3}$ in Figure 5), possibly due to unavailability of similar cases and/or the evolution of the viewpoints of the related agents. Also that case $ds/sel\_fin/34$ is used in both a position_pro and a position_con. This is due to different interpretation of the case by the two agents (*Cyclists_ Union agent* has also considered a childrenCase of $ds/sel\_fin/34$ - browsing $list\_pl\_12$ of abstractElements - that seems to better warrant his intended assertion). As shown in the last two figures, discussion is organized in a structured way, where entries (argumentation elements) are indexed according to their role and function. Among other relevant information, entries include references to the cases used as warrants and *primary_ keys* for the indexing of cases. Finally, references to the participating agents and their viewpoints are provided.

5 Concluding Remarks

Our main motivation for the framework suggested in this paper is to provide direct computer support for argumentation and negotiation with case-based reasoning, especially in weak domains. The argumentation part of the system is already implemented in Java, the aim being to deploy it on the web. What agents need to participate in a discussion is only a standard browser. Exploiting Web-based technology, our framework meets practical requirements such as relatively inexpensive access to a broad public, intuitive interfaces in order to be easily usable by inexperienced users, and availability on any prominent operating system and hardware platform. We focus on distributed, asynchronous collaboration, allowing agents to surpass the requirements of being in the same place and working at the same time.

Acknowledgements: We thank M. Jaczynski and the anonymous referees for their helpful comments and suggestions. Nikos Karacapilidis is financed by the Commission of the European Communities through the ERCIM Fellowship Programme.

References

1. Aamodt, A., Plaza, E.: Case-Based Reasoning: Foundational Issues, Methodological Variations and System Approaches. *AI Communications* 7(1), 1996.
2. Aamodt, A.: Explanation-driven Retrieval, Reuse, and Learning of Cases. In *Proceedings of EWCBR'93*, pp. 279-284, 1996.
3. Alterman, R., Griffin, D.: Remembering Episodes of Question Answering. In *Proceedings of EWCBR'94*, pp. 235-242, 1994.
4. Ashley, K.D, Mc Laren, B.M.: Reasoning with Reasons in Case-Based Comparisons. In M. Veloso & A. Aamodt (eds.) *Case-Based Reasoning: Research and Development*, LNAI 1010, Springer-Verlag, pp. 133-144, 1995.
5. Ashley, K.D.: Indexing and Analytical Models. In Hammond K.J. (ed.) *Proceedings of DARPA Workshop on CBR*, Morgan Kaufmann, pp. 197-202, 1989.
6. Brown, M., Watson, I., Filer, N.: Separating the Cases from the Data: Towards More Flexible Case-Based Reasoning. In *Proceedings of ICCBR'95*, LNAI 1010, Springer-Verlag, pp. 157-168, 1995.
7. Eemeren, F.H. van, Grootendorst, R., Snoeck Henkemans, F.: *Fundamentals of Argumentation Theory: A Handbook of Historical Backgrounds and Contemporary Developments.* Lawrence Erblaum Associates, 1996.
8. O'Hara, S.: A Blackboard Architecture for Case Re-interpretation of cases. In *Proceedings of EWCBR'94*, pp. 337-346, 1994.
9. Karacapilidis, N.I., Papadias, D., Gordon, T.: An Argumentation Based Framework for Defeasible and Qualitative Reasoning. In D. Borges & C. Kaestner (eds.) *Advances in Artificial Intelligence*, LNAI 1159, Springer-Verlag, pp. 1-10, 1996.
10. Karacapilidis, N.I., Papadias, D.: A Group Decision and Negotiation Support System for Argumentation Based Reasoning. In G. Antoniou & M. Truszczynski (eds.) *Learning and Reasoning with Complex Representations*, LNAI Series, Springer-Verlag, 1997. In Press.
11. Kolodner, J.: *Case-Based Reasoning*, Morgan Kaufmann, 1993.
12. Leake, D.B.: Focusing Construction and Selection of Abductive Hypotheses. In *Proceedings of the 11th IJCAI*, pp. 24-29, 1993.
13. Rumbaugh, J., Blaha, M., Premerlani, W., Eddy, F., Lorensen, W.: *Object-Oriented Modeling and Design.* Prentice-Hall, 1991.
14. Plaza, E., Arcos, J.L., Martin, F.: Cooperative Case-Based Reasoning. In G. Weiss (ed.) *Distributed Artificial Intelligence meets Machine Learning*, LNAI Series, Springer-Verlag, 1997. In press.
15. Rissland, E.L., Skalak, D.B.: CABARET: rule interpretation in a hybrid architecture. *Int. Journal Man-Machine Studies* 34, pp. 839-887, 1991.
16. Rissland, E.L., Skalak, D.B., Friedman, M.T.: Using Heuristic Search to Retrieve Cases that Support Arguments. In *Proceedings of CBR'93 Workshop*, AAAI Press, pp. 5-11, 1993.
17. Sycara, K.: Resolving Adversarial Conflicts: An Approach Integrating Case-Based and Analytic Methods. Ph.D. diss., School of Information and Computer Science, Georgia Institute of Technology, 1987.
18. Toulmin, S.E.: *The Uses of Argument.* Cambridge University Press, 1958.
19. Trousse, B., Christiaans, H.: Design as a Topos-based Argumentative Activity: A Protocol Analysis Study. In N. Cross et. al. (eds) *Analysing Design Activity*, J. Wiley & Sons, pp. 365-388, 1996.
20. Trousse, B., Orel, T., Rothenburger, B., Vogel, C., Charrel, P.J.: Models of Viewpoints Correlation, Technical Report D3 of R&T CNES-INRIA Study of Dynamic Viewpoints, 1996 (in french).

Maintaining Unstructured Case Bases

Kirsti Racine[1] and Qiang Yang[1]

School of Computing Science
Simon Fraser University
Burnaby BC V5A 1S6,
Canada
Email : kracine@cs.sfu.ca, qyang@cs.sfu.ca
Web : http://fas.sfu.ca/kracine

Abstract. With the dramatic proliferation of case based reasoning systems in commercial applications, many case bases are now becoming legacy systems. They represent a significant portion of an organization's assets, but they are large and difficult to maintain. One of the contributing factors is that these case bases are often large and yet unstructured; they are represented in natural language text. Adding to the complexity is the fact that the case bases are often authored and updated by different people from a variety of knowledge sources, making it highly likely for a case base to contain redundant and inconsistent knowledge.

In this paper, we present methods and a system for maintaining large and unstructured case bases. We focus on two difficult problems in case-base maintenance: redundancy and inconsistency detection. These two problems are particularly pervasive when one deals with an unstructured case base. We will discuss both algorithms and a system for solving these problems. As the ability to contain the knowledge acquisition problem is of paramount importance, our methods allow one to express relevant domain expertise for detecting both redundancy and inconsistency naturally and effortlessly. Empirical evaluations of the system prove the effectiveness of the methods in several large domains.

1 Introduction

A pervasive, yet relatively ignored, problem inherent in using case-based reasoning is that of case-base maintenance. A case base is usually constructed over a long period of time, during which cases that solve approximately the same range of problems are entered, by different case authors at different times. As well, a case base may be the result of the union of several different smaller case bases, or the result of "scanning in" raw material from large quantities of literature. Similarly, a company's use for any given case base may change with time. For example, the cases for fixing a certain type of printer in an organization will become outdated when the company acquires a fleet of new printers for replacement. As the case base grows, errors within the case base become increasingly difficult to detect. The result can be contradictions or inconsistencies within a case base. These problems can potentially harm the performance of a case based reasoning system. All these reasons contribute to the need to update and reorganize a case base during its lifetime.

A case-base maintainer must be responsible for several different tasks. First, as time passes, cases may become redundant simply because there are more powerful cases in the same case base. In addition, some cases may contain inconsistent information either with other parts of the same case or with the background knowledge. A need then arises for identifying these cases and deciding whether to eliminate them. Second, a large case base implies that the cases are not used uniformly. Some cases are used more often than others, and this usage distribution can be dependent on many different factors, including time, the company's asset distribution and business strategies. A dynamic case base requires constant reorganization, so its most frequently, most recently accessed cases are easily presentable to the user. This requirement suggests a hierarchical organization structure for the case base. A complex aspect is that this structure must respond to the continuous change in the user environment. A final aspect of case base maintenance is in the ability for a system to identify and suggest solutions to "inconsistent cases." A case consists of a description of a target problem and a solution. If the case description and solution contain errors, it may lead to contradiction in the solution of a case. This problem will render a case solution unusable by the user. Thus, a case-base maintenance system should have the ability to identify inconsistent cases and parts of a case that are inconsistent with each other.

The problem of case-base maintenance is akin to that of software maintenance. It is now well known that as a software system is constructed, a major portion of an organization's resources is devoted to "software maintenance" in its entire life cycle; estimates put this effort at 50 to 70 percent of the total cost for developing and using the software in its life cycle [MO83, LS81, LST78]. We conjecture that the same amount of effort will be experienced by organizations exploiting case base reasoning systems.

2   Previous Approaches

The previous research in maintaining case-base systems has addressed many different aspects of the cleaning problem. [Aha91], by David Aha, presents several case-based learning (CBL) algorithms which are tolerant of noise and irrelevant features. These algorithms can predict feature values in future cases and, thereby, detect anomalies or possible errors in the data. However, CBL algorithms make several assumptions about the structure of the data, including the requirement that an explicit structure consisting of feature-value pairs be given. Also, features must be uniformly important across all cases for these approaches to work. Moreover, these methods concentrate on local, single-case level solutions. Further research conducted in this area concentrates on detecting discontinuities in case bases [ST96]. However, this research is still focused on very well structured cases, the cases are actually stored in a relational database. Predicting that a case is discontinuous involves examining the relationships between attributes across all cases.

Another area of case-base maintenance is concerned with *optimization*. Smyth and Keane [SK95] suggested a competence-preserving deletion approach. The premise of this approach is that each case in the base should be classified according to its competence. These classifications are made according to two key concepts: *coverage* and *reachability*. Coverage refers to the set of problems that each case can solve. Reachability is the set of cases that can provide solutions for each current problem. Cases that represent unique ways to answer a specific query are *pivotal* cases. *Auxiliary* cases are those which are completely subsumed by other cases in the base. In between these two extremes are the *spanning* cases which link together areas covered by other cases and *support* cases which exist in groups that support an idea. The deletion algorithm then deletes cases in the order of their classifications : auxiliary, support, spanning and then pivotal cases.

An unresolved issue is how these auxiliary cases are identified, and *what* will be done once they are found. In addition, in our experience, we found that simply deleting cases from a legacy case base is a very dangerous endeavor; since cases represent significant assets of an organization, deleting them could represent a possible loss to the company. In addition, Smyth and Keane's theory does not address the issue of detecting erroneous cases.

3 The Case for Case Base Maintenance

In this section we further clarify the case-base maintenance problem using an industrially relevant domain — the computer printer trouble-shooting domain. We show through the use of this domain that case maintenance is a serious problem not only in theory, but also in practice.

3.1 Two Types of Cases

The majority of the work in case based reasoning has concentrated on cases with well defined features. These cases have a relational structure, where each feature is more or less a field in a relational database. In reality, however, formulating a case into a structured format requires extensive knowledge engineering. For a given domain, the user has to first determine the important features to use to represent each case. Then a decision has to be made on the type of values for each feature. The process of authoring knowledge in this feature-value format requires extensive maintenance when a new feature is discovered and inserted, or when an existing feature becomes irrelevant.

In industrial practice, a majority of the case bases come directly from either unstructured text documents, which are scanned in, or end-users' verbal description. These cases may have generic features such as *problem description* and *problem solution*, but each of these features probably will not be further partitioned down to a relational level. As an example, in a computer-printer repair domain, a case might be described as:

```
Problem: Paper continues jamming laser printer due to dirty
and/or sticky internals.
SOLUTION : The internal components of the laser printer are
dirty and perhaps gummed up. There is also a possibility the
paper
is sticking together. Running regular gummed labels through a
laser printer is a key source of the problem because the high
heat
melts the gum labels.
```

Structured, relational cases often lend themselves to maintenance. Each attribute is associated with a set of values. The cases can be scanned and values that appear infrequently for a particular attribute can be modified or brought to the user's attention. Alternatively, integrity constraints can be specified ensuring that each value entered is a legal one for that attribute. Unstructured cases, on the other hand, are more problematic. Often the cases can not be reduced to a set of variable value pairs so even range checking can be a complex problem. A case-base management agent must be able to account for unstructured cases as well as structured cases.

3.2 The Inconsistent-Case Problem

As a case base grows larger, the number of inconsistent cases will inevitably increase as well. A case can be inconsistent in two different ways:

1. A case can be inconsistent with the background knowledge in an application domain. For example, due to a mis-spelling, a case-base maintainer in a medical domain might have entered "the patient is 200 years old". This is inconsistent with the knowledge that all humans are no older than 115 (if the Guinness Book of World Records is to be believed!).
2. A case can be inconsistent because sections of the it contradict each other. For example, a case from printer-repair domain may have an inconsistent solution requiring the user to both repair and replace the printer.

The medical case-base example above presents an instance of a soft constraint violation. A *soft* constraint violation could occur when a uncommonly occurring feature value is found in a case. In this situation, a warning is desired to bring this item to the users' attention. The printer example, however, demonstrates a hard constraint violation. *Hard* constraint violations are logical contradictions. A self cleaning agent must be able to identify both types of constraint violations.

3.3 The Redundant-Case Problem

With a large legacy case base a need arises to detect if two cases are equal or if one case subsumes another by some criteria determined by the background knowledge. A special case is when two cases are considered equivalent; that is, all attribute values are identical.

An example of redundancy in the printer-repair domain is displayed in Table 1. It demonstrates the difficulty of identifying redundant cases when the cases are unstructured. A string comparison of the two cases presented will detect some similarities, but there are significant differences between the cases.

Case 1
CASE NAME: Envelopes jam laser printer due to glue. SOLUTION: Normal envelopes and laser printers do not get along together. Problems include poor glue heat tolerance.
Case 2
CASE NAME: Paper continues jamming printer due to sticky internals SOLUTION: Envelopes do not work very well with laser printers. The high heat melts the gummed labels.

Table 1. Example of redundant cases in the printer repair domain

4 Maintenance Algorithm

4.1 Overview

Our approach to solving the maintenance problem for unstructured case bases is to integrate an agent within a case based reasoning system. In order to minimize the knowledge acquisition bottleneck, the agent allows unstructured cases to be processed as well as the structured ones. We first use an information-retrieval based algorithm to parse the cases by mining key words and important keywords and key phrases from the unstructured text. These keywords and phrases will offer the basis for subsequent modules to operate on. After the information-retrieval step, we then use a specialized redundancy-detection and inconsistency-detection module to manage the case base.

4.2 Keyword and Phrase Retrieval from Unstructured Cases

We use information retrieval techniques to partially automate the normalization process. The specific steps in this process are:

1. Remove the stop words. Stop words are those words proven to be poor indexers, such as "the" and "of". They typically comprise between 40% - 60% of the words within a document[SM83].
2. Collapse words using a domain thesaurus. In this application, the thesaurus is used to standardize terms. For example, "sega unit" and "sega player" may both appear in a case-based reasoner designed to diagnose cable failure.

These can both be reduced to "sega player" in order to facilitate string matching.

3. Identify significant terms through statistical measures. Keywords are those words which appear frequently within a small set of cases and infrequently across all other cases[FBY92] [SM83]. The key word, the weight of the key word within the file and the documents in which the key word appears are retained.

4. Identify key phrases. Phrases are groups of more than one word which have high inter-case cohesion[SM83]; if one word appears in a case, then the other words have a very high probability of also appearing. Identified phrases must appear in > T cases, where T is a standard threshold or user specified.

5. Generate an inverted index for the entire case base and for the key words. Our inverted index is a list of the terms that appear in the case base, the document number in which the term appears and the weight of the term within the document. This last measure is the frequency of the term within the case.

An example of the information retrieval process applied to one case in the printer-repair domain is shown in Table 2.

Step 1: Read in Original Case
CASE NAME: The printed page is black.
CASE SOLUTION: The printed page is black due to an unseated toner cartridge Reseat the toner cartridge and reprint the document.
To reseat the toner cartridge:
1.) Turn the laser printer off.
2.) Open the top by pressing button to release latch.
NOTE: Some printers require removing the paper tray first.

Step 2: Case After Stop Words Removed
CASE NAME: printed page black
CASE SOLUTION: printed page black unseated toner cartridge reseat toner cartridge reprint document
reseat toner cartridge turn laser printer press button release latch
printers require removing paper tray first

Step 3: Key Words And Phrases
KEY WORDS: toner, cartridge, tray, press, button, release, latch
PHRASES: toner cartridge, page black, paper tray, reseat toner cartridge.

Table 2. Example of Information Retrieval Techniques Applied to Incoming Case

Information retrieval techniques facilitate the comparison of cases. Cases are "normalized" allowing the similarities or differences between cases to become more pronounced. The normalized representation of the case can be used by retrieval schemes also to better solve the user's problem.

4.3 Guidelines for Inconsistent Cases

Addressing the Knowledge Acquisition Problem We chose to use string based rules to represent guidelines. These rules are very close to natural language, and the matching with the underlying case base is done through a string-based fuzzy matching algorithm. This method offers medium speed, but string-based rules are easy for the user to understand and easy for the expert to supply. An additional advantage is that string based rules can be easily modified by the user in case of spelling errors, irrelevant information or difficult wording. For this reason, we call these rules "guidelines".

Guideline Representation String-based guidelines are simply impossible combinations of key words or phrases. Therefore if K represents the keyword set, rules can be expressed as $k_1 \wedge k_2 \wedge ... \wedge k_n$ where $\{k_i \in K | i = 0...n \wedge |K| = n\}$. An example guideline in the printer-repair domain is: {Guideline: laser printer black ribbon}

Laser printers do not use ribbons, so this combination of words should not appear in a case. Range inconsistencies can also be defined. These rules are referred to as adjacency rules: {Guideline : channel < 89}

Violations of string-based guidelines are detected by examining the inverted index of the incoming case. If all of the words within a guideline are detected within one case, that case is flagged as possibly violating the guideline. The case must then be examined to determine adjacency of the words within the guideline. In the second example, the word "channel" is located and then the word directly following is tested to determine if it is a number and it is greater than "89". If so, a 100% chance of contradiction is reported to the user. Using hashing functions greatly reduces the amount of time required to "test" a case for consistency.

4.4 Solving the Redundancy Problem

Once each case has been given a standard description or profile, redundancy and subsumption can be partially identified.

Equivalence and Pure Subsumption First consider the case where two cases have the exact same string representation - clearly they are equivalent for all intents and purposes. However, that is not the interesting situation. We also detect situations where both the descriptions and the solutions of two cases are close to each other by our nearest-neighbor similarity function. These cases are then presented to the user for further examination.

Cases can also be redundant because they are subsumed by others. The advantage of identifying pure subsumption is that the user can be presented with two redundant cases and the system can explain that Case 1 subsumes Case 2. In this way, the system can provide the user with information regarding which is the more powerful case. Consider *Subsumption Rule 1*:

Case 1 : Problems (p_1, p_2) Solution (s_1)
Case 2 : Problems (p_1, p_2, q_1) Solution (s_1)

q_1 can either be a keyword or a set of words containing a keyword. In this case, Case 1 subsumes Case 2. The sufficient conditions for solution s_1 have been established to be (p_1, p_2). The value of q_1 is irrelevant. Once the first two premises hold, the solution can be offered to the user. Once this scenario has been detected, the system allows the user to view both cases and highlights the unnecessary condition. As it is possible that Case 1 is an inconsistent case, the fact that it subsumes Case 2 does not mean that Case 2 should be summarily deleted from the case base. The user must examine both cases and decide on the suitable course of action.

Similarly, consider *Subsumption Rule 2*:

Case 1 : Problem: (p_1, p_2) Solution: (s_1)
Case 2 : Problem: (p_1, p_2) Solution: (s_1, s_2)

Similarly to the first example, s_2 can either be a key word or a set of words containing a key word. In this case, Case 1 again subsumes Case 2. If (s_1) is sufficient to solve Case 1, then it is sufficient to solve Case 2. Any additional information or suggested actions are extraneous.

There is one more possibility (*Subsumption Rule 3*):

Case 1 : Problem: (p_1) Solution: (s_1, s_2)
Case 2 : Problem: (p_1, p_2) Solution: (s_1)

In this instance, the system generates a third case:

System Generated Case : Problem (p_1) Solution (s_1)

This new case subsumes both Case 1 and Case 2 by the previous two subsumption rules.

Example We now present an example of how to apply the subsumption rules. Consider the two cases in Table 3. Both cases have the same solution, but Case 2 contains extraneous problem descriptions. By Rule2, Case 2 is subsumed by Case 1. With the end-user's authorization, Case 2 can then be eliminated from the case base.

5 Empirical Testing

We have implemented the agent architecture in the framework of the CaseAdvisor system[1] developed at Simon Fraser University.

---

[1] To get an evaluation copy, contact http://www.cs.sfu.ca/cbr.

Case 1
Problem : Envelopes jam laser printer due to glue.
Solution: Normal envelopes and laser printers do not get along well together. Problems include poor glue heat tolerance.

Case 2
Problem : Paper continues jamming printer due to glue in the internals. The gummed labels of the envelope have melted.
Solution: Envelopes do not work very well with laser printers. Problems include poor glue heat tolerance.

Table 3. Detecting Redundancy in the Printer Repair Domain. In this example, Case 2 is subsumed by Case 1

CaseAdvisor™ is a case-based reasoning system implemented in C++ and operates on both the PC and the Internet environments as either a stand alone system or a client/server system. It's advanced functionalities includes visual case authoring, interactive problem resolution, interactive planning using decision forests, and case adaptation for sales automation. For case bases, it supports both flat file structures and ODBC database structures. CaseAdvisor comes in both an application version for the Windows and UNIX environments, and an API (application programming interface) version. So far, CaseAdvisor has been successfully applied to many different help-desk applications in industrial settings (for example, call center applications and financial package suggestions).

Our tests are aimed at establishing the validity of the agent-based approach to case-base maintenance. We hope to confirm through the experiments the following conjectures:

- The information-retrieval approach for processing unstructured cases is feasible for large case bases.
- The redundancy-detection module is capable of detecting most redundant cases.
- The inconsistency-detection module is capable of detecting intra-case inconsistencies through the use of string-based guidelines.
- Finally, the knowledge-acquisition bottleneck problem is adequately addressed by the agent.

5.1 Testing the Information Retrieval Module

Even the one time cost of normalizing a case base is not that expensive. The time required to remove the stop words from all of the cases applying the user defined thesaurus, the time to extract keywords and phrases from the cases and the time to build the inverted file structure were all measured. The information retrieval module was applied to 5 different case bases containing different types of data.

Each case was on average 0.3 kilobytes in size. The Sheffield LISA collection is a database of abstracts and titles extracted from The Library and Information Science Abstracts database from Sheffield University. We performed empirical testing on different components of the Sheffield LISA collection varying the case size from 500 cases to 8000. In all instances, the information retrieval module finished processing in less than 120 seconds. This proves that the self cleaning module can handle large case bases in a reasonable amount of time. When applied to an actual case base designed to diagnose cable failures, the information retrieval module completed processing in less than one second. Testing was completed on large test files to illustrate how the information retrieval module scales.

5.2   Testing the Redundancy-detection Module

The redundancy module is responsible for testing an incoming case for possible redundancy. If there is no possible redundancy, the case is simply added to the existing case base. If there is, the case is presented to the user along with the case causing the possible conflict. The user then determines which, if any, of the cases should be deleted from the case base.

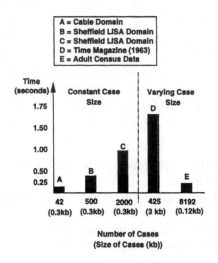

Fig. 1. CPU Time to Detect Redundancy

Figure 1 demonstrates that the algorithm to detect redundancy is efficient enough to be applied in a case authoring module. The average size of the case is also presented in the figure to illustrate the relative performance of the redundancy module is dependent on both the number of cases AND the typical case size. The case base with the largest number of cases, 8192, only needs approximately 0.25 seconds to check for redundancy due to the relatively small size of the cases. The results presented show that the redundancy module scales up to large case bases quite efficiently. Again, the case base containing, on average, three (3) kilobyte cases took the longest period of time to test for redundancy. However, the system still performed the redundancy check in less than two seconds.

The next experiment involved using blind subjects to type in cases from the same data sources. Five (5) subjects were required to input cases and submit them to be added to the case base. Approximately 50% of the required cases to enter were, in fact, redundant. The data sources used were in the form of decision trees, rather than cases, to introduce a level of indirection. One branch of the decision tree is equivalent to a case. Figure 2 presents the results of this experiment.

	Identified	Not Identified	
Redundant	97	6	103
Not Redundant	20	87	107
	117	93	

Fig. 2. Quality of Redundancy Module

Figure 2 demonstrates the efficacy of our redundancy module. 94% of the redundant cases were correctly identified by the application. Another encouraging statistic is that 83% of all cases identified as redundant were in fact redundant. Out of the 210 cases entered, 97 were correctly identified as redundant, 20 were falsely identified as redundant, 6 were falsely identified as not redundant and the remaining 87 were correctly classified. Using fuzzy string matching to determine redundancy allows for false positives. The threshold for identifying redundancy can be modified. However, this modification must be made at the expense of increasing the number of redundant cases that are not identified by the module.

5.3 System Design

The redundancy and inconsistency detection algorithms are now integrated as part of a larger case-base management module in CaseAdvisor system. Given a collection of text files containing case information, this module semi-automatically extracts the case base and performs redundancy and inconsistency testing and management. The module is also able to merge two case bases and accept a new case while detecting redundant and inconsistent cases.

6 Conclusions and Future Work

We maintain that case-base management should be taken seriously by every practitioner and researcher. Of high importance is the issue of how to contain knowledge acquisition costs while maintaining the case base. Our solution for this problem is a case base maintenance agent which can retrieve important information from a case base and then use this information to detect redundant and inconsistent cases. Our experiments confirmed that the approach can be used to address practical problems of large sizes.

One area of future work is conducting more experiments on the inconsistency detection algorithm. A first task of the experiments is to obtain more realistic guideline for inconsistency detection. These guidelines will be provided by the actual users of the system. With these guidelines we will be able to perform efficiency and usability analysis on the algorithm.

Acknowledgment

We wish to thank Christina Carrick, D. Edward Kim, Philip W.L. Fong and the other members of the Case based Reasoning Group at SFU for their comments. The authors are supported by grants from: Natural Sciences and Engineering Research Council of Canada (NSERC), BC Advanced Systems Institute and Canadian Cable Labs Fund.

References

[Aha91] D. Aha. Case-based learning algorithms. *Proceedings of the 1991 DARPA Case-Based Reasoning Workshop*, 1, 1991.

[FBY92] William B. Frakes and R. Baeza-Yates. *Information Retrieval: Data Structures and Algorithms*. Prentice-HALL, North Virginia, 1992.

[LS81] B. P. Lientz and B. E. Swanson. Problems in application software maintenance. *Communications of ACM*, 24(11):763–769, 1981.

[LST78] B. P. Lientz, E. B. Swanson, and G. E. Tompkins. Characteristics of application software maintenance. *Communications of ACM*, 21, June 1978.

[MO83] R. J. Martin and W. M. Osborne. Guidance on software maintenance. National Bureau of Standards Special Publication 500–106, Superintendent of Documents, Washington DC, 1983.

[SK95] B. Smyth and M. Keane. Remembering to forget : A competence-preserving case deletion policy for case-based reasoning systems. *International Joint Conference on Artificial Intelligence*, 1:377–382, 1995.

[SM83] G. Salton and M.J. McGill. *Introduction to Modern Information Retrieval*. Computer Science Series McGraw Hill Publishing Company, New York, 1983.

[ST96] H. Shimazu and Y. Takashima. Detecting discontinuities in case-bases. *Proceedings of the Thirteenth National Conference on Aritifical Intelligence*, 1:690–695, 1996.

An Analogical Theory of Creativity in Design

Sambasiva R. Bhatta[1] and Ashok K. Goel[2]

[1] NYNEX Science & Technology, 500 Westchester Ave., White Plains, NY 10604.
[2] College of Computing, Georgia Institute of Technology, Atlanta, GA 30332-0280.

Abstract. Creative design often involves large, complex modifications to the design topology. Making these modifications typically requires transfer of design configurations from different designs to the new problem. We describe an analogical theory of creative design called *model-based analogy* (MBA). In this theory, case-specific structure-behavior-function (SBF) models of past designs enable abstraction of *generic telelogical mechanisms* (GTMs) at storage time. The goal of adapting a specific design to address a new design problem leads to the retrieval of a relevant GTM and its instantiation in the context of the case-specific SBF model at transfer time. Thus GTMs learned from past designs mediate the transfer of abstract design configurations to a new problem.

1   Background, Motivations and Goals

Traditional case-based reasoning provides a process account of adaptive design in which the design modifications are small, simple and local. The process is characterized by reminding of a past design case based on its similarity to a given design problem, and direct transfer of the structure of the design case to the current problem. In earlier work (Goel 1991a), we showed that a Structure-Behavior-Function (SBF) ontology of physical devices provides a vocabulary for indexing known design cases and measures for determining the functional similarity of a past design with a given *function* → *structure* design problem. We also demonstrated that case-specific, hierarchically-organized SBF models give rise to an array of modification strategies that enable design modifications of two kinds: modifications to the parameters of design elements (i.e., subdesigns that are recursively decomposable into the primitive components and substances) in the structure of the known design, and replacement of design elements by functionally-similar elements. In addition, we showed that the SBF models enable evaluation of modified designs, and, if the evaluation succeeds, their storage in the case memory organized in function-oriented discrimination networks. We call this computational theory *adaptive modeling*.

   In this paper, we describe recent work on creative design characterized by large, complex modifications to the topology of a past design. In particular, we describe a computational theory of extracting, abstracting, and composing design configurations from different designs and composing them with a candidate design. In this theory, case-specific SBF models of past designs enable abstraction of generic behavior-function (BF) models. The goal of adapting a specific past design to address a new problem leads to the retrieval of a relevant generic

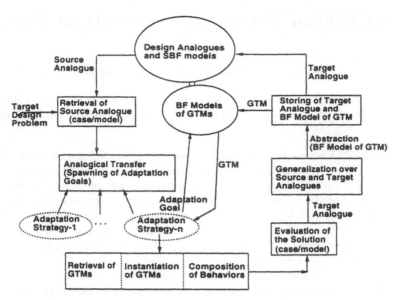

Fig. 1. IDEAL's partial process of Analogical Design via GTMs

model and its instantiation in the context of the case-specific SBF model of the past design. Thus the generic models mediate analogical transfer of design knowledge from familiar designs to the new design problem. We call this theory *model-based analogy* (MBA). IDEAL system instantiates and evaluates the MBA theory.

2 The Process of Model-Based Analogy

The computational process of MBA for design takes as input a specification of the functional and structural constraints on a desired design (i.e., the target design problem). and gives as output a structure (i.e., the solution) that realizes the specified function and also satisfies the structural constraints. MBA also gives an SBF model that explains how the structure realizes that function. A design case in this process specifies (1) the functions delivered by the past design. (2) the structure of the design, and (3) a pointer to the causal behaviors of the design (the case-specific SBF model). It indexes the design cases both by functions that the stored designs deliver and by the structural constraints they satisfy.

Figure 1 illustrates a portion of IDEAL's process of analogical design via one type of generic models called *generic teleological mechanisms* (GTMs). GTMs specify abstract, possibly complex, patterns of relations between output functions and internal behaviors for achieving the functions. They are "mechanisms" because they specify behaviors (or processes), "teleological" because they are in the service of functions, and "generic" because they pertain to classes of device domains. not just to a specific device or a particular device domain. Examples include cascading, feedback. and feedforward mechanisms.

When there are differences between the source and target problems, IDEAL spawns goals for adapting the source design. Different types of functional differences lead to different types of adaptation goals, some requiring only simple modifications (such as local parameter tweaks) and some others requiring more complex modifications (such as large topological changes). In order to control the reasoning involved in making large and complex modifications, IDEAL needs knowledge that can encapsulate the relationships between the modifications and their causal effects. In device design, GTMs provide such knowledge. Therefore, IDEAL uses the knowledge of GTMs in making some types of complex modifications that involve changes to the device topology in the similar past design and thus exhibiting creativity in design. In this paper, we focus on the subtasks of spawning of adaptation goals and achieving them by the use of GTMs.

Case-specific SBF Models. IDEAL represents its comprehension of specific design cases (i.e., case-specific device models) in the SBF language (Goel 1991b). This language provides conceptual primitives for representing and organizing knowledge of the structures, behaviors, and functions of a device. In this representation, the **structure** of a device is viewed as constituted of *components* and *substances*. Substances have *locations* in reference to the components in the device. They also have *behavioral properties,* such as *voltage* of *electricity,* and corresponding *parameters,* such as 1.5 volts, 3 volts, etc. Figure 2(a, b) illustrates the case-specific SBF model of a simple amplifier and Figure 2(c, d) that of an inverting amplifier. For each device, the structure, its function, and the behavior that achieves the function are shown.

A **function** in the SBF models is a behavioral abstraction and is represented as a schema that specifies the behavioral state the function takes as input, the behavioral state it gives as output, and a pointer to the internal causal behavior of the design that achieves the function. The pair of states indicated by GIVEN and MAKES in Fig. 2(b) shows the function "Amplify Electricity" of the simple amplifier. Both the input state and the output state are represented as *substance schemas.* Informally, the function specifies that the amplifier takes as input electricity of voltage V_{in} volts (i.e., 1) at i/p and gives as output electricity of voltage V_{out} volts (i.e., 100 ± 20 where 100 is the average value and 20 is the fluctuation around the average value) at o/p.

The internal causal **behaviors** in the SBF model of a device explicitly specify and explain how the functions of structural elements in the device get composed into device functions. The annotations on the state transitions express the *causal, structural,* and *functional contexts* in which the transformation of state variables, such as substance, location, properties, and parameters, can occur. Figure 2(b) shows the causal behavior that explains how electricity applied at the input location i/p of the simple amplifier is transformed at the output location o/p. The annotation USING-FUNCTION in $state_2 - state_3$ indicates that the transition occurs due to the primitive function "ALLOW electricity" of op-amp.

Generic Models. IDEAL represents its GTMs using the same SBF language as above. The SBF representation of a GTM encapsulates two types of knowledge:

568

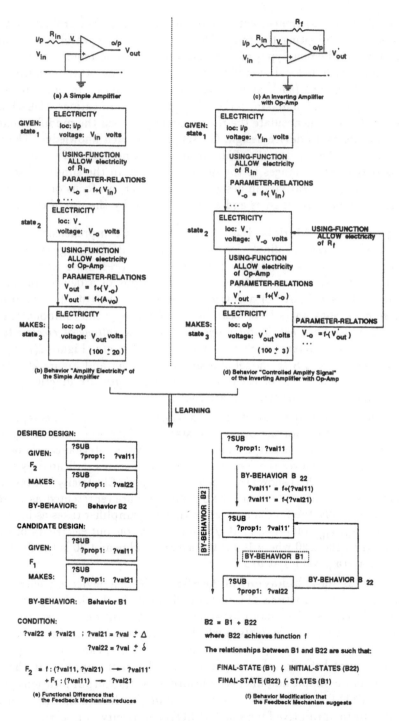

Fig. 2. Learning of Feedback Mechanism

knowledge about the patterns of differences between the functions of known designs and desired designs that the GTM can help reduce; and knowledge about patterns of modifications to the internal causal behaviors of the known designs that are necessary to reduce the differences. That is, it specifies relationships between patterns of functional differences and patterns of behavioral modifications to reduce those functional differences. For example, Fig. 2 (e) & Fig. 2(f) respectively show these two types of knowledge for a partial model of the feedback mechanism.[3] Figure 2(e) shows the patterns of functions F_1 and F_2 respectively of a candidate design available and the desired design, and the conditions under-which the mechanism is applicable. Because of the tasks for which they are used in MBA, the GTMs are indexed by the patterned functional differences such as shown in Fig. 2(e) (i.e., the fluctuations in the output substance property values are large vs. small). The model of the feedback indicates that the desired behavior (B_2) can be achieved by modifying the candidate behavior (B_1) through setting up the indicated causal relationships between the latter and the additional behaviors (that achieve the subfunctions of F_2 other than F_1 characterized in the conditions of the mechanism). In particular, the feedback mechanism suggests to add a causal relationship from a change in the output substance state to a change in an earlier state (input state or intermediate state) in the candidate behavior so that the effective input to the device is modified. Figure 2(f) shows (both diagrammatically and textually) the relationships in the generic model of the feedback mechanism that IDEAL learns from the two designs of amplifiers.

3 Acquisition of GTMs

Suppose that IDEAL's case memory contains the design of a simple amplifier (Fig. 2(a, b)). The output of this device is dependent on the open loop gain (A_{Vo}, a device parameter) of the op-amp and is typically very high (ideally ∞) and unstable. Consider that IDEAL is given the problem of designing an amplifier whose function (Fig. 2(d)) is to deliver a specific, controllable output electricity (which does not fluctuate much), i.e., an output electricity of voltage V'_{out} volts ($= 100 \pm 3$ where 100 is the average value and 3 is the fluctuation allowed around it) given an input electricity of V_{in} ($= 1$) volts. IDEAL uses the specified function as a probe into its memory of design cases and retrieves the design of the simple amplifier because the two functions are similar. Suppose now that IDEAL only has a simple strategy such as replacing a component in a past design to deliver new functions. Given the model of the simple amplifier shown in Fig. 2(b), IDEAL cannot localize the modification to reduce the difference between the source and the target and hence it fails. Then, if an oracle presents the correct design (whose structure is schematically shown in Fig. 2(c) and the case-specific SBF model in Fig. 2(d)), IDEAL can learn a generic model of the feedback mechanism (Fig. 2(e, f)). For details, see (Bhatta and Goel, 1996).

---

[3] Feedback can be open loop or closed loop. The feedback mechanism described here is one type of closed-loop feedback in which the output substance, fedback substance (i.e., controlling substance), and the input substance are all same.

4 Analogical Transfer via GTMs

Consider now a design problem IDEAL solves in the domain of mechanical controllers. Suppose that the new problem specifies a function that given the substance angular momentum of magnitude L_i and clockwise direction at an input location (gyroscope), the device needs to produce the angular momentum of magnitude L_O' proportional to the input and the same direction at a specified output location. It also specifies the constraint that the output cannot fluctuate much around an average value (i.e., $L_O' = L_{avg} \pm \delta$, where δ is small). This is the problem of designing a gyroscope follow-up (Hammond 1958).

Suppose also the design of a device (Fig. 3 (a, b, c)) which transfers angular momentum from a gyroscope to an output shaft location is available in IDEAL's case memory (or is given explicitly as part of the *adaptive* design problem). This device's function is that given an input angular momentum of magnitude L_i and clockwise direction at the input (gyroscope) location, it produces a proportional angular momentum of magnitude L_O and of clockwise direction at the output shaft location; however, L_O fluctuates over a large range, i.e., $L_O = L_{avg} \pm \Delta$, where Δ is large. IDEAL retrieves (if not given explicitly) this design because the desired function matches with this design's function.

Now, IDEAL's task is to modify the available design to deliver the desired function. Simple modifications such as replacing a component in the design case will not result in a device that solves the new problem because there is no single component in the device that seems responsible for the large fluctuations and that which may be selected for modification. Then the issue is if and how IDEAL can solve such a non-local adaptation problem.

The first step for IDEAL in abstraction-based analogical transfer is to retrieve the GTM. It uses the difference in the functions of the candidate and desired designs as a probe into its memory because it indexes the mechanisms by the functional differences and the decomposability conditions on the desired functions. It retrieves the feedback mechanism because the current functional difference, namely, the fluctuation in the output property is large vs. small (i.e., Δ vs. δ), matches with the difference that the feedback mechanism reduces which is specified in a device-independent manner. Then, it tries to match the decomposability condition on the desired function in the feedback mechanism (see Fig. 2(e) for the condition $F_2 = \ldots$) with the desired function in order to find the subfunctions f (or g) that need to be designed for and composed with the candidate function. By performing this match, as guided by the SBF language, IDEAL finds the subfunction $f{:}(L_i. L_O') - L_{ww}'$, i.e., it needs to design for a structure that takes two inputs. angular momentum of magnitude L_i and angular momentum of magnitude L_O', and gives as output an angular momentum of L_{ww}' in the opposite direction at the location of pivot in the candidate design.

The next step for IDEAL in this process is to transfer the retrieved GTM to the target design problem by instantiating it in the context of the problem. When the abstractions are GTMs, this process involves designing for the subfunction(s) determined by matching the applicability conditions of the mechanism and com-

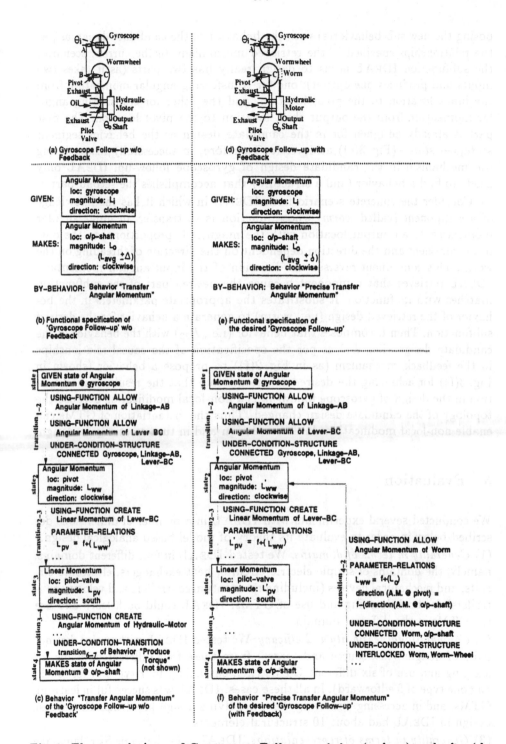

Fig. 3. The two designs of Gyroscope Follow-up *before* (a, b, c) and *after* (d. e, f) instantiating the Feedback Mechanism

posing the new sub-behavior(s) with the behavior of the candidate design as per the relationships specified in the retrieved mechanism. In the current scenario, the subfunction IDEAL needs to design really has two parts (as it takes two inputs and produces one output): one for transferring angular momentum from the input location to the pivot location, and the other for transferring angular momentum from the output shaft location to the pivot location. The first part is already designed for in the candidate design as the behavior segment $state_1 \rightarrow state_2$ (Fig. 3(c)) achieves it. Therefore, in successfully instantiating the mechanism in the candidate design of gyroscope follow-up, IDEAL only needs to find a behavior (and a structure) that accomplishes the second part.

Consider the concrete scenario from IDEAL in which it has the knowledge of a component (called *worm*) whose function is to transfer an input angular momentum to an output location with the magnitude proportional to the output component and the direction dependent on the direction of threading on the worm. This component reverses the direction of the input angular momentum. IDEAL retrieves that component because the desired part of the subfunction matches with its function. It substitutes the appropriate parameters in the behavior of the retrieved design (i.e., worm) to generate a behavior for the desired subfunction. Then it composes that behavior (i.e., B_{22}) with the behavior of the candidate design (i.e., B_1) as per the specification of the causal relationships in the feedback mechanism (as in Fig. 2(f)) to propose a behavior (shown in Fig. 3(f)) for achieving the desired function. Note that the resulting modification in the design of gyroscope follow-up is a non-local modification because the topology of the candidate design changed. Thus the instantiation of GTMs can enable non-local modifications in device design and in turn creativity in design.

5 Evaluation

We conducted several experiments with IDEAL in a number of dimensions described below in order to evaluate its theory of model-based analogical design.
(1) *Generality in terms of domains:* We tested IDEAL in four different domains, namely. the domains of simple electric circuits, heat exchangers, electronic circuits, and mechanical devices (including momentum controllers and velocity controllers) for both learning and use of GTMs. IDEAL could both learn and use the GTMs in the different domains.
(2) *Computational feasibility and efficacy:* We tested IDEAL with twelve distinct pairs of designs (i.e., source and target) from these four different domains for learning and use of six different GTMs (i.e., cascading, four types of feedback, and one type of feedforward). In all these cases, IDEAL was successful in learning GTMs. and in accessing and using them in solving design problems. The largest design in IDEAL had about 10 structural elements.
(3) *Generality in terms of representations:* IDEAL uses the same SBF language to represent both the case-specific models of devices and the case-independent models of GTMs.

(4) *Generality in terms of tasks:* IDEAL addresses multiple tasks, for example, both the learning and the use of GTMs in model-based analogical design.

6 Related Research

Much of the past work on case-based design has been limited to adaptive design in which the design modifications are small, simple and local. The relatively little research that explored creative design has focused on organization and exploration of case memory. IM-RECIDE (Gomes et al. 1996) and IMPROVISER (Wills and Kolodner 1996) are two recent examples of goal-directed exploration of the case memory. IDEAL's case memory is organized in multiple function-oriented discrimination networks. Also, each case is multiply indexed, both by the functional requirements and the structural constraints satisfied by the stored design. Case retrieval is goal-based while case storage is model-based; in the storage phase, the SBF model of the new design enables index learning.

Case-based theories typically involve direct transfer of the structure of familiar designs to new design situations. But in some case-based design systems, high-level abstractions do play an important role, especially in case indexing and case reminding. For example, KRITIK used functional abstractions of the stored design as case indices (Goel 1991a), and DEJA VU used them for hierarchical organization of the case memory (Smyth and Cunningham 1992). As mentioned earlier, IDEAL indexes cases by the functional requirements and structural constraints of the stored designs, and organizes them in discrimination networks based on a taxonomy of functions.

DSSUA (Qian and Gero 1992) is a recent analogical design system based on the notion of design prototypes. Like GTMs, design prototypes too specify functional relations and causal structures in a class of devices, but, unlike a GTM, a design prototype also specifies the generic physical structure of the device class. While a design prototype is a generalization over design cases such that a case is an instance of a prototype, a GTM is an abstraction over design prototypes such that a design prototype is a subclass of a design pattern. DSSUA uses an analogical process similar to that of the structure-mapping engine (SME) (Falkenhainer et al. 1989) to abstract causal behaviors at transfer time. In contrast, IDEAL abstracts GTMs at storage time for potential reuse. GTMs are indexed by the problem-solving goals stated in terms of functional differences between two design situations. This aspect of MBA shares the perspective of purpose-directed analogy (Kedar-Cabelli 1985).

Some recent work in case-based reasoning has explored the learning of adaptation knowledge from cases. For example, Leake (1995), and Hanney and Keane (1996) describe alternative methods for acquiring adaptation rules from adaptation cases. IDEAL too learns adaptation knowledge from cases (Bhatta and Goel 1996). Unlike other work on adaptation learning, the adaptation knowledge that IDEAL learns is declarative and demonstratably domain-independent.

7 Conclusions

Creative design involves large and complex modifications to the topology of known designs. These modifications are enabled by transfer and composition of design configurations from different designs to the new problem. MBA is a computational theory of this kind of analogy-based creative design. In MBA, case-specific SBF models of past designs enable abstraction of GTMs at storage time. The goal of adapting a specific similar past design to address a new design problem leads to the retrieval of a relevant GTM and its instantiation in the context of the case-specific SBF model of the past design. GTMs thus mediate the transfer of design knowledge across domains.

Acknowledgments

This paper has benefited from numerous discussions with members of the Intelligence and Design research group at Georgia Tech. This work has been supported in part by research grants from NSF (IRI-92-10925 and DMI-94-20405) and ONR (research contract N00014-92-J-1234).

References

Bhatta, S., Goel, A.: From design experiences to generic mechanisms: Model-based learning in analogical design. AI EDAM 10 (1996) 131–136

Falkenhainer, B., Forbus, K., Gentner, D.: The structure-mapping engine: Algorithm and examples. Artificial Intelligence 41 (1989) 1–63

Goel, A.: A model-based approach to case adaptation. In Proc. of the Thirteenth Annual Conf. of the Cog. Sci. Soc. (1991a) 143–148

Goel, A.: Model revision: A theory of incremental model learning. In Proc. of the Eighth Intl. Conf. on Machine Learning (1991b) 605–609

Gomes, P., Bento, C., Gago, P., Costa, E.: Towards a case-based model for creative design. In Proc. of 12th European Conf. on AI (1996)

Hammond, P. H.: Feedback Theory and Its Applications. (1958) The English Univ. Press Ltd., London, UK.

Hanney, K., Keane, M.: Learning adaptation rules from a case base. In Proc. of Third European Workshop on Case-Based Reasoning (1996)

Kedar-Cabelli, S. T.: Purpose-directed analogy. In Proc. of 7th Annual Conf. of the Cog. Sci. Soc. (1985) 150–159

Leake, D.: Combining rules and cases to learn case adaptation. In Proc. of 17th Annual Conf. of the Cog. Sci. Soc. (1995)

Qian, L., Gero, J. S.: A design support system using analogy. In J.S. Gero. editor, Proc. of the Second International Conference on AI in Design (1992) 795–813

Smyth, B., Cunningham, P.: Deja vu: A hierarchical case-based reasoning system for software design. In Proc. of 10th European Conf. on AI (1992)

Wills, L., Kolodner, J.: Towards more creative case-based design systems. In Case-Based Reasoning: Experiences, Lessons, and Future Directions, D. Leake (Ed.), (1996) 81–91. AAAI/MIT Press

Experimental Study of a Similarity Metric for Retrieving Pieces from Structured Plan Cases: Its Role in the Originality of Plan Case Solutions

Luís Macedo ([1,2]), Francisco C. Pereira ([2]), Carlos Grilo ([2]), Amílcar Cardoso ([2])

([1]) Instituto Superior de Engenharia de Coimbra, 3030 Coimbra, Portugal
(macedo@dei.uc.pt)
([2]) CISUC - Centro de Informática e Sistemas da Universidade de Coimbra, Polo II,
3030 Coimbra, Portugal
(francisco@alma.uc.pt, grilo@alma.uc.pt, amilcar@dei.uc.pt)

Abstract. This paper describes a quantitative similarity metric and its contribution to achieve original plan solutions. This similarity metric is used by an iterative process of piece retrieval from structured plan cases. Within our approach plan cases are tree-like networks of pieces (goals and actions). These case pieces are ill-related each other by links (explanations). These links may be classified as hierarchical or temporal, antecedent or consequent, and explicit or implicit. Besides links, each case piece has also information about its properties (the attributes-value pairs), its hierarchical and temporal position in the case (the address), and about its constraints in the relationship with others (the constraints). The similarity metric computes a similarity value between two case pieces taking into account similarities between these case piece's information types. Each time a problem is proposed, different weights are given to some of those similarities, with the aim of solving it with an original solution. This similarity metric is used by the system INSPIRER (ImagiNation taking as Source Past and Imperfectly REalated Reasonings). We illustrate the role of the similarity metric in the creativity of solutions, focusing specially their originality, with the presentation of the experimental results obtained in the musical composition domain, which is considered by us as a planning domain.

1 Introduction

The power of a Case-Based Reasoning (CBR) System (Kolodner and Riesbeck, 1986) is greatly determined by its capability to retrieve the relevant cases for the solution of a new problem. A nearest neighbour algorithm for case retrieval (Duda and Hart, 1973) searches through every case in memory, applies a similarity metric and returns the case or k cases with the past problem more similar to the new one. This similarity metric counts the number of facts that the past and the new problem have in common.

Knowledge-based retrieval systems (Koton, 1989) are a consequence of combining nearest neighbour and knowledge-guided techniques. These systems are characterised by the use of domain knowledge for the construction of explanations for why a problem had a particular solution in the past. Those explanations are necessary to similarity judgement (Barletta and Mark, 1989; Veloso, 1992; Bento and Costa, 1994): they are necessary to judge the relevance of the features comprising a past problem. In domains where a strong theory is not available but past experience is accessible, case explanations are imperfect (Bento, Macedo and Costa, 1994). CBR is appropriate for this kind of domains.

Although many CBR systems select out cases that are most similar to the new problem, other selection criteria may prove more effective. E.g., Kolodner (1989) has considered that the most useful cases are those that can address the reasoner's current goal, which means that they may not be the most similar ones. Particularly, this stands to reason when the goal is to achieve creative solutions, i.e., solutions required to be original but also appropriate (Macedo et al. 1996b, 1996c 1997a).

Considering cases as set of pieces (Barletta and Mark, 1988; Kolodner, 1988; Redmond, 1990; Sycara and Navinchandra, 1991; Veloso, 1992; Bento, Macedo and Costa, 1994) instead of monolithic entities, can improve the results of a CBR system in that solutions of problems may result from the contribution of multiple cases.

Moreover, structured representations of cases (Plaza, 1995) allow treating pieces of cases as full-fledged cases. This has two consequences: first, the similarity metric used by the nearest neighbour algorithm can be applied to them; second, the problems that appear when using parts of multiple monolithic cases are minimised, particularly, the lot of effort taken to find the useful parts in them.

A plan is a specific sequence of steps (or actions) with the aim of a goal achievement. Case-Based Planning (CBP) systems (Hammond, 1986; Veloso, 1992) reuse past sequences of actions from past plans to construct new ones. Some systems like CELIA (Redmond, 1990), JULIA (Kolodner, 1989), PRODIGY/ANALOGY (Veloso, 1992), etc., break up the goal into smaller sub-goals, enabling plan construction by composition of sub-plans. This leads to a hierarchical representation of plan cases (Macedo et al., 1996a). The case representation is similar to a tree where each node is a goal and its sons the sub-goals, or at the latest level, the actions of the plan. Each goal (or action) depends on other goals. This is particularly evident in structured domains.

In this paper we will focus on a similarity metric used by an iterative retrieval of case pieces from structured plan cases. This means that building a new plan case solution consists in an incremental association of case pieces, each one of these resulting from a retrieval process, which involves the application of a similarity metric to each candidate case piece present in memory. This means case pieces are treated as full-fledged cases. The similarity metric takes into account the address, context and attribute similarities between two case pieces. We propose a way to produce creative solutions, i.e., original but also appropriate solutions, based on applying the similarity metric giving different weights to its components, each time a problem is solved.

Our approach to case representation is presented in the next section. The retrieval and solution construction process are briefly presented in section 3. In section 4, we introduce the similarity metric. Section 5 focus the definition of creative solutions, and section 6 presents an application in the musical composition domain. The results obtained with our similarity metric function in this domain are presented in section 7. Finally, a conclusion about our work is made in section 8.

2 Case Representation

Within our approach a plan case is a set of goals and actions organised in a hierarchical way (Figure 1): a main goal (the main problem) is refined into sub-goals (the sub-problems), and so on, until reaching the actions (the leaf nodes of the tree) that satisfy the goals. It is worth noting that, although the actions are represented by the leaf nodes, some of their properties (attributes) are inherited from the attributes of their hierarchical ascendants.

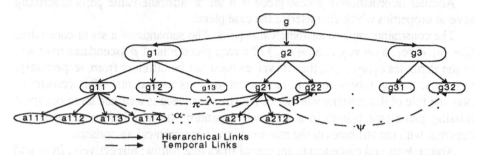

Figure 1 - Case structure. The g_i's represent the goals and the a_i's the actions.

In our model, each node of the hierarchical structure corresponds to a case piece. To complete the case structure, there are links between case pieces, representing causal justifications, or explanations. Some of these links maintain the hierarchical case structure, others reflect causal temporal relations between case pieces. Thus the existence of a case piece in a plan case is causally explained by several case pieces of the same plan case.

Considering the hierarchical links only (represented in Figure 1 by continuous arrows), the inherent meaning of the represented structure is: g, the main goal of the plan (or the main problem), is achieved by sequentially achieving sub-goals (sub-problems) $g1$, $g2$ and $g3$. Each one of these sub-goals is also broken up into other sub-goals. For example, $g1$ is broken up into $g11$, $g12$ and $g13$, and $g2$ into $g21$ and $g22$. To achieve the goal $g11$ the actions $a111$, $a112$, $a113$ and $a114$ must be sequentially executed by this temporal order.

Besides being explained by the goal-refinement process, through hierarchical links, a case piece may also be explained through temporal links (represented in Figure 1 by discontinuous arrows). For example, $g21$ (sub-goal of $g2$) is a consequence of case pieces $g11$ and $g12$, which is represented by the temporal links labelled α and λ, respectively.

A case piece has seven types of information describing its relevant aspects: a name that uniquely identifies the case piece, the name of the case to which the case piece belongs, the case piece address, the constraints, a set of attribute/value pairs, the antecedents and the consequents.

The address of a case piece in level n is represented by $N_n:N_{n-1}:...:N_0$, where each $N_i \in \aleph_0$ (from now on we will call offsets to the N_i's). An offset $L=N_i$, $0 \le i$ $<n$, means that the case piece with that address has a predecessor in level i of the tree which is the L-th son of its father (with the exception of the case piece in level

0, which has no ascendants and so its offset is always 0). The offset $J=N_n$ means that this case piece is the J-th son of its closer ascendant. Every case piece propagates its address to its descendants, that is, if the case piece's address is $N_n:...:N_0$, its M-th son's address will be $M:N_n:...:N_0$. This representation embeds in its syntax, explicitly, the position that a case piece and its ascendants occupy in the tree relatively to the others, and, implicitly, the hierarchical level that the case piece occupies in the tree.

Another information in a case piece is a set of attribute/value pairs describing several properties which characterise the case piece.

The constraints are also attribute/value pairs. The semantic of a set of constraints $C = \{a_1 = vc_1, a_2 = vc_2, ...,a_n = vc_n\}$ of a case piece p is: if p ascendants have any of the attributes $a_1, a_2, ...,a_n$, then its values must not be different from, respectively, vc_1, vc_2, ...,vc_n; otherwise, p is incoherent with its ascendants. Thus constraints play the role of determining whether or not the case piece is a candidate to occupy a missing piece (see below) in a solution, depending on whether or not they are coherent with the attributes of the missing piece's hierarchical ascendants.

Antecedents and consequents are causal links that follow, respectively, from and to other case pieces. Antecedent links show how a case piece is explained by the existence of other case pieces (e.g. in Figure 1, *g21* is explained by *g11* and *g12* through the links labelled α and λ, respectively, and by *g2* through a father link). Consequent links show how a case piece explains the existence of other case pieces (e.g., in Figure 1, *g21* partially explains *g22* and *g32* through links β and ψ, respectively, and *a211* and *a212* through father links).

Each antecedent or consequent link is classified into another two main kinds of links: hierarchical and temporal ones (described above).

Sometimes the type of relation between antecedent fact(s) and the consequent one may be unknown. This lack of a complete theory is common in CBR (Bento, Macedo and Costa, 1994). This idea leads to another classification of the links between case pieces: we say that a link between the case pieces *a* and *b* is explicit if we know it well and so we are able to represent it, and implicit if we can't represent it because we do not know it well, although we know it exists. In Figure 1, *g13* implicitly explains *g21*. There is not a concrete link between them, but it is coherent to assume that the existence of *g21* is partially due to the previous occurrence of *g13*. We may also say that *g* implicitly explains *g21*, although there is not a well known relation between them.

We call the case piece context to the set of case pieces that surround it. We distinguish eight types of contexts according to the kind of link existing between the case piece considered and the surrounding ones. Thus, each one of these surrounding case pieces is included in one of the contexts of the set C = {antecedent-hierarchical-implicit context, antecedent-hierarchical-explicit context, antecedent-temporal-implicit context, antecedent-temporal-explicit context, consequent-hierarchical-implicit context, consequent-hierarchical-explicit context, consequent-temporal-implicit context or consequent-temporal-explicit context}. Notice that the name of the context reflects the classification of the link to the case piece. For example, in Figure 1, the contexts of *g21* are: antecedent-hierarchical-implicit context = {*g*}; antecedent-hierarchical-explicit context = {*g2*}; antecedent-temporal-implicit context = {*g13*}; antecedent-temporal-explicit context = {*g11, g12*}; consequent-hierarchical-implicit context = {}; consequent-hierarchical-explicit context = {*a211, a212*}; consequent-temporal-implicit context = {*g31*}; consequent-temporal-explicit context = {*g22, g32*}.

Since there is not any direct link between implicitly related case pieces, it is necessary to define a frontier to limit the number of case pieces of the implicit contexts. We assume that this frontier involves the nearest case pieces.

3 Overview of the Retrieval Process and Solution Construction

The construction of an entire solution is performed by an iterative retrieval of case pieces from memory to fill the missing ones in the tree-like partially complete solution. This process is made level by level starting at the highest hierarchical level and ending at the lowest hierarchical level, and in each level, starting from the leftmost to the rightmost case piece.

The process of retrieving a case piece from memory is the following. Consider that π is the structured solution currently being constructed, and π_i a place on solution π in which a case piece is missing. The retrieval of a case piece to be placed in π_i involves the following steps:

(i) construction of the set of candidate case pieces by selecting those which belong to the same level of π_i;

(ii) application of a constraint based filter to the case pieces selected in (i), eliminating those which constraints are incompatible with the attributes of the π_i's ascendants. This step is performed as follows. Given a case piece p presented in memory, candidate to fill π_i, and given the set of constraints $L_c = \{c_1 = vc_1, c_2 = vc_2, ..., c_n = vc_n\}$ of case piece p, and the union of the sets of attribute-value pairs $L_a = \{a_1 = va_1, a_2 = va_2, ..., a_m = va_m\}$ of the hierarchical ascendants of π_i, then p is not filtered from the set of candidate case pieces to fill π_i if and only if: $\forall i \in \{1,2,...,n\}, \forall j \in \{1,2,...,m\}, \forall a_j = va_j \in L_a, \neg\exists c_i = vc_i \in L_c : c_i = a_j \land vc_i \neq va_j$

(iii) application of a similarity metric (function *CasePieceSim* presented below) to each candidate case piece;

(iv) ranking of the candidates case pieces by their similarity metric value;

(v) selection of the case piece with the highest similarity metric value;

(vi) validation of placing the selected case piece on π_i. This step comprises the verification of link incompatibilities between the selected case piece and the partially constructed solution for the given problem. Performing one of the following options solves these incompatibilities: (i) relaxing incompatibilities; (ii) selecting another case piece.

4 The Similarity Metric

The similarity metric computes similarities between two case pieces p and p' and is described as follows:

$$CasePieceSim(p, p') = \frac{\alpha \times AttrSim(p, p') + \phi \times AddrSim(p, p') + \lambda \times ContSim(p, p')}{\alpha + \phi + \lambda}$$

where *ContSim*, *AttrSim* and *AddrSim* are the functions that compute, respectively, the context, attribute and address similarities between p and p', as presented below, and α, ϕ and λ are the user assigned parameters that represent the weights given to those similarities, respectively.

AddrSim is the following:

$$AddrSim(p,p') = \frac{\phi_1 \times AbsASim(p_{ad},p'_{ad}) + \phi_2 \times AdYOSim(p_{ad},p'_{ad}) + \phi_3 \times AdSESim(p_{ad},p'_{ad})}{\phi_1 + \phi_2 + \phi_3}$$

where: *AbsAdSim* calculates the similarity between the addresses p_{ad} and p'_{ad}, respectively, of case piece p and p'; *AdYOSim* calculates the similarities between the component of the same addresses that contains the information about case pieces positions relatively to their old and young brothers; *AdSESim* calculates the similarities of the case pieces address relatively to the start and end of the case. The parameters ϕ_1, ϕ_2, and ϕ_3 represent the weights given to those similarities, respectively. These functions are presented as follows.

AbsAdSim is:

$$AbsAdSim(p_{ad},p'_{ad}) = \begin{cases} 1 \Leftarrow p_{ad} = p'_{ad} \\ 0 \Leftarrow p_{ad} \neq p'_{ad} \end{cases}$$

AdYOSim is:

$$AdYOSim(H:R,H':R') = 1 - \left(\frac{H}{NSons(R)} - \frac{H'}{NSons(R')} \right)$$

This function compares the mappings into the interval $(0,1)$ of the positions of each case piece relatively to its young and old brother. This mapping is done dividing the first offset of the case piece's address (H or H') by the number of sons of its father, whose value is given by the function *NSons*. Remember that the first offset H of the case piece's address H:R tells us that the case piece is the Hth son of its father, whose address is R.

AdSESim is:

$$AdSESim(H:R,H':R') = 1 - \left(\frac{H + Ha(H:R)}{NPiecesLevel(H:R)} - \frac{H' + Ha(H':R')}{NPiecesLevel(H':R')} \right)$$

This function is similar to the previous one. However, the mapping is done by first, summing the first offset of the case piece's address and the number of case pieces of the same level that are younger than it (this value is computed by the function *Ha*), and then, dividing this sum value by the number of case pieces of the same level of that case piece (this value is given by the function *NPiecesLevel*).

AttrSim is defined as follows:

$$AttrSim(p,p') = \frac{2 \times Length(p_a \cap p'_a)}{Length(p_a) + Length(p'_a)}$$

where p_a, p'_a are the sets of attributes of, respectively, p and p', and *Length* is the function that computes the length of a set.

ContSim is:

$$ContSim(p,p') = \frac{\sum_{i=1}^{8} \lambda_i \times F_i(p,p')}{\sum_{i=1}^{8} \lambda_i}$$

where each F_i is a function that computes similarities between two same types of contexts of two case pieces, as described below. Each λ_i is the weight given to each one of those similarities. The F_i functions is:

$$F_i(p,p') = \frac{\dfrac{2 \times Length(p_{c_i} \cap p'_{c_i})}{Length(p_{c_i}) + Length(p'_{c_i})} + SeqSim(p_{c_i}, p'_{c_i})}{2}$$

where c_i is the ith element of the set of contexts C (described above), and, p_{ci} and p'_{ci} are the c_i contexts of p and p', respectively. *SeqSim* is the function that computes the similarity between sequences of elements in both lists.

5 Creative Solutions

Creative solutions are undoubtedly mainly characterised by two properties: appropriateness and originality.

An appropriate solution is one that fulfills the goal(s) of the problem, i.e., that is useful by satisfying a need. A solution, to be appropriate, should also be coherent, without incompatibilities between its components, and also able to be executed (Macedo et al., 1996b, 1996c, 1997a).

An original solution is one that is different from previous ones, i.e., is one that stands apart from the solutions that the individual or other people has already produced. It is singular, novel and somehow unpredictable.

Originality of solutions is measured comparing the solution with the past solutions stored in memory. This comparison is made piece by piece, computing the number of new relations that a case piece has in the new solution in comparison with the relations it has in old solutions. Appropriateness is measured by experts taking into account the coherence and usefulness of solutions.

6 Musical Composition Domain

Balaban (1992) and others, state that any music can be represented by a hierarchy of temporal objects (objects with an associated temporal duration), in such a way that each one has, as descendants, a sequence of sub-objects that starts and ends at the same start and ending point as the object's. Figure 2 shows an example.

There are temporal causal relations in music (represented in Figure 2 by discontinuous arrows), since many musical objects may be causally explained, for instance, by transformations of some other object (e.g., repetition, variation, inversion, transposition, etc.). For example, in Figure 2, the temporal link between *theme* of *Part1* and *var1* of *Part2* may represent a variation transformation which, when applied to *theme* originates *var1*. These temporal relations are represented in the antecedents and consequents informations fields of a case piece.

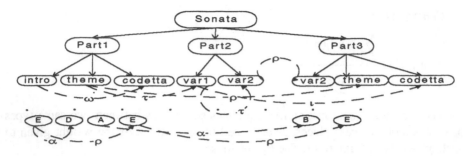

Figure 2 - A case in the music domain.

Each musical object has several properties which are represented in our approach by attribute/value pairs (e.g., {ton='I', meas=2/4} meaning that the tonality is 'I' and the measure is binary).

Additionally, each musical object has also a set of constraints, which are conditions that must be consistent with the attributes of its ascendants, when it is added to the new case (e.g., if a case piece has the set of constraints a = {meas=2/4, ton='II', etc} then it must not be a descendant of a case piece with tonality 'I', for instance). Thus the role of the constraints is to maintain the coherence of the new musical piece hierarchy, since they disallow the hierarchical association of case pieces with incompatible properties.

The goal of our application is to use analysis of music pieces from a seventeenth century composer as foundation for a restructuring process, providing a structured and constrained way of composing novel pieces, although keeping the essential traits of the composer's style. We use analysis of music pieces with six hierarchical levels. Each music piece is considered as a plan, since it is a sequence of musical objects with the aim of achieving a musical goal (e.g., a sonata).

7 Experimental Tests

7.1 Description and Results

The main aim of the tests performed with the similarity metric of INSPIRER in the musical composition domain is to evaluate its contribution to achieve original solutions. However, appropriateness is also guaranteed to a certain extent by the similarity metric since it disallows totally new solutions which may be inappropriate. Besides this, the tests also allow the formulation of conclusions about the accuracy of the INSPIRER's similarity metric.

We have made four tests (labelled Test #1, Test #2, Test #3 and Test #4) (Figure 3). In each test the values 0 or 1 were assigned to each parameter in the similarity metric function. In Test #1 the similarity metric is complete: it takes into account the attribute, address and context similarities (their parameters are assigned to 1). Test #2, #3 and #4 are similar to Test #1, with the difference of not taking into account, respectively, the context, the address and the attribute similarities in the similarity metric.

Test #1 has two variants: variant A (Figure 4) and variant B (Figure 5). Variant A corresponds to assigning different values (0 or 1) to the parameters of the sub-terms of the similarity metric address term. Variant B is similar to variant A, but relatively to the sub-terms of the context term of the similarity metric.

	α	φ	λ
Test #1	1	1	1
Test #2	1	1	0
Test #3	1	0	1
Test #4	0	1	1

Figure 3 - Test parameters.

Variant A	α	ϕ_1	ϕ_2	ϕ_3	λ
Test #A1	1	1	1	1	1
Test #A2	1	1	1	0	1
Test #A3	1	1	0	1	1
Test #A4	1	0	1	1	1

Figure 4 - Test parameters for variant A of Test #1.

Variant B	α	φ	λ_1	λ_2	λ_3	λ_4	λ_5	λ_6	λ_7	λ_8
Test #B1	1	1	1	1	1	1	1	1	1	1
Test #B2	1	1	1	1	1	1	1	1	1	0
Test #B3	1	1	1	1	1	1	1	1	0	1
Test #B4	1	1	1	1	1	1	1	0	1	1
Test #B5	1	1	1	1	1	1	0	1	1	1
Test #B6	1	1	1	1	1	0	1	1	1	1
Test #B7	1	1	1	1	0	1	1	1	1	1
Test #B8	1	1	1	0	1	1	1	1	1	1
Test #B9	1	1	0	1	1	1	1	1	1	1

Figure 5 - Test parameters for variant B of Test #1.

Each one of the Tests #2, #3, and #4, when compared with Test #1, allows to make conclusions about taking or not taking into account one term of the similarity metric. The same happen when comparing Tests #A2, #A3 and #A4 with Test #A1, and, Tests #B2, #B3,...,#B9 with Test #B1. This is based on the assumption that the best way to measure the relevance of x_k to y, when $y=f(x_1,..., x_{k-1}, x_k, x_{k+1},..., x_n)$, is by comparing $y_1=f(x_1,..., x_{k-1}, x_{k+1},..., x_n)$ with $y=f(x_1,..., x_{k-1}, x_k, x_{k+1},..., x_n)$.

Some test conditions were kept constant in all the tests: we used just one past case solution in memory (a musical symphony), because we want to test the performance of INSPIRER's similarity metric in the worst conditions to achieve original solutions; the problem proposed was always the same: to produce a new symphony; each test produced a new case solution (a new symphony), which was evaluated by three musical composition teachers of the Coimbra School of Music, about its appropriateness and originality, taking as reference the original composer's music piece, to which was given 100% of appropriateness.

Chart I of Figure 6 summarises the results obtained with the four tests. Chart II shows the results of variant A of Test #1, and Chart III, the results of variant B of Test #1.

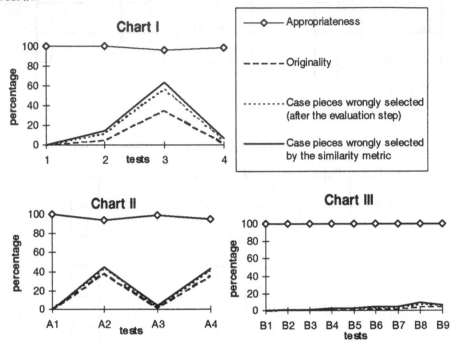

Figure 6 - Test results.

7.2 Analysis of Results

From Chart I (Figure 6) we may conclude that the address term is the most important one to the accuracy of the similarity metric. Actually, Test #3 has the highest number of wrongly selected case pieces. We consider that a case piece is wrongly selected if it is different from the one that would be selected from the past case solution, if we applied the complete similarity metric. The context term is the second most important one (Test #2), and the attribute term the third (Test #4).

From Chart II it can be seen that Test #A2 has the highest number of wrongly selected case pieces. This means the sub-term *AdSESim* is the most important to the accuracy of the similarity metric, followed closely by the sub-term *AbsAdSim* (Test #A4). The sub-term *AdYOSim* is not very relevant to the same accuracy (Test #A3).

Chart III shows that the sub-terms of the context term are almost equally relevant to the accuracy of the similarity metric. However, the antecedent contexts (Tests #B6, #B7, #B8 and #B9) are more important than consequent contexts (Tests #B2,

#B3, #B4 and #B5). This happens because a missing case piece of the partially constructed solution does not have consequent contexts. The hierarchical contexts (Tests #B4, #B5, #B8 and #B9) are more important than temporal contexts (Tests #B2, #B3, #B5 and #B6). This happens because every case piece has hierarchical links, while some of them may not have temporal links. Relatively to implicit and explicit contexts no relevant differences are identified.

From all of the charts we may conclude that the percentage number of wrongly selected case pieces by the similarity metric is, generally, greater than the percentage number of wrongly selected case pieces after applying the evaluation step. This is because the evaluation step rejects the case pieces that are given the highest similarity metric value but that, actually, are not the most similar, since the similarity metric does not takes into account all the terms.

In all the tests the appropriateness of the solutions is function of the originality: the more original is the solution, the less appropriate it is. However, there is no directly correlation between these two properties. Actually there are solutions with high originality but with an appropriateness almost equal to 100% (e.g., Test #3).

8 Conclusions

We have presented a similarity metric for retrieval of pieces from structured plan cases. This similarity metric is part of a iterative retrieval process for the construction of new case plans, which consists in an incremental association of case pieces from past plan cases.

Each plan case is a tree-like network, in which pieces (goals and actions) are linked to each other. Three main classifications of links were reported: implicit/explicit links; temporal/hierarchical links; and antecedent/consequent links. These link classifications determine eight types of case piece contexts. Besides links, case pieces have also represented information about its properties (the attributes) and about its position in the case (the address).

The similarity metric is based on similarities between same types of case piece's information. Creative solutions are achieved ignoring some of those similarities.

As shown, musical composition can be considered as a planning task and it is an appropriate domain to our approach. However, in this domain and other similar ones in which the solutions are required to be creative, we think it is important to assume that a useful case piece (or case) may not be the one with the highest similarity metric.

Acknowledgements

We would like to thank to Anabela Simões and António Andrade, teachers at the Coimbra School of Music for their valuable contribution.

References

Balaban, M., (1992). Musical Structures: Interleaving the Temporal and Hierarchical Aspects in Music. In Understanding Music with IA: Perspectives in Music Cognition, MIT Press.

Barletta, R., Mark, W., (1988). Breaking cases into pieces, in Proceedings of a Case-Based Reasoning Workshop, St. Paul, MN.

Barletta, R., Mark, W., (1989). Explanation-Based Indexing of Cases, in Proceedings of a Case-Based Reasoning Workshop, Morgan-Kaufmann.

Bento, C. and Costa, E., (1994). A Similarity Metric for Retrieval of Cases Imperfectly Explained, in First European Workshop on Case-Based Reasoning, Kaiserslautern.

Bento, C., Macedo, L. and Costa, E., (1994). RECIDE - Reasoning with Cases Imperfectly Described and Explained, in Second European Workshop on Case-Based Reasoning..

Duda, R., and Hart, P., (1973). Pattern Classification and Scene Analysis, New York: Wiley.

Hammond, K., (1986). Case Based Planning: An Integrated Theory of Planning, Learning and Memory, PhD Dissertation, Yale University.

Kolodner, J., and Riesbeck, C., (1986). Experience, Memory, and Reasoning, Lawrence Erlbaum Associates, Hillsdale, NJ.

Kolodner, J., (1988). Retrieving events from a Case Memory: a parallel implementation, in Proceedings of a Case-Based Reasoning Workshop, San Mateo, CA, Morgan-Kaufmann.

Kolodner, J., (1989). Judging Which is the "Best" Case for a Case-Based Reasoner, in Case-Based Reasoning: Proceedings of a Workshop, Florida, Morgan-Kaufmann.

Koton, P., (1989). Using Experience in Learning and Problem Solving, Massachusets Institute of Technology, Laboratory of Computer Science (Ph D diss.), MIT/LCS/TR-441.

Macedo, L., Pereira, F., Grilo, C. and Cardoso, M., (1996a). Plan Cases as Structured Networks of Hierarchical and Temporal Related Case Pieces, Third European Workshop on Case-Based Reasoning, Lausanne.

Macedo, L., Pereira, F., Grilo, C. and Cardoso, M., (1996b). Solving Planning Problems that Require Creative Solutions using a Hierarchical Case-Based Planning Approach, International Conference on Knowledge Based Computer Systems, India.

Macedo, L., Pereira, F., Grilo, C. and Cardoso, M., (1996c). A Case-Based Computational Model for Creative Planning, Proceedings of the First European Workshop on Cognitive Modeling, Berlim.

Macedo, L., Pereira, F., Grilo, C. and Cardoso, M., (1997a). A Computational Model for the Creative Planning Faculties of Mind, in Mind Modelling - A Cognitive Science Approach to Reasoning, Learning and Discover, Schmith, U., Krems, J.F., and Wysotzki, F., (Editors).(forthcomming)

Plaza, E., (1995). Cases as terms: A feature term approach to the structured representation of cases, in Proceedings of the First International Conference on Case-Based Reasoning, Sesimbra, Portugal .

Redmond, M., (1990). Distributed Cases for Case-Based Reasoning; Facilitating Use of Multiple Cases, In Proceedings of AAAI.

Sycara, K., Navinchandra, D., (1991). Influences: A Thematic Abstraction for Creative Use of Multiple Cases, in Proceedings of a Case-Based Reasoning Workshop.

Veloso, M., (1992). Learning by Analogical Reasoning in General Problem Solving, Ph D thesis, School of Computer Science, Carnegie Mellon University, Pittsburgh, PA.

Creative Design:
Reasoning and Understanding

Marin Simina and Janet Kolodner

College of Computing
Georgia Institute of Technology
Atlanta, GA 30332-0280
{marin, jlk}@cc.gatech.edu

Abstract. This paper investigates memory issues that influence long-term creative problem solving and design activity, taking a case-based reasoning perspective. Our exploration is based on a well-documented example: the invention of the telephone by Alexander Graham Bell. We abstract Bell's reasoning and understanding mechanisms that appear time and again in long-term creative design. We identify that the understanding mechanism is responsible for analogical anticipation of design constraints and analogical evaluation, beside case-based design. But an already understood design can satisfy opportunistically suspended design problems, still active in background. The new mechanisms are integrated in a computational model, ALEC[1], that accounts for some creative behavior in case-based design.

1 Introduction

This paper investigates memory mechanisms that influence long-term creative problem solving and design activity, from a case-based reasoning (CBR) (Kolodner [10]) perspective, by integrating elements of model-based reasoning (Goel [5]). Our exploration is based on a well documented example: the invention of the telephone (Notebooks[2]; US v. Bell [19]; Gorman [6]). Retrospectively, the obvious question related to the invention of the telephone is: what cognitive issues "delayed" the invention of the telephone till 1876? The *basic principles* of the telephone, electromagnetism and induction, had been known since 1831. Several inventors tried and failed to design the telephone, because they: (1) relied too much on prevalent telegraphy practice, (2) ignored the basic principles of electromagnetism, and (3) gave up too soon. It looks like these inventors applied CBR poorly: they stuck to minor adaptations of telegraphy rather than reassessing the problem and analyzing it from a new perspective. In contrast, Bell reassessed the telephone problem as being acoustical and not electrical. When Bell was stuck in electrical details, he analyzed his telephony experiments using acoustical experiences and expertise.

---

[1] Alec was Alexander Graham Bell's nickname, but serendipitously it is also an acronym for Analogical Learning by Explaining Cases ... more or less creatively.

[2] Alexander Graham Bell's Notebooks are available on-line at the following URL: *http://jefferson.village.virginia.edu/~meg3c/id/albell/homepage.html*

Bell's research plan, used to generate new learning goals, was much like that of other inventors. When Bell identified an unexpected function of a device, he tried to *understand* it in terms of his knowledge. When his understanding process failed, he generated new learning goals (Ram and Hunter [15]). But Bell brought a new perspective to the analysis of telephony by relying on his acoustical knowledge to generate new hypotheses. In analogy with acoustical sound transmission, Bell generated the electrical "undulatory current" hypothesis, essential for the design of the telephone. Bell frequently interpreted and remembered his electrical experiments in terms of acoustics, that he could easily *perceive* without supplementary equipment. Consequently, in some cases he could *recognize* opportunities to solve suspended problems while pursuing other problems (i.e., the "undulatory current" was recognized while working on the multiple telegraph problem, by noticing peculiar acoustical effects). But not all the recognized opportunities fell in the above category. Sometimes, working on several problems in the *same* period of time facilitated knowledge transfer among them without any special perceptual elaboration (i.e., interleaved work on both the telephone and phonautograph[3] inspired the microphone design for the telephone).

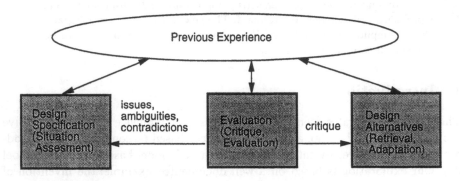

Fig. 1. Framework for Case-based Creative Design

Our exploration of creative design (Kolodner and Wills [11], Simina and Kolodner [18]) provides an initial framework (i.e., the IMPROVISER system) for a more enriched and dynamic CBR able to explain some of the reasoning issues involved in the invention of the telephone. In this framework a designer evolves concurrently the design specification and a pool of alternatives under consideration, relying on his previous experience (Fig. 1). Each new design alternative is evaluated mainly in relation to the *current goal* (i.e., the current design problem). But the Evaluation process may serendipitously generate state information relevant to other *suspended goals* (i.e., some related problems which

---

[3] The *phonautograph* is a device able to "visualize" speech (i.e., to represent graphically, as a function of time, the acoustical presure generated by speech).

could not be pursued and were postponed), in addition to critiquing the current design alternative and detecting ambiguities and contradictions in the design specification. Our model therefore has a mechanism for detecting opportunities and for activating the suspended goals to which they pertain.

Our previous framework handled most of Bell's control strategy during telephony work. Bell used to work on several open problems during the same period of time. When he got stuck on one problem, he switched to another one. Sooner or later Bell revisited the same problem, but this time from a new perspective. Indeed, working on other problems in the mean time seemed to refresh his memory. Interleaved work generated new learning goals and new background cues that were used to approach the same old problems in a new way. But the main processes in our framework (i.e., **Design Specification**, **Design Alternatives** and **Evaluation**) did not use effectively the available previous experience since they relied on *classical retrieval*[4] to explain some important parts of Bell's reasoning. In particular, Bell's understanding and interpretation processes seem far more complex than those handled by IMPROVISER. Bell used analogy when classical retrieval failed. When analogy also failed, Bell made new hypotheses by combining attributes of the (partial) design alternatives retrieved (i.e., analogical adaptation). This mechanism led to the famous hypothesis of the "undulatory current", by mixing properties of sound transmission and electrical currents. We realized that understanding is a memory issue that should play a more important role in our framework for creative design.

2 Creative Design

2.1 Issues

The task of a designer is to specify the structure of an artifact that delivers some functions and satisfies some constraints (see Chandrasekaran [2]). Creative design adds two supplementary constraints: the designed artifact should be both novel and useful. But this simplistic characterization of the creative design task provides no clues in the processes involved. A novel artifact implies a novel design specification and it is difficult to separate the evolution of the design solution from the evolution of the design specification. The evolution of the design specification can be viewed as another design process (Tong [21]) from an incomplete, contradictory and underconstrained specification to a better description, good enough for designing a novel artifact.

But how can designers get to an initial design specification? The exploration of the design space without a design specification (i.e., "tinkering"), can produce novel artifact ideas, but designers should be able to recognize and assess the

---

[4] *Classical retrieval* includes subprocesses for partial pattern matching and case storage, but not for analogical transfer (a pre-adaptation subprocess). Traditionally, explanation pattern (XP) instantiation (see Schank [17]) was responsible for analogical transfer, but analogical transfer is possible even in the absence of XPs.

usefulness of those ideas. However, recognizing opportunities is hard, especially when the domain is not well understood.

The prerequisite of opportunistic behavior is the existence of suspended goals, goals that cannot be pursued in the current context and are postponed. As an example, Bell realized that he needed to produce an "undulatory current" in order to design the telephone, but he had no clue of how to produce such a current. Later, Bell was able to recognize such an "undulatory current" while working on the multiple telegraph problem.

But where do the designer's goals come from? Scientific curiosity is the main source of open problems and suspended goals. A designer may notice an anomalous situation, while reasoning about an artifact (Ram [14] and Schank [17] have addressed this problem in the context of story understanding). If the anomalous situation is interesting (i.e., potentially, it is instrumental for satisfying higher goals), the designer may encode in memory a new goal to understand the anomaly. Later, he may recognize an opportunity to better understand the anomaly. The above process explains what happened when Bell encountered Helmholtz's Apparatus[5]. Bell was unable to understand some electrical details of the apparatus, but he returned to these details later when he recognized the opportunity to perform electrical experiments. By working on *several* related projects in the same period of time, creative designers incorporate "tinkering" opportunistically in long-term design: while working on the current project, they might recognize design ideas for new projects. In Bell's case, he generated the telephone idea while working on the multiple telegraph.

Once a designer has an initial design specification worth pursuing, he might generate and develop alternative design solutions. The most common methods for design use three subtasks: propose, critique, and modify (Chandrasekaran [2]). The issue here is how to implement these subtasks to explain creative behavior. We are interested to find out how designers use well-known designs in novel ways or how they engage in cross-domain transfer of abstract design ideas.

2.2 Case Representation

A case is a contextualized piece of knowledge representing an experience that teaches a lesson fundamental to achieving the goals of the reasoner (Kolodner [10]). In order to teach a lesson, a design case may be understood in terms of a more or less detailed *causal model*, by representing explicitly structural and behavioral relations (Goel [5]). In fact a reasoner can associate several causal models (e.g., acoustical, electrical) with a known case, by using analogical understanding.

The behavioral relations are essential also for representing evolving design specifications, used to retrieve and reason about known artifacts. Among the behavioral relations associated with an artifact, only the functional relations

---

[5] Helmholtz's Apparatus is an electro-magnetic artifact for synthesizing vowels, relevant to Bell's acoustic research.

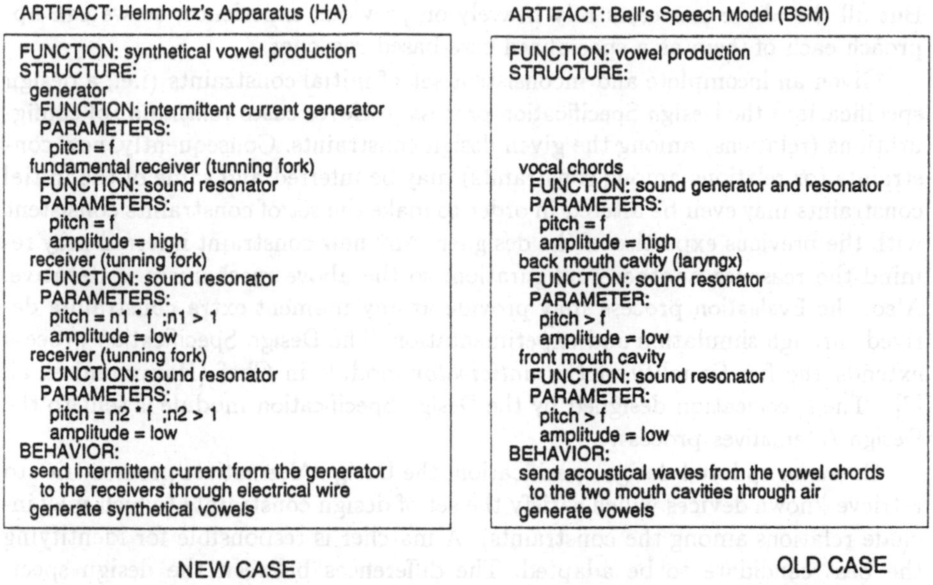

ARTIFACT: Helmholtz's Apparatus (HA)

```
FUNCTION: synthetical vowel production
STRUCTURE:
 generator
  FUNCTION: intermittent current generator
  PARAMETERS:
   pitch = f
 fundamental receiver (tunning fork)
  FUNCTION: sound resonator
  PARAMETERS:
   pitch = f
   amplitude = high
 receiver (tunning fork)
  FUNCTION: sound resonator
  PARAMETERS:
   pitch = n1 * f ;n1 > 1
   amplitude = low
 receiver (tunning fork)
  FUNCTION: sound resonator
  PARAMETERS:
   pitch = n2 * f ;n2 > 1
   amplitude = low
BEHAVIOR:
 send intermittent current from the generator
  to the receivers through electrical wire
 generate synthetical vowels
```

NEW CASE

ARTIFACT: Bell's Speech Model (BSM)

```
FUNCTION: vowel production
STRUCTURE:



 vocal chords
  FUNCTION: sound generator and resonator
  PARAMETERS:
   pitch = f
   amplitude = high
 back mouth cavity (laryngx)
  FUNCTION: sound resonator
  PARAMETER:
   pitch > f
   amplitude = low
 front mouth cavity
  FUNCTION: sound resonator
  PARAMETER:
   pitch > f
   amplitude = low
BEHAVIOR:
 send acoustical waves from the vowel chords
  to the two mouth cavities through air
 generate vowels
```

OLD CASE

Fig. 2. Matching Helmholtz's Apparatus and Bell's Speech Model

represent *predictive features* of the artifact (our framework relies on functional indexing; see Goel [5]).

The structural relations (configurations) associated with a known artifact represent important indexes for perceiving (Hinrichs [9]) and recognizing topological structures, while understanding a new design.

As an example, Fig. 2 shows a simplified case representation of Helmholtz Apparatus and of Bell's model for (human) speech production. The two artifacts have the same function, but different structures. Consequently, analogical reasoning can be used to infer more causal and structural relations about Helmholtz's Apparatus given a better known artifact (i.e., Bell's Speech Model).

2.3 Reasoning

Let's analyze the reasoning performed by each of the processes identified in Fig. 1, namely Design Specification, Design Alternatives and Evaluation. In our initial framework (IMPROVISER), Design Specification was mainly responsible for *situation assessment*, Design Alternatives was responsible mainly for *retrieval* and *adaptation*, while Evaluation was responsible mainly for *critique* and *evaluation*.

But all the above processes rely heavily on previous experience, so we can approach each of them as a specialized case-based reasoner.

Given an incomplete and inconsistent set of initial constraints (i.e., a design specification) the Design Specification process retrieves cases *reminding* of configurations (relations) among the given design constraints. Consequently, new constraints (or relations among constraints) may be inferred and some of the initial constraints may even be altered in order to make the set of constraints consistent with the previous expertise of the designer. Any new constraint inferred may remind the reasoner another configuration, so the above mechanism is iterative. Also, the Evaluation process may provide at any moment extra constraints derived through simulation and experimentation. The Design Specification process extends the functionality of the *anticipator* module in Chef (Hammond et al. [7]). The specification designed by the Design Specification module is sent to the Design Alternatives process.

Given an updated design specification, the Design Alternatives process tries to retrieve known devices which satisfy the set of design constraints (which may include relations among the constraints). A matcher is responsible for identifying the best candidate to be adapted. The differences between the design specification and the best retrieved candidate may be used to perform case-based adaptation (Bhatta and Goel [1]). But if the existing differences cannot be reduced in one step, planning a sequence of adaptation steps might be necessary. Finally, the adapted candidate artifact is sent to the Evaluation process.

Given a structural description of an artifact, the Evaluation process performs a qualitative simulation (Forbus [4]) to validate the design, if it has the prerequisite knowledge. Otherwise, evaluation by experimentation is performed. The Evaluation process may suggest new constraints to the Design Specification and Design Alternatives processes.

2.4 Understanding

All of the reasoning processes in our framework (see Fig. 1) rely on previous case-based experience. Our analysis of Bell's diaries suggest that this reliance on previous experience can be abstracted as an understanding subprocess involving both retrieval and analogical reasoning (Moorman and Ram [12], Bhatta and Goel [1]). While analogical reasoning has been used traditionally only by the Design Alternatives process, our contribution is to extend the use of analogical reasoning to the other processes in our framework, namely Evaluation and Design Specification.

The process of Design Specification perceives[6] and reasons about the relations among the given *behavioral* constraints. Once a set of constraints and consistent relations among them is proposed, analogical understanding may be used to remember a similar case (in a different domain) and infer more constraints through

---

[6] Hinrichs [9] addresses the complementary problem of perceiving *structural* constraints.

analogical transfer. This means that the Design Specification provides an *analogical anticipator* of constraints.

But what is the role of understanding in evaluation? When Bell came up with the initial theoretical design of the multiple telegraph, he evaluated an electrical device by using acoustical knowledge (since Bell did not have knowledge to evaluate electrical devices). Basically, Bell abstracted the acoustical functions of the electrical components, and he evaluated further an acoustical device. This means that Evaluation may rely on analogy beside retrieval. Consequently, the Evaluation process has to *understand* the candidate artifact at the right level of abstraction, by using the analogical mappings provided by the Design Alternatives process.

3 Computational Model

This section elaborates the initial creative design framework (presented in Fig. 1), by making explicit the role of understanding in design (see Fig. 3). The Design Specification, Evaluation and Design Alternatives processes use the Retrieval* algorithm (see Fig. 4) in order to access the previous experience to understand the current situation (one way to perform situation assessment). If understanding fails, the Retrieval* algorithm generates new learning goals, that are suspended in memory. ALEC, our evolved computational model, provides tools to model the reasoning that led Bell to the invention of the telephone. In particular it provided a solution to the issue of how pieces from different artifacts are combined in a new artifact.

3.1 Memory Architecture

The major component of our memory architecture (see Fig. 3), is a working memory (WM) which communicates with both long-term memory (LTM) and perceptual processes (Simina and Kolodner [18]). WM represents the activated part of LTM and keeps track of recent reasoning contexts. More precisely, the WM keeps track of: (1) the current problem context (i.e., the *Evolving Specification* and the pool of *Alternatives*), (2) the recent *Suspended Problems* and *Background Artifacts* (for simulating recency effects), (3) an *Opportunity Agenda* used by the control unit (not represented in Fig. 3) to select the next activity.

The set of *Suspended Problems* is characterized by non-elaborated design specifications (sketchy-specs), which cannot be understood successfully by ALEC. A suspended problem can be elaborated further when a *matching* algorithm (Forbus, Ferguson and Gentner [3]) recognizes opportunistically that something in the environment or created on the fly fulfills the requirements formulated in a sketchy-spec.

The set of *Background Artifacts* contains artifacts accessed recently, including design alternatives associated with *Suspended Problems*. While devices in LTM are indexed normally by their function, alternative designs for problems

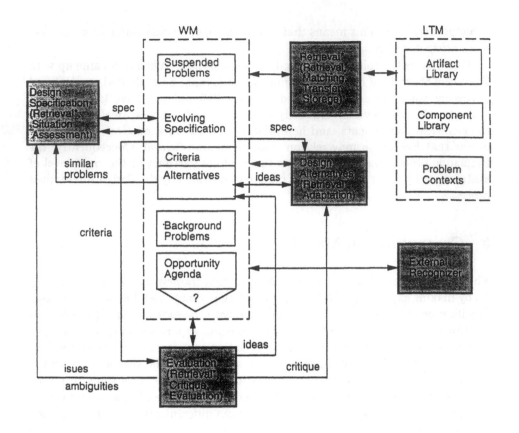

Fig. 3. Elaborated Framework for Creative Design (ALEC)

in *Background Artifacts* can be accessed also by structural and behavioral properties, due to recency effects. Bell's case study showed us that this is indeed the case. As an example, let's consider the episode when Bell had to design the microphone for the telephone:

> *"The problem that then arose in my mind was, how to move a piece of steel in the way that the air was moved by the action of the voice. While this problem was in my mind, I was carrying on experiments with the phonavtograph constructed from the human ear ... and it occurred to me that if such a thin and delicate membrane could move bones that were, relative to it, very massive indeed, why should not a larger and stouter membrane be able to move a piece of steel in the manner I desired? At once the conception of a membrane speaking telephone became complete in my mind; for I saw that a similar instrument to that used as a transmitter could also be employed as a receiver"* (US v. Bell [19]).

We notice here that the phonautograph design was recalled by a behavioral component (i.e. how to move heavy bones with a delicate membrane) which was not reflected in the phonautograph's function (i.e. record on paper the shape generated by different sounds). ALEC can replicate this reasoning when the phonautograph design is present in the *Background Artifacts*, due to its recent processing. This mechanism provides also an explanation of how pieces from an artifact (which cannot be retrieved independently, based on their usual functions) may be *selected* for synthesizing a new artifact. Design synthesis can be viewed as a sophisticated form of case-based adaptation.

Each of the processes in Fig. 3 (represented as gray rectangles) has the ability to inspect the *Opportunity Agenda*, to act upon relevant opportunities from the agenda, and to notice new opportunities for other processes, by recording them in the *Opportunity Agenda*. New opportunities can be created by the External Recognizer (exogenous opportunities) or by other internal process (endogenous opportunities). The control of our computational model is explicit, namely selection of opportunities from the agenda by using a *control plan* (Hayes-Roth [8]).

3.2 Processing Algorithms

Creative design usually evolves incrementally, during several design sessions. During each session, ALEC addresses some old issues/problems and it may raise other subproblems (see Figure 4a).

Our view of creative design includes two concurrent processes: one evolving Design Alternatives and another one evolving Design Specification. These two processes evolve under the control of a third process, Evaluation. Evaluation questions the advantages and disadvantages of each alternative and also the contradictions and ambiguities in the specification. The resolution of these questions serves to refine both the design specification and the pool of partial design alternatives. The output of a design session becomes the input of the next session and the structure of input/output becomes an invariant of the process (see Figure 4a). We call this invariant structure a *problem context*.

The three main processes involved in creative design rely heavily on the use of previous experience. Each of these processes has to understand the current situation by using the Retrieval* algorithm (see Fig. 4b), in order to act creatively. As a first step (1), Retrieval* performs *WM retrieval*, by matching the current *Evolving Specification* against the set of *Background Artifacts*. This is an *exhaustive* match (i.e., all the structural and internal behavioral properties are considered, beside the functional properties used for indexing in LTM). Since the *Alternatives* associated with a *Suspended Problem* are among the *Background Artifacts*, any match of the current *Evolving Specification* with one of the *Alternatives* associated with suspended problem (goal) *activates* that suspended problem. We notice that goal activation is an (opportunistic) side-effect of *WM retrieval*. If *WM retrieval* fails, the second step (2) is *LTM retrieval*, corresponding to the

TASK: Incremental Creative Design

INPUT:
- an agenda of opportunity
- an incomplete, contradictory and
  underconstrained design specification (goal)
  represented as a set of constraints (C_current)
- a set of design alternatives to build an artifact,
  satisfying C_current

OUTPUT:
- an updated opportunity agenda
- an evolved set of constraints (C_next)
  representing the evolved design specification
- an updated set of design alternatives
  (DA_next) for C_current

METHOD:

opportunity = pick the most relevant opportunity
CASE(recipient of opportunity) OF
  eval: Evaluate an artifact (DA) with respect to
        C_current
  alt: Design Alternatives (DA_next)
  spec: Design Specification (C_next)

Evaluate, Design Alternatives and Design
Specification use the Understanding subtask.

(a)

SUBTASK: Understanding

INPUT:
- artifact represented as a
  sketchy-spec (C_current)

OUTPUT:
- updated C_current
- design alternative (DA)
- analogical mappings

METHOD: Retrieval*

1. perform WM retrieval
2. if (1) fails, perform LTM retrieval
3. if matching succeds
   perform analogical transfer
   return
4. if matching fails
   relax design constraints
   goto (1)
5. otherwise, suspend the
   sketchy-spec in memory,
   indexed by C_current,
   and switch to another problem.

(b)

Fig. 4. Incremental Creative Design

classical CBR retrieval (includes detailed matching of the retrieved artifacts). If WM or LTM matching was successful, the third step (3) performs analogical transfer between the retrieved artifact and the current *Evolving Specification*. If retrieval failed (4), the algorithm attempts to relax the most specific design constraints to facilitate analogical reasoning (Forbus, Ferguson and Gentner [3]) and iterates step (1). Otherwise (5), the current problem context is suspended in WM (in *Suspended Problems*) and in LTM, by *predictively encoding* (Hammond et al. [7]) it in terms of its specification. We notice that any of the *Suspended Problems* is *exhaustively encoded* in WM, since the whole representation of its *Alternatives* is available for matching.

As an example, when Bell tried to understand an electrical device (i.e., Helmholtz's Apparatus) without having enough electrical experience, classical retrieval failed to retrieve useful electrical information from his memory. Next, he relaxed the constraints and looked for devices which performed the same acoustical functions (analogy). This time he could use his whole acoustical ex-pertize in understanding the electrical device. But sometimes this was not enough since the analogical mapping failed. When Bell made an analogy between speech transmission through air and sound transmission through electrical wires, standard analogy failed, since electrical currents could transmit only the pitch of the voice but not its amplitude. Sometimes it is possible to build dynamically a base within a given domain if the reasoner possesses some expertize in both target and intended base domain, by combining desirable attributes from several bases and evaluating the new base using knowledge from the target domain. Moorman and Ram ([12]) call such a technique *base-constructive analogy*. Essentially, base-constructive analogy is a form of case-based adaptation. Base-constructive analogy can be used to model the reasoning used by Bell in advancing the "undulatory current" hypothesis, by mixing properties of voice transmission through air and sound transmission through electrical wires. When base constructive analogy failed, Bell simply encoded predictively the understanding problem in memory and started working on another problem.

4 Conclusions

ALEC, our proposed computational model for creative design makes explicit the role of analogical understanding during design problem solving. Moorman and Ram ([12]) have addressed the complementary problem of making explicit the role of (mental) design during creative story understanding.

Our view of creative design includes both opportunistic and analogical aspects. On the opportunity recognition side, ALEC provides a mechanism for solving suspended problems (in WM or in LTM), while reasoning about the current design problem. In particular, the *Suspended Problems* in WM are more *active* than those suspended in LTM (i.e., a more detailed match and reasoning is performed for the recently *Suspended Problems*). The detailed internal behaviors associated with an artifact may be used to match the current design specification to *Background Artifacts* in WM, while the function of the artifact is used to match artifacts in LTM.

On the analogy side, ALEC proposes an *analogical anticipator* of design constraints and an *analogical evaluator* of proposed design solutions.

Our computational model represents work in progress, so we cannot say yet that it provides a correct or complete model of reasoning and understanding in creative design. Beside testing it on a wider variety of examples, we must also investigate more deeply the generation of new design goals and the synthesis of new artifacts from several existing design alternatives.

5 Acknowledgements

This research was was funded in part by NSF Grant No. IRI-8921256 and in part by ONR Grant No. N00014-92-J-1234. We thank Kenny Moorman, Ashwin Ram, Ashok Goel, Mike Gorman, Tom Hinrichs, Ron Ferguson, Ken Forbus, James Lawton and our anonymous reviewers for their comments on this research.

598

References

1. Bhatta, S., Goel A.: Learning Generic Mechanisms from Experiences for Analogical Reasoning. Proceedings of the Fifteenth Conference of the Cognitive Science Society. Lawrence Erlbaum Associates (1993) 237–242
2. Chandrasekaran, B.: Design Problem Solving: A Task Analysis. AI Magazine Volume 11, 4 (1990)
3. Forbus, K., Ferguson, R., Gentner, D.: Incremental Structure-Mapping. Proceedings of the Sixteenth Conference of the Cognitive Science Society. Lawrence Erlbaum Associates (1994) 313–318
4. Forbus, K.: Qualitative Process Theory. Artificial Intelligence **24** (1984) 85–168
5. Goel A.: Integrating Case-Based and Model-Based Reasoning: A Computational Model of Design Problem Solving. AI Magazine **13(2)** (1992) 50–54
6. Gorman, M.: Simulating Science: Heuristics, Mental Models and Technoscientific Thinking. Bloomington: Indiana University Press (1992)
7. Hammond K., Timothy C., Marks, M., Seifert C.: Opportunism and Learning. Machine Learning **10** (1993) 279–309
8. Hayes-Roth, B.: A Blackboard Architecture for Control. Artificial Intelligence, **26** (1985) , 251-321.
9. Hinrichs, T.: Some Limitations of Feature-Based Recognition in Case-Based Design. In Case-Based Reasoning Research and Development. Springer Verlag (1995) 471–480
10. Kolodner, J.: Case-Based Reasoning. Morgan Kaufmann (1993) 369–382
11. Kolodner, J., Wills, L.: Case-based Creative Design. AAAI Spring Symposium on AI and Creativity. Stanford, CA. (1993).
12. Moorman, K. & Ram, A.: A Model of Creative Understanding. In Proceedings of the Twelfth Annual AAAI Conference (1994)
13. Peterson, J., Mahesh, K., Goel, A.: Situating natural language understanding within experience-based design. International Journal of Human-Computer studies **41** (1994) 881-913
14. Ram, A.: A theory of Questions and Question Asking. The Journal of Learning Sciences, **1** (**3 & 4**) (1991) 273–318
15. Ram, A., Hunter, L.: The Use of Explicit Goals for Knowledge to Guide Inference and Learning. Journal of Applied Intelligence **2(1)** (1992) 47–73
16. Reich, Y., Fenves, S.: Inductive Learning of Synthesis Knowledge. International Journal of Expert Systems: Research and Applications **5(4)** (1992) 275-297
17. Schank, R.: Explanation Patterns. Lawrence Erlbaum Associates (1986)
18. Simina, M., Kolodner, J.: Opportunistic Reasoning: A Design Perspective. Proceedings of the Seventeenth Conference of the Cognitive Science Society. Lawrence Erlbaum Associates (1995) 78–83
19. US vs Bell: The Bell Telephone: The Deposition of Alexander Graham Bell. Boston: American Bell Telephone Company (1908)
20. Wills, L., Kolodner, J.: Explaining Serendipitous Recognition in Design. Proceedings of the Sixteenth Conference of the Cognitive Science Society. Lawrence Erlbaum Associates (1994) 940–945
21. Tong, C.: Knowledge-Based Circuit Design. Ph.D. Thesis. Rutgers Technical Report LCSR-TR-108 (1988)

Fuzzy Modelling of Case-Based Reasoning and Decision

Didier Dubois[1], Francesc Esteva[2], Pere Garcia[2], Lluís Godo[2],
Ramon L. de Màntaras[2] and Henri Prade[1]

[1] Institut de Recherche en Informatique de Toulouse (IRIT), Université Paul Sabatier, Bât. 1R3, 118 Route de Narbonne, 31062 Toulouse Cedex 4, France
emails: {dubois,prade}@irit.fr
[2] Institut d'Investigació en Intel·ligència Artificial (IIIA), Consejo Superior de Investigaciones Científicas(CSIC), Campus Universitat Autonoma de Barcelona, 08193 Bellaterra, Spain
emails: {esteva,pere,godo,mantaras}@iiia.csic.fr

Abstract. This paper is an attempt at providing a fuzzy set-based formalization of case-based reasoning. The proposed approach, which does not take into account the learning aspects of case-based reasoning, assumes a principle stating that "the more similar are the problem description attributes, the more similar are the outcome attributes". A weaker form of this principle is also considered. These two forms of the case-based reasoning principle are modelled in terms of fuzzy rules. Then an approximate reasoning machinery taking advantage of this principle enables us to apply the information stored in the memory of precedent cases to the current problem. A particular instance of case-based reasoning, named case-based decision, is especially investigated. A logical model of case-based inference is also described.

1 Introduction

Case-based reasoning amounts to inferring from known case(s) which are similar enough to a newly encountered situation, that what is true in the known case(s) might still be true, up to some suitable adaptation, in this new situation. Case-based reasoning may be viewed as a particular form of analogical reasoning, since an analogy is a relational statement of the form, "D is in the same relation w.r.t. C as B is w.r.t. A, which is usually seen as a way of *guessing* D, knowing A, B and C. Analogical reasoning has been investigated for a long time in Artificial Intelligence and the interest in this research has been considerably renewed by the development of case-based reasoning (Kolodner, 1993; Aamodt and Plaza, 1994). Any attempt to provide a general formalization of this common way of reasoning raises several critical issues, especially on such questions as

1. the definition and practical elicitation of similarity measures,
2. the retrieving of relevant cases,
3. the logical modelling of the inference mechanism,
4. the adaptation of the retrieved cases in order to extrapolate plausible values for the variable(s) of interest in the current situation,

5. the incomplete, imprecise, or even uncertain, description of available cases, or of the current problem.

Although these different steps apparently require some graded notion of similarity, there have been few attempts for introducing fuzzy set-based tools in case-based reasoning. Among them, some works have focused on the handling of fuzzy descriptions in the retrieval step (Jaczynski and Trousse, 1994), on the learning of fuzzy concepts from fuzzy examples (Plaza and Lopez de Mantaras, 1990), and very recently on the logical modelling of the inference mechanisms based on similarity measures (Plaza et al. 1996a). See (Dubois and Prade, 1994) for a general overview on similarity-based approximate reasoning.

This paper provides a more systematic investigation of the potentials of fuzzy logic-based approaches for the different issues mentioned above. It is also an attempt at formalizing the basic patterns of case-based reasoning and decision. Let us first specify how case-based reasoning is viewed in this paper. A *case* is viewed as a n-tuple of precise attribute values, this set of attributes being divided in two non-empty disjoint subsets: the problem description attributes subset and the solution or outcome attributes subset denoted by S and T respectively. These subsets are taken according to the problem we deal with. A case will be denoted as a tuple (s, t) where s and t stand for complete sets of precise attribute values of S and T respectively. In order to perform a case-based reasoning we assume that we have a finite set M of previously known cases, called *case base* or *memory* (M is thus a set of pairs (s, t)), and a current problem description, denoted by s_0, for which the precise values of all attributes belonging to S are known. Then case-based reasoning aims at extrapolating an estimate of the value t_0 of the attributes in T, for the current problem. It is therefore assumed everywhere in this paper that the memory only includes completely informed cases (with the exception of the conclusion section).

In the case-based reasoning setting it is also assumed that the attributes belonging to the outcome set can be related, in some way, to the problem description attributes. In the following, we assume that a *basic principle* stating that *"similar situations give (or may give) similar outcomes"* holds[3]. Therefore, a similarity measure S between problem descriptions and a similarity measure T between outcomes are needed and supposed to be given. We suppose that

---

[3] A similar idea has been emphasized for a long time in analogical reasoning. In particular, (Davies and Russell, 1987) have proposed to control the inference process by means of explicitly stated functional dependencies expressing that if two descriptions are identical with respect to the values of a set S of attributes, they should be also identical with respect to (an)other attribute(s) T. However, this form of meta-rule or principle is too restrictive for two kinds of reasons: i) perfect identity is required rather than (graded) similarity, and nothing is said in case of approximate identity, ii) the functional dependencies forbid to have identical cases w.r.t. to S which differ w.r.t. attributes in T, which is not very realistic in practice. Indeed two very similar second hand cars might be sold at different prices, for instance. In (Léa Sombé, 1990) some remedies to these two limitations have been suggested in terms of fuzzy functional dependencies.

these fuzzy relations are primitive notions and known in advance (although we might think of learning them from the set of precedents stored in the memory). Methods for obtaining fuzzy relations, or checking their adequacy are out of the scope of this paper[4]. Expressed in terms of the fuzzy relations S and T, the implicit *Case-Based Reasoning Principle* can be expressed by the following rule:

the more S-similar s_1 and s_2, the more T-similar t_1 and t_2

where $(s_1, t_1), (s_2, t_2) \in M$. A *problem* in the framework of our case-based reasoning model will be denoted by a 4-tuple $\langle M, S, T, s_0 \rangle$ where M stands for a case-base or memory, S and T stand for the similarity relations and s_0 stands for the current case. Throughout this paper we will refer to what we call *deterministic* case-based problems $\langle M, S, T, s_0 \rangle$ when the above principle is applicable, otherwise we will refer to *non-deterministic* problems (where only a weaker form of the principle, concluding only on the *possibility* that the outcome attributes are similar, can be used). We use the term "deterministic" since, as it will become clear in next section, when the principle holds, a problem description s_0 indeed determines the outcome t_0 (in the sense that two identical problem descriptions should be associated with the same outcome).

The paper is structured as follows. Section 2 describes the fuzzy set modelling of deterministic and non-deterministic case-based reasoning problems. Section 3 discusses case-based decision models. Section 4 provides a logical formalization of the deterministic case. Concluding remarks briefly discuss various extensions of the proposed approach.

2 A Fuzzy Set Framework for Case-Based Reasoning

2.1 Deterministic Problems

Fuzzy rules (see Dubois and Prade (1996) for an introduction) provide a tool for modelling the above expressions of the implicit Case-Based Reasoning Principle. We first consider the deterministic situation. In the deterministic setting, the above principle can be modelled by the constraint

$$\forall (s_1, t_1), (s_2, t_2) \in M, S(s_1, s_2) \leq T(t_1, t_2) \tag{1}$$

where S and T are fuzzy proximity relations ($S(s_1, s_2), T(t_1, t_2) \in [0, 1]$). S and T are supposed to be symmetric (i.e. $\forall s_1, \forall s_2, S(s_1, s_2) = S(s_2, s_1), T(t_1, t_2) = T(t_2, t_1)$), and reflexive ($\forall s_1, \forall s_2, S(s_1, s_1) = 1, T(t_1, t_1) = 1$). It is worth noticing that (1) should be understood in the following way: the similarity of s_1 and s_2 constrains the similarity of t_1 and t_2 at a minimum level, i.e., $S(s_1, s_2)$ is a lower bound of $T(t_1, t_2)$. In particular if $S(s_1, s_2) = 1$ then $T(t_1, t_2)$ should be also 1. Expression (1) corresponds to the representation of a gradual rule in the sense of (Dubois and Prade, 1992). In particular, $\forall \alpha \in (0, 1]$, we have

$$(s_1, s_2) \in S_\alpha \Rightarrow (t_1, t_2) \in T_\alpha \tag{2}$$

---

[4] See the long version of this paper (Dubois et al., 1997a) for a presentation of different types of fuzzy similarity relations and their properties.

where $S_\alpha = \{(s, s') \mid S(s, s') \geq \alpha\}$ is the α-cut of S and T_α is similarly defined. So (2) expresses that when s_1 and s_2 are close, t_1 and t_2 should be at least as close. Clearly, when $S(s_1, s_2) = 0$, $T(t_1, t_2)$ is no longer constrained. Moreover, if T is such that $T(t_1, t_2) = 1 \Leftrightarrow t_1 = t_2$ (separating property of T), then the classical functional dependency

$$s_1 = s_2 \Rightarrow t_1 = t_2 \tag{3}$$

is a consequence of (1) or (2) using the reflexivity of S. Constraint (1) is then clearly stronger than (3). In the paper, we always assume that T is separating in *deterministic problems* (this means that M agrees with the strong version of the Case-Based Reasoning Principle).

Let us know examine how (1) is used in the case-based inference process. Let $(s, t) \in M$, we have for the current situation s_0 the constraint $S(s, s_0) \leq T(t, t_0)$, where t_0 is unknown. Thus, the constraint defines a set of possible values for t_0, namely $\{t_0 \mid S(s, s_0) \leq T(t, t_0)\}$. Since, it applies for any (s, t) in M, we obtain the following set E of possible values for t_0

$$E = \bigcap_{(s,t) \in M} \{t' \in T \mid S(s, s_0) \leq T(t, t')\}. \tag{4}$$

When $E \neq \emptyset$, an interpolation mechanism is embedded in (4). The non-emptiness of E reflects the coherence of the case base M with the gradual rules associated with S and T in the sense of constraint (1); see (Dubois et al., 1997a) on this point. The interpolative nature of (4) will be made clearer in Section 4.2. Note that E may be empty if T is not permissive enough. For instance, assume that

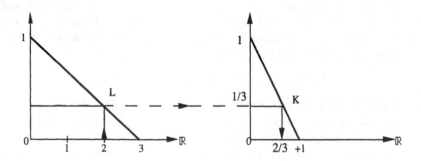

Fig. 1.

$S = T = \Re$, S and T are defined by $S_L(s, s') = L(|s - s'|)$, $T_K(t, t') = K(|t - t'|)$ with L and K given in Figure 1, $M = \{(7, 10), (3, 12)\}$ and $s_0 = 5$. Then $S_L(s_0, 7) = S_L(s_0, 3) = 1/3$. Thus, according to case $(7, 10)$, $t_0 \in [10 - 2/3, 10 + 2/3]$, while according to case $(3, 12)$, $t_0 \in [12 - 2/3, 12 + 2/3]$, and thus $E = \emptyset$.

2.2 Non-Deterministic Problems

Clearly, if we want to apply the principle expressed by (1), the case-base M should satisfy (1) for any pair of cases (s_1, t_1) and (s_2, t_2). This requirement may be felt to be too strong in some practical applications where M may for instance simultaneously include cases like (s, t) and (s, t') with $t \neq t'$, which violates (3), and thus (1). In such a case, we suggest to use a *weaker* version of the *Case-Based Reasoning Principle* stating that

"the more similar s_1 and s_2, the more possible t_1 and t_2 are similar".

The formal expression of this principle requires to clarify the intended meaning of *possible* in this meta-rule; this will be done in the next paragraph. A non-deterministic (fuzzy) dependency rule is thus of the form "*the more similar is s to s_0 (in the sense of S), the more possible is the similarity of t to t_0 (in the sense of T)*". It should be pointed out that this rule only concludes on the *possibility* of t_0 being similar to t. This acknowledges the fact that, often in practice, a database may contain cases which are rather similar with respect to the problem description attributes, but which are sensibly distinct with respect to outcome attribute(s). This emphasizes that case-based reasoning can only lead to cautious conclusions.

Rules of the form "the more X is A, the more possible Y is B" correspond to a particular kind of fuzzy rules called *possibility rules* (Dubois and Prade, 1996). They express that "the more X is A, the more possible B is a range for Y", which can be understood as "$\forall u$, if $X = u$, it is possible at least at the degree $A(u)$ that Y lies in B". When B is an ordinary subset, it clearly expresses that i) if $v \in B$, v is possible for Y at least at the level $A(u)$ if $X = u$, and ii) if $v \notin B$, nothing is said about the minimum possibility level of value v for Y. This leads to the following constraint on the conditional possibility distribution $\pi_{Y|X}$ representing the rule (where $\pi_{Y|X}(v, u)$ estimates to what extent $Y = v$ is possible when $X = u$), namely

$$\pi_{Y|X}(v, u) \geq A(u), \text{ if } v \in B; \ \pi_{Y|X}(v, u) \geq 0, \text{ if } v \notin B.$$

When both A and B are fuzzy sets it generalizes into

$$\forall u \in U, \forall v \in V, \min(A(u), B(v)) \leq \pi_{Y|X}(v, u). \tag{5}$$

This clearly gives back the above expression when $B(v) \in \{0, 1\}$. Since we apply the above *weak* principle, the fuzzy set of possible values t' for t_0 is given by

$$\pi_{t_0}(t') \geq \min(S(s, s_0), T(t, t')). \tag{6}$$

As it can be seen, what is obtained is the fuzzy set $T(t, \cdot) = \{t\} \circ T$ of values t' T-similar to t, *truncated* by the global degree $S(s, s_0)$ of similarity of s with s_0. The inequality in (5), which leads to a max-based aggregation of the contributions obtained from the comparison with each case (s, t) in the memory M of cases, acknowledges the fact that each new comparison may suggest new possible values for t_0. Since (6) applies to all the pairs $(s, t) \in M$, we obtain the following fuzzy set E of possible values t' for t_0 (i.e. $E(t') = \pi_{t_0}(t')$)

$$E(t') = \max_{(s,t) \in M} \min(S(s, s_0), T(t, t')). \tag{7}$$

When the relation T reduces to equality, (7) is nothing but the fuzzy set of values t associated with cases in M which are more or less similar to s_0.

3 Case-Based Decision

3.1 Gilboa and Schmeidler's Approach

Recently, Gilboa and Schmeidler (1995) have advocated a similarity-based approach to decision where a case is described as a triple $(problem, act, result)$ and where a decision-maker's non-negative utility function u assigns a numerical value $u(r)$ to a result r. When faced with a new situation s_0, the decision-maker is supposed to choose an act a which maximizes a counterpart of classical expected utility used in decision under uncertainty:

$$U_{s_0, M}(a) = \sum_{(s, a, r) \in M} S(s_0, s) \cdot u(r) \tag{8}$$

where S is a non-negative function which estimates the similarity of situations, here the similarity of the current situation s_0 against already encountered ones stored in M. Moreover it is assumed that $\forall s, \forall a, \exists! r$ such that $(s, a, r) \in M$ (i.e., results are uniquely determined by the act applied to the context of a given problem), and $\forall s, \exists! a$ such that $(s, a, r) \in M$ and $u(r) \neq 0$ (i.e., only the best act in context s is stored in the memory). Gilboa and Schmeidler (1995) give an axiomatic derivation of this U-maximization within a formal model.

In order to relate the case-based reasoning framework of the previous section to the above approach to decision problems, we consider the triples (s, a, r) as cases $((s, a), r)$ and we assume $S((s, a), (s_0, a)) = S(s, s_0)$. Under a rather special hypothesis on the contents of M, it is then possible to retrieve (8) by applying the approach of Section 2.1 in the deterministic case. Indeed let us try to estimate the utility $u(r_0)$ attached to the act a applied to the current problem description s_0. Then (4) yields

$$E_a = \bigcap_{(s, a, r) \in M} \{u(r') \mid S(s, s_0) \leq T(u(r), u(r'))\}. \tag{9}$$

Using results in (Dubois, Grabisch and Prade, 1994), it can be checked that under the hypothesis that M and S are such that for s_0, $\exists!(s_1, s_2)$ such that $(s_1, a, r_1) \in M$, $(s_2, a, r_2) \in M$, $S(s_0, s_1) > 0, S(s_0, s_2) > 0$ and moreover that $S(s_0, s_1) + S(s_0, s_2) = 1$, then E_a contains only one element e_a equal to

$$e_a = \frac{\sum_{(s, a, r) \in M} S(s, s_0) \cdot u(r)}{\sum_{(s, a, r) \in M} S(s, s_0)} \tag{10}$$

where we recognize (8) upto a normalization factor depending on the act a. An appropriate choice of T in (9) is also required in order to have (9) reducing to the value (10). This shows that for particular S and T, (9) embeds a linear interpolation mechanism. One way of satisfying the requirement of the above hypothesis when the problems s in M can be linearly ordered, is in fact to assume that a different S, say S_s, is associated with the neighborhood of each problem s, in such a way that $S(s, s')$ decreases to 0 when s' goes away from s and coincide with one of the two closest neighbors of s in M. Then it is easy to make $S_{s_1}(s_0, s_1) + S_{s_2}(s_0, s_2) = 1$.

Although (8) looks like an expected utility expression where probabilities are replaced by similarity degrees, its intuitive interpretation is quite different from the decision under uncertainty point of view. First, note that there is no constraint on the sum $\sum_s S(s, s_0)$, in particular it has not to sum to 1. The idea is rather to look for acts that in several similar situations had results with a high utility. However, a drawback of (8) is it unability to distinguish between a situation where there is only one case in M very similar to s_0 which led to a good result and a situation where there are many cases in M, all of them with a low degree of similarity to s_0 (which also led to good results); this may then yield estimates $U_{s_0, M}(a)$ which are very close. See (Dubois et al., 1997a) for a more detailed discussion. Moreover (8) somewhat compensates between good results r and bad results r' attached to the same act a for distinct problems s and s' which are both similar to s_0 (if we have both (s, a, r) and $(s', a, r') \in M$).

3.2 Alternative Approach

Another idea is to look for acts which for similar problems always gave good results. Then, for a given act a, we are interested in computing a degree of inclusion of the fuzzy set of problems which are similar to s_0 and where act a was experienced, into the fuzzy set of situations where act a led to good results. The function u, like S, is now supposed to range on the real interval $[0, 1]$, with the following interpretations: $S(s, s') = 1$ means perfect similarity of s and s', $S(s, s') = 0$ means that s and s' are not at all similar as previously, while $u(r) = 1$ means that the result r is among the best ones, while $u(r) = 0$ means that r is among the worst ones. Thus, the fuzzy set of situations similar to s_0 is represented by $S(\cdot, s_0) = \{s_0\} \circ S$, and u is the membership function of the fuzzy set of good results. The following degree of inclusion enables us to select the act(s) a, if any, which for problems similar to s_0 always gave good results:

$$U_{*s_0, M}(a) = \min_{(s, a, r) \in M} S(s, s_0) \to u(r) \qquad (11)$$

where $\to$ is a multiple-valued implication connective[5]. The fact of assuming
- $U_{*s_0, M}(a) = 1$ iff $\{s \mid (s, a, r) \in M, S(s, s_0) > 0\} \subseteq \{s \mid (s, a, r) \in M, u(r) = 1\}$
- $U_{*s_0, M}(a) = 0$ as soon as $\exists s, S(s, s_0) = 1, (s, a, r) \in M$ and $u(r) = 0$

leads to choose an implication $x \to y$ of the form $x \to y = n(x) \perp y$ where n is an

---

[5] $x \to y$ increases with y, decreases with x, and is the material implication on $\{0,1\}$.

involutive negation function and $\perp$ a disjunction operation. In case of a purely ordinal interpretation of $[0,1]$ where only the ordering of the levels is meaningful, we are led to use $x \to y = max(1 - x, y)$,[6] i.e.,

$$U_{*s_0,M}(a) = \min_{(s,r):(s,a,r)\in M} max(1 - S(s, s_0), u(r)) \tag{12}$$

which expresses that the existence of a case (s, a, r) in M does not penalize act a w.r.t. s_0 if r is a good result, or if s is not similar to s_0.

$U_{*s_0,M}$ is a rather drastic criterium since it requires that in all the problems similar to s_0, act a led in good results. A more *optimistic* behaviour can consist in selecting all the acts which led to a good result for at least one problem similar to s_0, i.e., the dual criteria

$$U_{s_0,M}^*(a) = \max_{(s,r):(s,a,r)\in M} min(u(r), S(s, s_0)). \tag{13}$$

Expressions (12) and (13) are similarity-based counterparts of qualitative utilities recently proposed in decision under uncertainty (Dubois and Prade, 1995). Moreover (12) and (13) can be seen as scalar summaries of the fuzzy set defined by (7) when T is the equality.

Remark. Expressions (12) and (13) make sense for case-based decision only when they take into account acts a that have been experienced in at least some situation s such that $S(s, s_0) = 1$. Otherwise, it could happen that $U_{*s_0,M}(a)$ would be very high while $S(s, s_0)$ is very low for all triples $(s, a, r) \in M$. To overcome this problem, a possible way is, for each act a, to renormalize[7] the fuzzy set $S(\cdot, s_0)$ over the situations s such that $(s, a, r) \in M$. But to keep track of the absence of situations very similar to s_0, a soft discount of (12) and (13) (once $S(\cdot, s_0)$ is already renormalized) should be also performed. Namely, letting $h_S(s_0) = max\{S(s, s_0) \mid (s, a, r) \in M\}$, we can define:

$$\overline{U}_{*s_0,M}(a) = min(h_S(s_0), U_{*s_0,M}^{\text{norm}}(a)),$$
$$\overline{U}_{s_0,M}^*(a) = max(1 - h_S(s_0), U_{s_0,M}^{*\text{norm}}(a)).$$

This preserves the inequality $U_{s_0,M}^* \geq U_{*s_0,M}$ between the pessimistic and the optimistic utilities, i.e $\overline{U}_{s_0,M}^* \geq \overline{U}_{*s_0,M}$. Thus $\overline{U}_{s_0,M}^*(a)$ is maximum as soon as (i) there exists a case corresponding to a problem completely similar to s_0 where the act a led to an excellent result, and (ii) act a has never been applied to a situation somewhat similar to s_0 (so if we are optimistic we should consider it). On the other hand, $\overline{U}_{*s_0,M}(a)$ is 0 when there is no situation similar to s_0 in M.

---

[6] since $max(1 - x, y) = 1$ if and only if $y = 1$ whenever $x > 0$. On an ordinal scale, $1 - (\cdot)$ is replaced by the order-reversing function of the scale.

[7] There are several ways of renormalizing a fuzzy set μ. If the scale is numerical the usual option is to define $\mu'(u) = \frac{\mu(u)}{max\{\mu(v)|v\in U\}}$, while if the scale is qualitative we may define $\mu''(u) = \mu(u)$ for $u \neq u_0$ and $\mu''(u_0) = 1$, where $\mu(u_0) = max\{\mu(v) \mid v \in U\}$.

4 A Similarity Logic Setting for Case-Based Reasoning

In this section we propose a setting which is closer to logical formalisms than the one described in Section 2.1, for the inference processes that take place in case-based reasoning systems when solving "deterministic" problems. The approach is inspired in the logical formulation of case-based inference proposed in Plaza et al. (1996), which in turn relies on two kinds of graded consequence relations that play a major role in similarity-based reasoning as shown in (Dubois et al., 1997b). The underlying assumption is that when a current problem description s_0 is compared with a precedent case (s, t) of the memory M, two basic steps are performed: (i) comparing s_0 with s, by means of the similarity relation, and (ii) extrapolating the problem solution t for s to s_0, according to their similarity degree computed in the previous step.

4.1 Background

Let $\mathcal{L}$ be a finite Boolean propositional language, Ω its set of interpretations and let S be a similarity relation on Ω. Ruspini (1991) defines the degree $I_S(p \mid w)$ to which an interpretation w is close to some model w' of a proposition p, written $w' \models p$, as

$$I_S(p \mid w) = \sup_{w' \models p} S(w, w'). \tag{14}$$

This defines, for each proposition p, the fuzzy set $[p^*]$ of interpretations which are close to p, by just considering $[p^*](w) = I_S(p \mid w)$. The fuzzy set $[p^*]$ is such that its α-level cuts $[p^*]_\alpha = \{w \mid [p^*](w) \geq \alpha\}$, for $\alpha \in (0, 1]$, define a family of nested approximations of the set $[p]$ of models of p, i.e., at each level α, $[p^*]_\alpha$ is the set of interpretations which are α-similar to p. Based on this idea, in Dubois et al. (1997b) the following graded *approximate entailment* is introduced:

$$w \models^\alpha p \quad \text{iff} \quad w \in [p^*]_\alpha \tag{15}$$

and thus $q \models^\alpha p$ iff $[q] \subseteq [p^*]_\alpha$. Equivalently, $q \models^\alpha p$ iff $I_S(p \mid q) \geq \alpha$, where $I_S(p \mid q) = \inf_{w \models q} I_S(p \mid w)$. For a context given under the form of some proposition K, it will be also useful to introduce the following notation:

$$q \models_K^\alpha p \quad \text{iff} \quad q \wedge K \models^\alpha p. \tag{16}$$

For modelling step (ii) above, we are viewing a case (p, q), where p and q are propositions of $\mathcal{L}$, as a kind of extrapolative entailment relation between p and q, with the following intended meaning: given a certain context K, p implies q in the classical sense, but moreover, if p is "close" to being true then q is also "close" to being true. In other words, in that context, the neighborhood of models of p should lie in the neighborhood of the models of q. This is in accordance with the view in Section 2.1 of a case as a gradual fuzzy rule "the more w in $[p^*]$, the more w in $[q^*]$", which is therefore expressed as

$$[p^*](w) \leq [q^*](w), \forall w \in [K]. \tag{17}$$

Furthermore, this notion of entailment, called *proximity entailment*, can be easily graded as well, just by noticing that $[p^*](w) \leq [q^*](w)$ iff $[p^*](w) \otimes \rightarrow [q^*](w) = 1$, $\otimes \rightarrow$ being the implication function defined by residuation[8] from any t-norm[9] $\otimes$. Given such an implication $\otimes \rightarrow$, it is natural to define

$$p \models_K^\alpha q \text{ iff } [p^*](w) \otimes \rightarrow [q^*](w) \geq \alpha, \forall w \in [K]. \tag{18}$$

When K is completely uninforamative, i.e. when $[K] = \Omega$, $\models_K^\alpha$ and $\models_K^\alpha$ coincide, but in general $\models_K^\alpha$ is stronger than $\models_K^\alpha$. Both approximate and proximity entailements can be related by means of the following inference pattern:

$$\text{from } p' \models^\alpha p \text{ and } p \models_K^\beta q \text{ infer } p' \models_K^{\alpha \otimes \beta} q \tag{19}$$

This inference pattern can be read as follows: if p' makes p α-true and, in a given context K, p extrapolatively entails q to the degree β then, in the same context K, p' makes q $(\alpha \otimes \beta)$-true.

4.2 Logical Modelling of Case-Based Inference

Now we make use of the logical framework just introduced in the previous subsection to reformulate the inference process involved in the case-based reasoning problems presented in Section 2.1 by means of formulating:
• step (i) above as computing the approximate entailment degree of s by s_0,
• each case (s, t) as a proximity entailment, given a suitable context K,
• step (ii) above as, due to the inference pattern (20), computing the approximate entailment degree of t given s_0 in the context K.

Let Ω_S and Ω_T denote the set of value assignments (interpretations) of attributes from S and T respectively, and define $\Omega = \Omega_S \times \Omega_T$. Assuming that the problem descriptions and outcomes are complete sets of precise attribute values for attributes in S and T, we can identify problem descriptions with interpretations of Ω_S and outcome descriptions with interpretations of Ω_T. According to the previous sections, we assume to have a similarity S on Ω_S and a similarity T on Ω_T.

Given a case base $M = \{(s_i, t_i)\}_{i \in I}$, and taking into account that problem and solution descriptions are indeed interpretations of Ω_S and Ω_T respectively, step (i) amounts to compute the similarity degree $S(s_i, s_0)$ between the current description and the precedent cases, while the context K needed to perform the extrapolative inference (i.e., the logical counterpart of our "deterministic principle") is assumed to be of the form $K = \{(s, t) \mid [s_i^*](s) \otimes \rightarrow [t_i^*](t) \geq \beta_i\} = \{(s, t) \mid S(s_i, s) \otimes \rightarrow T(t_i, t) \geq \beta_i\}$, where the parameters β_i are usually taken to be 1 (this is the situation that exactly corresponds to the expression (1) of

---

[8] The use of residuated implication $x \otimes \rightarrow y = \sup\{z \in [0,1] \mid x \otimes z \leq y\}$ is also in accordance with the semantics proposed in Dubois and Prade (1996) for the so-called gradual fuzzy rules.

[9] A t-norm is a monotonic semi-group operation in $[0, 1]$.

our deterministic principle[10]), but in general they could be assigned a lower value, denoting a weaker form of graduality between s_i and t_i. Then, the whole inference process described by (i) and (ii) can be formulated as the following inference pattern:

$$\frac{s_0 \models^{\alpha_i} s_i \ , \ s_i \models^{\beta_i}_K t_i}{s_0 \models^{\alpha_i \otimes \beta_i}_K t_i} \quad (20)$$

where $\alpha_i = S(s_0, si)$. In terms of the level-cuts, the inferred result is that $[s_0 \wedge K] \subseteq [t_i^*]_{\alpha_i \otimes \beta_i}$, for all $i \in I$. Therefore, the estimated solution t_0 for s_0 should verify

$$t_0 \in \bigcap_{(s_i, t_i) \in M} \{t \mid T(t_i, t) \geq \alpha_i \otimes \beta_i\} \quad (21)$$

which reduces to (4) when $\beta_i = 1$ for all $i \in I$.

5 Conclusions and Further Work

In this paper we have been concerned with the modelling of some aspects of case-based reasoning and decision using fuzzy set-based techniques. The basic tool is the use of fuzzy similarity relations both between problem descriptions and between outcomes of the cases. These similarity relations allow us to give a precise meaning to the implicit principle underlying "deterministic" case-based reasoning, i.e., "the more similar the problem descriptions, the more similar their outcomes", by interpreting each case in the memory as a gradual fuzzy rule. This interpretation has been also formalized in a logical setting by means of similarity-based graded consequence relations. Furthermore, a weaker form of the above principle has been proposed in order to cope with "non-deterministic" problems. Fuzzy possibility rules have then been used instead of gradual rules to model these non deterministic cases. We envisage to further develop these ideas in the near future in at least four different aspects.

1. Assesments of *dissimilarities* between cases and the current problem by means of different types of gradual rules allowing, for instance, to express generalized functional dependencies including prescribed dissimilarities as well as similarities in their statement.

2. *Dealing with cases whose attributes value are imprecise or unknown*: when the description of cases is pervaded by imprecision or uncertainty, we can no longer be sure about the identity or even the approximate equality of two feature values.

3. *Incorporating learning capabilities*: as we have already mentioned in the introduction, a possible approach could consist in looking for similarities and regularities inside the memory of cases by, for instance, clustering the cases into classes, and then building rules by induction which can be applied to the current problem s_0. The learning of the similarity relations from M may help to guarantee the coherence of the associated gradual rules w.r.t. M.

---

[10] The condition $S(s_i, s) \otimes \to T(t_i, t) \geq \beta_i$ is equivalent to $S(s_i, s) \otimes \beta_i \leq T(t_i, t)$, which is a more general constraint than expression (1)

4. *Using interpolation for case adaptation*: the fuzzy set-based model presented in Section 2.1 incorporates a natural interpolation mechanism (see Dubois et al., 1997b) which may be very helpful for the case adaptation step, specially when the outcome attribute domains are of numerical nature.

Acknowledgements. The authors are grateful to Enric Plaza and Adriana Zapico for valuable comments and discussions on preliminary drafts of this paper. The authors acknowledge partial support of the CSIC/CNRS grant called "Similarity based-reasoning and its applications".

References

1. Aamodt A., Plaza E. (1994) Case-based reasoning: Foundational issues, methodological varoations and system approaches. AI Communications, 7(1), 39-59.
2. Davies T.R., Russell S.J. (1987) A logical approach to reasoning by analogy. Proc. of the 10th Inter. Joint Conf. on Artificial Intelligence (IJCAI'87), 264-270.
3. Dubois D., Esteva F., Garcia P., Godo L., Prade H. (1997a) A logical approach to interpolation based on similarity relations. To appear in Int. J. of Approx. Reas.
4. Dubois D., Esteva F., Garcia P., Godo L., de Mantaras R.L., Prade H. (1997b) Fuzzy set-based models in case-based reasoning. In Tech. Rep. IRIT/96-54-R.
5. Dubois D., Grabisch M., Prade H. (1994) Gradual rules and the approximation of control laws. In: Theoretical aspects of fuzzy control (H.T. Nguyen et al. eds.), Wiley, 147-181.
6. Dubois D., Prade H. (1992) Gradual inference rules in approximate reasoning. Information Sciences, 61, 103-122.
7. Dubois D., Prade H. (1994) Similarity-based approximate reasoning. In: Computational Intelligence Imitating Life (Proc. IEEE Symp., Orlando, FL, June 27-July 1st, 1994) (J.M. Zurada et al., eds.), IEEE Press, New York, 69-80.
8. Dubois D., Prade H. (1995) Possibility theory as a basis for qualitative decision theory. Proc. of the 14th Inter. Joint Conf. on Artificial Intelligence (IJCAI'95), Montréal, Canada, Aug. 20-25, 1924-1930.
9. Dubois D., Prade H. (1996) What are fuzzy rules and how to use them. Fuzzy Sets and Systems, 84, 169-185.
10. Gilboa I., Schmeidler D. (1995) Case-based decision theory. The Quarterly J. of Economics, August, 607-639.
11. Jaczynski M., Trousse B. (1994) Fuzzy logic for the retrieval step of a case-based reasoner. Proc. of the EWCBR'94, 313-321.
12. Kolodner J. (1993) Case-Based Reasoning. Morgan Kaufmann, San Mateo, CA.
13. Léa Sombé (Group) (1990) Reasoning by analogy. In: Reasoning Under Incomplete Information in Artificial Intelligence. Wiley, New York, 418-424.
14. Plaza E., Esteva F., Garcia P., Godo L., López de Màntaras R. (1996) A logical approach to case-based reasoning using fuzzy similarity relations. To appear in Information Sciences.
15. Plaza E., Lopez de Mantaras R. (1990) A case-based apprentice that learns from fuzzy examples. In: Methodologies for Intelligent Systems, Vol. 5 (Z.W. Ras, M. Zemankova, M.L. Emrich, eds.), Elsevier, 420-427.
16. Ruspini E.H. (1991) On the semantics of fuzzy logic. Int. J. of Approximate Reasoning, 5, 45- 88.

Probabilistic Indexing for Case-Based Prediction

Boi Faltings

Artificial Intelligence Laboratory (LIA)
Computer Science Department (DI)
Swiss Federal Institute of Technology (EPFL)
IN-Ecublens, 1015 Lausanne, Switzerland

Abstract. The main assumption underlying case-based reasoning is that a problem with similar features as an earlier one is likely to have the same solution. However, this assumption has never been formally justified, and one can easily find practical situations where it is not true.

We use probablity theory to show that even if this fundamental assumption can be wrong for particular instances, it is guaranteed to be correct *on the average*, and this no matter what the probability distributions involved are. We define the concept of a *match weight* as a well-justified measure of similarity. We show how it is often possible to effectively compute a lower bound on match weight. We report on the performance of such bounds when used as a similarity measure in a simple example.

1 Introduction

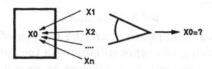

Fig. 1. *Task analyzed in this paper: predict the hidden result X_0.*

In this paper, we address the problem of predicting the value of an unobservable variable X_0 given the values of n observable and related variables $X_1, X_2, ..., X_n$, as illustrated in Figure 1. We call the observable variables *attributes* and the hidden one the *result*. Throughout the paper, we use upper case letters to denote variables, and corresponding lower case for their values; we refer to the observed values by $\hat{x}_1, \hat{x}_2, ..., \hat{x}_n$ and to the true value of the result as $\hat{x}_0$.

The relationship between attributes and result is known only through a set of representative *cases*. Each case is a record $C_i = (x_{i1}, x_{i2}, ..., x_{in}, x_{i0})$ containing the values of all attributes and the result for a particular previous experience.

The goal is to make an optimal prediction of the result given the observed attribute values and the case base. A simple example is prediction of credit risk, where $\{X_i\}$ are attributes describing the applicant and the desired loan and

$X_0 \in \{good, bad\}$. More generally, X_0 and also the attributes could be a vector of more complex values. This task is also assumed in [1, 3], and models most case-based reasoning systems.

We assume that the cases follow the same probability distributions as the scenarios presented for prediction. The optimal prediction is then the *maximum likelihood estimate*, i.e. $\hat{x}_0$ such that

$$pr(X_0 = \hat{x}_0 | X_1 = \hat{x}_1, ..., X_n = \hat{x}_n)$$

is maximal using the distribution of the precedent cases.

Recognition and Prediction The problem can pose itself in two forms, which we shall call *recognition* and *prediction*. In recognition, the observable attributes are a function of the class and some noise. A typical example of this is recognizing different animals given their features. Many statistical estimation techniques, including k-nearest neighbours, are designed for this model. It also implies that the attribute values are independent of one another given the class, so that the prediction problem can be solved using Bayesian inference ([7, 4]).

In prediction, it is the attributes which determine the result up to some noise. A typical example of this is predicting credit risk: presumably the different caracteristics of the loan will influence the course of events and lead to the credit being good or bad some time in the future. Now, it can no longer be assumed that the attributes are independent given the result: for example, the amount of the requested loan and the income of the applicant might well be statistically independent, but when it is known that the loan has been defaulted on it becomes far more likely that the amount was large with respect to income. A prediction using probabilistic inference would thus require the entire joint probability distribution

$$pr(X_0 | X_1, ..., X_n)$$

In the absence of background information, the number of examples required to estimate this distribution grows exponentially with the number of attributes. We assume here that the given data is insufficient to provide a sufficiently precise estimate of this distribution.

Prediction using base-based reasoning Case-based reasoning avoids the need for explicit probability distributions. Here, we find an earlier case which matches the current observations as closely as possible, and use its value of X_0 as the prediction. Thus, the problem is now no longer to find the maximum likelihood prediction, but to find the precedent which is most likely to have the same result as the observations, i.e. find a case X_i such that

$$pr(x_{i0} = \hat{x}_0 | x_{ij} = \hat{x}_j, x_{ik} = \hat{x}_k, ..., x_{il} = \hat{x}_l)$$

is maximized, where $j, k, ..., l$ are the indices of the matching attributes. We call this probability the *weight* associated with matching this set of attributes. The weight can be used as a similarity measure among cases: the higher the weight of a match, the larger the probability that it makes the correct prediction, and the more similar it is to the current situation. Whether the maximum weight match also gives the maximum likelihood prediction is an open research question.

A closer look at similarity The assumption underlying case-based reasoning is that the more similar a case is to the current problem, to more likely it is to provide the correct solution. Most measures of similarity have an ad-hoc character without formal justification, although analyses of certain measures have been proposed ([5, 9]). However, it is not always the case that higher similarity translates into higher prediction accuracy.

As an example, consider predicting the sucess of a company, characterized by two attributes:

- $X_1 = 1/0$ indicates that the company has/does not have debt
- $X_2 = 1/0$ indicates that it is a high-tech company or not

We would like to predict the value of attribute X_0 which is equal to 0 if the company is a failure, and 1 if it will be successful. Let the probability that $X_0 = 1$ given a certain combination of attributes values be given by the following table:

	$X_2 = 0$	$X_2 = 1$
$X_1 = 0$	0.9	0.6
$X_1 = 1$	0.4	0.5

and note that $pr(X_0 = 0) = 1 - pr(X_0 = 1)$. In a real application, this table would of course be unknown. Assume furthermore that all combinations of attribute values are equally likely, and that we have two sets of cases:

- set C_1: all cases where $X_1 = 0, X_2 = 1$
- set C_2: all cases where $X_1 = 0$

so that $C_2 \supseteq C_1$. We would like to predict the success of a company which has no debt and is a high-tech company, characterized by the vector $(\hat{x}_1 = 0, \hat{x}_2 = 1)$. A case in set C_1 provide a perfect match. Let's see if it also has the highest probability of a correct prediction. Using the table, we see that for our company, the real probability of success is 0.6, the probability of failure is 0.4. A case in C_1 predicts success and failure with the same probabilities, and thus the probability of its x_{10} making the correct prediction is:

$$pr(\hat{x}_0 = x_{10} = 0) + pr(\hat{x}_0 = x_{10} = 1) = 0.6^2 + 0.4^2 = 0.36 + 0.16 = 0.52$$

Now consider a arbitrary case in C_2. It predicts success with probability $0.5 \cdot (0.9+0.6) = 0.75$, failure with probability $1-0.75 = 0.25$. Hence, the probability of making the correct prediction when using an arbitrary case in C_2 is:

$$pr(\hat{x}_0 = x_{20} = 0) + pr(\hat{x}_0 = x_{20} = 1) = 0.6 \cdot 0.75 + 0.4 \cdot 0.25 = 0.45 + 0.1 = 0.55$$

Thus, using a case in C_2, obviously a worse match than a case in C_1, will on average result in a better prediction! Note that this characteristic is incompatible with many attempts at defining well-justified similarity metrics which are sensitive to particular values.

Notation Since the scenarios presented for prediction follow the same distribution as the cases themselves, they can be considered as additional members
of the case base for estimating the required probabilities. For the remainder of
this paper, we use underlines as a shorthand denoting matching arguments and
overlines as a shorthand for non-matching arguments of probablity distributions:

- $X_j = x_{ij}$ is written as $\underline{x_{ij}}$.
- $X_j = x_{ij}$ averaged over all possible values of x_{ij} is written as $\underline{X_j}$

The average is always taken over all value combinations of capitalized variables
in the formula. Thus, for example, we write:

$$pr(\underline{x_{50}}|\underline{x_{51}}, ..., \underline{x_{5n}}) \text{ for } pr(\hat{x}_0 = x_{50}|\hat{x}_1 = x_{51}, ..., \hat{x}_n = x_{5n})$$
$$pr(\underline{X_0}|\underline{X_1}, \underline{X_2}) \text{ for}$$
$$\sum_{x_{i0} \in X_0} \sum_{x_{i1} \in X_1} \sum_{x_{i2} \in X_2} pr(x_{i0}, x_{i1}, x_{i2}) \cdot pr(\hat{x}_0 = x_{i0}|\hat{x}_1 = x_{i1}, \hat{x}_2 = x_{i2})$$

2 Statistically independent attributes

Since it is unlikely that we will find a precedent which matches the observations
exactly, we will need to determine which partial match is most likely to give us
the best estimate of the classification. We define:

Definition 1. The *weight* of an attribute value $X_j = x_{ij}$ or a combination of
attribute values is the increase in the probability of correct prediction when the
attributes match over its a-priori value:

$$w(\underline{x_{ij}}) = pr(\underline{X_0}|\underline{x_{ij}}) - pr(\underline{X_0})$$
$$w(\underline{x_{ij}}, ..., \underline{x_{il}}) = pr(\underline{X_0}|\underline{x_{ij}}, ..., \underline{x_{il}}) - pr(\underline{X_0})$$

Under the assumption that the distribution of the precedents is the same as
the distribution of the observations, the weight can be computed from these as
follows:

$$w(\underline{x_{ij}}, ..., \underline{x_{il}}) = pr(\underline{X_0}|\underline{x_{ij}}, ..., \underline{x_{il}}) - pr(\underline{X_0})$$
$$= \sum_{x_{i0} \in X_0} pr(\underline{x_0}|\underline{x_{ij}}, ..., \underline{x_{il}})^2 - pr(\underline{x_0})^2$$

Applying these definitions to the example in the introduction, we find:

$$pr(\underline{X_0}) = (0.6^2 + 0.4^2) = 0.52$$
$$w(x_1 = 0) = 0.55 - 0.52 = 0.03$$
$$w(x_1 = 0, x_2 = 1) = 0.52 - 0.52 = 0$$

so that for these particular values the weight of only matching X_1 is indeed
higher than that of matching both X_1 and X_2!

Average weights A more intuitive result can be obtained if instead of considering the weights of matches or mismatches with *particular values*, we only consider the *average* weights of matches or mismatches in a certain attribute. We thus define:

Definition 2. The *average weight* $W(\underline{X})$ of matching an attribute X is the average of $w(X = x_i)$ over all possible values x_i of the attribute:

$$W(\underline{X}) = \sum_{x_i \in X} pr(X = x_i)w(X = x_i)$$

Applying these definitions to the example in the introduction, we now have:

$$W(\underline{X_1, X_2}) = \sum_{x_1, x_2 \in \{0,1\}} pr(X_1 = x_1, X_2 = x_2)w(X_1 = x_1, X_2 = x_2)$$

$$= 0.25 \cdot (0.9^2 + 0.1^2) + 0.25 \cdot (0.6^2 + 0.4^2) + 0.25 \cdot (0.4^2 + 0.6^2) +$$
$$0.25 \cdot (0.5^2 + 0.5^2) - (0.6^2 + 0.4^2)$$

$$= 0.205 + 0.13 + 0.13 + 0.125 - 0.52 = 0.59 - 0.52 = 0.07$$

as the average weight for matching both attributes, and

$$W(\underline{X_1}) = \sum_{x_1 \in \{0,1\}} pr(X_1 = x_1)w(\underline{x_1})$$

$$= 0.5 \cdot (0.75^2 + 0.25^2 - 0.52) + 0.5 \cdot (0.45^2 + 0.55^2 - 0.52)$$

$$= 0.045$$

as the average weight for matching X_1 only, so that *on average* also matching X_2 does produce better results!

Case-based reasoning works on the average It turns out that in fact, the intuition underlying case-based reasoning is in fact always correct as long as only *average* weights are considered:

Theorem 3. *Independently of the probability distributions, the average weight $W(\underline{X})$ of any attribute or combination of attributes X is always non-negative.*

Proof:
Observe that by Jensen's inequality and the convexity of squaring, for any x_0:

$$\sum_{x_i \in X} pr(X = x_i)pr(X_0 = x_0 | X = x_i)^2 \geq \left[\sum_{x_i \in X} pr(X = x_i)pr(X_0 = x_0 | X = x_i)\right]^2$$

$$= pr(X_0 = x_0)^2$$

so that:

$$W(\underline{X_i}) = \sum_{x_0 \in X_0} \left[\sum_{x_i \in X} pr(X = x_i)pr(X_0 = x_0 | X = x_i)^2\right] - pr(X_0 = x_0)^2$$

$$\geq \sum_{x_0 \in X_0} pr(X_0 = x_0)^2 - pr(X_0 = x_0)^2 = 0$$

and the theorem is proven.

QED

For independent attributes, we can show an even stronger theorem:

Theorem 4. *Given a sets of attributes A and an attribute B which is* statistically independent *of all attributes in A:*

$$W(\underline{A}) + W(\underline{B}) \leq W(\underline{A}, \underline{B})$$

Proof: Without loss of generality, we assume A to be single attribute; if A is a set of attributes, it can be regarded as a single vector-valued attribute. We prove the theorem by induction over the sets of possible values that the attributes A and B can take. For the base of the induction, assume that A can take only a single value, whereas B can take n values. Then, attribute A is always matched, thus $W(\underline{A}) = 0$ and $W(\underline{A}, \underline{B}) = W(\underline{B})$, and the theorem is true.

Now assume that the theorem holds for any A with up to k attribute values, and B takes n values. Let A be an attribute with $k+1$ values, labelled v_1 through v_{k+1}. Define a new attribute A' with k values v_1' through v_k' such that:

$$v_i' = v_i, i = 1..k - 1$$
$$v_k' = v_k \vee v_{k+1}$$

so that A' takes the same values as A except that it takes values v_k' whenever A takes values v_k or v_{k+1}. We define the following shorthand notation:

$$p = pr(A = v_k)$$
$$q = pr(A = v_{k+1})$$
$$r = pr(\underline{X_0}|A = v_k, B = x_j)$$
$$s = pr(\underline{X_0}|A = v_{k+1}, B = x_j)$$
$$t = \sum_{x_j \in B} pr(B = x_j)pr(\underline{X_0}|A = v_k, B = x_j)$$
$$u = \sum_{x_j \in B} pr(B = x_j)pr(\underline{X_0}|A = v_{k+1}, B = x_j)$$

Since most terms in the weight calculations involving A and A' are identical, the following differences only involve the terms referring to v_k and v_{k+1}; we have:

$W(\underline{A}, \underline{B}) - W(\underline{A'}, \underline{B})$

$$= \sum_{x_0 \in X_0} \sum_{x_j \in B} pr(B = x_j)pr^2 + qs^2 - \frac{1}{p+q}[(pr)^2 + (qs)^2]$$

$$= \sum_{x_0 \in X_0} \sum_{x_j \in B} pr(B = x_j)\frac{1}{p+q}\left\{p^2r^2 + pqr^2 + pqs^2 + q^2s^2 - p^2r^2 - q^2s^2\right\}$$

$$= \sum_{x_0 \in X_0} \sum_{x_j \in B} pr(B = x_j)\frac{pq}{p+q}(r^2 + s^2)$$

and:

$$W(\underline{A}) - W(\underline{A'}) = \sum_{x_0 \in X_0} pt^2 + qu^2 - \frac{1}{p+q}[(pt)^2 + (qu)^2]$$

$$= \sum_{x_0 \in X_0} \frac{pq}{p+q}(t^2 + u^2)$$

so that:

$$[W(\underline{A}, \underline{B}) - W(\underline{A}) - W(\underline{B})] - [W(\underline{A'}, \underline{B}) - W(\underline{A'}) - W(\underline{B})] =$$

$$\sum_{x_0 \in X_0} \frac{pq}{p+q} \left\{ [\sum_{x_j \in B} pr(B = x_j)(r^2 + s^2)] - (t^2 + u^2) \right\} =$$

$$\sum_{x_0 \in X_0} \frac{pq}{p+q} \left\{ [\sum_{x_j \in B} pr(B = x_j)r^2] - t^2 + [\sum_{x_j \in B} pr(B = x_j)s^2] - u^2 \right\}$$

$$\geq 0$$

since by Jensen's inequality:

$$[\sum_{x_j \in B} pr(B = x_j)r^2] - t^2$$

$$= [\sum_{x_j \in B} pr(B = x_j)r^2] - \left\{ \sum_{x_j \in B} pr(B = x_j)pr(\underline{X_0}|A = v_k, B = x_j) \right\}^2$$

$$\geq [\sum_{x_j \in B} pr(B = x_j)r^2] - [\sum_{x_j \in B} pr(B = x_j)pr(\underline{X_0}|A = v_k, B = x_j)^2]$$

$$= \sum_{x_j \in B} pr(B = x_j)(r^2 - r^2) = 0$$

and similarly

$$[\sum_{x_j \in B} pr(B = x_j)s^2] - u^2 \geq 0$$

Since the theorem is satisfied for A', which has only k values, it is also satisfied for A. This completes the induction, and the theorem is proven.
QED

3 Dealing with dependent attributes

With the exception of Theorem 3, all results so far have assumed that attributes are statistically independent of one another. In reality, such independence will occur only very rarely. This can have dramatic effects. For example, let X and Y be two attributes such that always $X = Y$. Thus, whenever X matches, Y will also match, and the weight $W(\underline{X}, \underline{Y}) = W(\underline{X}) = W(\underline{Y})$!

Practical experience has shown that in many practical problems, attribute dependence can be modelled using probabilistic networks ([7, 2]). A probabilistic network is a directed acyclic graph whose nodes are attributes and whose arcs indicate statistical dependencies between nodes. Nodes are statistically dependent only on their direct parents, i.e. if node x has parents $y_0, .., y_k$, then for any other set of nodes Z:

$$pr(x|y_0, ..., y_k, Z) = pr(x|y_0, ..., y_k)$$

More important than the links which are present in the network are those which are absent; these indicate independence relations. More precisely, any pair of nodes x_1 and x_2 with parents Z_1 and Z_2 and not having a path between them is statistically independent given $Z_1 \cup Z_2$, i.e.:

$$pr(x_1|x_2, Z_1 \cup Z_2, Y) = pr(x_1|Z_1 \cup Z_2)$$

This result was proven by Olmsted ([6]); it also figures as Corrolary 4 on page 120 of [7]. Thus, two variables X and Y which have no direct link between them are *conditionally independent* given the values of their common ancestors Z:

$$pr(X = x, Y = y|Z) = pr(X = x|Z) \cdot pr(Y = y|Z)$$

Conditional weights We define the *conditional weight* of a set of matching or mismatching attributes A given a set of matching or mismatching attributes B:

$$W(\underline{A}|\underline{B}) = W(\underline{A}, \underline{B}) - W(\underline{B})$$

We can now prove:

Theorem 5. *Assume that X and Y are conditionally independent given an attribute or set of attributes Z. Then:*

$$W(\underline{X}|\underline{Z}) + W(\underline{Y}|\underline{Z}) \leq W(\underline{XY}|\underline{Z})$$

Proof: We apply the following transformations:

$$W(\underline{X}|\underline{Z}) = W(\underline{X}, \underline{Z}) - W(\underline{Z})$$
$$= \sum_{z \in Z} pr(z) \cdot [pr(\underline{X_0}|\underline{X}, z) - pr(\underline{X_0}|z)]$$

$$W(\underline{Y}|\underline{Z}) = \sum_{z \in Z} pr(z) \cdot [pr(\underline{X_0}|\underline{Y}, z) - pr(\underline{X_0}|z)]$$

$$W(\underline{X}, \underline{Y}|\underline{Z}) = \sum_{z \in Z} pr(z) \cdot [pr(\underline{X_0}|\underline{X}, \underline{Y}, z) - pr(\underline{X_0}|z)]$$

We now prove the theorem by showing that the inequality holds for every z, i.e. we show that:

$$pr(\underline{X_0}|\underline{X}, z) - pr(\underline{X_0}|z) + pr(\underline{X_0}|\underline{Y}, z) - pr(\underline{X_0}|z) \leq pr(\underline{X_0}|\underline{X}, \underline{Y}, z) - pr(\underline{X_0}|z)$$

Let $p_z(\cdot)$ be the probability distribution $pr(\cdot)$ conditioned on $\underline{z}$. By the assumption of conditional independence, $p_z(\underline{X_0}, \underline{X})$ and $p_z(\underline{X_0}, \underline{Y})$ are independent probability distributions. Also define $W_z(\cdot) = p_z(\underline{X_0}|\cdot) - p_z(\underline{X_0})$, so that we have:

$$W_z(\underline{X}) + W_z(\underline{Y}) \leq W_z(\underline{X}, \underline{Y})$$

Since X and Y are independent with respect to this weight calculation, this inequality is true by Theorem 4, and so the theorem is proven. QED.

4 Using weights as similarity metrics

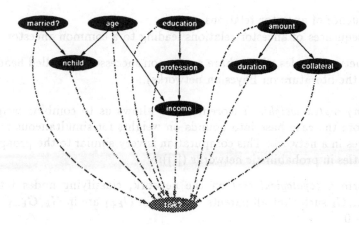

Fig. 2. *Example of assessing credit risk.*

Since match weights give the probability that a case makes the correct prediction, they would make an ideal similarity metric for indexing cases. This requires in particular an efficient way of computing match weights for any combination of features. Note that estimating match weights for large combinations of features directly from the case base will give inaccurate values due to an insufficient number of examples. Conditional independence relations provide a way to obtain a lower bound on the match weight given the match weights for small combinations of features. This lower bound could be used as a similarity metric, and we now give an algorithm for computing it.

A synthetic example of assessing credit risk is used to illustrate. It has 9 attributes whose dependencies are accurately characterized by the graph shown in Figure 2. Credit risk (good/bad) is computed as a deterministic function of all attributes. As an example, assume that we want to know the weight of matching a case in attributes X_3, X_4, X_5, X_6, X_7 and X_8.

Bounding match weights The algorithm for bounding match weights has the following steps:

1. reduce the probabilistic network for all attributes to one which contains only those that participate in the match.
2. perform a topological sort, ordering the nodes in the network so that every node is only connected to predecessors in this ordering.
3. approximate the conditional match weights for all attributes and arcs in the network by counting out in the case base.
4. compute the weight of the combined match by composition.

In general, it will be very rare for *all* attributes in the case description to match the observations. The first step is thus to construct a *reduced* probabilistic network containing only attributes which participate in the match. In this new network, paths through nodes which have been eliminated are replaced by direct links. Such direct links must be created for all paths which are either:

- a sequence of ancestor relations, or
- two sequences of ancestor relations leading to a common ancestor.

but not between nodes which share a common successor (so-called head-to-head nodes in the literature on Bayesian networks).

Combining match weights Theorem 4 now allows us to combine weights estimated from the case base into bounds on weights for simultaneous matches of all features in a network. This computation is very similar to the proapgation of probabilities in probabilistic networks ([7]):

1. perform a *topological sort* on the network, classifying nodes into classes $G_0, ..., G_k$ such that all parents of nodes in G_{k+1} are in $G_k, G_{k-1}, ..., G_0$.
2. $W \leftarrow 0$
3. for i $\leftarrow$ 0 to k do
   - for all $X \in G_i$ with ancestors Y: estimate $W(\underline{X}|\underline{Y})$ from the case base and set $W \leftarrow W + W(\underline{X}|\underline{Y})$

In this example, we have two classes: $G_0 = \{X_3, X_6, X_7\}$ and $G_1 = \{X_4, X_5, X_8\}$. Thus, we require the weights $W(\underline{X_3}), W(\underline{X_6})$ and $W(\underline{X_7})$ as well as the conditional weights $W(\underline{X_4}|\underline{X_3}), W(\underline{X_5}|\underline{X_4}, \underline{X_6})$ and $W(\underline{X_8}|\underline{X_7})$.

Approximating match weights from the case base Average weights can be precomputed by counting out all pairs of matching cases. For computing the weight of the combination $W(\underline{X_k}, \underline{X_l}, ..., \underline{X_m})$, the algorithm would be as follows:

1. $W_t \leftarrow 0, W_f \leftarrow 0$
2. for all pairs of cases C_i, C_j
   matching in $X_k, X_l, ..., X_m$ do

   if $x_{0i} = x_{0j}$ then $W_t \leftarrow W_t + 1$
   else $W_f \leftarrow W_f + 1$.

3. return $\frac{W_i}{W_j+W_i}$

This algorithm can also be used to estimate several match weights in parallel during a single pass over all case combinations. Conditional match weights are best computed using the formula:

$$W(\underline{A}|\underline{B}) = W(\underline{A}, \underline{B}) - W(\underline{B})$$

Dealing with inexact matches Weights are computed only for attributes which match exactly. For attributes with a large number or values, such as numbers, this will rarely be the case. It would be desirable to take into account imprecise matches in such attributes as well.

Plaza ([8]) has studied similarity measures where attribute values are grouped into a hierarchy such that all values in a group share some similarities. For example, an attribute taking as values real numbers between 0 and 10 could be represented by a hierarchy of intervals:

- level 0: [0..10]
- level 1: [0..4], [5..10]
- level 2: [0..2],[3..4],[5..7],[8..10]
- level 3: 0,1,2,3,4,5,6,7,8,9,10

Now, a match can occur at different levels. For example, values 2 and 5 would match at level 0, whereas 5 and 7 would match at level 2. Depending on the level of the match, its contribution to the total similarity can be smaller or greater.

Such hierarchies can be applied to weight computations as well and significantly improve accuracy. Now, we consider every level in the hierarchy a separate attribute, and compute weights for matches at all levels in the hierarchy. This results in much higher weights and thus greater confidence in the prediction.

5 Discussion

Most existing theoretical analyses of statistical prediction have considered the *classification* problem, where attributes can be assumed to provide independent evidence to the classification; examples of this are work in Bayesian inference ([7, 2]) as well as k-nearest neighbour classifiers.

In this paper, we have instead considered the *prediction* problem, where the contributions of attributes are not independent. The case-based reasoning approach is promising for this problem class because it does not require any assumptions about the nature of the relationship between attributes and the result. owever, assumptions about the attribute-class relationship are often introduced in the similarity measure used for case indexing. The analysis in this paper does not require any such assumption.

The main novel results of this paper are that on average, increased similarity does indeed lead to improved prediction *independently of how attributes and classes are distributed*, and that furthermore it is possible to compute lower bounds on the true probability of correct prediction.

In practice, these lower bounds seem to provide very powerful similarity metrics, although our experiments are still too rudimentary to give definite conclusions. The sum of the weight and the a-priori probability of correct prediction is equal to the probability that the case makes the correct prediction. If it is close to 1, which is often the case in our synthetic example, this provides a good confidence measure for using the particular case. In applications where bounds are always much smaller than 1, this is an indication that either the case base is really much too sparse, or that the attributes used are not the right ones for classification. In this case, the bounds may also help in guiding the search for attributes which would allow more accurate classification.

Acknowledgements

Part of this work was carried out while the author was on leave at NEC Research Institute, Princeton, NJ; the generous support is gratefully acknowledged. I would also like to thank Marek Blaszczyk for the implementation example.

References

1. **R.H. Creecy, B.M. Masand, S.J. Smith, D.L.Waltz**: "Trading MIPS and Memory for Knowledge Engineering," *Communications of the ACM* 35(8), August 1992
2. **D. Heckerman**: "Probabilistic Similarity Networks," *MIT Press*, 1990
3. **S. Kasif, S. Salzberg, D. Waltz, J. Rachlin, D. Aha**: "Towards a Framework for Memory-Based Reasoning," NECI Technical Report 95-132, December 1995
4. **P. Myllymäki, H. Tirri**: "Massively Parralel Case-Based Reasoning with Probabilistic Similarity Metrics," *Proceedings of the 1st European Workshop on Case-based Reasoning*, Lecture Notes in Artificial Intelligence 837, pp. 145-154, Springer Verlag, 1993
5. **S. Okamoto, K. Satoh**: "An Average-Case Analysis of k-Nearest Neighbor Classifier," *Proceedings of the 1st International Confernce on Case-based Reasoning*, Lecture Notes in Artificial Intelligence 1010, pp. 253-264, Springer Verlag, 1995
6. **S. Olmsted**: "On representing and solving decision problems," Ph.D. Thesis, Department of Engineering - Economic Systems, Stanford University, 1983
7. **J. Pearl**: "Probabilistic Reasoning in Intelligent Systems," Morgan-Kaufmann, 1988
8. **E. Plaza, R. López de Mántaras, E. Armengol**: "On the Importance of Similitude: An Entropy-Based Assessment," *Proceedings of the 3rd European Workshop on Case-based Reasoning*, Lecture Notes in Computer Science 1168, pp. 324-338, Springer Verlag, 1996
9. **M.M. Richter**: "On the Notion of Similarity in Case-Based Reasoning," in G. della Riccia et al (eds.): *Mathematical and Statistical Methods in Artificial Intelligence*, Springer Verlag 1995, pp. 171-184

A Probabilistic Model for Case-Based Reasoning

Andrés F. Rodríguez1, Sunil Vadera[1] and L. Enrique Sucar[2]

[1] University of Salford
Department of Mathematics and Computer Science
Salford, M5 4WT,
{A.Rodriguez / S.Vadera}@cms.salford.ac.uk
[2] ITESM - Campus Morelos
AP C-99, Cuernavaca, Mor., 62020, Mexico
esucar@campus.mor.itesm.mx

Abstract. An exemplar-based model with foundations in Bayesian networks is described. The proposed model utilises two Bayesian networks: one for indexing of categories, and another for identifying exemplars within categories. Learning is incrementally conducted each time a new case is classified. The representation structure dynamically changes each time a new case is classified and a coverage function is used as a basis for selecting suitable exemplars. Finally, a simple example is given to illustrate the concepts in the model.

1 Introduction

Organizing and indexing cases in memory is a fundamental part of *case-based reasoning* (CBR) that involves learning and reasoning processes. This problem can be divided into two parts. The first is the selection of the features of the cases that can be used to index and retrieve the cases. The second is the organisation of the case memory so that the case retrieval process is efficient and accurate.

One approach that has been used to address this problem has been to store all the cases and develop algorithms to partition the search space for retrieving similar cases. So for example, systems like REMIND provide a tree induction algorithm that can be used to avoid examining all the cases. This kind of approach is particularly useful when large databases of cases are already available. However, when cases are not available in advance, and the domain is not well defined this approach is more difficult to apply.

An alternative approach, that is perhaps more applicable to such situations, is to store only prototypical cases. This approach, known as the *exemplar-based* model has its basis in cognitive theories, which postulate that concepts can be represented by exemplars [14, 15, 9]. However, previous implementations of the exemplar-based models have struggled to produce systems that can be justified in a rational manner. For example, the Protos system [3] uses many heuristics and mechanisms for combining evidence that are hard to justify independently of its original application.

Hence, this paper attempts to develop an exemplar-based model with foundations that utilise Bayesian models. First, it describes the main problems that need to be solved to achieve exemplar-based reasoning. Then, a new exemplar-based model is proposed. Both learning and classification algorithms for the proposed model are presented and illustrated with an example.

2 Exemplar-based models: the problem

An exemplar-based model is thought to be particularly appropriate for weak domains [13], where it is difficult to define categories by explicitly using classical membership constraints [4]. For such situations, which can be common in real applications, an exemplar-based model may provide a better representation of the categories. Figure 1 illustrates the idea of a weak domain together with cases, exemplars, and categories. It shows two categories, A, B (the solid lines), that each have exemplars that represent regions (the dashed lines) that contain cases (the dots).

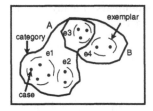

Fig. 1. Cases, exemplars and categories in a weak domain.

To illustrate the problem, suppose that the category A is represented by the exemplars e_1, e_2, and e_3 and the category B is represented by the exemplars e_3 and e_4. Also suppose that the exemplars e_1, e_2, e_3, and e_4 currently represent 4, 2, 3, and 2 cases respectively. Now suppose that a new case is given. The following two functions must be provided by an exemplar-based model:

1. Determine the exemplar that best classifies the new case given the available information.
2. Determine how knowing the new instance and its classification it can be used to improve the accuracy of the model.

The first of these functions is a classification task, while the second can be viewed as a supervised learning task [1]. The next section describes the representation used, and section 4 presents the classification and learning algorithms.

3 Representation

In the proposed model, the case memory (CB) is represented by a set of categories $\{C_1, \cdots, C_n\}$ which are not necessarily disjoint. A *category* C_j is represented by a set of exemplars $\{e_{1j}, \cdots, e_{mj}\}$. An exemplar e_{ij}, which depicts a set of "similar" cases, is represented by a set of features $\{f_a, \cdots, f_g\}$. A *case* c_{kij} is represented by a set of features $\{f_1, \cdots, f_p\}$ and a *feature* is a term that represents a binary variable.

The model uses two *Bayesian networks* [8] as shown Fig. 2.

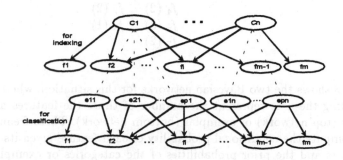

Fig. 2. Bayesian networks for indexing and classification.

The first Bayesian network (BN) is used as an index structure to categories. The second BN defines the relationships between the features and the exemplars. These networks are used in two stages as follows:

1. Given the features of a new case, the first network is used to determine the probability of each category $P(C_j|nc)$. This information ranks the order in which the categories can be searched for a similar exemplar.
2. Each category can then be investigated, in order of rank, to find an exemplar that is "similar" to a new case. That is, within a selected category, the second network is used to calculate the probability of each exemplar given the features of the new case. Thus, "similarity" is interpreted as the probability that an exemplar represents a case.

The decision of when to stop investigating is normally application dependent. A user may want to stop as soon as an exemplar with a *high* probability (e.g., above 0.9) is found, or the user may prefer to obtain all the exemplars with a probability above a threshold value.

To illustrate the representation, suppose we continue with the example of Fig. 1. Suppose each category is defined as shown below. The numbers in the exemplars indicate the actual cases that have been classified (or are represented) by the exemplar and the numbers in the features indicate the frequency of the feature in the exemplar. So, for example, e_1 is known to represent four actual cases and the feature f_1 occurs three times. Notice that the exemplar e_3 is in both categories.

category : A   exemplars : e_1 (4) e_2 (2) e_3 (3)

features : f_1 (3) f_2 (2) f_2 (1)
             f_2 (4) f_4 (2) f_4 (2)
             f_3 (2) f_5 (1) f_6 (3)
                                         f_7 (2)

category : B   exemplars : e_3 (3) e_4 (2)

features : f_2 (1) f_2 (2)
             f_4 (2) f_7 (2)
             f_6 (3) f_8 (1)
             f_7 (2)

Figure 3 shows the two Bayesian networks for this situation, where the numbers labelling the arcs represent the number of times the features are true in a category (top network) or exemplar (bottom network). These frequencies are used to compute the conditional probability of each feature given its categories or exemplars and the prior probabilities of the categories or exemplars in the Bayesian networks.

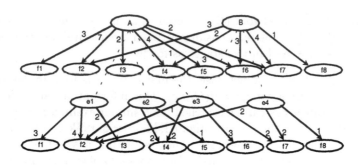

Fig. 3. The organisation structure.

4   Classification and learning

This section presents the classification and learning algorithms. Figure 4 shows the classification algorithm of the proposed model. For simplicity and conciseness, we present a version that stops as soon as an exemplar is found whose conditional probability is above a user defined threshold.

The first step of the algorithm computes the conditional probabilities of the categories given the features. This computation is carried out by propagation

```
Classify(nc, e_c, CL)

Input: A new case described by a set of features nc = {f_a, · · · , f_i}
Results: The category list CL, and the exemplar e_c that is "similar".

The following local variables are used:
    H is a list sorted of categories
    E is a list sorted of exemplars
    C_c is the current category
    done is a boolean variable

Step 1. Rank the Categories

    Compute conditional probabilities in the first BN, i.e., the category-features BN

    Compute P(C_j|nc)        ∀C_j ∈ CB
    Set H to the list of categories ranked in descending order of P(C_j|nc)

Step 2. Determination of an Exemplar

    e_c = nil
    C_c = first(H)              The list H returns ∅ at the end
    done = false

    while (not done) and (C_c ≠ ∅) do begin

        Compute conditional probabilities in the second BN, i.e., the exemplar-features BN

        Compute P(e_i|nc)      ∀e_i ∈ C_c
        Set E to the list of exemplars in C_c ranked in descending order of P(e_i|nc)

        e_c = first(E)
        if P(e_c|nc) > threshold then
            done = true
        else
            C_c = next(H)
            end(if)
    end(while)

    if done then
        CL = all categories that contain (e_c)
    else
        e_c = nil
        CL = ∅
    end(if)
```

Fig. 4. Classification algorithm

techniques used for singly connected networks developed by Pearl [12]. These probabilities are then used to rank the categories. The second step then searches through the ranked list of categories for the first exemplar whose conditional probability is above the threshold. Then the exemplar confirms the hypothesis and the search process finishes.

Figure 5 shows the learning algorithm. It uses a training case and its categories[3] in an attempts to improve the accuracy of the model.

Input: A training case described by a set of features $nc = \{f_a, \cdots, f_i\}$ and
a set of categories $L = (C_o, \cdots, C_p)$ to which it *jointly* belongs.
Results: Updating model for CBR.

The following local variables are used:
CL is a list of categories that classify the nc
e_c is the exemplar that classifies the nc

$Classify(nc, e_c, CL)$

if $(CL = \emptyset)$ then
    $e_c = nc$
    for each category $C_k \in L$ do begin
        add_exemplar(e_c, C_k)
        return;
end(if)

Learning
if $L = CL$ then
    $e_c = coverage(e_c, nc)$
else
    $e_c = nc$
    add_exemplar(e_c, C_k) $\forall C_k \in L$
end(if)

Fig. 5. Learning algorithm

The learning procedure works as follows. First it obtains the behaviour of the current model by using the classification procedure to return the categories which would jointly classify the training example. If no categories are found by classifying ($CL = \emptyset$), then the training case is added as an exemplar to all its categories[4]. If classifying does return a list of categories, there are two situations. First, if the returned list is not the same as the training case's categories, then the case is added as an exemplar to each of its categories. Notice, that the test is for equivalence since the training case's categories are viewed as a joint category. Alternatively, if the predicted list of categories corresponds to the actual joint categories then we have to consider whether to retaining the training instance as an exemplar, and whether it should replace the exemplar that was used to classify it. But how can we decide whether the new case is a better exemplar? To answer this, we need to return to the definition of a prototype. Usually, by a prototype, we mean a representative case that denotes a set of cases bound together by family resemblance [14] . In the situation under consideration, a

---

[3] An exemplar can be in several categories
[4] This may also involve creating categories

good exemplar will be one that represents a region consisting of cases that have roughly the same kind of features (i.e. family resemblance). Further, a case is a good prototype if it is a focal point of its category [5]. By this, we mean the case must share most of its features with many of the cases in its category. Hence, one measure of "goodness" of an exemplar is the number of times its features occur amongst the other cases in the same category. This function can be defined as the coverage:

Definition 1: Coverage

Given an set of similar cases $\{c_1, \cdots, c_s\}$
each one represented by a set of features $\{f_1, \cdots, f_p\}$

$$Coverage\ c_i = \sum_{n=1}^{p}\ frequency(f_n)$$

Now, returning to the earlier example, suppose that we have the following new training case: $c_{12} = \{f_4, f_6, f_7, f_9\}$ and it is correctly classified by exemplar e_3. Its features and their frequencies are summarised in Table 1.

Table 1. Coverage of cases in a updated set of similar cases

	c_3	c_{12}	frequency
	f_2		1
	f_4	f_4	3
	f_6	f_6	4
	f_7	f_7	3
		f_9	2
coverage		11	12

Then, since c_{12} gives greater coverage, the model changes as shown in Fig. 6.

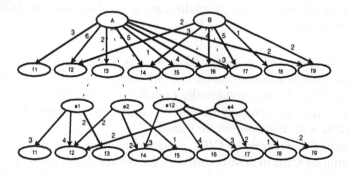

Fig. 6. The updated organisation structure.

5 Related work

The proposed model uses Bayesian networks for an incremental exemplar-based classification. The related work can therefore be classified in three groups. (i) inductive models with supervised learning, (ii) exemplar-based models, and (iii) use of Bayesian models in CBR.

Each of these groups has been extensively covered in the literature. The first group includes work such as that on *instance-based learning* (IBL) algorithms [1], and explanation based learning [10]. The work on exemplar-based models includes that of Biberman, who examined the role of prototypicality [5], and the work on Protos [3]. The use of Bayesian networks in CBR is increasing rapidly and includes the work of Aha and Chang [2], Myllymäki and Tirri [11],Breese and Heckerman [6], Chang and Harrison [7]. For conciseness, this section summarises the relationship with Protos, and only some of the main aspects of other systems that use Bayesian networks. The reader is referred to the work by Aha and Chang [2] for a more detailed account of other approaches to the use of Bayesian neetworks in CBR.

Protos is perhaps the best known exemplar-based system [3]. It is available for academic use for experimental purposes and has therefore been well studied. In terms of the stages, Protos is quite similar to the proposed model. However, there are three significant differences. First, in Protos, an exemplar is represented by a prototypical case while in the proposed model, an exemplar is represented by a Bayesian network, where the random variables of the network are determined by the prototypical case. Second, the proposed model uses Bayesian networks in the retrieval process instead of heuristics for setting up and using indices (e.g., remindings, difference links, censors) thereby providing a better foundation for the proposed model. Thirdly, in the learning phase, Protos learns the importance of its indices by explanation while the proposed model learns directly from the data. Also, Protos retains those cases that are not correctly classified as new exemplars. Cases that are correctly classified result in an increase of an exemplar's prototypicality but are discarded. In contrast, the proposed model attempts to use the notion of prototypicality to determine if a new case, that is correctly classified, would make a better exemplar.

The following summarises the main aspects of other work on CBR that uses Bayesian networks.

- The model proposed by Myllymäki and Tirri [11] integrates Bayesian reasoning and CBR in a connectionist network for case matching and adaptation. This model is limited to mutually exclusive case set and the cases must be complete (i.e. are not polymorphic). Namely, all the cases have the same attributes with their respective values
- A Bayesian framework for CBR, proposed by Tirri et al [16], uses Bayesian reasoning for CBR in data-intensive tasks. Although the goals of this model is similar to the proposed model, their approach is different in that it performs *unsupervised* learning and required a large database of fixed format cases.

- Breese and Heckerman [6] integrated the Bayesian and CBR approaches for diagnostic purposes. They used a three-layer Bayes net to link the causes of cases (called, *issues*) with observable *symptoms*. Then, when some evidence is available, it is propagated in the networks to identify the most probable cases. The most probable cases are then used as a basis for diagnosing the fault and determining a cost-effective solution.
- Chang and Harrison [7] used a Bayesian approach to guide retrieval and indexing as part of an experimental testbed that includes other techniques. Their case representation was a flat set of features and they allow a user to experiment with different instance selection algorithms. The instance selection schemes have similar goals to exemplar selection but are not based on notions of protypicality or focality as in the proposed model.
- Aha and Chang [2] use a Bayesian network and CBR to work cooperatively on multiagent planning tasks. The Bayesian networks are used to characterize actions selection whereas CBR is used to determine how to implement actions. That, is unlike the proposed model, their model does not aim to utilize Bayesian networks for CBR, but instead combines the mutual strengths to solve a particular task.

6 Conclusion and future work

This paper proposes an exemplar-based model with foundations in Bayesian networks. The model utilises two networks: one for ranking categories, and another for identifying exemplars within categories. This view of exemplar-based models leads to the notion of assessing similarity by conditional probabilities. Thus in classification, one can obtain the probability of an exemplar given the features of the new case.

Learning is incrementally conducted each time a new case is classified. When a new training case is well classified the model determines whether the new case will make a better exemplar than the one used to classify it. This is achieved by the utilising the notion of prototypicality and focality to suggest a the "goodness" of an exemplar measure that is called coverage. When a new case is not properly classified, it is simply added to all the categories to which it belongs. Both situations update the representation structure to improve the accuracy of the model.

Current work is carrying out an empirical evaluation which would be available in the near future. Future work will consider dependencies among features in order to increase the expressivity of the model.

7 Acknowledgements

The authors are grateful to David Aha, whose comments on earlier versions of this work and directions to related references have been most valuable.

References

1. D.W. Aha. Case-based learning algorithms. In *Proc. of the DARPA Case-Based Reasoning Workshop*, pages 147–158, Washington, D.C.: Morgan Kaufmann, 1991.
2. D.W. Aha and L.W. Chang. Cooperative bayesian and case-based reasoning for solving multiagent planning tasks. Technical Report AIC-96-005, Navy Center for Applied Research in AI Naval Research Laboratory, Washington, DC, U.S.A., 1996.
3. R. Bareiss. *Exemplar-based knowledge acquisition. A unified approach to concept representation, classification, and learning.* Academic Press Inc., Harcourt Brace Jovanovich Publishers, San Diego, Calif., U.S.A., 1989.
4. H.W. Beck, T. Anwar, and S.B. Navathe. A conceptual clustering algorithm for database schema design. *IEEE Transaction on Knowledge and Data Engineering*, 6(3):396–411, 1994.
5. Y. Biberman. The role of prototypicality in exemplar-based learning. In Nada Lavrač and Stefan Wrobel, editors, *Proc. Machine Learning: ECML-95, 8th European Conference on Machine Learning*, pages 77–91, Heraclion, Crete, Greece, 1995.
6. J.S. Breese and D. Heckerman. Decision-theoretic case-based reasoning. In *Proc. of the Fifth International Workshop on Artificial Intelligence and Statistics*, pages 56–63, Ft. Lauderdale, U.S.A., 1995.
7. L. Chang and P. Harrison. A case-based reasoning testbed for experiments in adaptive memory retrieval and indexing. In D.H. Aha and A. Ram, editors, *Proc. of the AAAI fall Symposium on Adaptation of Knowledge for Reuse*, Menlo Park: AAAI Press., 1995.
8. T. Dean, J. Allen, and Y. Aloimonos. *Artificial Intelligence theory and practice.* The Benjamin/Cummings Publishing Company, Inc., Redwood City, Calif., U.S.A., 1995.
9. D.L. Medin and M.M. Schaffer. Contex theory of clasification learning. *Psychological Review*, 85:207–238, 1978.
10. S. Minton, J.G. Carbonell, C.A. Knoblock, D.R. Kuokka, O. Etzioni, and Y. Gil. Explanation-based learning: a problem solving perspective. In Jaime Carbonell, editor, *Machine Learning: Paradigms and Methods*, pages 63–118. MIT/Elsevier Science, Cambridge, Massachusetts, U.S.A., 1990.
11. P. Myllymäki and H. Tirri. Massively parallel case-based reasoning with probabilistic similarity metrics. In Klauss-Dieter Althoff Stefan Wess and Michael M. Ritcher, editors, *Topics in Case-Based Reasoning*, pages 144–154. Volume 837, Lecture Notes in Artificial Intelligence. Springer Verlag, 1994.
12. J. Pearl. *Probabilistic reasoning in intelligent systems.* Morgan Kaufmann, Palo Alto, Calif., U.S.A., 1988.
13. B.W. Porter, R. Bareiss, and R.C. Holte. Concept learning and heuristic classification in weak-theory domains. *Artificial Intelligence, University of Texas, Austin Texas, U.S.A.*, (45):229–263, 1990.
14. E. Rosch and C.B. Mervis. Family resemblance studies in the internal structure of categories. *Cognitive Psychology*, (7):573–605, 1975.
15. E. Smith and D. Medin. *Categories and concepts.* Cambride: Harvard University Press, U.S.A., 1981.
16. H. Tirri, P. Kontkanen, and P. Myllymäki. A bayesian framework for case-based reasoning. In *Proc. of the 3rd European Workshop on Case-based Reasoning*, Lausanne, Switzerland, 1996.

Case Based Reasoning, Fuzzy Systems Modeling and Solution Composition

Ronald R. Yager
Machine Intelligence Institute, Iona College
New Rochelle, NY 10801

Abstract

Fuzzy systems modeling technique and the case based reasoning methodology are briefly described. It is then shown that these two approaches can be viewed as essentially involving the same process, a matching step and a solution composition step. It is noted that in the typical case based reasoning application the solution composition step is more difficult. Two techniques are suggested to help in the solution composition task in case based reasoning. The first, the weighted median, is useful in domains in which the action space consists of an ordered collection of alternatives. The second, a variation of reinforcement learning, is useful in domains in which the resulting actions involve a sequence of steps.

Keywords: Fuzzy modeling, reinforcement learning, matching, solution composition

1. Introduction

Fuzzy systems modeling (FSM) [1] and case based reasoning (CBR) [2] are two technologies useful for reasoning about new situations using information about previous situations. This information is contained in a knowledge base. In this work we show that the reasoning process used in FSM and CBR are the same. One distinction between the two is that fuzzy modeling has been generally used in environments in which the required solutions are numeric values, whereas the case based methodology has a more ambitious agenda regarding the domain of the possible solutions. This more ambitious agenda comes at the price of not always having available the necessary operations to combine solutions. In an attempt to address this issue we first introduce the weighted median [3-5] to help provide appropriate operations for some classes of problems in which the resulting actions are not necessarily the determination of a numeric value. We also introduce a variation of reinforcement learning [6] to help provide appropriate operations in domains in which the output actions involve a sequence of steps.

2. Fuzzy Systems Modeling

In this section we provide a brief overview of the FSM technology [1]. Assume $V_1, V_2, ..., V_p$ are a collection of variables taking their values in the spaces $X_j, j = 1, ..., p$. Typically these spaces are subsets of the real line. We call these the antecedent variables. Furthermore, let U be another variable, called the consequent variable, which takes its value in the space Y. Again in most applications Y is typically some subset of the real line.

A fuzzy systems model is a knowledge based model, very much in the spirit of an expert system, consisting of a collection of n rules of the form

$$\text{if } V_1 \text{ is } L_{i1} \text{ and } V_2 \text{ is } L_{i2} \text{ and. . . and } V_p \text{ is } L_{ip} \text{ then } U \text{ is } M_i.$$

The L_{ij}'s and M_i's are linguistic values associated with the corresponding variables. Thus a typical manifestation of such a rule is

if temperature is <u>low</u> and pressure is <u>high</u> then new engine speed setting is <u>moderate</u>.

An important feature which distinguishes fuzzy system models from expert systems is that a semantics is provided for the linguistic values associated with variables. This semantics is provided via fuzzy subsets. In particular, we associate with each of the linguistic terms, L_{ij}, a fuzzy subset A_{ij} over the space X_j providing a definition for that concept L_{ij}. Thus for each $x_j \in X_j$ the membership grade $A_{ij}(x_j)$ indicates the degree to which x_j is compatible with the concept L_{ij}. In similar way we associated with each of the linguistic terms M_i a fuzzy subset B_i over the space Y.

One approach used for the construction of such models is to derive the rules from observations on the variables [1]. Under this method the observations are clustered and the centers of these clusters essentially become the focus of the fuzzy rules in the knowledge base. In this spirit we see that the rule base is essentially a condensation and homogenization of the observations. A second method [1] is to obtain the rules directly from the experts. However, in this environment the rules are also obtained from a condensation of observation, although implicitly. For the construction of the rules by the expert can be seen to result from the experts observation on the system over time.

Once having constructed such a knowledge base the next step is to use it to obtain values for the consequent or action variable U. Assume we have an object whose values are $V_j = x_j^*$. The process for calculating the value of U is as follows. For each rule we calculate the degree to which it is applicable to the current situation. For the ith rule we calculate the $A_{ij}(x_j^*)$'s, then since the antecedents are connected by an "and" operation we calculate the relevance of the rule, its firing level, as $\lambda_i = \underset{j = 1, ..., p}{\text{Min}} A_{ij}(x_j^*)$. The next step is to use these firing levels to find a weighted aggregation (union) of the individual rule consequents. In particular, we calculate $F = \cup_i (\lambda_i \wedge B_i)$ thus $F(y) = \text{Max}_i [\lambda_i \wedge B_i]$. The end result of this provides a fuzzy subset F over the space Y where the membership grade $F(y)$ indicates the strength to which the model suggests y is the appropriate value for U.

3. Case Based Reasoning

In this section we shall review the case based reasoning technology [2]. The central component of a case based reasoning (CBR) system is a library of remembered cases. Each case in the library can be identified by an index of corresponding features. In addition each case has an associated action. More formally we can let $(V_1, V_2, ..., V_n)$ be a collection of attributes used to index the cases and let U be the variable corresponding to the action. A particular case can be represented by a $p + 1$ tuple $(x_{i1}, x_{i2}, ..., x_{in}, u_i)$ where x_{ij} corresponds to the value of V_j for this case and u_i corresponds to the action.

In case based reasoning we are generally given a new case and are required to determine the appropriate action based upon our library of historical cases. These new cases can be represented by a probe consisting of a n-tuple $p = (p_1, ..., p_n)$ in which p_i corresponds to the value of the attribute V_i. Using the probe we must search the case library for relevant cases. The solutions to these relevant cases can then be used to help find a solution to the current case.

The process of selecting the relevant cases from the library can be seen to consist of essentially two steps. In the first step, the individual attributes of a case are matched to the corresponding attribute in the probe. This step results, for the case being matched, in a collection $[m_{i1}, ..., m_{in}]$, where $m_{ij} \in [0, 1]$ is a measure of the compatibility of the attribute value x_{ij} with the probe value for the attribute, p_j. This step will be denoted as attribute matching. The second step is the aggregation of these individual scores to obtain an overall matching value of the case to the probe. This second step is called score aggregation. These overall scores are then used to select the relevant cases.

In the following we shall describe some of the approaches useful for the construction of individual feature matching techniques. A distinction must be made between attributes whose values are numeric and those that are linguistic. For those that are numeric initially we shall discuss two classes of approaches. The first approach is based upon a generalizing of the library case's attribute values. The central idea here is to extend the features of a case from its specific values to a neighborhood about these values. For a given library case assume the jth attribute is a number x_{ij}. We can generalize x_{ij} by turning it into a fuzzy subset D_{ij}, corresponding to the value $near\ x_{ij}$. The idea here is that the solution to the case, u_i, is still valid for values of V_i near x_{ij}. Having obtained the generalization of the case value in terms of the fuzzy subset D_{ij} we can obtain the degree of matching of the probe to this feature, m_{ij}, as the membership grade of the probe value p_j in the fuzzy subset D_{ij}, this is denoted $D_{ij}(p_i)$.

The second approach to numeric attribute matching is based upon the consideration that $similar$ values for the attributes should yield similar solutions. An implementation of this idea is based upon the use of a similarity relation [7] over the domain of the attribute. Assume V_j is an attribute taking its value in the set X_j. A similarity measure S is a mapping $S: X_j \times X_j \rightarrow [0, 1]$ such that 1. $S(x, x) = 1$ 2. $S(x, y) = S(y, x)$ 3. $S(x, z) = Max_y[S(x, y) * S(y, z)]$ where $*$ is any t-norm [8]. Having such a similarity relation, given a probe value p_i and a case value x_{ij} we get $m_{ij} = S(p_i, x_{ij})$.

In situations where the attribute values are words, linguistic values, the problem becomes more complex. In these situations we are faced with a fundamental problem of uncertainty management. In many cases words correspond to sets of values rather then specific points. For example $tall$ corresponds to a collection of heights and red corresponds to a set of frequencies. In order to match words we must focus on techniques that allow us to compare sets of values with other sets of values. Assume for the attribute V_j the probe value p_j, and the case value x_{ij} are linguistic values. The first step involves transforming these into fuzzy subsets representing the range of values corresponding to these linguistic entities. Let X_j be the universe of discourse on which these fuzzy subsets are defined and let P_j and A_{ij} be the fuzzy subsets representing these linguistic values. The problem becomes that of finding the degree of matching of these two fuzzy subsets. A number of techniques are available for the determination of the degree of matching of two fuzzy subsets. Let us describe some of these techniques. The first approach involves the use of a measure of possibility [9]. In this method $m_{ij} = \text{Poss} [P_j/A_{ij}] = \text{Max}_x[P_j(x) \wedge A_{ij}(x)]$ ($\wedge = \text{Min}$). The idea here is that if two words have some degree of overlap in their meaning then the possibility exists that their solutions should have some overlap. This can be seen as a soft kind of matching of these concepts.

Anther approach is to use the idea of entailment. With this idea we are saying that if the probe is a special case of a library case then the library case should be relevant. A measure that has been developed in the theory of fuzzy logic to capture this kind of measure is the measure of certainty [9]. In this approach

$$m_{ij} = \text{Cert} [P_j/A_{ij}] = \text{Min}_x[\overline{P_j}(x) \vee A_{ij}(x)] \qquad (\vee = \text{Max})$$

where $\overline{P_j}(x) = 1 - P_j(x)$. The measure of certainty can be seen as a hard measure of matching. Taken together the measures of certainty and possibility can be viewed as lower and upper bounds on the truth of the statement "*word* P_j *matches word* A_{ij}".

As a result of the matching step, for a given case in the library, we obtain a vector of values $[m_{ij}, ..., m_{in}]$ indicating the degree to which each of the features has been matched. The next problem faced by the system builder is to aggregate these individual scores to obtain an overall score for the matching of the case and the probe. We consider the problem of aggregation as one of multi-criteria decision making. Given a probe containing an attributes, V_j, $j = 1, ..., n$, one can consider that the attribute value is a criteria that must be satisfied for the case to be relevant for this probe. In particular the score m_{ij} is the degree of satisfaction or truth of the criteria, G_j,

the attribute V_j of the probe is matched by the attribute value V_j of the library case.

The problem of aggregation becomes that of combining these individual criteria satisfactions to find the overall satisfaction of the case to the probe. This problem can be viewed as finding some function F such that $M_i = F(m_{i1}, m_{i2}, ..., m_{in})$ where M_i is the overall score of the library case. In formulating F we need to take into account the relationship that the system builder believes exists between the criteria. Is is desired that all attributes must be matched or can some portion of them be matched? Are some attributes more important then other? If one attribute is very strongly matched can we allow a weaker matching of some other attribute?

Consider the situation where we have n attributes in the index. Let G_j be the criteria "the probe and the case match on attribute j" and let m_{ij} be the satisfaction of this criteria. One typical situation is that the user requires that <u>all</u> the criteria be satisfied. In this case the overall selection function F can be seen to be equivalent to the logical statement: $F = G_1$ *and* G_2 *and* G_3 ... *and* G_n. In the preceding we see that the connection between the individual criteria is based upon the use of the logical *and* one tool for implementing the logical *and* in this environment is the t-norm. The t-norm operator provides a general class of multi-valued logic implementations for the logical *and*. Two examples of the t-norm are the min and product operator, using these operators we would get for our overall satisfaction $M_i = Min_j[m_{ij}]$ or $M_i = \Pi_j[m_{ij}]$.

At the other extreme is the situation where all that is desired for the matching of the probe and the case is that *at least one* attribute is matched. In this case the structure of the overall matching function is $G = G_1$ *or* G_2 *or* G_3 ... *or* G_n. One tool for implementing this type of *or* aggregation is to use the dual of the t-norms, the t-conorm [8] family of operators. Examples of this operator are: $M_i = Max_j[M_j]$, $M_i = Min[1, \Sigma_j m_j]$ and $M_i = 1 - \Pi_j[(1 - m_{ij})]$.

In most settings of CBR systems neither of these two extreme forms of aggregation captures the real desire of the system builder. A more representative formulation of the aggregation would be that a case is relevant

if <u>most</u> of the attributes of the probe and the case are matched.

The underlined term *most* is an example of a linguistic quantifier [10] lying somewhere between the extremes of *for all* (and) and *at least one* (or). In [11] Yager called such aggregations quantifier guided aggregations. Yager [12] introduced a family of operators, called OWA operators, to model these kinds of aggregations. These OWA operators provide a family of aggregation operators which have the *and* operator at one extreme and the *or* operator at the other extreme. It also has the simple average as a special case.

Definition: An OWA operator of dimension n is a function F, F: $[0, 1]^n \rightarrow [0, 1]$, that has associated with it a set of weights $W = [w_1 w_2 \ . \ . \ . \ w_n]$ such that (1) $w_i \in [0, 1]$ and (2) $\Sigma_i w_i = 1$, where for any argument $< m_{i1}, ..., m_{in} >$

$$F_W(m_{i1}, ..., m_{in}) = \Sigma_j b_j * w_j$$

with b_j being the jth largest of the m's.

A number of special cases of this OWA operator are worth pointing out. In [12] Yager shows that for the special operator, which he denotes F^*, where $w_1 = 1$ and $w_j = 0$ for $j > 1$, we get $F^*(m_{i1}, ..., m_{in}) = Max_j[m_{ij}]$. This operator performs as a pure *or* operator. Another special case, denoted F_*, where $w_n = 1$ and $w_j = 0$ for $j < n$, we get $F_*(m_{i1}, ..., m_{in}) = Min_j[m_{ij}]$. Thus this operator performs as a pure *and*.

Another special case of these operators, denoted F_A, is the case where $w_j = 1/n$ for all j. Using these weights we get $F_A(m_{i1}, ..., m_{in}) = \frac{1}{n} \Sigma_j m_{ij}$, which is the simple average operator.

For any OWA operator F, $Min_i[m_i] \leq F(m_1, ..., m_n) \leq Max_i[m_i]$. Thus this operator provides a whole family aggregations lying between the extremes of *anding* and *oring* the individual attributes satisfactions.

In [12] Yager shows the close relationship between OWA operators and linguistic quantifiers, he suggested a methodology for associating linguistic quantifiers with an OWA operator. Using this methodology one can convert a statement such as "almost all of the attributes should be matched' into a formal aggregation function F.

As a result of using the preceding techniques we associated with each case in the library a measure $M_i \in [0, 1]$ indicating the relevance of this case to the current case.

Since each case has an associated solution u_i the scores M_i essentially provide a measure of appropriateness of the solution u_i to the current case.

At this point let us look at some of the similarities and differences between the fuzzy modeling and case based reasoning technologies. In both technologies we have a knowledge case to help us find the appropriate answer. In the CBR method our knowledge base consists of a library or collection of previous cases. In the fuzzy modeling technology our knowledge base consists of a collection of rules. However, the rules as we previous noted are constructed by combining past observations on the system. So we see that in the CBR approach our knowledge base is made up of the "raw" observations, the previous cases, while in the fuzzy modeling method the raw cases have been coalesced into rules. Essentially the rules in the fuzzy modeling technique can be viewed as prototypical or generalized cases. So that at some level the objects in both knowledge bases can be viewed as the same type of objects, individual cases in CBR and prototypical cases in fuzzy model. We shall refer to these objects as *specimens*.

The rules in the fuzzy model are made up of two components the antecedent and the consequent. For a given input the antecedent portion is matched to give us a firing level of the rule. these firing levels are used to weight the consequent in an aggregation that results in a function, fuzzy subset, indicating the strength of each element in the output space as the appropriate action.

The cases in the CBR model are also make up of two components, the index values and the action values. For a given new case the indexed values are matched with those of the cases and this results in a weighted associated with the action.

4. Solution Composition

In both CBR and FSM, as a result of the matching process, we end up with a weighting function, a fuzzy set over the space of actions, indicating the appropriate of each action. The next step in this process is to use this information to compose a prescribed action.

Formally we have a set Y of possible actions and an associated fuzzy subset F over Y where for every $y \in Y$, $F(y)$ indicates the degree to which the matching suggests y is the appropriate action. Our problem then is to use this information to obtain a unique action to pursue. The nature of the procedure we use to accomplish this task strongly depends upon the characteristics of the elements in the space Y.

We first consider the case in which the action space Y is some sub-interval of the real line. This is the case which normally holds in the applications of fuzzy modeling. In [1] a number of approaches to this problem which is commonly called defuzzification are described.

The usual method used for defuzzification is the COA method, where the defuzzified value is $y^* = \Sigma_y \, y \, f(y) / \Sigma_y \, f(y)$. Denoting $w_i = f(y_i) / \Sigma_y \, f(y)$ as the normalized weight associated with y_i then $y^* = \Sigma_i \, w_i \, y_i$, which is essentially a weighted average. In [1] the authors provided a probabilistic interpretation of this approach. They suggested defuzzification corresponds to a process in which we transform the fuzzy subset F into a probability distribution where $p(y_i) = f(y_i) / \Sigma_y \, f(y)$ and the defuzzified value is the expected value of this probability distribution $y^* = \Sigma_i\, p(y_i)\, y_i$.

An alternative approach to defuzzification is the mean of maxima method. In this approach we let Z be the subset of elements in that have the maximum membership grade and then calculate $y^* = \dfrac{1}{\text{card}\,(Z)} \displaystyle\sum_{y\, \in\, Z} y$

In many environments where CBR is used and some situations where fuzzy modeling is used, the underlying structure of the action space is not as rich as the real line and therefore doesn't allow the composition of solutions used in the previous defuzzification methods. In the following we shall consider a situation in which the action space is discrete $Y = \{y_1, y_2, ..., y_n\}$, essentially we can't form new solutions but must pick one of the elements in Y. We shall also assume that their exists a natural ordering on the objects in the output space $y_j > y_i$ if $j < i$. A prototypical example of this occurs when the problem is to determine the setting position of a dial which has n discrete settings, where we assume that settings are ordered regarding the effect of the action, that is y_j is a stronger action then y_i if $j < i$.

In [5] Yager and Rybalov introduced an aggregation operation called the weighted median. This operation has been shown to be similar in spirit to the weighted average but is implementable in the type of discrete environments just described. In the following we briefly describe this method. Assume (w_i, a_i) $i = 1, 2, ..., n$ are a collection of pairs where $w_i \in [0, 1]$ and $\displaystyle\sum_{i\,=\,1}^{n} w_i = 1$ and the a_i are values drawn from the set Y, which has at least an ordering on its elements. To calculate $y^* =$ Weighted Median$_i\,((w_i, a_i))$ we proceed as follows:

1. Order the (w_i, a_i) in descending order according to the a_i values. This gives us the collection of pairs (u_j, b_j) where $b_k \geq b_j$ if $k < j$. We note that u_j is the weight associated with the a_i that becomes b_j.

2. Calculate the index i^* such that

$$T_{i^*\,-\,1} = \sum_{j\,=\,1}^{i^*\,-\,1} u_j < 0.5 \text{ and } T_{i^*} = \sum_{j\,=\,1}^{i^*} u_j \geq 0.5$$

(i^* is the index where the sum of the ordered weights crosses 0.5)

3. Then the weighted median in this case is $y^* = b_i{}^*$

As the following example illustrates we can use this aggregation to implement action selection in an ordinal environment.

Example: Assume we have a fuzzy systems model whose action space is
$$Y = \{\text{Set }(1), \text{Set }(2), \text{Set }(3), \text{Set }(4), \text{Set }(5)\}$$
where Set (i) indicates the setting of a dial should be at position i.

Assume we have a rule base describing the appropriate situations in which to set the dial to each of the positions:

$$\text{If V is } A_i \text{ then U is } \{\tfrac{1}{y_i}\} \qquad i = 1, 2, 3, 4, 5$$

where $y_i =$ Set (i). We note here the rules have been indexed such that $y_i > y_j$ if $i < j$.

Consider an input to the system $V = x^*$ which gives the following firing values $\lambda_1 = A_1(x^*) = 0.7$, $\lambda_2 = A_2(x^*) = 0.4$, $\lambda_3 = A_3(x^*) = 0.3$, $\lambda_4 = A_4(x^*) = 0.2$, $\lambda_5 = A_5(x^*) = 0$. In this case $w_i = \dfrac{\lambda_i}{\displaystyle\sum_{i=1}^{n} \lambda_i} = \dfrac{\lambda_i}{1.6}$ and hence $w_1 = 0.44$, $w_2 = 0.25$, $w_3 = 0.19$, $w_4 = 0.12$, $w_5 = 0$.

Since we have assumed that the arguments are ordered in the appropriate manner we see that $T_1 = \displaystyle\sum_{i=1}^{1} w_i = 0.44$ and $T_2 = \displaystyle\sum_{i=1}^{2} w_i = 0.69$ and hence $i^* = 2$ and therefore $y^* = y_2 = $ Set (2).

While we have illustrated the weighted median in the case of fuzzy modeling it can be easily seen to be useful in case based reasoning.

5. Reinforcement Learning for Process Based Cases

One environment where it is particularly difficult to compose a solution to a probe case is when the solution involves some process built from a number of steps. Assume we have a relevant collection of cases some of which provided good answers and some bad answers to the case at hand. It is usually very difficult to determine which were the steps in the process that accounted for the solution being a good or bad solution to the problem. A prototypical example of this is a chess game. After a losing game we would like to analyze our moves to determine which moves caused us to lose. A technique has been described in the neural network literature called reinforcement learning [6] which attempts to address this problem. We feel that this technology may have some potential applications in the case based reasoning paradigm.

In the following we shall briefly described the basic ideas inherent in the reinforcement learning approach which we feel can be useful in composing solutions in case based reasoning. Assume the solution to some problem can be described by a process consisting of a number of actions where the choice of the next action is dependent upon where we are, the current state. Formally we can describe our environment with a state model. Let $S = \{S_1, S_2, ...S_q\}$ be a collection of states any one of which we can be in during the performance of this process. Associated with state S_j is a collection of actions $A_j = \{a_{ij}\}$ which we can take in this state. Furthermore, we have a state transition function $S' = F(S, a)$ which indicates the new state S' if we perform action a in state S. In this environment a solution to a given case consists of a string of actions which result in either a good or bad solution.

In trying to use such a model to compose a solution starting from some initial state we need some information as to the appropriateness of a given action in a state. One form in which to have this information is to have, for each state, a probability distribution over the set of possible actions available in the state where p_{ij} indicates the probability that action a_{ij} is the appropriate action to take in state j. Having such a probability distribution we select an action in a state based upon the probability associated with the actions in available in that state.

The key to using this model to construct new process type solutions is the availability of the probabilities associated with the actions allowable in each state. We shall now describe a procedure, based upon the idea of reinforcement learning, for obtaining these probabilities. In the following we shall use the term *a manifestation* to indicate the list of actions starting from some initial state and ending with either a good/successful (+1) or bad/unsuccessful (-1) result. Essentially a manifestation is a string of actions, a process, that constitutes a solution to a case in our library. The key aspect of the reinforcement learning paradigm is the use of these manifestations to help in the learning of the probabilities associated with the actions in the states. This learning is accomplished by positively reinforcing actions made in successful cases and negatively reinforcing actions made in unsuccessful cases. We now describe the learning mechanism. Assume that in a given successful case which passed through state S_j we took action a_{kj} in that state. Let $\{a_{1j}, a_{2j}, ..., a_{nj}\}$ be the set of possible actions available in that state, with p_{ij} their respective probabilities. Since this was a successful case we desire to reinforce the action a_{kj}. The reinforcement is accomplished by changing the probabilities p_{ij} to $\hat{p}_{ij}$ in the manner described below

$$\hat{p}_{kj} = p_{kj} + \alpha \sum_{i \neq k} p_{ij}$$

$$\hat{p}_{ij} = p_{ij} - \alpha\, p_{ij} \qquad i \neq k$$

where $\alpha \in [0, 1]$ is our learning rate. We have essentially increased the probability associated with a good move.

On the other hand if the action a_{kj} was associated with an unsuccessful case we diminish its associated probability as follows:

$$\hat{p}_{kj} = (1 - \beta)\, p_{kj}$$

$$\hat{p}_{ij} = \hat{p}_{kj} + \frac{\beta p_{kj} \cdot p_{ij}}{\sum_{i \neq k} p_{ij}} \qquad k \neq j$$

where $\beta \in [0, 1]$ is the learning rate. By using all the manifestation we then learn, in a probabilistic sense, the correct move in each state.

It appears that this methodology can be applied with some modification to the case based reasoning paradigm. Assume we have a library of cases, each case consisting of an index and a solution which is a process. As we shall subsequently see the solution will play the role of the manifestation in the above. Assume we have a probe, new case, whose solution we desire. We now match the library cases to the probe and get an aggregate match score M for each case. We then select the relevant cases, highest scoring, to build our state network in the manner described above. It appears that we should modify the learning process slightly in this environment. In particular cases which are closer the probe, higher M, should play a more important role in the learning process. With this in mind we suggest using a modification learning rate, $\alpha^* = \alpha M$ and $\beta^* = \beta M$, so that cases closer allow more change.

Once having constructed the state space with its associated probabilities from the relevant cases we can use it to generate potential solutions.

6. Conclusion

We showed the fundamental similarity between CBR and FSM. Both use a knowledge base of specimens whose form is a set of conditions and an associated action. In the CBR approach these specimens are raw cases while in FSM they are "rules". The reasoning process is basically the same. A new situation is matched to the specimens, resulting in a relevance measure of that specimen. These matching scores are then associated with the action indicated in the specimen. The effective action is then obtained by combining the weighted individual specimen actions. In FSM the rule actions are generally associated with the assignment of a numeric value to some variable. This numeric framework allows the use of simple aggregation techniques, such as the weighted average. In the case based reasoning environment the associated actions are typical drawn from a space not as mathematically rich as the number system, the actions are more sophisticated. This situation does not make it as easy to combine the weighted actions. We have introduced the weighted median as a tool for extending the applicability of the CBR method, it provides for aggregations in situations where the action space has only an ordering on the objects.. This does not always solve the aggregation problems in CBR applications, there is a need to develop techniques which can be used for specifuc kinds of action spaces encountered in CBR.

7. References

[1]. Yager, R. R. and Filev, D. P., Essentials of Fuzzy Modeling and Control, John Wiley: New York, 1994.

[2]. Kolodner, J., Case-Based Reasoning, Morgan Kaufmann: San Mateo, CA, 1993.

[3]. Yager, R. R., "Information fusion and weighted median aggregation," Proceedings 5th International CIFT Workshop Trento, Italy, 209-219, 1995.

[4]. Yager, R. R., "Fusion of ordinal information using weighted median aggregation," Technical Report# MII-1520 Machine Intelligence Institute, Iona College, 1995.

[5]. Yager, R. R. and Rybalov, A., "Understanding the Median as a Fusion Operator," International Journal of General Systems, (To Appear).

[6]. Barto, A. G., Sutton, R. S. and Anderson, C. W., "Neuronlike adaptive elements that can solve difficult learning control problems," IEEE Transactions on Systems, Man and Cybernetics 13, 834-846, 1983.

[7]. Zadeh, L. A., "Similarity relations and fuzzy orderings," Inf. Sci. 3, 177-200, 1971.

[8]. Dubois, D. and Prade, H., "A review of fuzzy sets aggregation connectives," Information Sciences 36, 85 - 121, 1985.

[9]. Zadeh, L. A., "Fuzzy sets and information granularity," in Advances in Fuzzy Set Theory and Applications, Gupta, M.M., Ragade, R.K. & Yager, R.R. (eds.), Amsterdam: North-Holland, 3-18, 1979.

[10]. Zadeh, L. A., "A computational approach to fuzzy quantifiers in natural languages," Computing and Mathematics with Applications 9, 149-184, 1983.

[11]. Yager, R. R., "Quantifier guided aggregation using OWA operators," International Journal of Intelligent Systems 11, 49-73, 1996.

[12]. Yager, R. R., "On ordered weighted averaging aggregation operators in multi-criteria decision making," IEEE Trans. on Sys, Man and Cyber. 18, 183-190, 1988.

List of Presentations

Talk Presentations

Poster Presentations

Author Index

Lecture Notes in Artificial Intelligence (LNAI)

Lecture Notes in Computer Science